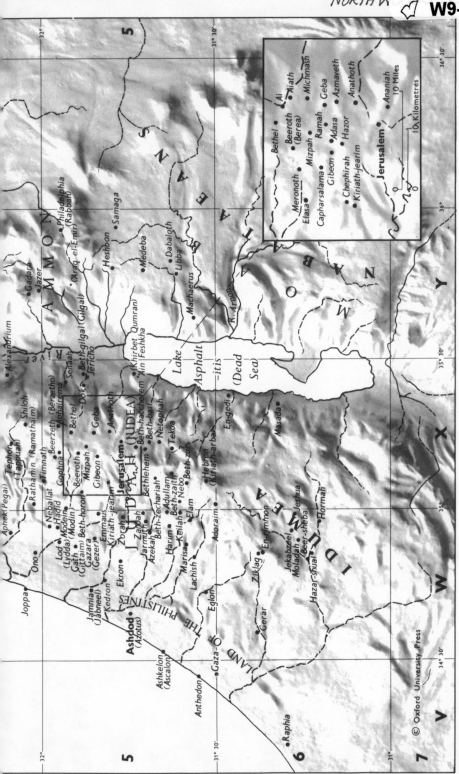

Inset map (top right):

Ai
Aiath
Bethel
Michmash
Beeroth (Berea)
Geba
Azmaveth
Anathoth
Ananiah
Meronoth
Mizpah
Ramah
Adasa
Hazor
Elasa
Gibeon
Chephirah
Kiriath-jearim
Capharsalama
Jerusalem

10 Miles
10 Kilometres

Main map labels:

32°   31° 30′   36° 30′   36°   35° 30′   35°

AMMON
S...ANS (Beth-saida/region label)
Philadelphia (Rabbah)
Gadara
Jazer
'Araq el-Emir
Samaga
Heshbon
Medeba
Dabaloth
Libba
Machaerus
R. Arnon
NABATAEANS
MOW (desert label)
N

Alexandrium
Aphek (Pegai)
River (Jordan)
Beth-gilgal (Gilgal)
Seraah
Dok
(Khirbet Qumran)
'Ain Feshkha
Jericho
Lake Asphalt-itis (Dead Sea)
En-gedi
Masada

Tephon (Tappuah)
Rathamin (Ramathaim)
Timnath
Shiloh
Beerzeth (Berzetho)
Aphairema
Bethel
Geba
Anathoth
Tekoa
Beth-haccherem
Beth-basi
Netophah
JUDEA (JUDAH)

Lod (Lydda) (Modin)
Nebalat
Hadid
Modin
Beth-horon
Beeroth
Mizpah
Gophna
Gibeon
Jerusalem
Bethlehem
Beth-zechariah
Beth-zaith
Beth-zur
Nebo
Hebron (Kiriath-arba)

Gath (Gittaim)
Gazara (Gezer)
Emmaus
Kiriath-jearim
Zorah
Zanoah
Jarmuth
Adullam
Elam
Adoraim

Oro
Joppa
Jamnia (Jabneel)
Kedron
Ekron
Azekah
Harim
Keilah
Marisa
Lachish
Eglon

Ashdod (Azotus)
THE PHILISTINES
Ashkelon (Ascalon)
Anthedon
Gaza
Gerar
Ziklag
En-rimmon
Jekabzeel
Moladah
Beer-sheba
Jeshua
Hazar-shual
Hormah
IDUMEA
LAND OF THE PHILISTINES
Raphia

© Oxford University Press

5   6   7
V   W   X   Y

" Your Faith Journey"

THE NEW
OXFORD ANNOTATED
APOCRYPHA

The Apocryphal/Deuterocanonical Books
of the Old Testament

Edited by

BRUCE M. METZGER   ROLAND E. MURPHY

NEW REVISED STANDARD
VERSION

New York
OXFORD UNIVERSITY PRESS

OXFORD UNIVERSITY PRESS

Oxford   New York   Toronto
Delhi   Bombay   Calcutta   Madras   Karachi
Petaling Jaya   Singapore   Hong Kong   Tokyo
Nairobi   Dar es Salaam   Cape Town
Melbourne   Auckland

and associated companies in
Berlin   Ibadan

Published by Oxford University Press, Inc.
200 Madison Avenue, New York, New York 10016

1 3 5 7 9 8 6 4 2

Printed in the United States of America
on acid-free paper

*courage is fear that
has said its prayers.*

CONTENTS

THE APOCRYPHAL/DEUTEROCANONICAL BOOKS

The Apocryphal/Deuterocanonical Books are listed here in four groupings, as follows:

(a) Books and Additions to Esther and Daniel that are in the Roman Catholic, Greek, and Slavonic Bibles

(b) Books in the Greek and Slavonic Bibles; not in the Roman Catholic Canon

(c) In the Slavonic Bible and in the Latin Vulgate Appendix

(d) In an Appendix to the Greek Bible

ABBREVIATIONS

The following abbreviations are used for the Apocryphal/Deuterocanonical Books

Tob	Tobit	1 Esd	1 Esdras	Bel	Bel and the Dragon
Jdt	Judith	2 Esd	2 Esdras	1 Macc	1 Maccabees
Add Esth	Additions to Esther	Let Jer	Letter of Jeremiah	2 Macc	2 Maccabees
Wis	Wisdom	Song of Thr·	Prayer of	3 Macc	3 Maccabees
Sir	Sirach (Ecclesiasticus)		Azariah and the Song	4 Macc	4 Maccabees
Bar	Baruch		of the Three Jews	Pr Man	Prayer of Manasseh
		Sus	Susanna		

In the notes to the Apocryphal/Deuterocanonical Books the following abbreviations are used:

Ch, chs Chapter, chapters
Cn   Correction; made where the text has suffered in transmission and the versions provide no satisfactory restoration but where the Standard Bible Committee agrees with the judgment of competent scholars as to the most probable reconstruction of the original text.
Gk   Septuagint, Greek version of the Old Testament
Heb   Hebrew of the Qumran, Masada, and Cairo Geniza texts
Lat   Latin versions of the Apocryphal/Deuterocanonical Books
Macc   The book(s) of the Maccabees
Ms(s)   Manuscript(s)
Q Ms(s) Manuscript(s) found at Qumran by the Dead Sea
Syr   Syriac Version of the Old Testament
Syr H   Syriac Version of Origen's Hexapla
Vg   Vulgate, Latin Version of the Old Testament

TITLES GIVEN TO BOOKS ASSOCIATED WITH
EZRA AND NEHEMIAH IN SELECTED VERSIONS

Version \ Document	Old Testament book of Ezra	Old Testament book of Nehemiah	Paraphrase of 2 Chronicles chs 35—36; the whole book of Ezra; Nehemiah 7.38—8.12; plus a tale about Darius' bodyguards	A Latin Apocalypse
Greek Bible (Septuagint)	2 Esdras		1 Esdras	
Latin Vulgate Bible	1 Esdras	2 Esdras	3 Esdras	4 Esdras
Many later Latin Manuscripts	1 Esdras		3 Esdras	2 Esdras = chs 1—2 4 Esdras = chs 3—14 5 Esdras = chs 15—16
Douay English Version (1609–1610)	1 Esdras	2 Esdras	3 Esdras	4 Esdras
Russian Bible, Moscow Patriarchate (1956)	1 Esdras	Nehemiah	2 Esdras	3 Esdras
King James and New Revised Standard Versions	Ezra	Nehemiah	1 Esdras	2 Esdras

TO THE READER

This preface is addressed to you by the Committee of translators, who wish to explain, as briefly as possible, the origin and character of our work. The publication of our revision is yet another step in the long, continual process of making the Bible available in the form of the English language that is most widely current in our day. To summarize in a single sentence: the New Revised Standard Version of the Bible is an authorized revision of the Revised Standard Version, published in 1952, which was a revision of the American Standard Version, published in 1901, which, in turn, embodied earlier revisions of the King James Version, published in 1611.

In the course of time, the King James Version came to be regarded as "the Authorized Version." With good reason it has been termed "the noblest monument of English prose," and it has entered, as no other book has, into the making of the personal character and the public institutions of the English-speaking peoples. We owe to it an incalculable debt.

Yet the King James Version has serious defects. By the middle of the nineteenth century, the development of biblical studies and the discovery of many biblical manuscripts more ancient than those on which the King James Version was based made it apparent that these defects were so many as to call for revision. The task was begun, by authority of the Church of England, in 1870. The (British) Revised Version of the Bible was published in 1881–1885; and the American Standard Version, its variant embodying the preferences of the American scholars associated with the work, was published, as was mentioned above, in 1901. In 1928 the copyright of the latter was acquired by the International Council of Religious Education and thus passed into the ownership of the churches of the United States and Canada that were associated in this Council through their boards of education and publication.

The Council appointed a committee of scholars to have charge of the text of the American Standard Version and to undertake inquiry concerning the need for further revision. After studying the questions whether or not revision should be undertaken, and if so, what its nature and extent should be, in 1937 the Council authorized a revision. The scholars who served as members of the Committee worked in two sections, one dealing with the Old Testament and one with the New Testament. In 1946 the Revised Standard Version of the New Testament was published. The publication of the Revised Standard Version of the Bible, containing the Old and New Testaments, took place on September 30, 1952. A translation of the Apocryphal/Deuterocanonical Books of the Old Testament followed in 1957. In 1977 this collection was issued in an expanded edition, containing three additional texts received by Eastern Orthodox communions (3 and 4 Maccabees and Psalm 151). Thereafter the Revised Standard Version gained the distinction of being officially authorized for use by all major Christian churches: Protestant, Anglican, Roman Catholic, and Eastern Orthodox.

The Revised Standard Version Bible Committee is a continuing body, comprising about thirty members, both men and women. Ecumenical in representation, it includes scholars affiliated with various Protestant denominations, as well as several Roman Catholic members, an Eastern Orthodox member, and a Jewish member who serves in the Old Testament section. For a period of time the Committee included several members from Canada and from England. In 1974 the Policies Committee of the Revised Standard Version, which is a standing committee of the National Council of the Churches of Christ in the U.S.A., authorized the preparation of a revision of the entire RSV Bible.

For the Apocryphal/Deuterocanonical Books of the Old Testament the Committee has made use of a number of texts. For most of these books the basic Greek text from which the present translation was made is the edition of the Septuagint prepared by Alfred Rahlfs and published by the Württemberg Bible Society (Stuttgart, 1935). For several of the books the more recently published individual volumes of the Göttingen Septuagint project were utilized. For the book of Tobit it was decided to follow the form of the Greek text found in codex Sinaiticus (supported as it is by evidence from Qumran); where this text is defective, it was supplemented and corrected by other Greek manuscripts. For the three Additions to Daniel (namely, Susanna, the Prayer of Azariah and the Song of the Three Jews, and Bel and the Dragon) the Committee continued to use the Greek version attributed to Theodotion (the so-called "Theodotion-Daniel"). In translating Ecclesiasticus (Sirach), while constant reference was made to the Hebrew fragments of a large portion of this book (those discovered at Qumran and Masada as well those recovered from the Cairo Geniza), the Committee generally followed the Greek text (including verse numbers) published by Joseph Ziegler in the Göttingen Septuagint (1965). But in many places the Committee has translated the Hebrew text when this provides a reading that is clearly superior to the Greek; the Syriac and Latin versions were also consulted throughout and occasionally adopted. The basic text adopted in rendering 2 Esdras is the Latin version given in *Biblia Sacra,* edited by Robert Weber (Stuttgart, 1971). This was supplemented by consulting the Latin text as edited by R. L. Bensly (1895) and by Bruno Violet (1910), as well as by taking into account the several Oriental versions of 2 Esdras, namely, the Syriac, Ethiopic, Arabic (two forms, referred to as Arabic 1 and Arabic 2), Armenian, and Georgian versions. Finally, since the Additions to the Book of Esther are disjointed and quite unintelligible as they stand in most editions of the Apocrypha, we have provided them with their original context by translating the whole of the Greek version of Esther from Robert Hanhart's Göttingen edition (1983).

As for the style of English adopted for the present revision, among the mandates given to the Committee in 1980 by the Division of Education and Ministry of the National Council of Churches of Christ (which now holds the copyright of the RSV Bible) was the directive to continue in the tradition of the King James Bible, but to introduce such changes as are warranted on the basis of accuracy, clarity, euphony, and current English usage. Within the constraints set by the original texts and by the mandates of the Division, the Committee has followed the maxim, "As literal as possible, as free as necessary." As a consequence, the New Revised Standard Version (NRSV) remains essentially a literal translation. Paraphrastic renderings have been adopted only sparingly, and then chiefly to compensate for a deficiency in the English language—the lack of a common gender third person singular pronoun.

During the almost half a century since the publication of the RSV, many in the churches have become sensitive to the danger of linguistic sexism arising from the inherent bias of the English language towards the masculine gender, a bias that in the case of the Bible has often restricted or obscured the meaning of the original text. The mandates from the Division specified that, in references to men and women, masculine-oriented language should be eliminated as far as this can be done without altering passages that reflect the historical situation of ancient patriarchal culture. As can be appreciated, more than once the Committee found that the several mandates stood in tension and even in conflict. The various concerns had to be balanced case by case in order to provide a faithful and acceptable rendering withut using contrived English. Only very occasionally has the pronoun "he" or "him" been retained in passages where the reference may have been to a woman as well as to a man; for example, in several legal texts in Leviticus and Deuteronomy. In such instances of formal, legal language, the options of either putting the passage in the plural or of introducing additional nouns to avoid masculine pronouns in English seemed to the Committee to obscure the historic structure and literary character of the original. In the vast majority of cases, however, inclusiveness has been attained by simple rephrasing or by introducing plural forms when this does not distort the meaning of the passage. Of course, in narrative and in parable no attempt was made to generalize the sex of individual persons.

This new version seeks to preserve all that is best in the English Bible as it has been known and used through the years. It is intended for use in public reading and congregational worship, as well as in private study, instruction, and meditation. We have resisted the temptation to introduce terms and phrases that merely reflect current moods, and have tried to put the message of the Scriptures in simple, enduring words and expressions that are worthy to stand in the great tradition of the King James Bible and its predecessors.

For the Committee,
BRUCE M. METZGER

THE EDITORS' PREFACE

The recent publication of the Apocryphal/Deuterocanonical Books of the Old Testament in the New Revised Standard Version of the Bible makes it opportune not only to adjust the annotations on the wording of the new version, but also to introduce many other changes as well. All of the introductions and annotations of the Apocryphal/Deuterocanonical Books have been reviewed, either by the original contributor or, in most instances, by another scholar. In some cases relatively few changes were called for; in others, where many advances have occurred, there was greater need for revision.

In the following list of contributors the name of the original writer is followed by the name of the reviewer; when the reviewer was also the original writer, the name occurs only once. It is understood that the editors have also introduced a certain number of modifications throughout.

1 Esdras, WALTER J. HARRELSON; 2 Esdras, BRUCE M. METZGER/WALTER J. HARRELSON; Tobit and Judith, ROBERT C. DENTAN/CAREY A. MOORE; Esther (Greek), †FLOYD V. FILSON/CAREY A. MOORE; Wisdom of Solomon, †FLOYD V. FILSON/ROLAND E. MURPHY; Ecclesiasticus (Sirach), BRUCE M. METZGER/ROLAND E. MURPHY; Baruch and the Letter of Jeremiah, HERBERT G. MAY/JAMES A. SANDERS; The Additions to the Book of Daniel and the Prayer of Manasseh, BRUCE M. METZGER/JAMES A. SANDERS; 1 and 2 Maccabees, SHERMAN E. JOHNSON/MARY C. CALLAWAY; 3 Maccabees, DEMETRIOS J. CONSTANTELOS/JOHN BRECK; 4 Maccabees, SHERMAN E. JOHNSON/JOHN BRECK; and Psalm 151, BRUCE M. METZGER/JAMES A. SANDERS. The introduction to the Aprocryphal/Deuterocanonical Books is by BRUCE M. METZGER, and the general article on "The Additions to the Greek Book of Daniel" is by JAMES A. SANDERS.

The editors express their gratitude to all who are mentioned above, as well as to the staff and artisans of the Oxford University Press, who, under the careful guidance of Donald Kraus, have assisted in producing this annotated edition of the Apocryphal/Deuterocanonical Books.

BRUCE M. METZGER,
ROLAND E. MURPHY

ACKNOWLEDGMENTS

Many people contributed to this volume. Among them were: Herbert J. Addison, Elizabeth M. Edman, Kelly Gallagher, June Gunden, Deborah Jenks, Susan Kraus, Estella Pate, Leslie Phillips, Lynn Stanley, Mildred and Frederick Tripp. The publisher expresses thanks to these and all others who had a part in bringing this work to completion.

H

Chronological Tables of Rulers

THE SELEUCID DYNASTY

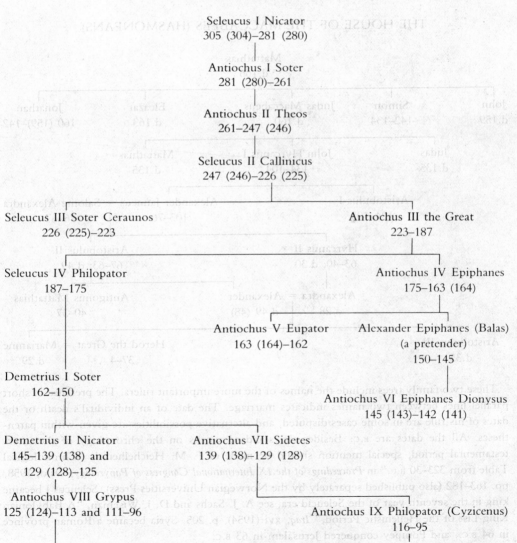

Seleucus I Nicator
305 (304)–281 (280)

Antiochus I Soter
281 (280)–261

Antiochus II Theos
261–247 (246)

Seleucus II Callinicus
247 (246)–226 (225)

Seleucus III Soter Ceraunos
226 (225)–223

Antiochus III the Great
223–187

Seleucus IV Philopator
187–175

Antiochus IV Epiphanes
175–163 (164)

Antiochus V Eupator
163 (164)–162

Alexander Epiphanes (Balas)
(a pretender)
150–145

Demetrius I Soter
162–150

Antiochus VI Epiphanes Dionysus
145 (143)–142 (141)

Demetrius II Nicator
145–139 (138) and
129 (128)–125

Antiochus VII Sidetes
139 (138)–129 (128)

Antiochus VIII Grypus
125 (124)–113 and 111–96

Antiochus IX Philopator (Cyzicenus)
116–95

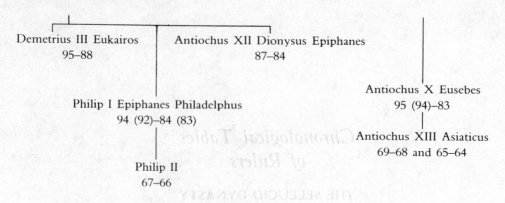

Demetrius III Eukairos
95–88

Antiochus XII Dionysus Epiphanes
87–84

Antiochus X Eusebes
95 (94)–83

Philip I Epiphanes Philadelphus
94 (92)–84 (83)

Antiochus XIII Asiaticus
69–68 and 65–64

Philip II
67–66

THE HOUSE OF THE MACCABEES (HASMONEANS)

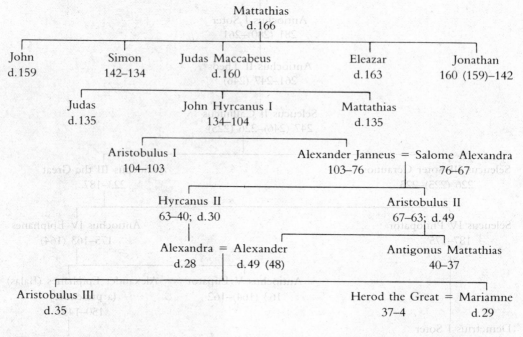

Mattathias
d.166

John
d.159

Simon
142–134

Judas Maccabeus
d.160

Eleazar
d.163

Jonathan
160 (159)–142

Judas
d.135

John Hyrcanus I
134–104

Mattathias
d.135

Aristobulus I
104–103

Alexander Janneus = Salome Alexandra
103–76   76–67

Hyrcanus II
63–40; d.30

Aristobulus II
67–63; d.49

Alexandra = Alexander
d.28   d.49 (48)

Antigonus Mattathias
40–37

Aristobulus III
d.35

Herod the Great = Mariamne
37–4   d.29

These two family trees include the names of the more important rulers. The presence of short parallel lines between two names indicates marriage. The date of an individual's death or the dates of his rule are in some cases disputed, and alternative possibilities are given within parentheses. All the dates are B.C. Besides the standard works on the chronology of the intertestamental period, special mention should be made of F. M. Heichelheim's "Chronological Table from 323–30 B.C." in *Proceedings of the IX International Congress of Papyrology*, Oslo, 1958, pp. 163–182 (also published separately by the Norwegian Universities Press). Seleucus I became king in the seventh year of the Seleucid era; see A. J. Sachs and D. J. Wiseman, "A Babylonian King List of the Hellenistic Period," *Iraq*, xvi (1954), p. 205. Syria became a Roman province in 64 B.C., and Pompey conquered Jerusalem in 63 B.C.

Introduction to the Apocryphal/Deuterocanonical Books

MEANINGS AND USAGE OF THE TERMS "APOCRYPHAL" AND "DEUTEROCANONICAL"

The word "apocrypha" is used in a variety of ways that can be confusing to the general reader. Confusion arises partly from the ambiguity of the ancient usage of the word, and partly from the modern application of the term to different groups of books. Etymologically the word means "things that are hidden," but why it was chosen to describe certain books is not clear. Some have suggested that the books were "hidden" or withdrawn from common use because they were deemed to contain mysterious or esoteric lore, too profound to be communicated to any except the initiated (compare 2 Esd 14.45–46). Others have suggested that the term was employed by those who held that such books deserved to be "hidden" because they were spurious or heretical. Thus it appears that in antiquity the term had an honorable significance as well as a derogatory one, depending upon the point of view of those who made use of the word.

According to traditional usage "Apocrypha" has been the designation applied to the fifteen books, or portions of books, listed below. (In many earlier editions of the Apocrypha, the Letter of Jeremiah is incorporated as the final chapter of the Book of Baruch; hence in these editions there are fourteen books.)

Tobit

Judith

The Additions to the Book of Esther
(contained in the Greek version of Esther)

The Wisdom of Solomon

Ecclesiasticus,
or the Wisdom of Jesus son of Sirach

Baruch

The Letter of Jeremiah

The Prayer of Azariah and the Song of the Three Jews

Susanna

Bel and the Dragon

1 Maccabees

2 Maccabees

1 Esdras

The Prayer of Manasseh

2 Esdras

In addition, the present expanded edition includes the following three texts that are of special interest to Eastern Orthodox readers (see p. iv):

3 Maccabees   4 Maccabees   Psalm 151

None of these books is included in the Hebrew canon of Holy Scripture. All of them, however, with the exception of 2 Esdras, are present in copies of the Greek version of the Old Testament known as the Septuagint. The Old Latin translations of the Old Testament, made from the Septuagint, also include them, along with 2 Esdras. As a consequence, many of the early Church Fathers quoted most of these books as authoritative Scripture (see p. vi AP).

At the end of the fourth century Pope Damasus commissioned Jerome, the most learned biblical scholar of his day, to prepare a standard Latin version of the Scriptures (the Latin Vulgate). In the Old Testament Jerome followed the Hebrew canon and by means of prefaces called the reader's attention to the separate category of the apocryphal books. Subsequent copyists of the Latin Bible, however, were not always careful to transmit Jerome's prefaces, and during the medieval period the Western Church generally regarded these books as part of the holy Scriptures. In 1546 the Council of Trent decreed that the canon of the Old Testament includes them (except the Prayer of Manasseh and 1 and 2 Esdras). Subsequent editions of the Latin Vulgate text, officially approved by the Roman Catholic Church, contain these books incorporated within the sequence of the Old Testament books. Thus Tobit and Judith stand after Nehemiah; the Wisdom of Solomon and Ecclesiasticus stand after the Song of Solomon; Baruch (with the Letter of Jeremiah as chapter 6) stands after Lamentations; and 1 and 2 Maccabees conclude the books of the Old Testament. An appendix after the New Testament contains the Prayer of Manasseh and 1 and 2 Esdras, without implying canonical status.

Editions of the Bible prepared by Protestants have followed the Hebrew canon. The disputed books have generally been placed in a separate section, usually bound between the Old and New Testaments, but occasionally placed after the close of the New Testament.

Modern Roman Catholic scholars commonly employ a distinction introduced by Sixtus of Sienna in 1566 to designate the two groups of books. The terms "protocanonical" and "deuterocanonical" are used to signify respectively those books of Scripture that were received by the entire Church from the beginning as inspired, and those whose inspiration came to be recognized later, after the matter had been disputed by certain Fathers and local churches. Thus Roman Catholics accept as fully canonical those books and parts of books that Protestants call the Apocrypha (except the Prayer of Manasseh and 1 and 2 Esdras, which both groups regard as apocryphal). In short, as a popular Roman Catholic Catechism puts it, "*Deuterocanonical* does not mean *Apocryphal,* but simply 'later added to the canon.' "

The Eastern Orthodox Churches recognize several other books as authoritative. Editions of the Old Testament approved by the Holy Synod of the Greek Orthodox Church contain, besides the Deuterocanonical books, 1 Esdras, Psalm 151, the Prayer of Manasseh, and 3 Maccabees, while 4 Maccabees stands in an appendix. Slavonic Bibles approved by the Russian Orthodox Church contain, besides the Deuterocanonical books, 1 and 2 Esdras (called 2 and 3 Esdras), Psalm 151, and 3 Maccabees.

Besides the books that are included in the present edition, many other Jewish and Jewish-Christian works have survived from the period between about 200 B.C. to about A.D. 200. Since most of these profess to have been written by ancient worthies of Israel, who lived long before the books were actually composed, they are generally called "pseudepigrapha," meaning writings "falsely ascribed." (For a description of several of the more noteworthy pseudepigrapha, see pp. xi–xii AP.)

KINDS OF LITERATURE

The apocryphal/deuterocanonical books represent several different literary genres, including the historical, novelistic, didactic, devotional, epistolary, and apocalyptic types. Though several of the books combine material belonging to more than one of these genres, most of the books can be classified as predominantly of one type or another. Thus 1 Esdras, 1 Maccabees, and, in a certain sense, 2 Maccabees belong to the genre of historical writing. Second Maccabees, which is characterized by bombastic rhetoric, fiery arguments, exaggerated numbers, and superabundant use of invectives against the enemies of Jewish orthodoxy, falls more precisely into the category, then so popular in the Hellenistic world, known as "pathetic history"—a type of literature that uses all possible means to strike the imagination and move the emotions of the reader.

Ostensibly historical but actually quite imaginative are the books of Tobit, Judith, Susanna, and Bel and the Dragon, which may be called moralistic novels. In fact, the last two are noteworthy as ancient examples of the detective story.

Of a serious and didactic nature are the two treatises on wisdom, the Wisdom of Solomon and Ecclesiasticus, or the Wisdom of Jesus son of Sirach. The latter shows particularly close connections with the style and content of the Old Testament book of Proverbs, from which it is a natural development.

The Prayer of Manasseh takes its place with devotional literature of a relatively high order. The psalmody of the Prayer of Azariah and the Song of the Three Jews is of a decidedly liturgical cast.

The Old Testament contains no books that are in the form of a letter, but twenty-one of the twenty-seven books of the New Testament are in epistolary form. The Letter of Jeremiah, which dates from inter-testamental times, may have provided later writers with an example of how this literary form could be used for religious purposes, a form that offers the possibility of combining profound theological content with a direct personal approach to the reader.

Finally, 2 Esdras, a book that purports to reveal the future, is a specimen of the type of literature called apocalyptic (see "Apocalyptic Literature," pp. 362–363 NT). An apocalypse is literally "an unveiling." Like the last six chapters of Daniel in the Old Testament and the book of Revelation in the New Testament, which also are apocalypses, 2 Esdras includes many symbols involving mysterious numbers, strange beasts, and the disclosure of hitherto hidden truths through angelic visitants.

Despite the diversities of literary form, most of which are parallel to, or developments from, similar genres in the Old Testament, the attentive reader of the Apocrypha will be struck by the absence of the prophetic element. From first to last these books bear testimony to the assertion of the Jewish historian Josephus (*Against Apion,* i.8), that "the exact succession of the prophets" had been broken after the close of the Hebrew canon of the Old Testament. Sometimes there is a direct confession that the gift of prophecy had departed (1 Macc 9.27); at other times a hope is expressed that it might one day return (1 Macc 4.46; 14.41). When a writer imitates the prophetic character, as in the book of Baruch, he repeats with slight modifications the language of the older prophets. But the introductory phrase, "Thus says the LORD," which occurs so frequently in the Old Testament, is conspicuous by its absence from the apocryphal/deuterocanonical books.

DIVERGENT ATTITUDES IN THE CHRISTIAN CHURCH

Ecclesiastical opinions concerning the nature and worth of the books of the Apocrypha have varied with age and place.

None of the authors of the books of the New Testament makes a direct quotation from any of the fifteen books of the Apocrypha, though frequent quotations occur from most of the thirty-nine books of the Hebrew canon of the Old Testament. On the other hand, several New Testament writers make occasional allusions to one or more apocryphal books. For example, what seem to be literary echoes from the Wisdom of Solomon are present in Paul's Letter to the Romans (compare Rom 1.20–29 with Wis 13.5,8; 14.24,27; and Rom 9.20–23 with Wis 12.12,20; 15.7) and in his correspondence with the Corinthians (compare 2 Cor 5.1,4 with Wis 9.15). The short Letter of James, a typical bit of "wisdom literature" in the New Testament, contains allusions not only to the Old Testament book of Proverbs but to gnomic sayings in Sirach as well (compare Jas 1.19 with Sir 5.11; and Jas 1.13 with Sir 15.11–12).

During the early Christian centuries most Greek and Latin Church Fathers, such as Irenaeus, Tertullian, Clement of Alexandria, and Cyprian (none of whom knew any Hebrew), quoted passages from the Greek text of apocryphal/deuterocanonical books as "Scripture," "divine Scripture," "inspired," and the like. In this period only an occasional Father made an effort to learn the limits of the Palestinian Jewish canon (as Melito of Sardis) or to distinguish between the Hebrew text of Daniel and the addition of the story of Susanna in the Greek version (as Africanus).

In the fourth century many Greek Fathers (including Eusebius, Athanasius, Cyril of Jerusalem, Gregory of Nazianzus, Amphilochius, and Epiphanius) came to recognize a distinction between the books in the Hebrew canon and the rest, though the latter were still customarily cited as Scripture. During the following centuries usage fluctuated in the East, but at the important Synod of Jerusalem in 1672 the books of Tobit, Judith, Ecclesiasticus, and Wisdom were expressly designated as canonical.

In the Latin Church, on the other hand, though opinion has not been unanimous, a generally high regard for these books has prevailed. More than one local synodical council (e.g. Hippo, A.D. 393, and Carthage, 397 and 419) justified and authorized their use as Scripture. The so-called *Decretum Gelasianum,* a Latin document handed down most frequently under the name of Pope Gelasius (A.D. 492–496), but in some manuscripts as the work of Damasus (366–384) or Hormisdas (514–523), contains, among other material, lists of the books to be read as divine Scripture and of books to be avoided as apocryphal. The former list, which is not present in all the manuscripts, includes among the biblical books Tobit, Judith, Wisdom, Ecclesiasticus, and 1 and 2 Maccabees. Irrespective of the problem of its authorship (many scholars today believe it to be the work of a cleric who lived in south Gaul), the list without doubt reflects the views of the Roman Church at the beginning of the sixth century.

There were, however, occasional voices raised to question the legitimacy of regarding the disputed books as Scripture. At the close of the fourth century, Jerome spoke out decidedly for the Hebrew canon, declaring unreservedly that books that were outside that canon should be classed as apocryphal. When he prepared his celebrated revision of the Latin Bible, the Vulgate, he scrupulously separated the apocryphal Additions to Daniel and Esther, marking them with prefatory notes as absent from the original Hebrew. But, as was remarked above, subsequent scribes were not always careful to transmit Jerome's explanatory material, and during the Middle Ages most readers of the Latin Bible made no distinction between the two classes of books. It is noteworthy, however, that throughout these centuries more than one highly respected ecclesiastical writer (such as Gregory the Great, Walafrid Strabo, Hugh of St. Victor, Hugh of St. Cher, and Nicholas of Lyra), being influenced by the great authority of Jerome, raised theoretical doubts about the disputed books.

Toward the close of the fourteenth century John Wyclif ("the father of English prose") and his disciples, Nicholas of Hereford and John Purvey, produced the first English version of the Bible (see "English Versions of the Bible," pp. 400–406). This translation, having been rendered from the Latin Vulgate, included all of the disputed books, with the exception of 2 Esdras. In the Prologue to the Old Testament, however, a distinction is made between the books of the Hebrew canon, which are thereupon enumerated, and the others which, the writer says, "shal be set among apocrifa, that is, with outen autorite of bileue." In the case of the books of Esther and Daniel, the translators included a rendering of Jerome's notes calling the reader's attention to the additions.

In the controversies that arose at the time of the Reformation, Protestant leaders soon recognized the need to distinguish between books that were authoritative for the establishment of doctrine and those that were not. Thus, disputes over the doctrines of Purgatory and of the efficacy of prayers and Masses for the dead inevitably involved discussion concerning the authority of 2 Maccabees, which contains what was held to be scriptural warrant for them (12.43–45).

The first extensive discussion of the canon from the Protestant point of view was a treatise in Latin, *De Canonicis Scripturis Libellus,* published at Wittenberg in 1520 by Andreas Bodenstein, who is commonly known as Carlstadt, the name of his birthplace. Besides distinguishing the canonical books of the Hebrew Old Testament from the books of the Apocrypha, Carlstadt classified the latter into two divisions. Of one group, containing Wisdom, Ecclesiasticus, Judith, Tobit, and 1 and 2 Maccabees, he says, "These are Apocrypha, that is, are outside the Hebrew canon; yet they are holy writings" (sect. 114). In explaining his view of the status and worth of such books as Tobit, Wisdom, and Ecclesiasticus, he writes:

> What they contain is not to be despised at once; still it is not right that Christians should relieve, much less slake, their thirst with them. . . . Before all things the best books must be read, that is, those that are canonical beyond all controversy; afterwards, if one has the time, it is allowed to peruse the controverted books, provided that you have the set purpose of comparing and collating the non-canonical books with those which are truly canonical (sect. 118).

The second group of apocryphal books, namely 1 and 2 Esdras, Baruch, Prayer of Manasseh, and the Additions to Daniel, Carlstadt declared to be filled with ridiculous puerilities worthy of the censor's ban, and therefore to be contemptuously discarded.

The first Bible in a modern vernacular to segregate the apocryphal books from the others was the Dutch Bible published by Jacob van Liesveldt in 1526 at Antwerp. After Malachi there follows a section embodying the Apocrypha, which is entitled, "The books which are not in the canon, that is to say, which one does not find among the Jews in the Hebrew."

The first edition of the Swiss-German Bible, prepared by ministers of the Church in Zurich, was published in six volumes (Zurich, 1527–29), the fifth of which contains the Apocrypha. The title page of this volume states, "These are the books which are not reckoned as biblical by the ancients, nor are found among the Hebrews." A one-volume edition of the Zurich Bible, which appeared in 1530, contains the apocryphal books grouped together after the New Testament. In commenting on the attitude of Protestants respecting the disputed books, Œcolampadius, perhaps on the whole the best representative of the Swiss Reformers, declared in a formal statement issued in 1530: "We do not despise Judith, Tobit, Ecclesiasticus, Baruch, the last two books of Esdras, the three books of Maccabees, the Additions to Daniel; but we do not allow them divine authority with the others."

In reaction to Protestant criticism of the disputed books, on April 8, 1546, the Council of Trent gave what is regarded by Roman Catholics as the first infallible and effectually promulgated declaration on the canon of the Holy Scriptures. After enumerating the books, which in the Old Testament include Tobit, Judith, Wisdom, Ecclesiasticus, Baruch, and the two books of Maccabees, the decree pronounces an anathema upon anyone who "does not accept as sacred and canonical the aforesaid books in their entirety and with all their parts, as they have been accustomed to be read in the Catholic Church and as they are contained in the old Latin Vulgate Edition" (trans. by Father H. J. Schroeder). The reference to "books in their entirety and with all their parts" is intended to cover the Letter of Jeremiah as chapter 6 of Baruch, the Additions to Esther, and the chapters in Daniel concerning the Song of the Three Jews, Susanna, and Bel and the Dragon. It is noteworthy, however, that the Prayer of Manasseh and 1 and 2 Esdras, though included in some manuscripts of the Latin Vulgate, were denied canonical status by the Council. In the official edition of the Vulgate, published in 1592, these three are printed as an appendix after the New Testament, "lest they should perish altogether."

In England, though Protestants were unanimous in declaring that the apocryphal books were not to be used to establish any doctrine, differences arose as to the proper use and place of non-canonical books. The milder view prevailed in the Church of England, and the lectionary attached to the Book of Common Prayer, from 1549 onward, has always contained prescribed lessons from the Apocrypha. In reply to those who urged the discontinuance of reading lessons from apocryphal books, as being inconsistent with the sufficiency of Scripture, the bishops at the Savoy Conference, held in 1661, replied that the same objection could be raised against the preaching of sermons, and that it was much to be desired that all sermons should give as useful instruction as did the chapters selected from the Apocrypha.

A more strict point of view was taken by the Puritans, who felt uneasy that there should be any books included within the covers of the Bible besides those that they regarded as authoritative. In time this aversion to associating merely human books with those acknowledged as the only sacred and canonical ones found a natural expression in the publication of editions of the Bible from which the section devoted to the Apocrypha was omitted. The earliest copies of the English Bible that excluded the Apocrypha are certain Geneva Bibles printed in 1599 mainly in the Low Countries. The omission of the sheets containing the Apocrypha was presumably due to those responsible for binding the copies, for the titles of the apocryphal books occur in the table of contents at the beginning of the edition.

It would seem that the practice of issuing copies of the Bible without the Apocrypha continued, for in 1615 George Abbot, Archbishop of Canterbury, who had been one of the translators of the King James Version of 1611, directed public notices to be given that no Bibles were to be bound up and sold without the Apocrypha on pain of a whole year's imprisonment. Despite the severe penalty, however, not a few printings of the King James Version appeared in London and Cambridge without the Apocrypha; copies lacking the disputed books are dated 1616, 1618, 1620, 1622, 1626, 1627, 1629, 1630, and 1633. Like the copies of the Geneva Bible of 1599, these seem to have been the work of publishers who wished to satisfy a growing demand for less bulky and less expensive editions of the Bible.

During subsequent centuries the editions of Bibles that lacked the books of the Apocrypha came to outnumber by far those that included them, and soon it became difficult to obtain ordinary editions of the King James Version containing the Apocrypha.

THE PERVASIVE INFLUENCE OF THESE BOOKS

Most readers will probably be surprised to learn how pervasive the influence of the Apocrypha has been over the centuries. Not only have these books inspired homilies, meditations, and liturgical forms, but poets, dramatists, composers, and artists have drawn freely upon them for subject matter. Common proverbs and familiar names are derived from their pages. Even the discovery of the New World was due in part to the influence of a passage in 2 Esdras upon Christopher Columbus. In what follows the reader will find a representative selection of such examples, most of them chosen from *An Introduction to the Apocrypha* by B. M. Metzger (Oxford University Press), and arranged under the headings of (*a*) English Literature, (*b*) Music, (*c*) Art, and (*d*) Miscellaneous.

(*a*) English Literature. Sometime during the ninth or the tenth century an unknown poet, using the West-Saxon dialect, turned the story of Judith into an Old English epic of twelve cantos, transforming at the same time the heroine into a Christian. It is thought that the poem was written to celebrate the prowess of Æthelflæd, "The Lady of the Mercians," who, like the indomitable Judith, delivered her people from the fury of invaders, the heathen Northmen.

During the fourteenth and fifteenth centuries a poem called "The Pistill [i.e. Epistle] of Swete Susan" circulated in Scotland. Written in stanzas of thirteen lines and characterized by an unusual combination of alliteration and rhyme, the ancient apocryphal story was adorned with many imaginative details by the author, thought to have been a certain Huchown (Hugh) of Ayrshire in western Scotland.

How conversant Shakespeare was with the contents of the Bible is a question that, like many another concerning the bard of Avon, has been keenly debated. In any case, it is a fact that two of the poet's daughters bore the names of two of the chief heroines of the Apocrypha—Susanna and Judith—and, what is of greater significance, allusions to about eighty passages from eleven books of the Apocrypha have been identified in his plays.

Noteworthy among American writers who have drawn upon the Apocrypha for themes as well as subject matter is Henry Wadsworth Longfellow. His *New England Tragedies* contains references to 1 and 2 Maccabees, and the chief episodes of the courageous Maccabean uprising are included in his poetic dramatization, *Judas Maccabaeus*.

(*b*) Music. More than one hymn writer has drawn inspiration, as well as, in some cases, the words themselves, from the Apocrypha. For example, the exalted hymn of thanksgiving, "Nun danket alle Gott," written by Pastor Martin Rinkart about 1636 when the devastating Thirty Years War was nearing its end, is dependent upon Luther's translation of Sir 50.22–24. Two stanzas of the hymn, as translated by Catherine Winkworth, will show the amount of borrowing (here printed in italics):

Now thank we all our God
  With heart and hands and voices,
Who wondrous things hath done,
  In whom His world rejoices;
Who, from our mother's arms,
  Hath blessed us on our way
With countless gifts of love,
  And still is ours today.

O may this bounteous God
  Through all our life be near us,
With ever joyful hearts
  And blessed peace to cheer us;
And keep us in His grace,
  And guide us when perplexed,
And free us from all ills
  In this world and the next.

Strange though it may seem, ideas included in the Christmas hymn, "It Came upon the Midnight Clear," are traceable to the Old Testament Apocrypha. In the New Testament accounts of the Nativity, nothing is said of the exact time of Jesus' birth. The subsequent identification of the hour of his birth as midnight is doubtless due to the influence of a remarkable passage in the Wisdom of Solomon. At an early century in the Christian era the imagination of more than one Church Father was caught by pseudo-Solomon's vivid reference to the time when

God's "all-powerful word [the Logos] leaped from heaven, from the royal throne," namely when "night in its swift course was now half gone" (Wis 18.14–15). Despite the context of the passage, which speaks of the destruction of the first-born Egyptians at the time of the Exodus, the words were interpreted as referring to the Incarnation of the eternal Word of God, Jesus Christ. Thus by a curious, not to say ironical, twist of fortune, a passage that tells of a stern warrior with a sharp sword filling a doomed land with death has had a share in fixing popular traditions concerning the time and circumstances of the birth of the Prince of Peace.

The influence of the Apocrypha can also be traced in many an anthem, cantata, oratorio, and opera. Handel's oratorios *Susanna* and *Judas Maccabaeus,* as well as his *Alexander Balus,* an historical sequel to the latter, will occur at once to music lovers. At an early date in operatic history the stirring story of Judith was found to lend itself admirably to dramatic presentation. Italian and German operas on this theme were written by Andrea Salvadori, Marco da Gagliano, Martin Opitz, and Joachim Beccau. In the nineteenth century the noted Russian pianist and composer, Anton Rubenstein, published *The Maccabees,* an opera of monumental proportions, the libretto of which was written by one of his collaborators, Dr. H. S. von Mosenthal.

(*c*) Art. During the Renaissance and later, many painters chose subjects from the deuterocanonical books. Almost every large gallery in Europe and America has one or more works of the old masters depicting Judith, Tobit, or Susanna, who were the three most popular subjects from these books.

Besides paintings, down through the ages artists in almost every other medium have chosen themes from the Apocrypha. Were space available here for an inventory, examples could be cited from such divergent types of *objets d'art* as mosaics, frescoes, gems, ivories, sarcophagi, enameled plaques, terra cottas, stained glass, manuscript illumination, sculpture, and tapestries.

(*d*) Miscellaneous. The influence of the Apocrypha in everyday life can be observed in the currency of such names as Edna, Susanna (or one of its many derivatives, such as Susan, Suzanne, and Sue), Judith (or Judy), Raphael, and Tobias (or Toby).

The word "macabre," according to the opinion of several lexicographers, may be derived ultimately from "Maccabee," alluding to the grisly and gruesome tortures inflicted upon the Jewish martyrs.

Some of the most common expressions and proverbs have come from the Apocrypha. The sententious sayings, "A good name endures forever" and "You can't touch pitch without being defiled," are derived from Sir 41.13 and 13.1. The noble affirmation in 1 Esd 4.41, "Great is Truth, and mighty above all things" (King James Version), or its Latin form, *Magna est veritas et praevalet,* has been used frequently as a motto or maxim in a wide variety of contexts.

A passage from the Apocrypha encouraged Christopher Columbus in the enterprise that resulted in his discovery of the New World. To be sure, the verse in 2 Esdras is an erroneous comment upon the Genesis narrative of creation, and Columbus was mistaken in attributing its authority to the "prophet Ezra" of the Old Testament, but—for all that—it played a significant part in pushing back the earth's horizons, both figuratively and literally. The words of 2 Esd 6.42 concerning God's work of creation ("On the third day you commanded the waters to be gathered together in a seventh part of the earth; six parts you dried up and kept so that some of them might be planted and cultivated and be of service before you") led Columbus to reason that, if only one-seventh of the earth's surface is covered with water, the ocean between the west coast of Europe and the east coast of Asia could be no great width and might be navigated in a few days with a fair wind. It was partly by quoting this verse from what was regarded as an authoritative book that Columbus managed to persuade Ferdinand and Isabella of Spain to provide the necessary financial support for his voyage.

OTHER APOCRYPHAL AND PSEUDEPIGRAPHICAL LITERATURE

Besides the fifteen books or parts of books that are traditionally called the Apocrypha, there are many other Jewish or Jewish-Christian works, dating from the centuries immediately before and after the beginning of the Christian era, which for a time were popular among certain groups of Jews and in early Eastern Churches. It is customary (though not entirely appropriate) to classify these writings as Palestinian pseudepigrapha (those composed in Hebrew or Aramaic) and Alexandrian pseudepigrapha (those composed in Greek). Of the scores of such documents that are known to have circulated more or less widely, the following have been chosen as representative examples. (For a definition of pseudepigrapha, see p. iv AP.)

(a) Palestinian pseudepigrapha. The Book of Jubilees is a legendary expansion of Gen 1.1–Ex 12.47, written in Hebrew not long before 100 B.C. by an unknown author of nationalist and rigoristic outlook, who deplored contemporary laxity. It attempts to show that the Mosaic law, with its prescriptions about festivals, the Sabbath offerings, abstinence from blood and from fornication (which for the writer includes intermarriage with Gentiles), was promulgated in patriarchal times, and indeed existed eternally with God in heaven. Events recorded in Genesis are dated exactly (but fictitiously) according to the jubilee (every forty-nine years) and its subdivisions. The book has been transmitted in its entirety in an Ethiopic translation, and portions of the text survive in Greek, Latin, and Syriac versions. At about the middle of the present century five fragmentary manuscripts of Jubilees, written in a good style of Hebrew, were discovered at Qumran by the Dead Sea. These manuscripts, which preserve portions of fifteen of the fifty chapters of the book, show that the Latin and Ethiopic versions are faithful translations of the original.

In addition to the 150 psalms comprising the Book of Psalms in the Hebrew Bible, during the intertestamental period other psalms were composed in Hebrew and in other languages. One of these, which celebrates the prowess of young David in slaying Goliath, is appended (as Ps 151) to the Psalter in Greek manuscripts. Part of this psalm (see pp. 283–284 AP) came to be incorporated in the Ethiopian coronation ritual.

The Psalms of Solomon is a collection of eighteen songs of generally exalted sentiments, composed in Hebrew during the last century B.C. They are extant today in Greek and Syriac. The author, who is usually thought to reflect Pharisaic polemic against Sadducean dominance in the religious ceremonial of his day, looked forward to the time when the Messiah would reign as king at Jerusalem. According to an extended description of the coming Messiah (chs 17–18), he is to be sinless, strong through the spirit of holiness, gaining his wisdom from God, shepherding the flock of the Lord with fidelity and righteousness, and conquering the entire heathen world without warfare, "by the word of his mouth."

The book of Enoch, also called 1 Enoch or Ethiopic Enoch, is a heterogeneous collection of apocalypses and other material written by several authors in Aramaic (or Hebrew) during the last two centuries B.C. It embodies a series of revelations, of which Enoch is the professed recipient, on such matters as the origin of evil, the angels and their destinies, the nature of Gehenna and Paradise, and the pre-existent Messiah. Interspersed throughout the lengthy and rambling work are sections that have been called "the book of celestial physics." These sections, which are one of the curiosities of ancient pseudo-scientific literature, set forth contemporary speculations concerning such meteorological and astronomical phenomena as lightning, hail, snow, the twelve winds, the heavenly luminaries, and the like. The entire work is preserved in an Ethiopic translation, which includes what have been thought to be Christian interpolations in chs 37–71, where the Messiah is called the Son of Man. Portions of the book are extant in Greek and Latin; recently eight manuscripts of part of the work (but not chs 37–71) have turned up in Aramaic at Qumran. It is of interest that a quotation from the book of Enoch (1.9) occurs in the New Testament letter of Jude (vv. 14–15).

(*b*) Alexandrian pseudepigrapha. Third Maccabees is a religious novel written in Greek by an Alexandrian Jew sometime between 100 B.C. and A.D. 70. The title is a misnomer, for the book has nothing to do with the Maccabees. With many legendary embellishments the author recounts three stories of conflict between Ptolemy IV (221–203 B.C.) and the Jews of Egypt. The most dramatic section describes how the Jews were herded into the hippodrome near Alexandria, to be trampled under the feet of intoxicated elephants. After the king's purpose had been several times providentially delayed, it was finally foiled by a vision of angels which turned the elephants upon the persecutors.

Fourth Maccabees is a Greek philosophical treatise addressed to Jews on the supremacy of devout reason over the passions of body and soul. In the form of a Stoic diatribe, or popular address, the author begins with a philosophical exposition of his theme, which he then illustrates with examples drawn from 2 Maccabees. He describes at length the gruesome tortures that tested the fortitude of Eleazar, the seven brothers, and their mother, all of whom preferred death to committing apostasy. The book was probably written by a Hellenistic Jew of Alexandria at some time later than 2 Maccabees and before A.D. 70. In early Christianity the Maccabean martyrs were eventually canonized and accorded a yearly festival in the ecclesiastical calendar (August 1).

From what has been said above the reader will be able to form some opinion of the importance of apocryphal and pseudepigraphical literature, both for its own sake as well as for the information it supplies concerning the development of Jewish life and thought just prior to the beginning of the Christian era. The stirring political fortunes of the Jews in the time of the Maccabees; the rise of what has been called normative Judaism, and the emergence of the sects of the Pharisees and the Sadducees; the lush growth of popular belief in the activities of angels and demons, and the use of apotropaic magic to avert the malevolent influence of the latter; the growing preoccupation concerning original sin and its relation to the "evil inclination" present in every person; the blossoming of apocalyptic hopes relating to the coming Messiah, the resurrection of the body, and the vindication of the righteous—all these and many other topics receive welcome light from the apocryphal/deuterocanonical books.

(a) The following books and parts of books are recognized as Deuterocanonical Scripture by the Roman Catholic, Greek, and Russian Orthodox Churches.

Tobit

The book of Tobit is named after a generous and God-fearing Jew whose blindness and poverty in Nineveh are the direct result of his performing one of his most characteristic good deeds, namely, burying an executed fellow-Jew. Thanks to the courageous efforts of his devoted son Tobias, who is assisted by the angel Raphael disguised as Azariah, Tobit not only recovers his sight and fortune but also gains a pious daughter-in-law, Sarah. From her, Tobias exorcises Asmodeus, the demon who had claimed the lives of her seven previous husbands on their wedding night. On his deathbed, Tobit has Tobias promise to move the family from Nineveh to Ecbatana, where Tobias lives to a rich old age.

Despite all its trappings as an historical account, Tobit is best understood as a romance of Diaspora Judaism, relating the outcome of a successful quest. The tale is intended to entertain as well as to inspire faith in God and human effort. Without Tobias' own devotion and courage, neither Tobit nor Sarah would have been delivered, the help of Raphael notwithstanding.

The author created his narrative out of three well-known secular folktales: (1) the tale of the Grateful Dead (the story about a man who is impoverished but ultimately rewarded for burying an abused corpse); (2) the tale of the Monster in the Bridal Chamber (the story of a demon who kills the bride's husbands on their wedding night); and (3) the tale of Ahiqar (the account of a wise courtier who, though falsely incriminated by his adopted son, is vindicated).

The distinctive structure, images, and spirit of the book come, however, from the Hebrew Bible. Although only Amos and Nahum are actually mentioned, other biblical books are far more influential for the story, notably Genesis (with its stories of the betrothals of Isaac and Jacob), Job, and Isaiah (especially with regard to the Exile and the Return). Deuteronomy's doctrine of retribution (i.e. ultimately the righteous are rewarded and the wicked punished) provides the basic theology for Tobit.

Even though there is a strong cultic concern in chs 1–3 and a vision of a new and greater Jerusalem and temple in chs 13–14, the book's primary emphasis is on the everyday practical, moral, and sapiental aspects of being and doing good. The entire book—its plot, characters, and message—is ironic, since the reader's knowledge of the situation of the characters is greater than that of the characters themselves. Tobit's name ("God is my good") and those of the other major human characters are ironic, especially at the height of their personal anguish. The book's irony is purchased at the cost of a loss of suspense, the reader assured by ch 3 that Tobit and Sarah will be delivered; and by ch 6, how.

The author effectively uses a wide variety of literary techniques to express his religious ideas: monologue and dialogue, prayers and hymns, demonology and angelology, wisdom sayings, and death-bed testimony. The personalities of the main characters are clearly and individually developed. Despite their individual shortcomings, they are good but quite ordinary people, with none of the heroic stature of such other exilic characters as Daniel, Esther, or Judith.

The author of Tobit was a Jew, writing originally in Hebrew or Aramaic (copies of it in those languages have been found at Qumran), probably somewhere between 225–175 B.C., and, possibly, in Palestine.

Tobit is represented by three major Greek recensions and two Latin translations. Unlike the RSV, the NRSV of Tobit is based upon the Sinaiticus family as supplemented by the Old Latin. There are also some late Hebrew translations, which are based upon a Greek text, as are the older Syriac, Ethiopic, and Sahidic versions.

1 This book tells the story of Tobit son of Tobiel son of Hananiel son of Aduel son of Gabael son of Raphael^a of the descendants of Asiel, of the tribe of Naphtali, ²who in the days of King Shalmaneser^b of the Assyrians was taken into captivity from Thisbe, which is to the south of Kedesh Naphtali in Upper Galilee, above Asher toward the west, and north of Phogor.

3 I, Tobit, walked in the ways of truth and righteousness all the days of my life. I performed many acts of charity for my kindred and my people who had gone with me in exile to Nineveh in the land of the Assyrians. ⁴When I was in my own country, in the land of Israel, while I was still a young man, the whole tribe of my ancestor Naphtali deserted the house of David and Jerusalem. This city had been chosen from among all the tribes of Israel, where all the tribes of Israel should offer sacrifice and where the temple, the dwelling of God, had been consecrated and established for all generations forever.

5 All my kindred and our ancestral house of Naphtali sacrificed to the calf^c that King Jeroboam of Israel had erected in Dan and on all the mountains of Galilee. ⁶But I alone went often to Jerusalem for the festivals, as it is prescribed for all Israel by an everlasting decree. I would hurry off to Jerusalem with the first fruits of the crops and the firstlings of the flock, the tithes of the cattle, and the first shearings of the sheep. ⁷I would give these to the priests, the sons of Aaron, at the altar; likewise the tenth of the grain, wine, olive oil, pomegranates, figs, and the rest of the fruits to the sons of Levi who ministered at Jerusalem. Also for six years I would save up a second tenth in money and go and distribute it in Jerusalem. ⁸A third tenth^d I would give to the orphans and widows and to the converts who had attached themselves to Israel. I would bring it and give it to them in the third year, and we would eat it according to the ordinance decreed concerning it in the law of Moses and according to the instructions of Deborah, the mother of my father Tobiel,^e for my father had died and left me an orphan. ⁹When I be-

a Other ancient authorities lack *son of Raphael son of Raguel*   b Gk *Enemessaros*   c Other ancient authorities read *heifer*   d *A third tenth* added from other ancient authorities   e Lat: Gk *Hananiel*

1.1–2: **Title. 2**: *Shalmaneser* (or rather Sargon; see v. 15 n.) took Samaria, the capital of Israel, in 722 B.C. and transported a large part of the population to Assyria (2 Kings 17.1–6). *Thisbe* is unidentified. *Kedesh Naphtali*, 2 Kings 15.29. *Asher* is probably Hazor; *Phogor* is unknown.
1.3–3.6: **Tobit's own account of his virtuous life and unhappy fate.**
1.3–22: **Tobit's piety brings him into conflict with the king. 3**: *Nineveh* was the capital of Assyria. **4**: Since the rebellion of the northern tribes against Jerusalem (1 Kings 12.19–20) occurred about 922 B.C., Tobit could not have been *still a young man*, or even born, when it happened. Such chronological, topographical, and other historical difficulties make it clear that the story is fiction (compare v. 15 n., 6.2 n., 9.2 n.). **5**: *Calf*, 1 Kings 12.28–29. **6–8**: During the apostasy, Tobit alone remains loyal to the divinely-appointed temple in Jerusalem. **6**: *An everlasting decree*, Deut 12.11, 13–14. **9**: The name *Tobias* means "God is my good."
1.10–12: Even in captivity among Gentiles Tobit refuses to violate the dietary laws. **14**: *Media* is the northern part of modern Iran, east of Assyria. *Ten talents,* while impossible

came a man I married a woman,*f* a member of our own family, and by her I became the father of a son whom I named Tobias.

10 After I was carried away captive to Assyria and came as a captive to Nineveh, everyone of my kindred and my people ate the food of the Gentiles, 11 but I kept myself from eating the food of the Gentiles. 12 Because I was mindful of God with all my heart, 13 the Most High gave me favor and good standing with Shalmaneser,*g* and I used to buy everything he needed. 14 Until his death I used to go into Media, and buy for him there. While in the country of Media I left bags of silver worth ten talents in trust with Gabriel, the brother of Gabri. 15 But when Shalmaneser*g* died, and his son Sennacherib reigned in his place, the highways into Media became unsafe and I could no longer go there.

16 In the days of Shalmaneser*g* I performed many acts of charity to my kindred, those of my tribe. 17 I would give my food to the hungry and my clothing to the naked; and if I saw the dead body of any of my people thrown out behind the wall of Nineveh, I would bury it. 18 I also buried any whom King Sennacherib put to death when he came fleeing from Judea in those days of judgment that the king of heaven executed upon him because of his blasphemies. For in his anger he put to death many Israelites; but I would secretly remove the bodies and bury them. So when Sennacherib looked for them he could not find them. 19 Then one of the Ninevites went and informed the king about me, that I was burying them; so I hid myself. But when I real-ized that the king knew about me and that I was being searched for to be put to death, I was afraid and ran away. 20 Then all my property was confiscated; nothing was left to me that was not taken into the royal treasury except my wife Anna and my son Tobias.

21 But not forty*h* days passed before two of Sennacherib's*i* sons killed him, and they fled to the mountains of Ararat, and his son Esar-haddon*j* reigned after him. He appointed Ahikar, the son of my brother Hanael*k* over all the accounts of his kingdom, and he had authority over the entire administration. 22 Ahikar interceded for me, and I returned to Nineveh. Now Ahikar was chief cupbearer, keeper of the signet, and in charge of administrations of the accounts under King Sennacherib of Assyria; so Esar-haddon*j* reappointed him. He was my nephew and so a close relative.

2 Then during the reign of Esar-haddon*j* I returned home, and my wife Anna and my son Tobias were restored to me. At our festival of Pentecost, which is the sacred festival of weeks, a good dinner was prepared for me and I reclined to eat. 2 When the table was set for me and an abundance of food placed before me, I said to my son Tobias, "Go, my child, and bring whatever poor person you may find of our people among the exiles in Nineveh, who is wholeheartedly mindful of God,*l* and he

---

f Other ancient authorities add *Anna*
g Gk *Enemessaros*   *h* Other ancient authorities read either *forty-five* or *fifty*   *i* Gk *his*
j Gk *Sacherdonos*   *k* Other authorities read *Hananael*   *l* Lat: Gk *wholeheartedly mindful*

---

to equate to present-day purchasing power, it was a substantial sum of money. **1.15–20:** Tobit arouses Sennacherib's wrath and flees the country. **15:** *Shalmaneser* actually died before the fall of Samaria, which was taken by Sargon II. *Sennacherib* succeeded his father Sargon II in 705 B.C. **17:** It was for the Jews a great calamity that a dead body should lie unburied. **21–22:** Under a new king, *Esar-haddon* (681–669 B.C.), Tobit is able to return. **21:** *Ahikar* is patterned after Ahiqar, a legendary ancient wise man whose story survives in several Near-Eastern or Semitic languages. An Aramaic version of his adventures, dating from the fifth century B.C., was found among the Jewish papyri at Elephantine in upper Egypt (see also 14.10 n.).

2.1–14: Another act of charity results in Tobit's blindness and impoverishment. 1: The name *Anna* means "grace." *Pentecost* is approximately *seven weeks* after passover (Lev 23.15–21; Deut 16.9–11). **2:** Generosity toward the poor is one of the virtues taught by this book (4.7–11, 16). **3:** *Strangled,* presum-

shall eat together with me. I will wait for
you, until you come back." [3]So Tobias
went to look for some poor person of our
people. When he had returned he said,
"Father!" And I replied, "Here I am, my
child." Then he went on to say, "Look,
father, one of our own people has been
murdered and thrown into the market
place, and now he lies there strangled."
[4]Then I sprang up, left the dinner before
even tasting it, and removed the body[m]
from the square[n] and laid it[m] in one of
the rooms until sunset when I might
bury it.[m] [5]When I returned, I washed
myself and ate my food in sorrow.
[6]Then I remembered the prophecy of
Amos, how he said against Bethel,[o]

"Your festivals shall be turned
into mourning,
and all your songs into
lamentation."

And I wept.

7 When the sun had set, I went and
dug a grave and buried him. [8]And my
neighbors laughed and said, "Is he still
not afraid? He has already been hunted
down to be put to death for doing this,
and he ran away; yet here he is again
burying the dead!" [9]That same night I
washed myself and went into my courtyard and slept by the wall of the courtyard; and my face was uncovered because of the heat. [10]I did not know that
there were sparrows on the wall; their
fresh droppings fell into my eyes and
produced white films. I went to physicians to be healed, but the more they
treated me with ointments the more my
vision was obscured by the white films,
until I became completely blind. For four
years I remained unable to see. All my
kindred were sorry for me, and Ahikar
took care of me for two years before he
went to Elymais.

11 At that time, also, my wife Anna
earned money at women's work. [12]She
used to send what she made to the owners and they would pay wages to her.
One day, the seventh of Dystrus, when
she cut off a piece she had woven and sent
it to the owners, they paid her full wages
and also gave her a young goat for a
meal. [13]When she returned to me, the
goat began to bleat. So I called her and
said, "Where did you get this goat? It is
surely not stolen, is it? Return it to the
owners; for we have no right to eat anything stolen." [14]But she said to me, "It
was given to me as a gift in addition to
my wages." But I did not believe her,
and told her to return it to the owners. I
became flushed with anger against her
over this. Then she replied to me,
"Where are your acts of charity? Where
are your righteous deeds? These things
are known about you!"[p]

3 Then with much grief and anguish
of heart I wept, and with groaning
began to pray:

2 "You are righteous, O Lord,
and all your deeds are just;
all your ways are mercy and truth;
you judge the world.[q]
3 And now, O Lord, remember me
and look favorably upon me.
Do not punish me for my sins
and for my unwitting offenses
and those that my ancestors
committed before you.
They sinned against you,
4 and disobeyed your
commandments.
So you gave us over to plunder,
exile, and death,
to become the talk, the byword,
and an object of reproach
among all the nations among

---

m Gk *him* *n* Other ancient authorities lack *from the square* *o* Other ancient authorities read *against Bethlehem* *p* Or *to you;* Gk *with you* *q* Other ancient authorities read *you render true and righteous judgment forever*

---

ably executed (compare 1.18). Leaving the body unburied was intended as additional punishment, so Tobit's act of charity was an act of defiance toward the king. **5:** *Washed myself,* ceremonially, after touching a corpse (Num 19.11–13).

2.6: *Prophecy of Amos,* see Am 8.10. **10:** *Elymais,* a city, or possibly a region, in Persia (1 Macc 6.1). **12:** *Dystrus,* the Greek name for the Semitic month of Adar (February-March).

3.1–6: Tobit's prayer.

whom you have dispersed
us.
5 And now your many judgments
are true
in exacting penalty from me for
my sins.
For we have not kept your
commandments
and have not walked in
accordance with truth
before you.
6 So now deal with me as you will;
command my spirit to be taken
from me,
so that I may be released from
the face of the earth and
become dust.
For it is better for me to die than
to live,
because I have had to listen to
undeserved insults,
and great is the sorrow within
me.
Command, O Lord, that I be
released from this distress;
release me to go to the eternal
home,
and do not, O Lord, turn your
face away from me.
For it is better for me to die
than to see so much distress in
my life
and to listen to insults."

7 On the same day, at Ecbatana in
Media, it also happened that Sarah, the
daughter of Raguel, was reproached by
one of her father's maids. [8]For she had
been married to seven husbands, and the
wicked demon Asmodeus had killed
each of them before they had been with
her as is customary for wives. So the
maid said to her, "You are the one who
kills[r] your husbands! See, you have already been married to seven husbands
and have not borne the name of[s] a single

one of them. [9]Why do you beat us? Because your husbands are dead? Go with
them! May we never see a son or daughter of yours!"

10 On that day she was grieved in
spirit and wept. When she had gone up
to her father's upper room, she intended
to hang herself. But she thought it over
and said, "Never shall they reproach my
father, saying to him, 'You had only one
beloved daughter but she hanged herself
because of her distress.' And I shall bring
my father in his old age down in sorrow
to Hades. It is better for me not to hang
myself, but to pray the Lord that I may
die and not listen to these reproaches
anymore." [11]At that same time, with
hands outstretched toward the window,
she prayed and said,

"Blessed are you, merciful God!
Blessed is your name forever;
let all your works praise you
forever.
12 And now, Lord,[t] I turn my face
to you,
and raise my eyes toward you.
13 Command that I be released from
the earth
and not listen to such reproaches
any more.
14 You know, O Master, that I am
innocent
of any defilement with a man,
15 and that I have not disgraced my
name
or the name of my father in the
land of my exile.
I am my father's only child;
he has no other child to be his
heir;
and he has no close relative or
other kindred

r Other ancient authorities read *strangles*
s Other ancient authorities read *have had no
benefit from*   t Other ancient authorities lack
Lord

**3.7–17: God hears the prayer of Tobit,
and also of Sarah, plagued by a demon-
lover.** From this point on the story is told in
the third person, thereby enabling the narrator to know even the thoughts of the characters in the books. **7–10:** Sarah ("Mistress")

contemplates suicide. **7:** *Ecbatana,* capital of
Media, in Persia. **8:** The name *Asmodeus*
means "destroyer" in Hebrew, but he may
represent the Persian demon Aeshma Daeva.
   3.11–15: Sarah's prayer. **11:** *Blessed are you*
is the traditional beginning of a Jewish prayer

for whom I should keep myself
as wife.
Already seven husbands of mine
have died.
Why should I still live?
But if it is not pleasing to you,
O Lord, to take my life,
hear me in my disgrace."
16 At that very moment, the prayers of both of them were heard in the glorious presence of God. 17 So Raphael was sent to heal both of them: Tobit, by removing the white films from his eyes, so that he might see God's light with his eyes; and Sarah, daughter of Raguel, by giving her in marriage to Tobias son of Tobit, and by setting her free from the wicked demon Asmodeus. For Tobias was entitled to have her before all others who had desired to marry her. At the same time that Tobit returned from the courtyard into his house, Sarah daughter of Raguel came down from her upper room.

4 That same day Tobit remembered the money that he had left in trust with Gabael at Rages in Media, 2 and he said to himself, "Now I have asked for death. Why do I not call my son Tobias and explain to him about the money before I die?" 3 Then he called his son Tobias, and when he came to him he said, "My son, when I die, *u* give me a proper burial. Honor your mother and do not abandon her all the days of her life. Do whatever pleases her, and do not grieve

her in anything. 4 Remember her, my son, because she faced many dangers for you while you were in her womb. And when she dies, bury her beside me in the same grave.

5 "Revere the Lord all your days, my son, and refuse to sin or to transgress his commandments. Live uprightly all the days of your life, and do not walk in the ways of wrongdoing; 6 for those who act in accordance with truth will prosper in all their activities. To all those who practice righteousness *v* 7 give alms from your possessions, and do not let your eye begrudge the gift when you make it. Do not turn your face away from anyone who is poor, and the face of God will not be turned away from you. 8 If you have many possessions, make your gift from them in proportion; if few, do not be afraid to give according to the little you have. 9 So you will be laying up a good treasure for yourself against the day of necessity. 10 For almsgiving delivers from death and keeps you from going into the Darkness. 11 Indeed, almsgiving, for all who practice it, is an excellent offering in the presence of the Most High.

12 "Beware, my son, of every kind of fornication. First of all, marry a woman

u Lat v The text of codex Sinaiticus goes directly from verse 6 to verse 19, reading To those who practice righteousness 19the Lord will give good counsel. In order to fill the lacuna verses 7 to 18 are derived from other ancient authorities

---

(compare 8.5, 15 and see Jdt 13.17). **16–17:** The angel Raphael is sent in answer to both the prayers (see 12.12–15 n.). **17:** The name *Raphael* means "God heals." *Entitled to have her,* 6.12. The phrase *at the same time* is a dramatic device which heightens the interest of the story.

4.1–21: Preparing to send his son for the trust-money, Tobit imparts his philosophy of life. 1: *The money . . . at Rages, Rages* was an important city whose ruins are located about five miles southeast of modern Teheran. **5–19:** This section of general ethical counsel epitomizes the moral teaching of the book. There are many close parallels with other biblical books of wisdom, such as Proverbs and Sirach, as well as with wisdom literature of other nations and peoples of the an-

cient Near East. **6:** Morality guarantees prosperity; a dogma of orthodox Hebrew wisdom (Ps 1.1–3; Prov 10.27–30). **7–11:** The value of almsgiving; the emphasis is typical of the books, as well as of the period (12.8–9; 14.10–11; Sir 3.30; 35.2; Mt 6.2–4).

4.12–13: One should marry within his own family group; this is a keynote of the book (1.9; 3.15; 6.11–12). **13:** *Pride,* Prov 16.18. *Idleness,* Prov 19.15; Sir 22.1–2. **14:** Lev 19.13. **15:** *What you hate, do not do,* the Golden Rule (Mt 7.12) which was enunciated also by the great Jewish teacher, Hillel (flourished in the time of Herod the Great, 37–4 B.C.). *Wine,* Prov 23.29–35; Sir 31.29–31. **16:** Compare vv. 7–11. **17:** Placing food on graves was a pagan practice, forbidden in the Hebrew Bible (Deut 26.14) and

from among the descendants of your ancestors; do not marry a foreign woman, who is not of your father's tribe; for we are the descendants of the prophets. Remember, my son, that Noah, Abraham, Isaac, and Jacob, our ancestors of old, all took wives from among their kindred. They were blessed in their children, and their posterity will inherit the land. 13 So now, my son, love your kindred, and in your heart do not disdain your kindred, the sons and daughters of your people, by refusing to take a wife for yourself from among them. For in pride there is ruin and great confusion. And in idleness there is loss and dire poverty, because idleness is the mother of famine.

14 "Do not keep over until the next day the wages of those who work for you, but pay them at once. If you serve God you will receive payment. "Watch yourself, my son, in everything you do, and discipline yourself in all your conduct. 15 And what you hate, do not do to anyone. Do not drink wine to excess or let drunkenness go with you on your way. 16 Give some of your food to the hungry, and some of your clothing to the naked. Give all your surplus as alms, and do not let your eye begrudge your giving of alms. 17 Place your bread on the grave of the righteous, but give none to sinners. 18 Seek advice from every wise person and do not despise any useful counsel. 19 At all times bless the Lord God, and ask him that your ways may be made straight and that all your paths and plans may prosper. For none of the nations has understanding, but the Lord himself will give them good counsel; but if he chooses otherwise, he casts down to deepest Hades. So now, my child, remember these commandments, and do not let them be erased from your heart.

20 "And now, my son, let me explain to you that I left ten talents of silver in trust with Gabael son of Gabrias, at Rages in Media. 21 Do not be afraid, my son, because we have become poor. You have great wealth if you fear God and flee from every sin and do what is good in the sight of the Lord your God."

5 Then Tobias answered his father Tobit, "I will do everything that you have commanded me, father; 2 but how can I obtain the money *w* from him, since he does not know me and I do not know him? What evidence *x* am I to give him so that he will recognize and trust me, and give me the money? Also, I do not know the roads to Media, or how to get there." 3 Then Tobit answered his son Tobias, "He gave me his bond and I gave him my bond. I *y* divided his in two; we each took one part, and I put one with the money. And now twenty years have passed since I left this money in trust. So now, my son, find yourself a trustworthy man to go with you, and we will pay him wages until you return. But get back the money from Gabael." *z*

4 So Tobias went out to look for a man to go with him to Media, someone who was acquainted with the way. He went out and found the angel Raphael standing in front of him; but he did not perceive that he was an angel of God. 5 Tobias *a* said to him, "Where do you come from, young man?" "From your kindred, the Israelites," he replied, "and I have come here to work." Then Tobias *b* said to him, "Do you know the way to go to Media?" 6 "Yes," he replied, "I have been there many times; I am acquainted with it and know all the roads.

w Gk *it*   x Gk *sign*   y Other authorities read *He*   z Gk *from him*   a Gk *He*   b Gk *he*

---

deprecated by many Jews (compare Sir 30.18). Some interpret the verse as a reference to the meals provided the mourners at funerals (compare Jer 16.7; Ezek 24.17); more likely, since this practice is also found in the proverbs of the Aramaic Ahiqar, the passage here is an echo of that proverb. **19**: A sound moral life needs to be sustained by prayer.

5.1–22: Raphael, in the disguise of Azariah, is employed as Tobias' guide. **4**: Tobias *did not perceive that he was an angel,* as frequently in folklore, where angels (or gods) traveling in disguise are a favorite theme (compare Gen ch 18; Heb 13.2). **6**: *A journey of two days,* the distance between Rages and Ecbatana is actually 185 miles.

I have often traveled to Media, and would stay with our kinsman Gabael who lives in Rages of Media. It is a journey of two days from Ecbatana to Rages; for it lies in a mountainous area, while Ecbatana is in the middle of the plain." 7 Then Tobias said to him, "Wait for me, young man, until I go in and tell my father; for I do need you to travel with me, and I will pay you your wages." 8 He replied, "All right, I will wait; but do not take too long."

9 So Tobias*c* went in to tell his father Tobit and said to him, "I have just found a man who is one of our own Israelite kindred!" He replied, "Call the man in, my son, so that I may learn about his family and to what tribe he belongs, and whether he is trustworthy enough to go with you."

10 Then Tobias went out and called him, and said, "Young man, my father is calling for you." So he went in to him, and Tobit greeted him first. He replied, "Joyous greetings to you!" But Tobit retorted, "What joy is left for me any more? I am a man without eyesight; I cannot see the light of heaven, but I lie in darkness like the dead who no longer see the light. Although still alive, I am among the dead. I hear people but I cannot see them." But the young man*c* said, "Take courage; the time is near for God to heal you; take courage." Then Tobit said to him, "My son Tobias wishes to go to Media. Can you accompany him and guide him? I will pay your wages, brother." He answered, "I can go with him and I know all the roads, for I have often gone to Media and have crossed all its plains, and I am familiar with its mountains and all of its roads."

11 Then Tobit*c* said to him, "Brother, of what family are you and from what tribe? Tell me, brother." 12 He replied, "Why do you need to know my tribe?" But Tobit*c* said, "I want to be sure, brother, whose son you are and what

your name is." 13 He replied, "I am Azariah, the son of the great Hananiah, one of your relatives." 14 Then Tobit said to him, "Welcome! God save you, brother. Do not feel bitter toward me, brother, because I wanted to be sure about your ancestry. It turns out that you are a kinsman, and of good and noble lineage. For I knew Hananiah and Nathan,*d* the two sons of Shemeliah,*e* and they used to go with me to Jerusalem and worshiped with me there, and were not led astray. Your kindred are good people; you come of good stock. Hearty welcome!"

15 Then he added, "I will pay you a drachma a day as wages, as well as expenses for yourself and my son. So go with my son, 16 and*f* I will add something to your wages." Raphael*g* answered, "I will go with him; so do not fear. We shall leave in good health and return to you in good health, because the way is safe." 17 So Tobit*c* said to him, "Blessings be upon you, brother."

Then he called his son and said to him, "Son, prepare supplies for the journey and set out with your brother. May God in heaven bring you safely there and return you in good health to me; and may his angel, my son, accompany you both for your safety."

Before he went out to start his journey, he kissed his father and mother. Tobit then said to him, "Have a safe journey."

18 But his mother*h* began to weep, and said to Tobit, "Why is it that you have sent my child away? Is he not the staff of our hand as he goes in and out before us? 19 Do not heap money upon money, but let it be a ransom for our child. 20 For the life that is given to us by the Lord is enough for us." 21 Tobit*g* said

c Gk *he*   *d* Other ancient authorities read *Jathan* or *Nathamiah*   *e* Other ancient authorities read *Shemaiah*   *f* Other ancient authorities add *when you return safely*   *g* Gk *He*   *h* Other ancient authorities add *Anna*

5.13: In Hebrew *Azariah* means "God helps." 15: Evidently a *drachma* was the normal day's wage for an artisan.

5.22: Pleasing irony here (and in v. 17); Tobit does not know that Raphael is the *good angel.*

to her, "Do not worry; our child will leave in good health and return to us in good health. Your eyes will see him on the day when he returns to you in good health. Say no more! Do not fear for them, my sister. 22For a good angel will accompany him; his journey will be successful, and he will come back in good

6 health." 1So she stopped weeping.

The young man went out and the angel went with him; 2and the dog came out with him and went along with them. So they both journeyed along, and when the first night overtook them they camped by the Tigris river. 3Then the young man went down to wash his feet in the Tigris river. Suddenly a large fish leaped up from the water and tried to swallow the young man's foot, and he cried out. 4But the angel said to the young man, "Catch hold of the fish and hang on to it!" So the young man grasped the fish and drew it up on the land. 5Then the angel said to him, "Cut open the fish and take out its gall, heart, and liver. Keep them with you, but throw away the intestines. For its gall, heart, and liver are useful as medicine." 6So after cutting open the fish the young man gathered together the gall, heart, and liver; then he roasted and ate some of the fish, and kept some to be salted.

The two continued on their way together until they were near Media.*i* 7Then the young man questioned the angel and said to him, "Brother Azariah, what medicinal value is there in the fish's heart and liver, and in the gall?" 8He replied, "As for the fish's heart and liver, you must burn them to make a smoke in the presence of a man or woman afflicted by a demon or evil spirit, and every affliction will flee away and never remain

with that person any longer. 9And as for the gall, anoint a person's eyes where white films have appeared on them; blow upon them, upon the white films, and the eyes*j* will be healed."

10 When he entered Media and already was approaching Ecbatana, *k* 11Raphael said to the young man, "Brother Tobias." "Here I am," he answered. Then Raphael*l* said to him, "We must stay this night in the home of Raguel. He is your relative, and he has a daughter named Sarah. 12He has no male heir and no daughter except Sarah only, and you, as next of kin to her, have before all other men a hereditary claim on her. Also it is right for you to inherit her father's possessions. Moreover, the girl is sensible, brave, and very beautiful, and her father is a good man." 13He continued, "You have every right to take her in marriage. So listen to me, brother; tonight I will speak to her father about the girl, so that we may take her to be your bride. When we return from Rages we will celebrate her marriage. For I know that Raguel can by no means keep her from you or promise her to another man without incurring the penalty of death according to the decree of the book of Moses. Indeed he knows that you, rather than any other man, are entitled to marry his daughter. So now listen to me, brother, and tonight we shall speak concerning the girl and arrange her engagement to you. And when we return from Rages we will take her and bring her back with us to your house."

14 Then Tobias said in answer to Raphael, "Brother Azariah, I have heard

*i Other ancient authorities read Ecbatana
j Gk they   k Other ancient authorities read Rages   l Gk he*

6.1–9: **On the journey, Raphael instructs Tobias in obtaining magical medicines from a fish.** 2: *The dog,* which in some versions is mentioned in 5.17 as Tobias' pet, is evidently a part of the folktale in an earlier form (see 11.4 n.). *The Tigris* is actually west of Nineveh, so they would not have crossed

it going to Persia (see 1.4 n.). 6–9: Belief in the healing properties of the fish's organs is typical of folklore.

6.10–18: **Raphael prepares Tobias to seek the hand of Sarah.** 13: *According to the decree of the book of Moses,* presumably Num 36.6–8, although there is no mention of a

that she already has been married to seven husbands and that they died in the bridal chamber. On the night when they went in to her, they would die. I have heard people saying that it was a demon that killed them. ¹⁵It does not harm her, but it kills anyone who desires to approach her. So now, since I am the only son my father has, I am afraid that I may die and bring my father's and mother's life down to their grave, grieving for me—and they have no other son to bury them."

16 But Raphael^m said to him, "Do you not remember your father's orders when he commanded you to take a wife from your father's house? Now listen to me, brother, and say no more about this demon. Take her. I know that this very night she will be given to you in marriage. ¹⁷When you enter the bridal chamber, take some of the fish's liver and heart, and put them on the embers of the incense. An odor will be given off; ¹⁸the demon will smell it and flee, and will never be seen near her any more. Now when you are about to go to bed with her, both of you must first stand up and pray, imploring the Lord of heaven that mercy and safety may be granted to you. Do not be afraid, for she was set apart for you before the world was made. You will save her, and she will go with you. I presume that you will have children by her, and they will be as brothers to you. Now say no more!" When Tobias heard the words of Raphael and learned that she was his kinswoman,ⁿ related through his father's lineage, he loved her very much, and his heart was drawn to her.

7 Now when they^o entered Ecbatana, Tobias^m said to him, "Brother Azariah, take me straight to our brother Raguel." So he took him to Raguel's house, where they found him sitting beside the courtyard door. They greeted him first, and he replied, "Joyous greetings, brothers; welcome and good health!" Then he brought them into his house. ²He said to his wife Edna, "How much the young man resembles my kinsman Tobit!" ³Then Edna questioned them, saying, "Where are you from, brothers?" They answered, "We belong to the descendants of Naphtali who are exiles in Nineveh." ⁴She said to them, "Do you know our kinsman Tobit?" And they replied, "Yes, we know him." Then she asked them, "Is he^p in good health?" ⁵They replied, "He is alive and in good health." And Tobias added, "He is my father!" ⁶At that Raguel jumped up and kissed him and wept. ⁷He also spoke to him as follows, "Blessings on you, my child, son of a good and noble father!"^q "O most miserable of calamities that such an upright and beneficent man has become blind!" He then embraced his kinsman Tobias and wept. ⁸His wife Edna also wept for him, and their daughter Sarah likewise wept. ⁹Then Raguel^m slaughtered a ram from the flock and received them very warmly.

When they had bathed and washed themselves and had reclined to dine, Tobias said to Raphael, "Brother Azariah,

m Gk *he*   n Gk *sister*   o Other ancient authorities read *he*   p Other ancient authorities add *alive and*   q Other ancient authorities add *When he heard that Tobit had lost his sight, he was stricken with grief and wept. Then he said,*

---

death penalty. **15:** *To bury them,* one of the chief concerns of this book (see 1.17 n.; 4.3–4; 14.10). **18:** *Pray, imploring the Lord,* magic is not enough; prayer is necessary too. *Before the world was made,* "marriages are made in heaven" (compare Gen 24.14).

7.1–9a: Tobias and Raphael arrive at the home of Sarah's father. The following conversation implies that Sarah and her family had not previously been aware of Tobias' existence. **2:** *Edna* ("Pleasure"), again,

an ironic name. **4–5:** The Syriac and Latin Vulgate omit the conversation about Tobit health, possibly on account of his blindness.

7.9b–16: Tobias proposes and the wedding takes place. 12: *Took her by the hand,* like a modern parent "giving away the bride," he marries her to Tobias. **13:** Signing the *contract* was the only other ceremony required, although there is no such reference to it in the Hebrew Bible.

8.1–9a: On the wedding night, Tobias

ask Raguel to give me my kinswoman'
Sarah." [10] But Raguel overheard it and
said to the lad, "Eat and drink, and be
merry tonight. For no one except you,
brother, has the right to marry my
daughter Sarah. Likewise I am not at liberty to give her to any other man than
yourself, because you are my nearest relative. But let me explain to you the true
situation more fully, my child. [11] I have
given her to seven men of our kinsmen,
and all died on the night when they went
in to her. But now, my child, eat and
drink, and the Lord will act on behalf of
you both." But Tobias said, "I will neither eat nor drink anything until you settle the things that pertain to me." So Raguel said, "I will do so. She is given to
you in accordance with the decree in the
book of Moses, and it has been decreed
from heaven that she be given to you.
Take your kinswoman;' from now on
you are her brother and she is your sister.
She is given to you from today and forever. May the Lord of heaven, my child,
guide and prosper you both this night
and grant you mercy and peace." [12] Then
Raguel summoned his daughter Sarah.
When she came to him he took her by the
hand and gave her to Tobias,' saying,
"Take her to be your wife in accordance
with the law and decree written in the
book of Moses. Take her and bring her
safely to your father. And may the God
of heaven prosper your journey with his
peace." [13] Then he called her mother and
told her to bring writing material; and he
wrote out a copy of a marriage contract,
to the effect that he gave her to him as
wife according to the decree of the law of
Moses. [14] Then they began to eat and
drink.

[15] Raguel called his wife Edna and
said to her, "Sister, get the other room
ready, and take her there." [16] So she went
and made the bed in the room as he had
told her, and brought Sarah' there. She

wept for her daughter.' Then, wiping
away the tears," she said to her, "Take
courage, my daughter; the Lord of heav-
en grant you joy*' in place of your sorrow. Take courage, my daughter." Then
she went out.

8 When they had finished eating and
drinking they wanted to retire; so
they took the young man and brought
him into the bedroom. [2] Then Tobias remembered the words of Raphael, and he
took the fish's liver and heart out of the
bag where he had them and put them on
the embers of the incense. [3] The odor of
the fish so repelled the demon that he fled
to the remotest parts*' of Egypt. But Raphael followed him, and at once bound
him there hand and foot.

[4] When the parents*' had gone out
and shut the door of the room, Tobias
got out of bed and said to Sarah,' "Sister, get up, and let us pray and implore
our Lord that he grant us mercy and safety." [5] So she got up, and they began to
pray and implore that they might be kept
safe. Tobias*' began by saying,

"Blessed are you, O God of our
        ancestors,
    and blessed is your name in all
        generations forever.
Let the heavens and the whole
        creation bless you forever.
[6] You made Adam, and for him
        you made his wife Eve
    as a helper and support.
    From the two of them the
        human race has sprung.
You said, 'It is not good that the
        man should be alone;
    let us make a helper for him like
        himself.'

---

r Gk *sister*   s Gk *him*   t Gk *her*   u Other
ancient authorities read *the tears of her daughter*
v Other ancient authorities read *favor*
w Or *fled through the air to the parts*   x Gk *they*
y Gk *He*

---

routs the demon. 3: *Egypt* was the traditional home of magic and witchcraft (compare Ex
7.11). **4**: See 6.18 n. **5–8**: Tobias and Sarah
join in prayer before consummating the marriage, although according to the Vulgate they
waited until the end of the third night to con-
summate their marriage. **5**: *Blessed are you*, see
3.11 n.

7 I now am taking this kinswoman
    of mine,
  not because of lust,
  but with sincerity.
Grant that she and I may find
    mercy
  and that we may grow old
    together."
8 And they both said, "Amen, Amen."
9 Then they went to sleep for the night.

But Raguel arose and called his servants to him, and they went and dug a grave, 10 for he said, "It is possible that he will die and we will become an object of ridicule and derision." 11 When they had finished digging the grave, Raguel went into his house and called his wife, 12 saying, "Send one of the maids and have her go in to see if he is alive. But if he is dead, let us bury him without anyone knowing it." 13 So they sent the maid, lit a lamp, and opened the door; and she went in and found them sound asleep together. 14 Then the maid came out and informed them that he was alive and that nothing was wrong. 15 So they blessed the God of heaven, and Raguel[z] said,

"Blessed are you, O God, with
    every pure blessing;
  let all your chosen ones bless
    you.[a]
  Let them bless you forever.
16 Blessed are you because you have
    made me glad.
  It has not turned out as I
    expected,
  but you have dealt with us
    according to your great
    mercy.

17 Blessed are you because you had
    compassion
  on two only children.
Be merciful to them, O Master,
  and keep them safe;
  bring their lives to fulfillment
    in happiness and mercy."
18 Then he ordered his servants to fill in the grave before daybreak.

19 After this he asked his wife to bake many loaves of bread; and he went out to the herd and brought two steers and four rams and ordered them to be slaughtered. So they began to make preparations. 20 Then he called for Tobias and swore on oath to him in these words:[b] "You shall not leave here for fourteen days, but shall stay here eating and drinking with me; and you shall cheer up my daughter, who has been depressed. 21 Take at once half of what I own and return in safety to your father; the other half will be yours when my wife and I die. Take courage, my child. I am your father and Edna is your mother, and we belong to you as well as to your wife[c] now and forever. Take courage, my child."

9 Then Tobias called Raphael and said to him, 2 "Brother Azariah, take four servants and two camels with you and travel to Rages. Go to the home of Gabael, give him the bond, get the money, and then bring him with you to the wedding celebration. 4 For you know that my father must be counting the

---

z Gk *they*   a Other ancient authorities lack this line   b Other ancient authorities read *Tobias and said to him*   c Gk *sister*

8.9b–21: Raguel's fears are happily disappointed and he provides an extended wedding feast. 9b: *Dug a grave,* because he did not, of course, know that Tobias was provided with an effective means to drive away the demon. **20:** For joy Raguel doubles the usual length of a wedding feast (11.18; Judg 14.12). The oath complicates Tobias' affairs and makes necessary Raphael's solitary mission in 9.3–5, although Tobias' sending Raphael for the money shows how much Tobias trusts him.

9.1–6: Raphael goes to Rages and obtains the money from Gabael. 2: From Ecbatana to *Rages* was a journey which, according to the ancient historian Arrian (*Anabasis,* III. 19–20), took Alexander's army eleven days of forced marches; the author evidently supposed it to be much shorter (see 1.4 n.). **3:** *Has sworn,* 8.20. **4:** Tobias' tender concern for his father is typical of the spirit of the book. The son's unwillingness to prolong his visit is thoroughly justified by the touching description of his parent's uneasiness in

days, and if I delay even one day I will upset him very much. [3] You are witness to the oath Raguel has sworn, and I cannot violate his oath." *d* [5] So Raphael with the four servants and two camels went to Rages in Media and stayed with Gabael. Raphael*e* gave him the bond and informed him that Tobit's son Tobias had married and was inviting him to the wedding celebration. So Gabael*f* got up and counted out to him the money bags, with their seals intact; then they loaded them on the camels.*g* [6] In the morning they both got up early and went to the wedding celebration. When they came into Raguel's house they found Tobias reclining at table. He sprang up and greeted Gabael,*h* who wept and blessed him with the words, "Good and noble son of a father good and noble, upright and generous! May the Lord grant the blessing of heaven to you and your wife, and to your wife's father and mother. Blessed be God, for I see in Tobias the very image of my cousin Tobit."

10 Now, day by day, Tobit kept counting how many days Tobias*f* would need for going and for returning. And when the days had passed and his son did not appear, [2] he said, "Is it possible that he has been detained? Or that Gabael has died, and there is no one to give him the money?" [3] And he began to worry. [4] His wife Anna said, "My child has perished and is no longer among the living." And she began to weep and mourn for her son, saying, [5] "Woe to me, my child, the light of my eyes, that I let you make the journey." [6] But Tobit kept saying to her, "Be quiet and stop worrying, my dear;*i* he is all right. Probably something unexpected has happened there. The man who went

with him is trustworthy and is one of our own kin. Do not grieve for him, my dear;*i* he will soon be here." [7] She answered him, "Be quiet yourself! Stop trying to deceive me! My child has perished." She would rush out every day and watch the road her son had taken, and would heed no one.*j* When the sun had set she would go in and mourn and weep all night long, getting no sleep at all.

Now when the fourteen days of the wedding celebration had ended that Raguel had sworn to observe for his daughter, Tobias came to him and said, "Send me back, for I know that my father and mother do not believe that they will see me again. So I beg of you, father, to let me go so that I may return to my own father. I have already explained to you how I left him." [8] But Raguel said to Tobias, "Stay, my child, stay with me; I will send messengers to your father Tobit and they will inform him about you." [9] But he said, "No! I beg you to send me back to my father." [10] So Raguel promptly gave Tobias his wife Sarah, as well as half of all his property: male and female slaves, oxen and sheep, donkeys and camels, clothing, money, and household goods. [11] Then he saw them safely off; he embraced Tobias*h* and said, "Farewell, my child; have a safe journey. The Lord of heaven prosper you and your wife Sarah, and may I see children of yours before I die." [12] Then he kissed his daughter Sarah and said to her, "My daughter, honor your father-in-law and

d In other ancient authorities verse 3 precedes verse 4   *e* Gk *He*   *f* Gk *he*   *g* Other ancient authorities lack *on the camels*   *h* Gk *him*   *i* Gk *sister*   *j* Other ancient authorities read *and she would eat nothing*

10.1–7. **5–6:** Like all the other characters in the book (except the demon), Gabael shows himself to be a loving and trustworthy person.

10.1–7a: Tobias' father and mother grow anxious at their son's absence. 1: In *counting . . . days,* Tobit had naturally made no allowance for a two-week wedding celebration. **4:** *My child has perished,* Anna's ten-

dency to suspect the worst and her husband's courageous attempts to console her illustrate the author's fine sensitivity to a broad spectrum of human reactions to the same events.

10.7b–13: Tobias and Sarah start for home. 11: *The Lord of heaven* was a favorite name for Israel's God in the Persian period and later (Jdt 5.8; Ezra 1.2).

your mother-in-law,*k* since from now on they are as much your parents as those who gave you birth. Go in peace, daughter, and may I hear a good report about you as long as I live." Then he bade them farewell and let them go. Then Edna said to Tobias, "My child and dear brother, the Lord of heaven bring you back safely, and may I live long enough to see children of you and of my daughter Sarah before I die. In the sight of the Lord I entrust my daughter to you; do nothing to grieve her all the days of your life. Go in peace, my child. From now on I am your mother and Sarah is your beloved wife.*l* May we all prosper together all the days of our lives." Then she kissed them both and saw them safely off. 13 Tobias parted from Raguel with happiness and joy, praising the Lord of heaven and earth, King over all, because he had made his journey a success. Finally, he blessed Raguel and his wife Edna, and said, "I have been commanded by the Lord to honor you all the days of my life."*m*

11 When they came near to Kaserin, which is opposite Nineveh, Raphael said, 2 "You are aware of how we left your father. 3 Let us run ahead of your wife and prepare the house while they are still on the way." 4 As they went on together Raphael*n* said to him, "Have the gall ready." And the dog*o* went along behind them.

5 Meanwhile Anna sat looking intently down the road by which her son would come. 6 When she caught sight of him coming, she said to his father, "Look, your son is coming, and the man who went with him!"

7 Raphael said to Tobias, before he had approached his father, "I know that his eyes will be opened. 8 Smear the gall of the fish on his eyes; the medicine will make the white films shrink and peel off

from his eyes, and your father will regain his sight and see the light."

9 Then Anna ran up to her son and threw her arms around him, saying, "Now that I have seen you, my child, I am ready to die." And she wept. 10 Then Tobit got up and came stumbling out through the courtyard door. Tobias went up to him, 11 with the gall of the fish in his hand, and holding him firmly, he blew into his eyes, saying, "Take courage, father." With this he applied the medicine on his eyes, 12 and it made them smart.*m* 13 Next, with both his hands he peeled off the white films from the corners of his eyes. Then Tobit*n* saw his son and*p* threw his arms around him, 14 and he wept and said to him, "I see you, my son, the light of my eyes!" Then he said,

"Blessed be God,
   and blessed be his great name,
   and blessed be all his holy
      angels.
May his holy name be blessed*q*
   throughout all the ages.
15 Though he afflicted me,
   he has had mercy upon me.*r*
Now I see my son Tobias!"

So Tobit went in rejoicing and praising God at the top of his voice. Tobias reported to his father that his journey had been successful, that he had brought the money, that he had married Raguel's daughter Sarah, and that she was, indeed, on her way there, very near to the gate of Nineveh.

16 Then Tobit, rejoicing and praising God, went out to meet his daughter-in-law at the gate of Nineveh. When the

k Other ancient authorities lack parts of *Then . . . mother-in-law*   l Gk *sister*   m Lat: Meaning of Gk uncertain   n Gk *he*   o Codex Sinaiticus reads *And the Lord*   p Other ancient authorities lack *saw his son and*   q Codex Sinaiticus reads *May his great name be upon us and blessed be all the angels*   r Lat: Gk lacks this line

---

11.1–15: Tobias and Raphael precede Sarah into the city and heal Tobit's blindness. 4: *The dog* appears again for the first time since 6.2; perhaps his presence in the

story is a survival from an older folktale, in which he had a real function.

11.16–18: Tobit meets his daughter-in-law and celebrates the marriage. 18: *Ahi-*

people of Nineveh saw him coming, walking along in full vigor and with no one leading him, they were amazed. [17]Before them all, Tobit acknowledged that God had been merciful to him and had restored his sight. When Tobit met Sarah the wife of his son Tobias, he blessed her saying, "Come in, my daughter, and welcome. Blessed be your God who has brought you to us, my daughter. Blessed be your father and your mother, blessed be my son Tobias, and blessed be you, my daughter. Come in now to your home, and welcome, with blessing and joy. Come in, my daughter." So on that day there was rejoicing among all the Jews who were in Nineveh. [18]Ahikar and his nephew Nadab were also present to share Tobit's joy. With merriment they celebrated Tobias's wedding feast for seven days, and many gifts were given to him.[s]

12 When the wedding celebration was ended, Tobit called his son Tobias and said to him, "My child, see to paying the wages of the man who went with you, and give him a bonus as well." [2]He replied, "Father, how much shall I pay him? It would do no harm to give him half of the possessions brought back with me. [3]For he has led me back to you safely, he cured my wife, he brought the money back with me, and he healed you. How much extra shall I give him as a bonus?" [4]Tobit said, "He deserves, my child, to receive half of all that he brought back." [5]So Tobias[t] called him and said, "Take for your wages half of all that you brought back, and farewell."

[6]Then Raphael[t] called the two of them privately and said to them, "Bless God and acknowledge him in the presence of all the living for the good things he has done for you. Bless and sing praise to his name. With fitting honor declare to all people the deeds[u] of God. Do not be slow to acknowledge him. [7]It is good to conceal the secret of a king, but to acknowledge and reveal the works of God, and with fitting honor to acknowledge him. Do good and evil will not overtake you. [8]Prayer with fasting[v] is good, but better than both is almsgiving with righteousness. A little with righteousness is better than wealth with wrongdoing.[w] It is better to give alms than to lay up gold. [9]For almsgiving saves from death and purges away every sin. Those who give alms will enjoy a full life, [10]but those who commit sin and do wrong are their own worst enemies.

[11]"I will now declare the whole truth to you and will conceal nothing from you. Already I have declared it to you when I said, 'It is good to conceal the secret of a king, but to reveal with due honor the works of God.' [12]So now when you and Sarah prayed, it was I who brought and read[x] the record of your prayer before the glory of the Lord, and likewise whenever you would bury the dead. [13]And that time when you did not hesitate to get up and leave your dinner to go and bury the dead, [14]I was sent to

s Other ancient authorities lack parts of this sentence   t Gk he   u Gk words; other ancient authorities read words of the deeds   v Codex Sinaiticus with sincerity   w Lat   x Lat: Gk lacks and read

---

kar . . . *Nadab,* see 14.10 n. *Seven days,* apparently the normal period of a wedding celebration (see 8.20 n.).

12.1–22: Raphael, being offered his wages, gives good advice and discloses his true identity. 1–5: Tobias generously wishes to reward Raphael far beyond the amount agreed upon (5.15). **6–10:** In the style of a Jewish teacher of wisdom, Raphael delivers a brief exhortation on the good life, similar to that of Tobit in ch 4. **8:** *Prayer . . . fasting . . . almsgiving . . .* and *righteousness* ("piety")

are mentioned together also in Mt 6.1–18 (on almsgiving, compare 4.7–11 and see Sir 3.30 n.).

12.11: Verse 7. **12–15:** Raphael reveals himself as an angelic intercessor who brings the prayers of mortals into the presence of God. From v. 15 we learn that there are six others. "Uriel" is named in 2 Esd 4.1; "Gabriel" and "Michael," respectively, in Dan 9.21 and 10.13. The growth of angelology was characteristic of the Judaism of the period; this was partly due to an increasing sense of God's

you to test you. And at the same time God sent me to heal you and Sarah your daughter-in-law. [15] I am Raphael, one of the seven angels who stand ready and enter before the glory of the Lord."

16 The two of them were shaken; they fell face down, for they were afraid. [17] But he said to them, "Do not be afraid; peace be with you. Bless God forevermore. [18] As for me, when I was with you, I was not acting on my own will, but by the will of God. Bless him each and every day; sing his praises. [19] Although you were watching me, I really did not eat or drink anything—but what you saw was a vision. [20] So now get up from the ground,[y] and acknowledge God. See, I am ascending to him who sent me. Write down all these things that have happened to you." And he ascended. [21] Then they stood up, and could see him no more. [22] They kept blessing God and singing his praises, and they acknowledged God for these marvelous deeds of his, when an angel of God had appeared to them.

13 Then Tobit[z] said: "Blessed be God who lives forever, because his kingdom[a] lasts throughout all ages.

2 For he afflicts, and he shows mercy; he leads down to Hades in the lowest regions of the earth, and he brings up from the great abyss,[b] and there is nothing that can escape his hand.

3 Acknowledge him before the nations, O children of Israel;

for he has scattered you among them.

4 He has shown you his greatness even there. Exalt him in the presence of every living being, because he is our Lord and he is our God; he is our Father and he is God forever.

5 He will afflict[c] you for your iniquities, but he will again show mercy on all of you. He will gather you from all the nations among whom you have been scattered.

6 If you turn to him with all your heart and with all your soul, to do what is true before him, then he will turn to you and will no longer hide his face from you. So now see what he has done for you; acknowledge him at the top of your voice. Bless the Lord of righteousness, and exalt the King of the ages.[d] In the land of my exile I acknowledge him, and show his power and majesty to a nation of sinners:

[y] Other ancient authorities read *now bless the Lord on earth*   [z] Gk *he*   [a] Other ancient authorities read *forever, and his kingdom*   [b] Gk *from destruction*   [c] Other ancient authorities read *He afflicted*   [d] The lacuna in codex Sinaiticus, verses 6b to 10a, is filled in from other ancient authorities

---

transcendence and partly, perhaps, to Persian influences. **17**: *Do not be afraid,* compare Mt 28.5, 10.

13.1–17: Tobit's hymn of praise. Some scholars believe that chs 13 and 14 were added to the book much later in order to give substance to the words of 12.22a and to round out the account of Tobit's life. The hymn contains numerous echoes of Old Testament

passages, especially Isa 40–55, and has no particular appropriateness to Tobit's personal situation. On the other hand, while Tobit and his family have been delivered, the other exiles have not; therefore chs 13–14 can be seen as completing the story of Israel's deliverance. **1–6**: Exhortation to the exiles. **2**: 1 Sam 2.6–8; Lk 1.52–53. **4**: *Our Father,* Isa 63.16; 64.8; Sir 23.1, 4; Mt 6.9.

'Turn back, you sinners, and do
what is right before him;
perhaps he may look with favor
upon you and show you
mercy.'

7 As for me, I exalt my God,
and my soul rejoices in the King
of heaven.

8 Let all people speak of his majesty,
and acknowledge him in
Jerusalem.

9 O Jerusalem, the holy city,
he afflicted*e* you for the deeds
of your hands,*f*
but will again have mercy on
the children of the
righteous.

10 Acknowledge the Lord, for he is
good,*g*
and bless the King of the ages,
so that his tent*h* may be rebuilt
in you in joy.
May he cheer all those within you
who are captives,
and love all those within you
who are distressed,
to all generations forever.

11 A bright light will shine to all the
ends of the earth;
many nations will come to you
from far away,
the inhabitants of the remotest
parts of the earth to your
holy name,
bearing gifts in their hands for
the King of heaven.
Generation after generation will
give joyful praise in you,
the name of the chosen city will
endure forever.

12 Cursed are all who speak a harsh
word against you;
cursed are all who conquer you
and pull down your walls,
all who overthrow your towers
and set your homes on fire.
But blessed forever will be all
who revere you.*i*

13 Go, then, and rejoice over the
children of the righteous,
for they will be gathered
together
and will praise the Lord of the
ages.

14 Happy are those who love you,
and happy are those who rejoice
in your prosperity.
Happy also are all people who
grieve with you
because of your afflictions;
for they will rejoice with you
and witness all your glory
forever.

15 My soul blesses*j* the Lord, the
great King!

16 For Jerusalem will be built*k* as
his house for all ages.
How happy I will be if a remnant
of my descendants should
survive
to see your glory and
acknowledge the King of
heaven.
The gates of Jerusalem will be
built with sapphire and
emerald,
and all your walls with precious
stones.
The towers of Jerusalem will be
built with gold,
and their battlements with pure
gold.
The streets of Jerusalem will be
paved
with ruby and with stones of
Ophir.

17 The gates of Jerusalem will sing
hymns of joy,
and all her houses will cry,
'Hallelujah!
Blessed be the God of Israel!'

e Other ancient authorities read *will afflict*
f Other ancient authorities read *your children*
g Other ancient authorities read *Lord worthily*
h Or *tabernacle*   i Other ancient authorities
read *who build you up*   j Or *O my soul, bless*
k Other ancient authorities add *for a city*

13.8–17: God's favor to Jerusalem. 10:
Tent, temple. 16–17: That *Jerusalem will be*
built with precious stones is an echo of Isa
54.11–12 (compare Rev 21.18–21).

and the blessed will bless the
holy name forever and
ever."

14 So ended Tobit's words of praise.
2 Tobit[l] died in peace when he
was one hundred twelve years old, and
was buried with great honor in Nineveh.
He was sixty-two[m] years old when he
lost his eyesight, and after regaining it he
lived in prosperity, giving alms and continually blessing God and acknowledging God's majesty.

3 When he was about to die, he called
his son Tobias and the seven sons of Tobias[n] and gave this command: "My son,
take your children 4and hurry off to Media, for I believe the word of God that
Nahum spoke about Nineveh, that all
these things will take place and overtake
Assyria and Nineveh. Indeed, everything that was spoken by the prophets of
Israel, whom God sent, will occur. None
of all their words will fail, but all will
come true at their appointed times. So it
will be safer in Media than in Assyria and
Babylon. For I know and believe that
whatever God has said will be fulfilled
and will come true; not a single word of
the prophecies will fail. All of our kindred, inhabitants of the land of Israel,
will be scattered and taken as captives
from the good land; and the whole land
of Israel will be desolate, even Samaria
and Jerusalem will be desolate. And the
temple of God in it will be burned to the
ground, and it will be desolate for a
while.[o]

5 "But God will again have mercy on
them, and God will bring them back into
the land of Israel; and they will rebuild
the temple of God, but not like the first
one until the period when the times of
fulfillment shall come. After this they all
will return from their exile and will rebuild Jerusalem in splendor; and in it the

temple of God will be rebuilt, just as the
prophets of Israel have said concerning
it. 6Then the nations in the whole world
will all be converted and worship God in
truth. They will all abandon their idols,
which deceitfully have led them into
their error; 7and in righteousness they
will praise the eternal God. All the Israelites who are saved in those days and are
truly mindful of God will be gathered
together; they will go to Jerusalem and
live in safety forever in the land of Abraham, and it will be given over to them.
Those who sincerely love God will rejoice, but those who commit sin and injustice will vanish from all the earth.
8,9So now, my children, I command
you, serve God faithfully and do what is
pleasing in his sight. Your children are
also to be commanded to do what is right
and to give alms, and to be mindful of
God and to bless his name at all times
with sincerity and with all their strength.
So now, my son, leave Nineveh; do not
remain here. 10On whatever day you
bury your mother beside me, do not stay
overnight within the confines of the city.
For I see that there is much wickedness
within it, and that much deceit is practiced within it, while the people are without shame. See, my son, what Nadab did
to Ahikar who had reared him. Was he
not, while still alive, brought down into
the earth? For God repaid him to his face
for this shameful treatment. Ahikar came
out into the light, but Nadab went into
the eternal darkness, because he tried to
kill Ahikar. Because he gave alms, Ahikar[p] escaped the fatal trap that Nadab
had set for him, but Nadab fell into it

l Gk He   m Other ancient authorities read
fifty-eight   n Lat: Gk lacks *and the seven sons of
Tobias*   o Lat: Other ancient authorities read
*of God will be in distress and will be burned for a
while*   p Gk he; other ancient authorities read
Manasses

**14.1–15: Tobit's final counsel and
death. 3–9**: He advises his son to leave Nineveh, which is to be destroyed, and predicts
the future course of Israel's history. **4**: *The
word . . . Nahum spoke,* see Nahum 1.1; 2.8–
10, 13; 3.18–19. **6**: That *the nations . . . will all*

be converted to Judaism was a characteristic
belief of the post-exilic age (e.g. Zech 8.20–
23). **10**: *Nadab* (also Nasbas or Nadin) is the
villain of the *Ahikar* story (see 1.21 n.). *Gave
alms,* 4.7–11.

himself, and was destroyed. [11] So now, my children, see what almsgiving accomplishes, and what injustice does—it brings death! But now my breath fails me."

Then they laid him on his bed, and he died; and he received an honorable funeral. [12] When Tobias's mother died, he buried her beside his father. Then he and his wife and children[q] returned to Media and settled in Ecbatana with Raguel his father-in-law. [13] He treated his parents-in-law[r] with great respect in their old age, and buried them in Ecbatana of Media. He inherited both the property of Raguel and that of his father Tobit. [14] He died highly respected at the age of one hundred seventeen[s] years. [15] Before he died he heard[t] of the destruction of Nineveh, and he saw its prisoners being led into Media, those whom King Cyaxares[u] of Media had taken captive. Tobias[v] praised God for all he had done to the people of Nineveh and Assyria; before he died he rejoiced over Nineveh, and he blessed the Lord God forever and ever. Amen.[w]

q Codex Sinaiticus lacks *and children*
r Gk *them*   s Other authorities read other numbers   t Codex Sinaiticus reads *saw and heard*   u Cn: Codex Sinaiticus *Ahikar*; other ancient authorities read *Nebuchadnezzar and Ahasuerus*   v Gk *He*   w Other ancient authorities lack *Amen*

Judith

No other biblical book, in either its parts or its totality, is as quintessentially ironic as Judith. All its important scenes, as well as its major and minor characters, are ironic. Able to defeat mighty nations in both the East and the West (chs 1–7), the Assyrian army of Nebuchadnezzar, under the command of Holofernes, is routed by Bethulia, a small Samaritan town blocking the army's route to Jerusalem and the temple (chs 8–16). Even more ironic, Holofernes, the "invincible" head of the Assyrian army, is beheaded by Judith, a beautiful and wealthy Israelite widow who is known for her piety and self-denial. The book of Judith, then, is about a saint who risks her life to slay the enemy of her people.

Often characterized as a novel, Judith is best understood as a folktale about a pious widow who, strengthened by her faith in the God of Israel, takes matters into her own hands and so saves her people and Jerusalem. The story's characters are vividly drawn and take on a life of their own. Their speeches, conversations, and prayers, as well as the story's plot, clearly and effectively express the storyteller's theology and ethics.

As for the book's religious ideas, neither God's titles nor attributes are in any way unusual, let alone objectionable. Moreover, the importance of Jerusalem, the efficacy of prayer, fasting and the wearing of sackcloth, the importance of observing dietary laws—all are unquestioned. With the exception of almsgiving and the baptizing of Gentile converts, virtually all the traditional practices of Maccabean Pharisaism are mentioned. God's covenant with Israel is interpreted largely in Deuteronomistic terms. Finally, the atmosphere of the tale is entirely realistic, with no aura of the miraculous.

And yet, the book bristles with problems, as its struggles for canonicity so clearly attest. Although the book purports to be an historical account, it abounds in serious problems concerning both history and geography (chs 1–2). Despite the wealth of geographical and topographical clues throughout the story, the location of Bethulia, the principal scene of the action, is unknown.

Moreover, many readers, past and present, have censured Judith's character and conduct. For though the reader is assured by the narrator that Judith was diligent in prayer and fasting, strict in observing dietary laws, forever celibate after her husband's death, ever fearing the Lord and always honored by all, the discerning reader also recognizes that in Judith's dealings with Holofernes she showed herself to be a shameless flatterer, a bold-faced liar, and a ruthless assassin.

The basis of the Greek version of Judith was certainly Hebrew. The author of the Semitic version was probably a Palestinian Jew.

Despite the story's post-exilic setting and a significant number of Persian nouns and names, it also has unmistakable Hellenistic features, as well as distinctively Maccabean/Hasmonean elements, notably the worshiping of a king as god, the sweeping political and military powers of the high priest, and the supremacy of the Jerusalem council.

Other elements in the story are reminiscent of the general circumstances, terminology, spirit, and tradition of the days of Judas Maccabeus (167–161 B.C.) and his defeat of Nicanor, the general under the infamous Antiochus IV Epiphanes (175–163 B.C.), as narrated in 1 Macc 7.43–50. The book was probably composed sometime during the reign of John Hyrcanus I (135–105 B.C.).

The story is extant in four slightly different Greek versions, two Latin ones, a Syriac one, as well as several later Hebrew recensions. The tale has inspired numerous works of painting, sculpture, and literature, including an Anglo-Saxon epic (see p. ix AP).

1 It was the twelfth year of the reign of Nebuchadnezzar, who ruled over the Assyrians in the great city of Nineveh. In those days Arphaxad ruled over the Medes in Ecbatana. ²He built walls around Ecbatana with hewn stones three cubits thick and six cubits long; he made the walls seventy cubits high and fifty cubits wide. ³At its gates he raised towers one hundred cubits high and sixty cubits wide at the foundations. ⁴He made its gates seventy cubits high and forty cubits wide to allow his armies to march out in force and his infantry to form their ranks. ⁵Then King Nebuchadnezzar made war against King Arphaxad in the great plain that is on the borders of Ragau. ⁶There rallied to him all the people of the hill country and all those who lived along the Euphrates, the Tigris, and the Hydaspes, and, on the plain, Arioch, king of the Elymeans. Thus, many nations joined the forces of the Chaldeans. ᵃ

7 Then Nebuchadnezzar, king of the Assyrians, sent messengers to all who lived in Persia and to all who lived in the west, those who lived in Cilicia and Damascus, Lebanon and Antilebanon, and all who lived along the seacoast, ⁸and those among the nations of Carmel and Gilead, and Upper Galilee and the great plain of Esdraelon, ⁹and all who were in Samaria and its towns, and beyond the Jordan as far as Jerusalem and Bethany and Chelous and Kadesh and the river of Egypt, and Tahpanhes and Raamses and the whole land of Goshen, ¹⁰even beyond Tanis and Memphis, and all who lived in Egypt as far as the borders of Ethiopia. ¹¹But all who lived in the whole region disregarded the summons of Nebuchadnezzar, king of the Assyrians, and refused to join him in the war; for they were not afraid of him, but regarded him as only one man. ᵇ So they sent back his messengers empty-handed and in disgrace.

12 Then Nebuchadnezzar became very angry with this whole region, and swore by his throne and kingdom that he would take revenge on the whole territory of Cilicia and Damascus and Syria, that he would kill with his sword also all the inhabitants of the land of Moab, and the people of Ammon, and all Judea, and every one in Egypt, as far as the coasts of the two seas.

13 In the seventeenth year he led his forces against King Arphaxad and defeated him in battle, overthrowing the whole army of Arphaxad and all his cavalry and all his chariots. ¹⁴Thus he took possession of his towns and came to Ecbatana, captured its towers, plundered its markets, and turned its glory into disgrace. ¹⁵He captured Arphaxad in the

a Syr: Gk *Cheleoudites*   *b* Or *a man*

1.1–6: Nebuchadnezzar declares war on Arphaxad, king of Media. 1: *Nebuchadnezzar* (605 [or 604]–562 B.C.) was second ruler over the Neo-Babylonian Empire (not *over the Assyrians*). It was he who destroyed Jerusalem in 587–86 B.C. and carried the Jews off into their Babylonian Exile (2 Kings 24.1–25.26). The author of the book of Judith, in complete disregard of history, represents him as flourishing after the Exile (4.3; 5.19). Some scholars believe that the historical confusion of the book, of which this is but one example, is deliberate, intended to stamp the work unmistakably as fiction. *Arphaxad* is unknown. *The Medes* inhabited the northern part of modern Iran and had their capital at *Ecbatana* (Tob 3.7). **5:** *Ragau,* the Median city where Arphaxad was later slain (v. 15), located 200 miles northeast of Ecbatana and six miles southwest of modern Teheran. **6:** *Euphrates . . . Tigris,* the principal rivers of Mesopotamia (modern Iraq). *Hydaspes,* a river in India, but here evidently placed in Mesopotamia. *Arioch,* unknown. *Elymeans,* possibly the inhabitants of Elyma, a Persian district (Polybius v. 44.9). *Chaldeans,* the Neo-Babylonians (see v. 1 n.).

1.7–11: The Persians and the western nations refuse Nebuchadnezzar's plea for help. 7–10: The nations enumerated correspond to modern Syria, Lebanon, Palestine, and Egypt. **7:** *Persia,* the southern part of modern Iran.

1.12–16: Angry at the western nations, Nebuchadnezzar defeats Arphaxad without their assistance. 12: *The two seas,* unclear, possibly the Red and the Mediterranean.

mountains of Ragau and struck him down with his spears, thus destroying him once and for all. [16] Then he returned to Nineveh, he and all his combined forces, a vast body of troops; and there he and his forces rested and feasted for one hundred twenty days.

2 In the eighteenth year, on the twenty-second day of the first month, there was talk in the palace of Nebuchadnezzar, king of the Assyrians, about carrying out his revenge on the whole region, just as he had said. [2] He summoned all his ministers and all his nobles and set before them his secret plan and recounted fully, with his own lips, all the wickedness of the region. [c] [3] They decided that every one who had not obeyed his command should be destroyed.

4 When he had completed his plan, Nebuchadnezzar, king of the Assyrians, called Holofernes, the chief general of his army, second only to himself, and said to him, [5] "Thus says the Great King, the lord of the whole earth: Leave my presence and take with you men confident in their strength, one hundred twenty thousand foot soldiers and twelve thousand cavalry. [6] March out against all the land to the west, because they disobeyed my orders. [7] Tell them to prepare earth and water, for I am coming against them in my anger, and will cover the whole face of the earth with the feet of my troops, to whom I will hand them over to be plundered. [8] Their wounded shall fill their ravines and gullies, and the swelling river shall be filled with their dead. [9] I will lead them away captive to the ends of the whole earth. [10] You shall go and seize all their territory for me in advance. They must yield themselves to you, and you shall hold them for me until the day of their punishment. [11] But to those who resist show no mercy, but hand them over to slaughter and plunder throughout your whole region. [12] For as I live, and by the power of my kingdom, what I have spoken I will accomplish by my own hand. [13] And you—take care not to transgress any of your lord's commands, but carry them out exactly as I have ordered you; do it without delay."

14 So Holofernes left the presence of his lord, and summoned all the commanders, generals, and officers of the Assyrian army. [15] He mustered the picked troops by divisions as his lord had ordered him to do, one hundred twenty thousand of them, together with twelve thousand archers on horseback, [16] and he organized them as a great army is marshaled for a campaign. [17] He took along a vast number of camels and donkeys and mules for transport, and innumerable sheep and oxen and goats for food; [18] also ample rations for everyone, and a huge amount of gold and silver from the royal palace.

19 Then he set out with his whole army, to go ahead of King Nebuchadnezzar and to cover the whole face of the earth to the west with their chariots and cavalry and picked foot soldiers. [20] Along with them went a mixed crowd like a swarm of locusts, like the dust[d] of the earth—a multitude that could not be counted.

c Meaning of Gk uncertain   d Gk sand

2.1–13: **Nebuchadnezzar orders Holofernes to lead a punitive expedition against the West. 4**: Next to Judith, *Holofernes* is the principal character of the book. So far as is known, Nebuchadnezzar had no such general, but the name is found in classical authors of a much later period. His career may have been suggested by memories of a Persian general of similar name who was a leader in the expedition which invaded the West under Artaxerxes III about 350 B.C. (Diodorus Siculus, *Hist.* XXXI. 19; see 12.11 n.).

2.7: *Earth and water* were characteristic signs of submission demanded by Persian (not Assyrian or Babylonian) kings (Herodotus, *Hist.* VI. 48).

2.14–27: **Holofernes brings an enormous army to Damascus. 21**: The *three days* march is impossible, since *Nineveh,* the capital of Assyria, is at least three hundred miles from *Bectileth* (an unidentified site), which is described as *north of Upper Cilicia.* Cilicia is in southeastern Asia Minor.

21 They marched for three days from Nineveh to the plain of Bectileth, and camped opposite Bectileth near the mountain that is to the north of Upper Cilicia. 22From there Holofernes*e* took his whole army, the infantry, cavalry, and chariots, and went up into the hill country. 23He ravaged Put and Lud, and plundered all the Rassisites and the Ishmaelites on the border of the desert, south of the country of the Chelleans. 24Then he followed*f* the Euphrates and passed through Mesopotamia and destroyed all the fortified towns along the brook Abron, as far as the sea. 25He also seized the territory of Cilicia, and killed everyone who resisted him. Then he came to the southern borders of Japheth, facing Arabia. 26He surrounded all the Midianites, and burned their tents and plundered their sheepfolds. 27Then he went down into the plain of Damascus during the wheat harvest, and burned all their fields and destroyed their flocks and herds and sacked their towns and ravaged their lands and put all their young men to the sword.

28 So fear and dread of him fell upon all the people who lived along the seacoast, at Sidon and Tyre, and those who lived in Sur and Ocina and all who lived in Jamnia. Those who lived in Azotus and Ascalon feared him greatly.

3 They therefore sent messengers to him to sue for peace in these words: 2"We, the servants of Nebuchadnezzar, the Great King, lie prostrate before you. Do with us whatever you will. 3See, our buildings and all our land and all our wheat fields and our flocks and herds and all our encampments*g* lie before you; do with them as you please. 4Our towns and their inhabitants are also your slaves; come and deal with them as you see fit."

5 The men came to Holofernes and told him all this. 6Then he went down to the seacoast with his army and stationed garrisons in the fortified towns and took picked men from them as auxiliaries. 7These people and all in the countryside welcomed him with garlands and dances and tambourines. 8Yet he demolished all their shrines*h* and cut down their sacred groves; for he had been commissioned to destroy all the gods of the land, so that all nations should worship Nebuchadnezzar alone, and that all their dialects and tribes should call upon him as a god.

e Gk *he*   *f* Or *crossed*   *g* Gk *all the sheepfolds of our tents*   *h* Syr: Gk *borders*

2.23: *Put and Lud,* probably in Asia Minor. *Rassisites,* unknown. *Ishmaelites,* Arabs (Gen 16.11–12). *Chelleans,* unknown. 24: The geography here is confused. *Abron,* unknown. The natural line of march would be directly south from Cilicia to Damascus. 26: *Midianites,* archaic for Arabs (Judg 6.1–6). 27: *Damascus,* the ancient and beautiful capital of Syria, was noted for its fertile surroundings.
2.28–3.8: **Through fear the people of the seacoast submit voluntarily.** 2.28: *Sidon and Tyre,* on the Phoenician coast, west of Damascus. *Sur and Ocina,* unknown. *Jamnia,* just north of *Azotus* (Ashdod) *and Ascalon* (Ashkelon), important (and at one time Philistine) cities in southwest Palestine.
3.8: Holofernes seems here to go beyond his original commission, which was merely punitive; now he seeks to impose religious unity by forcing all peoples to worship Nebuchadnezzar alone. The language is suggested directly by such passages as Dan chs 3 and 6, and indirectly by the persecutions of Antiochus Epiphanes as related in 1 Macc 1.10–2.26 and 2 Macc chs 6–7. Holofernes' invasion thus becomes a threat to Israel's religious integrity as well as the people's national security.

3.9–4.15: **When Holofernes reaches the soil of Palestine, the Jews prepare to resist.** 3.9: *Esdraelon* is the great plain which cuts across Palestine just north of Mt. Carmel. *Dothan* is a short distance south of the plain. *Scythopolis* is identical with Beth-shan, located at the junction of Esdraelon and the Jordan Valley. 4.3: The statement that *they had only recently returned from exile* is flagrantly anachronistic, since it was Nebuchadnezzar who had begun the captivity (compare 1.1 n.), and the return took place nearly fifty years later under the Persian Empire, which had succeeded the Babylonian (Ezra 1.1–3). 4: The inclusion of *Samaria* is puzzling, since the people of Judea (v. 1) and the Samaritans were separate and increasingly hostile communities in the post-exilic era. 6: The name of the high priest, *Joakim,* is probably derived from Neh 12.26. The identification of *Bethulia,* the center of the story's action, is one of the major problems of the book; the most

9 Then he came toward Esdraelon, near Dothan, facing the great ridge of Judea; [10]he camped between Geba and Scythopolis, and remained for a whole month in order to collect all the supplies for his army.

4 When the Israelites living in Judea heard of everything that Holofernes, the general of Nebuchadnezzar, the king of the Assyrians, had done to the nations, and how he had plundered and destroyed all their temples, [2]they were therefore greatly terrified at his approach; they were alarmed both for Jerusalem and for the temple of the Lord their God. [3]For they had only recently returned from exile, and all the people of Judea had just now gathered together, and the sacred vessels and the altar and the temple had been consecrated after their profanation. [4]So they sent word to every district of Samaria, and to Kona, Beth-horon, Belmain, and Jericho, and to Choba and Aesora, and the valley of Salem. [5]They immediately seized all the high hilltops and fortified the villages on them and stored up food in preparation for war—since their fields had recently been harvested.

6 The high priest, Joakim, who was in Jerusalem at the time, wrote to the people of Bethulia and Betomesthaim, which faces Esdraelon opposite the plain near Dothan, [7]ordering them to seize the mountain passes, since by them Judea could be invaded; and it would be easy to stop any who tried to enter, for the approach was narrow, wide enough for only two at a time to pass.

8 So the Israelites did as they had been ordered by the high priest Joakim and the senate of the whole people of Israel, in session at Jerusalem. [9]And every man of Israel cried out to God with great fervor, and they humbled themselves with much fasting. [10]They and their wives and their children and their cattle and every resident alien and hired laborer and purchased slave—they all put sackcloth around their waists. [11]And all the Israelite men, women, and children living at Jerusalem prostrated themselves before the temple and put ashes on their heads and spread out their sackcloth before the Lord. [12]They even draped the altar with sackcloth and cried out in unison, praying fervently to the God of Israel not to allow their infants to be carried off and their wives to be taken as booty, and the towns they had inherited to be destroyed, and the sanctuary to be profaned and desecrated to the malicious joy of the Gentiles.

13 The Lord heard their prayers and had regard for their distress; for the people fasted many days throughout Judea and in Jerusalem before the sanctuary of the Lord Almighty. [14]The high priest Joakim and all the priests who stood before the Lord and ministered to the Lord, with sackcloth around their loins, offered the daily burnt offerings, the votive offerings, and freewill offerings of the people. [15]With ashes on their turbans, they cried out to the Lord with all their might to look with favor on the whole house of Israel.

5 It was reported to Holofernes, the general of the Assyrian army, that the people of Israel had prepared for war and had closed the mountain passes and fortified all the high hilltops and set up barricades in the plains. [2]In great anger he called together all the princes of Moab and the commanders of Ammon and all the governors of the coastland, [3]and said

---

probable suggestion is that it is a pseudonym for Shechem (see 6.11 n.; 7.18 n.; and 10.10 n.).

4.8: *Senate,* an anachronism of the author (see 1.1 n. and 1 Macc 12.6 n.). **14:** *The daily burnt offerings* were the prescribed sacrifices (Ex 29.38–42); the *freewill offerings* were presented voluntarily as occasion required (Lev 22.18–30).

5.1–24: Holofernes is advised by Achior that the Jews are invincible as long as they keep God's law. 2: *Moab* was the region directly east of the Dead Sea, while *Ammon* lay north and east of it. Both nations were traditional enemies of the Jews (Judg 3.12–30; 2 Sam 10–12; 2 Kings 3.4–27; 24.2). **3:** The circumstance that Israel inhabited the rugged *hill country* had often helped her to

to them, "Tell me, you Canaanites, what people is this that lives in the hill country? What towns do they inhabit? How large is their army, and in what does their power and strength consist? Who rules over them as king and leads their army? ⁴And why have they alone, of all who live in the west, refused to come out and meet me?"

5 Then Achior, the leader of all the Ammonites, said to him, "May my lord please listen to a report from the mouth of your servant, and I will tell you the truth about this people that lives in the mountain district near you. No falsehood shall come from your servant's mouth. ⁶These people are descended from the Chaldeans. ⁷At one time they lived in Mesopotamia, because they did not wish to follow the gods of their ancestors who were in Chaldea. ⁸Since they had abandoned the ways of their ancestors, and worshiped the God of heaven, the God they had come to know, their ancestorsⁱ drove them out from the presence of their gods. So they fled to Mesopotamia, and lived there for a long time. ⁹Then their God commanded them to leave the place where they were living and go to the land of Canaan. There they settled, and grew very prosperous in gold and silver and very much livestock. ¹⁰When a famine spread over the land of Canaan they went down to Egypt and lived there as long as they had food. There they became so great a multitude that their race could not be counted. ¹¹So the king of Egypt became hostile to them; he exploited them and forced them to make bricks. ¹²They cried out to their

God, and he afflicted the whole land of Egypt with incurable plagues. So the Egyptians drove them out of their sight. ¹³Then God dried up the Red Sea before them, ¹⁴and he led them by the way of Sinai and Kadesh-barnea. They drove out all the people of the desert, ¹⁵and took up residence in the land of the Amorites, and by their might destroyed all the inhabitants of Heshbon; and crossing over the Jordan they took possession of all the hill country. ¹⁶They drove out before them the Canaanites, the Perizzites, the Jebusites, the Shechemites, and all the Gergesites, and lived there a long time.

17 "As long as they did not sin against their God they prospered, for the God who hates iniquity is with them. ¹⁸But when they departed from the way he had prescribed for them, they were utterly defeated in many battles and were led away captive to a foreign land. The temple of their God was razed to the ground, and their towns were occupied by their enemies. ¹⁹But now they have returned to their God, and have come back from the places where they were scattered, and have occupied Jerusalem, where their sanctuary is, and have settled in the hill country, because it was uninhabited.

20 "So now, my master and lord, if there is any oversight in this people and they sin against their God and we find out their offense, then we can go up and defeat them. ²¹But if they are not a guilty nation, then let my lord pass them by; for their Lord and God will defend them,

i Gk *they*

---

preserve her independence in the past. **5–21:** To explain the character of the Israelites, Achior summarizes their entire history from Abraham to the return from exile. **6–9:** The migration of Abraham and the prosperity of his descendants (Gen 11.27–37.1). **6:** *Chaldeans,* Abraham came from Ur of the Chaldees (Gen 11.27–31). **7:** *Mesopotamia* here is the region in the north around Haran (Gen 11.31). Late Jewish tradition ascribed the migration of Abraham's family to a desire to escape the influence of polytheism.

5.8: *The God (or Lord) of heaven* was a favorite name for Israel's God during the Persian period and later (Tob 10.11; Ezra 1.2). **10–13:** The descent into Egypt and the Exodus (Gen 37.2–Ex 18.27). **14:** *Sinai,* Ex 19.1–Num 10.10. *Kadesh-barnea,* Num 20.1. **15–16:** The conquests in Transjordan and Canaan (Num 20.14–Josh 11.23). **15:** *Amorites . . . Heshbon,* Num 21.21–32.

5.17: *They prospered,* the philosophy of Deuteronomy (28.1–14). **18:** The exile (see 1.1 n.). **19:** The return from exile (Ezra chs 1–

and we shall become the laughingstock of the whole world."

22 When Achior had finished saying these things, all the people standing around the tent began to complain; Holofernes' officers and all the inhabitants of the seacoast and Moab insisted that he should be cut to pieces. 23 They said, "We are not afraid of the Israelites; they are a people with no strength or power for making war. 24 Therefore let us go ahead, Lord Holofernes, and your vast army will swallow them up."

6 When the disturbance made by the people outside the council had died down, Holofernes, the commander of the Assyrian army, said to Achior*j* in the presence of all the foreign contingents:
2 "Who are you, Achior and you mercenaries of Ephraim, to prophesy among us as you have done today and tell us not to make war against the people of Israel because their God will defend them? What god is there except Nebuchadnezzar? He will send his forces and destroy them from the face of the earth. Their God will not save them; 3 we the king's*k* servants will destroy them as one man. They cannot resist the might of our cavalry. 4 We will overwhelm them;*l* their mountains will be drunk with their blood, and their fields will be full of their dead. Not even their footprints will survive our attack; they will utterly perish. So says King Nebuchadnezzar, lord of the whole earth. For he has spoken; none of his words shall be in vain.

5 "As for you, Achior, you Ammonite mercenary, you have said these words in a moment of perversity; you shall not see my face again from this day until I take revenge on this race that came out of Egypt. 6 Then at my return the sword of my army and the spear*m* of my servants shall pierce your sides, and you shall fall among their wounded. 7 Now my slaves are going to take you back into the hill country and put you in one of the towns beside the passes. 8 You will not die until you perish along with them. 9 If you really hope in your heart that they will not be taken, then do not look downcast! I have spoken, and none of my words shall fail to come true."

10 Then Holofernes ordered his slaves, who waited on him in his tent, to seize Achior and take him away to Bethulia and hand him over to the Israelites. 11 So the slaves took him and led him out of the camp into the plain, and from the plain they went up into the hill country and came to the springs below Bethulia. 12 When the men of the town saw them,*n* they seized their weapons and ran out of the town to the top of the hill, and all the slingers kept them from coming up by throwing stones at them. 13 So having taken shelter below the hill, they bound Achior and left him lying at the foot of the hill, and returned to their master.

14 Then the Israelites came down from their town and found him; they untied him and brought him into Bethulia and placed him before the magistrates of their town, 15 who in those days were Uzziah son of Micah, of the tribe of Simeon, and Chabris son of Gothoniel, and Charmis son of Melchiel. 16 They called together all the elders of the town, and all their young men and women ran to the assembly. They set Achior in the midst of all their people, and Uzziah questioned him about what had happened. 17 He answered and told them what had taken place at the council of Holofernes, and all that he had said in the presence of the Assyrian leaders, and all that Holo-

j Other ancient authorities add *and to all the Moabites*   *k* Gk *his*   *l* Other ancient authorities add *with it*   *m* Lat Syr: Gk *people*   *n* Other ancient authorities add *on the top of the hill*

---

3); see 4.3 n. **22–24**: Holofernes' other advisers oppose the view of Achior.

6.1–21: For his presumption, Achior is handed over to the Jews to perish with them in the fall of Bethulia. 1–9: Holofernes' denunciation of Achior. **10–13**: Achior is

left bound in sight of the inhabitants of Bethulia. **11**: With whatever place the mysterious Bethulia may be identified (see 4.6 n.), it is clearly pictured as a city on a hill with *springs* below it.

6.14–21: The Israelites bring Achior inside

fernes had boasted he would do against the house of Israel. 18 Then the people fell down and worshiped God, and cried out:

19 "O Lord God of heaven, see their arrogance, and have pity on our people in their humiliation, and look kindly today on the faces of those who are consecrated to you."

20 Then they reassured Achior, and praised him highly. 21 Uzziah took him from the assembly to his own house and gave a banquet for the elders; and all that night they called on the God of Israel for help.

7 The next day Holofernes ordered his whole army, and all the allies who had joined him, to break camp and move against Bethulia, and to seize the passes up into the hill country and make war on the Israelites. 2 So all their warriors marched off that day; their fighting forces numbered one hundred seventy thousand infantry and twelve thousand cavalry, not counting the baggage and the foot soldiers handling it, a very great multitude. 3 They encamped in the valley near Bethulia, beside the spring, and they spread out in breadth over Dothan as far as Balbaim and in length from Bethulia to Cyamon, which faces Esdraelon.

4 When the Israelites saw their vast numbers, they were greatly terrified and said to one another, "They will now strip clean the whole land; neither the high mountains nor the valleys nor the hills will bear their weight." 5 Yet they all seized their weapons, and when they had kindled fires on their towers, they remained on guard all that night.

6 On the second day Holofernes led out all his cavalry in full view of the Israelites in Bethulia. 7 He reconnoitered the approaches to their town, and visited the

springs that supplied their water; he seized them and set guards of soldiers over them, and then returned to his army.

8 Then all the chieftains of the Edomites and all the leaders of the Moabites and the commanders of the coastland came to him and said, 9 "Listen to what we have to say, my lord, and your army will suffer no losses. 10 This people, the Israelites, do not rely on their spears but on the height of the mountains where they live, for it is not easy to reach the tops of their mountains. 11 Therefore, my lord, do not fight against them in regular formation, and not a man of your army will fall. 12 Remain in your camp, and keep all the men in your forces with you; let your servants take possession of the spring of water that flows from the foot of the mountain, 13 for this is where all the people of Bethulia get their water. So thirst will destroy them, and they will surrender their town. Meanwhile, we and our people will go up to the tops of the nearby mountains and camp there to keep watch to see that no one gets out of the town. 14 They and their wives and children will waste away with famine, and before the sword reaches them they will be strewn about in the streets where they live. 15 Thus you will pay them back with evil, because they rebelled and did not receive you peaceably."

16 These words pleased Holofernes and all his attendants, and he gave orders to do as they had said. 17 So the army of the Ammonites moved forward, together with five thousand Assyrians, and they encamped in the valley and seized the water supply and the springs of the Israelites. 18 And the Edomites and Ammonites went up and encamped in the

the city, which then hears the story of Holofernes' arrogance.

7.1–7: Holofernes and his allies advance to Bethulia and survey the situation. 1–3: The line of march is south from Esdraelon. **3:** *Beside the spring,* see 6.11 n. *Dothan,* see 3.9 n. *Balbaim* and *Cyamon* are unknown. *Esdraelon,* see 3.9 n.

7.8–18: They cut off the city's water supply by seizing the springs. 8: The

Edomites, not previously mentioned in the narrative, were located southeast of the Dead Sea; they were traditional enemies of the Israelites (see e.g. Ob 18 and 1 Macc 5.1–5). **18:** The localities of *Egrebeh* and *Chusi* and the valley of *Mochmur* have all been identified (with varying degrees of probability) with sites in the neighborhood of Shechem (see 4.6 n.).

hill country opposite Dothan; and they sent some of their men toward the south and the east, toward Egrebeh, which is near Chusi beside the Wadi Mochmur. The rest of the Assyrian army encamped in the plain, and covered the whole face of the land. Their tents and supply trains spread out in great number, and they formed a vast multitude.

19 The Israelites then cried out to the Lord their God, for their courage failed, because all their enemies had surrounded them, and there was no way of escape from them. 20 The whole Assyrian army, their infantry, chariots, and cavalry, surrounded them for thirty-four days, until all the water containers of every inhabitant of Bethulia were empty; 21 their cisterns were going dry, and on no day did they have enough water to drink, for their drinking water was rationed. 22 Their children were listless, and the women and young men fainted from thirst and were collapsing in the streets of the town and in the gateways; they no longer had any strength.

23 Then all the people, the young men, the women, and the children, gathered around Uzziah and the rulers of the town and cried out with a loud voice, and said before all the elders, 24 "Let God judge between you and us! You have done us a great injury in not making peace with the Assyrians. 25 For now we have no one to help us; God has sold us into their hands, to be strewn before them in thirst and exhaustion. 26 Now summon them and surrender the whole town as booty to the army of Holofernes and to all his forces. 27 For it would be better for us to be captured by them. o We shall indeed become slaves, but our lives will be spared, and we shall not witness our little ones dying before our eyes, and our wives and children drawing their last breath. 28 We call to witness

against you heaven and earth and our God, the Lord of our ancestors, who punishes us for our sins and the sins of our ancestors; do today the things that we have described!"

29 Then great and general lamentation arose throughout the assembly, and they cried out to the Lord God with a loud voice. 30 But Uzziah said to them, "Courage, my brothers and sisters!p Let us hold out for five days more; by that time the Lord our God will turn his mercy to us again, for he will not forsake us utterly. 31 But if these days pass by, and no help comes for us, I will do as you say."

32 Then he dismissed the people to their various posts, and they went up on the walls and towers of their town. The women and children he sent home. In the town they were in great misery.

8 Now in those days Judith heard about these things: she was the daughter of Merari son of Ox son of Joseph son of Oziel son of Elkiah son of Ananias son of Gideon son of Raphain son of Ahitub son of Elijah son of Hilkiah son of Eliab son of Nathanael son of Salamiel son of Sarasadai son of Israel. 2 Her husband Manasseh, who belonged to her tribe and family, had died during the barley harvest. 3 For as he stood overseeing those who were binding sheaves in the field, he was overcome by the burning heat, and took to his bed and died in his town Bethulia. So they buried him with his ancestors in the field between Dothan and Balamon. 4 Judith remained as a widow for three years and four months 5 at home where she set up a tent for herself on the roof of her house. She put sackcloth around her waist and dressed in widow's clothing. 6 She fasted

o Other ancient authorities add *than to die of thirst*   p Gk *Courage, brothers*

7.19–28: Driven to desperation, the citizens of Bethulia urge their leaders to capitulate. 23: *Uzziah*, 6.15.

7.29–32: Uzziah advises a delay of five days.

8.1–8: The character of Judith. 1: The

name *Judith* means "Jewess." Her ancestors cannot be identified: some of the names are unparalleled in the Old Testament. **2–3**: Her husband had died of sunstroke (compare 2 Kings 4.18–20). **6**: Judith's rigorous fasting, which the author obviously approves of, is in

all the days of her widowhood, except the day before the sabbath and the sabbath itself, the day before the new moon and the day of the new moon, and the festivals and days of rejoicing of the house of Israel. 7 She was beautiful in appearance, and was very lovely to behold. Her husband Manasseh had left her gold and silver, men and women slaves, livestock, and fields; and she maintained this estate. 8 No one spoke ill of her, for she feared God with great devotion.

9 When Judith heard the harsh words spoken by the people against the ruler, because they were faint for lack of water, and when she heard all that Uzziah said to them, and how he promised them under oath to surrender the town to the Assyrians after five days, 10 she sent her maid, who was in charge of all she possessed, to summon Uzziah and *q* Chabris and Charmis, the elders of her town. 11 They came to her, and she said to them,

"Listen to me, rulers of the people of Bethulia! What you have said to the people today is not right; you have even sworn and pronounced this oath between God and you, promising to surrender the town to our enemies unless the Lord turns and helps us within so many days. 12 Who are you to put God to the test today, and to set yourselves up in the place of*r* God in human affairs? 13 You are putting the Lord Almighty to the test, but you will never learn anything! 14 You cannot plumb the depths of the human heart or understand the workings of the human mind; how do you expect to search out God, who made all these things, and find out his mind or comprehend his thought? No, my brothers, do not anger the Lord our God. 15 For if he does not choose to help us

within these five days, he has power to protect us within any time he pleases, or even to destroy us in the presence of our enemies. 16 Do not try to bind the purposes of the Lord our God; for God is not like a human being, to be threatened, or like a mere mortal, to be won over by pleading. 17 Therefore, while we wait for his deliverance, let us call upon him to help us, and he will hear our voice, if it pleases him.

18 "For never in our generation, nor in these present days, has there been any tribe or family or people or town of ours that worships gods made with hands, as was done in days gone by. 19 That was why our ancestors were handed over to the sword and to pillage, and so they suffered a great catastrophe before our enemies. 20 But we know no other god but him, and so we hope that he will not disdain us or any of our nation. 21 For if we are captured, all Judea will be captured and our sanctuary will be plundered; and he will make us pay for its desecration with our blood. 22 The slaughter of our kindred and the captivity of the land and the desolation of our inheritance—all this he will bring on our heads among the Gentiles, wherever we serve as slaves; and we shall be an offense and a disgrace in the eyes of those who acquire us. 23 For our slavery will not bring us into favor, but the Lord our God will turn it to dishonor.

24 "Therefore, my brothers, let us set an example for our kindred, for their lives depend upon us, and the sanctuary—both the temple and the altar—rests upon us. 25 In spite of everything let us give thanks to the Lord our

---

q Other ancient authorities lack *Uzziah and* (see verses 28 and 35) *r* Or *above*

---

accord with the practices of the Pharisees. She omits fasting only on days when it is forbidden. **7**: In the eyes of some biblical narrators, beauty and wealth are normal elements in the character of a romantic heroine.

8.9–27: Judith presents sound theological arguments against Uzziah's proposal. 12: Note the neat balance of her antitheses:

it is not for us to *put God to the test* (Deut 6.16); he is (v. 25) putting us to the test. **16**: *God is not like a human being,* Num 23.19; 1 Sam 15.29.

8.18: The people are safe because they have been entirely loyal to God (compare 5.21). Judith's optimistic judgment of her contemporaries stands in sharp contrast to the atti-

God, who is putting us to the test as he did our ancestors. ²⁶Remember what he did with Abraham, and how he tested Isaac, and what happened to Jacob in Syrian Mesopotamia, while he was tending the sheep of Laban, his mother's brother. ²⁷For he has not tried us with fire, as he did them, to search their hearts, nor has he taken vengeance on us; but the Lord scourges those who are close to him in order to admonish them."

28 Then Uzziah said to her, "All that you have said was spoken out of a true heart, and there is no one who can deny your words. ²⁹Today is not the first time your wisdom has been shown, but from the beginning of your life all the people have recognized your understanding, for your heart's disposition is right. ³⁰But the people were so thirsty that they compelled us to do for them what we have promised, and made us take an oath that we cannot break. ³¹Now since you are a God-fearing woman, pray for us, so that the Lord may send us rain to fill our cisterns. Then we will no longer feel faint from thirst."

32 Then Judith said to them, "Listen to me. I am about to do something that will go down through all generations of our descendants. ³³Stand at the town gate tonight so that I may go out with my maid; and within the days after which you have promised to surrender the town to our enemies, the Lord will deliver Israel by my hand. ³⁴Only, do not try to find out what I am doing; for I will not tell you until I have finished what I am about to do."

35 Uzziah and the rulers said to her,

"Go in peace, and may the Lord God go before you, to take vengeance on our enemies." ³⁶So they returned from the tent and went to their posts.

9 Then Judith prostrated herself, put ashes on her head, and uncovered the sackcloth she was wearing. At the very time when the evening incense was being offered in the house of God in Jerusalem, Judith cried out to the Lord with a loud voice, and said,

2 "O Lord God of my ancestor Simeon, to whom you gave a sword to take revenge on those strangers who had torn off a virgin's clothing^s to defile her, and exposed her thighs to put her to shame, and polluted her womb to disgrace her; for you said, 'It shall not be done'—yet they did it. ³So you gave up their rulers to be killed, and their bed, which was ashamed of the deceit they had practiced, was stained with blood, and you struck down slaves along with princes, and princes on their thrones. ⁴You gave up their wives for booty and their daughters to captivity, and all their booty to be divided among your beloved children who burned with zeal for you and abhorred the pollution of their blood and called on you for help—O God, my God, hear me also—a widow.

5 "For you have done these things and those that went before and those that followed. You have designed the things that are now, and those that are to come. What you had in mind has happened; ⁶the things you decided on presented themselves and said, 'Here we are!' For all your ways are prepared in advance,

---

^{s} Cn: Gk *loosed her womb*

---

tude of the great prophets, but is similar to that of the author of Ps 44.17–18. **27**: Their present sufferings are not punitive, but educative.

8.28–35: Answering Uzziah's plea, she personally pledges to deliver the city. 30–31: The vow, though wrong, as Judith said, had been made and its consequences could be avoided only by an act of God.

8.33: Judith promises that God will act through her.

9.1–14: Judith's prayer. 1: *Evening incense,* Ex 30.8; Ps 141.2. It may have become customary to offer prayer regularly at this time of day. **2**: *My ancestor Simeon,* the patriarch, son of Jacob, who, with Levi, avenged their sister Dinah (Gen 34.25–26). **4**: God's special care for the *widow* was an article of Israel's faith (Deut 10.18; Ps 146.9).

9.5–6: God's absolute foreknowledge and control of history, both past and future (Isa 44.6–8). **10**: The author of the book apparent-

and your judgment is with foreknowledge.

7 "Here now are the Assyrians, a greatly increased force, priding themselves in their horses and riders, boasting in the strength of their foot soldiers, and trusting in shield and spear, in bow and sling. They do not know that you are the Lord who crushes wars; the Lord is your name. 8 Break their strength by your might, and bring down their power in your anger; for they intend to defile your sanctuary, and to pollute the tabernacle where your glorious name resides, and to break off the horns*t* of your altar with the sword. 9 Look at their pride, and send your wrath upon their heads. Give to me, a widow, the strong hand to do what I plan. 10 By the deceit of my lips strike down the slave with the prince and the prince with his servant; crush their arrogance by the hand of a woman.

11 "For your strength does not depend on numbers, nor your might on the powerful. But you are the God of the lowly, helper of the oppressed, upholder of the weak, protector of the forsaken, savior of those without hope. 12 Please, please, God of my father, God of the heritage of Israel, Lord of heaven and earth, Creator of the waters, King of all your creation, hear my prayer! 13 Make my deceitful words bring wound and bruise on those who have planned cruel things against your covenant, and against your sacred house, and against Mount Zion, and against the house your children possess. 14 Let your whole na-

tion and every tribe know and understand that you are God, the God of all power and might, and that there is no other who protects the people of Israel but you alone!"

10 When Judith*u* had stopped crying out to the God of Israel, and had ended all these words, 2 she rose from where she lay prostrate. She called her maid and went down into the house where she lived on sabbaths and on her festal days. 3 She removed the sackcloth she had been wearing, took off her widow's garments, bathed her body with water, and anointed herself with precious ointment. She combed her hair, put on a tiara, and dressed herself in the festive attire that she used to wear while her husband Manasseh was living. 4 She put sandals on her feet, and put on her anklets, bracelets, rings, earrings, and all her other jewelry. Thus she made herself very beautiful, to entice the eyes of all the men who might see her. 5 She gave her maid a skin of wine and a flask of oil, and filled a bag with roasted grain, dried fig cakes, and fine bread;*v* then she wrapped up all her dishes and gave them to her to carry.

6 Then they went out to the town gate of Bethulia and found Uzziah standing there with the elders of the town, Chabris and Charmis. 7 When they saw her transformed in appearance and dressed differently, they were very

t Syr: Gk *horn*   *u* Gk *she*   *v* Other ancient authorities add *and cheese*

---

ly feels no moral inconsistency in having Judith pray for divine help in practicing *deceit* (see v. 13 n.). That an enemy should be destroyed *by the hand of a woman* would be not only remarkable, but, in the thinking of the time, particularly ignominious (Judg 9.54). **11:** *Your strength does not depend on numbers,* Judg 7.2; 1 Sam 14.6.

9.12: *King of all your creation,* a favorite late Jewish title for God. **13:** This prayer for God's blessing on a lie has been frequently criticized as a serious, and basic, moral blemish in the book. While Judith's conduct may, in the abstract, seem indefensible, it has often been imitated by both Jews and Christians in criti-

cal or life-threatening circumstances. The moral question is complex and the practical solution sometimes agonizing.

10.1–5: Judith beautifies herself. 2: *Went down into the house,* from the roof where she apparently lived (presumably in a tent) except on the sabbath and festivals. **4:** The Latin version states that God gave her a supernatural beauty because her motive in adorning herself was virtuous, not sensual. **5:** *Dishes,* for cooking her food in accordance with Jewish dietary laws.

10.6–10: She leaves the city with the elders' blessing. 8: *She bowed down to God,* prayer and acts of piety accompany every one

greatly astounded at her beauty and said to her, 8 "May the God of our ancestors grant you favor and fulfill your plans, so that the people of Israel may glory and Jerusalem may be exalted." She bowed down to God.

9 Then she said to them, "Order the gate of the town to be opened for me so that I may go out and accomplish the things you have just said to me." So they ordered the young men to open the gate for her, as she requested. 10 When they had done this, Judith went out, accompanied by her maid. The men of the town watched her until she had gone down the mountain and passed through the valley, where they lost sight of her.

11 As the women[w] were going straight on through the valley, an Assyrian patrol met her 12 and took her into custody. They asked her, "To what people do you belong, and where are you coming from, and where are you going?" She replied, "I am a daughter of the Hebrews, but I am fleeing from them, for they are about to be handed over to you to be devoured. 13 I am on my way to see Holofernes the commander of your army, to give him a true report; I will show him a way by which he can go and capture all the hill country without losing one of his men, captured or slain."

14 When the men heard her words, and observed her face—she was in their eyes marvelously beautiful—they said to her, 15 "You have saved your life by hurrying down to see our lord. Go at once to his tent; some of us will escort you and hand you over to him. 16 When you stand before him, have no fear in your heart, but tell him what you have just said, and he will treat you well."

17 They chose from their number a hundred men to accompany her and her maid, and they brought them to the tent of Holofernes. 18 There was great excitement in the whole camp, for her arrival was reported from tent to tent. They came and gathered around her as she stood outside the tent of Holofernes, waiting until they told him about her. 19 They marveled at her beauty and admired the Israelites, judging them by her. They said to one another, "Who can despise these people, who have women like this among them? It is not wise to leave one of their men alive, for if we let them go they will be able to beguile the whole world!"

20 Then the guards of Holofernes and all his servants came out and led her into the tent. 21 Holofernes was resting on his bed under a canopy that was woven with purple and gold, emeralds and other precious stones. 22 When they told him of her, he came to the front of the tent, with silver lamps carried before him. 23 When Judith came into the presence of Holofernes[x] and his servants, they all marveled at the beauty of her face. She prostrated herself and did obeisance to him, but his slaves raised her up.

11 Then Holofernes said to her, "Take courage, woman, and do not be afraid in your heart, for I have never hurt anyone who chose to serve Nebuchadnezzar, king of all the earth. 2 Even now, if your people who live in the hill country had not slighted me, I would never have lifted my spear against them. They have brought this on themselves. 3 But now tell me why you have

w Gk *they*   x Gk *him*

of her decisive acts. **10:** *Down the mountain . . . through the valley,* the geographical location of Bethulia, on the mountain with the "Assyrian" camp at the entrance of the valley leading up to it, could hardly be described more clearly.

10.11–23: Arriving at the enemy lines, she is brought into Holofernes' presence. **13:** *I will show him a way,* the first of her "deceitful words" (see 9.13 n.). **10.21:** The *canopy* was some kind of deco-

rated mosquito net. The Anglo-Saxon poem of Judith describes it thus: "There was hung/All golden a fair fly-net round the bed/Of the folk-leader, that the baleful one,/The chief of warriors, might look through on each/Child of the brave who came therein, and none/Might look on him. . . ."

11.1–4: Holofernes graciously receives her.

fled from them and have come over to us. In any event, you have come to safety. Take courage! You will live tonight and ever after. ⁴No one will hurt you. Rather, all will treat you well, as they do the servants of my lord King Nebuchadnezzar."

5 Judith answered him, "Accept the words of your slave, and let your servant speak in your presence. I will say nothing false to my lord this night. ⁶If you follow out the words of your servant, God will accomplish something through you, and my lord will not fail to achieve his purposes. ⁷By the life of Nebuchadnezzar, king of the whole earth, and by the power of him who has sent you to direct every living being! Not only do human beings serve him because of you, but also the animals of the field and the cattle and the birds of the air will live, because of your power, under Nebuchadnezzar and all his house. ⁸For we have heard of your wisdom and skill, and it is reported throughout the whole world that you alone are the best in the whole kingdom, the most informed and the most astounding in military strategy.

9 "Now as for Achior's speech in your council, we have heard his words, for the people of Bethulia spared him and he told them all he had said to you. ¹⁰Therefore, lord and master, do not disregard what he said, but keep it in your mind, for it is true. Indeed our nation cannot be punished, nor can the sword prevail against them, unless they sin against their God.

11 "But now, in order that my lord may not be defeated and his purpose frustrated, death will fall upon them, for a sin has overtaken them by which they are about to provoke their God to anger when they do what is wrong. ¹²Since their food supply is exhausted and their water has almost given out, they have planned to kill their livestock and have determined to use all that God by his laws has forbidden them to eat. ¹³They have decided to consume the first fruits of the grain and the tithes of the wine and oil, which they had consecrated and set aside for the priests who minister in the presence of our God in Jerusalem— things it is not lawful for any of the people even to touch with their hands. ¹⁴Since even the people in Jerusalem have been doing this, they have sent messengers there in order to bring back permission from the council of the elders. ¹⁵When the response reaches them and they act upon it, on that very day they will be handed over to you to be destroyed.

16 "So when I, your slave, learned all this, I fled from them. God has sent me to accomplish with you things that will astonish the whole world wherever people shall hear about them. ¹⁷Your servant is indeed God-fearing and serves the God of heaven night and day. So, my lord, I will remain with you; but every night your servant will go out into the valley and pray to God. He will tell me when they have committed their sins. ¹⁸Then I will come and tell you, so that you may go out with your whole army, and not one of them will be able to withstand you. ¹⁹Then I will lead you through Judea, until you come to Jerusalem; there I

11.5–23: Judith's explanation of her flight commends her to the general and his advisers. With the exception of v. 6 (which the narrator intends to be ironic) and vv. 9–10, every verse contains an equivocation, half-truth, or misrepresentation. **6:** The idea that God can work through heathen kings and their armies is fairly common in the Old Testament (Isa 10.5; 44.28; Jer 25.9). **7:** This verse is as obscure in the Greek as in the English.

11.9: *Achior's speech,* compare 5.5–21. **11–**

15: It is not true to say that the imminent fall of Bethulia is due to the circumstance that its citizens are about to appropriate to common use food that the Mosaic law assigned to God and the temple. **13:** *First fruits,* Ex 23.19. *Tithes,* Lev 27.30. **14:** *Council of the elders,* the Sanhedrin, the supreme religious authority of later Judaism. **17:** *God of heaven,* see 5.8 n. By telling him that *every night* she *will go out into the valley* Judith is preparing a ruse for her eventual escape (13.10).

will set your throne. *y* You will drive them like sheep that have no shepherd, and no dog will so much as growl at you. For this was told me to give me foreknowledge; it was announced to me, and I was sent to tell you."

20 Her words pleased Holofernes and all his servants. They marveled at her wisdom and said, 21 "No other woman from one end of the earth to the other looks so beautiful or speaks so wisely!" 22 Then Holofernes said to her, "God has done well to send you ahead of the people, to strengthen our hands and bring destruction on those who have despised my lord. 23 You are not only beautiful in appearance, but wise in speech. If you do as you have said, your God shall be my God, and you shall live in the palace of King Nebuchadnezzar and be renowned throughout the whole world."

12 Then he commanded them to bring her in where his silver dinnerware was kept, and ordered them to set a table for her with some of his own delicacies, and with some of his own wine to drink. 2 But Judith said, "I cannot partake of them, or it will be an offense; but I will have enough with the things I brought with me." 3 Holofernes said to her, "If your supply runs out, where can we get you more of the same? For none of your people are here with us." 4 Judith replied, "As surely as you live, my lord, your servant will not use up the supplies I have with me before the Lord carries out by my hand what he has determined."

5 Then the servants of Holofernes brought her into the tent, and she slept until midnight. Toward the morning watch she got up 6 and sent this message to Holofernes: "Let my lord now give orders to allow your servant to go out and pray." 7 So Holofernes commanded his guards not to hinder her. She remained in the camp three days. She went out each night to the valley of Bethulia, and bathed at the spring in the camp. *z* 8 After bathing, she prayed the Lord God of Israel to direct her way for the triumph of his *a* people. 9 Then she returned purified and stayed in the tent until she ate her food toward evening.

10 On the fourth day Holofernes held a banquet for his personal attendants only, and did not invite any of his officers. 11 He said to Bagoas, the eunuch who had charge of his personal affairs, "Go and persuade the Hebrew woman who is in your care to join us and to eat and drink with us. 12 For it would be a disgrace if we let such a woman go without having intercourse with her. If we do not seduce her, she will laugh at us."

13 So Bagoas left the presence of Holofernes, and approached her and said, "Let this pretty girl not hesitate to come to my lord to be honored in his presence, and to enjoy drinking wine with us, and to become today like one of the Assyrian women who serve in the palace of Nebuchadnezzar." 14 Judith replied, "Who am I to refuse my lord? Whatever pleases him I will do at once, and it will be a joy

y Or *chariot*   *z* Other ancient authorities lack *in the camp*   *a* Other ancient authorities read *her*

12.1–9: For three days Judith remains and establishes a pattern of conduct. 2: Once again the narrative stresses Judith's meticulous observance of the Jewish dietary laws, even in the presence of Gentiles. Her behavior contrasts markedly with that of Esther (Esth 2.20; compare Dan 1.8). **4:** *Before the Lord carries out by my hand* is a skillful foreshadowing of the murder. **6–7:** Since she had gone out every night, her departure after Holofernes' assassination would occasion no surprise. **8:** Her prayer was genuine enough, but not for the purpose previously announced (11.17).

12.10–20: Judith invited to Holofernes' banquet. 11: *Bagoas* is a well-known Persian name, spelled "Bigvai" in Ezra 2.2 and the Elephantine papyri. Diodorus Siculus (*Hist.* XVI. 47) mentions an officer Bagoas in the army of Artaxerxes III (see 2.4 n.). In oriental kingdoms the officer in charge of the women was normally a *eunuch;* eunuchs often attained also to positions of considerable responsibility in the state (Dan 1.3; Acts 8.27).

to me until the day of my death." ¹⁵So she proceeded to dress herself in all her woman's finery. Her maid went ahead and spread for her on the ground before Holofernes the lambskins she had received from Bagoas for her daily use in reclining.

16 Then Judith came in and lay down. Holofernes' heart was ravished with her and his passion was aroused, for he had been waiting for an opportunity to seduce her from the day he first saw her. ¹⁷So Holofernes said to her, "Have a drink and be merry with us!" ¹⁸Judith said, "I will gladly drink, my lord, because today is the greatest day in my whole life." ¹⁹Then she took what her maid had prepared and ate and drank before him. ²⁰Holofernes was greatly pleased with her, and drank a great quantity of wine, much more than he had ever drunk in any one day since he was born.

13 When evening came, his slaves quickly withdrew. Bagoas closed the tent from outside and shut out the attendants from his master's presence. They went to bed, for they all were weary because the banquet had lasted so long. ²But Judith was left alone in the tent, with Holofernes stretched out on his bed, for he was dead drunk.

3 Now Judith had told her maid to stand outside the bedchamber and to wait for her to come out, as she did on the other days; for she said she would be going out for her prayers. She had said the same thing to Bagoas. ⁴So everyone went out, and no one, either small or great, was left in the bedchamber. Then Judith, standing beside his bed, said in her heart, "O Lord God of all might, look in this hour on the work of my

hands for the exaltation of Jerusalem. ⁵Now indeed is the time to help your heritage and to carry out my design to destroy the enemies who have risen up against us."

6 She went up to the bedpost near Holofernes' head, and took down his sword that hung there. ⁷She came close to his bed, took hold of the hair of his head, and said, "Give me strength today, O Lord God of Israel!" ⁸Then she struck his neck twice with all her might, and cut off his head. ⁹Next she rolled his body off the bed and pulled down the canopy from the posts. Soon afterward she went out and gave Holofernes' head to her maid, ¹⁰who placed it in her food bag.

Then the two of them went out together, as they were accustomed to do for prayer. They passed through the camp, circled around the valley, and went up the mountain to Bethulia, and came to its gates. ¹¹From a distance Judith called out to the sentries at the gates, "Open, open the gate! God, our God, is with us, still showing his power in Israel and his strength against our enemies, as he has done today!"

12 When the people of her town heard her voice, they hurried down to the town gate and summoned the elders of the town. ¹³They all ran together, both small and great, for it seemed unbelievable that she had returned. They opened the gate and welcomed them. Then they lit a fire to give light, and gathered around them. ¹⁴Then she said to them with a loud voice, "Praise God, O praise him! Praise God, who has not withdrawn his mercy from the house of Israel, but has destroyed our enemies by my hand this very night!"

12.14: Judith's words *Who am I to refuse my lord? Whatever pleases him I will do at once* are a masterpiece of irony; for Holofernes thinks that he is her lord, but the reader knows otherwise.

13.1–10a: Judith beheads Holofernes. 4–7: The irony is that Holofernes is mastered by the very person he thought he had mastered—and with his own sword. Judith's prayer before she decapitates the enemy of

her people is the most dramatic, horrifying, and ironic moment in the story, for the pious woman prays for strength to slay the tyrant. **9:** *Pulled down the canopy* (10.21) and carried it off as a trophy (v. 15). **10a:** Even the bag in which she brought her food (10.5) is now seen to have been part of a well-laid plan. **13.10b–20: She escapes and returns to her own people. 10b:** Her established habit of leaving the camp each night for prayer

15 Then she pulled the head out of the bag and showed it to them, and said, "See here, the head of Holofernes, the commander of the Assyrian army, and here is the canopy beneath which he lay in his drunken stupor. The Lord has struck him down by the hand of a woman. 16 As the Lord lives, who has protected me in the way I went, I swear that it was my face that seduced him to his destruction, and that he committed no sin with me, to defile and shame me."

17 All the people were greatly astonished. They bowed down and worshiped God, and said with one accord, "Blessed are you our God, who have this day humiliated the enemies of your people."

18 Then Uzziah said to her, "O daughter, you are blessed by the Most High God above all other women on earth; and blessed be the Lord God, who created the heavens and the earth, who has guided you to cut off the head of the leader of our enemies. 19 Your praise[b] will never depart from the hearts of those who remember the power of God. 20 May God grant this to be a perpetual honor to you, and may he reward you with blessings, because you risked your own life when our nation was brought low, and you averted our ruin, walking in the straight path before our God." And all the people said, "Amen. Amen."

14 Then Judith said to them, "Listen to me, my friends. Take this head and hang it upon the parapet of your wall. 2 As soon as day breaks and the sun rises on the earth, each of you take up your weapons, and let every able-bodied man go out of the town; set a captain over them, as if you were going down to the plain against the Assyrian outpost; only do not go down. 3 Then they will seize their arms and go into the camp and rouse the officers of the Assyrian army. They will rush into the tent of Holofernes and will not find him. Then panic will come over them, and they will flee before you. 4 Then you and all who live within the borders of Israel will pursue them and cut them down in their tracks. 5 But before you do all this, bring Achior the Ammonite to me so that he may see and recognize the man who despised the house of Israel and sent him to us as if to his death."

6 So they summoned Achior from the house of Uzziah. When he came and saw the head of Holofernes in the hand of one of the men in the assembly of the people, he fell down on his face in a faint. 7 When they raised him up he threw himself at Judith's feet, and did obeisance to her, and said, "Blessed are you in every tent of Judah! In every nation those who hear your name will be alarmed. 8 Now tell me what you have done during these days."

So Judith told him in the presence of the people all that she had done, from the day she left until the moment she began speaking to them. 9 When she had finished, the people raised a great shout and made a joyful noise in their town. 10 When Achior saw all that the God of Israel had done, he believed firmly in God. So he was circumcised, and joined the house of Israel, remaining so to this day.

b Other ancient authorities read *hope*

(11.17; 12.7) permits her an easy escape. **17:** *Blessed are you our God,* is the most common formula of late Jewish prayers (see Tob 3.11 n.). **18:** Uzziah's words are reminiscent of those spoken concerning Jael under similar circumstances (Judg 5.24); also of Melchizedek's greeting to Abraham (Gen 14.19–20). **14.1–10: Achior identifies the head of Holofernes and is converted to Judaism. 1–4:** Judith suggests tactics that will put the enemy to flight with minimum effort by the Jewish forces. In the Latin version, v. 5 is omitted and vv. 6–7, more logically, precede vv. 1–4. **5:** *Achior,* the Ammonite leader whom Holofernes had left to be destroyed with the Jews (5.5–6.21). The full irony of the situation is evident when one remembers that Achior had been told he would see that face again only on the day of Holofernes' vengeance (6.5). **10:** The fact that the conversion of an Ammonite to Judaism is strictly forbidden by the law (Deut 23.3) may explain why

11 As soon as it was dawn they hung the head of Holofernes on the wall. Then they all took their weapons, and they went out in companies to the mountain passes. 12 When the Assyrians saw them they sent word to their commanders, who then went to the generals and the captains and to all their other officers. 13 They came to Holofernes' tent and said to the steward in charge of all his personal affairs, "Wake up our lord, for the slaves have been so bold as to come down against us to give battle, to their utter destruction."

14 So Bagoas went in and knocked at the entry of the tent, for he supposed that he was sleeping with Judith. 15 But when no one answered, he opened it and went into the bedchamber and found him sprawled on the floor dead, with his head missing. 16 He cried out with a loud voice and wept and groaned and shouted, and tore his clothes. 17 Then he went to the tent where Judith had stayed, and when he did not find her, he rushed out to the people and shouted, 18 "The slaves have tricked us! One Hebrew woman has brought disgrace on the house of King Nebuchadnezzar. Look, Holofernes is lying on the ground, and his head is missing!"

19 When the leaders of the Assyrian army heard this, they tore their tunics and were greatly dismayed, and their loud cries and shouts rose up throughout the camp.

15 When the men in the tents heard it, they were amazed at what had happened. 2 Overcome with fear and trembling, they did not wait for one another, but with one impulse all rushed out and fled by every path across the plain and through the hill country. 3 Those who had camped in the hills around Bethulia also took to flight. Then the Israelites, everyone that was a soldier, rushed out upon them. 4 Uzziah sent men to Betomasthaim ͨ and Choba and Kola, and to all the frontiers of Israel, to tell what had taken place and to urge all to rush out upon the enemy to destroy them. 5 When the Israelites heard it, with one accord they fell upon the enemy, ͩ and cut them down as far as Choba. Those in Jerusalem and all the hill country also came, for they were told what had happened in the camp of the enemy. The men in Gilead and in Galilee outflanked them with great slaughter, even beyond Damascus and its borders. 6 The rest of the people of Bethulia fell upon the Assyrian camp and plundered it, acquiring great riches. 7 And the Israelites, when they returned from the slaughter, took possession of what remained. Even the villages and towns in the hill country and in the plain got a great amount of booty, since there was a vast quantity of it.

8 Then the high priest Joakim and the elders of the Israelites who lived in Jerusalem came to witness the good things that the Lord had done for Israel, and to see Judith and to wish her well. 9 When they met her, they all blessed her with one accord and said to her, "You are the glory of Jerusalem, you are the great boast of Israel, you are the great pride of our nation! 10 You have done all this with your own hand; you have done great good to Israel, and God is well pleased

c Other ancient authorities add *and Bebai*
d Gk *them*

---

the book of Judith was never canonized by the Jews.

14.11–19: The enemy discovers Holofernes' death. 11–13: As Judith had planned, the threatening movements of the Jews lead to the discovery of Holofernes' body.

15.1–7: The Assyrians, fleeing in panic, are slaughtered and despoiled by the Jews. 3: *Those who had camped in the hills* were the Edomites and Ammonites (7.18). **4:** As with so many place names in this book, *Betomasthaim and Choba and Kola* have never been satisfactorily identified. **5:** *Gilead,* which was situated in the northern part of Transjordan, and *Galilee,* in the north of Palestine proper, lay on either flank of the enemy's northeastward flight through *Damascus* and back toward Assyria.

15.8–13: Judith is led in triumph to Jerusalem. 11: The *thirty days* of plundering is

with it. May the Almighty Lord bless you forever!" And all the people said, "Amen."

11 All the people plundered the camp for thirty days. They gave Judith the tent of Holofernes and all his silver dinnerware, his beds, his bowls, and all his furniture. She took them and loaded her mules and hitched up her carts and piled the things on them.

12 All the women of Israel gathered to see her, and blessed her, and some of them performed a dance in her honor. She took ivy-wreathed wands in her hands and distributed them to the women who were with her; 13 and she and those who were with her crowned themselves with olive wreaths. She went before all the people in the dance, leading all the women, while all the men of Israel followed, bearing their arms and wearing garlands and singing hymns.

14 Judith began this thanksgiving before all Israel, and all the people loudly

16 sang this song of praise. 1 And Judith said,
Begin a song to my God with
tambourines,
sing to my Lord with cymbals.
Raise to him a new psalm;*e*
exalt him, and call upon his
name.
2 For the Lord is a God who
crushes wars;
he sets up his camp among his
people;
he delivered me from the hands
of my pursuers.

3 The Assyrian came down from the
mountains of the north;
he came with myriads of his
warriors;
their numbers blocked up the
wadis,
and their cavalry covered the
hills.
4 He boasted that he would burn up
my territory,
and kill my young men with the
sword,
and dash my infants to the
ground,
and seize my children as booty,
and take my virgins as spoil.

5 But the Lord Almighty has foiled
them
by the hand of a woman.*f*
6 For their mighty one did not fall
by the hands of the young
men,
nor did the sons of the Titans
strike him down,
nor did tall giants set upon him;
but Judith daughter of Merari
with the beauty of her
countenance undid him.

7 For she put away her widow's
clothing
to exalt the oppressed in Israel.

e Other ancient authorities read *a psalm and
praise*   *f* Other ancient authorities add *he has
confounded them*

---

obviously unrealistic. While the people apparently intend that Judith herself shall have Holofernes' treasure, she accepts the gifts only with the intention of dedicating them to God (16.19). **12**: *A dance,* compare 1 Sam 18.6; Ps 149.3–9. *Ivy-wreathed wands,* Ps 118.27; 1 Macc 13.51; 2 Macc 10.7. **13**: The reference to *olive wreaths* seems to indicate a late date for the book, for the custom is Greek, not Jewish. The destination of the procession is the temple in Jerusalem (16.18).
16.1–17: Judith's thanksgiving psalm.
In the book of Tobit (ch 13) a prayer composed by Tobit occupies a similar position at the end of the story. It is Israel, personified as

a woman, who sings the hymn; Judith herself is referred to only in the third person (v. 7). **1–2**: A call to praise (compare Ex 15.21; Judg 5.2). **1**: The phrase "a new" psalm (compare v. 13) is a cliché drawn from the Psalter (e.g. Pss 96.1; 98.1). **3–12**: Description of the victory. **6**: *Sons of the Titans* is Greek; perhaps the Semitic original had "sons of Rephaim" (compare Deut 3.11). **13–16**: A general hymn of praise. **13**: *I will sing . . . a new song,* Ps 144.9. The hymn begins in the next line. **14**: Pss 33.6; 104.30. **16**: *Every sacrifice . . . is a small thing;* to compare sacrifice unfavorably with moral obedience ("to fear the Lord") is a commonplace of Old Testament religion,

She anointed her face with
      perfume;
8 she fastened her hair with a tiara
      and put on a linen gown to
      beguile him.
9 Her sandal ravished his eyes,
      her beauty captivated his mind,
      and the sword severed his neck!
10 The Persians trembled at her
      boldness,
   the Medes were daunted at her
      daring.

11 Then my oppressed people
      shouted;
   my weak people cried out,^g and
      the enemy^h trembled;
   they lifted up their voices, and
      the enemy^h were turned
      back.
12 Sons of slave girls pierced them
      through
   and wounded them like the
      children of fugitives;
   they perished before the army of
      my Lord.

13 I will sing to my God a new song:
   O Lord, you are great and
      glorious,
   wonderful in strength,
      invincible.
14 Let all your creatures serve you,
      for you spoke, and they were
      made.
   You sent forth your spirit,ⁱ and it
      formed them;^j
   there is none that can resist your
      voice.
15 For the mountains shall be shaken
      to their foundations with
      the waters;
   before your glance the rocks
      shall melt like wax.

But to those who fear you
      you show mercy.
16 For every sacrifice as a fragrant
      offering is a small thing,
   and the fat of all whole burnt
      offerings to you is a very
      little thing;
   but whoever fears the Lord is
      great forever.

17 Woe to the nations that rise up
      against my people!
   The Lord Almighty will take
      vengeance on them in the
      day of judgment;
   he will send fire and worms into
      their flesh;
   they shall weep in pain forever.

18 When they arrived at Jerusalem, they worshiped God. As soon as the people were purified, they offered their burnt offerings, their freewill offerings, and their gifts. 19 Judith also dedicated to God all the possessions of Holofernes, which the people had given her; and the canopy that she had taken for herself from his bedchamber she gave as a votive offering. 20 For three months the people continued feasting in Jerusalem before the sanctuary, and Judith remained with them.

21 After this they all returned home to their own inheritances. Judith went to Bethulia, and remained on her estate. For the rest of her life she was honored throughout the whole country. 22 Many desired to marry her, but she gave herself to no man all the days of her life after her husband Manasseh died and was gath-

g Other ancient authorities read *feared*
h Gk *they*   i Or *breath*   j Other ancient
authorities read *they were created*

especially in later times (1 Sam 15.22; Pss 40.6–8; 50.8–15; 51.16–17; Hos 6.6; compare Sir 34.18–19). **17:** Concluding anathema on Israel's enemies (compare Judg 5.31). *Fire and worms,* Isa 66.24; Sir 7.17. As in Dan 12.2, the punishment of the wicked is eternal.
16.18–20: A victory celebration in Je-

rusalem. **20:** *Three months,* Syriac, "a month of days."
16.21–25: Judith remains a widow and dies at a ripe old age. 24: She *distributed her property,* according to the Mosaic law (Num 27.11).

ered to his people. 23 She became more and more famous, and grew old in her husband's house, reaching the age of one hundred five. She set her maid free. She died in Bethulia, and they buried her in the cave of her husband Manasseh; 24 and the house of Israel mourned her for seven days. Before she died she distributed her property to all those who were next of kin to her husband Manasseh, and to her own nearest kindred. 25 No one ever again spread terror among the Israelites during the lifetime of Judith, or for a long time after her death.

NOTE. The deuterocanonical portions of the Book of Esther are several additional passages found in the Greek translation of the Hebrew Book of Esther, a translation that differs also in other respects from the Hebrew text (the latter is translated in the NRSV Old Testament). The disordered chapter numbers come from the displacement of the additions to the end of the canonical Book of Esther by Jerome in his Latin translation and from the subsequent division of the Bible into chapters by Stephen Langton, who numbered the additions consecutively as though they formed a direct continuation of the Hebrew text. So that the additions may be read in their proper context, the whole of the Greek version is here translated, though certain familiar names are given according to their Hebrew rather than their Greek form; for example, Mordecai and Vashti instead of Mardocheus and Astin. The order followed is that of the Greek text, but the chapter and verse numbers conform to those of the King James or Authorized Version. The additions, conveniently indicated by the letters A–F, are located as follows: A, before 1.1; B, after 3.13; C and D, after 4.17; E, after 8.12; F, after 10.3.

Esther

(*The Greek Version Containing the Additional Chapters*)

The Additions to the book of Esther comprise 107 verses. Their contents are as follows: Addition A: Mordecai's dream (11.2–12) and his discovery of a plot against the king (12.1–6); Addition B: The royal edict dictated by Haman, announcing a pogrom against the Jews (13.1–7); Addition C: The prayers of Mordecai (13.8–18) and Esther (14.1–19); Addition D: Esther's appearing, unsummoned, before the king (15.4–19); and Addition E: The royal edict dictated by Mordecai, counteracting the edict sent by Haman (16.1–24); and Addition F: The interpretation of Mordecai's dream (10.4–13) and the colophon (an inscription at the end of a manuscript) to the Greek version (11.1).

There is no mention of God in the Hebrew narrative, but in the Greek Additions the words "Lord" or "God" appear more than fifty times. In fact, occasionally God is mentioned also in the portions of the Greek version that correspond to the canonical Hebrew text, as when Mordecai instructs Esther prior to her becoming queen that she should "fear God and keep his laws" (2.20) and then later urges her to "call upon the Lord" (4.8) before appearing, unsummoned and unannounced, before the king. We also read in the Greek text: "That night the Lord took sleep from the king" (compare the Hebrew at 6.1). Likewise, Haman's wife and his friends caution Haman that if Mordecai be Jewish, then "the living God is with him" (compare the Hebrew at 6.13).

The additions are clearly intrusive and secondary, for they contradict the Hebrew at a number of points. They sometimes make the characters and events more vivid or dramatic, and they always give the narrative an explicitly religious character that is lacking in the Hebrew.

Moreover, the additions provide their authors with an opportunity to express their own particular theological views. Additions A and F especially emphasize God's providential care for the people Israel in a universally hostile world. Addition C attests to the efficacy of prayer and well expresses Queen Esther's abhorrence at being married to a Gentile, her loathing of all things worldly and courtly, and her strict observance of dietary laws—none of which are so much as hinted at in the Hebrew. Thanks in part to Addition D, the climax of the Greek version is reached when God miraculously changes to gentleness the king's "fierce anger" at Esther's unannounced entrance. This is lacking in the Hebrew. Taken together, the six additions de-emphasize the establishment of Purim and express a strong anti-Gentile spirit.

Originally, A, C, D, and F were probably composed in either Hebrew or Aramaic and, if so, were already part of that particular Semitic text used by the Greek translator. B and E are so florid and rhetorical that they must have been originally composed in Greek.

The additions were not composed at the same time. The latest possible date for B, C, D, and E is A.D. 93. The colophon's location (11.1) immediately after F suggests that A as well as F were part of the Semitic text at the time that Lysimachus of Jerusalem made his Greek translation of it, about 114 B.C. It is impossible to say who composed the Semitic or Greek Additions.

Additions B and E may have been composed in a sophisticated Greek Jewish center, such as Alexandria, but a Palestinian provenance for the others is likely.

ADDITION A

11 *a* 2 In the second year of the reign of Artaxerxes the Great, on the first day of Nisan, Mordecai son of Jair son of Shimei *b* son of Kish, of the tribe of Benjamin, had a dream. 3 He was a Jew living in the city of Susa, a great man, serving in the court of the king. 4 He was one of the captives whom King Nebuchadnezzar of Babylon had brought from Jerusalem with King Jeconiah of Judea. And this was his dream: 5 Noises *c* and confusion, thunders and earthquake, tumult on the earth! 6 Then two great dragons came forward, both ready to fight, and they roared terribly. 7 At their roaring every nation prepared for war, to fight against the righteous nation. 8 It was a day of darkness and gloom, of tribulation and distress, affliction and great tu-mult on the earth! 9 And the whole righteous nation was troubled; they feared the evils that threatened them, *d* and were ready to perish. 10 Then they cried out to God; and at their outcry, as though from a tiny spring, there came a great river, with abundant water; 11 light came, and the sun rose, and the lowly were exalted and devoured those held in honor.

12 Mordecai saw in this dream what God had determined to do, and after he awoke he had it on his mind, seeking all day to understand it in every detail.

12 Now Mordecai took his rest in the courtyard with Gabatha and Tharra, the two eunuchs of the king who kept watch in the courtyard. 2 He overheard their conversation and inquired

a Chapters 11.2–12.6 correspond to chapter A 1–17 in some translations.   *b* Gk *Semeios*
c Or *Voices*   *d* Gk *their own evils*

11.2–12: Mordecai's dream of impending conflict between two *dragons* (Mordecai and Haman; compare 10.7) pictures how the *righteous nation* Israel, threatened with annihilation, is delivered by God. **2:** *Artaxerxes,* the Greek name used throughout the Greek version of Esther and to be identified with Heb Ahasuerus, which is Xerxes I (486 [or 485]–465 B.C.). His *second year* was 485 [or 484] B.C. As the first month of the new year, Nisan (Babylonian name for March–April) is the appropriate time for a new and significant dream for Mordecai. All the month names in the book are of Babylonian derivation. **4:** This verse dates Mordecai's captivity in 597 B.C. (2 Kings 24.15); v. 2 dates his dream 112 years later. **7:** *The righteous nation,* that is,

the Jews. **10:** The expressions *tiny spring* and *great river* refer to Esther (10.6). **12:** Mordecai knows that the *dream* forecasts God's action, but does not yet grasp the interpretation given in 10.6–12.

12.1–6: Mordecai saves the king's life when two eunuchs posted to protect the king plot instead to kill him. It is unclear whether this plot is the same as the one in Esth 2.19–23 of the Hebrew text or is an earlier one. **5:** The king rewards Mordecai (in Esth 6.3, however, it is said later that "You have not done anything for him"). **6:** It is implied that Haman shared in the plot and so resented Mordecai's action. *Bougean* represents a term of reproach, which in Esth 3.1 translates the Hebrew word Agagite (compare 1 Sam 15.8).

into their purposes, and learned that they were preparing to lay hands on King Artaxerxes; and he informed the king concerning them. ³Then the king examined the two eunuchs, and after they had confessed it, they were led away to execution. ⁴The king made a permanent record of these things, and Mordecai wrote an account of them. ⁵And the king ordered Mordecai to serve in the court, and rewarded him for these things. ⁶But Haman son of Hammedatha, a Bougean, who was in great honor with the king, determined to injure Mordecai and his people because of the two eunuchs of the king.

END OF ADDITION A

1 It was after this that the following things happened in the days of Artaxerxes, the same Artaxerxes who ruled over one hundred twenty-seven provinces from India to Ethiopia.ᵉ ²In those days, when King Artaxerxes was enthroned in the city of Susa, ³in the third year of his reign, he gave a banquet for his Friends and other persons of various nations, the Persians and Median nobles, and the governors of the provinces. ⁴After this, when he had displayed to them the riches of his kingdom and the splendor of his bountiful celebration during the course of one hundred eighty days, ⁵at the end of the festivityᶠ the king gave a drinking party for the people of various nations who lived in the city. This was held for six days in the courtyard of the royal palace, ⁶which was adorned with curtains of fine linen and cotton, held by

cords of purple linen attached to gold and silver blocks on pillars of marble and other stones. Gold and silver couches were placed on a mosaic floor of emerald, mother-of-pearl, and marble. There were coverings of gauze, embroidered in various colors, with roses arranged around them. ⁷The cups were of gold and silver, and a miniature cup was displayed, made of ruby, worth thirty thousand talents. There was abundant sweet wine, such as the king himself drank. ⁸The drinking was not according to a fixed rule; but the king wished to have it so, and he commanded his stewards to comply with his pleasure and with that of the guests.

9 Meanwhile, Queen Vashtiᵍ gave a drinking party for the women in the palace where King Artaxerxes was.

10 On the seventh day, when the king was in good humor, he told Haman, Bazan, Tharra, Boraze, Zatholtha, Abataza, and Tharaba, the seven eunuchs who served King Artaxerxes, ¹¹to escort the queen to him in order to proclaim her as queen and to place the diadem on her head, and to have her display her beauty to all the governors and the people of various nations, for she was indeed a beautiful woman. ¹²But Queen Vashtiᵍ refused to obey him and would not come with the eunuchs. This offended the king and he became furious. ¹³He said to his Friends, "This is how Vashtiᵍ has answered me.ʰ Give therefore your ruling and judgment on this matter." ¹⁴Arkesaeus, Sarsathaeus, and Malesear, then

e Other ancient authorities lack *to Ethiopia*
f Gk *marriage feast*   g Gk *Astin*   h Gk *Astin has said thus and so*

1.1–9: Artaxerxes' banquet. The king gives a lavish seven-day drinking party to celebrate his marriage. **2:** That the king *was enthroned* underscores that he now rules securely, having successfully put down earlier uprisings throughout his empire. **5:** *The festivity* (literally, "the marriage feast"), in the Hebrew text there is no mention of this being a marriage feast (but see 1.11 of the Greek). Here, the Greek speaks of *six days* of partying; but it has "seven" in 1.10 (so also 1.5, 10 of the Hebrew). **7:** The Hebrew text makes no mention of the fabulously expensive *miniature cup*.

1.10–22: The dismissal of Queen Vashti, the result of her refusing to appear before the king and his guests. **11:** *To proclaim her as queen,* here, Vashti's coronation is the purpose of her appearance and not, as in the Hebrew, merely for the king to display her fabled beauty to his drunken friends. **14:** In place of the seven privy counselors named in the Hebrew text, three *governors* are named here: *Arkesaeus, Sarsathaeus, and Malesear.*

the governors of the Persians and Medes who were closest to the king— Arkesaeus, Sarsathaeus, and Malesear, who sat beside him in the chief seats— came to him [15] and told him what must be done to Queen Vashti[i] for not obeying the order that the king had sent her by the eunuchs. [16] Then Muchaeus said to the king and the governors, "Queen Vashti[i] has insulted not only the king but also all the king's governors and officials" [17] (for he had reported to them what the queen had said and how she had defied the king). "And just as she defied King Artaxerxes, [18] so now the other ladies who are wives of the Persian and Median governors, on hearing what she has said to the king, will likewise dare to insult their husbands. [19] If therefore it pleases the king, let him issue a royal decree, inscribed in accordance with the laws of the Medes and Persians so that it may not be altered, that the queen may no longer come into his presence; but let the king give her royal rank to a woman better than she. [20] Let whatever law the king enacts be proclaimed in his kingdom, and thus all women will give honor to their husbands, rich and poor alike." [21] This speech pleased the king and the governors, and the king did as Muchaeus had recommended. [22] The king sent the decree into all his kingdom, to every province in its own language, so that in every house respect would be shown to every husband.

2 After these things, the king's anger abated, and he no longer was concerned about Vashti[i] or remembered what he had said and how he had condemned her. [2] Then the king's servants said, "Let beautiful and virtuous girls be sought out for the king. [3] The king shall appoint officers in all the provinces of his kingdom, and they shall select beautiful young virgins to be brought to the harem in Susa, the capital. Let them be entrusted to the king's eunuch who is in charge of the women, and let ointments and whatever else they need be given them. [4] And the woman who pleases the king shall be queen instead of Vashti.[i] This pleased the king, and he did so.

5 Now there was a Jew in Susa the capital whose name was Mordecai son of Jair son of Shimei[j] son of Kish, of the tribe of Benjamin; [6] he had been taken captive from Jerusalem among those whom King Nebuchadnezzar of Babylon had captured. [7] And he had a foster-child, the daughter of his father's brother, Aminadab, and her name was Esther. When her parents died, he brought her up to womanhood as his own. The girl was beautiful in appearance. [8] So, when the decree of the king was proclaimed, and many girls were gathered in Susa the capital in custody of Gai, Esther also was brought to Gai, who had custody of the women. [9] The girl pleased him and won his favor, and he quickly provided her with ointments and her portion of food,[k] as well as seven maids chosen from the palace; he treated her and her maids with special favor in the harem. [10] Now Esther had not disclosed her people or country, for Mordecai had commanded her not to make it known. [11] And every day Mordecai walked in the courtyard of the harem, to see what would happen to Esther.

12 Now the period after which a girl was to go to the king was twelve months. During this time the days of beautification are completed—six months while they are anointing themselves with oil of myrrh, and six months with spices and ointments for women. [13] Then she goes in to the king; she is handed to the person appointed, and goes with him from the harem to the

i Gk *Astin*   *j* Gk *Semeios*   *k* Gk lacks *of food*

2.1–18: Esther becomes the new queen by following carefully the instructions of her foster-father Mordecai and the harem etiquette as offered by Gai, the eunuch in charge of the harem. **7:** *Esther,* whose Hebrew name ("Hadassah") is lacking here, is the daughter of *Aminadab* ("Abihail" in Hebrew at 2.15). **2.16:** Esther went in to the king *in the twelfth*

king's palace. [14]In the evening she enters and in the morning she departs to the second harem, where Gai the king's eunuch is in charge of the women; and she does not go in to the king again unless she is summoned by name.

15 When the time was fulfilled for Esther daughter of Aminadab, the brother of Mordecai's father, to go in to the king, she neglected none of the things that Gai, the eunuch in charge of the women, had commanded. Now Esther found favor in the eyes of all who saw her. [16]So Esther went in to King Artaxerxes in the twelfth month, which is Adar, in the seventh year of his reign. [17]And the king loved Esther and she found favor beyond all the other virgins, so he put on her the queen's diadem. [18]Then the king gave a banquet lasting seven days for all his Friends and the officers to celebrate his marriage to Esther; and he granted a remission of taxes to those who were under his rule.

19 Meanwhile Mordecai was serving in the courtyard. [20]Esther had not disclosed her country—such were the instructions of Mordecai; but she was to fear God and keep his laws, just as she had done when she was with him. So Esther did not change her mode of life.

21 Now the king's eunuchs, who were chief bodyguards, were angry because of Mordecai's advancement, and they plotted to kill King Artaxerxes. [22]The matter became known to Mordecai, and he warned Esther, who in turn revealed the plot to the king. [23]He investigated the two eunuchs and hanged them. Then the king ordered a memorandum to be deposited in the royal library in praise of the goodwill shown by Mordecai.

3 After these events King Artaxerxes promoted Haman son of Hammedatha, a Bougean, advancing him and granting him precedence over all the king's[l] Friends. [2]So all who were at court used to do obeisance to Haman,[m] for so the king had commanded to be done. Mordecai, however, did not do obeisance. [3]Then the king's courtiers said to Mordecai, "Mordecai, why do you disobey the king's command?" [4]Day after day they spoke to him, but he would not listen to them. Then they informed Haman that Mordecai was resisting the king's command. Mordecai had told them that he was a Jew. [5]So when Haman learned that Mordecai was not doing obeisance to him, he became furiously angry, [6]and plotted to destroy all the Jews under Artaxerxes' rule.

7 In the twelfth year of King Artaxerxes Haman[n] came to a decision by casting lots, taking the days and the months one by one, to fix on one day to destroy the whole race of Mordecai. The lot fell on the fourteenth[o] day of the month of Adar.

8 Then Haman[n] said to King Artax-

---

l Gk *all his*   *m* Gk *him*   *n* Gk *he*
o Other ancient witnesses read *thirteenth*; see 8.12

---

month . . . *Adar* (March–April), but the Hebrew at 2.16 has "tenth month . . . Tebeth" (December–January). **17**: *The queen's diadem,* the actual queen of Xerxes was Amestris (Herodotus, *Hist.* VII, 61), a Persian woman. **18**: *Granted a remission of taxes,* Hebrew "granted a holiday."

2.19–23: A plot to kill King Artaxerxes. According to the Greek text this is a second plot discovered and reported by Mordecai (see Addition A [12.1–6]). **20**: *She was to fear God and keep his laws* is lacking in the Hebrew. *Esther did not change her mode of life,* there is no hint of this in the Hebrew, where she is a Jew more by ethnicity than religious faith or observance. **21**: *Angry because of Mor-*

decai's advancement, the Hebrew offers no motive for the bodyguards' anger against the king.

3.1–7: Mordecai refuses to do obeisance to Haman, thereby earning the latter's determination to destroy Mordecai and his people. **7**: In keeping with the Greek's playing down the establishing of the festival of Purim, here (in contrast to 3.7 of the Hebrew) no clue is given until 9.26 that this *casting lots* will provide the name for the festival of Purim ("Lots"). Instead of *fourteenth day,* 8.12 of the Greek and the Hebrew rightly have "the thirteenth."

3.8–13: The royal decree against the Jews, instigated by Haman, is empire-wide

erxes, "There is a certain nation scattered among the other nations in all your kingdom; their laws are different from those of every other nation, and they do not keep the laws of the king. It is not expedient for the king to tolerate them. [9]If it pleases the king, let it be decreed that they are to be destroyed, and I will pay ten thousand talents of silver into the king's treasury." [10]So the king took off his signet ring and gave it to Haman to seal the decree[p] that was to be written against the Jews. [11]The king told Haman, "Keep the money, and do whatever you want with that nation."

12 So on the thirteenth day of the first month the king's secretaries were summoned, and in accordance with Haman's instructions they wrote in the name of King Artaxerxes to the magistrates and the governors in every province from India to Ethiopia. There were one hundred twenty-seven provinces in all, and the governors were addressed each in his own language. [13]Instructions were sent by couriers throughout all the empire of Artaxerxes to destroy the Jewish people on a given day of the twelfth month, which is Adar, and to plunder their goods.

ADDITION B

13 [q] This is a copy of the letter: "The Great King, Artaxerxes, writes the following to the governors of the hundred twenty-seven provinces from India to Ethiopia and to the officials under them:

2 "Having become ruler of many na-

tions and master of the whole world (not elated with presumption of authority but always acting reasonably and with kindness), I have determined to settle the lives of my subjects in lasting tranquility and, in order to make my kingdom peaceable and open to travel throughout all its extent, to restore the peace desired by all people.

3 "When I asked my counselors how this might be accomplished, Haman— who excels among us in sound judgment, and is distinguished for his unchanging goodwill and steadfast fidelity, and has attained the second place in the kingdom— [4]pointed out to us that among all the nations in the world there is scattered a certain hostile people, who have laws contrary to those of every nation and continually disregard the ordinances of kings, so that the unifying of the kingdom that we honorably intend cannot be brought about. [5]We understand that this people, and it alone, stands constantly in opposition to every nation, perversely following a strange manner of life and laws, and is ill-disposed to our government, doing all the harm they can so that our kingdom may not attain stability.

6 "Therefore we have decreed that those indicated to you in the letters written by Haman, who is in charge of affairs and is our second father, shall all—wives and children included—be utterly destroyed by the swords of their enemies, without pity or restraint, on the four-

p Gk lacks *the decree*   q Chapter 13.1-7 corresponds to chapter B 1-7 in some translations.

---

and fixed for the thirteenth of Adar. **8:** *Their laws are different*, i.e. the Mosaic law. **13:** *Instructions were sent*, the Greek omits the Hebrew's hyperbolic claim "to every province in its own script and every people in its own language" (3.12). Aramaic was normally used for such official correspondence. *To destroy the Jewish people* is a tame rendering of the Hebrew's far more explicitly brutal "to destroy, to kill, and to annihilate all Jews, young and old, women and children." *On a*

given day, i.e. the thirteenth (so 8.12 of the Greek and of the Hebrew).
13.1–7: The king's letter ordering the massacre of the Jews. This addition follows Esth 3.1–13, in which Haman has induced Artaxerxes to send a letter to all provinces of his kingdom, ordering complete annihilation of *a certain hostile people,* the Jews, because they observe *a strange manner of life and laws;* they observe the Mosaic law. **6:** *Our second father* implies that Haman ranked second only

teenth day of the twelfth month, Adar, of this present year, 7so that those who have long been hostile and remain so may in a single day go down in violence to Hades, and leave our government completely secure and untroubled hereafter."

END OF ADDITION B

3 14Copies of the document were posted in every province, and all the nations were ordered to be prepared for that day. 15The matter was expedited also in Susa. And while the king and Haman caroused together, the city of Susa*r* was thrown into confusion.

4 When Mordecai learned of all that had been done, he tore his clothes, put on sackcloth, and sprinkled himself with ashes; then he rushed through the street of the city, shouting loudly: "An innocent nation is being destroyed!" 2He got as far as the king's gate, and there he stopped, because no one was allowed to enter the courtyard clothed in sackcloth and ashes. 3And in every province where the king's proclamation had been posted there was a loud cry of mourning and lamentation among the Jews, and they put on sackcloth and ashes. 4When the queen's*s* maids and eunuchs came and told her, she was deeply troubled by what she heard had happened, and sent some clothes to Mordecai to put on instead of sackcloth; but he would not consent. 5Then Esther summoned Hachratheus, the eunuch who attended her, and ordered him to get accurate information for her from Mordecai.*t*

7 So Mordecai told him what had happened and how Haman had promised to pay ten thousand talents into the royal treasury to bring about the destruction of the Jews. 8He also gave him a copy of what had been posted in Susa for their destruction, to show to Esther; and he told him to charge her to go in to the king and plead for his favor in behalf of the people. "Remember," he said, "the days when you were an ordinary person, being brought up under my care—for Haman, who stands next to the king, has spoken against us and demands our death. Call upon the Lord; then speak to the king in our behalf, and save us from death."

9 Hachratheus went in and told Esther all these things. 10And she said to him, "Go to Mordecai and say, 11'All nations of the empire know that if any man or woman goes to the king inside the inner court without being called, there is no escape for that person. Only the one to whom the king stretches out the golden scepter is safe—and it is now thirty days since I was called to go to the king.' "

12 When Hachratheus delivered her entire message to Mordecai, 13Mordecai told him to go back and say to her, "Esther, do not say to yourself that you alone among all the Jews will escape alive. 14For if you keep quiet at such a time as this, help and protection will come to the Jews from another quarter, but you and your father's family will perish. Yet, who knows whether it was not for such a time as this that you were made queen?" 15Then Esther gave the messenger this answer to take back to Mordecai: 16"Go and gather all the Jews who are in Susa and fast on my behalf;

r Gk *the city* *s* Gk *When her* *t* Other ancient witnesses add *6So Hachratheus went out to Mordecai in the street of the city opposite the city gate.*

---

to the king. *Fourteenth day,* according to 16.20 (and Esth 3.13; 8.12; 9.1) it was the thirteenth day. *Adar,* February–March.

3.14–15: The letter is delivered and panic ensues.

4.1–17: Mordecai seeks Esther's aid. He orders her to risk her life by going, unsummoned, before the king to ask him to spare her people. **8:** *Call upon the Lord,* Mordecai makes no such request in the Hebrew.

4.11: Although *without being called, there is no escape* is simply a security precaution, it effectively sets the stage for Esther's dramatic appearance in Addition D. **14:** *Help . . . from another quarter,* in contrast to the Hebrew, here there can be no doubt that divine help is

for three days and nights do not eat or drink, and my maids and I will also go without food. After that I will go to the king, contrary to the law, even if I must die." [17] So Mordecai went away and did what Esther had told him to do.

ADDITION C

13 [8][u] Then Mordecai[v] prayed to the Lord, calling to remembrance all the works of the Lord.

[9] He said, "O Lord, Lord, you rule as King over all things, for the universe is in your power and there is no one who can oppose you when it is your will to save Israel, [10] for you have made heaven and earth and every wonderful thing under heaven. [11] You are Lord of all, and there is no one who can resist you, the Lord. [12] You know all things; you know, O Lord, that it was not in insolence or pride or for any love of glory that I did this, and refused to bow down to this proud Haman; [13] for I would have been willing to kiss the soles of his feet to save Israel! [14] But I did this so that I might not set human glory above the glory of God, and I will not bow down to anyone but you, who are my Lord; and I will not do these things in pride. [15] And now, O Lord God and King, God of Abraham, spare your people; for the eyes of our foes are upon us[w] to annihilate us, and they desire to destroy the inheritance that has been yours from the beginning. [16] Do not neglect your portion, which you redeemed for yourself out of the land of Egypt. [17] Hear my prayer, and have mercy upon your inheritance; turn our mourning into feasting that we may

live and sing praise to your name, O Lord; do not destroy the lips[x] of those who praise you."

[18] And all Israel cried out mightily, for their death was before their eyes.

14 Then Queen Esther, seized with deadly anxiety, fled to the Lord. [2] She took off her splendid apparel and put on the garments of distress and mourning, and instead of costly perfumes she covered her head with ashes and dung, and she utterly humbled her body; every part that she loved to adorn she covered with her tangled hair. [3] She prayed to the Lord God of Israel, and said: "O my Lord, you only are our king; help me, who am alone and have no helper but you, [4] for my danger is in my hand. [5] Ever since I was born I have heard in the tribe of my family that you, O Lord, took Israel out of all the nations, and our ancestors from among all their forebears, for an everlasting inheritance, and that you did for them all that you promised. [6] And now we have sinned before you, and you have handed us over to our enemies [7] because we glorified their gods. You are righteous, O Lord! [8] And now they are not satisfied that we are in bitter slavery, but they have covenanted with their idols [9] to abolish what your mouth has ordained, and to destroy your inheritance, to stop the mouths of those who praise you and to quench your altar and the glory of your house, [10] to open the mouths of the nations for the

---

u Chapters 13.8—15.16 correspond to chapters C 1-30 and D 1-16 in some translations.
v Gk *he*   *w* Gk *for they are eying us*
x Gk *mouth*

---

meant. 16: *Fast on my behalf,* the act of fasting is also here in the Hebrew; it is the only religious activity explicitly mentioned in the Hebrew text (see 4.3, 14; 9.31).
13.8–14.19: The prayers of Mordecai and Esther. The canonical book of Esther never mentions God or prayer or calls Israel God's chosen people. These prayers are added to give the book an explicitly religious tone. They call God *Lord* and *King* and *Lord God of Abraham.* He is righteous, has created and rules all things, has redeemed his people Israel

from Egypt, answers prayer, and can save them now.
13.12–14: Mordecai did not *bow down* to Haman, as the king's other servants did (Esth 3.2), because such homage is due only to God. **18:** All Israel echoed Mordecai's prayer.
14.1–19: Esther joins in her people's prayer for deliverance. 1–2: She discards every trace of queenly attire and elegance and prays as an unworthy member of Israel. **6–7:** Her people's captivity is due to their sinfulness and idolatry while living in Palestine

praise of vain idols, and to magnify forever a mortal king.

11 "O Lord, do not surrender your scepter to what has no being; and do not let them laugh at our downfall; but turn their plan against them, and make an example of him who began this against us. 12 Remember, O Lord; make yourself known in this time of our affliction, and give me courage, O King of the gods and Master of all dominion! 13 Put eloquent speech in my mouth before the lion, and turn his heart to hate the man who is fighting against us, so that there may be an end of him and those who agree with him. 14 But save us by your hand, and help me, who am alone and have no helper but you, O Lord. 15 You have knowledge of all things, and you know that I hate the splendor of the wicked and abhor the bed of the uncircumcised and of any alien. 16 You know my necessity—that I abhor the sign of my proud position, which is upon my head on days when I appear in public. I abhor it like a filthy rag, and I do not wear it on the days when I am at leisure. 17 And your servant has not eaten at Haman's table, and I have not honored the king's feast or drunk the wine of libations. 18 Your servant has had no joy since the day that I was brought here until now, except in you, O Lord God of Abraham. 19 O God, whose might is over all, hear the voice of the despairing, and save us from the hands of evildoers. And save me from my fear!"

END OF ADDITION C

ADDITION D

15 On the third day, when she ended her prayer, she took off the garments in which she had worshiped, and arrayed herself in splendid attire. 2 Then, majestically adorned, after invoking the aid of the all-seeing God and Savior, she took two maids with her; 3 on one she leaned gently for support, 4 while the other followed, carrying her train. 5 She was radiant with perfect beauty, and she looked happy, as if beloved, but her heart was frozen with fear. 6 When she had gone through all the doors, she stood before the king. He was seated on his royal throne, clothed in the full array of his majesty, all covered with gold and precious stones. He was most terrifying.

7 Lifting his face, flushed with splendor, he looked at her in fierce anger. The queen faltered, and turned pale and faint, and collapsed on the head of the maid who went in front of her. 8 Then God changed the spirit of the king to gentleness, and in alarm he sprang from his throne and took her in his arms until she came to herself. He comforted her with soothing words, and said to her, 9 "What is it, Esther? I am your husband. *y* Take courage; 10 You shall not die, for our law applies only to our subjects. *z* Come near."

11 Then he raised the golden scepter and touched her neck with it; 12 he embraced her, and said, "Speak to me." 13 She said to him, "I saw you, my lord, like an angel of God, and my heart was

y Gk *brother*   *z* Meaning of Gk uncertain

(Dan 9.16); Israel does not deserve to be saved.

14.11: Esther begs God not to allow pagan idols, which have no real existence, to rule the world. **16–18:** Esther says that she hates her position as queen and wife of the king, and has never *eaten at Haman's table* or *honored the king's feast* (but compare Esth 2.18, as well as Esth 5.5 and 7.1).

15.1–16: Esther risks her life to appeal to the king. This passage expands and exaggerates Esth 5.1–2, bringing out religious elements absent from the Hebrew text. **1–2:** *She had worshiped . . . invoking the aid of the all-seeing God and Savior* is lacking in the Hebrew. Anyone who entered the king's presence without his summons or permission was put to death, unless the king forgave the intrusion (Esth 4.11). To avoid personal danger and to induce the king to reverse his decree, Esther enhanced her charm by splendid attire; then with fearful heart she entered the king's presence.

15.8: That *God changed the spirit of the king*

shaken with fear at your glory. ¹⁴For you are wonderful, my lord, and your countenance is full of grace." ¹⁵And while she was speaking, she fainted and fell. ¹⁶Then the king was agitated, and all his servants tried to comfort her.

END OF ADDITION D

5 ᵃ ³The king said to her, "What do you wish, Esther? What is your request? It shall be given you, even to half of my kingdom." ⁴And Esther said, "Today is a special day for me. If it pleases the king, let him and Haman come to the dinner that I shall prepare today." ⁵Then the king said, "Bring Haman quickly, so that we may do as Esther desires." So they both came to the dinner that Esther had spoken about. ⁶While they were drinking wine, the king said to Esther, "What is it, Queen Esther? It shall be granted you." ⁷She said, "My petition and request is: ⁸if I have found favor in the sight of the king, let the king and Haman come to the dinner that I shall prepare them, and tomorrow I will do as I have done today."

9 So Haman went out from the king joyful and glad of heart. But when he saw Mordecai the Jew in the courtyard, he was filled with anger. ¹⁰Nevertheless, he went home and summoned his friends and his wife Zosara. ¹¹And he told them about his riches and the honor that the king had bestowed on him, and how he had advanced him to be the first in the kingdom. ¹²And Haman said, "The queen did not invite anyone to the dinner with the king except me; and I am invited again tomorrow. ¹³But these things give

me no pleasure as long as I see Mordecai the Jew in the courtyard." ¹⁴His wife Zosara and his friends said to him, "Let a gallows be made, fifty cubits high, and in the morning tell the king to have Mordecai hanged on it. Then, go merrily with the king to the dinner." This advice pleased Haman, and so the gallows was prepared.

6 That night the Lord took sleep from the king, so he gave orders to his secretary to bring the book of daily records, and to read to him. ²He found the words written about Mordecai, how he had told the king about the two royal eunuchs who were on guard and sought to lay hands on King Artaxerxes. ³The king said, "What honor or dignity did we bestow on Mordecai?" The king's servants said, "You have not done anything for him." ⁴While the king was inquiring about the goodwill shown by Mordecai, Haman was in the courtyard. The king asked, "Who is in the courtyard?" Now Haman had come to speak to the king about hanging Mordecai on the gallows that he had prepared. ⁵The servants of the king answered, "Haman is standing in the courtyard." And the king said, "Summon him." ⁶Then the king said to Haman, "What shall I do for the person whom I wish to honor?" And Haman said to himself, "Whom would the king wish to honor more than me?" ⁷So he said to the king, "For a person whom the king wishes to honor, ⁸let the king's servants bring out the fine linen robe that the king has worn, and the horse on which the king rides, ⁹and let

a In Greek, Chapter D replaces verses 1 and 2 in Hebrew.

---

is in no way indicated in the Hebrew text. **13:** *You . . . like an angel of God,* lacking in Hebrew, is pure flattery.
    5.3–8: Esther before the king. 3: *To half of my kingdom* (also 7.2) is a customary hyperbole (compare Mk 6.23). **4, 8:** No subtle reason need be sought for the first and second *dinner,* nor for Haman's being the only guest; these are but literary embellishments needful for the story.

    5.9–14: Haman's plot against Mordecai will, temporarily, assuage his anger against Mordecai. **14:** *Gallows . . . fifty cubits high* (more than 75 feet high) is a hyperbole for literary effect.
    6.1–13: Mordecai's generous reward from the king is, ironically, proposed by Haman himself. **1:** *The Lord took sleep from the king,* Heb "The king could not sleep." **3:** *You have not done anything for him,* in contrast to the

both be given to one of the king's honored Friends, and let him robe the person whom the king loves and mount him on the horse, and let it be proclaimed through the open square of the city, saying, 'Thus shall it be done to everyone whom the king honors.' " ¹⁰Then the king said to Haman, "You have made an excellent suggestion! Do just as you have said for Mordecai the Jew, who is on duty in the courtyard. And let nothing be omitted from what you have proposed." ¹¹So Haman got the robe and the horse; he put the robe on Mordecai and made him ride through the open square of the city, proclaiming, "Thus shall it be done to everyone whom the king wishes to honor." ¹²Then Mordecai returned to the courtyard, and Haman hurried back to his house, mourning and with his head covered. ¹³Haman told his wife Zosara and his friends what had befallen him. His friends and his wife said to him, "If Mordecai is of the Jewish people, and you have begun to be humiliated before him, you will surely fall. You will not be able to defend yourself, because the living God is with him."

14 While they were still talking, the eunuchs arrived and hurriedly brought Haman to the banquet that Esther had prepared. ¹So the king and Haman went in to drink with the queen. ²And the second day, as they were drinking wine, the king said, "What is it, Queen Esther? What is your petition and what is your request? It shall be granted to you, even to half of my kingdom." ³She answered and said, "If I have found favor with the king, let my life be granted me at my petition, and my people at

my request. ⁴For we have been sold, I and my people, to be destroyed, plundered, and made slaves—we and our children—male and female slaves. This has come to my knowledge. Our antagonist brings shame on*ᵇ* the king's court." ⁵Then the king said, "Who is the person that would dare to do this thing?" ⁶Esther said, "Our enemy is this evil man Haman!" At this, Haman was terrified in the presence of the king and queen.

7 The king rose from the banquet and went into the garden, and Haman began to beg for his life from the queen, for he saw that he was in serious trouble. ⁸When the king returned from the garden, Haman had thrown himself on the couch, pleading with the queen. The king said, "Will he dare even assault my wife in my own house?" Haman, when he heard, turned away his face. ⁹Then Bugathan, one of the eunuchs, said to the king, "Look, Haman has even prepared a gallows for Mordecai, who gave information of concern to the king; it is standing at Haman's house, a gallows fifty cubits high." So the king said, "Let Haman be hanged on that." ¹⁰So Haman was hanged on the gallows he had prepared for Mordecai. With that the anger of the king abated.

8 On that very day King Artaxerxes granted to Esther all the property of the persecutor*ᶜ* Haman. Mordecai was summoned by the king, for Esther had told the king*ᵈ* that he was related to her. ²The king took the ring that had been taken from Haman, and gave it to Mor-

---

b Gk *is not worthy of*   c Gk *slanderer*
d Gk *him*

---

king's rewarding Mordecai for his information concerning the first plot (see Addition A [12.5]). **13**: *Because the living God is with him* foreshadows for the reader Haman's sure and certain demise.

6.14–7.6: At Esther's second banquet Haman is caught unawares by her and is revealed for the evil counselor he is.

7.7–10: Haman's punishment of being hanged on the gallows he had erected for Mordecai is poetic justice. **8**: *Even assault my*

wife, by even touching Esther's couch to beg for his life Haman is violating harem law and committing a capital offense. **9**: *Bugathan,* Heb "Harbona."

8.1–12: The king's favor toward the Jews is proved by Mordecai's being invested with all the powers of Haman and by having Haman's royal edict against the Jews neutralized by a new royal edict. **2**: *The king took the ring . . . from Haman,* this transference of the signet ring to Mordecai indicates his promo-

decai; and Esther set Mordecai over everything that had been Haman's.

3 Then she spoke once again to the king and, falling at his feet, she asked him to avert all the evil that Haman had planned against the Jews. [4]The king extended his golden scepter to Esther, and she rose and stood before the king. [5]Esther said, "If it pleases you, and if I have found favor, let an order be sent rescinding the letters that Haman wrote and sent to destroy the Jews in your kingdom. [6]How can I look on the ruin of my people? How can I be safe if my ancestral nation[e] is destroyed?" [7]The king said to Esther, "Now that I[f] have granted all of Haman's property to you and have hanged him on a tree because he acted against the Jews, what else do you request? [8]Write in my name what you think best and seal it with my ring; for whatever is written at the king's command and sealed with my ring cannot be contravened."

9 The secretaries were summoned on the twenty-third day of the first month, that is, Nisan, in the same year; and all that he commanded with respect to the Jews was given in writing to the administrators and governors of the provinces from Media to Ethiopia, one hundred twenty-seven provinces, to each province in its own language. [10]The edict was written[g] with the king's authority and sealed with his ring, and sent out by couriers. [11]He ordered the Jews in every city to observe their own laws, to defend themselves, and to act as they wished against their opponents and enemies [12]on a certain day, the thirteenth of the twelfth month, which is Adar, throughout all the kingdom of Artaxerxes.

"The Great King, Artaxerxes, to the governors of the provinces from India to Ethiopia, one hundred twenty-seven provinces, and to those who are loyal to our government, greetings.

2 "Many people, the more they are honored with the most generous kindness of their benefactors, the more proud do they become, [3]and not only seek to injure our subjects, but in their inability to stand prosperity, they even undertake to scheme against their own benefactors. [4]They not only take away thankfulness from others, but, carried away by the boasts of those who know nothing of goodness, they even assume that they will escape the evil-hating justice of God, who always sees everything. [5]And often many of those who are set in places of authority have been made in part responsible for the shedding of innocent blood, and have been involved in irremediable calamities, by the persuasion of friends who have been entrusted with the administration of public affairs, [6]when these persons by the false trickery of their evil natures beguile the sincere goodwill of their sovereigns.

7 "What has been wickedly accomplished through the pestilent behavior of those who exercise authority unworthily can be seen, not so much from the more ancient records that we hand on, as from investigation of matters close at hand.[i] [8]In the future we will take care to render our kingdom quiet and peaceable for all, [9]by changing our methods and always judging what comes before our eyes with more equitable consideration. [10]For Haman son of Hammedatha, a Macedonian (really an alien to the Persian blood, and quite devoid of our kindliness), having become our guest, [11]enjoyed so fully the

ADDITION E

16 [h] The following is a copy of this letter:

e Gk *country*   *f* Gk *If I*
g Gk *It was written*   *h* Chapter 16.1-24
corresponds to chapter E 1-24 in some
translations.   *i* Gk *matters beside* (your) *feet*

tion to the rank of grand vizier. **3:** *Spoke once again to the king* but with none of the "weeping and pleading" in 8.3 of the Hebrew. **8:** *Whatever is written . . . cannot be contravened* (see

1.19), this belief in the immutability of Persian law, a literary invention for effect, also appears in Dan 6.8.

8.9: *First month . . . Nisan,* Hebrew "third

goodwill that we have for every nation that he was called our father and was continually bowed down to by all as the person second to the royal throne. 12 But, unable to restrain his arrogance, he undertook to deprive us of our kingdom and our life,*j* 13 and with intricate craft and deceit asked for the destruction of Mordecai, our savior and perpetual benefactor, and of Esther, the blameless partner of our kingdom, together with their whole nation. 14 He thought that by these methods he would catch us undefended and would transfer the kingdom of the Persians to the Macedonians.

15 "But we find that the Jews, who were consigned to annihilation by this thrice-accursed man, are not evildoers, but are governed by most righteous laws 16 and are children of the living God, most high, most mighty,*k* who has directed the kingdom both for us and for our ancestors in the most excellent order.

17 "You will therefore do well not to put in execution the letters sent by Haman son of Hammedatha, 18 since he, the one who did these things, has been hanged at the gate of Susa with all his household—for God, who rules over all things, has speedily inflicted on him the punishment that he deserved.

19 "Therefore post a copy of this letter publicly in every place, and permit the Jews to live under their own laws. 20 And give them reinforcements, so that on the thirteenth day of the twelfth month, Adar, on that very day, they may defend themselves against those who attack them at the time of oppres-

sion. 21 For God, who rules over all things, has made this day to be a joy for his chosen people instead of a day of destruction for them.

22 "Therefore you shall observe this with all good cheer as a notable day among your commemorative festivals, 23 so that both now and hereafter it may represent deliverance for you*l* and the loyal Persians, but that it may be a reminder of destruction for those who plot against us.

24 "Every city and country, without exception, that does not act accordingly shall be destroyed in wrath with spear and fire. It shall be made not only impassable for human beings, but also most hateful to wild animals and birds for all time.

END OF ADDITION E

---

8 13 "Let copies of the decree be posted conspicuously in all the kingdom, and let all the Jews be ready on that day to fight against their enemies."

14 So the messengers on horseback set out with all speed to perform what the king had commanded; and the decree was published also in Susa. 15 Mordecai went out dressed in the royal robe and wearing a gold crown and a turban of purple linen. The people in Susa rejoiced on seeing him. 16 And the Jews had light and gladness 17 in every city and province

j Gk *our spirit*   *k* Gk *greatest*   *l* Other ancient authorities read *for us*

---

month . . . Sivan [May-June]." **11:** This explicit permission for the *Jews . . . to observe their own laws,* which is a distinctly religious concern, is lacking in the Hebrew.

16.1–24: The king's second letter, denouncing Haman and directing his subjects to help the Jews.

16.10–14: Haman, already executed (Esth 7.6–10), is (falsely) called a *Macedonian* trying to overthrow Persian rule.

16.15–16: The king commends the Mosaic *laws,* praises the Jews, and recognizes God's rule. All Persian subjects are commanded to ignore Haman's letter (according to 13.1–6 it

was really the king's letter) and help the Jews defend themselves on the thirteenth day of Adar, the prescribed day of annihilation. **18:** *Hanged . . . with all his household* contradicts 7.10 of the Hebrew, where only Haman is hanged (see also 9.6–10, 14 of the Greek text). **24:** Destruction faces every place that does not defend and respect the Jews.

8.13–17: Dispatch and posting of the king's decree. 15: Mordecai appears in his state robes. **17:** *A banquet and a holiday* contrast with the mourning and lamentation of 4.3. *Gentiles were circumcised,* the Hebrew says merely "professed to be Jews."

wherever the decree was published; wherever the proclamation was made, the Jews had joy and gladness, a banquet and a holiday. And many of the Gentiles were circumcised and became Jews out of fear of the Jews.

9 Now on the thirteenth day of the twelfth month, which is Adar, the decree written by the king arrived. 2On that same day the enemies of the Jews perished; no one resisted, because they feared them. 3The chief provincial governors, the princes, and the royal secretaries were paying honor to the Jews, because fear of Mordecai weighed upon them. 4The king's decree required that Mordecai's name be held in honor throughout the kingdom. *m* 6Now in the city of Susa the Jews killed five hundred people, 7including Pharsannestain, Delphon, Phasga, 8Pharadatha, Barea, Sarbacha, 9Marmasima, Aruphaeus, Arsaeus, Zabutheus, 10the ten sons of Haman son of Hammedatha, the Bougean, the enemy of the Jews—and they indulged*n* themselves in plunder.

11 That very day the number of those killed in Susa was reported to the king. 12The king said to Esther, "In Susa, the capital, the Jews have destroyed five hundred people. What do you suppose they have done in the surrounding countryside? Whatever more you ask will be done for you." 13And Esther said to the king, "Let the Jews be allowed to do the same tomorrow. Also, hang up the bodies of Haman's ten sons." 14So he permitted this to be done, and handed over to the Jews of the city the bodies of Haman's sons to hang up. 15The Jews who

were in Susa gathered on the fourteenth and killed three hundred people, but took no plunder.

16 Now the other Jews in the kingdom gathered to defend themselves, and got relief from their enemies. They destroyed fifteen thousand of them, but did not engage in plunder. 17On the fourteenth day they rested and made that same day a day of rest, celebrating it with joy and gladness. 18The Jews who were in Susa, the capital, came together also on the fourteenth, but did not rest. They celebrated the fifteenth with joy and gladness. 19On this account then the Jews who are scattered around the country outside Susa keep the fourteenth of Adar as a joyful holiday, and send presents of food to one another, while those who live in the large cities keep the fifteenth day of Adar as their joyful holiday, also sending presents to one another.

20 Mordecai recorded these things in a book, and sent it to the Jews in the kingdom of Artaxerxes both near and far, 21telling them that they should keep the fourteenth and fifteenth days of Adar, 22for on these days the Jews got relief from their enemies. The whole month (namely, Adar), in which their condition had been changed from sorrow into gladness and from a time of distress to a holiday, was to be celebrated as a time for feasting*o* and gladness and

m Meaning of Gk uncertain. Some ancient authorities add verse 5, *So the Jews struck down all their enemies with the sword, killing and destroying them, and they did as they pleased to those who hated them.*   *n* Other ancient authorities read *did not indulge*   *o* Gk *of weddings*

9.1–19: Victory of the Jews over their enemies on the thirteenth of Adar is total throughout the empire, with the exception of Susa, which has complete success the next day (v. 15). Therefore, Jews outside of Susa celebrate their victory on the fourteenth of Adar; those in Susa on the fifteenth. **2:** That *no one resisted,* which contradicts the Hebrew ("no one could withstand them"), is patently false; for thousands did (see 9.11, 16). **9.10:** That *the ten sons of Haman* were killed

on the thirteenth of Adar agrees with the Hebrew but contradicts Addition E (16.18). *Indulged themselves in plunder* contradicts the Hebrew. **16:** *Destroyed fifteen thousand,* Hebrew "seventy-five thousand."

9.20–10.3: The festival of Purim, ordered first by Mordecai and then later confirmed by Queen Esther, is to be celebrated by all Jews on the fourteenth and fifteenth of Adar.

for sending presents of food to their friends and to the poor.

23 So the Jews accepted what Mordecai had written to them [24]—how Haman son of Hammedatha, the Macedonian,[p] fought against them, how he made a decree and cast lots[q] to destroy them, [25] and how he went in to the king, telling him to hang Mordecai; but the wicked plot he had devised against the Jews came back upon himself, and he and his sons were hanged. [26] Therefore these days were called "Purim," because of the lots (for in their language this is the word that means "lots"). And so, because of what was written in this letter, and because of what they had experienced in this affair and what had befallen them, Mordecai established this festival,[r] [27] and the Jews took upon themselves, upon their descendants, and upon all who would join them, to observe it without fail.[s] These days of Purim should be a memorial and kept from generation to generation, in every city, family, and country. [28] These days of Purim were to be observed for all time, and the commemoration of them was never to cease among their descendants.

29 Then Queen Esther daughter of Aminadab along with Mordecai the Jew wrote down what they had done, and gave full authority to the letter about Purim.[t] [31] And Mordecai and Queen Esther established this decision on their own responsibility, pledging their own well-being to the plan.[s] [32] Esther established it by a decree forever, and it was written for a memorial.

10 The king levied a tax upon his kingdom both by land and sea. [2] And as for his power and bravery, and the wealth and glory of his kingdom, they were recorded in the annals of the kings of the Persians and the Medes.

[3] Mordecai acted with authority on behalf of King Artaxerxes and was great in the kingdom, as well as honored by the Jews. His way of life was such as to make him beloved to his whole nation.

ADDITION F

[4][u] And Mordecai said, "These things have come from God; [5] for I remember the dream that I had concerning these matters, and none of them has failed to be fulfilled. [6] There was the little spring that became a river, and there was light and sun and abundant water—the river is Esther, whom the king married and made queen. [7] The two dragons are Haman and myself. [8] The nations are those that gathered to destroy the name of the Jews. [9] And my nation, this is Israel, who cried out to God and were saved. The Lord has saved his people; the Lord has rescued us from all these evils; God has done great signs and wonders, wonders that have never happened among the nations. [10] For this purpose he made two lots, one for the people of God and one for all the nations, [11] and these two lots came to the hour and moment and day of decision before God and among all the nations. [12] And God remembered his people and vindicated his inheritance. [13] So they will observe these days in the month of Adar, on the fourteenth and fifteenth[v] of that month, with an assembly and joy and gladness before God,

p Other ancient witnesses read *the Bougean*
q Gk *a lot*   r Gk *he established* (it)
s Meaning of Gk uncertain   t Verse 30 in Heb is lacking in Gk: *Letters were sent to all the Jews, to the one hundred twenty-seven provinces of the kingdom of Ahasuerus, in words of peace and truth.*
u Chapter 10.4–13 and 11.1 correspond to chapter F1–11 in some translations.   v Other ancient authorities lack *and fifteenth*

9.23: Here, *the Macedonian* ("the Agagite" in 9.24 of the Hebrew) is a pejorative epithet. **26**: *In their language,* "Purim" is the Hebrew cognate of the Akkadian word for "lots." **10.4–13**: **Mordecai's dream interpreted.** This passage interprets the dream of 11.5–11. The threat to Israel is here ascribed not to one man, Haman, as in the canonical Esther, but to a general anti-Semitic hostility against the Jews. **11**: *Two lots,* not mentioned in Addition A, but mentioned here because of the word Purim ("lots"). **13**: As in Esth 9.20–22, Israel is to celebrate this deliverance annually.

from generation to generation forever among his people Israel." [1] In the fourth year of the reign of Ptolemy and Cleopatra, Dositheus, who said that he was a priest and a Levite, [w] and his son Ptolemy brought to Egypt [x] the preceding Letter about Purim, which they said was authentic and had been translat-

11

ed by Lysimachus son of Ptolemy, one of the residents of Jerusalem.

END OF ADDITION F

w Or *priest, and Levitas*   *x* Cn: Gk *brought in*

11.1: The book of Esther attested as genuine. 1: *Fourth year,* that is 114–113 B.C. *The preceding Letter,* a reference not merely to Mordecai's letter (Esth 9.20–22) but to the entire book of Esther, including, probably, some of the Additions. *Lysimachus* is a Greek name; on his work of translating the Hebrew book of Esther into Greek, see the Introduction.

The Wisdom of Solomon

This book is attributed to Solomon, though his name never appears (even in 9.8). But 7.1–14 and 8.17–9.18 deliberately reflect his prayer for wisdom as found in 1 Kings 3.6–9 and 2 Chr 1.8–10. The work was composed in Greek by an unknown Hellenistic Jew, probably at Alexandria, the largest Jewish center in the Diaspora (the "dispersion," the name for the Jewish communities outside the land of Israel). The date is uncertain, probably the latter part of the first century B.C. The literary genre is generally described as protreptic, a form of didactic exhortation. It is clearly a product of Hellenistic culture, as indicated by the mention of the four cardinal virtues in 8.7 and the philosophical treatment of the knowledge of God in 13.1–9. There is also a wide range of Greek vocabulary in the work. At the same time, it is intensely Jewish. The author has borrowed phraseology from the Septuagint, the Greek translation that would have been the Bible of his Jewish compatriots, and it is written in the poetic parallelism characteristic of the Hebrew Bible.

Chapters 1–5 deal with the gift of immortality, and this constitutes a breakthrough in biblical thought (see also Dan 12.2–3); righteousness is undying (1.15; see also 3.1–5). When the wicked behold the just person before the throne of God, they realize their mistake; the just one is numbered among the children of God and given the portion of the holy ones in the heavenly court (5.5). In chs 6–9 pseudo-Solomon speaks to the "judges" of the earth (in reality to the Jews) concerning Wisdom (a spirit and personified as in Prov 8; Sir 24) and her attributes. Unlike other wisdom books, which usually leave the sacred history unmentioned, this work portrays wisdom as a savior of Israel's ancestors (10.1–21). In chs 11–19 there is presented an elaborate system of contrasts between God's treatment of the Israelites and of the Egyptians at the time of the plagues. The theme is spelled out in 11.5: Israel was benefited through the very things that punished their enemies (thus, water from the rock, instead of the plague of the Nile, for instance); in the same way, "one is punished by the very things by which one sins" (11.16). Interspersed in this meditation on the Egyptian plagues are several digressions about God's power and mercy (11.17–12.22), false worship (13.1–15.17), and other matters.

To the Jews of the dispersion the Wisdom of Solomon offered strength and consolation. Theirs was a true wisdom, which surpassed even that of the Greeks. Theirs was immortality (a gift of God to the righteous, not the result of having an immortal or spiritual "soul"). Their Lord was the "author of beauty" (13.3); to know him was complete righteousness and to know his power was the root of immortality (15.3), for his immortal spirit was in all things (12.1).

1 Love righteousness, you rulers of
    the earth,
think of the Lord in goodness
and seek him with sincerity of
    heart;
2 because he is found by those who
    do not put him to the test,
and manifests himself to those
    who do not distrust him.
3 For perverse thoughts separate
    people from God,
and when his power is tested, it
    exposes the foolish;
4 because wisdom will not enter a
    deceitful soul,
or dwell in a body enslaved to sin.
5 For a holy and disciplined spirit
    will flee from deceit,
and will leave foolish thoughts
    behind,
and will be ashamed at the
    approach of
    unrighteousness.

6 For wisdom is a kindly spirit,
but will not free blasphemers from
    the guilt of their words;
because God is witness of their
    inmost feelings,
and a true observer of their hearts,
    and a hearer of their
    tongues.
7 Because the spirit of the Lord has
    filled the world,
and that which holds all things
    together knows what is
    said,
8 therefore those who utter
    unrighteous things will not
    escape notice,
and justice, when it punishes, will
    not pass them by.

9 For inquiry will be made into the
    counsels of the ungodly,
and a report of their words will
    come to the Lord,
to convict them of their lawless
    deeds;
10 because a jealous ear hears all
    things,
and the sound of grumbling does
    not go unheard.
11 Beware then of useless grumbling,
and keep your tongue from
    slander;
because no secret word is without
    result, *a*
and a lying mouth destroys the
    soul.

12 Do not invite death by the error
    of your life,
or bring on destruction by the
    works of your hands;
13 because God did not make death,
and he does not delight in the
    death of the living.
14 For he created all things so that
    they might exist;
the generative forces *b* of the
    world are wholesome,
and there is no destructive poison
    in them,
and the dominion *c* of Hades is not
    on earth.
15 For righteousness is immortal.

16 But the ungodly by their words
    and deeds summoned
    death; *d*

a Or *will go unpunished*   *b* Or *the creatures*
c Or *palace*   *d* Gk *him*

1.1–6.25: **Commendation of wisdom as
guide to happiness and immortality. 1.1–
5:** *Rulers* (compare 6.1) are urged to *love righteousness* and seek God. *Wisdom* dwells only in
a sincere, holy, and disciplined soul.
    1.6–11: **The ungodly will not escape
punishment;** God knows their unrighteous
thoughts, words, and deeds and will judge
them. **6:** *A kindly spirit,* literally "a philan-
thropic spirit," i.e. loving humankind; wisdom's concern for human welfare will not

tolerate blasphemous or unrighteous words.
    1.12–15: **God has made human beings
for immortality. 15:** *Immortal* is literally
"undying." Immortality is seen as a gift of
God; it is not due to the nature of the soul, but
to *righteousness,* the vital relationship of persons to God.
    1.16–2.24: **The reasoning of the materi-
alist or sensualist. 2.1–5:** The ungodly say
that life is *short,* birth the result of *mere chance,*
life without real meaning, and physical death

considering him a friend, they
pined away
and made a covenant with him,
because they are fit to belong to
his company.

2 For they reasoned unsoundly,
saying to themselves,
"Short and sorrowful is our life,
and there is no remedy when a life
comes to its end,
and no one has been known to
return from Hades.
2 For we were born by mere
chance,
and hereafter we shall be as
though we had never been,
for the breath in our nostrils is
smoke,
and reason is a spark kindled by
the beating of our hearts;
3 when it is extinguished, the body
will turn to ashes,
and the spirit will dissolve like
empty air.
4 Our name will be forgotten in
time,
and no one will remember our
works;
our life will pass away like the
traces of a cloud,
and be scattered like mist
that is chased by the rays of the
sun
and overcome by its heat.
5 For our allotted time is the passing
of a shadow,
and there is no return from our
death,
because it is sealed up and no one
turns back.

6 "Come, therefore, let us enjoy the
good things that exist,
and make use of the creation to
the full as in youth.
7 Let us take our fill of costly wine
and perfumes,

and let no flower of spring pass us
by.
8 Let us crown ourselves with
rosebuds before they
wither.
9 Let none of us fail to share in our
revelry;
everywhere let us leave signs of
enjoyment,
because this is our portion, and
this our lot.
10 Let us oppress the righteous poor
man;
let us not spare the widow
or regard the gray hairs of the
aged.
11 But let our might be our law of
right,
for what is weak proves itself to
be useless.

12 "Let us lie in wait for the
righteous man,
because he is inconvenient to us
and opposes our actions;
he reproaches us for sins against
the law,
and accuses us of sins against our
training.
13 He professes to have knowledge of
God,
and calls himself a child*e* of the
Lord.
14 He became to us a reproof of our
thoughts;
15 the very sight of him is a burden
to us,
because his manner of life is unlike
that of others,
and his ways are strange.
16 We are considered by him as
something base,
and he avoids our ways as
unclean;

e Or *servant*

---

the end of existence. **6–9:** They encourage
one another to live lives of sensual satisfaction
before death snuffs out existence.
2.10–20: They urge one another to oppress *righteous,* helpless folk, whose godly
words and lives reproach them, and to persecute, torture, and kill those who call *God* their
father.

he calls the last end of the
    righteous happy,
and boasts that God is his father.
17 Let us see if his words are true,
    and let us test what will happen at
        the end of his life;
18 for if the righteous man is God's
        child, he will help him,
    and will deliver him from the
        hand of his adversaries.
19 Let us test him with insult and
        torture,
so that we may find out how
        gentle he is,
and make trial of his forbearance.
20 Let us condemn him to a shameful
        death,
for, according to what he says, he
        will be protected."

21 Thus they reasoned, but they were
        led astray,
for their wickedness blinded them,
22 and they did not know the secret
        purposes of God,
nor hoped for the wages of
        holiness,
nor discerned the prize for
        blameless souls;
23 for God created us for
        incorruption,
and made us in the image of his
        own eternity,*f*
24 but through the devil's envy death
        entered the world,
and those who belong to his
        company experience it.

3 But the souls of the righteous are
        in the hand of God,
and no torment will ever touch
        them.

2 In the eyes of the foolish they
        seemed to have died,
and their departure was thought to
        be a disaster,
3 and their going from us to be
        their destruction;
but they are at peace.
4 For though in the sight of others
        they were punished,
their hope is full of immortality.
5 Having been disciplined a little,
        they will receive great
        good,
because God tested them and
        found them worthy of
        himself;
6 like gold in the furnace he tried
        them,
and like a sacrificial burnt offering
        he accepted them.
7 In the time of their visitation they
        will shine forth,
and will run like sparks through
        the stubble.
8 They will govern nations and rule
        over peoples,
and the Lord will reign over them
        forever.
9 Those who trust in him will
        understand truth,
and the faithful will abide with
        him in love,
because grace and mercy are upon
        his holy ones,
and he watches over his elect.*g*

10 But the ungodly will be punished
        as their reasoning deserves,

f Other ancient authorities read *nature*   *g* Text
of this line uncertain; omitted by some ancient
authorities. Compare 4.15

2.21–24: Such false reasoning arises from
wickedness and consequent failure to know
God. Human beings were made in the divine
image for immortality, but *the devil's envy*
(compare 1.16) brought *death* into *the world*.
    **3.1–9: The blessed estate of the righ-
teous.** Though affliction, suffering, and the
early death of *the righteous* may seem to be
divine punishment, after death they are forever safe and at *peace* with God; they enjoy sure

immortality. **7–9:** Their discipline and testing
will be followed by a divine *visitation;* God
will vindicate them, let them share in his rule
over all peoples, and give them understanding of his ways.
    **3.10–4.6: The punishment of the un-
godly.** The *ungodly* will meet a sad end because, disregarding what *the righteous* could
teach them, they *rebelled against the Lord*
(v. 10). In Israel the possession of many chil-

those who disregarded the
righteous[h]
and rebelled against the Lord;
11 for those who despise wisdom and
instruction are miserable.
Their hope is vain, their labors are
unprofitable,
and their works are useless.
12 Their wives are foolish, and their
children evil;
13 their offspring are accursed.
For blessed is the barren woman
who is undefiled,
who has not entered into a sinful
union;
she will have fruit when God
examines souls.
14 Blessed also is the eunuch whose
hands have done no lawless
deed,
and who has not devised wicked
things against the Lord;
for special favor will be shown
him for his faithfulness,
and a place of great delight in the
temple of the Lord.
15 For the fruit of good labors is
renowned,
and the root of understanding does
not fail.
16 But children of adulterers will not
come to maturity,
and the offspring of an unlawful
union will perish.
17 Even if they live long they will be
held of no account,
and finally their old age will be
without honor.
18 If they die young, they will have
no hope
and no consolation on the day of
judgment.
19 For the end of an unrighteous
generation is grievous.

4 Better than this is childlessness
with virtue,
for in the memory of virtue[i] is
immortality,
because it is known both by God
and by mortals.
2 When it is present, people imitate[j]
it,
and they long for it when it has
gone;
throughout all time it marches,
crowned in triumph,
victor in the contest for prizes that
are undefiled.
3 But the prolific brood of the
ungodly will be of no use,
and none of their illegitimate
seedlings will strike a deep
root
or take a firm hold.
4 For even if they put forth boughs
for a while,
standing insecurely they will be
shaken by the wind,
and by the violence of the winds
they will be uprooted.
5 The branches will be broken off
before they come to
maturity,
and their fruit will be useless,
not ripe enough to eat, and good
for nothing.
6 For children born of unlawful
unions
are witnesses of evil against their
parents when God examines
them.[k]
7 But the righteous, though they die
early, will be at rest.
8 For old age is not honored for
length of time,

h Or *what is right*   i Gk *it*   j Other ancient
authorities read *honor*   k Gk *at their examination*

---

dren and a long life were often considered
proof of God's favor. But the *barren woman*
and the *eunuch* are also blessed by God
(vv. 13–14); a virtuous life is what counts, for
it alone leads to *immortality*. The wicked, even
if they *live long* (v. 17) and have many children (4.3), have *no* justified *hope* for the future; their children usually die early, are *of no*
account, and attest their parents' wickedness
(3.16–18).
   **4.7–19: The blessedness of the righ-
teous despite premature death.** The righteous who die young *will be at rest* with God
(v. 7). *A blameless life* means more than long
years; and early death ends the danger of falling into evil.

or measured by number of years;

9 but understanding is gray hair for
anyone,
and a blameless life is ripe old age.

10 There were some who pleased
God and were loved by
him,
and while living among sinners
were taken up.

11 They were caught up so that evil
might not change their
understanding
or guile deceive their souls.

12 For the fascination of wickedness
obscures what is good,
and roving desire perverts the
innocent mind.

13 Being perfected in a short time,
they fulfilled long years;

14 for their souls were pleasing to the
Lord,
therefore he took them quickly
from the midst of
wickedness.

15 Yet the peoples saw and did not
understand,
or take such a thing to heart,
that God's grace and mercy are
with his elect,
and that he watches over his holy
ones.

16 The righteous who have died will
condemn the ungodly who
are living,
and youth that is quickly
perfected[l] will condemn
the prolonged old age of
the unrighteous.

17 For they will see the end of the
wise,
and will not understand what the
Lord purposed for them,
and for what he kept them safe.

18 The unrighteous[m] will see, and
will have contempt for
them,

but the Lord will laugh them to
scorn.
After this they will become
dishonored corpses,
and an outrage among the dead
forever;

19 because he will dash them
speechless to the ground,
and shake them from the
foundations;
they will be left utterly dry and
barren,
and they will suffer anguish,
and the memory of them will
perish.

20 They will come with dread when
their sins are reckoned up,
and their lawless deeds will
convict them to their face.

5 Then the righteous will stand with
great confidence
in the presence of those who have
oppressed them
and those who make light of their
labors.

2 When the unrighteous[n] see them,
they will be shaken with
dreadful fear,
and they will be amazed at the
unexpected salvation of the
righteous.

3 They will speak to one another in
repentance,
and in anguish of spirit they will
groan, and say,

4 "These are persons whom we once
held in derision
and made a byword of
reproach—fools that we
were!
We thought that their lives were
madness
and that their end was without
honor.

l Or ended   m Gk They   n Gk they

4.10–15: Enoch is an example of a good
man *perfected in a short time;* he lived 365 years,
several hundred years less than any other listed in Gen ch 5. **14–15:** *The peoples . . . did not*
understand, they fail to recognize God's providence in an early death (compare v. 17).
4.20–5.23: The judgment. In contrast to
their arrogant speech in 1.16–2.24, the un-

5 Why have they been numbered
    among the children of God?
And why is their lot among the
    saints?
6 So it was we who strayed from
    the way of truth,
and the light of righteousness did
    not shine on us,
and the sun did not rise upon us.
7 We took our fill of the paths of
    lawlessness and destruction,
and we journeyed through
    trackless deserts,
but the way of the Lord we have
    not known.
8 What has our arrogance profited
    us?
And what good has our boasted
    wealth brought us?

9 "All those things have vanished
    like a shadow,
and like a rumor that passes by;
10 like a ship that sails through the
    billowy water,
and when it has passed no trace
    can be found,
no track of its keel in the waves;
11 or as, when a bird flies through
    the air,
no evidence of its passage is
    found;
the light air, lashed by the beat of
    its pinions
and pierced by the force of its
    rushing flight,
is traversed by the movement of
    its wings,
and afterward no sign of its
    coming is found there;
12 or as, when an arrow is shot at a
    target,
the air, thus divided, comes
    together at once,
so that no one knows its pathway.
13 So we also, as soon as we were

born, ceased to be,
and we had no sign of virtue to
    show,
but were consumed in our
    wickedness."
14 Because the hope of the ungodly is
    like thistledown*o* carried by
    the wind,
and like a light frost*p* driven away
    by a storm;
it is dispersed like smoke before
    the wind,
and it passes like the remembrance
    of a guest who stays but a
    day.

15 But the righteous live forever,
and their reward is with the Lord;
the Most High takes care of them.
16 Therefore they will receive a
    glorious crown
and a beautiful diadem from the
    hand of the Lord,
because with his right hand he will
    cover them,
and with his arm he will shield
    them.
17 The Lord*q* will take his zeal as his
    whole armor,
and will arm all creation to repel*r*
    his enemies;
18 he will put on righteousness as a
    breastplate,
and wear impartial justice as a
    helmet;
19 he will take holiness as an
    invincible shield,
20 and sharpen stern wrath for a
    sword,
and creation will join with him to
    fight against his frenzied
    foes.

o Other ancient authorities read *dust*   *p* Other
ancient authorities read *spider's web*   *q* Gk He
r Or *punish*

---

godly are now filled with remorse at their
own folly. **5.5**: *Among the children of God . . .
among the saints*: that is, the righteous are to be
counted in the heavenly court, with God's
family (angels). **6–7**: The *way of the Lord* is
contrasted with the *paths of lawlessness*. **9–14**:

The examples of *ship, bird,* and *arrow,* which
leave *no trace,* underscore the folly of the unrighteous.
5.15–16: The *reward* of the righteous is a
glorious crown and divine protection. **17–22**:
The *punishment* of the Lord's enemies is

21 Shafts of lightning will fly with
    true aim,
and will leap from the clouds to
    the target, as from a
    well-drawn bow,
22 and hailstones full of wrath will be
    hurled as from a catapult;
the water of the sea will rage
    against them,
and rivers will relentlessly
    overwhelm them;
23 a mighty wind will rise against
    them,
and like a tempest it will winnow
    them away.
Lawlessness will lay waste the
    whole earth,
and evil-doing will overturn the
    thrones of rulers.

6 Listen therefore, O kings, and
    understand;
learn, O judges of the ends of the
    earth.
2 Give ear, you that rule over
    multitudes,
and boast of many nations.
3 For your dominion was given you
    from the Lord,
and your sovereignty from the
    Most High;
he will search out your works and
    inquire into your plans.
4 Because as servants of his
    kingdom you did not rule
    rightly,
or keep the law,
or walk according to the purpose
    of God,
5 he will come upon you terribly
    and swiftly,
because severe judgment falls on
    those in high places.

6 For the lowliest may be pardoned
    in mercy,
but the mighty will be mightily
    tested.
7 For the Lord of all will not stand
    in awe of anyone,
or show deference to greatness;
because he himself made both
    small and great,
and he takes thought for all alike.
8 But a strict inquiry is in store for
    the mighty.
9 To you then, O monarchs, my
    words are directed,
so that you may learn wisdom and
    not transgress.
10 For they will be made holy who
    observe holy things in
    holiness,
and those who have been taught
    them will find a defense.
11 Therefore set your desire on my
    words;
long for them, and you will be
    instructed.

12 Wisdom is radiant and unfading,
and she is easily discerned by
    those who love her,
and is found by those who seek
    her.
13 She hastens to make herself
    known to those who desire
    her.
14 One who rises early to seek her
    will have no difficulty,
for she will be found sitting at the
    gate.
15 To fix one's thought on her is
    perfect understanding,
and one who is vigilant on her
    account will soon be free
    from care,

---

reminiscent of Isa 59.16–19; see also Eph
6.14–17. **23**: The statement that *evil-doing*
overthrows *thrones* recalls 1.1 and prepares for
6.1–11.
    6.1–25: Exhortation to seek wisdom.
1–11: Further admonition to rulers (see 1.1),
who receive their authority from God and
must answer for lawless, godless acts; God

treats alike lowly and *mighty*, . . . *small and
great* (vv. 6–7). *Monarchs* need *wisdom* and will
receive it if they desire it (vv. 9–11).
    6.12–16: Wisdom is personified as a wom-
an, as in Prov 8. She is easily found, for she
seeks out those who *desire her,* and pseudo-
Solomon will seek her out as a bride (8.2).

16 because she goes about seeking
those worthy of her,
and she graciously appears to them
in their paths,
and meets them in every thought.

17 The beginning of wisdom*s* is the
most sincere desire for
instruction,
and concern for instruction is love
of her,
18 and love of her is the keeping of
her laws,
and giving heed to her laws is
assurance of immortality,
19 and immortality brings one near
to God;
20 so the desire for wisdom leads to a
kingdom.

21 Therefore if you delight in thrones
and scepters, O monarchs
over the peoples,
honor wisdom, so that you may
reign forever.
22 I will tell you what wisdom is and
how she came to be,
and I will hide no secrets from
you,
but I will trace her course from
the beginning of creation,
and make knowledge of her clear,
and I will not pass by the truth;
23 nor will I travel in the company of
sickly envy,
for envy*t* does not associate with
wisdom.
24 The multitude of the wise is the
salvation of the world,
and a sensible king is the stability
of any people.

25 Therefore be instructed by my
words, and you will profit.

7 I also am mortal, like everyone
else,
a descendant of the first-formed
child of earth;
and in the womb of a mother I
was molded into flesh,
2 within the period of ten months,
compacted with blood,
from the seed of a man and the
pleasure of marriage.
3 And when I was born, I began to
breathe the common air,
and fell upon the kindred earth;
my first sound was a cry, as is
true of all.
4 I was nursed with care in
swaddling cloths.
5 For no king has had a different
beginning of existence;
6 there is for all one entrance into
life, and one way out.
7 Therefore I prayed, and
understanding was given
me;
I called on God, and the spirit of
wisdom came to me.
8 I preferred her to scepters and
thrones,
and I accounted wealth as nothing
in comparison with her.
9 Neither did I liken to her any
priceless gem,
because all gold is but a little sand
in her sight,
and silver will be accounted as
clay before her.

s Gk *Her beginning*   *t* Gk *this*

6.17–21: The steps from the love of wisdom to immortality; a sorites (a form of logic much used by the Stoics), tracing the path from *desire* for wisdom to its results in *immortality* and being *near to God*. 20: A *kingdom*, God's eternal kingdom, in which rulers and others who truly desire wisdom participate. 21–25: An invitation to learn of wisdom from Solomon. As in 1.1 and 6.1, *kings* are addressed, but the real audience is the Jewish community.

7.1–8.21: A description of wisdom and Solomon's quest for her. 7.1–22a: Recognizing his need for wisdom, Solomon *prayed* for and received wisdom, valuing it above every other gift (1 Kings 3.5–15). With the gift of wisdom he received *all good things, friendship with God,* and *unerring knowledge* of the world, the heavenly bodies, and plant and animal life. This is the encyclopedic knowledge that was particularly cultivated in the Hellenistic world.

10 I loved her more than health and
  beauty,
and I chose to have her rather than
  light,
because her radiance never ceases.
11 All good things came to me along
  with her,
and in her hands uncounted
  wealth.
12 I rejoiced in them all, because
  wisdom leads them;
but I did not know that she was
  their mother.
13 I learned without guile and I
  impart without grudging;
I do not hide her wealth,
14 for it is an unfailing treasure for
  mortals;
those who get it obtain friendship
  with God,
commended for the gifts that
  come from instruction.

15 May God grant me to speak with
  judgment,
and to have thoughts worthy of
  what I have received;
for he is the guide even of
  wisdom
and the corrector of the wise.
16 For both we and our words are in
  his hand,
as are all understanding and skill
  in crafts.
17 For it is he who gave me unerring
  knowledge of what exists,
to know the structure of the world
  and the activity of the
  elements;
18 the beginning and end and middle
  of times,
the alternations of the solstices and
  the changes of the seasons,
19 the cycles of the year and the
  constellations of the stars,
20 the natures of animals and the
  tempers of wild animals,

the powers of spirits^u and the
  thoughts of human beings,
the varieties of plants and the
  virtues of roots;
21 I learned both what is secret and
  what is manifest,
22 for wisdom, the fashioner of all
  things, taught me.

There is in her a spirit that is
  intelligent, holy,
unique, manifold, subtle,
mobile, clear, unpolluted,
distinct, invulnerable, loving the
  good, keen,
irresistible, 23 beneficent, humane,
steadfast, sure, free from anxiety,
all-powerful, overseeing all,
and penetrating through all spirits
that are intelligent, pure, and
  altogether subtle.
24 For wisdom is more mobile than
  any motion;
because of her pureness she
  pervades and penetrates all
  things.
25 For she is a breath of the power of
  God,
and a pure emanation of the glory
  of the Almighty;
therefore nothing defiled gains
  entrance into her.
26 For she is a reflection of eternal
  light,
a spotless mirror of the working
  of God,
and an image of his goodness.
27 Although she is but one, she can
  do all things,
and while remaining in herself, she
  renews all things;
in every generation she passes into
  holy souls
and makes them friends of God,
  and prophets;

u Or *winds*

7.22b–8.1: **The nature and beneficial
works of wisdom. 22b–23**: Wisdom's
twenty-one (3 × 7) attributes. **24**: She is a
pure, freely moving, and all penetrating *spirit*

(see 1.6; 9.12). **25–26**: She emanates from
God; her *power, glory,* purity, *light,* and *goodness* are expressed through her (see also Jn
1.1–14; Heb 1.1–3).

28 for God loves nothing so much as
    the person who lives with
    wisdom.
29 She is more beautiful than the sun,
    and excels every constellation of
    the stars.
    Compared with the light she is
    found to be superior,
30 for it is succeeded by the night,
    but against wisdom evil does not
    prevail.

8 She reaches mightily from one end
    of the earth to the other,
    and she orders all things well.
2 I loved her and sought her from
    my youth;
    I desired to take her for my bride,
    and became enamored of her
    beauty.
3 She glorifies her noble birth by
    living with God,
    and the Lord of all loves her.
4 For she is an initiate in the
    knowledge of God,
    and an associate in his works.
5 If riches are a desirable possession
    in life,
    what is richer than wisdom, the
    active cause of all things?
6 And if understanding is effective,
    who more than she is fashioner of
    what exists?
7 And if anyone loves righteousness,
    her labors are virtues;
    for she teaches self-control and
    prudence,
    justice and courage;
    nothing in life is more profitable
    for mortals than these.
8 And if anyone longs for wide
    experience,
    she knows the things of old, and
    infers the things to come;
    she understands turns of speech
    and the solutions of riddles;

    she has foreknowledge of signs
    and wonders
    and of the outcome of seasons and
    times.
9 Therefore I determined to take her
    to live with me,
    knowing that she would give me
    good counsel
    and encouragement in cares and
    grief.
10 Because of her I shall have glory
    among the multitudes
    and honor in the presence of the
    elders, though I am young.
11 I shall be found keen in judgment,
    and in the sight of rulers I shall be
    admired.
12 When I am silent they will wait
    for me,
    and when I speak they will give
    heed;
    if I speak at greater length,
    they will put their hands on their
    mouths.
13 Because of her I shall have
    immortality,
    and leave an everlasting
    remembrance to those who
    come after me.
14 I shall govern peoples,
    and nations will be subject to me;
15 dread monarchs will be afraid of
    me when they hear of me;
    among the people I shall show
    myself capable, and
    courageous in war.
16 When I enter my house, I shall
    find rest with her;
    for companionship with her has
    no bitterness,
    and life with her has no pain, but
    gladness and joy.
17 When I considered these things
    inwardly,
    and pondered in my heart

7.27–8.1: She is everywhere, *orders all
things all well,* and *can do all things.* She enters
holy souls and makes them *friends of God; evil*
cannot defeat her.
**8.2–21: Solomon desires wisdom as his
bride and teacher. 4–6:** She is God's *associate in his works,* and his agent in making all

things (Prov 8.22–30; see also Jn 1.3; Col
1.16; Heb 1.2). **7:** She *teaches self-control, prudence, justice,* and *courage,* which (according to
Plato and the Stoics) are the four cardinal
virtues. **8:** She knows the past and the future,
and so can give good counsel.
8.10–16: *Because of her* Solomon will re-

that in kinship with wisdom there
 is immortality,
18 and in friendship with her, pure
 delight,
 and in the labors of her hands,
 unfailing wealth,
 and in the experience of her
 company, understanding,
 and renown in sharing her words,
 I went about seeking how to get
 her for myself.
19 As a child I was naturally gifted,
 and a good soul fell to my lot;
20 or rather, being good, I entered an
 undefiled body.
21 But I perceived that I would not
 possess wisdom unless God
 gave her to me—
 and it was a mark of insight to
 know whose gift she was—
 so I appealed to the Lord and
 implored him,
 and with my whole heart I said:

9 "O God of my ancestors and Lord
 of mercy,
 who have made all things by your
 word,
2 and by your wisdom have formed
 humankind
 to have dominion over the
 creatures you have made,
3 and rule the world in holiness and
 righteousness,
 and pronounce judgment in
 uprightness of soul,
4 give me the wisdom that sits by
 your throne,
 and do not reject me from among
 your servants.
5 For I am your servant*v* the son of
 your serving girl,
 a man who is weak and
 short-lived,
 with little understanding of
 judgment and laws;
6 for even one who is perfect among
 human beings

will be regarded as nothing
 without the wisdom that
 comes from you.
7 You have chosen me to be king of
 your people
 and to be judge over your sons
 and daughters.
8 You have given command to build
 a temple on your holy
 mountain,
 and an altar in the city of your
 habitation,
 a copy of the holy tent that you
 prepared from the
 beginning.
9 With you is wisdom, she who
 knows your works
 and was present when you made
 the world;
 she understands what is pleasing in
 your sight
 and what is right according to
 your commandments.
10 Send her forth from the holy
 heavens,
 and from the throne of your glory
 send her,
 that she may labor at my side,
 and that I may learn what is
 pleasing to you.
11 For she knows and understands all
 things,
 and she will guide me wisely in
 my actions
 and guard me with her glory.
12 Then my works will be
 acceptable,
 and I shall judge your people
 justly,
 and shall be worthy of the throne*w*
 of my father.
13 For who can learn the counsel of
 God?
 Or who can discern what the Lord
 wills?

v Gk *slave*   *w* Gk *thrones*

---

ceive *honor* and respect, *immortality,* a great
empire, *rest* and *joy.* **19–20:** The Platonic view
of the soul as pre-existent seems to be reflected here, but unlike Plato's view, there is
union with an *undefiled body.*

9.1–18: Solomon's prayer for wisdom
(1 Kings 3.6–9). **1–2:** God *made all* things by
word and *wisdom* (Jn 1.1–3); here "word" and
"wisdom" are synonymous. **9:** Compare 8.3–
4 and Prov 8.27–30.

14 For the reasoning of mortals is
      worthless,
   and our designs are likely to fail;
15 for a perishable body weighs
      down the soul,
   and this earthy tent burdens the
      thoughtful^x mind.
16 We can hardly guess at what is on
      earth,
   and what is at hand we find with
      labor;
   but who has traced out what is in
      the heavens?
17 Who has learned your counsel,
   unless you have given wisdom
   and sent your holy spirit from on
      high?
18 And thus the paths of those on
      earth were set right,
   and people were taught what
      pleases you,
   and were saved by wisdom."

10 Wisdom^y protected the
      first-formed father of the
      world, when he alone had
      been created;
   she delivered him from his
      transgression,
2 and gave him strength to rule all
      things.
3 But when an unrighteous man
      departed from her in his
      anger,
   he perished because in rage he
      killed his brother.
4 When the earth was flooded
      because of him, wisdom
      again saved it,
   steering the righteous man by a
      paltry piece of wood.

5 Wisdom^y also, when the nations
      in wicked agreement had
      been put to confusion,
   recognized the righteous man and
      preserved him blameless
      before God,
   and kept him strong in the face of
      his compassion for his
      child.

6 Wisdom^y rescued a righteous man
      when the ungodly were
      perishing;
   he escaped the fire that descended
      on the Five Cities.^z
7 Evidence of their wickedness still
      remains:
   a continually smoking wasteland,
   plants bearing fruit that does not
      ripen,
   and a pillar of salt standing as a
      monument to an
      unbelieving soul.
8 For because they passed wisdom
      by,
   they not only were hindered from
      recognizing the good,
   but also left for humankind a
      reminder of their folly,
   so that their failures could never
      go unnoticed.

9 Wisdom rescued from troubles
      those who served her.
10 When a righteous man fled from
      his brother's wrath,
   she guided him on straight paths;
   she showed him the kingdom of
      God,

x Or anxious   y Gk She   z Or on Pentapolis

9.13–15: The *perishable body,* though not called evil (8.20), *burdens* and hampers the *mind.* 16–17: Even earthly things we know imperfectly; only through *wisdom,* also called *the holy spirit,* can we learn heavenly things (1 Cor 2.7–12). 18: *Wisdom* guides, teaches, and saves her followers. This is illustrated in ch 10 in the lives of the righteous ancestors. 10.1–11.4: **Seven historical illustrations** of the saving power of wisdom. 10.1–2: Adam (Gen 1.26–5.5). 3: Cain (Gen 4.1–6). *Perished,* spiritual death. 4: Noah (Gen 5.28–9.29). 5: Abraham (Gen 11.26–15.10); he is linked with the *nations* of Gen 11.1–9.

10.6–8: *A righteous man,* Lot (Gen 19.23–26); throughout this chapter personal names are deliberately replaced by the category of "righteous." 9–12: Jacob (Gen 25.19–49.33,

and gave him knowledge of holy
    things;
she prospered him in his labors,
    and increased the fruit of his toil.
11 When his oppressors were
    covetous,
she stood by him and made him
    rich.
12 She protected him from his
    enemies,
and kept him safe from those who
    lay in wait for him;
in his arduous contest she gave
    him the victory,
so that he might learn that
    godliness is more powerful
    than anything else.

13 When a righteous man was sold,
    wisdom*a* did not desert
    him,
but delivered him from sin.
She descended with him into the
    dungeon,
14 and when he was in prison she did
    not leave him,
until she brought him the scepter
    of a kingdom
and authority over his masters.
Those who accused him she
    showed to be false,
and she gave him everlasting
    honor.

15 A holy people and blameless race
wisdom delivered from a nation of
    oppressors.
16 She entered the soul of a servant
    of the Lord,
and withstood dread kings with
    wonders and signs.
17 She gave to holy people the
    reward of their labors;
she guided them along a
    marvelous way,
and became a shelter to them by
    day,

and a starry flame through the
    night.
18 She brought them over the Red
    Sea,
and led them through deep waters;
19 but she drowned their enemies,
and cast them up from the depth
    of the sea.
20 Therefore the righteous plundered
    the ungodly;
they sang hymns, O Lord, to your
    holy name,
and praised with one accord your
    defending hand;
21 for wisdom opened the mouths of
    those who were mute,
and made the tongues of infants
    speak clearly.

11 Wisdom*b* prospered their
    works by the hand of a
    holy prophet.
2 They journeyed through an
    uninhabited wilderness,
and pitched their tents in
    untrodden places.
3 They withstood their enemies and
    fought off their foes.
4 When they were thirsty, they
    called upon you,
and water was given them out of
    flinty rock,
and from hard stone a remedy for
    their thirst.
5 For through the very things by
    which their enemies were
    punished,
they themselves received benefit in
    their need.
6 Instead of the fountain of an
    ever-flowing river,
stirred up and defiled with blood
7 in rebuke for the decree to kill the
    infants,

a Gk *she*   *b* Gk *She*

---

especially ch 28). **13–14:** Joseph (Gen 39;
41.39–47).
    10.15–11.4: Through Moses, *a holy prophet*
(11.1), wisdom delivered Israel from Egypt
(Ex 1.1–15.21, especially chs 14–15), leading

the people *through an uninhabited wilderness* (Ex
15.22–17.6).
    **11.5–19.22: The writer composes an his-
torical meditation,** consisting of comparisons between Israel and Egypt. **11.5:** The prin-

you gave them abundant water
  unexpectedly,
8 showing by their thirst at that
    time
how you punished their enemies.
9 For when they were tried, though
    they were being disciplined
    in mercy,
they learned how the ungodly
    were tormented when
    judged in wrath.
10 For you tested them as a parent*c*
    does in warning,
but you examined the ungodly*d* as
    a stern king does in
    condemnation.
11 Whether absent or present, they
    were equally distressed,
12 for a twofold grief possessed
    them,
and a groaning at the memory of
    what had occurred.
13 For when they heard that through
    their own punishments
the righteous*e* had received
    benefit, they perceived it
    was the Lord's doing.
14 For though they had mockingly
    rejected him who long
    before had been cast out
    and exposed,
at the end of the events they
    marveled at him,
when they felt thirst in a different
    way from the righteous.

15 In return for their foolish and
    wicked thoughts,
which led them astray to worship
    irrational serpents and
    worthless animals,
you sent upon them a multitude of
    irrational creatures to
    punish them,

16 so that they might learn that one
    is punished by the very
    things by which one sins.
17 For your all-powerful hand,
    which created the world out of
    formless matter,
did not lack the means to send
    upon them a multitude of
    bears, or bold lions,
18 or newly-created unknown beasts
    full of rage,
or such as breathe out fiery breath,
or belch forth a thick pall of
    smoke,
or flash terrible sparks from their
    eyes;
19 not only could the harm they did
    destroy people,*f*
but the mere sight of them could
    kill by fright.
20 Even apart from these, people*e*
    could fall at a single breath
when pursued by justice
and scattered by the breath of
    your power.
But you have arranged all things
    by measure and number
    and weight.

21 For it is always in your power to
    show great strength,
and who can withstand the might
    of your arm?
22 Because the whole world before
    you is like a speck that tips
    the scales,
and like a drop of morning dew
    that falls on the ground.
23 But you are merciful to all, for
    you can do all things,
and you overlook people's sins, so
    that they may repent.

c Gk *a father*   *d* Gk *those*   *e* Gk *they*
f Gk *them*

---

ciple behind all the comparisons: *through the very things by which* Egypt *was punished,* Israel *received benefit.*

11.6–17: Instead of the Nile plague, Israel received water from the rock (vv. 4, 7; Ex 17.1–7), but Egypt was afflicted with the small animals. **7:** *You,* refers to the Lord, in the direct address which continues to 19.22.

15: *Irrational creatures,* such as the frogs and flies, etc. (Ex chs 8 and 10), in accordance with the principle enunciated in v. 16 (see also Ps 7.15–16). **11.17–12.2: God's mercy and love for all. 11.17:** *Formless matter,* a concept derived from Greek philosophy, is used to describe the chaos of Gen 1.2.

24 For you love all things that exist,
 and detest none of the things that
  you have made,
 for you would not have made
  anything if you had hated
  it.
25 How would anything have
  endured if you had not
  willed it?
 Or how would anything not called
  forth by you have been
  preserved?
26 You spare all things, for they are
  yours, O Lord, you who
  love the living.

12 For your immortal spirit is in
  all things.
2 Therefore you correct little by
  little those who trespass,
 and you remind and warn them of
  the things through which
  they sin,
 so that they may be freed from
  wickedness and put their
  trust in you, O Lord.

3 Those who lived long ago in your
  holy land
4 you hated for their detestable
  practices,
 their works of sorcery and unholy
  rites,
5 their merciless slaughter*g* of
  children,
 and their sacrificial feasting on
  human flesh and blood.
 These initiates from the midst of a
  heathen cult,*h*
6 these parents who murder helpless
  lives,
 you willed to destroy by the hands
  of our ancestors,
7 so that the land most precious of
  all to you
 might receive a worthy colony of
  the servants*i* of God.

8 But even these you spared, since
  they were but mortals,
 and sent wasps*j* as forerunners of
  your army
 to destroy them little by little,
9 though you were not unable to
  give the ungodly into the
  hands of the righteous in
  battle,
 or to destroy them at one blow by
  dread wild animals or your
  stern word.
10 But judging them little by little
  you gave them an
  opportunity to repent,
 though you were not unaware that
  their origin*k* was evil
 and their wickedness inborn,
 and that their way of thinking
  would never change.
11 For they were an accursed race
  from the beginning,
 and it was not through fear of
  anyone that you left them
  unpunished for their sins.

12 For who will say, "What have you
  done?"
 Or will resist your judgment?
 Who will accuse you for the
  destruction of nations that
  you made?
 Or who will come before you to
  plead as an advocate for the
  unrighteous?
13 For neither is there any god
  besides you, whose care is
  for all people,
 to whom you should prove that
  you have not judged
  unjustly;

---

g Gk *slaughterers*   h Meaning of Gk uncertain
i Or *children*   j Or *hornets*   k Or *nature*
l Or *all things*

12.3–11: Even the Canaanites were objects of divine leniency. Despite their evil *practices,* God judged them *little by little* (v. 8; see Ex 23.29–30), giving them *an opportunity to repent* (v. 10; compare 2 Esd 9.11; Heb 12.17).

12.12–18: God's supreme power delights in benevolence. God, *sovereign,* all-powerful, is answerable to no one; he is *righteous,* condemns no one unjustly, and judges with *mildness* and *forbearance.* He cares for all people (v. 13) and rules all things (v. 15).

14 nor can any king or monarch
     confront you about those
     whom you have punished.
15 You are righteous and you rule all
     things righteously,
  deeming it alien to your power
  to condemn anyone who does not
     deserve to be punished.
16 For your strength is the source of
     righteousness,
  and your sovereignty over all
     causes you to spare all.
17 For you show your strength when
     people doubt the
     completeness of your
     power,
  and you rebuke any insolence
     among those who know
     it. *m*
18 Although you are sovereign in
     strength, you judge with
     mildness,
  and with great forbearance you
     govern us;
  for you have power to act
     whenever you choose.

19 Through such works you have
     taught your people
  that the righteous must be kind,
  and you have filled your children
     with good hope,
  because you give repentance for
     sins.
20 For if you punished with such
     great care and indulgence *n*
  the enemies of your servants *o* and
     those deserving of death,
  granting them time and
     opportunity to give up their
     wickedness,
21 with what strictness you have
     judged your children,

to whose ancestors you gave oaths
     and covenants full of good
     promises!
22 So while chastening us you
     scourge our enemies ten
     thousand times more,
  so that, when we judge, we may
     meditate upon your
     goodness,
  and when we are judged, we may
     expect mercy.

23 Therefore those who lived
     unrighteously, in a life of
     folly,
  you tormented through their own
     abominations.
24 For they went far astray on the
     paths of error,
  accepting as gods those animals
     that even their enemies *p*
     despised;
  they were deceived like foolish
     infants.
25 Therefore, as though to children
     who cannot reason,
  you sent your judgment to mock
     them.
26 But those who have not heeded
     the warning of mild
     rebukes
  will experience the deserved
     judgment of God.
27 For when in their suffering they
     became incensed
  at those creatures that they had
     thought to be gods, being
     punished by means of
     them,

m Meaning of Gk uncertain   n Other ancient
authorities lack and indulgence; others read and
entreaty   o Or children   p Gk they

**12.19–22: God's mercy is an example to
Israel.** Israel may think that God has *judged*
them strictly (v. 21), but he *scourges* Israel's
enemies far *more;* God chastens Israel in *mercy*
and for their own good.
**12.23–27: Further comments on the
punishment of the Egyptians** (in accord
with the principle set forth in 11.16). The
Egyptians were tormented by the *animals* that
they worshiped. **27:** Though the Egyptians
recognized Israel's God as *the true God,* they
refused to let Israel go. *The utmost condemnation,* i.e. the death of their firstborn sons and
the disaster at the Red Sea.

they saw and recognized as the
true God the one whom
they had before refused to
know.
Therefore the utmost
condemnation came upon
them.

13 For all people who were
ignorant of God were
foolish by nature;
and they were unable from the
good things that are seen to
know the one who exists,
nor did they recognize the artisan
while paying heed to his
works;

2 but they supposed that either fire
or wind or swift air,
or the circle of the stars, or
turbulent water,
or the luminaries of heaven were
the gods that rule the
world.

3 If through delight in the beauty of
these things people assumed
them to be gods,
let them know how much better
than these is their Lord,
for the author of beauty created
them.

4 And if people*q* were amazed at
their power and working,
let them perceive from them
how much more powerful is the
one who formed them.

5 For from the greatness and beauty
of created things
comes a corresponding perception
of their Creator.

6 Yet these people are little to be
blamed,

for perhaps they go astray
while seeking God and desiring to
find him.

7 For while they live among his
works, they keep searching,
and they trust in what they see,
because the things that are
seen are beautiful.

8 Yet again, not even they are to be
excused;

9 for if they had the power to know
so much
that they could investigate the
world,
how did they fail to find sooner
the Lord of these things?

10 But miserable, with their hopes set
on dead things, are those
who give the name "gods" to the
works of human hands,
gold and silver fashioned with
skill,
and likenesses of animals,
or a useless stone, the work of an
ancient hand.

11 A skilled woodcutter may saw
down a tree easy to handle
and skillfully strip off all its bark,
and then with pleasing
workmanship
make a useful vessel that serves
life's needs,

12 and burn the cast-off pieces of his
work
to prepare his food, and eat his
fill.

13 But a cast-off piece from among
them, useful for nothing,
a stick crooked and full of knots,

q Gk *they*

13.1–15.17: A digression on false worship. 13.1–9: Nature worship is the least culpable form of false worship. The implication is that God can be known apart from revelation *from the good things that are seen*. He is *the author of beauty*, and from *his works* he is known by analogy (*a corresponding perception of their Creator*). **6–7:** The writer partly excuses such idolatry as arising from an honest search for God. **8–9:** But such people are not

to be excused; they should have discerned *the Lord* of created *things*.
13.10–19: The folly of image-worship. The polemic against idols is frequent in the Bible; see Isa 44.9–20; Jer 10.1–16; Ps 135.15–18. This is a satirical description of how a *woodcutter* fells a *tree*, makes of some knotty *cast-off* piece a *likeness* of *a human being* or *animal*, and calls it his god, though it cannot stand or act and has no life.

he takes and carves with care in
  his leisure,
and shapes it with skill gained in
  idleness;[r]
he forms it in the likeness of a
  human being,
14 or makes it like some worthless
  animal,
giving it a coat of red paint and
  coloring its surface red
and covering every blemish in it
  with paint;
15 then he makes a suitable niche for
  it,
and sets it in the wall, and fastens
  it there with iron.
16 He takes thought for it, so that it
  may not fall,
because he knows that it cannot
  help itself,
for it is only an image and has
  need of help.
17 When he prays about possessions
  and his marriage and
  children,
he is not ashamed to address a
  lifeless thing.
18 For health he appeals to a thing
  that is weak;
for life he prays to a thing that is
  dead;
for aid he entreats a thing that is
  utterly inexperienced;
for a prosperous journey, a thing
  that cannot take a step;
19 for money-making and work and
  success with his hands
he asks strength of a thing whose
  hands have no strength.

14 Again, one preparing to sail
  and about to voyage over
  raging waves
calls upon a piece of wood more
  fragile than the ship that
  carries him.

2 For it was desire for gain that
  planned that vessel,
and wisdom was the artisan who
  built it;
3 but it is your providence,
  O Father, that steers its
  course,
because you have given it a path
  in the sea,
and a safe way through the waves,
4 showing that you can save from
  every danger,
so that even a person who lacks
  skill may put to sea.
5 It is your will that works of your
  wisdom should not be
  without effect;
therefore people trust their lives
  even to the smallest piece of
  wood,
and passing through the billows
  on a raft they come safely
  to land.
6 For even in the beginning, when
  arrogant giants were
  perishing,
the hope of the world took refuge
  on a raft,
and guided by your hand left to
  the world the seed of a new
  generation.
7 For blessed is the wood by which
  righteousness comes.

8 But the idol made with hands is
  accursed, and so is the one
  who made it—
he for having made it, and the
  perishable thing because it
  was named a god.
9 For equally hateful to God are the
  ungodly and their
  ungodliness;

r Other ancient authorities read *with intelligent skill*

**14.1–14: The folly of the seafarer who
trusts in the wooden image on the ship's
prow.** It is the *providence* of the *Father* that is
responsible for a safe voyage.
  14.6–7: The reference is to Noah, *the hope*
of the world. The *wood* refers not (as some have
thought) to the cross of Christ, but to Noah's
ark, which carried forward God's righteous
will. In contrast to the *blessed wood* is the *ac-*
cursed idolator.

10 for what was done will be
   punished together with the
   one who did it.
11 Therefore there will be a visitation
   also upon the heathen idols,
   because, though part of what God
   created, they became an
   abomination,
   snares for human souls
   and a trap for the feet of the
   foolish.

12 For the idea of making idols was
   the beginning of
   fornication,
   and the invention of them was the
   corruption of life;
13 for they did not exist from the
   beginning,
   nor will they last forever.
14 For through human vanity they
   entered the world,
   and therefore their speedy end has
   been planned.

15 For a father, consumed with grief
   at an untimely
   bereavement,
   made an image of his child, who
   had been suddenly taken
   from him;
   he now honored as a god what
   was once a dead human
   being,
   and handed on to his dependents
   secret rites and initiations.
16 Then the ungodly custom, grown
   strong with time, was kept
   as a law,
   and at the command of monarchs
   carved images were
   worshiped.
17 When people could not honor
   monarchs[s] in their
   presence, since they lived at
   a distance,

they imagined their appearance far
   away,
and made a visible image of the
   king whom they honored,
so that by their zeal they might
   flatter the absent one as
   though present.

18 Then the ambition of the artisan
   impelled
even those who did not know the
   king to intensify their
   worship.
19 For he, perhaps wishing to please
   his ruler,
skillfully forced the likeness to
   take more beautiful form,
20 and the multitude, attracted by the
   charm of his work,
now regarded as an object of
   worship the one whom
   shortly before they had
   honored as a human being.
21 And this became a hidden trap for
   humankind,
because people, in bondage to
   misfortune or to royal
   authority,
bestowed on objects of stone or
   wood the name that ought
   not to be shared.

22 Then it was not enough for them
   to err about the knowledge
   of God,
but though living in great strife
   due to ignorance,
they call such great evils peace.
23 For whether they kill children in
   their initiations, or celebrate
   secret mysteries,
or hold frenzied revels with
   strange customs,

s Gk *them*

14.15–21: The origins of idolatry. The cult of the dead is traced to a grief-stricken *father* who made and *worshiped* an *image* of his *dead* child (vv. 15–16). Ruler worship is explained by the subjects who lived at a distance, and worshiped *a visible image* of their king (v. 17); moreover skilled craftsmen made the image *more beautiful* than the king (vv. 18–20). (Euhemerus, about 300 B.C., taught that all gods were deified rulers). **14.22–31: The evil results of idolatry** (Rom 1.24–32). Ignorance of God, *strife,*

24 they no longer keep either their
  lives or their marriages
  pure,
but they either treacherously kill
  one another, or grieve one
  another by adultery,
25 and all is a raging riot of blood
  and murder, theft and
  deceit, corruption,
  faithlessness, tumult,
  perjury,
26 confusion over what is good,
  forgetfulness of favors,
defiling of souls, sexual
  perversion,
disorder in marriages, adultery,
  and debauchery.
27 For the worship of idols not to be
  named
is the beginning and cause and end
  of every evil.
28 For their worshipers[t] either rave
  in exultation,
or prophesy lies, or live
  unrighteously, or readily
  commit perjury;
29 for because they trust in lifeless
  idols
they swear wicked oaths and
  expect to suffer no harm.
30 But just penalties will overtake
  them on two counts:
because they thought wrongly
  about God in devoting
  themselves to idols,
and because in deceit they swore
  unrighteously through
  contempt for holiness.
31 For it is not the power of the
  things by which people
  swear,[u]
but the just penalty for those who
  sin,
that always pursues the
  transgression of the
  unrighteous.

15 But you, our God, are kind
  and true,
patient, and ruling all things[v] in
  mercy.
2 For even if we sin we are yours,
  knowing your power;
but we will not sin, because we
  know that you
  acknowledge us as yours.
3 For to know you is complete
  righteousness,
and to know your power is the
  root of immortality.
4 For neither has the evil intent of
  human art misled us,
nor the fruitless toil of painters,
a figure stained with varied colors,
5 whose appearance arouses yearning
  in fools,
so that they desire[w] the lifeless
  form of a dead image.
6 Lovers of evil things and fit for
  such objects of hope[x]
are those who either make or
  desire or worship them.

7 A potter kneads the soft earth
and laboriously molds each vessel
  for our service,
fashioning out of the same clay
both the vessels that serve clean
  uses
and those for contrary uses,
  making all alike;
but which shall be the use of each
  of them
the worker in clay decides.
8 With misspent toil, these workers
  form a futile god from the
  same clay—
these mortals who were made of
  earth a short time before

t Gk *they*   *u* Or *of the oaths people swear*
v Or *ruling the universe*   *w* Gk *and he desires*
x Gk *such hopes*

moral wrong, and perversion (v. 26) will
bring sure punishment.
  15.1–17: The contrast between the wor-
shipers of the true God and idolaters. 1–5:
Speaking to God (vv. 1–3; see also 11.26–
12.2), the writer notes the purifying influence
of the worship of the true God on the life of

Israel. **3**: *To know* God is *righteousness* and
eternal life (Jn 17.3).
  15.6–17: The folly and wickedness of
making and worshiping clay idols. For financial profit *a potter* molds from one mass of *clay*
both useful *vessels* and *counterfeit gods;* cheap
imitations of gold, silver, and copper *images.*

and after a little while go to the
earth from which all
mortals are taken,
when the time comes to return the
souls that were borrowed.

9 But the workers are not concerned
that mortals are destined to
die
or that their life is brief,
but they compete with workers in
gold and silver,
and imitate workers in copper;
and they count it a glorious thing
to mold counterfeit gods.

10 Their heart is ashes, their hope is
cheaper than dirt,
and their lives are of less worth
than clay,

11 because they failed to know the
one who formed them
and inspired them with active
souls
and breathed a living spirit into
them.

12 But they considered our existence
an idle game,
and life a festival held for profit,
for they say one must get money
however one can, even by
base means.

13 For these persons, more than all
others, know that they sin
when they make from earthy
matter fragile vessels and
carved images.

14 But most foolish, and more
miserable than an infant,
are all the enemies who oppressed
your people.

15 For they thought that all their
heathen idols were gods,
though these have neither the use
of their eyes to see with,
nor nostrils with which to draw
breath,
nor ears with which to hear,

nor fingers to feel with,
and their feet are of no use for
walking.

16 For a human being made them,
and one whose spirit is borrowed
formed them;
for none can form gods that are
like themselves.

17 People are mortal, and what they
make with lawless hands is
dead;
for they are better than the objects
they worship,
since[y] they have life, but the
idols[z] never had.

18 Moreover, they worship even the
most hateful animals,
which are worse than all others
when judged by their lack
of intelligence;

19 and even as animals they are not
so beautiful in appearance
that one would desire them,
but they have escaped both the
praise of God and his
blessing.

16 Therefore those people[a] were
deservedly punished
through such creatures,
and were tormented by a
multitude of animals.

2 Instead of this punishment you
showed kindness to your
people,
and you prepared quails to eat,
a delicacy to satisfy the desire of
appetite;

3 in order that those people, when
they desired food,
might lose the least remnant of
appetite[b]
because of the odious creatures
sent to them,

y Other ancient authorities read *of which*
z Gk *but they*   a Gk *they*   b Gk *loathed
the necessary appetite*

14–17: The stupidity of Israel's *enemies,* who
worship useless, lifeless images.
  **15.18–16.4: Resumption of the topic of
the plague of animals** (11.15). **16.1–4:** The

Egyptians, *tormented* by the *animals* they wor-
shiped (Ex chs 8 and 10), lost all appetite; the
Israelites, after brief hunger, enjoyed quails
(Num ch 11).

while your people,^c after suffering
 want a short time,
might partake of delicacies.
4 For it was necessary that upon
 those oppressors inescapable
 want should come,
 while to these others it was merely
 shown how their enemies
 were being tormented.

5 For when the terrible rage of wild
 animals came upon your
 people^d
and they were being destroyed by
 the bites of writhing
 serpents,
your wrath did not continue to the
 end;
6 they were troubled for a little
 while as a warning,
and received a symbol of
 deliverance to remind them
 of your law's command.

7 For the one who turned toward it
 was saved, not by the thing
 that was beheld,
but by you, the Savior of all.
8 And by this also you convinced
 our enemies
that it is you who deliver from
 every evil.
9 For they were killed by the bites
 of locusts and flies,
and no healing was found for
 them,
because they deserved to be
 punished by such things.
10 But your children were not
 conquered even by the
 fangs of venomous
 serpents,
for your mercy came to their help
 and healed them.

11 To remind them of your oracles
 they were bitten,
and then were quickly delivered,
so that they would not fall into
 deep forgetfulness
and become unresponsive^e to
 your kindness.
12 For neither herb nor poultice
 cured them,
but it was your word, O Lord,
 that heals all people.
13 For you have power over life and
 death;
you lead mortals down to the
 gates of Hades and back
 again.
14 A person in wickedness kills
 another,
but cannot bring back the departed
 spirit,
or set free the imprisoned soul.

15 To escape from your hand is
 impossible;
16 for the ungodly, refusing to know
 you,
were flogged by the strength of
 your arm,
pursued by unusual rains and hail
 and relentless storms,
and utterly consumed by fire.
17 For—most incredible of all—in
 water, which quenches all
 things,
the fire had still greater effect,
for the universe defends the
 righteous.
18 At one time the flame was
 restrained,
so that it might not consume the
 creatures sent against the
 ungodly,

c Gk *they*   d Gk *them*   e Meaning of Gk
uncertain

16.5–14: Another contrast between Egyptians and Israelites. The Egyptians were killed by bites of locusts and flies; Israel, bitten by serpents (Num 21.6–9), suffered briefly as a *warning* (vv. 6, 11) but were quickly healed by God's word (vv. 11–12), not by the bronze serpent.
 16.13–14: God has *power* to bestow *life* or lead to *death,* in contrast to the wicked, who cannot free the soul *imprisoned* by the gates of *Hades,* or Sheol (1 Sam 2.6; Ps 9.13).
 16.15–29: The elements combine to punish the Egyptians and to serve Israel. The food of angels is manna, suited to the taste of each Israelite (vv. 20–21, 25).

but that seeing this they might
    know
that they were being pursued by
    the judgment of God;
19 and at another time even in the
    midst of water it burned
    more intensely than fire,
to destroy the crops of the
    unrighteous land.
20 Instead of these things you gave
    your people food of angels,
and without their toil you supplied
    them from heaven with
    bread ready to eat,
providing every pleasure and
    suited to every taste.
21 For your sustenance manifested
    your sweetness toward your
    children;
and the bread, ministering*f* to the
    desire of the one who took
    it,
was changed to suit everyone's
    liking.
22 Snow and ice withstood fire
    without melting,
so that they might know that the
    crops of their enemies
were being destroyed by the fire
    that blazed in the hail
and flashed in the showers of rain;
23 whereas the fire,*g* in order that the
    righteous might be fed,
even forgot its native power.

24 For creation, serving you who
    made it,
exerts itself to punish the
    unrighteous,
and in kindness relaxes on behalf
    of those who trust in you.
25 Therefore at that time also,
    changed into all forms,
it served your all-nourishing
    bounty,

according to the desire of those
    who had need,*h*
26 so that your children, whom you
    loved, O Lord, might learn
that it is not the production of
    crops that feeds humankind
but that your word sustains those
    who trust in you.
27 For what was not destroyed by
    fire
was melted when simply warmed
    by a fleeting ray of the sun,
28 to make it known that one must
    rise before the sun to give
    you thanks,
and must pray to you at the
    dawning of the light;
29 for the hope of an ungrateful
    person will melt like wintry
    frost,
and flow away like waste water.

17 Great are your judgments and
    hard to describe;
therefore uninstructed souls have
    gone astray.
2 For when lawless people supposed
    that they held the holy
    nation in their power,
they themselves lay as captives of
    darkness and prisoners of
    long night,
shut in under their roofs, exiles
    from eternal providence.
3 For thinking that in their secret
    sins they were unobserved
behind a dark curtain of
    forgetfulness,
they were scattered, terribly*i*
    alarmed,
and appalled by specters.

f Gk *and it, ministering*   *g* Gk *this*
h Or *who made supplication*   *i* Other ancient
authorities read *unobserved, they were darkened
behind a dark curtain of forgetfulness, terribly*

16.22–27: The *fire* God sent executed his
judgment; now he kept fire from melting
snow and ice (a poetical expression for the
manna; 19.21); now *a fleeting ray of the sun*
melted it (Ex 16.21). The fire and manna
show how *creation* serves God (5.17), so that
Israel might learn that it is sustained by God's

word (v. 26). **28–29:** One should *rise* at dawn
to thank God, for God's blessing escapes the
ungrateful person as fast as the rising sun melts
wintry frost.
17.1–18.4: **The contrast between the
plague of darkness and the pillar of fire.**
1–7: God's judgment made the *lawless* Egyp-

4 For not even the inner chamber
    that held them protected
    them from fear,
but terrifying sounds rang out
    around them,
and dismal phantoms with gloomy
    faces appeared.
5 And no power of fire was able to
    give light,
nor did the brilliant flames of the
    stars
avail to illumine that hateful night.
6 Nothing was shining through to
    them
except a dreadful, self-kindled fire,
and in terror they deemed the
    things that they saw
to be worse than that unseen
    appearance.
7 The delusions of their magic art
    lay humbled,
and their boasted wisdom was
    scornfully rebuked.
8 For those who promised to drive
    off the fears and disorders
    of a sick soul
were sick themselves with
    ridiculous fear.
9 For even if nothing disturbing
    frightened them,
yet, scared by the passing of wild
    animals and the hissing of
    snakes
10 they perished in trembling fear,
refusing to look even at the air,
    though it nowhere could be
    avoided.
11 For wickedness is a cowardly
    thing, condemned by its
    own testimony;*j*
distressed by conscience, it has
    always exaggerated*k* the
    difficulties.
12 For fear is nothing but a giving up
    of the helps that come from
    reason;
13 and hope, defeated by this inward
    weakness,

prefers ignorance of what causes
    the torment.
14 But throughout the night, which
    was really powerless
and which came upon them from
    the recesses of powerless
    Hades,
they all slept the same sleep,
15 and now were driven by
    monstrous specters,
and now were paralyzed by their
    souls' surrender;
for sudden and unexpected fear
    overwhelmed them.
16 And whoever was there fell down,
and thus was kept shut up in a
    prison not made of iron;
17 for whether they were farmers or
    shepherds
or workers who toiled in the
    wilderness,
they were seized, and endured the
    inescapable fate;
for with one chain of darkness
    they all were bound.
18 Whether there came a whistling
    wind,
or a melodious sound of birds in
    wide-spreading branches,
or the rhythm of violently rushing
    water,
19 or the harsh crash of rocks hurled
    down,
or the unseen running of leaping
    animals,
or the sound of the most savage
    roaring beasts,
or an echo thrown back from a
    hollow of the mountains,
it paralyzed them with terror.
20 For the whole world was
    illumined with brilliant
    light,
and went about its work
    unhindered,

j Meaning of Gk uncertain
k Other ancient authorities read *anticipated*

tians the terrified *captives of darkness,* unaided by their *magic art* or *boasted wisdom* (Ex 1.21–23).
17.11: *Conscience,* in the moral sense, occurs only here in the Greek Old Testament. **12:** A remarkable description of fear. **18–19:** The *terror* of the Egyptians is illustrated by seven incidents.

21 while over those people alone
  heavy night was spread,
an image of the darkness that was
  destined to receive them;
but still heavier than darkness
  were they to themselves.

18 But for your holy ones there
  was very great light.
Their enemies[l] heard their voices
  but did not see their forms,
and counted them happy for not
  having suffered,
2 and were thankful that your holy
  ones,[m] though previously
  wronged, were doing them
  no injury;
and they begged their pardon for
  having been at variance
  with them.[m]
3 Therefore you provided a flaming
  pillar of fire
as a guide for your people's[n]
  unknown journey,
and a harmless sun for their
  glorious wandering.
4 For their enemies[o] deserved to be
  deprived of light and
  imprisoned in darkness,
those who had kept your children
  imprisoned,
through whom the imperishable
  light of the law was to be
  given to the world.

5 When they had resolved to kill the
  infants of your holy ones,
and one child had been abandoned
  and rescued,
you in punishment took away a
  multitude of their children;
and you destroyed them all
  together by a mighty flood.
6 That night was made known
  beforehand to our
  ancestors,
so that they might rejoice in sure

knowledge of the oaths in
  which they trusted.
7 The deliverance of the righteous
  and the destruction of their
  enemies
were expected by your people.
8 For by the same means by which
  you punished our enemies
you called us to yourself and
  glorified us.
9 For in secret the holy children of
  good people offered
  sacrifices,
and with one accord agreed to the
  divine law,
so that the saints would share alike
  the same things,
both blessings and dangers;
and already they were singing the
  praises of the ancestors.[p]
10 But the discordant cry of their
  enemies echoed back,
and their piteous lament for their
  children was spread abroad.
11 The slave was punished with the
  same penalty as the master,
and the commoner suffered the
  same loss as the king;
12 and they all together, by the one
  form[q] of death,
had corpses too many to count.
For the living were not sufficient
  even to bury them,
since in one instant their most
  valued children had been
  destroyed.
13 For though they had disbelieved
  everything because of their
  magic arts,
yet, when their firstborn were
  destroyed, they
  acknowledged your people
  to be God's child.

l Gk They   m Meaning of Gk uncertain
n Gk their   o Gk those persons   p Other
ancient authorities read dangers, the ancestors
already leading the songs of praise   q Gk name

18.1: *Your holy ones:* the Israelites. **3–4:** *Pillar of fire . . . a harmless sun,* Ex 13.21–22. *Light of the law,* in contrast to the *light* and *darkness* of their enemies.
18.5–25: **The contrast between the**
tenth plague and the fate of the Israelites.
5: *Resolved,* Ex 1.16. *Abandoned and rescued,* Ex 2.1–10. *A multitude of their children,* the Egyptian firstborn (Ex 12.29). *That night,* the first passover.

14 For while gentle silence enveloped
        all things,
   and night in its swift course was
        now half gone,
15 your all-powerful word leaped
        from heaven, from the
        royal throne,
   into the midst of the land that was
        doomed,
   a stern warrior
16 carrying the sharp sword of your
        authentic command,
   and stood and filled all things with
        death,
   and touched heaven while standing
        on the earth.
17 Then at once apparitions in
        dreadful dreams greatly
        troubled them,
   and unexpected fears assailed
        them;
18 and one here and another there,
        hurled down half dead,
   made known why they were
        dying;
19 for the dreams that disturbed them
        forewarned them of this,
   so that they might not perish
        without knowing why they
        suffered.

20 The experience of death touched
        also the righteous,
   and a plague came upon the
        multitude in the desert,
   but the wrath did not long
        continue.
21 For a blameless man was quick to
        act as their champion;
   he brought forward the shield of
        his ministry,
   prayer and propitiation by incense;
   he withstood the anger and put an
        end to the disaster,
   showing that he was your servant.
22 He conquered the wrath* not by
        strength of body,

   not by force of arms,
   but by his word he subdued the
        avenger,
   appealing to the oaths and
        covenants given to our
        ancestors.
23 For when the dead had already
        fallen on one another in
        heaps,
   he intervened and held back the
        wrath,
   and cut off its way to the living.
24 For on his long robe the whole
        world was depicted,
   and the glories of the ancestors
        were engraved on the four
        rows of stones,
   and your majesty was on the
        diadem upon his head.
25 To these the destroyer yielded,
        these he* feared;
   for merely to test the wrath was
        enough.

19 But the ungodly were assailed
        to the end by pitiless anger,
   for God* knew in advance even
        their future actions:
2 how, though they themselves had
        permitted* your people to
        depart
   and hastily sent them out,
   they would change their minds
        and pursue them.
3 For while they were still engaged
        in mourning,
   and were lamenting at the graves
        of their dead,
   they reached another foolish
        decision,
   and pursued as fugitives those
        whom they had begged and
        compelled to leave.

r Cn: Gk *multitude*   s Other ancient authorities
read *they*   t Gk *he*   u Other ancient
authorities read *had changed their minds to permit*

18.15: God's *all-powerful word* (Greek "lo-
gos"), as a *stern warrior, leaped from heaven*
and carried out God's judgment (this recalls
Rev 19.13 rather than Jn 1.1–18). **20–25**:
When *a plague* struck Israel *in the desert*, Aaron
stopped the destroying angel from inflicting
further death (Num 16.41–50). **24**: From Ex
28.15–21, and Jewish tradition.
   19.1–22: **God judged the Egyptians and
delivered Israel at the Red Sea. 1–5**: The

4 For the fate they deserved drew
    them on to this end,
and made them forget what had
    happened,
in order that they might fill up the
    punishment that their
    torments still lacked,
5 and that your people might
    experience[v] an incredible
    journey,
but they themselves might meet a
    strange death.

6 For the whole creation in its
    nature was fashioned anew,
complying with your commands,
so that your children[w] might be
    kept unharmed.
7 The cloud was seen
    overshadowing the camp,
and dry land emerging where
    water had stood before,
an unhindered way out of the Red
    Sea,
and a grassy plain out of the
    raging waves,
8 where those protected by your
    hand passed through as one
    nation,
after gazing on marvelous
    wonders.
9 For they ranged like horses,
and leaped like lambs,
praising you, O Lord, who
    delivered them.
10 For they still recalled the events of
    their sojourn,
how instead of producing animals
    the earth brought forth
    gnats,

and instead of fish the river
    spewed out vast numbers of
    frogs.
11 Afterward they saw also a new
    kind[x] of birds,
when desire led them to ask for
    luxurious food;
12 for, to give them relief, quails
    came up from the sea.

13 The punishments did not come
    upon the sinners
without prior signs in the violence
    of thunder,
for they justly suffered because of
    their wicked acts;
for they practiced a more bitter
    hatred of strangers.
14 Others had refused to receive
    strangers when they came
    to them,
but these made slaves of guests
    who were their benefactors.
15 And not only so—but, while
    punishment of some sort
    will come upon the former
for having received strangers with
    hostility,
16 the latter, having first received
    them with festal
    celebrations,
afterward afflicted with terrible
    sufferings
those who had already shared the
    same rights.
17 They were stricken also with loss
    of sight—

---

v Other ancient authorities read accomplish
w Or servants   x Or production

Egyptians' foolish decision to pursue Israel and enslave them again. **6–12:** As before (16.24), creation serves God's purposes. **7:** *Cloud,* Ex 13.21–22. *Dry land,* Ex 14.21–22. **10:** Ex 8.1–24. **11–12:** Ex 16.13 and Num 11.4, 20, 31–32.
19.13–17: The Egyptians treated *strangers* worse than did the inhabitants of Sodom, and so deserved greater *punishment.* **14:** *Others,* those of Sodom (Gen 19.1–11). *These,* the Egyptians. *Guests,* Israel had been invited to

Egypt (Gen 45.16–20). **17:** Gen 19.11; Ex 10.21–23. **18–21:** In the plagues and at the Red Sea nature and *animals* changed their customary action to effect God's redemptive purpose (16.24). **19:** *Land animals,* apparently a reference to Israel and their cattle crossing the Red Sea. *Creatures that swim,* frogs (Ex 8.1–7). **20–21:** 16.17. *Heavenly food,* the manna. **22:** This abrupt ending gives the lesson of the historical survey: God's *help* for this people.

just as were those at the door of
the righteous man—
when, surrounded by yawning
darkness,
all of them tried to find the way
through their own doors.

18 For the elements changed[y] places
with one another,
as on a harp the notes vary the
nature of the rhythm,
while each note remains the
same.[z]
This may be clearly inferred from
the sight of what took
place.
19 For land animals were transformed
into water creatures,
and creatures that swim moved
over to the land.

20 Fire even in water retained its
normal power,
and water forgot its fire-quenching
nature.
21 Flames, on the contrary, failed to
consume
the flesh of perishable creatures
that walked among them,
nor did they melt[a] the crystalline,
quick-melting kind of
heavenly food.

22 For in everything, O Lord, you
have exalted and glorified
your people,
and you have not neglected to
help them at all times and
in all places.

y Gk *changing*   z Meaning of Gk uncertain
a Cn: Gk *nor could be melted*

Solomon asked for wisdom from God.

Ecclesiasticus,
or the Wisdom of Jesus Son of
Sirach

This work is known as Ecclesiasticus, or the Wisdom of Ben Sira, or simply Sirach (the Greek spelling of Sira). "Ecclesiasticus" suggests its use as a "church book" in the early Christian community, which accepted it into its canon. The Jewish community, followed by the Reformers, excluded it from the canon. This explains the extraordinary history of its text. The original Hebrew text was lost to the western world from about 400 to 1900; the book survived in Greek, Latin, Syriac, and other translations. Since about 1900, extensive fragments of copies of the Hebrew have been discovered in various places: Cairo, Qumran, and Masada, so that now two-thirds of the Hebrew text exists. The translation here is one of a critically established text, using both Hebrew and other witnesses to the original. The reader will occasionally find a slightly different verse numbering from that in traditional renderings, since the NRSV follows the numbering of the critical Greek text edited by J. Ziegler.

Ben Sira signs his name (50.27), describes his profession (39.1–11), and invites students to his school (51.23). Sometime before 180 B.C. and the ensuing Maccabean revolt, he committed his wisdom to writing, probably in Jerusalem (see his description in 50.1–24 of Simeon II, who was high priest from 219–196). Sometime after 132 (see the Prologue) his grandson translated the original Hebrew into Greek. The grandson rightly stresses the profound knowledge that Sirach had of Hebrew traditions ("the Law and the Prophets and the other books"—already the three-fold division of the Hebrew Bible was in the process of formation).

Although Sirach lacks any clear structure, it resembles the book of Proverbs in many ways. It stresses characteristic wisdom teachings: proper speech, riches and poverty, honesty, diligence, choice of friends, sin and death, retribution, and wisdom itself. Unlike Proverbs 10ff., individual proverbs are not set apart, but are incorporated into smooth-flowing poems of some length (often in accordance with the number of letters in the Hebrew alphabet). The doctrine is surprisingly traditional, almost as if Job and Ecclesiastes had never been written. Sirach is not unaware of the problem of suffering (2.1–6; 11.4; 40.1–10), but he is a firm believer in the justice of divine retribution. God will reward everyone according to one's deserts (15.11–16.23). There is no intimation of a future life with God in the Hebrew text; rather, all go to Sheol (14.12–19; 38.16–23). This is the usual Hebrew teaching, which understood immortality only in terms of one's progeny and good name (44.13–15). Traditionally, wisdom literature never appealed to Israel's sacred history or covenant. Sirach is an outstanding exception, in view of his "Praise of the Ancestors" (chs 44–50) and his identification of personified wisdom with the Torah or Law (24.23). At the same time, his book belongs definitely to the genre of wisdom literature, with its stress on the lessons of experience and on the "fear of the Lord" (1.11–30; 25.10–11; 40.25–27).

Many great teachings have been given to us through the Law and the Prophets and the others *a* that followed them, and for these we should praise Israel for instruction and wisdom. Now, those who read the scriptures must not only themselves understand them, but must also as lovers of learning be able through the spoken and written word to help the outsiders. So my grandfather Jesus, who had devoted himself especially to the reading of the Law and the Prophets and the other books of our ancestors, and had acquired considerable proficiency in them, was himself also led to write something pertaining to instruction and wisdom, so that by becoming familiar also with his book *b* those who love learning might make even greater progress in living according to the law.

You are invited therefore to read it with goodwill and attention, and to be indulgent in cases where, despite our diligent labor in translating, we may seem to have rendered some phrases imperfectly. For what was originally expressed in Hebrew does not have exactly the same sense when translated into another language. Not only this book, but even the Law itself, the Prophecies, and the rest of the books differ not a little when read in the original.

When I came to Egypt in the thirty-eighth year of the reign of Euergetes and stayed for some time, I found opportunity for no little instruction. *c* It seemed highly necessary that I should myself devote some diligence and labor to the translation of this book. During that time I have applied my skill day and night to complete and publish the book for those living abroad who wished to gain learning and are disposed to live according to the law.

1 All wisdom is from the Lord,
  and with him it remains forever.
2 The sand of the sea, the drops of
    rain,
  and the days of eternity—who
    can count them?
3 The height of heaven, the breadth
    of the earth,
  the abyss, and wisdom *d*—who
    can search them out?
4 Wisdom was created before all
    other things,
  and prudent understanding from
    eternity. *e*
6 The root of wisdom—to whom
    has it been revealed?
  Her subtleties—who knows
    them? *f*
8 There is but one who is wise,
    greatly to be feared,
  seated upon his throne—the
    Lord.
9 It is he who created her;
  he saw her and took her
    measure;
  he poured her out upon all his
    works,
10 upon all the living according to his
    gift;
  he lavished her upon those who
    love him. *g*

11 The fear of the Lord is glory and
    exultation,

a Or *other books*   b Gk *with these things*
c Other ancient authorities read *I found a copy
affording no little instruction*   d Other ancient
authorities read *the depth of the abyss*   e Other
ancient authorities add as verse 5, *The source of
wisdom is God's word in the highest heaven, and her
ways are the eternal commandments.*   f Other
ancient authorities add as verse 7, *The knowledge
of wisdom—to whom was it manifested? And her
abundant experience—who has understood it?*
g Other ancient authorities add *Love of the Lord
is glorious wisdom; to those to whom he appears he
apportions her, that they may see him.*

1.1–10: The personification of Wisdom (see also ch 24; Job 28; Prov 8). **1:** *From the Lord,* a divine origin, as in 24.3; Prov 8.22–25. **2–3:** Illustrations of the impossibility of fathoming the depths of divine wisdom (18.4–7; Rom 11.33). **4:** Prov 8.22–31. **6–10:** Only with God is Wisdom to be found (Job 28); yet God has *lavished* her upon *all the living,* i.e. Jews and Gentiles, but especially upon *those who love him* (Israel).

1.11–30: A poem that identifies wisdom and fear of the Lord (vv. 11–14, 16, 18,

and gladness and a crown of
rejoicing.

12 The fear of the Lord delights the
heart,
and gives gladness and joy and
long life. *h*

13 Those who fear the Lord will have
a happy end;
on the day of their death they
will be blessed.

14 To fear the Lord is the beginning
of wisdom;
she is created with the faithful in
the womb.

15 She made *i* among human beings
an eternal foundation,
and among their descendants she
will abide faithfully.

16 To fear the Lord is fullness of
wisdom;
she inebriates mortals with her
fruits;

17 she fills their *j* whole house with
desirable goods,
and their *j* storehouses with her
produce.

18 The fear of the Lord is the crown
of wisdom,
making peace and perfect health
to flourish. *k*

19 She rained down knowledge and
discerning comprehension,
and she heightened the glory of
those who held her fast.

20 To fear the Lord is the root of
wisdom,
and her branches are long life. *l*

22 Unjust anger cannot be justified,
for anger tips the scale to one's
ruin.

23 Those who are patient stay calm
until the right moment,
and then cheerfulness comes
back to them.

24 They hold back their words until
the right moment;

then the lips of many tell of
their good sense.

25 In the treasuries of wisdom are
wise sayings,
but godliness is an abomination
to a sinner.

26 If you desire wisdom, keep the
commandments,
and the Lord will lavish her
upon you.

27 For the fear of the Lord is wisdom
and discipline,
fidelity and humility are his
delight.

28 Do not disobey the fear of the
Lord;
do not approach him with a
divided mind.

29 Do not be a hypocrite before
others,
and keep watch over your lips.

30 Do not exalt yourself, or you may
fall
and bring dishonor upon
yourself.
The Lord will reveal your secrets
and overthrow you before the
whole congregation,
because you did not come in the
fear of the Lord,
and your heart was full of
deceit.

2 My child, when you come to
serve the Lord,
prepare yourself for testing. *m*

h Other ancient authorities add *The fear of the
Lord is a gift from the Lord; also for love he makes
firm paths.*   *i* Gk *made as a nest*   *j* Other
ancient authorities read *her*   *k* Other ancient
authorities add *God for peace; glory
opens out for those who love him. He saw her and
took her measure.*   *l* Other ancient authorities
add as verse 21, *The fear of the Lord drives away
sins; and where it abides, it will turn away all anger.*
m Or *trials*

20–21, 25, 27–28, 30). **12:** *Long life,* typical of
wisdom teaching; see v. 20; Prov 3.16. **14:**
Prov 1.7; 9.10; Job 28.28; Ps 111.10.

2.1–17: A poem on trusting God. 1–6:
The testing of faith is a common biblical
theme (Gen 22; Job 1–2; Jas 1.2–4; Luke

2 Set your heart right and be steadfast,
and do not be impetuous in time of calamity.
3 Cling to him and do not depart,
so that your last days may be prosperous.
4 Accept whatever befalls you,
and in times of humiliation be patient.
5 For gold is tested in the fire,
and those found acceptable, in the furnace of humiliation.[n]
6 Trust in him, and he will help you;
make your ways straight, and hope in him.

7 You who fear the Lord, wait for his mercy;
do not stray, or else you may fall.
8 You who fear the Lord, trust in him,
and your reward will not be lost.
9 You who fear the Lord, hope for good things,
for lasting joy and mercy.[o]
10 Consider the generations of old and see:
has anyone trusted in the Lord and been disappointed?
Or has anyone persevered in the fear of the Lord[p] and been forsaken?
Or has anyone called upon him and been neglected?
11 For the Lord is compassionate and merciful;
he forgives sins and saves in time of distress.

12 Woe to timid hearts and to slack hands,
and to the sinner who walks a double path!
13 Woe to the faint-hearted who have no trust!
Therefore they will have no shelter.
14 Woe to you who have lost your nerve!
What will you do when the Lord's reckoning comes?

15 Those who fear the Lord do not disobey his words,
and those who love him keep his ways.
16 Those who fear the Lord seek to please him,
and those who love him are filled with his law.
17 Those who fear the Lord prepare their hearts,
and humble themselves before him.
Let us fall into the hands of the Lord,
but not into the hands of mortals;
for equal to his majesty is his mercy,
and equal to his name are his works.[q]

3 Listen to me your father, O children;
act accordingly, that you may be kept in safety.
2 For the Lord honors a father above his children,
and he confirms a mother's right over her children.
3 Those who honor their father atone for sins,

n Other ancient authorities add *in sickness and poverty put your trust in him*
o Other ancient authorities add *For his reward is an everlasting gift with joy.* *p* Gk *of him*
q Syr: Gk lacks this line

11.4). **7–9**: Vv. 15–17. **9**: *Joy*, in this life, not in the next.
2.10–11: Israel's history shows the efficacy of trust in God, who is *compassionate and merciful* (Ex 34.6–7; Ps 103.8–9; Jon 4.2). **17**: 2 Sam 24.14; 1 Chr 21.13.
3.1–16: **Filial duty and its reward** (Ex 20.12; Deut 5.16; Eph 6.1–3). In accord with

4 and those who respect their
   mother are like those who
   lay up treasure.
5 Those who honor their father will
   have joy in their own
   children,
   and when they pray they will be
   heard.
6 Those who respect their father
   will have long life,
   and those who honor*r* their
   mother obey the Lord;
7   they will serve their parents as
   their masters.*s*
8 Honor your father by word and
   deed,
   that his blessing may come
   upon you.
9 For a father's blessing strengthens
   the houses of the children,
   but a mother's curse uproots
   their foundations.
10 Do not glorify yourself by
   dishonoring your father,
   for your father's dishonor is no
   glory to you.
11 The glory of one's father is one's
   own glory,
   and it is a disgrace for children
   not to respect their mother.

12 My child, help your father in his
   old age,
   and do not grieve him as long
   as he lives;
13 even if his mind fails, be patient
   with him;
   because you have all your
   faculties do not despise
   him.
14 For kindness to a father will not
   be forgotten,
   and will be credited to you
   against your sins;

15 in the day of your distress it will
   be remembered in your
   favor;
   like frost in fair weather, your
   sins will melt away.
16 Whoever forsakes a father is like a
   blasphemer,
   and whoever angers a mother is
   cursed by the Lord.

17 My child, perform your tasks with
   humility;*t*
   then you will be loved by those
   whom God accepts.
18 The greater you are, the more you
   must humble yourself;
   so you will find favor in the
   sight of the Lord.*u*
20 For great is the might of the Lord;
   but by the humble he is
   glorified.
21 Neither seek what is too difficult
   for you,
   nor investigate what is beyond
   your power.
22 Reflect upon what you have been
   commanded,
   for what is hidden is not your
   concern.
23 Do not meddle in matters that are
   beyond you,
   for more than you can
   understand has been shown
   you.
24 For their conceit has led many
   astray,
   and wrong opinion has impaired
   their judgment.

r Heb: Other ancient authorities read *comfort*
s In other ancient authorities this line is preceded
by *Those who fear the Lord honor their father,*
t Heb: Gk *meekness*   u Other ancient
authorities add as verse 19, *Many are lofty and
renowned, but to the humble he reveals his secrets.*

---

the Jewish doctrine that the observance of the
Mosaic law is meritorious, Sirach teaches that
the keeping of the commandment to honor
one's parents (Ex 20.12) *atones for sins* (vv. 3,
14–15).
   3.14: *Kindness,* literally "righteousness,"
which came to be centered in almsgiving as

the characteristic sign (3.10–4.6; 7.10; 29.8–
13; Tob 14.10–11).
   3.17–24: On humility. A frequent topic
in wisdom instruction (Prov 11.2; 15.33;
22.4; and Sir 7.16–17; 10.28). **21–24:** Perhaps
Sirach is warning against Greek learning. **21:**
Ps 131; Eccl 7.24.

25 Without eyes there is no light;
   without knowledge there is no
      wisdom. *v*

26 A stubborn mind will fare badly at
      the end,
   and whoever loves danger will
      perish in it.

27 A stubborn mind will be burdened
      by troubles,
   and the sinner adds sin to sins.

28 When calamity befalls the proud,
      there is no healing,
   for an evil plant has taken root
      in him.

29 The mind of the intelligent
      appreciates proverbs,
   and an attentive ear is the desire
      of the wise.

30 As water extinguishes a blazing
      fire,
   so almsgiving atones for sin.

31 Those who repay favors give
      thought to the future;
   when they fall they will find
      support.

4 My child, do not cheat the poor
   of their living,
   and do not keep needy eyes
      waiting.

2 Do not grieve the hungry,
   or anger one in need.

3 Do not add to the troubles of the
      desperate,
   or delay giving to the needy.

4 Do not reject a suppliant in
      distress,
   or turn your face away from the
      poor.

5 Do not avert your eye from the
      needy,
   and give no one reason to curse
      you;

6 for if in bitterness of soul some
      should curse you,
   their Creator will hear their
      prayer.

7 Endear yourself to the
      congregation;
   bow your head low to the great.

8 Give a hearing to the poor,
   and return their greeting
      politely.

9 Rescue the oppressed from the
      oppressor;
   and do not be hesitant in giving
      a verdict.

10 Be a father to orphans,
   and be like a husband to their
      mother;
   you will then be like a son of the
      Most High,
   and he will love you more than
      does your mother.

11 Wisdom teaches *w* her children
   and gives help to those who
      seek her.

12 Whoever loves her loves life,
   and those who seek her from
      early morning are filled
      with joy.

13 Whoever holds her fast inherits
      glory,
   and the Lord blesses the place
      she *x* enters.

14 Those who serve her minister to
      the Holy One;
   the Lord loves those who love
      her.

15 Those who obey her will judge
      the nations,
   and all who listen to her will
      live secure.

16 If they remain faithful, they will
      inherit her;
   their descendants will also
      obtain her.

17 For at first she will walk with
      them on tortuous paths;

---

v Heb: Other ancient authorities lack verse 25
w Heb Syr: Gk *exalts*   *x* Or *he*

3.25–29: On docility. The *stubborn* (literally "heavy heart") refuse the lessons of wisdom.
3.30–4.10: On almsgiving. See 3.14 n.
4.6: Ex 22.22. **9–10:** 34.21–27; see 35.14–
15 n. Orphans and widows were particularly indigent (Ex 22.21–23).
4.11–19: The rewards of Wisdom. Personified Wisdom (1.10; ch 24) loves her followers, but also tests them. **14:** Service of

she will bring fear and dread
    upon them,
and will torment them by her
    discipline
until she trusts them, *y*
and she will test them with her
    ordinances.
¹⁸ Then she will come straight back
    to them again and gladden
    them,
and will reveal her secrets to
    them.
¹⁹ If they go astray she will forsake
    them,
and hand them over to their
    ruin.

²⁰ Watch for the opportune time, and
    beware of evil,
and do not be ashamed to be
    yourself.
²¹ For there is a shame that leads to
    sin,
and there is a shame that is
    glory and favor.
²² Do not show partiality, to your
    own harm,
or deference, to your downfall.
²³ Do not refrain from speaking at
    the proper moment, *z*
and do not hide your wisdom. *a*
²⁴ For wisdom becomes known
    through speech,
and education through the
    words of the tongue.
²⁵ Never speak against the truth,
but be ashamed of your
    ignorance.
²⁶ Do not be ashamed to confess
    your sins,
and do not try to stop the
    current of a river.
²⁷ Do not subject yourself to a fool,
or show partiality to a ruler.
²⁸ Fight to the death for truth,

and the Lord God will fight for
    you.
²⁹ Do not be reckless in your speech,
or sluggish and remiss in your
    deeds.
³⁰ Do not be like a lion in your
    home,
or suspicious of your servants.
³¹ Do not let your hand be stretched
    out to receive
and closed when it is time to
    give.

5 Do not rely on your wealth,
    or say, "I have enough."
² Do not follow your inclination
    and strength
in pursuing the desires of your
    heart.
³ Do not say, "Who can have power
    over me?"
for the Lord will surely punish
    you.
⁴ Do not say, "I sinned, yet what
    has happened to me?"
for the Lord is slow to anger.
⁵ Do not be so confident of
    forgiveness *b*
that you add sin to sin.
⁶ Do not say, "His mercy is great,
    he will forgive *c* the multitude
    of my sins,"
for both mercy and wrath are with
    him,
and his anger will rest on
    sinners.
⁷ Do not delay to turn back to the
    Lord,

y Or *until they remain faithful in their heart*
z Heb: Gk *at a time of salvation*   *a* So some
Gk Mss and Heb Syr Lat: Other Gk Mss lack
and do not hide your wisdom   *b* Heb: Gk
atonement   *c* Heb: Gk *he* (or *it*) *will atone for*

---

wisdom is service of God, and God will love
those who love her (Prov 8.17). **17–18:** Prov
3.11–12.
    4.20–5.8: Precepts for everyday life.
20–28: True and false shame (20.22–23;
41.14–42.8). **26:** It is as futile to hide one's
sins from God as to try to stop a river from

flowing. **30:** *A lion,* wild, relentless, destructive. **31:** *Hand,* Deut 15.7–8; Acts 20.35.
    5.1–8: A poem against presumption. **5:**
Sin to sin, presumption is the added sin. **6:**
16.11–12. The Lord is a God of both *mercy and
wrath.*

and do not postpone it from day
to day;
for suddenly the wrath of the Lord
will come upon you,
and at the time of punishment
you will perish.
8 Do not depend on dishonest
wealth,
for it will not benefit you on
the day of calamity.

9 Do not winnow in every wind,
or follow every path. *d*
10 Stand firm for what you know,
and let your speech be
consistent.
11 Be quick to hear,
but deliberate in answering.
12 If you know what to say, answer
your neighbor;
but if not, put your hand over
your mouth.

13 Honor and dishonor come from
speaking,
and the tongue of mortals may
be their downfall.
14 Do not be called double-tongued*e*
and do not lay traps with your
tongue;
for shame comes to the thief,
and severe condemnation to the
double-tongued.
15 In great and small matters cause
no harm,*f*

6 1 and do not become an enemy
instead of a friend;
for a bad name incurs shame and
reproach;
so it is with the double-tongued
sinner.

2 Do not fall into the grip of
passion,*g*

or you may be torn apart as by
a bull. *h*
3 Your leaves will be devoured and
your fruit destroyed,
and you will be left like a
withered tree.
4 Evil passion destroys those who
have it,
and makes them the
laughingstock of their
enemies.

5 Pleasant speech multiplies friends,
and a gracious tongue multiplies
courtesies.
6 Let those who are friendly with
you be many,
but let your advisers be one in a
thousand.
7 When you gain friends, gain them
through testing,
and do not trust them hastily.
8 For there are friends who are such
when it suits them,
but they will not stand by you
in time of trouble.
9 And there are friends who change
into enemies,
and tell of the quarrel to your
disgrace.
10 And there are friends who sit at
your table,
but they will not stand by you
in time of trouble.
11 When you are prosperous, they
become your second self,
and lord it over your servants;
12 but if you are brought low, they
turn against you,
and hide themselves from you.

d Gk adds *so it is with the double-tongued sinner*
(see 6.1)   *e* Heb: Gk *a slanderer*   *f* Heb Syr:
Gk *be ignorant*   *g* Heb: Meaning of Gk
uncertain   *h* Meaning of Gk uncertain

5.9–6.1: Honesty and sincerity. 9: A
condemnation of duplicity. **12:** *Hand . . .
mouth,* to keep silence, since one has no
competency to speak. **13:** The topic of the
tongue (use and abuse) is taken up frequently;
see 19.6–17; 20.16–20; 22.27–23.15; 28.12–
26.
6.2–4: Self-control; a warning against

lustful passions (18.30–19.3).
6.5–17: True and false friendship. A
frequent topic (see 11.29–12.18; 22.19–26;
37.1–6). Friends are to be tested, lest they
turn out to be "fair weather" friends (vv. 5–
12). True friends are a *treasure,* a gift from
God (vv. 13–17).

13 Keep away from your enemies,
and be on guard with your
friends.

14 Faithful friends are a sturdy
shelter:
whoever finds one has found a
treasure.

15 Faithful friends are beyond price;
no amount can balance their
worth.

16 Faithful friends are life-saving
medicine;
and those who fear the Lord
will find them.

17 Those who fear the Lord direct
their friendship aright,
for as they are, so are their
neighbors also.

18 My child, from your youth choose
discipline,
and when you have gray hair
you will still find wisdom.

19 Come to her like one who plows
and sows,
and wait for her good harvest.
For when you cultivate her you
will toil but little,
and soon you will eat of her
produce.

20 She seems very harsh to the
undisciplined;
fools cannot remain with her.

21 She will be like a heavy stone to
test them,
and they will not delay in
casting her aside.

22 For wisdom is like her name;
she is not readily perceived by
many.

23 Listen, my child, and accept my
judgment;
do not reject my counsel.

24 Put your feet into her fetters,
and your neck into her collar.

25 Bend your shoulders and carry
her,
and do not fret under her
bonds.

26 Come to her with all your soul,
and keep her ways with all your
might.

27 Search out and seek, and she will
become known to you;
and when you get hold of her,
do not let her go.

28 For at last you will find the rest
she gives,
and she will be changed into joy
for you.

29 Then her fetters will become for
you a strong defense,
and her collar a glorious robe.

30 Her yoke[i] is a golden ornament,
and her bonds a purple cord.

31 You will wear her like a glorious
robe,
and put her on like a splendid
crown.[j]

32 If you are willing, my child, you
can be disciplined,
and if you apply yourself you
will become clever.

33 If you love to listen you will gain
knowledge,
and if you pay attention you
will become wise.

34 Stand in the company of the
elders.
Who is wise? Attach yourself to
such a one.

35 Be ready to listen to every godly
discourse,

i Heb: Gk *Upon her*   *j* Heb: Gk *crown of
gladness*

6.18–37: Encouragement to seek Wisdom. *Discipline* (Hebrew "musar"; see 1.27; 4.17; 22.6; 23.2; 26.14; 32.14) is needed (vv. 18–22). There is a wordplay on "musar," which can also mean "withdrawn," and thus *not readily perceived by many* (v. 22).
6.23–31: Ben Sira often speaks to *my child,* in the style of the sages (Prov 4.10). One is to submit to the *yoke* of Wisdom, which is in reality a *golden ornament.* **32–37:** One way of becoming wise is to seek out the intelligent and frequent their company. Attaining wisdom means fidelity to the Law (v. 37; see also 15.1; 19.20; 23.27; 24.23).

and let no wise proverbs escape
you.
36 If you see an intelligent person,
rise early to visit him;
let your foot wear out his
doorstep.
37 Reflect on the statutes of the Lord,
and meditate at all times on his
commandments.
It is he who will give insight to[k]
your mind,
and your desire for wisdom will
be granted.

7 Do no evil, and evil will never
overtake you.
2 Stay away from wrong, and it will
turn away from you.
3 Do[l] not sow in the furrows of
injustice,
and you will not reap a
sevenfold crop.

4 Do not seek from the Lord high
office,
or the seat of honor from the
king.
5 Do not assert your righteousness
before the Lord,
or display your wisdom before
the king.
6 Do not seek to become a judge,
or you may be unable to root
out injustice;
you may be partial to the
powerful,
and so mar your integrity.
7 Commit no offense against the
public,
and do not disgrace yourself
among the people.

8 Do not commit a sin twice;
not even for one will you go
unpunished.

9 Do not say, "He will consider the
great number of my gifts,
and when I make an offering to
the Most High God, he will
accept it."
10 Do not grow weary when you
pray;
do not neglect to give alms.
11 Do not ridicule a person who is
embittered in spirit,
for there is One who humbles
and exalts.
12 Do not devise[m] a lie against your
brother,
or do the same to a friend.
13 Refuse to utter any lie,
for it is a habit that results in no
good.
14 Do not babble in the assembly of
the elders,
and do not repeat yourself when
you pray.
15 Do not hate hard labor
or farm work, which was
created by the Most High.
16 Do not enroll in the ranks of
sinners;
remember that retribution does
not delay.
17 Humble yourself to the utmost,
for the punishment of the
ungodly is fire and
worms.[n]

18 Do not exchange a friend for
money,
or a real brother for the gold of
Ophir.
19 Do not dismiss[o] a wise and good
wife,

k Heb: Gk *will confirm*   *l* Gk *My child, do*
m Heb: Gk *plow*   *n* Heb *for the expectation of*
mortals is worms   *o* Heb: Gk *deprive yourself of*

7.1–17: Various ethical maxims. 1–3:
Avoidance of sin. **4–7:** Proper conduct in
public life. **9:** One cannot buy off God. **11:**
11.4. The role of God is emphasized also in
1 Sam 2.8. **14:** Eccl 5.1 [2]; Mt 6.8. **16:** In the
context of v. 15, this means to consider oneself better than others. **17:** *Worms,* or corruption in the grave, awaits all (not "fire and
worms" as the Greek has it).
 7.18–36: Various duties. 18: *Ophir,* on
the coast of southern Arabia or eastern Africa,
was famous for its gold (1 Kings 9.28). **19:**

for her charm is worth more
than gold.
20 Do not abuse slaves who work
faithfully,
or hired laborers who devote
themselves to their task.
21 Let your soul love intelligent
slaves;*p*
do not withhold from them
their freedom.

22 Do you have cattle? Look after
them;
if they are profitable to you,
keep them.
23 Do you have children? Discipline
them,
and make them obedient*q* from
their youth.
24 Do you have daughters? Be
concerned for their
chastity,*r*
and do not show yourself too
indulgent with them.
25 Give a daughter in marriage, and
you complete a great task;
but give her to a sensible man.
26 Do you have a wife who pleases
you?*s* Do not divorce her;
but do not trust yourself to one
whom you detest.

27 With all your heart honor your
father,
and do not forget the birth
pangs of your mother.
28 Remember that it was of your
parents*t* you were born;
how can you repay what they
have given to you?

29 With all your soul fear the Lord,
and revere his priests.

30 With all your might love your
Maker,
and do not neglect his ministers.
31 Fear the Lord and honor the
priest,
and give him his portion, as you
have been commanded:
the first fruits, the guilt offering,
the gift of the shoulders,
the sacrifice of sanctification,
and the first fruits of the
holy things.

32 Stretch out your hand to the poor,
so that your blessing may be
complete.
33 Give graciously to all the living;
do not withhold kindness even
from the dead.
34 Do not avoid those who weep,
but mourn with those who
mourn.
35 Do not hesitate to visit the sick,
because for such deeds you will
be loved.
36 In all you do, remember the end
of your life,
and then you will never sin.

8 Do not contend with the
powerful,
or you may fall into their hands.
2 Do not quarrel with the rich,
in case their resources outweigh
yours;
for gold has ruined many,
and has perverted the minds of
kings.
3 Do not argue with the loud of
mouth,

p Heb Love a wise slave as yourself
*q Gk bend their necks   r Gk body   s Heb Syr
lack who pleases you   t Gk them*

Such a *wife* is not to be divorced; on wives,
see 9.1; 26.1–18; 36.27–31. **21**: After six years
of service a Hebrew slave was entitled to *freedom* (Ex 21.2; Lev 25.9–43).
 7.24–25: On *daughters,* see 42.9–14.
 7.29–31: In supporting and showing hon-
or to the priests one indirectly honors God
himself; for the priestly portion, see Num
18.9–20. **31**: *As . . . commanded,* Ex 29.27; Lev

7.31–34; Num 18.8–20; Deut 18.3. **33**: *Kindness,* probably provision for an honorable
burial (30.18; Tob 1.17). **34**: Rom 12.15. **36**:
The realization that the end of a sinner is
bound to be a sad one should serve as a deter-
rence from sin.
 8.1–19: **Advice about various types of
people. 1–2**: The *gold* of the *rich* can function
as a bribe. **5–7**: Have respect for the penitent,

and do not heap wood on their
   fire.

4 Do not make fun of one who is
   ill-bred,
  or your ancestors may be
   insulted.
5 Do not reproach one who is
   turning away from sin;
  remember that we all deserve
   punishment.
6 Do not disdain one who is old,
  for some of us are also growing
   old.
7 Do not rejoice over any one's
   death;
  remember that we must all die.

8 Do not slight the discourse of the
   sages,
  but busy yourself with their
   maxims;
  because from them you will learn
   discipline
  and how to serve princes.
9 Do not ignore the discourse of the
   aged,
  for they themselves learned
   from their parents;*u*
  from them you learn how to
   understand
  and to give an answer when the
   need arises.

10 Do not kindle the coals of sinners,
  or you may be burned in their
   flaming fire.
11 Do not let the insolent bring you
   to your feet,
  or they may lie in ambush
   against your words.
12 Do not lend to one who is
   stronger than you;
  but if you do lend anything,
   count it as a loss.
13 Do not give surety beyond your
   means;

but if you give surety, be
  prepared to pay.

14 Do not go to law against a judge,
  for the decision will favor him
   because of his standing.
15 Do not go traveling with the
   reckless,
  or they will be burdensome to
   you;
  for they will act as they please,
  and through their folly you will
   perish with them.
16 Do not pick a fight with the
   quick-tempered,
  and do not journey with them
   through lonely country,
  because bloodshed means nothing
   to them,
  and where no help is at hand,
   they will strike you down.
17 Do not consult with fools,
  for they cannot keep a secret.
18 In the presence of strangers do
   nothing that is to be kept
   secret,
  for you do not know what they
   will divulge.*v*
19 Do not reveal your thoughts to
   anyone,
  or you may drive away your
   happiness.*w*

9 Do not be jealous of the wife of
   your bosom,
  or you will teach her an evil
   lesson to your own hurt.
2 Do not give yourself to a woman
  and let her trample down your
   strength.
3 Do not go near a loose woman,
  or you will fall into her snares.
4 Do not dally with a singing girl,
  or you will be caught by her
   tricks.

u Or *ancestors*   *v* Or *it will bring forth*
w Heb: Gk *and let him not return a favor to you*

---

the aged, and the departed. **8–9:** Learn from
people with experience. **10:** Lighting *coals* is
an image for arousing passion. **12–13:** Sirach
is cautious about loans and surety, but not
opposed to them (29.1–7), in contrast to Prov

6.1–5; 11.15. **17–19:** The dangers of confiding
in people.
   9.1–9: Conduct with women. 1–2: Do
not be jealous (v.1), but be firm (v.2). **3:** *Loose,*
on the "strange" woman, see Prov 2.16; 5.3,

⁵ Do not look intently at a virgin,
    or you may stumble and incur
        penalties for her.
⁶ Do not give yourself to
        prostitutes,
    or you may lose your
        inheritance.
⁷ Do not look around in the streets
        of a city,
    or wander about in its deserted
        sections.
⁸ Turn away your eyes from a
        shapely woman,
    and do not gaze at beauty
        belonging to another;
many have been seduced by a
    woman's beauty,
    and by it passion is kindled like
        a fire.
⁹ Never dine with another man's
        wife,
    or revel with her at wine;
    or your heart may turn aside to
        her,
    and in blood*ˣ* you may be
        plunged into destruction.

¹⁰ Do not abandon old friends,
    for new ones cannot equal
        them.
    A new friend is like new wine;
    when it has aged, you can drink
        it with pleasure.
¹¹ Do not envy the success of
        sinners,
    for you do not know what their
        end will be like.
¹² Do not delight in what pleases the
        ungodly;
    remember that they will not be
        held guiltless all their lives.
¹³ Keep far from those who have
        power to kill,
    and you will not be haunted by
        the fear of death.

But if you approach them, make
    no misstep,
    or they may rob you of your
        life.
Know that you are stepping
    among snares,
    and that you are walking on the
        city battlements.

¹⁴ As much as you can, aim to know
    your neighbors,
    and consult with the wise.
¹⁵ Let your conversation be with
    intelligent people,
    and let all your discussion be
        about the law of the Most
        High.
¹⁶ Let the righteous be your dinner
    companions,
    and let your glory be in the fear
        of the Lord.

¹⁷ A work is praised for the skill of
    the artisan;
    so a people's leader is proved
        wise by his words.
¹⁸ The loud of mouth are feared in
    their city,
    and the one who is reckless in
        speech is hated.

10 A wise magistrate educates his
    people,
    and the rule of an intelligent
        person is well ordered.
² As the people's judge is, so are his
    officials;
    as the ruler of the city is, so are
        all its inhabitants.
³ An undisciplined king ruins his
    people,
    but a city becomes fit to live in
        through the understanding
        of its rulers.
⁴ The government of the earth is in
    the hand of the Lord,

x Heb: Gk *by your spirit*

20; 7.5. **4–9:** The following prohibitions have
various motive clauses, mostly practical.
  **9.10–16: Precepts about various types
of persons.**

9.17–10.5: Concerning rulers. 10.4: *For
the right time.*
  **10.6–18: Concerning arrogance and
pride,** especially in rulers (Prov 16, 18). Si-

and over it he will raise up the
    right leader for the time.

5 Human success is in the hand of
    the Lord,
  and it is he who confers honor
    upon the lawgiver. *y*

6 Do not get angry with your
    neighbor for every injury,
  and do not resort to acts of
    insolence.

7 Arrogance is hateful to the Lord
    and to mortals,
  and injustice is outrageous to
    both.

8 Sovereignty passes from nation to
    nation
  on account of injustice and
    insolence and wealth. *z*

9 How can dust and ashes be proud?
  Even in life the human body
    decays. *a*

10 A long illness baffles the
    physician; *b*
  the king of today will die
    tomorrow.

11 For when one is dead
  he inherits maggots and
    vermin *c* and worms.

12 The beginning of human pride is
    to forsake the Lord;
  the heart has withdrawn from
    its Maker.

13 For the beginning of pride is sin,
  and the one who clings to it
    pours out abominations.
  Therefore the Lord brings upon
    them unheard-of calamities,
  and destroys them completely.

14 The Lord overthrows the thrones
    of rulers,
  and enthrones the lowly in their
    place.

15 The Lord plucks up the roots of
    the nations, *d*
  and plants the humble in their
    place.

16 The Lord lays waste the lands of
    the nations,
  and destroys them to the
    foundations of the earth.

17 He removes some of them and
    destroys them,
  and erases the memory of them
    from the earth.

18 Pride was not created for human
    beings,
  or violent anger for those born
    of women.

19 Whose offspring are worthy of
    honor?
  Human offspring.
  Whose offspring are worthy of
    honor?
  Those who fear the Lord.
  Whose offspring are unworthy of
    honor?
  Human offspring.
  Whose offspring are unworthy of
    honor?
  Those who break the
    commandments.

20 Among family members their
    leader is worthy of honor,
  but those who fear the Lord are
    worthy of honor in his
    eyes. *e*

22 The rich, and the eminent, and the
    poor—
  their glory is the fear of the
    Lord.

23 It is not right to despise one who
    is intelligent but poor,
  and it is not proper to honor
    one who is sinful.

y Heb: Gk *scribe*   *z* Other ancient authorities
add here or after verse 9a, *Nothing is more wicked
than one who loves money, for such a person puts his
own soul up for sale.*   *a* Heb: Meaning of Gk
uncertain   *b* Heb Lat: Meaning of Gk
uncertain   *c* Heb: Gk *wild animals*   *d* Other
ancient authorities read *proud nations*
e Other ancient authorities add as verse 21, *The
fear of the Lord is the beginning of acceptance;
obduracy and pride are the beginning of rejection.*

---

rach may have in mind certain Ptolemaic or
Seleucid kings, but several verses apply to
ordinary people (vv. 12, 18).

**10.19–11.6: True honor is fear of the
Lord. 19:** This key verse is developed in what
follows. **28:** See 3.17 n. Humility is not false

24 The prince and the judge and the
ruler are honored,
  but none of them is greater than
  the one who fears the Lord.
25 Free citizens will serve a wise
servant,
  and an intelligent person will
  not complain.

26 Do not make a display of your
wisdom when you do your
work,
  and do not boast when you are
  in need.
27 Better is the worker who has
goods in plenty
  than the boaster who lacks
  bread.

28 My child, honor yourself with
humility,
  and give yourself the esteem
  you deserve.
29 Who will acquit those who
condemn*f* themselves?
  And who will honor those who
  dishonor themselves?*g*
30 The poor are honored for their
knowledge,
  while the rich are honored for
  their wealth.
31 One who is honored in poverty,
how much more in wealth!
  And one dishonored in wealth,
  how much more in
  poverty!

11 The wisdom of the humble lifts
their heads high,
  and seats them among the great.
2 Do not praise individuals for their
good looks,
  or loathe anyone because of
  appearance alone.

3 The bee is small among flying
creatures,
  but what it produces is the best
  of sweet things.
4 Do not boast about wearing fine
clothes,
  and do not exalt yourself when
  you are honored;
for the works of the Lord are
wonderful,
  and his works are concealed
  from humankind.
5 Many kings have had to sit on the
ground,
  but one who was never thought
  of has worn a crown.
6 Many rulers have been utterly
disgraced,
  and the honored have been
  handed over to others.

7 Do not find fault before you
investigate;
  examine first, and then criticize.
8 Do not answer before you listen,
  and do not interrupt when
  another is speaking.
9 Do not argue about a matter that
does not concern you,
  and do not sit with sinners
  when they judge a case.

10 My child, do not busy yourself
with many matters;
  if you multiply activities, you
  will not be held blameless.
If you pursue, you will not
overtake,
  and by fleeing you will not
  escape.
11 There are those who work and
struggle and hurry,

f Heb: Gk *sin against*   *g* Heb Lat: Gk *their own
life*

---

grovelling. **30–31:** *Wealth* does make a difference, even for the wise, *honored for their knowledge.*
  11.2–4: Do not judge by appearances,
whether *looks,* or size, or *clothes.*
  **11.7–9: Six prohibitions against hasty
and rash actions.**
  11.10–13: Avoidance of anxiety.
  11.14–19: All things come from the

Lord, both good and evil (Isa 45.7; Job
1.21). **19:** Lk 12.19.
  11.20–28: Retribution. 20–26: God's reward or punishment occurs in this life, down
to the very end. **27–28:** The *close of one's life*
revives memories of the past, and is a test of
one's life; see 7.36 n.
  **11.29–12.18: Choosing companions. 29–
34:** Sirach advises extreme care.

but are so much the more in want.

12 There are others who are slow and need help,
who lack strength and abound in poverty;
but the eyes of the Lord look kindly upon them;
he lifts them out of their lowly condition
13 and raises up their heads to the amazement of the many.

14 Good things and bad, life and death,
poverty and wealth, come from the Lord. *h*
17 The Lord's gift remains with the devout,
and his favor brings lasting success.
18 One becomes rich through diligence and self-denial,
and the reward allotted to him is this:
19 when he says, "I have found rest, and now I shall feast on my goods!"
he does not know how long it will be
until he leaves them to others and dies.

20 Stand by your agreement and attend to it,
and grow old in your work.
21 Do not wonder at the works of a sinner,
but trust in the Lord and keep at your job;
for it is easy in the sight of the Lord
to make the poor rich suddenly, in an instant.
22 The blessing of the Lord is *i* the reward of the pious,
and quickly God causes his blessing to flourish.
23 Do not say, "What do I need, and what further benefit can be mine?"
24 Do not say, "I have enough,

and what harm can come to me now?"
25 In the day of prosperity, adversity is forgotten,
and in the day of adversity, prosperity is not remembered.
26 For it is easy for the Lord on the day of death
to reward individuals according to their conduct.
27 An hour's misery makes one forget past delights,
and at the close of one's life one's deeds are revealed.
28 Call no one happy before his death;
by how he ends, a person becomes known. *j*

29 Do not invite everyone into your home,
for many are the tricks of the crafty.
30 Like a decoy partridge in a cage, so is the mind of the proud,
and like spies they observe your weakness; *k*
31 for they lie in wait, turning good into evil,
and to worthy actions they attach blame.
32 From a spark many coals are kindled,
and a sinner lies in wait to shed blood.
33 Beware of scoundrels, for they devise evil,
and they may ruin your reputation forever.
34 Receive strangers into your home and they will stir up trouble for you,
and will make you a stranger to your own family.

h Other ancient authorities add as verses 15 and 16, 15 Wisdom, understanding, and knowledge of the law come from the Lord; affection and the ways of good works come from him. 16 Error and darkness were created with sinners; evil grows old with those who take pride in malice. i Heb: Gk is in j Heb: Gk and through his children a person becomes known k Heb: Gk downfall

12 If you do good, know to
whom you do it,
and you will be thanked for
your good deeds.
2 Do good to the devout, and you
will be repaid—
if not by them, certainly by the
Most High.
3 No good comes to one who
persists in evil
or to one who does not give
alms.
4 Give to the devout, but do not
help the sinner.
5 Do good to the humble, but do
not give to the ungodly;
hold back their bread, and do not
give it to them,
for by means of it they might
subdue you;
then you will receive twice as
much evil
for all the good you have done
to them.
6 For the Most High also hates
sinners
and will inflict punishment on
the ungodly.*l*
7 Give to the one who is good, but
do not help the sinner.
8 A friend is not known*m* in
prosperity,
nor is an enemy hidden in
adversity.
9 One's enemies are friendly*n* when
one prospers,
but in adversity even one's
friend disappears.
10 Never trust your enemy,
for like corrosion in copper, so
is his wickedness.
11 Even if he humbles himself and
walks bowed down,
take care to be on your guard
against him.
Be to him like one who polishes a
mirror,

to be sure it does not become
completely tarnished.
12 Do not put him next to you,
or he may overthrow you and
take your place.
Do not let him sit at your right
hand,
or else he may try to take your
own seat,
and at last you will realize the
truth of my words,
and be stung by what I have
said.
13 Who pities a snake charmer when
he is bitten,
or all those who go near wild
animals?
14 So no one pities a person who
associates with a sinner
and becomes involved in the
other's sins.
15 He stands by you for a while,
but if you falter, he will not be
there.
16 An enemy speaks sweetly with his
lips,
but in his heart he plans to
throw you into a pit;
an enemy may have tears in his
eyes,
but if he finds an opportunity he
will never have enough of
your blood.
17 If evil comes upon you, you will
find him there ahead of
you;
pretending to help, he will trip
you up.
18 Then he will shake his head, and
clap his hands,
and whisper much, and show
his true face.

*l Other ancient authorities add and he is keeping
them for the day of their punishment*
m Other ancient authorities read punished
n Heb: Gk grieved

12.1–7: While Sirach's advice is positive, it
is also self-serving. The contrast between the
sinners and the *devout* is sharply drawn. As
sinner, the *ungodly* one deserves rejection by

God (v. 6, "hate" is not a mere emotion).
8–18: A warning against false friends (see
6.5–17).
13.1–14.2: Warnings about associates. 1:

13 Whoever touches pitch gets dirty,
and whoever associates with a proud person becomes like him.
2 Do not lift a weight too heavy for you,
or associate with one mightier and richer than you.
How can the clay pot associate with the iron kettle?
The pot will strike against it and be smashed.
3 A rich person does wrong, and even adds insults;
a poor person suffers wrong, and must add apologies.
4 A rich person[o] will exploit you if you can be of use to him,
but if you are in need he will abandon you.
5 If you own something, he will live with you;
he will drain your resources without a qualm.
6 When he needs you he will deceive you,
and will smile at you and encourage you;
he will speak to you kindly and say, "What do you need?"
7 He will embarrass you with his delicacies,
until he has drained you two or three times,
and finally he will laugh at you.
Should he see you afterwards, he will pass you by
and shake his head at you.

8 Take care not to be led astray and humiliated when you are enjoying yourself.[p]
9 When an influential person invites you, be reserved,
and he will invite you more insistently.
10 Do not be forward, or you may be rebuffed;
do not stand aloof, or you will be forgotten.
11 Do not try to treat him as an equal,
or trust his lengthy conversations;
for he will test you by prolonged talk,
and while he smiles he will be examining you.
12 Cruel are those who do not keep your secrets;
they will not spare you harm or imprisonment.
13 Be on your guard and very careful,
for you are walking about with your own downfall.[q]
15 Every creature loves its like,
and every person the neighbor.
16 All living beings associate with their own kind,
and people stick close to those like themselves.
17 What does a wolf have in common with a lamb?
No more has a sinner with the devout.
18 What peace is there between a hyena and a dog?
And what peace between the rich and the poor?
19 Wild asses in the wilderness are the prey of lions;
likewise the poor are feeding grounds for the rich.
20 Humility is an abomination to the proud;
likewise the poor are an abomination to the rich.

o Gk *He*   p Other ancient authorities read *in your folly*   q Other ancient authorities add as verse 14, *When you hear these things in your sleep, wake up! During all your life love the Lord, and call on him for your salvation.*

This maxim is developed in the following sayings. **3–7:** Wealth makes a difference; rich and poor are not treated alike (see 10.31). **13.9–13:** Caution in dealing with the powerful.

13.13–23: "Like loves like," and inequalities between the rich and the poor (vv. 20–23) are obvious (see vv. 3–7). **24:** 11.10; 31.8. **25:** The exterior appearance reflects what is within.

21 When the rich person totters, he is
supported by friends,
but when the humble' falls, he
is pushed away even by
friends.
22 If the rich person slips, many
come to the rescue;
he speaks unseemly words, but
they justify him.
If the humble person slips, they
even criticize him;
he talks sense, but is not given a
hearing.
23 The rich person speaks and all are
silent;
they extol to the clouds what he
says.
The poor person speaks and they
say, "Who is this fellow?"
And should he stumble, they
even push him down.
24 Riches are good if they are free
from sin;
poverty is evil only in the
opinion of the ungodly.

25 The heart changes the
countenance,
either for good or for evil. ʳ
26 The sign of a happy heart is a
cheerful face,
but to devise proverbs requires
painful thinking.

14 Happy are those who do not
blunder with their lips,
and need not suffer remorse for
sin.
2 Happy are those whose hearts do
not condemn them,
and who have not given up
their hope.

3 Riches are inappropriate for a
small-minded person;
and of what use is wealth to a
miser?
4 What he denies himself he collects
for others;

and others will live in luxury on
his goods.
5 If one is mean to himself, to
whom will he be generous?
He will not enjoy his own
riches.
6 No one is worse than one who is
grudging to himself;
this is the punishment for his
meanness.
7 If ever he does good, it is by
mistake;
and in the end he reveals his
meanness.
8 The miser is an evil person;
he turns away and disregards
people.
9 The eye of the greedy person is
not satisfied with his share;
greedy injustice withers the
soul.
10 A miser begrudges bread,
and it is lacking at his table.

11 My child, treat yourself well,
according to your means,
and present worthy offerings to
the Lord.
12 Remember that death does not
tarry,
and the decreeᵗ of Hades has
not been shown to you.
13 Do good to friends before you
die,
and reach out and give to them
as much as you can.
14 Do not deprive yourself of a day's
enjoyment;
do not let your share of desired
good pass by you.
15 Will you not leave the fruit of
your labors to another,
and what you acquired by toil
to be divided by lot?

r Other ancient authorities read *poor*
s Other ancient authorities add *and a glad heart makes
a cheerful countenance*   t Heb Syr: Gk *covenant*

**14.3–19: The proper use of wealth. 3–
10:** A description of the *miser* and his fate.
14.11–19: In contrast to vv. 3–10, riches are
to be used generously because there will be no
opportunity after death (vv. 12, 16), which is
inevitable (vv. 17–19).

16 Give, and take, and indulge
yourself,
because in Hades one cannot
look for luxury.
17 All living beings become old like a
garment,
for the decree*u* from of old is,
"You must die!"
18 Like abundant leaves on a
spreading tree
that sheds some and puts forth
others,
so are the generations of flesh and
blood:
one dies and another is born.
19 Every work decays and ceases to
exist,
and the one who made it will
pass away with it.

20 Happy is the person who
meditates on*v* wisdom
and reasons intelligently,
21 who*w* reflects in his heart on her
ways
and ponders her secrets,
22 pursuing her like a hunter,
and lying in wait on her paths;
23 who peers through her windows
and listens at her doors;
24 who camps near her house
and fastens his tent peg to her
walls;
25 who pitches his tent near her,
and so occupies an excellent
lodging place;
26 who places his children under her
shelter,
and lodges under her boughs;
27 who is sheltered by her from the
heat,
and dwells in the midst of her
glory.

15 Whoever fears the Lord will do
this,

and whoever holds to the law
will obtain wisdom. *x*
2 She will come to meet him like a
mother,
and like a young bride she will
welcome him.
3 She will feed him with the bread
of learning,
and give him the water of
wisdom to drink.
4 He will lean on her and not fall,
and he will rely on her and not
be put to shame.
5 She will exalt him above his
neighbors,
and will open his mouth in the
midst of the assembly.
6 He will find gladness and a crown
of rejoicing,
and will inherit an everlasting
name.
7 The foolish will not obtain her,
and sinners will not see her.
8 She is far from arrogance,
and liars will never think of her.
9 Praise is unseemly on the lips of a
sinner,
for it has not been sent from the
Lord.
10 For in wisdom must praise be
uttered,
and the Lord will make it
prosper.
11 Do not say, "It was the Lord's
doing that I fell away";
for he does not do*y* what he
hates.
12 Do not say, "It was he who led
me astray";
for he has no need of the sinful.
13 The Lord hates all abominations;

---

u Heb: Gk *covenant*   *v* Other ancient
authorities read *dies in*   *w* The structure adopted
in verses 21–27 follows the Heb   *x* Gk *her*
y Heb: Gk *you ought not do*

**14.20–15.10: The search for Wisdom
and her blessings. 14.20–27:** One should
pursue Wisdom as a beloved, with intensity
and resolution.

15.1–10: Wisdom's response to those who
seek her, and hold *to the law.*
15.11–20: Free will. 11–13: God cannot be
blamed for human sinfulness. **14–17:** Al-

such things are not loved by
those who fear him.

14 It was he who created humankind
in the beginning,
and he left them in the power of
their own free choice.

15 If you choose, you can keep the
commandments,
and to act faithfully is a matter
of your own choice.

16 He has placed before you fire and
water;
stretch out your hand for
whichever you choose.

17 Before each person are life and
death,
and whichever one chooses will
be given.

18 For great is the wisdom of the
Lord;
he is mighty in power and sees
everything;

19 his eyes are on those who fear
him,
and he knows every human
action.

20 He has not commanded anyone to
be wicked,
and he has not given anyone
permission to sin.

16 Do not desire a multitude of
worthless *z* children,
and do not rejoice in ungodly
offspring.

2 If they multiply, do not rejoice in
them,
unless the fear of the Lord is in
them.

3 Do not trust in their survival,
or rely on their numbers;*a*

for one can be better than a
thousand,
and to die childless better than
to have ungodly children.

4 For through one intelligent person
a city can be filled with
people,
but through a clan of outlaws it
becomes desolate.

5 Many such things my eye has
seen,
and my ear has heard things
more striking than these.

6 In an assembly of sinners a fire is
kindled,
and in a disobedient nation
wrath blazes up.

7 He did not forgive the ancient
giants
who revolted in their might.

8 He did not spare the neighbors of
Lot,
whom he loathed on account of
their arrogance.

9 He showed no pity on the
doomed nation,
on those dispossessed because of
their sins;*b*

10 or on the six hundred thousand
foot soldiers
who assembled in their
stubbornness.*c*

z Heb: Gk *unprofitable*   *a* Other ancient
authorities add *For you will groan in untimely
mourning, and will know of their sudden end.*
b Other ancient authorities add *All these things he
did to the hard-hearted nations, and by the multitude
of his holy ones he was not appeased.*   *c* Other
ancient authorities add *Chastising, showing mercy,
striking, healing, the Lord persisted in mercy and
discipline.*

---

though the Bible affirms human responsibility, it does not speak of "free will," which is
the meaning of "yeṣer" in v. 14 (*free choice*).
The Hebrew word is a technical term, sometimes used in a good sense (Isa 26.3; 1 Chr
29.18); but usually it refers to an evil tendency
or inclination toward sin (Gen 6.5; 8.21; compare 2 Esd 4.30–31). In post-biblical times the
doctrine arose of a good and an evil "yeṣer"
that every person possesses. **16:** *Fire and water,*
representing opposite extremes. *Fire* here has

no eschatological significance. **17:** Deut 30.19;
Jer 21.8. **18–20:** The divine attributes mentioned here reaffirm the point of vv. 11–13.
   **16.1–4: The misfortune of having un-
godly children** (40.15–16; 41.5–13).
   **16.5–23: The certainty of punishment
for sin. 6–8:** Sirach refers to the fate of Korah, Dathan, and Abiram (v. 6; Num 16), *the
ancient giants* of Gen 6.4, and the people of
Sodom (v. 8; Ezek 16.49–50; Gen 19).
   16.9: The Canaanites are meant. **10:** The

11 Even if there were only one
     stiff-necked person,
   it would be a wonder if he
     remained unpunished.
   For mercy and wrath are with the
     Lord;*d*
   he is mighty to forgive—but he
     also pours out wrath.
12 Great as his mercy, so also is his
     chastisement;
   he judges a person according to
     one's deeds.
13 The sinner will not escape with
     plunder,
   and the patience of the godly
     will not be frustrated.
14 He makes room for every act of
     mercy;
   everyone receives in accordance
     with one's deeds.*e*

17 Do not say, "I am hidden from
     the Lord,
   and who from on high has me
     in mind?
   Among so many people I am
     unknown,
   for what am I in a boundless
     creation?
18 Lo, heaven and the highest
     heaven,
   the abyss and the earth, tremble
     at his visitation!*f*
19 The very mountains and the
     foundations of the earth
   quiver and quake when he looks
     upon them.
20 But no human mind can grasp
     this,
   and who can comprehend his
     ways?
21 Like a tempest that no one can
     see,

so most of his works are
     concealed.*g*
22 Who is to announce his acts of
     justice?
   Or who can await them? For his
     decree*h* is far off."*i*
23 Such are the thoughts of one
     devoid of understanding;
   a senseless and misguided
     person thinks foolishly.

24 Listen to me, my child, and
     acquire knowledge,
   and pay close attention to my
     words.
25 I will impart discipline precisely*j*
   and declare knowledge
     accurately.

26 When the Lord created*k* his works
     from the beginning,
   and, in making them,
     determined their
     boundaries,
27 he arranged his works in an
     eternal order,
   and their dominion*l* for all
     generations.
   They neither hunger nor grow
     weary,

d Gk *him*   *e* Other ancient authorities
add *15The Lord hardened Pharaoh so that
he did not recognize him, in order that his works
might be known under heaven. 16His mercy is
manifest to the whole of creation, and he divided his
light and darkness with a plumb line.*   *f* Other
ancient authorities add *The whole world past and
present is in his will.*   *g* Meaning of Gk
uncertain: Heb Syr *If I sin, no eye can see me, and
if I am disloyal all in secret, who is to know?*
h Heb *the decree:* Gk *the covenant*   *i* Other
ancient authorities add *and a scrutiny for all comes
at the end*   *j* Gk *by weight*   *k* Heb: Gk *judged*
l Or *elements*

600,000 are the Israelites in the desert (see
46.8; Num 14). **11**: *Mercy and wrath*, 5.6. **12–
14**: Good works are efficacious, and God
judges accordingly, as Sirach frequently affirms (3.3, 14–16; 11.26; 15.19; 29.11–12).
   16.17–23: Let no one think it is possible to
escape God's attention in the immense and
mysterious realm of creation! In v. 23 Sirach

expresses his judgment on the ideas expressed
in vv. 17–22.
   **16.24–17.14: Divine wisdom seen in
creation. 26–30**: The order and harmony of
created things. God provides for all *living beings*, and eventually they return to the earth
(17.1; 40.11; Gen 3.19).

and they do not abandon their
tasks.

28 They do not crowd one another,
and they never disobey his
word.

29 Then the Lord looked upon the
earth,
and filled it with his good
things.

30 With all kinds of living beings he
covered its surface,
and into it they must return.

17 The Lord created human beings
out of earth,
and makes them return to it
again.

2 He gave them a fixed number of
days,
but granted them authority over
everything on the earth. *m*

3 He endowed them with strength
like his own, *n*
and made them in his own
image.

4 He put the fear of them *o* in all
living beings,
and gave them dominion over
beasts and birds. *p*

6 Discretion and tongue and eyes,
ears and a mind for thinking he
gave them.

7 He filled them with knowledge
and understanding,
and showed them good and
evil.

8 He put the fear of him into *q* their
hearts
to show them the majesty of his
works. *r*

10 And they will praise his holy
name,

9 to proclaim the grandeur of his
works.

11 He bestowed knowledge upon
them,

and allotted to them the law of
life. *s*

12 He established with them an
eternal covenant,
and revealed to them his
decrees.

13 Their eyes saw his glorious
majesty,
and their ears heard the glory of
his voice.

14 He said to them, "Beware of all
evil."
And he gave commandment to
each of them concerning
the neighbor.

15 Their ways are always known to
him;
they will not be hid from his
eyes. *t*

17 He appointed a ruler for every
nation,
but Israel is the Lord's own
portion. *u*

19 All their works are as clear as the
sun before him,
and his eyes are ever upon their
ways.

20 Their iniquities are not hidden
from him,

m Lat: Gk *it*   *n* Lat: Gk *proper to them*
o Syr: Gk *him*   *p* Other ancient authorities add
as verse 5, *They obtained the use of the five faculties
of the Lord; as sixth he distributed to them the gift of mind,
and as seventh, reason, the interpreter of one's faculties.*
q Other ancient authorities read *He set his eye upon*
r Other ancient authorities add *and he gave them
to boast of his marvels forever*   *s* Other ancient
authorities add *so that they may know that they who
are alive now are mortal*
t Other ancient authorities add *16Their ways from
youth tend toward evil, and they are unable to make
for themselves hearts of flesh in place of their stony
hearts. 17For in the division of the nations of the
whole earth, he appointed*   *u* Other ancient
authorities add as verse 18, *whom, being his
firstborn, he brings up with discipline, and allotting to
him the light of his love, he does not neglect him.*

17.1–14: The creation of *human beings* is a
reason for praise, because of God's gracious
gifts, especially the *law of life*, the *covenant*,
and *commandment* (3–14).
17.15–24: The divine judge. God knows
the good (especially *almsgiving*, v. 22) and the
sinful actions of humans, and will requite accordingly. **17:** See Deut 32.8–9, an allusion to
Israel's special position. **24:** *A return*, to God's
favor.

and all their sins are before the
    Lord. *ᵛ*

22 One's almsgiving is like a
    signet-ring with the Lord, *ʷ*
  and he will keep a person's
    kindness like the apple of
    his eye. *ˣ*

23 Afterward he will rise up and
    repay them,
  and he will bring their
    recompense on their heads.

24 Yet to those who repent he grants
    a return,
  and he encourages those who
    are losing hope.

25 Turn back to the Lord and forsake
    your sins;
  pray in his presence and lessen
    your offense.

26 Return to the Most High and turn
    away from iniquity, *ʸ*
  and hate intensely what he
    abhors.

27 Who will sing praises to the Most
    High in Hades
  in place of the living who give
    thanks?

28 From the dead, as from one who
    does not exist, thanksgiving
    has ceased;
  those who are alive and well
    sing the Lord's praises.

29 How great is the mercy of the
    Lord,
  and his forgiveness for those
    who return to him!

30 For not everything is within
    human capability,
  since human beings are not
    immortal.

31 What is brighter than the sun? Yet
    it can be eclipsed.
  So flesh and blood devise evil.

32 He marshals the host of the height
    of heaven;

but all human beings are dust
  and ashes.

18 He who lives forever created
    the whole universe;
2   the Lord alone is just. *ᶻ*

4 To none has he given power to
    proclaim his works;
  and who can search out his
    mighty deeds?

5 Who can measure his majestic
    power?
  And who can fully recount his
    mercies?

6 It is not possible to diminish or
    increase them,
  nor is it possible to fathom the
    wonders of the Lord.

7 When human beings have finished,
    they are just beginning,
  and when they stop, they are
    still perplexed.

8 What are human beings, and of
    what use are they?
  What is good in them, and what
    is evil?

9 The number of days in their life is
    great if they reach one
    hundred years. *ᵃ*

10 Like a drop of water from the sea
    and a grain of sand,
  so are a few years among the
    days of eternity.

v Other ancient authorities add as verse 21, *But
the Lord, who is gracious and knows how they are
formed, has neither left them nor abandoned them, but
has spared them.*   *w* Gk *him*   *x* Other
ancient authorities add *apportioning repentance to
his sons and daughters*   *y* Other ancient
authorities add *for he will lead you out of darkness
to the light of health.*   *z* Other ancient
authorities add *and there is no other beside him; ³he
steers the world with the span of his hand, and all
things obey his will; for he is king of all things by his
power, separating among them the holy things from
the profane.*   *a* Other ancient authorities add *but
the death of each one is beyond the calculation of all*

**17.25–32: Exhortation to turn to God.
27–28:** One reason for repentance is that
there is no loving contact with God in *Hades*
(Sheol); see Pss 6.5; 30.9; 88.5; 115.17–18; Isa
38.18–19; Bar 2.17. By repentance, one can
be *alive,* and *sing the Lord's praises.* **31:** If the *sun*

can suffer an eclipse, a mere human can also
fail.
18.1–14: A hymn to God's majesty. Although the Lord is transcendent (vv. 1–7), and
humans are weak and short-lived (vv. 8–10), God
is *patient* and merciful to them (vv. 11–14).

11 That is why the Lord is patient
with them
and pours out his mercy upon
them.
12 He sees and recognizes that their
end is miserable;
therefore he grants them
forgiveness all the more.
13 The compassion of human beings
is for their neighbors,
but the compassion of the Lord
is for every living thing.
He rebukes and trains and teaches
them,
and turns them back, as a
shepherd his flock.
14 He has compassion on those who
accept his discipline
and who are eager for his
precepts.

15 My child, do not mix reproach
with your good deeds,
or spoil your gift by harsh
words.
16 Does not the dew give relief from
the scorching heat?
So a word is better than a gift.
17 Indeed, does not a word surpass a
good gift?
Both are to be found in a
gracious person.
18 A fool is ungracious and abusive,
and the gift of a grudging giver
makes the eyes dim.

19 Before you speak, learn;
and before you fall ill, take care
of your health.
20 Before judgment comes, examine
yourself;
and at the time of scrutiny you
will find forgiveness.
21 Before falling ill, humble yourself;
and when you have sinned,
repent.
22 Let nothing hinder you from
paying a vow promptly,

and do not wait until death to
be released from it.
23 Before making a vow, prepare
yourself;
do not be like one who puts the
Lord to the test.
24 Think of his wrath on the day of
death,
and of the moment of
vengeance when he turns
away his face.
25 In the time of plenty think of the
time of hunger;
in days of wealth think of
poverty and need.
26 From morning to evening
conditions change;
all things move swiftly before
the Lord.

27 One who is wise is cautious in
everything;
when sin is all around, one
guards against wrongdoing.
28 Every intelligent person knows
wisdom,
and praises the one who finds
her.
29 Those who are skilled in words
become wise themselves,
and pour forth apt proverbs. *b*

SELF-CONTROL *c*
30 Do not follow your base desires,
but restrain your appetites.
31 If you allow your soul to take
pleasure in base desire,
it will make you the
laughingstock of your
enemies.
32 Do not revel in great luxury,
or you may become
impoverished by its
expense.

b Other ancient authorities add *Better is confidence
in the one Lord than clinging with a dead heart to a
dead one.*   *c* This heading is included in the Gk
text.

**18.15–19.19: Various warnings and ob-
servations. 18.15–18:** Do not humiliate the re-
ceiver of charity (v. 16; see also 43.22); be a
gracious giver. **19–21:** The need of foresight.

22–26: Be careful in making vows. **27–29:**
Characteristics of the *wise*.
18.30–19.4: An exhortation to self-
control. **19.5–12:** Warnings against gossip. **8:**

33 Do not become a beggar by
feasting with borrowed
money,
when you have nothing in your
purse. *d*

19 The one who does this*e* will
not become rich;
one who despises small things
will fail little by little.
2 Wine and women lead intelligent
men astray,
and the man who consorts with
prostitutes is reckless.
3 Decay and worms will take
possession of him,
and the reckless person will be
snatched away.

4 One who trusts others too quickly
has a shallow mind,
and one who sins does wrong to
oneself.
5 One who rejoices in wickedness*f*
will be condemned,*g*
6 but one who hates gossip has
less evil.
7 Never repeat a conversation,
and you will lose nothing at all.
8 With friend or foe do not report
it,
and unless it would be a sin for
you, do not reveal it;
9 for someone may have heard you
and watched you,
and in time will hate you.
10 Have you heard something? Let it
die with you.
Be brave, it will not make you
burst!
11 Having heard something, the fool
suffers birthpangs
like a woman in labor with a
child.
12 Like an arrow stuck in a person's
thigh,
so is gossip inside a fool.

13 Question a friend; perhaps he did
not do it;

or if he did, so that he may not
do it again.
14 Question a neighbor; perhaps he
did not say it;
or if he said it, so that he may
not repeat it.
15 Question a friend, for often it is
slander;
so do not believe everything
you hear.
16 A person may make a slip without
intending it.
Who has not sinned with his
tongue?
17 Question your neighbor before
you threaten him;
and let the law of the Most
High take its course. *h*

20 The whole of wisdom is fear of
the Lord,
and in all wisdom there is the
fulfillment of the law. *i*
22 The knowledge of wickedness is
not wisdom,
nor is there prudence in the
counsel of sinners.
23 There is a cleverness that is
detestable,
and there is a fool who merely
lacks wisdom.
24 Better are the God-fearing who
lack understanding
than the highly intelligent who
transgress the law.

d Other ancient authorities add *for you will be
plotting against your own life*   *e* Heb: Gk
A worker who is a drunkard   *f* Other ancient
authorities read *heart*   *g* Other ancient
authorities add *but one who withstands pleasures
crowns his life. 6One who controls the tongue will live
without strife,*   *h* Other ancient authorities
add *and do not be angry. 18The fear of the Lord
is the beginning of acceptance, and wisdom obtains
his love. 19The knowledge of the Lord's commandments
is life-giving discipline; and those who do what is pleasing
to him enjoy the fruit of the tree of immortality.*
i Other ancient authorities add *and the knowledge of
his omnipotence. 21When a slave says to his master, "I
will not act as you wish," even if later he does it, he
angers the one who supports him.*

Unless by keeping silent *it would be a sin.* **16–
18**: On administering reproof. Note that v. 18
is in note *h*.

19.20–30: **Wisdom and craftiness contrasted. 23**: *Who merely lacks wisdom,* and is
guileless.

25 There is a cleverness that is exact
  but unjust,
    and there are people who abuse
      favors to gain a verdict.
26 There is the villain bowed down
  in mourning,
    but inwardly he is full of deceit.
27 He hides his face and pretends not
  to hear,
    but when no one notices, he
      will take advantage of you.
28 Even if lack of strength keeps him
  from sinning,
    he will nevertheless do evil
      when he finds the
        opportunity.
29 A person is known by his
  appearance,
    and a sensible person is known
      when first met, face to face.
30 A person's attire and hearty
  laughter,
    and the way he walks, show
      what he is.

20 There is a rebuke that is
    untimely,
  and there is the person who is
    wise enough to keep silent.
2 How much better it is to rebuke
  than to fume!
3 And the one who admits his fault
  will be kept from failure.
4 Like a eunuch lusting to violate a
  girl
    is the person who does right
      under compulsion.
5 Some people keep silent and are
  thought to be wise,
    while others are detested for
      being talkative.
6 Some people keep silent because
  they have nothing to say,
    while others keep silent because
      they know when to speak.
7 The wise remain silent until the
  right moment,

but a boasting fool misses the
  right moment.
8 Whoever talks too much is
  detested,
    and whoever pretends to
      authority is hated.*j*

9 There may be good fortune for a
  person in adversity,
    and a windfall may result in a
      loss.
10 There is the gift that profits you
  nothing,
    and the gift to be paid back
      double.
11 There are losses for the sake of
  glory,
    and there are some who have
      raised their heads from
        humble circumstances.
12 Some buy much for little,
  but pay for it seven times over.
13 The wise make themselves
  beloved by only few
    words,*k*
      but the courtesies of fools are
        wasted.
14 A fool's gift will profit you
  nothing,*l*
    for he looks for recompense
      sevenfold.*m*
15 He gives little and upbraids much;
  he opens his mouth like a town
    crier.
      Today he lends and tomorrow he
        asks it back;
          such a one is hateful to God and
            humans.*n*
16 The fool says, "I have no friends,

j Other ancient authorities add *How good it is to show
repentance when you are reproved, for so you will
escape deliberate sin!*   *k* Heb: Gk *by words*
l Other ancient authorities add *so it is with the
envious who give under compulsion*   *m* Syr: Gk *he
has many eyes instead of one*   *n* Other ancient
authorities lack *to God and humans*

19.26–30: Appearances can be both de-
ceiving and revealing.
20.1–8: Times for speech and silence. 4:
The point of the comparison is that one cannot be compelled to do what is *right*. **5–6:**

Prov 17.27–28. **7:** *The right moment,* Prov
15.23; 25.17.
**20.9–17: Paradoxes in the appearances
of things.**

and I get no thanks for my
good deeds.
Those who eat my bread are
evil-tongued."
17 How many will ridicule him, and
how often![o]

18 A slip on the pavement is better
than a slip of the tongue;
the downfall of the wicked will
occur just as speedily.
19 A coarse person is like an
inappropriate story,
continually on the lips of the
ignorant.
20 A proverb from a fool's lips will
be rejected,
for he does not tell it at the
proper time.

21 One may be prevented from
sinning by poverty;
so when he rests he feels no
remorse.
22 One may lose his life through
shame,
or lose it because of human
respect.[p]
23 Another out of shame makes
promises to a friend,
and so makes an enemy for
nothing.

24 A lie is an ugly blot on a person;
it is continually on the lips of
the ignorant.
25 A thief is preferable to a habitual
liar,
but the lot of both is ruin.
26 A liar's way leads to disgrace,
and his shame is ever with him.

PROVERBIAL SAYINGS[q]

27 The wise person advances himself
by his words,
and one who is sensible pleases
the great.
28 Those who cultivate the soil heap
up their harvest,
and those who please the great
atone for injustice.
29 Favors and gifts blind the eyes of
the wise;
like a muzzle on the mouth they
stop reproofs.
30 Hidden wisdom and unseen
treasure,
of what value is either?
31 Better are those who hide their
folly
than those who hide their
wisdom.[r]

21 Have you sinned, my child? Do
so no more,
but ask forgiveness for your
past sins.
2 Flee from sin as from a snake;
for if you approach sin, it will
bite you.
Its teeth are lion's teeth,
and can destroy human lives.
3 All lawlessness is like a two-edged
sword;
there is no healing for the
wound it inflicts.

4 Panic and insolence will waste
away riches;
thus the house of the proud will
be laid waste.[s]

o Other ancient authorities add *for he has not honestly received what he has, and what he does not have is unimportant to him*
p Other ancient authorities read *his foolish look*
q This heading is included in the Gk text.
r Other ancient authorities add [32]*Unwearied endurance in seeking the Lord is better than a masterless charioteer of one's own life.*
s Other ancient authorities read *uprooted*

20.18–20: Inappropriate speech. 19: Syriac: "As the fat tail of a sheep [Ex 29.22], eaten without salt, so is a word spoken out of season."
20.21–23: Reflections on poverty and shame. 23: The *promises* are either insincere or impossible.
20.24–26: Lying (7.13; 25.2; Prov 6.16–19; 12.22).
20.27–31: Recommendations for wisdom. 29: The danger of *gifts,* or bribes.
21.1–10: Warnings against sin. 2–3: The characteristics of sin are subtlety, strength, and deadliness. **5:** 35.17–21.

5 The prayer of the poor goes from
  their lips to the ears of
  God,^{t}
and his judgment comes
  speedily.
6 Those who hate reproof walk in
  the sinner's steps,
but those who fear the Lord
  repent in their heart.
7 The mighty in speech are widely
  known;
when they slip, the sensible
  person knows it.

8 Whoever builds his house with
  other people's money
is like one who gathers stones
  for his burial mound.^{u}
9 An assembly of the wicked is like
  a bundle of tow,
and their end is a blazing fire.
10 The way of sinners is paved with
  smooth stones,
but at its end is the pit of
  Hades.

11 Whoever keeps the law controls
  his thoughts,
and the fulfillment of the fear of
  the Lord is wisdom.
12 The one who is not clever cannot
  be taught,
but there is a cleverness that
  increases bitterness.
13 The knowledge of the wise will
  increase like a flood,
and their counsel like a
  life-giving spring.
14 The mind^v of a fool is like a
  broken jar;
it can hold no knowledge.

15 When an intelligent person hears a
  wise saying,

he praises it and adds to it;
when a fool^w hears it, he laughs
  at^x it
and throws it behind his back.
16 A fool's chatter is like a burden on
  a journey,
but delight is found in the
  speech of the intelligent.
17 The utterance of a sensible person
  is sought in the assembly,
and they ponder his words in
  their minds.

18 Like a house in ruins is wisdom to
  a fool,
and to the ignorant, knowledge
  is talk that has no meaning.
19 To a senseless person education is
  fetters on his feet,
and like manacles on his right
  hand.
20 A fool raises his voice when he
  laughs,
but the wise^y smile quietly.
21 To the sensible person education is
  like a golden ornament,
and like a bracelet on the right
  arm.

22 The foot of a fool rushes into a
  house,
but an experienced person waits
  respectfully outside.
23 A boor peers into the house from
  the door,
but a cultivated person remains
  outside.
24 It is ill-mannered for a person to
  listen at a door;

t Gk *his ears*   *u* Other ancient authorities
read *for the winter*   *v* Syr Lat: Gk *entrails*
w Syr: Gk *reveler*   *x* Syr: Gk *dislikes*
y Syr Lat: Gk *clever*

21.7b: An ironic comment on the *mighty talker*, who is unaware of his errors. **8:** That is, by oppression of others, he prepares for his own destruction. **9:** The image of *fire* is meant to suggest punishment in this life (see v. 10). **10:** *Hades,* Sheol; see 17.27 n.
21.11–28: A series of contrasts between the wise and fools. 13–14: The contrast is

between a *spring* and a *broken jar* (or cistern, Jer 2.13), which holds no water. All the comparisons that follow are in favor of the wise: increasing wisdom (v. 15), giving *delight* (v. 16), a *golden ornament* (v. 21), courtesy (vv. 22–24), careful *words* (vv. 25–26). **27:** *Curses himself,* in the sense that the curse recoils upon him.

the discreet would be grieved by
the disgrace.

25 The lips of babblers speak of what
is not their concern. *z*
but the words of the prudent are
weighed in the balance.
26 The mind of fools is in their
mouth,
but the mouth of the wise is in *a*
their mind.
27 When an ungodly person curses an
adversary, *b*
he curses himself.
28 A whisperer degrades himself
and is hated in his
neighborhood.

22 The idler is like a filthy stone,
and every one hisses at his
disgrace.
2 The idler is like the filth of
dunghills;
anyone that picks it up will
shake it off his hand.

3 It is a disgrace to be the father of
an undisciplined son,
and the birth of a daughter is a
loss.
4 A sensible daughter obtains a
husband of her own,
but one who acts shamefully is a
grief to her father.
5 An impudent daughter disgraces
father and husband,
and is despised by both.
6 Like music in time of mourning is
ill-timed conversation,
but a thrashing and discipline
are at all times wisdom. *c*

9 Whoever teaches a fool is like one
who glues potsherds
together,

or who rouses a sleeper from
deep slumber.
10 Whoever tells a story to a fool
tells it to a drowsy man;
and at the end he will say,
"What is it?"
11 Weep for the dead, for he has left
the light behind;
and weep for the fool, for he
has left intelligence behind.
Weep less bitterly for the dead, for
he is at rest;
but the life of the fool is worse
than death.
12 Mourning for the dead lasts seven
days,
but for the foolish or the
ungodly it lasts all the days
of their lives.

13 Do not talk much with a senseless
person
or visit an unintelligent person. *d*
Stay clear of him, or you may
have trouble,
and be spattered when he shakes
himself off.
Avoid him and you will find rest,
and you will never be wearied
by his lack of sense.
14 What is heavier than lead?
And what is its name except
"Fool"?
15 Sand, salt, and a piece of iron
are easier to bear than a stupid
person.

z Other ancient authorities read *of strangers speak of these things*   a Other ancient authorities omit *in*   b Or *curses Satan*   c Other ancient authorities add *7Children who are brought up in a good life, conceal the lowly birth of their parents. 8Children who are disdainfully and boorishly haughty stain the nobility of their kindred.*
d Other ancient authorities add *For being without sense he will despise everything about you*

22.1–18: Concerning laziness and foolishness. 1: *Filthy stone,* a stone used in lieu of toilet paper; see v. 2. **3–6:** These verses deal with wicked offspring. **3b:** This reflects the misogyny of the age.
22.7: A thankless task. **11–12:** One can *weep for a fool* more than for the *dead; seven days* was

the usual period of mourning (Gen 50.10).
22.13–18: Avoid fools. **13:** *Shakes himself off,* as would an animal, to remove filth. **14–15:** 21.16; the fool is difficult *to bear.* The *mind* of the wise is contrasted with the *resolve* of the fool.

16 A wooden beam firmly bonded
   into a building
   is not loosened by an
      earthquake;
   so the mind firmly resolved after
      due reflection
   will not be afraid in a crisis.

17 A mind settled on an intelligent
      thought
   is like stucco decoration that
      makes a wall smooth.

18 Fences^e set on a high place
   will not stand firm against the
      wind;
   so a timid mind with a fool's
      resolve
   will not stand firm against any
      fear.

19 One who pricks the eye brings
      tears,
   and one who pricks the heart
      makes clear its feelings.

20 One who throws a stone at birds
      scares them away,
   and one who reviles a friend
      destroys a friendship.

21 Even if you draw your sword
      against a friend,
   do not despair, for there is a
      way back.

22 If you open your mouth against
      your friend,
   do not worry, for reconciliation
      is possible.
   But as for reviling, arrogance,
      disclosure of secrets, or a
      treacherous blow—
   in these cases any friend will
      take to flight.

23 Gain the trust of your neighbor in
      his poverty,
   so that you may rejoice with
      him in his prosperity.
   Stand by him in time of distress,

so that you may share with him
   in his inheritance.^f

24 The vapor and smoke of the
      furnace precede the fire;
   so insults precede bloodshed.

25 I am not ashamed to shelter a
      friend,
   and I will not hide from him.

26 But if harm should come to me
      because of him,
   whoever hears of it will beware
      of him.

27 Who will set a guard over my
      mouth,
   and an effective seal upon my
      lips,
   so that I may not fall because of
      them,
   and my tongue may not destroy
      me?

23 O Lord, Father and Master of
   my life,
   do not abandon me to their
      designs,
   and do not let me fall because of
      them!

2 Who will set whips over my
      thoughts,
   and the discipline of wisdom
      over my mind,
   so as not to spare me in my
      errors,
   and not overlook my^g sins?

3 Otherwise my mistakes may be
      multiplied,
   and my sins may abound,
   and I may fall before my
      adversaries,
   and my enemy may rejoice over
      me.^h

e Other ancient authorities read *Pebbles*
f Other ancient authorities add *For one should not
always despise restricted circumstances, or admire a rich
person who is stupid.*   g Gk *their*
h Other ancient authorities add *From them
the hope of your mercy is remote*

22.19–26: **The preservation of friendship. 19:** As the *eye* can weep, the *heart* can
show *feelings.* **20–22:** The things that destroy
friendship. **23–26:** Fidelity in friendship.

22.27–23.27: **A prayer for self-control,
with reflections on adultery. 22.27–23.1:**
Sins of the *tongue,* which is also the topic of
23.7–15.

4 O Lord, Father and God of my
life,
do not give me haughty eyes,
5 and remove evil desire from me.
6 Let neither gluttony nor lust
overcome me,
and do not give me over to
shameless passion.

DISCIPLINE OF THE TONGUE *i*

7 Listen, my children, to instruction
concerning the mouth;
the one who observes it will
never be caught.
8 Sinners are overtaken through
their lips;
by them the reviler and the
arrogant are tripped up.
9 Do not accustom your mouth to
oaths,
nor habitually utter the name of
the Holy One;
10 for as a servant who is constantly
under scrutiny
will not lack bruises,
so also the person who always
swears and utters the Name
will never be cleansed *j* from
sin.
11 The one who swears many oaths
is full of iniquity,
and the scourge will not leave
his house.
If he swears in error, his sin
remains on him,
and if he disregards it, he sins
doubly;
if he swears a false oath, he will
not be justified,
for his house will be filled with
calamities.

12 There is a manner of speaking
comparable to death; *k*
may it never be found in the
inheritance of Jacob!

Such conduct will be far from the
godly,
and they will not wallow in
sins.
13 Do not accustom your mouth to
coarse, foul language,
for it involves sinful speech.
14 Remember your father and mother
when you sit among the great,
or you may forget yourself in
their presence,
and behave like a fool through
bad habit;
then you will wish that you had
never been born,
and you will curse the day of
your birth.
15 Those who are accustomed to
using abusive language
will never become disciplined as
long as they live.

16 Two kinds of individuals multiply
sins,
and a third incurs wrath.
Hot passion that blazes like a fire
will not be quenched until it
burns itself out;
one who commits fornication with
his near of kin
will never cease until the fire
burns him up.
17 To a fornicator all bread is sweet;
he will never weary until he
dies.
18 The one who sins against his
marriage bed
says to himself, "Who can see
me?
Darkness surrounds me, the walls
hide me,

i This heading is included in the Gk text.
j Syr *be free*   *k* Other ancient authorities read
clothed about with death

23.2–6: Sins of passion, especially lust,
which is the topic of 23.16–26. 11: *Doubly,*
because he not only swears rashly, but *disregards* the oath by failing to keep it.
23.12: *Comparable to death,* a reference to
blasphemy (Lev 24.11–16).

23.16–17: This numerical saying singles
out three kinds of lechers: the dissolute, the
incestuous, and the adulterer. 17: *All bread is
sweet,* a euphemism for the adulterer's search
for a partner.
23.18–21: Reflections about the adulterer.

and no one sees me. Why
should I worry?
The Most High will not
remember sins."

19 His fear is confined to human eyes
and he does not realize that the
eyes of the Lord
are ten thousand times brighter
than the sun;
they look upon every aspect of
human behavior
and see into hidden corners.

20 Before the universe was created, it
was known to him,
and so it is since its completion.

21 This man will be punished in the
streets of the city,
and where he least suspects it,
he will be seized.

22 So it is with a woman who leaves
her husband
and presents him with an heir
by another man.

23 For first of all, she has disobeyed
the law of the Most High;
second, she has committed an
offense against her husband;
and third, through her fornication
she has committed adultery
and brought forth children by
another man.

24 She herself will be brought before
the assembly,
and her punishment will extend
to her children.

25 Her children will not take root,
and her branches will not bear
fruit.

26 She will leave behind an accursed
memory
and her disgrace will never be
blotted out.

27 Those who survive her will
recognize

that nothing is better than the
fear of the Lord,
and nothing sweeter than to heed
the commandments of the
Lord. *l*

THE PRAISE OF WISDOM *m*

24 Wisdom praises herself,
and tells of her glory in the
midst of her people.

2 In the assembly of the Most High
she opens her mouth,
and in the presence of his hosts
she tells of her glory:

3 "I came forth from the mouth of
the Most High,
and covered the earth like a
mist.

4 I dwelt in the highest heavens,
and my throne was in a pillar of
cloud.

5 Alone I compassed the vault of
heaven
and traversed the depths of the
abyss.

6 Over waves of the sea, over all
the earth,
and over every people and
nation I have held sway. *n*

7 Among all these I sought a resting
place;
in whose territory should I
abide?

8 "Then the Creator of all things
gave me a command,
and my Creator chose the place
for my tent.
He said, 'Make your dwelling in
Jacob,

l Other ancient authorities add as verse 28, *It is a
great honor to follow God, and to be received by him
is long life.*   *m* This heading is included in the
Gk text   *n* Other ancient authorities read
I have acquired a possession

20: God knows things even before creation.
22–26: Reflections about the adulteress. **27**:
A conclusion.
24.1–34: Praise of Lady Wisdom (Prov
8). **1–2**: Introduction of Wisdom, speaking to
the people and to members of the heavenly

court (*assembly of the Most High*). **3–7**: Wisdom's speech describes her divine origin and
her search for a resting place, though she rules
both in *heavens* and on *the earth*.
24.8–12: She obeys the divine command
to dwell in *Jacob,* and there eternal Wisdom

and in Israel receive your
inheritance.'
9 Before the ages, in the beginning,
he created me,
and for all the ages I shall not
cease to be.
10 In the holy tent I ministered
before him,
and so I was established in
Zion.
11 Thus in the beloved city he gave
me a resting place,
and in Jerusalem was my
domain.
12 I took root in an honored people,
in the portion of the Lord, his
heritage.

13 "I grew tall like a cedar in
Lebanon,
and like a cypress on the heights
of Hermon.
14 I grew tall like a palm tree in
En-gedi,[o]
and like rosebushes in Jericho;
like a fair olive tree in the field,
and like a plane tree beside
water[p] I grew tall.
15 Like cassia and camel's thorn I
gave forth perfume,
and like choice myrrh I spread
my fragrance,
like galbanum, onycha, and stacte,
and like the odor of incense in
the tent.
16 Like a terebinth I spread out my
branches,
and my branches are glorious
and graceful.
17 Like the vine I bud forth delights,
and my blossoms become
glorious and abundant
fruit.[q]

19 "Come to me, you who desire
me,
and eat your fill of my fruits.
20 For the memory of me is sweeter
than honey,
and the possession of me
sweeter than the
honeycomb.
21 Those who eat of me will hunger
for more,
and those who drink of me will
thirst for more.
22 Whoever obeys me will not be put
to shame,
and those who work with me
will not sin."

23 All this is the book of the
covenant of the Most High
God,
the law that Moses commanded
us
as an inheritance for the
congregations of Jacob.[r]
25 It overflows, like the Pishon, with
wisdom,
and like the Tigris at the time of
the first fruits.
26 It runs over, like the Euphrates,
with understanding,
and like the Jordan at harvest
time.
27 It pours forth instruction like the
Nile,[s]
like the Gihon at the time of
vintage.
28 The first man did not know

o Other ancient authorities read *on the beaches*
p Other ancient authorities omit *beside water*
q Other ancient authorities add as verse 18, *I am the mother of beautiful love, of fear, of knowledge, and of holy hope; being eternal, I am given to all my children, to those who are named by him.*
r Other ancient authorities add as verse 24, *"Do not cease to be strong in the Lord, cling to him so that he may strengthen you; the Lord Almighty alone is God, and besides him there is no savior."*
s Syr: Gk *It makes instruction shine forth like light*

(vv. 9–10) ministers to the Lord in the Jerusalem temple. **24.13–17:** Her majesty is compared to trees, plants, and exotic aromatics. **19–22:** She concludes her speech with an invitation to her unusual meal, which increases one's hunger, and keeps from sin; see Prov 9.5; 8.35. **24.23–29:** Sirach identifies Wisdom with the Torah that *overflows . . . with wisdom*

wisdom¹ fully,
  nor will the last one fathom her.
29 For her thoughts are more
    abundant than the sea,
  and her counsel deeper than the
    great abyss.

30 As for me, I was like a canal from
    a river,
  like a water channel into a
    garden.
31 I said, "I will water my garden
    and drench my flower-beds."
  And lo, my canal became a river,
    and my river a sea.
32 I will again make instruction shine
    forth like the dawn,
  and I will make it clear from far
    away.
33 I will again pour out teaching like
    prophecy,
  and leave it to all future
    generations.
34 Observe that I have not labored
    for myself alone,
  but for all who seek wisdom. ¹

25 I take pleasure in three things,
  and they are beautiful in the
    sight of God and of
    mortals:"
  agreement among brothers and
    sisters, friendship among
    neighbors,
  and a wife and a husband who
    live in harmony.
2 I hate three kinds of people,
  and I loathe their manner of life:
  a pauper who boasts, a rich person
    who lies,
  and an old fool who commits
    adultery.

3 If you gathered nothing in your
    youth,
  how can you find anything in
    your old age?
4 How attractive is sound judgment
    in the gray-haired,
  and for the aged to possess good
    counsel!
5 How attractive is wisdom in the
    aged,
  and understanding and counsel
    in the venerable!
6 Rich experience is the crown of
    the aged,
  and their boast is the fear of the
    Lord.

7 I can think of nine whom I would
    call blessed,
  and a tenth my tongue
    proclaims:
  a man who can rejoice in his
    children;
  a man who lives to see the
    downfall of his foes.
8 Happy the man who lives with a
    sensible wife,
  and the one who does not plow
    with ox and ass together. ⁿ
  Happy is the one who does not
    sin with the tongue,
  and the one who has not served
    an inferior.
9 Happy is the one who finds a
    friend, ʷ
  and the one who speaks to
    attentive listeners.

t Gk *her*   *u* Syr Lat: Gk *In three things I was*
beautiful and I stood in beauty before the Lord and
mortals.   *v* Heb Syr: Gk lacks *and the one who does*
not plow with ox and ass together   *w* Lat Syr: Gk
good sense

(vv. 23–24). **28:** Just as the *first man* (Adam)
did not know her (since the Torah was given
first to Moses), so the *last one* will never ex-
haust such profound wisdom.
  24.30–34: Sirach describes how in chan-
neling this wisdom in his book, he has become indeed a *river,* a veritable *sea* whose
instruction (comparable to *prophecy*) reaches
all future generations.
  25.1–2: A numerical saying about
three beautiful and three hateful things.
  25.3–6: The attractiveness of wisdom
in the aged.
  25.7–11: A numerical saying of ten
blessings.
  25.13–26.27: Wicked and virtuous
women. 13–15: The wickedness of the *wife* is
heightened by the perils inherent in polygamy (*vengeance, wrath*).

10 How great is the one who finds
   wisdom!
   But none is superior to the one
   who fears the Lord.
11 Fear of the Lord surpasses
   everything;
   to whom can we compare the
   one who has it?[x]

13 Any wound, but not a wound of
   the heart!
   Any wickedness, but not the
   wickedness of a woman!
14 Any suffering, but not suffering
   from those who hate!
   And any vengeance, but not the
   vengeance of enemies!
15 There is no venom[y] worse than a
   snake's venom,[y]
   and no anger worse than a
   woman's[z] wrath.

16 I would rather live with a lion and
   a dragon
   than live with an evil woman.
17 A woman's wickedness changes
   her appearance,
   and darkens her face like that of
   a bear.
18 Her husband sits[a] among the
   neighbors,
   and he cannot help sighing[b]
   bitterly.
19 Any iniquity is small compared to
   a woman's iniquity;
   may a sinner's lot befall her!
20 A sandy ascent for the feet of the
   aged—
   such is a garrulous wife to a
   quiet husband.
21 Do not be ensnared by a woman's
   beauty,
   and do not desire a woman for
   her possessions.[c]
22 There is wrath and impudence and
   great disgrace

when a wife supports her
   husband.
23 Dejected mind, gloomy face,
   and wounded heart come from
   an evil wife.
   Drooping hands and weak knees
   come from the wife who does
   not make her husband
   happy.
24 From a woman sin had its
   beginning,
   and because of her we all die.
25 Allow no outlet to water,
   and no boldness of speech to an
   evil wife.
26 If she does not go as you direct,
   separate her from yourself.

26 Happy is the husband of a
   good wife;
   the number of his days will be
   doubled.
2 A loyal wife brings joy to her
   husband,
   and he will complete his years
   in peace.
3 A good wife is a great blessing;
   she will be granted among the
   blessings of the man who
   fears the Lord.
4 Whether rich or poor, his heart is
   content,
   and at all times his face is
   cheerful.
5 Of three things my heart is
   frightened,
   and of a fourth I am in great
   fear:[d]

x Other ancient authorities add as verse 12,
*The fear of the Lord is the beginning of love
for him, and faith is the beginning of clinging to him.*
y Syr: Gk *head*   z Other ancient
authorities read *an enemy's*   a Heb Syr: Gk
loses heart   b Other ancient authorities read *and
listening he sighs*   c Heb Syr: Other Gk
authorities read *for her beauty*
d Syr: Meaning of Gk uncertain

25.19: *Sinner's lot,* by her being married to
a sinner. **24:** Chronologically, the *woman* in
Eden sinned first.
   25.26b: Literally, "cut her off from your
flesh," that is, divorce her (Deut 24.1); hitherto they had been "one flesh" (Gen 2.24).
   26.5–6: A numerical saying that illustrates
the problems of polygamy (v. 5, the cul-
minating evil, *worse than death*).

Slander in the city, the gathering
of a mob,
and false accusation—all these
are worse than death.
6 But it is heartache and sorrow
when a wife is jealous of a
rival,
and a tongue-lashing makes it
known to all.
7 A bad wife is a chafing yoke;
taking hold of her is like
grasping a scorpion.
8 A drunken wife arouses great
anger;
she cannot hide her shame.
9 The haughty stare betrays an
unchaste wife;
her eyelids give her away.

10 Keep strict watch over a
headstrong daughter,
or else, when she finds liberty,
she will make use of it.
11 Be on guard against her impudent
eye,
and do not be surprised if she
sins against you.
12 As a thirsty traveler opens his
mouth
and drinks from any water near
him,
so she will sit in front of every
tent peg
and open her quiver to the
arrow.

13 A wife's charm delights her
husband,
and her skill puts flesh on his
bones.
14 A silent wife is a gift from the
Lord,
and nothing is so precious as her
self-discipline.
15 A modest wife adds charm to
charm,
and no scales can weigh the
value of her chastity.
16 Like the sun rising in the heights
of the Lord,
so is the beauty of a good wife
in her well-ordered home.

17 Like the shining lamp on the holy
lampstand,
so is a beautiful face on a stately
figure.
18 Like golden pillars on silver bases,
so are shapely legs and steadfast
feet.

Other ancient authorities add
verses 19–27:

19 *My child, keep sound the bloom of*
your youth,
and do not give your strength to
strangers.
20 *Seek a fertile field within the whole*
plain,
and sow it with your own seed,
trusting in your fine stock.
21 *So your offspring will prosper,*
and, having confidence in their good
descent, will grow great.
22 *A prostitute is regarded as spittle,*
and a married woman as a tower of
death to her lovers.
23 *A godless wife is given as a portion to*
a lawless man,
but a pious wife is given to the man
who fears the Lord.
24 *A shameless woman constantly acts*
disgracefully,
but a modest daughter will even be
embarrassed before her
husband.
25 *A headstrong wife is regarded as a*
dog,
but one who has a sense of shame
will fear the Lord.
26 *A wife honoring her husband will*
seem wise to all,
but if she dishonors him in her
pride she will be known to all
as ungodly.
Happy is the husband of a good
wife;
for the number of his years will be
doubled.
27 *A loud-voiced and garrulous wife is*
like a trumpet sounding the
charge,
and every person like this lives in
the anarchy of war.

28 At two things my heart is grieved,
   and because of a third anger
      comes over me:
   a warrior in want through
      poverty,
   intelligent men who are treated
      contemptuously,
   and a man who turns back from
      righteousness to sin—
   the Lord will prepare him for
      the sword!

29 A merchant can hardly keep from
      wrongdoing,
   nor is a tradesman innocent of
      sin.

27 Many have committed sin for
      gain,*e*
   and those who seek to get rich
      will avert their eyes.

2 As a stake is driven firmly into a
      fissure between stones,
   so sin is wedged in between
      selling and buying.

3 If a person is not steadfast in the
      fear of the Lord,
   his house will be quickly
      overthrown.

4 When a sieve is shaken, the refuse
      appears;
   so do a person's faults when he
      speaks.

5 The kiln tests the potter's vessels;
   so the test of a person is in his
      conversation.

6 Its fruit discloses the cultivation of
      a tree;
   so a person's speech discloses
      the cultivation of his mind.

7 Do not praise anyone before he
      speaks,
   for this is the way people are
      tested.

8 If you pursue justice, you will
      attain it

and wear it like a glorious robe.

9 Birds roost with their own kind,
   so honesty comes home to those
      who practice it.

10 A lion lies in wait for prey;
   so does sin for evildoers.

11 The conversation of the godly is
      always wise,
   but the fool changes like the
      moon.

12 Among stupid people limit your
      time,
   but among thoughtful people
      linger on.

13 The talk of fools is offensive,
   and their laughter is wantonly
      sinful.

14 Their cursing and swearing make
      one's hair stand on end,
   and their quarrels make others
      stop their ears.

15 The strife of the proud leads to
      bloodshed,
   and their abuse is grievous to
      hear.

16 Whoever betrays secrets destroys
      confidence,
   and will never find a congenial
      friend.

17 Love your friend and keep faith
      with him;
   but if you betray his secrets, do
      not follow after him.

18 For as a person destroys his
      enemy,
   so you have destroyed the
      friendship of your
      neighbor.

19 And as you allow a bird to escape
      from your hand,
   so you have let your neighbor
      go, and will not catch him
      again.

e Other ancient authorities read *a trifle*

26.28–28.26: **Miscellaneous observations.** 26.28: *A warrior,* Syriac, "a wealthy man."
26.29–27.3: The moral dangers in commercial activities. 27.1: Prov 28.21. 4–7: Tests in life.

27.8–10: Reward and retribution. 11–15: Kinds of talk.
27.16–21: Against disclosing secrets (Prov 20.19; 25.8–10). 21: *Without hope,* of reconciliation (22.22).

²⁰ Do not go after him, for he is too
  far off,
  and has escaped like a gazelle
    from a snare.
²¹ For a wound may be bandaged,
  and there is reconciliation after
    abuse,
  but whoever has betrayed
    secrets is without hope.

²² Whoever winks the eye plots
    mischief,
  and those who know him will
    keep their distance.
²³ In your presence his mouth is all
    sweetness,
  and he admires your words;
  but later he will twist his speech
  and with your own words he
    will trip you up.
²⁴ I have hated many things, but him
    above all;
  even the Lord hates him.
²⁵ Whoever throws a stone straight
    up throws it on his own
    head,
  and a treacherous blow opens
    up many wounds.
²⁶ Whoever digs a pit will fall into it,
  and whoever sets a snare will be
    caught in it.
²⁷ If a person does evil, it will roll
    back upon him,
  and he will not know where it
    came from.
²⁸ Mockery and abuse issue from the
    proud,
  but vengeance lies in wait for
    them like a lion.
²⁹ Those who rejoice in the fall of
    the godly will be caught in
    a snare,
  and pain will consume them
    before their death.

³⁰ Anger and wrath, these also are
    abominations,

yet a sinner holds on to them.

28 The vengeful will face the
    Lord's vengeance,
  for he keeps a strict account of*ᶠ*
    their sins.
² Forgive your neighbor the wrong
    he has done,
  and then your sins will be
    pardoned when you pray.
³ Does anyone harbor anger against
    another,
  and expect healing from the
    Lord?
⁴ If one has no mercy toward
    another like himself,
  can he then seek pardon for his
    own sins?
⁵ If a mere mortal harbors wrath,
  who will make an atoning
    sacrifice for his sins?
⁶ Remember the end of your life,
    and set enmity aside;
  remember corruption and death,
    and be true to the
    commandments.
⁷ Remember the commandments,
    and do not be angry with
    your neighbor;
  remember the covenant of the
    Most High, and overlook
    faults.

⁸ Refrain from strife, and your sins
    will be fewer;
  for the hot-tempered kindle
    strife,
⁹ and the sinner disrupts friendships
  and sows discord among those
    who are at peace.
¹⁰ In proportion to the fuel, so will
    the fire burn,
  and in proportion to the
    obstinacy, so will strife
    increase;*ᵍ*

f Other ancient authorities read *for he firmly
establishes*   *g* Other ancient authorities read
burn

27.22–27: Hypocrisy and punishment.
22: *Winks*, with insincerity (Prov 6.13;
10.10). 25–27: Evil actions beget evil results
(Ps 7.14–16; 9.15–16; Prov 26.27; Eccl 10.8).
27.28–28.1: *Vengeance* comes upon the

evil, ultimately from the Lord. 28.2–7: Forgiveness for oneself is contingent upon showing forgiveness to others (Mt 6.12, 14; Mk
11.25).
28.8–11: Quarreling. 12–26: Evils of the

in proportion to a person's
   strength will be his anger,
and in proportion to his wealth
   he will increase his wrath.
11 A hasty quarrel kindles a fire,
   and a hasty dispute sheds blood.
12 If you blow on a spark, it will
      glow;
   if you spit on it, it will be put
      out;
   yet both come out of your
      mouth.

13 Curse the gossips and the
      double-tongued,
   for they destroy the peace of
      many.
14 Slander*h* has shaken many,
   and scattered them from nation
      to nation;
   it has destroyed strong cities,
   and overturned the houses of
      the great.
15 Slander*i* has driven virtuous
      women from their homes,
   and deprived them of the fruit
      of their toil.
16 Those who pay heed to slander*j*
      will not find rest,
   nor will they settle down in
      peace.
17 The blow of a whip raises a welt,
   but a blow of the tongue
      crushes the bones.
18 Many have fallen by the edge of
      the sword,
   but not as many as have fallen
      because of the tongue.
19 Happy is the one who is protected
      from it,
   who has not been exposed to its
      anger,
   who has not borne its yoke,
   and has not been bound with its
      fetters.

20 For its yoke is a yoke of iron,
   and its fetters are fetters of
      bronze;
21 its death is an evil death,
   and Hades is preferable to it.
22 It has no power over the godly;
   they will not be burned in its
      flame.
23 Those who forsake the Lord will
      fall into its power;
   it will burn among them and
      will not be put out.
   It will be sent out against them
      like a lion;
   like a leopard it will mangle
      them.
24a As you fence in your property
      with thorns,
25b   so make a door and a bolt for
      your mouth.
24b As you lock up your silver and
      gold,
25a   so make balances and scales for
      your words.
26 Take care not to err with your
      tongue,*k*
   and fall victim to one lying in
      wait.

29 The merciful lend to their
      neighbors;
   by holding out a helping hand
      they keep the
      commandments.
2 Lend to your neighbor in his time
      of need;
   repay your neighbor when a
      loan falls due.
3 Keep your promise and be honest
      with him,
   and on every occasion you will
      find what you need.

h Gk *A third tongue*   *i* Gk *a third tongue*
j Gk *it*   *k* Gk *with it*

---

tongue. **12:** *Mouth,* see 5.13; Prov 15.1; Jas
3.9–10.
   28.17: Prov 25.15. **21:** *Hades* (Sheol) is *preferable* to the living *death* inflicted by the *evil*
tongue. **24–25:** Just as one protects valuables,
one should be careful about one's *words.*
   29:1–20: **Loans, Alms, Surety. 1–7:** Ex

22.25; loans were given without charging interest (Ex 22.24), but interest was permitted
if one loaned to a Gentile (Deut 23.20–21). **3:**
If a loan is repaid on time, one can count on
receiving a future loan. **4–7:** Warnings about
abuses in borrowing.

4 Many regard a loan as a windfall,
  and cause trouble to those who
      help them.
5 One kisses another's hands until
      he gets a loan,
  and is deferential in speaking of
      his neighbor's money;
  but at the time for repayment he
      delays,
  and pays back with empty
      promises,
  and finds fault with the time.
6 If he can pay, his creditor[l] will
      hardly get back half,
  and will regard that as a
      windfall.
  If he cannot pay, the borrower[l]
      has robbed the other of his
      money,
  and he has needlessly made him
      an enemy;
  he will repay him with curses and
      reproaches,
  and instead of glory will repay
      him with dishonor.
7 Many refuse to lend, not because
      of meanness,
  but from fear[m] of being
      defrauded needlessly.

8 Nevertheless, be patient with
      someone in humble
      circumstances,
  and do not keep him waiting for
      your alms.
9 Help the poor for the
      commandment's sake,
  and in their need do not send
      them away empty-handed.
10 Lose your silver for the sake of a
      brother or a friend,
  and do not let it rust under a
      stone and be lost.
11 Lay up your treasure according to
      the commandments of the
      Most High,
  and it will profit you more than
      gold;

12 Store up almsgiving in your
      treasury,
  and it will rescue you from
      every disaster;
13 better than a stout shield and a
      sturdy spear,
  it will fight for you against the
      enemy.

14 A good person will be surety for
      his neighbor,
  but the one who has lost all
      sense of shame will fail
      him.
15 Do not forget the kindness of
      your guarantor,
  for he has given his life for you.
16 A sinner wastes the property of
      his guarantor,
17 and the ungrateful person
      abandons his rescuer.
18 Being surety has ruined many
      who were prosperous,
  and has tossed them about like
      waves of the sea;
  it has driven the influential into
      exile,
  and they have wandered among
      foreign nations.
19 The sinner comes to grief through
      surety;
  his pursuit of gain involves him
      in lawsuits.
20 Assist your neighbor to the best of
      your ability,
  but be careful not to fall
      yourself.

21 The necessities of life are water,
      bread, and clothing,
  and also a house to assure
      privacy.
22 Better is the life of the poor under
      their own crude roof

---

l Gk *he*   *m* Other ancient authorities
read *many refuse to lend, therefore, because of
such meanness; they are afraid*

29.8–13: As regards the poor, almsgiving
is a duty (see 40.1–6). **9:** *For the commandment's
sake,* Deut 15.7–11.

29.14–20: The dangers in guaranteeing a
loan for another (see 8.12–13 n.); Sirach advises caution.

than sumptuous food in the
house of others.

23 Be content with little or much,
and you will hear no reproach
for being a guest."

24 It is a miserable life to go from
house to house;
as a guest you should not open
your mouth;

25 you will play the host and provide
drink without being
thanked,
and besides this you will hear
rude words like these:

26 "Come here, stranger, prepare the
table;
let me eat what you have
there."

27 "Be off, stranger, for an honored
guest is here;
my brother has come for a visit,
and I need the
guest-room."

28 It is hard for a sensible person to
bear
scolding about lodging° and the
insults of the moneylender.

CONCERNING CHILDREN *p*

30 He who loves his son will whip
him often,
so that he may rejoice at the
way he turns out.

2 He who disciplines his son will
profit by him,
and will boast of him among
acquaintances.

3 He who teaches his son will make
his enemies envious,
and will glory in him among his
friends.

4 When the father dies he will not
seem to be dead,
for he has left behind him one
like himself,

5 whom in his life he looked upon
with joy
and at death, without grief.

6 He has left behind him an avenger
against his enemies,
and one to repay the kindness of
his friends.

7 Whoever spoils his son will bind
up his wounds,
and will suffer heartache at
every cry.

8 An unbroken horse turns out
stubborn,
and an unchecked son turns out
headstrong.

9 Pamper a child, and he will
terrorize you;
play with him, and he will
grieve you.

10 Do not laugh with him, or you
will have sorrow with him,
and in the end you will gnash
your teeth.

11 Give him no freedom in his
youth,
and do not ignore his errors.

12 Bow down his neck in his youth, *q*
and beat his sides while he is
young,
or else he will become stubborn
and disobey you,
and you will have sorrow of
soul from him. *r*

13 Discipline your son and make his
yoke heavy, *s*
so that you may not be offended
by his shamelessness.

n Lat: Gk *reproach from your family*; other ancient
authorities lack this line   *o* Or *scolding from the
household*   *p* This heading is included in the
Gk text.   *q* Other ancient authorities lack this
line and the preceding line   *r* Other ancient
authorities lack this line   *s* Heb: Gk *take pains
with him*

29.21–28: Frugality. 21: The basic necessities are expanded in 39.26. **24–28:** Do not
live beyond your means so that you do not
become dependent upon others.

30.1–13: Training of children. 1: Physical punishment is taken for granted (22.6;
Prov 13.24; 19.18; 23.13–14; 29.15). **4:** The
child is the image of the *father;* see Tob 9.6.
6: *An avenger,* as in Ps 127.5.

30.7–13: Dangers that result if discipline is
not applied.

14 Better off poor, healthy, and fit
than rich and afflicted in body.
15 Health and fitness are better than
any gold,
and a robust body than
countless riches.
16 There is no wealth better than
health of body,
and no gladness above joy of
heart.
17 Death is better than a life of
misery,
and eternal sleep*t* than chronic
sickness.

CONCERNING FOODS *u*
18 Good things poured out upon a
mouth that is closed
are like offerings of food placed
upon a grave.
19 Of what use to an idol is a
sacrifice?
For it can neither eat nor smell.
So is the one punished by the
Lord;
20 he sees with his eyes and groans
as a eunuch groans when
embracing a girl. *v*

21 Do not give yourself over to
sorrow,
and do not distress yourself
deliberately.
22 A joyful heart is life itself,
and rejoicing lengthens one's life
span.
23 Indulge yourself*w* and take
comfort,
and remove sorrow far from
you,
for sorrow has destroyed many,
and no advantage ever comes
from it.
24 Jealousy and anger shorten life,
and anxiety brings on premature
old age.

25 Those who are cheerful and merry
at table
will benefit from their food.

31 Wakefulness over wealth wastes
away one's flesh,
and anxiety about it drives away
sleep.
2 Wakeful anxiety prevents slumber,
and a severe illness carries off
sleep. *x*
3 The rich person toils to amass a
fortune,
and when he rests he fills
himself with his dainties.
4 The poor person toils to make a
meager living,
and if ever he rests he becomes
needy.

5 One who loves gold will not be
justified;
one who pursues money will be
led astray*y* by it.
6 Many have come to ruin because
of gold,
and their destruction has met
them face to face.
7 It is a stumbling block to those
who are avid for it,
and every fool will be taken
captive by it.
8 Blessed is the rich person who is
found blameless,
and who does not go after gold.
9 Who is he, that we may praise
him?
For he has done wonders among
his people.

t Other ancient authorities lack *eternal sleep*
u This heading is included in the Gk text; other
ancient authorities place the heading before
verse 16   *v* Other ancient authorities add *So
is the person who does right under compulsion*
w Other ancient authorities read *Beguile yourself*
x Other ancient authorities read *sleep carries off
a severe illness*   *y* Heb Syr: Gk *pursues destruction
will be filled*

30.14–20: Concerning health. 17: Job
3.11, 13, 17; Tob 3.6, 10, 13. **18:** Let Jer 27.28;
Bel 3 (compare Ps 115.5–7).
30.21–25: Cheerfulness.

31.1–11: Right attitude toward wealth.
Sirach has strict views concerning the rich
(vv. 5–7; 11.11), and the implication of verses
8–11 is that few rich people are also just.

10 Who has been tested by it and
   been found perfect?
   Let it be for him a ground for
   boasting.
   Who has had the power to
   transgress and did not
   transgress,
   and to do evil and did not do it?
11 His prosperity will be
   established,*z*
   and the assembly will proclaim
   his acts of charity.

12 Are you seated at the table of the
   great?*a*
   Do not be greedy at it,
   and do not say, "How much
   food there is here!"
13 Remember that a greedy eye is a
   bad thing.
   What has been created more
   greedy than the eye?
   Therefore it sheds tears for any
   reason.
14 Do not reach out your hand for
   everything you see,
   and do not crowd your
   neighbor*b* at the dish.
15 Judge your neighbor's feelings by
   your own,
   and in every matter be
   thoughtful.
16 Eat what is set before you like a
   well brought-up person,*c*
   and do not chew greedily, or
   you will give offense.
17 Be the first to stop, as befits good
   manners,
   and do not be insatiable, or you
   will give offense.
18 If you are seated among many
   persons,
   do not help yourself*d* before
   they do.

19 How ample a little is for a
   well-disciplined person!

He does not breathe heavily
   when in bed.
20 Healthy sleep depends on
   moderate eating;
   he rises early, and feels fit.
   The distress of sleeplessness and of
   nausea
   and colic are with the glutton.
21 If you are overstuffed with food,
   get up to vomit, and you will
   have relief.
22 Listen to me, my child, and do
   not disregard me,
   and in the end you will
   appreciate my words.
   In everything you do be
   moderate,*e*
   and no sickness will overtake
   you.
23 People bless the one who is liberal
   with food,
   and their testimony to his
   generosity is trustworthy.
24 The city complains of the one
   who is stingy with food,
   and their testimony to his
   stinginess is accurate.

25 Do not try to prove your strength
   by wine-drinking,
   for wine has destroyed many.
26 As the furnace tests the work of
   the smith,*f*
   so wine tests hearts when the
   insolent quarrel.
27 Wine is very life to human beings
   if taken in moderation.
   What is life to one who is without
   wine?
   It has been created to make
   people happy.

*z Other ancient authorities add because of this
a Heb Syr: Gk at a great table   b Gk him
c Heb: Gk like a human being   d Gk reach out
your hand   e Heb Syr: Gk industrious   f Heb:
Gk tests the hardening of steel by dipping*

**31.12–31: Temperance in food and
drink.** One should be particularly aware of
the need of politeness and kindness when eating with others. **13:** *Greedy eye,* as in 14.10.
   31.25–26: Excessive drinking is not a
proof of a person's worth. As metal is tested
by *fire,* so *hearts* are tested by *wine;* see vv. 29–
30. **27–28:** Wine is a staple food in Mediterranean countries (Ps 104.15).

28 Wine drunk at the proper time and
   in moderation
 is rejoicing of heart and gladness
   of soul.
29 Wine drunk to excess leads to
   bitterness of spirit,
 to quarrels and stumbling.
30 Drunkenness increases the anger of
   a fool to his own hurt,
 reducing his strength and adding
   wounds.
31 Do not reprove your neighbor at a
   banquet of wine,
 and do not despise him in his
   merrymaking;
 speak no word of reproach to
   him,
 and do not distress him by
   making demands of him.

32 If they make you master of the
   feast, do not exalt yourself;
 be among them as one of their
   number.
 Take care of them first and then
   sit down;
2 when you have fulfilled all your
   duties, take your place,
 so that you may be merry along
   with them
 and receive a wreath for your
   excellent leadership.

3 Speak, you who are older, for it is
   your right,
 but with accurate knowledge,
   and do not interrupt the
   music.
4 Where there is entertainment, do
   not pour out talk;
 do not display your cleverness
   at the wrong time.
5 A ruby seal in a setting of gold
 is a concert of music at a
   banquet of wine.
6 A seal of emerald in a rich setting
   of gold

is the melody of music with
   good wine.

7 Speak, you who are young, if you
   are obliged to,
 but no more than twice, and
   only if asked.
8 Be brief; say much in few words;
 be as one who knows and can
   still hold his tongue.
9 Among the great do not act as
   their equal;
 and when another is speaking,
   do not babble.
10 Lightning travels ahead of the
   thunder,
 and approval goes before one
   who is modest.
11 Leave in good time and do not be
   the last;
 go home quickly and do not
   linger.
12 Amuse yourself there to your
   heart's content,
 but do not sin through proud
   speech.
13 But above all bless your Maker,
 who fills you with his good
   gifts.

14 The one who seeks God[g] will
   accept his discipline,
 and those who rise early to seek
   him[h] will find favor.
15 The one who seeks the law will be
   filled with it,
 but the hypocrite will stumble
   at it.
16 Those who fear the Lord will
   form true judgments,
 and they will kindle righteous
   deeds like a light.
17 The sinner will shun reproof,

g Heb: Gk *who fears the Lord*   h Other ancient
authorities lack *to seek him*

32.1–13: Proper behavior at a banquet.
1–2: The *master of the feast* had to care for the
needs of those at the table. **3–10**: Directions
to the *older* people and the *young*. **11–13**: These
words are meant for all.

**32.14–33.6: The God-fearing man con-
trasted with the sinner. 32.14:** *Discipline,*
Hebrew "musar," is a frequent topic (see
6.18 n.). **17:** *A decision,* i.e. an interpretation
(of the law).

and will find a decision
according to his liking.

18 A sensible person will not
overlook a thoughtful
suggestion;
an insolent[i] and proud person
will not be deterred by
fear.[j]

19 Do nothing without deliberation,
but when you have acted, do
not regret it.

20 Do not go on a path full of
hazards,
and do not stumble at an
obstacle twice.[k]

21 Do not be overconfident on a
smooth[l] road,

22 and give good heed to your
paths.[m]

23 Guard[n] yourself in every act,
for this is the keeping of the
commandments.

24 The one who keeps the law
preserves himself,[o]
and the one who trusts the Lord
will not suffer loss.

33 No evil will befall the one who
fears the Lord,
but in trials such a one will be
rescued again and again.

2 The wise will not hate the law,
but the one who is hypocritical
about it is like a boat in a
storm.

3 The sensible person will trust in
the law;
for such a one the law is as
dependable as a divine
oracle.

4 Prepare what to say, and then you
will be listened to;
draw upon your training, and
give your answer.

5 The heart of a fool is like a cart
wheel,
and his thoughts like a turning
axle.

6 A mocking friend is like a stallion
that neighs no matter who the
rider is.

7 Why is one day more important
than another,
when all the daylight in the year
is from the sun?

8 By the Lord's wisdom they were
distinguished,
and he appointed the different
seasons and festivals.

9 Some days he exalted and
hallowed,
and some he made ordinary
days.

10 All human beings come from the
ground,
and humankind[p] was created
out of the dust.

11 In the fullness of his knowledge
the Lord distinguished them
and appointed their different
ways.

12 Some he blessed and exalted,
and some he made holy and
brought near to himself;
but some he cursed and brought
low,
and turned them out of their
place.

13 Like clay in the hand of the
potter,
to be molded as he pleases,

---

i Heb: Gk *alien* *j* Meaning of Gk uncertain.
Other ancient authorities add *and after acting,*
with him, without deliberation *k* Heb: Gk *stumble*
on stony ground *l* Or *an unexplored* *m* Heb
Syr: Gk *and beware of your children* *n* Heb Syr:
Gk *Trust* *o* Heb: Gk *who believes the law heeds*
the commandments *p* Heb: Gk *Adam*

33.2: Hebrew, "He that hates the law is not
wise, and is tossed about like a boat in a
storm." **3**: *Urim,* 45.10; Ex 28.30; Num
27.21; 1 Sam 14.41–42.
33.7–15: **Divinely ordained opposites
in creation.** Corresponding to wise (righteous) and foolish (sinner) are the polarities to
be found in life, such as holy days and *ordinary*
days (v. 9), the blessed and the cursed (v. 12).
13: *Clay . . . potter,* a common biblical image
(Isa 29.16; 45.8; 64.8; Jer 18.4, 6; Wis 15.7–8;
Rom 9.21) that underscores divine determi-

so all are in the hand of their
  Maker,
    to be given whatever he decides.

14 Good is the opposite of evil,
    and life the opposite of death;
    so the sinner is the opposite of
      the godly.
15 Look at all the works of the Most
    High;
    they come in pairs, one the
      opposite of the other.

16 Now I was the last to keep vigil;
    I was like a gleaner following
      the grape-pickers;
17 by the blessing of the Lord I
    arrived first,
    and like a grape-picker I filled
      my wine press.
18 Consider that I have not labored
    for myself alone,
    but for all who seek instruction.
19 Hear me, you who are great
      among the people,
    and you leaders of the
      congregation, pay heed!

20 To son or wife, to brother or
    friend,
    do not give power over
      yourself, as long as you
      live;
    and do not give your property to
      another,
    in case you change your mind
      and must ask for it.
21 While you are still alive and have
    breath in you,
    do not let anyone take your
      place.
22 For it is better that your children
    should ask from you
    than that you should look to the
      hand of your children.
23 Excel in all that you do;

bring no stain upon your honor.
24 At the time when you end the
    days of your life,
    in the hour of death, distribute
      your inheritance.

25 Fodder and a stick and burdens for
    a donkey;
    bread and discipline and work
      for a slave.
26 Set your slave to work, and you
    will find rest;
    leave his hands idle, and he will
      seek liberty.
27 Yoke and thong will bow the
    neck,
    and for a wicked slave there are
      racks and tortures.
28 Put him to work, in order that he
    may not be idle,
29 for idleness teaches much evil.
30 Set him to work, as is fitting for
    him,
    and if he does not obey, make
      his fetters heavy.
    Do not be overbearing toward
      anyone,
    and do nothing unjust.

31 If you have but one slave, treat
    him like yourself,
    because you have bought him
      with blood.
    If you have but one slave, treat
      him like a brother,
    for you will need him as you
      need your life.
32 If you ill-treat him, and he leaves
    you and runs away,
33 which way will you go to seek
    him?

34 The senseless have vain and
    false hopes,
    and dreams give wings to fools.

---

nism at the same time that human free will is
affirmed (15.11–20). **14–15:** A summary
statement of the theme.
  **33.16–19: The author's qualifications as
a teacher.** See also 24.30–34; 39.12–13;
51.13–28.

**33.20–24: On preserving financial in-
dependence.**
  33.25–33: On the treatment of slaves.
Slavery is taken for granted as a feature of
society. Although Sirach's words are strong,
especially for the lazy (vv.25–29), he urges

2 As one who catches at a shadow
   and pursues the wind,
   so is anyone who believes in*q*
   dreams.
3 What is seen in dreams is but a
   reflection,
   the likeness of a face looking at
   itself.
4 From an unclean thing what can
   be clean?
   And from something false what
   can be true?
5 Divinations and omens and
   dreams are unreal,
   and like a woman in labor, the
   mind has fantasies.
6 Unless they are sent by
   intervention from the Most
   High,
   pay no attention to them.
7 For dreams have deceived many,
   and those who put their hope in
   them have perished.
8 Without such deceptions the law
   will be fulfilled,
   and wisdom is complete in the
   mouth of the faithful.

9 An educated*r* person knows many
   things,
   and one with much experience
   knows what he is talking
   about.
10 An inexperienced person knows
   few things,
11   but he that has traveled acquires
   much cleverness.
12 I have seen many things in my
   travels,
   and I understand more than I
   can express.

13 I have often been in danger of
   death,
   but have escaped because of
   these experiences.

14 The spirit of those who fear the
   Lord will live,
15   for their hope is in him who
   saves them.
16 Those who fear the Lord will not
   be timid,
   or play the coward, for he is
   their hope.
17 Happy is the soul that fears the
   Lord!
18   To whom does he look? And
   who is his support?
19 The eyes of the Lord are on those
   who love him,
   a mighty shield and strong
   support,
   a shelter from scorching wind and
   a shade from noonday sun,
   a guard against stumbling and a
   help against falling.
20 He lifts up the soul and makes the
   eyes sparkle;
   he gives health and life and
   blessing.

21 If one sacrifices ill-gotten goods,
   the offering is blemished;*s*
22   the gifts*t* of the lawless are not
   acceptable.
23 The Most High is not pleased
   with the offerings of the
   ungodly,

q Syr: Gk *pays heed to*   *r* Other ancient
author ities read *A traveled*   *s* Other ancient
authorities read *is made in mockery*   *t* Other
ancient author ities read *mockeries*

---

justice (v.30). The rights of a slave are defined in the law codes (Ex 21.2–6, 20–21,
26–27; Lev 25.46; Deut 15.12–18).
   **34.1–8: The vanity of dreams and
omens** (Deut 13.2–5; 18.9–14; Eccl 5.7; Jer
29.8). **2:** *Pursues the wind,* the image as in Hos
12.1; Eccl 1.14; and often. **3:** *Dreams* have no
reality; they are a reflection of one's concerns.
4: Job 14.4. **6:** Allowance is made for God-
given dreams, (Gen 37.5ff.; Judg 7.13ff.; Job
33.15–18).

   **34.9–13: Learning from experience
and travel.**
   **34.14–20: The blessings of those who
fear God. 19:** *Shelter,* Ps 61.2–4; 91.1–4; Isa
25.4; the *scorching wind* is the well known
sirocco in spring and autumn.
   34.21–31: Unacceptable sacrifices (1 Sam
15.22; Ps 51.16–19; Prov 15.8; 21.3; Hos
6.6: Am 5.21–24; Mt 23.23). Sirach strikes
out against abuses and against *offerings of the
ungodly* (v. 22).

nor for a multitude of sacrifices
    does he forgive sins.
24 Like one who kills a son before
    his father's eyes
  is the person who offers a
    sacrifice from the property
    of the poor.
25 The bread of the needy is the life
    of the poor;
  whoever deprives them of it is a
    murderer.
26 To take away a neighbor's living
    is to commit murder;
27   to deprive an employee of
    wages is to shed blood.

28 When one builds and another tears
    down,
  what do they gain but hard
    work?
29 When one prays and another
    curses,
  to whose voice will the Lord
    listen?
30 If one washes after touching a
    corpse, and touches it
    again,
  what has been gained by
    washing?
31 So if one fasts for his sins,
  and goes again and does the
    same things,
  who will listen to his prayer?
  And what has he gained by
    humbling himself?

35 The one who keeps the law
    makes many offerings;
2   one who heeds the commandments
    makes an offering of
    well-being.
3 The one who returns a kindness
  offers choice flour,

4 and one who gives alms
    sacrifices a thank offering.
5 To keep from wickedness is
    pleasing to the Lord,
  and to forsake unrighteousness
    is an atonement.
6 Do not appear before the Lord
    empty-handed,
7 for all that you offer is in
    fulfillment of the
    commandment.
8 The offering of the righteous
    enriches the altar,
  and its pleasing odor rises before
    the Most High.
9 The sacrifice of the righteous is
    acceptable,
  and it will never be forgotten.
10 Be generous when you worship
    the Lord,
  and do not stint the first fruits
    of your hands.
11 With every gift show a cheerful
    face,
  and dedicate your tithe with
    gladness.
12 Give to the Most High as he has
    given to you,
  and as generously as you can
    afford.
13 For the Lord is the one who
    repays,
  and he will repay you sevenfold.
14 Do not offer him a bribe, for he
    will not accept it;
15 and do not rely on a dishonest
    sacrifice;
  for the Lord is the judge,
  and with him there is no
    partiality.
16 He will not show partiality to the
    poor,
  but he will listen to the prayer
    of one who is wronged.

34.28: *One builds,* i.e. the poor person victimized by the rich man, who *tears down;* both of them lose. **29**: The rich man *prays* hypocritically, and the poor *curses* him, but it is clear that the Lord will listen to the *voice* of the poor (35.20–21). **30–31**: The futility of purificatory acts by an unrepentant sinner.
35.1–13: Acceptable sacrifices (Isa 1.11–

18; Mic 6.6–8; Mk 12.33). **1–2**: Keeping the law (especially almsgiving) is equivalent to *many offerings.*
35.6–13: The spirit with which one should offer sacrifices.
35.14–26: A warning against exploitation of the poor. 14: *Dishonest sacrifice,* i.e. one made possible by injustice (34.21). *No*

17 He will not ignore the supplication
of the orphan,
or the widow when she pours
out her complaint.

18 Do not the tears of the widow run
down her cheek

19 as she cries out against the one
who causes them to fall?

20 The one whose service is pleasing
to the Lord will be
accepted,
and his prayer will reach to the
clouds.

21 The prayer of the humble pierces
the clouds,
and it will not rest until it
reaches its goal;
it will not desist until the Most
High responds

22 and does justice for the
righteous, and executes
judgment.
Indeed, the Lord will not delay,
and like a warrior[u] will not be
patient
until he crushes the loins of the
unmerciful

23 and repays vengeance on the
nations;
until he destroys the multitude of
the insolent,
and breaks the scepters of the
unrighteous;

24 until he repays mortals according
to their deeds,
and the works of all according
to their thoughts;

25 until he judges the case of his
people
and makes them rejoice in his
mercy.

26 His mercy is as welcome in time
of distress

as clouds of rain in time of
drought.

36 Have mercy upon us, O God[v]
of all,

2 and put all the nations in fear of
you.

3 Lift up your hand against foreign
nations
and let them see your might.

4 As you have used us to show your
holiness to them,
so use them to show your glory
to us.

5 Then they will know,[w] as we have
known
that there is no God but you,
O Lord.

6 Give new signs, and work other
wonders;

7 make your hand and right arm
glorious.

8 Rouse your anger and pour out
your wrath;

9 destroy the adversary and wipe
out the enemy.

10 Hasten the day, and remember the
appointed time,[x]
and let people recount your
mighty deeds.

11 Let survivors be consumed in the
fiery wrath,
and may those who harm your
people meet destruction.

12 Crush the heads of hostile rulers
who say, "There is no one but
ourselves."

u Heb: Gk *and with them*   *v* Heb: Gk *O Master,*
the God   *w* Heb: Gk *And let them know*
you   *x* Other ancient authorities read *remember*
your oath

---

partiality, Deut 10.17; Job 34.19; Wis 6.7; Acts
10.34; Gal 2.6. **17–18:** The orphan and the
widow in particular need help since there is
no one to plead their cause (except God).

35.22–26: This serves as an introduction
to the prayer in 36.1–19; Sirach has in mind
the oppression of the chosen people by pagan
oppressors.

36.1–22: A prayer for the deliverance

and restoration of Israel. 1: *God of all,* not
just of Israel. **2:** *All the nations,* the Seleucids
in particular are meant; they had power over
Palestine after 198 B.C. **4:** As God showed his
holiness by punishing Israel (Ezek 20.41;
28.25), so now he shows his *glory* by punishing the Gentiles. **10:** *The appointed time,* the
coming of the Messianic era.

¹³ Gather all the tribes of Jacob, *y*
¹⁶   and give them their inheritance,
        as at the beginning.
¹⁷ Have mercy, O Lord, on the
        people called by your
        name,
    on Israel, whom you have
        named *z* your firstborn,
¹⁸ Have pity on the city of your
        sanctuary, *a*
    Jerusalem, the place of your
        dwelling. *b*
¹⁹ Fill Zion with your majesty, *c*
    and your temple *d* with your
        glory.
²⁰ Bear witness to those whom you
        created in the beginning,
    and fulfill the prophecies spoken
        in your name.
²¹ Reward those who wait for you
    and let your prophets be found
        trustworthy.
²² Hear, O Lord, the prayer of your
        servants, according to your
        goodwill toward *e* your
        people,
    and all who are on the earth will
        know
    that you are the Lord, the God
        of the ages.

²³ The stomach will take any food,
    yet one food is better than
        another.
²⁴ As the palate tastes the kinds of
        game,
    so an intelligent mind detects
        false words.
²⁵ A perverse mind will cause grief,
    but a person with experience
        will pay him back.
²⁶ A woman will accept any man as
        a husband,
    but one girl is preferable to
        another.

²⁷ A woman's beauty lights up a
        man's face,
    and there is nothing he desires
        more.
²⁸ If kindness and humility mark her
        speech,
    her husband is more fortunate
        than other men.
²⁹ He who acquires a wife gets his
        best possession, *f*
    a helper fit for him and a pillar
        of support. *g*
³⁰ Where there is no fence, the
        property will be plundered;
    and where there is no wife, a
        man will become a fugitive
        and a wanderer. *h*
³¹ For who will trust a nimble
        robber
    that skips from city to city?
    So who will trust a man that has
        no nest,
    but lodges wherever night
        overtakes him?

37 Every friend says, "I too am a
        friend";
    but some friends are friends
        only in name.
² Is it not a sorrow like that for
        death itself
    when a dear friend turns into an
        enemy?
³ O inclination to evil, why were
        you formed

y Owing to a dislocation in the Greek Mss of
Sirach, the verse numbers 14 and 15 are not
used in chapter 36, though no text is missing.
z Other ancient authorities read *you have
likened to*   *a* Or *on your holy city*   *b* Heb:
Gk *your rest*   *c* Heb Syr: Gk *the celebration of
your wondrous deeds*   *d* Heb Syr: Gk Lat *people*
e Heb and two Gk witnesses: Lat and most Gk
witnesses read *according to the blessing of Aaron for*
f Heb: Gk *enters upon a possession*   *g* Heb: Gk
rest   *h* Heb: Gk *wander about and sigh*

36.23–31: Concerning discrimination
(vv. 23–25, in general; vv. 26–31, in choosing a wife). **26:** *Will accept,* because the marriage was arranged by her father (see 7.25).
29: *A helper fit for him,* Gen 2.18.
37.1–6: False friends (6.7–13). **3:** *Inclination to evil,* the evil "yeṣer" (see 15.14 n.). **4:**

Happiness, arising from feasting (see v. 5).
37.7–15: Concerning counselors. 14:
Sentinels, probably astrologers.
37.16–26: True and false wisdom.
37.27–31: Temperance (see 31.12–
32.13).

to cover the land with deceit?

4 Some companions rejoice in the
    happiness of a friend,
  but in time of trouble they are
    against him.
5 Some companions help a friend
    for their stomachs' sake,
  yet in battle they will carry his
    shield.
6 Do not forget a friend during the
    battle,ⁱ
  and do not be unmindful of him
    when you distribute your
    spoils.^j

7 All counselors praise the counsel
    they give,
  but some give counsel in their
    own interest.
8 Be wary of a counselor,
  and learn first what is his interest,
  for he will take thought for
    himself.
  He may cast the lot against you
9 and tell you, "Your way is
    good,"
  and then stand aside to see what
    happens to you.
10 Do not consult the one who
    regards you with suspicion;
  hide your intentions from those
    who are jealous of you.
11 Do not consult with a woman
    about her rival
  or with a coward about war,
  with a merchant about business
  or with a buyer about selling,
  with a miser about generosity^k
  or with the merciless about
    kindness,
  with an idler about any work
  or with a seasonal laborer about
    completing his work,
  with a lazy servant about a big
    task—
  pay no attention to any advice
    they give.
12 But associate with a godly person
  whom you know to be a keeper
    of the commandments,
  who is like-minded with yourself,
  and who will grieve with you if
    you fail.

13 And heed^l the counsel of your
    own heart,
  for no one is more faithful to
    you than it is.
14 For our own mind sometimes
    keeps us better informed
  than seven sentinels sitting high
    on a watchtower.
15 But above all pray to the Most
    High
  that he may direct your way in
    truth.

16 Discussion is the beginning of
    every work,
  and counsel precedes every
    undertaking.
17 The mind is the root of all
    conduct;
18   it sprouts four branches,^m
  good and evil, life and death;
  and it is the tongue that
    continually rules them.
19 Some people may be clever
    enough to teach many,
  and yet be useless to themselves.
20 A skillful speaker may be hated;
  he will be destitute of all food,
21 for the Lord has withheld the gift
    of charm,
  since he is lacking in all
    wisdom.
22 If a person is wise to his own
    advantage,
  the fruits of his good sense will
    be praiseworthy.ⁿ
23 A wise person instructs his own
    people,
  and the fruits of his good sense
    will endure.
24 A wise person will have praise
    heaped upon him,
  and all who see him will call
    him happy.
25 The days of a person's life are
    numbered,
  but the days of Israel are
    without number.

i Heb: Gk *in your heart*   *j* Heb: Gk *him in
your wealth*   *k* Heb: Gk *gratitude*   *l* Heb: Gk
establish   *m* Heb: Gk *As a clue to changes of
heart four kinds of destiny appear*   *n* Other
ancient witnesses read *trustworthy*

26 One who is wise among his
people will inherit honor, [o]
and his name will live forever.

27 My child, test yourself while you
live;
see what is bad for you and do
not give in to it.

28 For not everything is good for
everyone,
and no one enjoys everything.

29 Do not be greedy for every
delicacy,
and do not eat without restraint;

30 for overeating brings sickness,
and gluttony leads to nausea.

31 Many have died of gluttony,
but the one who guards against
it prolongs his life.

38 Honor physicians for their
services,
for the Lord created them;

2 for their gift of healing comes
from the Most High,
and they are rewarded by the
king.

3 The skill of physicians makes
them distinguished,
and in the presence of the great
they are admired.

4 The Lord created medicines out of
the earth,
and the sensible will not despise
them.

5 Was not water made sweet with a
tree
in order that its[p] power might
be known?

6 And he gave skill to human beings
that he[q] might be glorified in
his marvelous works.

7 By them the physician[r] heals and
takes away pain;

8 the pharmacist makes a mixture
from them.
God's[s] works will never be
finished;

and from him health[t] spreads
over all the earth.

9 My child, when you are ill, do
not delay,
but pray to the Lord, and he
will heal you.

10 Give up your faults and direct
your hands rightly,
and cleanse your heart from all
sin.

11 Offer a sweet-smelling sacrifice,
and a memorial portion of
choice flour,
and pour oil on your offering,
as much as you can
afford.[u]

12 Then give the physician his place,
for the Lord created him;
do not let him leave you, for
you need him.

13 There may come a time when
recovery lies in the hands of
physicians,[v]

14 for they too pray to the Lord
that he grant them success in
diagnosis[w]
and in healing, for the sake of
preserving life.

15 He who sins against his Maker,
will be defiant toward the
physician.[x]

16 My child, let your tears fall for
the dead,
and as one in great pain begin
the lament.
Lay out the body with due
ceremony,
and do not neglect the burial.

17 Let your weeping be bitter and
your wailing fervent;

o Other ancient authorities read *confidence*
p Or *his*   q Or *they*   r Heb: Gk *he*
s Gk *His*   t Or *peace*   u Heb: Lat lacks *as
much as you can afford*; Meaning of Gk uncertain
v Gk *in their hands*   w Heb: Gk *rest*
x Heb: Gk *may he fall into the hands of the
physician*

38.1–15: Concerning physicians. Their
work is a continuation of God's creative work
(v. 8).

38.16–23: On mourning for the dead
(22.11–12).

make your mourning worthy of
the departed,
for one day, or two, to avoid
criticism;
then be comforted for your
grief.
18 For grief may result in death,
and a sorrowful heart saps one's
strength.
19 When a person is taken away,
sorrow is over;
but the life of the poor weighs
down the heart.
20 Do not give your heart to grief;
drive it away, and remember
your own end.
21 Do not forget, there is no coming
back;
you do the dead[y] no good, and
you injure yourself.
22 Remember his[z] fate, for yours is
like it;
yesterday it was his,[a] and today
it is yours.
23 When the dead is at rest, let his
remembrance rest too,
and be comforted for him when
his spirit has departed.

24 The wisdom of the scribe depends
on the opportunity of
leisure;
only the one who has little
business can become wise.
25 How can one become wise who
handles the plow,
and who glories in the shaft of a
goad,
who drives oxen and is occupied
with their work,
and whose talk is about bulls?
26 He sets his heart on plowing
furrows,
and he is careful about fodder
for the heifers.

27 So too is every artisan and master
artisan
who labors by night as well as
by day;
those who cut the signets of seals,
each is diligent in making a
great variety;
they set their heart on painting a
lifelike image,
and they are careful to finish
their work.
28 So too is the smith, sitting by the
anvil,
intent on his iron-work;
the breath of the fire melts his
flesh,
and he struggles with the heat
of the furnace;
the sound of the hammer deafens
his ears,[b]
and his eyes are on the pattern
of the object.
He sets his heart on finishing his
handiwork,
and he is careful to complete its
decoration.
29 So too is the potter sitting at his
work
and turning the wheel with his
feet;
he is always deeply concerned
over his products,
and he produces them in
quantity.
30 He moulds the clay with his arm
and makes it pliable with his
feet;
he sets his heart to finish the
glazing,
and he takes care in firing[c] the
kiln.

y Gk *him*   *z* Heb: Gk *my*   *a* Heb: Gk
mine   *b* Cn: Gk *renews his ear*   *c* Cn: Gk
cleaning

38.24–39.11: Various craftsmen contrasted with the scribe, a student of divine
wisdom. Sirach shows high regard for the
farmer and seal-maker, the *smith* and the *potter,* and he describes their work with enthusi-
asm. But the highest vocation is that of the
scribe (v. 24) who is concerned with the *law,*
wisdom (i.e. the Writings), and *prophecies;* this
reflects the threefold division of the Hebrew
Bible (39.1–3; see also the prologue by his
grandson).

31 All these rely on their hands,
    and all are skillful in their own
        work.
32 Without them no city can be
        inhabited,
    and wherever they live, they
        will not go hungry. *d*
    Yet they are not sought out for
        the council of the people, *e*
33   nor do they attain eminence in
        the public assembly.
    They do not sit in the judge's seat,
        nor do they understand the
        decisions of the courts;
    they cannot expound discipline or
        judgment,
    and they are not found among
        the rulers. *f*
34 But they maintain the fabric of the
        world,
    and their concern is for *g* the
        exercise of their trade.

How different the one who
        devotes himself
    to the study of the law of the
        Most High!

39 He seeks out the wisdom of all
        the ancients,
    and is concerned with
        prophecies;
2 he preserves the sayings of the
        famous
    and penetrates the subtleties of
        parables;
3 he seeks out the hidden meanings
        of proverbs
    and is at home with the
        obscurities of parables.
4 He serves among the great
    and appears before rulers;
    he travels in foreign lands
    and learns what is good and evil
        in the human lot.
5 He sets his heart to rise early
    to seek the Lord who made
        him,
    and to petition the Most High;

he opens his mouth in prayer
    and asks pardon for his sins.

6 If the great Lord is willing,
    he will be filled with the spirit
        of understanding;
    he will pour forth words of
        wisdom of his own
    and give thanks to the Lord in
        prayer.
7 The Lord *h* will direct his counsel
        and knowledge,
    as he meditates on his mysteries.
8 He will show the wisdom of what
        he has learned,
    and will glory in the law of the
        Lord's covenant.
9 Many will praise his
        understanding;
    it will never be blotted out.
    His memory will not disappear,
    and his name will live through
        all generations.
10 Nations will speak of his wisdom,
    and the congregation will
        proclaim his praise.
11 If he lives long, he will leave a
        name greater than a
        thousand,
    and if he goes to rest, it is
        enough *i* for him.

12 I have more on my mind to
        express;
    I am full like the full moon.
13 Listen to me, my faithful children,
        and blossom
    like a rose growing by a stream
        of water.
14 Send out fragrance like incense,
    and put forth blossoms like a
        lily.

d Syr: Gk *and people can neither live nor walk there*
e Most ancient authorities lack this line
f Cn: Gk *among parables*   g Syr: Gk *prayer is in*
h Gk *He himself*   i Cn: Meaning of Gk
uncertain

39.12–35: A hymn of praise about the
goodness and purposefulness of creation (see
vv. 16, 21, 33–35). Both *good* and *bad* things
are used by God for the divine purpose
(vv. 25–31). See 33.7–15.

Scatter the fragrance, and sing a
   hymn of praise;
 bless the Lord for all his works.
15 Ascribe majesty to his name
   and give thanks to him with
      praise,
 with songs on your lips, and with
      harps;
   this is what you shall say in
      thanksgiving:

16 "All the works of the Lord are
      very good,
   and whatever he commands will
      be done at the appointed
      time.
17 No one can say, 'What is this?' or
   'Why is that?'—
   for at the appointed time all
      such questions will be
      answered.
 At his word the waters stood in a
      heap,
   and the reservoirs of water at
      the word of his mouth.
18 When he commands, his every
      purpose is fulfilled,
   and none can limit his saving
      power.
19 The works of all are before him,
   and nothing can be hidden from
      his eyes.
20 From the beginning to the end of
      time he can see everything,
   and nothing is too marvelous
      for him.
21 No one can say, 'What is this?' or
   'Why is that?'—
   for everything has been created
      for its own purpose.

22 "His blessing covers the dry land
      like a river,
   and drenches it like a flood.
23 But his wrath drives out the
      nations,
   as when he turned a watered
      land into salt.
24 To the faithful his ways are
      straight,
   but full of pitfalls for the
      wicked.

25 From the beginning good things
      were created for the good,
   but for sinners good things and
      bad.*j*
26 The basic necessities of human life
      are water and fire and iron and
      salt
 and wheat flour and milk and
      honey,
   the blood of the grape and oil
      and clothing.
27 All these are good for the godly,
   but for sinners they turn into
      evils.

28 "There are winds created for
      vengeance,
   and in their anger they can
      dislodge mountains;*k*
 on the day of reckoning they will
      pour out their strength
   and calm the anger of their
      Maker.
29 Fire and hail and famine and
      pestilence,
   all these have been created for
      vengeance;
30 the fangs of wild animals and
      scorpions and vipers,
   and the sword that punishes the
      ungodly with destruction.
31 They take delight in doing his
      bidding,
   always ready for his service on
      earth;
 and when their time comes they
      never disobey his
      command."

32 So from the beginning I have been
      convinced of all this
   and have thought it out and left
      it in writing:
33 All the works of the Lord are
      good,
   and he will supply every need in
      its time.
34 No one can say, "This is not as
      good as that,"

j Heb Lat: Gk *sinners bad things*   *k* Heb Syr:
Gk *can scourge mightily*

for everything proves good in
  its appointed time.
35 So now sing praise with all your
    heart and voice,
  and bless the name of the Lord.

40 Hard work was created for
      everyone,
  and a heavy yoke is laid on the
    children of Adam,
  from the day they come forth
      from their mother's womb
  until the day they return to *l* the
    mother of all the living. *m*
2 Perplexities and fear of heart are
    theirs,
  and anxious thought of the day
    of their death.
3 From the one who sits on a
    splendid throne
  to the one who grovels in dust
    and ashes,
4 from the one who wears purple
    and a crown
  to the one who is clothed in
    burlap,
5 there is anger and envy and
    trouble and unrest,
  and fear of death, and fury and
    strife.
  And when one rests upon his bed,
  his sleep at night confuses his
    mind.
6 He gets little or no rest;
  he struggles in his sleep as he
    did by day. *n*
  He is troubled by the visions of
    his mind
  like one who has escaped from
    the battlefield.
7 At the moment he reaches safety
    he wakes up,
  astonished that his fears were
    groundless.
8 To all creatures, human and
    animal,
  but to sinners seven times more,

9 come death and bloodshed and
    strife and sword,
  calamities and famine and ruin
    and plague.
10 All these were created for the
    wicked,
  and on their account the flood
    came.
11 All that is of earth returns to
    earth,
  and what is from above returns
    above. *o*
12 All bribery and injustice will be
    blotted out,
  but good faith will last forever.
13 The wealth of the unjust will dry
    up like a river,
  and crash like a loud clap of
    thunder in a storm.
14 As a generous person has cause to
    rejoice,
  so law-breakers will utterly fail.
15 The children of the ungodly put
    out few branches;
  they are unhealthy roots on
    sheer rock.
16 The reeds by any water or river
    bank
  are plucked up before any grass;
17 but kindness is like a garden of
    blessings,
  and almsgiving endures forever.

18 Wealth and wages make life
    sweet, *p*
  but better than either is finding
    a treasure.
19 Children and the building of a city
    establish one's name,
  but better than either is the one
    who finds wisdom.

l Other Gk and Lat authorities read *are
buried in*   *m* Heb: Gk *of all*   *n* Arm: Meaning
of Gk uncertain   *o* Heb Syr: Gk Lat *from the
waters returns to the sea*   *p* Heb: Gk *Life is sweet
for the self-reliant worker*

**40.1–41.13: Reflections on the human
condition,** its miseries (40.1–17; 40.28–
41.13) and its joys (40.18–27). **40.10:** A typical
expression of the traditional view of retribution (39.29–31).

40.11: *What is from above,* the life-breath of
God (Gen 2.7; Eccl 12.7). **27:** The climax of
the ten "better"-sayings is *fear of the Lord* (see
1.11–30).

Cattle and orchards make one
prosperous;*q*
but a blameless wife is
accounted better than
either.

20 Wine and music gladden the heart,
but the love of friends*r* is better
than either.

21 The flute and the harp make sweet
melody,
but a pleasant voice is better
than either.

22 The eye desires grace and beauty,
but the green shoots of grain
more than either.

23 A friend or companion is always
welcome,
but a sensible wife*s* is better
than either.

24 Kindred and helpers are for a time
of trouble,
but almsgiving rescues better
than either.

25 Gold and silver make one stand
firm,
but good counsel is esteemed
more than either.

26 Riches and strength build up
confidence,
but the fear of the Lord is better
than either.
There is no want in the fear of the
Lord,
and with it there is no need to
seek for help.

27 The fear of the Lord is like a
garden of blessing,
and covers a person better than
any glory.

28 My child, do not lead the life of a
beggar;
it is better to die than to beg.

29 When one looks to the table of
another,
one's way of life cannot be
considered a life.

One loses self-respect with another
person's food,
but one who is intelligent and
well instructed guards
against that.

30 In the mouth of the shameless
begging is sweet,
but it kindles a fire inside him.

41 O death, how bitter is the
thought of you
to the one at peace among
possessions,
who has nothing to worry about
and is prosperous in
everything,
and still is vigorous enough to
enjoy food!

2 O death, how welcome is your
sentence
to one who is needy and failing
in strength,
worn down by age and anxious
about everything;
to one who is contrary, and has
lost all patience!

3 Do not fear death's decree for you;
remember those who went
before you and those who
will come after.

4 This is the Lord's decree for all
flesh;
why then should you reject the
will of the Most High?
Whether life lasts for ten years or
a hundred or a thousand,
there are no questions asked in
Hades.

5 The children of sinners are
abominable children,
and they frequent the haunts of
the ungodly.

q Heb Syr: Gk lacks *but better . . . prosperous*
r Heb: Gk *wisdom*   s Heb Compare Syr: Gk
wife with her husband

41.3–4: Resignation to death is characteristic of Old Testament thought (see 14.11–19; 17.25–28; 38.16–23). **5–13:** A contrast between the fate of the virtuous and the wicked.

Verses 8–10 show that Sirach has in mind those who abandon the Law for another, perhaps Greek, way of life.

6 The inheritance of the children of
sinners will perish,
and on their offspring will be a
perpetual disgrace.
7 Children will blame an ungodly
father,
for they suffer disgrace because
of him.
8 Woe to you, the ungodly,
who have forsaken the law of
the Most High God!
9 If you have children, calamity will
be theirs;
you will beget them only for
groaning.
When you stumble, there is lasting
joy;*
and when you die, a curse is
your lot.
10 Whatever comes from earth
returns to earth;
so the ungodly go from curse to
destruction.

11 The human body is a fleeting
thing,
but a virtuous name will never
be blotted out.*
12 Have regard for your name, since
it will outlive you
longer than a thousand hoards
of gold.
13 The days of a good life are
numbered,
but a good name lasts forever.

14 My children, be true to your
training and be at peace;
hidden wisdom and unseen
treasure—
of what value is either?
15 Better are those who hide their
folly
than those who hide their
wisdom.
16 Therefore show respect for my
words;

for it is not good to feel shame in
every circumstance,
nor is every kind of abashment
to be approved.*

17 Be ashamed of sexual immorality,
before your father or
mother;
and of a lie, before a prince or a
ruler;
18 of a crime, before a judge or
magistrate;
and of a breach of the law,
before the congregation and
the people;
of unjust dealing, before your
partner or your friend;
19 and of theft, in the place where
you live.
Be ashamed of breaking an oath or
agreement,*
and of leaning on your elbow at
meals;
of surliness in receiving or giving,
20 and of silence, before those who
greet you;
of looking at a prostitute,
21 and of rejecting the appeal of a
relative;
of taking away someone's portion
or gift,
and of gazing at another man's
wife;
22 of meddling with his servant
girl—
and do not approach her bed;
of abusive words, before friends—
and do not be insulting after
making a gift.

42 Be ashamed of repeating what
you hear,

---

t Heb: Meaning of Gk uncertain   *u* Heb: Gk
*People grieve over the death of the body, but the bad
name of sinners will be blotted out*   *v* Heb: Gk *and
not everything is confidently esteemed by everyone*
w Heb: Gk *before the truth of God and the covenant*

41.14–42.8: A poem on true shame
(41.16–42.1) **and false shame** (42.2–8).
**42.9–14: A father's concern for his
daughter** (7.24–25; 25.13–26.18).

**42.15–43.33: In praise of God, the om-
nipotent and omniscient Creator. 42.15:**
The *works of the Lord* in creation are meant.

and of betraying secrets.
Then you will show proper shame,
and will find favor with
everyone.

Of the following things do not be
ashamed,
and do not sin to save face:

2 Do not be ashamed of the law of
the Most High and his
covenant,
and of rendering judgment to
acquit the ungodly;

3 of keeping accounts with a partner
or with traveling
companions,
and of dividing the inheritance
of friends;

4 of accuracy with scales and
weights,
and of acquiring much or little;

5 of profit from dealing with
merchants,
and of frequent disciplining of
children,
and of drawing blood from the
back of a wicked slave.

6 Where there is an untrustworthy
wife, a seal is a good thing;
and where there are many
hands, lock things up.

7 When you make a deposit, be sure
it is counted and weighed,
and when you give or receive,
put it all in writing.

8 Do not be ashamed to correct the
stupid or foolish
or the aged who are guilty of
sexual immorality.
Then you will show your sound
training,
and will be approved by all.

9 A daughter is a secret anxiety to
her father,
and worry over her robs him of
sleep;
when she is young, for fear she
may not marry,
or if married, for fear she may
be disliked;

10 while a virgin, for fear she may be
seduced
and become pregnant in her
father's house;
or having a husband, for fear she
may go astray,
or, though married, for fear she
may be barren.

11 Keep strict watch over a
headstrong daughter,
or she may make you a
laughingstock to your
enemies,
a byword in the city and the
assembly of[x] the people,
and put you to shame in public
gatherings.[y]
See that there is no lattice in her
room,
no spot that overlooks the
approaches to the house.[z]

12 Do not let her parade her beauty
before any man,
or spend her time among
married women;[a]

13 for from garments comes the moth,
and from a woman comes
woman's wickedness.

14 Better is the wickedness of a man
than a woman who does
good;
it is woman who brings shame
and disgrace.

15 I will now call to mind the works
of the Lord,
and will declare what I have
seen.
By the word of the Lord his
works are made;
and all his creatures do his
will.[b]

16 The sun looks down on
everything with its light,
and the work of the Lord is full
of his glory.

x Heb: Meaning of Gk uncertain   *y* Heb: Gk
to shame before the great multitude   *z* Heb: Gk
lacks *See . . . house*   *a* Heb: Meaning of Gk
uncertain   *b* Syr Compare Heb: most Gk
witnesses lack *and all . . . will*

17 The Lord has not empowered
even his holy ones
to recount all his marvelous
works,
which the Lord the Almighty has
established
so that the universe may stand
firm in his glory.
18 He searches out the abyss and the
human heart;
he understands their innermost
secrets.
For the Most High knows all that
may be known;
he sees from of old the things
that are to come. *c*
19 He discloses what has been and
what is to be,
and he reveals the traces of
hidden things.
20 No thought escapes him,
and nothing is hidden from
him.
21 He has set in order the splendors
of his wisdom;
he is from all eternity one and
the same.
Nothing can be added or taken
away,
and he needs no one to be his
counselor.
22 How desirable are all his works,
and how sparkling they are to
see! *d*
23 All these things live and remain
forever;
each creature is preserved to
meet a particular need. *e*
24 All things come in pairs, one
opposite the other,
and he has made nothing
incomplete.
25 Each supplements the virtues of
the other.
Who could ever tire of seeing
his glory?

43 The pride of the higher realms
is the clear vault of the sky,
as glorious to behold as the
sight of the heavens.
2 The sun, when it appears,
proclaims as it rises
what a marvelous instrument it
is, the work of the Most
High.
3 At noon it parches the land,
and who can withstand its
burning heat?
4 A man tending *f* a furnace works
in burning heat,
but three times as hot is the sun
scorching the mountains;
it breathes out fiery vapors,
and its bright rays blind the
eyes.
5 Great is the Lord who made it;
at his orders it hurries on its
course.
6 It is the moon that marks the
changing seasons, *g*
governing the times, their
everlasting sign.
7 From the moon comes the sign for
festal days,
a light that wanes when it
completes its course.
8 The new moon, as its name
suggests, renews itself; *h*
how marvelous it is in this
change,
a beacon to the hosts on high,
shining in the vault of the
heavens!
9 The glory of the stars is the
beauty of heaven,

c Heb: Gk *he sees the sign(s) of the age*   *d* Meaning
of Gk uncertain   *e* Heb: Gk *forever for every need,
and all are obedient*   *f* Other ancient authorities
read *blowing upon g* Heb: Meaning of Gk
uncertain   *h* Heb: Gk *The month is named after
the moon*

42.17: *Holy ones,* the members of the heavenly court, or angels, as in Job 5.1; 15.15; Ps 89.8. Even the angels are unable adequately to declare God's *marvelous works.*
42.18–21: The divine omniscience extends to the *abyss* and its chaotic forces, and to the human heart (see Prov 15.11), to past and future (v. 19), because God is *everlasting* (v. 21). **22–25:** The beauty and splendor of his *works* are increased by their purposefulness (v. 23), and their polarity (v. 24; see 33.15).

a glittering array in the heights
of the Lord.

10 On the orders of the Holy One
they stand in their
appointed places;
they never relax in their
watches.

11 Look at the rainbow, and praise
him who made it;
it is exceedingly beautiful in its
brightness.

12 It encircles the sky with its
glorious arc;
the hands of the Most High
have stretched it out.

13 By his command he sends the
driving snow
and speeds the lightnings of his
judgment.

14 Therefore the storehouses are
opened,
and the clouds fly out like birds.

15 In his majesty he gives the clouds
their strength,
and the hailstones are broken in
pieces.

17a The voice of his thunder rebukes
the earth;

16 when he appears, the mountains
shake.
At his will the south wind blows;

17b so do the storm from the north
and the whirlwind.
He scatters the snow like birds
flying down,
and its descent is like locusts
alighting.

18 The eye is dazzled by the beauty
of its whiteness,
and the mind is amazed as it
falls.

19 He pours frost over the earth like
salt,
and icicles form like pointed
thorns.

20 The cold north wind blows,
and ice freezes on the water;
it settles on every pool of water,
and the water puts it on like a
breastplate.

21 He consumes the mountains and
burns up the wilderness,
and withers the tender grass like
fire.

22 A mist quickly heals all things;
the falling dew gives
refreshment from the heat.

23 By his plan he stilled the deep
and planted islands in it.

24 Those who sail the sea tell of its
dangers,
and we marvel at what we hear.

25 In it are strange and marvelous
creatures,
all kinds of living things, and
huge sea-monsters.

26 Because of him each of his
messengers succeeds,
and by his word all things hold
together.

27 We could say more but could
never say enough;
let the final word be: "He is the
all."

28 Where can we find the strength to
praise him?
For he is greater than all his
works.

29 Awesome is the Lord and very
great,
and marvelous is his power.

30 Glorify the Lord and exalt him as
much as you can,
for he surpasses even that.
When you exalt him, summon all
your strength,
and do not grow weary, for you
cannot praise him enough.

43.1–12: The splendor of heavenly phenomena: *sky, sun, moon* (the Jews followed
a lunar calendar), *stars,* and *rainbow.*
43.13–26: A list of various things in nature
that fulfill the divine will. **23–25:** The *deep*
or *sea* occurs frequently in the Bible as the
personified power of chaos with which Rahab
or Leviathan are associated (Ps 104.24–26).
27: *He is the all,* in the sense that all creatures
reveal the divine presence.

31 Who has seen him and can
describe him?
Or who can extol him as he is?
32 Many things greater than these lie
hidden,
for I[i] have seen but few of his
works.
33 For the Lord has made all things,
and to the godly he has given
wisdom.

HYMN IN HONOR OF OUR ANCESTORS[j]

44 Let us now sing the praises of
famous men,
our ancestors in their
generations.
2 The Lord apportioned to them[k]
great glory,
his majesty from the beginning.
3 There were those who ruled in
their kingdoms,
and made a name for themselves
by their valor;
those who gave counsel because
they were intelligent;
those who spoke in prophetic
oracles;
4 those who led the people by their
counsels
and by their knowledge of the
people's lore;
they were wise in their words of
instruction;
5 those who composed musical
tunes,
or put verses in writing;
6 rich men endowed with resources,
living peacefully in their
homes—
7 all these were honored in their
generations,
and were the pride of their
times.
8 Some of them have left behind a
name,

so that others declare their
praise.
9 But of others there is no memory;
they have perished as though
they had never existed;
they have become as though they
had never been born,
they and their children after
them.
10 But these also were godly men,
whose righteous deeds have not
been forgotten;
11 their wealth will remain with their
descendants,
and their inheritance with their
children's children.[l]
12 Their descendants stand by the
covenants;
their children also, for their
sake.
13 Their offspring will continue
forever,
and their glory will never be
blotted out.
14 Their bodies are buried in peace,
but their name lives on
generation after generation.
15 The assembly declares[m] their
wisdom,
and the congregation proclaims
their praise.

16 Enoch pleased the Lord and was
taken up,
an example of repentance to all
generations.

17 Noah was found perfect and
righteous;
in the time of wrath he kept the
race alive;[n]

i Heb: Gk *we*   j This title is included in the
Gk text.   k Heb: Gk *created*   l Heb Compare
Lat Syr: Meaning of Gk uncertain   m Heb: Gk
Peoples declare   n Heb: Gk *was taken in exchange*

44.1–50.24: In praise of famous men.
Sirach celebrates the covenant with the patriarchs and Israel by commenting on the heroes
of Israel's history.
44.1–15: Introduction. **1:** *Famous men,* Hebrew and Syriac, "men of piety." **3–7:** Sirach

lists twelve classes of heroes who were *the
pride of their times,* and will be exemplified in
the names to follow. **9–10:** Some good people
have left no memorial, but they will not be
forgotten (by God).
44.16–18: Enoch. The popularity of spec-

therefore a remnant was left on
the earth
when the flood came.
18 Everlasting covenants were made
with him
that all flesh should never again
be blotted out by a flood.

19 Abraham was the great father of a
multitude of nations,
and no one has been found like
him in glory.
20 He kept the law of the Most
High,
and entered into a covenant
with him;
he certified the covenant in his
flesh,
and when he was tested he
proved faithful.
21 Therefore the Lord*o* assured him
with an oath
that the nations would be
blessed through his
offspring;
that he would make him as
numerous as the dust of the
earth,
and exalt his offspring like the
stars,
and give them an inheritance from
sea to sea
and from the Euphrates*p* to the
ends of the earth.
22 To Isaac also he gave the same
assurance
for the sake of his father
Abraham.
The blessing of all people and the
covenant
23 he made to rest on the head of
Jacob;
he acknowledged him with his
blessings,

and gave him his inheritance;
he divided his portions,
and distributed them among
twelve tribes.

From his descendants the Lord*o*
brought forth a godly man,
who found favor in the sight of
all

45 1 and was beloved by God and
people,
Moses, whose memory is
blessed.
2 He made him equal in glory to the
holy ones,
and made him great, to the
terror of his enemies.
3 By his words he performed swift
miracles;*q*
the Lord*o* glorified him in the
presence of kings.
He gave him commandments for
his people,
and revealed to him his glory.
4 For his faithfulness and meekness
he consecrated him,
choosing him out of all
humankind.
5 He allowed him to hear his voice,
and led him into the dark cloud,
and gave him the commandments
face to face,
the law of life and knowledge,
so that he might teach Jacob the
covenant,
and Israel his decrees.

6 He exalted Aaron, a holy man like
Moses*r*
who was his brother, of the
tribe of Levi.

o Gk *he*   p Syr: Heb Gk *River*   q Heb: Gk
caused signs to cease   r Gk *him*

ulation about *Enoch* in Sirach's time may be
the reason he heads the list (although the
name is lacking in several ancient witnesses),
and closes it in 49.14. *Noah* deserves early
mention as the second founder of the human
race after the flood.
**44.19–47.11: Others with whom God
has made a covenant:** Abraham, Isaac, Ja-
cob/Israel, Moses, Aaron, Phinehas, and David. The glorification of Aaron reflects the
ascendancy of the high priesthood in Sirach's
day. Much more space is given to him and
Phinehas (and then to Simeon the high priest
in ch 50) than to Moses; note the prayer for
high priests in 45.26.

7 He made an everlasting covenant
   with him,
   and gave him the priesthood of
   the people.
   He blessed him with stateliness,
   and put a glorious robe on him.
8 He clothed him in perfect splendor,
   and strengthened him with the
   symbols of authority,
   the linen undergarments, the
   long robe, and the ephod.
9 And he encircled him with
   pomegranates,
   with many golden bells all
   around,
   to send forth a sound as he walked,
   to make their ringing heard in
   the temple
   as a reminder to his people;
10 with the sacred vestment, of gold
   and violet
   and purple, the work of an
   embroiderer;
   with the oracle of judgment, Urim
   and Thummim;
11 with twisted crimson, the work
   of an artisan;
   with precious stones engraved like
   seals,
   in a setting of gold, the work of
   a jeweler,
   to commemorate in engraved
   letters
   each of the tribes of Israel;
12 with a gold crown upon his
   turban,
   inscribed like a seal with
   "Holiness,"
   a distinction to be prized, the
   work of an expert,
   a delight to the eyes, richly
   adorned.
13 Before him such beautiful things
   did not exist.
   No outsider ever put them on,
   but only his sons
   and his descendants in
   perpetuity.
14 His sacrifices shall be wholly
   burned
   twice every day continually.
15 Moses ordained him,
   and anointed him with holy oil;

it was an everlasting covenant for
   him
   and for his descendants as long
   as the heavens endure,
   to minister to the Lord*s* and serve
   as priest
   and bless his people in his name.
16 He chose him out of all the living
   to offer sacrifice to the Lord,
   incense and a pleasing odor as a
   memorial portion,
   to make atonement for the*t*
   people.
17 In his commandments he gave him
   authority and statutes and*u*
   judgments,
   to teach Jacob the testimonies,
   and to enlighten Israel with his
   law.
18 Outsiders conspired against him,
   and envied him in the
   wilderness,
   Dathan and Abiram and their
   followers
   and the company of Korah, in
   wrath and anger.
19 The Lord saw it and was not
   pleased,
   and in the heat of his anger they
   were destroyed;
   he performed wonders against them
   to consume them in flaming fire.
20 He added glory to Aaron
   and gave him a heritage;
   he allotted to him the best of the
   first fruits,
   and prepared bread of first fruits
   in abundance;
21 for they eat the sacrifices of the
   Lord,
   which he gave to him and his
   descendants.
22 But in the land of the people he
   has no inheritance,
   and he has no portion among
   the people;
   for the Lord*v* himself is his*w*
   portion and inheritance.

s Gk *him*   *t* Other ancient authorities read *his*
or *your*   *u* Heb: Gk *authority in covenants of*
v Gk *he*   *w* Other ancient authorities read
your

23 Phinehas son of Eleazar ranks
    third in glory
  for being zealous in the fear of
    the Lord,
  and standing firm, when the
    people turned away,
    in the noble courage of his soul;
  and he made atonement for
    Israel.
24 Therefore a covenant of friendship
    was established with him,
    that he should be leader of the
    sanctuary and of his people,
  that he and his descendants should
    have
    the dignity of the priesthood
    forever.
25 Just as a covenant was established
    with David
    son of Jesse of the tribe of
    Judah,
  that the king's heritage passes only
    from son to son,
  so the heritage of Aaron is for
    his descendants alone.
26 And now bless the Lord
    who has crowned you with
    glory. *x*
  May the Lord *y* grant you wisdom
    of mind
    to judge his people with
    justice,
  so that their prosperity may not
    vanish,
  and that their glory may endure
    through all their generations.

46 Joshua son of Nun was mighty
    in war,
  and was the successor of Moses
    in the prophetic office.
He became, as his name implies,
    a great savior of God's *z* elect,
  to take vengeance on the enemies
    that rose against them,

  so that he might give Israel
    its inheritance.
2 How glorious he was when he
    lifted his hands
  and brandished his sword
    against the cities!
3 Who before him ever stood so
    firm?
  For he waged the wars of the
    Lord.
4 Was it not through him that the
    sun stood still
  and one day become as long as
    two?
5 He called upon the Most High,
    the Mighty One,
  when enemies pressed him on
    every side,
  and the great Lord answered him
    with hailstones of mighty
    power.
6 He overwhelmed that nation in
    battle,
  and on the slope he destroyed
    his opponents,
  so that the nations might know his
    armament,
    that he was fighting in the sight
    of the Lord;
  for he was a devoted follower of
    the Mighty One.
7 And in the days of Moses he
    proved his loyalty,
  he and Caleb son of Jephunneh:
  they opposed the congregation, *a*
  restrained the people from sin,
  and stilled their wicked
    grumbling.
8 And these two alone were spared
    out of six hundred thousand
    infantry,
  to lead the people *b* into their
    inheritance,

x Heb: Gk lacks *who . . . glory*   *y* Gk *he*
z Gk *his*   *a* Other ancient authorities read
the enemy   *b* Gk *them*

46.1–20: Joshua (vv.1–7), **Caleb** (vv.7–10), **the judges** (vv.11–12), **and Samuel** (vv.13–20). **1:** *His name* means "The Lord is salvation." **2–8:** Josh chs 6–11. **4:** Josh 10.12–14. **6:** Josh 10.11. **7:** Num 14.6–10; 1 Macc 2.55–56. **8:** Num 11.21; 14.38; 26.65. **9:** Josh 14.6–11.

46.12: *Bones send forth new life* (49.10), the meaning is to be interpreted in the light of the last line of the verse. **13:** *Anointed rulers,* 1 Sam 10.1; 16.13. **15:** 1 Sam 3.19–20. **16–18:** 1 Sam 7.9–11. **19:** 1 Sam 12.3. **20:** 1 Sam 28.18–19.

the land flowing with milk and
honey.
9 The Lord gave Caleb strength,
which remained with him in his
old age,
so that he went up to the hill
country,
and his children obtained it for
an inheritance,
10 so that all the Israelites might see
how good it is to follow the
Lord.

11 The judges also, with their
respective names,
whose hearts did not fall into
idolatry
and who did not turn away from
the Lord—
may their memory be blessed!
12 May their bones send forth new
life from where they lie,
and may the names of those
who have been honored
live again in their children!

13 Samuel was beloved by his Lord;
a prophet of the Lord, he
established the kingdom
and anointed rulers over his
people.
14 By the law of the Lord he judged
the congregation,
and the Lord watched over
Jacob.
15 By his faithfulness he was proved
to be a prophet,
and by his words he became
known as a trustworthy
seer.
16 He called upon the Lord, the
Mighty One,
when his enemies pressed him
on every side,
and he offered in sacrifice a
suckling lamb.

17 Then the Lord thundered from
heaven,
and made his voice heard with a
mighty sound;
18 he subdued the leaders of the
enemy[c]
and all the rulers of the
Philistines.
19 Before the time of his eternal
sleep,
Samuel[d] bore witness before the
Lord and his anointed:
"No property, not so much as a
pair of shoes,
have I taken from anyone!"
And no one accused him.
20 Even after he had fallen asleep, he
prophesied
and made known to the king his
death,
and lifted up his voice from the
ground
in prophecy, to blot out the
wickedness of the people.

47 After him Nathan rose up
to prophesy in the days of
David.
2 As the fat is set apart from the
offering of well-being,
so David was set apart from the
Israelites.
3 He played with lions as though
they were young goats,
and with bears as though they
were lambs of the flock.
4 In his youth did he not kill a
giant,
and take away the people's
disgrace,
when he whirled the stone in the
sling
and struck down the boasting
Goliath?
5 For he called on the Lord, the
Most High,

c Heb: Gk *leaders of the people of Tyre*
d Gk *he*

47.1–22: Nathan (v.1), **David** (vv.2–11),
and Solomon (vv.12–22). **1:** 2 Sam 7.2–3;
12.1; 1 Chr 17.1. **2:** *The fat,* the portion reserved for sacrifice (Lev 3.3–5). **3:** 1 Sam 17.34.
4: 1 Sam 17.49–51.

and he gave strength to his right
 arm
to strike down a mighty warrior,
 and to exalt the power*e* of his
 people.
6 So they glorified him for the tens
 of thousands he conquered,
 and praised him for the
 blessings bestowed by the
 Lord,
 when the glorious diadem was
 given to him.
7 For he wiped out his enemies on
 every side,
 and annihilated his adversaries
 the Philistines;
 he crushed their power*e* to our
 own day.
8 In all that he did he gave thanks
 to the Holy One, the Most
 High, proclaiming his
 glory;
 he sang praise with all his heart,
 and he loved his Maker.
9 He placed singers before the altar,
 to make sweet melody with
 their voices.*f*
10 He gave beauty to the festivals,
 and arranged their times
 throughout the year,*g*
 while they praised God's*h* holy
 name,
 and the sanctuary resounded
 from early morning.
11 The Lord took away his sins,
 and exalted his power*e* forever;
 he gave him a covenant of
 kingship
 and a glorious throne in Israel.

12 After him a wise son rose up
 who because of him lived in
 security:*i*
13 Solomon reigned in an age of
 peace,
 because God made all his
 borders tranquil,

so that he might build a house in
 his name
 and provide a sanctuary to stand
 forever.
14 How wise you were when you
 were young!
 You overflowed like the Nile*j*
 with understanding.
15 Your influence spread throughout
 the earth,
 and you filled it with proverbs
 having deep meaning.
16 Your fame reached to far-off
 islands,
 and you were loved for your
 peaceful reign.
17 Your songs, proverbs, and
 parables,
 and the answers you gave
 astounded the nations.
18 In the name of the Lord God,
 who is called the God of Israel,
you gathered gold like tin
 and amassed silver like lead.
19 But you brought in women to lie
 at your side,
 and through your body you
 were brought into
 subjection.
20 You stained your honor,
 and defiled your family line,
so that you brought wrath upon
 your children,
 and they were grieved*k* at your
 folly,
21 because the sovereignty was
 divided
 and a rebel kingdom arose out
 of Ephraim.
22 But the Lord will never give up
 his mercy,
 or cause any of his works to
 perish;

*e Gk horn   f Other ancient authorities add
and daily they sing his praises   g Gk to completion
h Gk his   i Heb: Gk in a broad place   j Heb:
Gk a river   k Other ancient authorities read I
was grieved*

47.6: 1 Sam 18.7. 7: 2 Sam 5.7; 8.1. 9:
1 Chr 16.4. 11: 2 Sam 12.13. 13–17: 1 Kings
4.21–32.

47.14: Compare the address to Elijah in
48.4–11. 18: 1 Kings 10.21, 27. 19: 1 Kings
11.1. 21: 1 Kings 12.15–20. 22: 2 Sam 7.15; Ps

he will never blot out the
   descendants of his chosen
     one,
or destroy the family line of
   him who loved him.
So he gave a remnant to Jacob,
   and to David a root from his
     own family.

23 Solomon rested with his ancestors,
   and left behind him one of his
     sons,
broad in*l* folly and lacking in
     sense,
Rehoboam, whose policy drove
   the people to revolt.
Then Jeroboam son of Nebat led
     Israel into sin
and started Ephraim on its sinful
     ways.
24 Their sins increased more and
     more,
until they were exiled from their
     land.
25 For they sought out every kind of
     wickedness,
until vengeance came upon
     them.

48 Then Elijah arose, a prophet
   like fire,
and his word burned like a
     torch.
2 He brought a famine upon them,
   and by his zeal he made them
     few in number.
3 By the word of the Lord he shut
   up the heavens,
and also three times brought
     down fire.
4 How glorious you were, Elijah, in
   your wondrous deeds!
   Whose glory is equal to yours?

5 You raised a corpse from death
   and from Hades, by the word of
     the Most High.
6 You sent kings down to
     destruction,
and famous men, from their
     sick-beds.
7 You heard rebuke at Sinai
   and judgments of vengeance at
     Horeb.
8 You anointed kings to inflict
     retribution,
and prophets to succeed you.*m*
9 You were taken up by a
   whirlwind of fire,
   in a chariot with horses of fire.
10 At the appointed time, it is
     written, you are destined*n*
to calm the wrath of God before
     it breaks out in fury,
to turn the hearts of parents to
     their children,
and to restore the tribes of
     Jacob.
11 Happy are those who saw you
   and were adorned*o* with your
     love!
   For we also shall surely live.*p*

12 When Elijah was enveloped in the
     whirlwind,
Elisha was filled with his spirit.
He performed twice as many
     signs,
   and marvels with every
     utterance of his mouth.*q*
Never in his lifetime did he
     tremble before any ruler,

---

l Heb (with a play on the name Rehoboam)
Syr: Gk *the people's*   *m* Heb: Gk *him*   *n* Heb:
Gk *are for reproofs*   *o* Other ancient authorities
read *and have died*   *p* Text and meaning of
Gk uncertain   *q* Heb: Gk lacks *He performed . . .
mouth*

89.33. *Or . . . perish,* Hebrew "He will let
none of his words fall to the ground."
47.23–48.14: Kings and prophets. Solomon's son, Rehoboam, and Jeroboam in the
northern kingdom are mentioned briefly, and
the deeds of Elijah and Elisha are described in
detail. **23:** 1 Kings 11.43; 12.10–14; for Jeroboam, 1 Kings 12.28–30. **24:** 2 Kings 17.6,
18.

48.1: 1 Kings 17.1. *Torch,* Hebrew "furnace." **2:** Jas 5.17. **3:** 1 Kings 18.38; 2 Kings
1.10–12. **5:** 1 Kings 17.21–22. **6:** 2 Kings
1.16.
48.7: 1 Kings 19.8. **8:** 1 Kings 19.15–16. **9:**
2 Kings 2.11. **10:** Mal 4.5–6. **12:** 2 Kings 2.9,
13. **13:** 2 Kings 13.20–21. **15:** 2 Kings 18.11–
12.
48.15–49.13: In the kingdom of Judah,

nor could anyone intimidate
him at all.

13 Nothing was too hard for him,
and when he was dead, his body
prophesied.

14 In his life he did wonders,
and in death his deeds were
marvelous.

15 Despite all this the people did not
repent,
nor did they forsake their sins,
until they were carried off as
plunder from their land,
and were scattered over all the
earth.
The people were left very few in
number,
but with a ruler from the house
of David.

16 Some of them did what was right,
but others sinned more and
more.

17 Hezekiah fortified his city,
and brought water into its
midst;
he tunneled the rock with iron
tools,
and built cisterns for the water.

18 In his days Sennacherib invaded
the country;
he sent his commander[r] and
departed;
he shook his fist against Zion,
and made great boasts in his
arrogance.

19 Then their hearts were shaken and
their hands trembled,
and they were in anguish, like
women in labor.

20 But they called upon the Lord
who is merciful,
spreading out their hands
toward him.

The Holy One quickly heard them
from heaven,
and delivered them through
Isaiah.

21 The Lord[s] struck down the camp
of the Assyrians,
and his angel wiped them out.

22 For Hezekiah did what was
pleasing to the Lord,
and he kept firmly to the ways
of his ancestor David,
as he was commanded by the
prophet Isaiah,
who was great and trustworthy
in his visions.

23 In Isaiah's[t] days the sun went
backward,
and he prolonged the life of the
king.

24 By his dauntless spirit he saw the
future,
and comforted the mourners in
Zion.

25 He revealed what was to occur to
the end of time,
and the hidden things before
they happened.

49 The name[u] of Josiah is like
blended incense
prepared by the skill of the
perfumer;
his memory[v] is as sweet as honey
to every mouth,
and like music at a banquet of
wine.

2 He did what was right by
reforming the people,
and removing the wicked
abominations.

r Other ancient authorities add *from Lachish*
s Gk *He*   t Gk *his*   u Heb: Gk *memory*
v Heb: Gk *it*

the heroes are Hezekiah and Isaiah, followed
by Jeremiah, Ezekiel (and Job; see Ezek 14.14),
and the twelve prophets, which probably
constituted a corpus of writings by the time
of Sirach. The heroes of the restoration are
Zerubbabel, Jeshua, and Nehemiah, with
Ezra being notably absent. **48.17**: 2 Kings

20.20. **18**: 2 Kings 18.13, 17; Isa 36.1. *Made
. . . boasts,* Hebrew and Syriac read "blas-
phemed God." **20**: 2 Kings 19.15–20.
48.21: 2 Kings 19.35; Isa 37.36; 1 Macc
7.41. **22**: 2 Kings 18.3. **23**: 2 Kings 20.10–11;
Isa 38.8. **24–25**: Isa 40.1; 42.9.
49.2a: Hebrew, "For he was grieved over

3 He kept his heart fixed on the
    Lord;
  in lawless times he made
    godliness prevail.

4 Except for David and Hezekiah
    and Josiah,
  all of them were great sinners,
  for they abandoned the law of the
    Most High;
  the kings of Judah came to an
    end.
5 They^w gave their power to others,
  and their glory to a foreign
    nation,
6 who set fire to the chosen city of
    the sanctuary,
  and made its streets desolate,
  as Jeremiah had foretold.^{x}
7 For they had mistreated him,
  who even in the womb had
    been consecrated a prophet,
  to pluck up and ruin and destroy,
  and likewise to build and to
    plant.

8 It was Ezekiel who saw the vision
    of glory,
  which God^y showed him above
    the chariot of the cherubim.
9 For God^z also mentioned Job
  who held fast to all the ways of
    justice.^{a}
10 May the bones of the Twelve
    Prophets
  send forth new life from where
    they lie,
  for they comforted the people of
    Jacob
  and delivered them with
    confident hope.

11 How shall we magnify
    Zerubbabel?
  He was like a signet-ring on the
    right hand,
12 and so was Jeshua son of
    Jozadak;

in their days they built the house
  and raised a temple^b holy to the
    Lord,
  destined for everlasting glory.
13 The memory of Nehemiah also is
    lasting;
  he raised our fallen walls,
  and set up gates and bars,
  and rebuilt our ruined houses.

14 Few have^c ever been created on
    earth like Enoch,
  for he was taken up from the
    earth.
15 Nor was anyone ever born like
    Joseph;^{d}
  even his bones were cared for.
16 Shem and Seth and Enosh were
    honored,^{e}
  but above every other created
    living being was Adam.

50 The leader of his brothers and
    the pride of his people^f
  was the high priest, Simon son
    of Onias,
  who in his life repaired the house,
  and in his time fortified the
    temple.
2 He laid the foundations for the
    high double walls,
  the high retaining walls for the
    temple enclosure.
3 In his days a water cistern was
    dug,^{g}
  a reservoir like the sea in
    circumference.
4 He considered how to save his
    people from ruin,

w Heb *He*   x Gk *by the hand of Jeremiah*
y Gk *He*   z Gk *he*   a Heb Compare Syr:
Meaning of Gk uncertain   b Other ancient
authorities read *people*   c Heb Syr: Gk *No one
has*   d Heb Syr: Gk adds *the leader of his
brothers, the support of the people*   e Heb: Gk
Shem and Seth were honored by people
f Heb Syr: Gk lacks this line. Compare 49.15
g Heb: Meaning of Gk uncertain

---

our backslidings" (2 Kings 22.11–13). **3:**
2 Kings 23.3, 25. **5–7:** 2 Chr 36.17–19. *Jeremiah,* Jer 1.5–10; 39.8.
49.8–9: Ezek 1.3–15; 13.11; 38.9, 16, 22.

10: *Bones,* see 46.12 n. **11:** Ezra 3.2; Hag 2.23.
12: Ezra 3.2; Hag 1.12; 2.2; Zech 3.1. **13:** Neh
7.1.
49.14–16: Conclusion. The mention of

and fortified the city against
   siege.
5 How glorious he was, surrounded
   by the people,
   as he came out of the house of
      the curtain.
6 Like the morning star among the
   clouds,
   like the full moon at the festal
      season; *h*
7 like the sun shining on the temple
   of the Most High,
   like the rainbow gleaming in
      splendid clouds;
8 like roses in the days of first
   fruits,
   like lilies by a spring of water,
   like a green shoot on Lebanon
      on a summer day;
9 like fire and incense in the censer,
   like a vessel of hammered gold
   studded with all kinds of
      precious stones;
10 like an olive tree laden with fruit,
   and like a cypress towering in
      the clouds.
11 When he put on his glorious robe
   and clothed himself in perfect
      splendor,
   when he went up to the holy
      altar,
   he made the court of the
      sanctuary glorious.

12 When he received the portions
   from the hands of the
      priests,
   as he stood by the hearth of the
      altar
   with a garland of brothers around
      him,
   he was like a young cedar on
      Lebanon
   surrounded by the trunks of
      palm trees.
13 All the sons of Aaron in their
   splendor

held the Lord's offering in their
   hands
before the whole congregation
   of Israel.
14 Finishing the service at the altars, *i*
   and arranging the offering to the
      Most High, the Almighty,
15 he held out his hand for the cup
   and poured a drink offering of
      the blood of the grape;
   he poured it out at the foot of the
      altar,
   a pleasing odor to the Most
      High, the king of all.
16 Then the sons of Aaron shouted;
   they blew their trumpets of
      hammered metal;
   they sounded a mighty fanfare
   as a reminder before the Most
      High.
17 Then all the people together
   quickly
   fell to the ground on their faces
   to worship their Lord,
   the Almighty, God Most High.
18 Then the singers praised him with
   their voices
   in sweet and full-toned
      melody. *j*
19 And the people of the Lord Most
   High offered
   their prayers before the Merciful
      One,
   until the order of worship of the
      Lord was ended,
   and they completed his ritual.
20 Then Simon *k* came down and
   raised his hands
   over the whole congregation of
      Israelites,
   to pronounce the blessing of the
      Lord with his lips,

h Heb: Meaning of Gk uncertain   *i* Other
ancient authorities read *altar*   *j* Other ancient
authorities read *in sweet melody throughout*
the house   *k* Gk *he*

Enoch (see also 44.16) and Joseph along with
Shem, Seth, and Enosh leads back to Adam.
14: Gen 5.24; Heb 11.5. **15:** Gen 39.1ff.;
50.25–26. **16:** Gen 5.3, 32.

50.1–24: Simon, son of Onias. 1: Simon II was high priest about 219–196 (Josephus, *Antiquities,* XII. iv. 10). *Onias* is the
Greek form of Johanan. *The house,* of God.

and to glory in his name;
21 and they bowed down in worship
a second time,
to receive the blessing from the
Most High.

22 And now bless the God of all,
who everywhere works great
wonders,
who fosters our growth from
birth,
and deals with us according to
his mercy.
23 May he give us[l] gladness of heart,
and may there be peace in our[m]
days
in Israel, as in the days of old.
24 May he entrust to us his mercy,
and may he deliver us in our[n]
days!

25 Two nations my soul detests,
and the third is not even a
people:
26 Those who live in Seir,[o] and the
Philistines,
and the foolish people that live
in Shechem.

27 Instruction in understanding and
knowledge
I have written in this book,
Jesus son of Eleazar son of Sirach[p]
of Jerusalem,
whose mind poured forth
wisdom.
28 Happy are those who concern
themselves with these
things,
and those who lay them to heart
will become wise.
29 For if they put them into practice,
they will be equal to
anything,
for the fear[q] of the Lord is their
path.

PRAYER OF JESUS SON OF SIRACH[r]

51 I give you thanks, O Lord and
King,
and praise you, O God my
Savior.
I give thanks to your name,
2 for you have been my protector
and helper
and have delivered me from
destruction
and from the trap laid by a
slanderous tongue,
from lips that fabricate lies.
In the face of my adversaries
you have been my helper 3 and
delivered me,
in the greatness of your mercy
and of your name,
from grinding teeth about to
devour me,
from the hand of those seeking
my life,
from the many troubles I
endured,
4 from choking fire on every side,
and from the midst of fire that I
had not kindled,
5 from the deep belly of Hades,
from an unclean tongue and
lying words—
6 the slander of an unrighteous
tongue to the king.
My soul drew near to death,
and my life was on the brink of
Hades below.
7 They surrounded me on every
side,
and there was no one to help
me;

l Other ancient authorities read *you* *m* Other ancient authorities read *your* *n* Other ancient authorities read *his* *o* Heb Compare Lat: Gk *on the mountain of Samaria* *p* Heb: Meaning of Gk uncertain *q* Heb: Other ancient authorities read *light* *r* This title is included in the Gk text.

50.16: *Trumpets,* Num 10.2; 31.6. **20**: *The blessing,* namely Num 6.24–27. *His name,* only the high priest (and only once a year, on the Day of Atonement) could utter the ineffable name, YHWH.
50.22–24: Doxology. **24**: Hebrew, "May his love abide upon Simeon, and may he keep in him the covenant of Phinehas; may one never be cut off from him; and as for his offspring, (may it be) as the days of heaven."
50.25–26: **An invective** against Edomites (*Seir*), pagans or Hellenists (*Philistines*), and Samaritans (*Shechem*).
50.27–29: **A postscript,** probably the

I looked for human assistance,
and there was none.
8 Then I remembered your mercy,
O Lord,
and your kindness[s] from of old,
for you rescue those who wait for
you
and save them from the hand of
their enemies.
9 And I sent up my prayer from the
earth,
and begged for rescue from
death.
10 I cried out, "Lord, you are my
Father;[t]
do not forsake me in the days of
trouble,
when there is no help against
the proud.
11 I will praise your name
continually,
and will sing hymns of
thanksgiving."
My prayer was heard,
12 for you saved me from
destruction
and rescued me in time of
trouble.
For this reason I thank you and
praise you,
and I bless the name of the
Lord.

———————

Heb adds:
*Give thanks to the Lord, for he is
good,
for his mercy endures forever;*

*Give thanks to the God of praises,
for his mercy endures forever;*

*Give thanks to the guardian of Israel,
for his mercy endures forever;*

*Give thanks to him who formed all
things,
for his mercy endures forever;*

*Give thanks to the redeemer of Israel,
for his mercy endures forever;*

*Give thanks to him who gathers the
dispersed of Israel,
for his mercy endures forever;*

*Give thanks to him who rebuilt his
city and his sanctuary,
for his mercy endures forever;*

*Give thanks to him who makes a
horn to sprout for the house of
David,
for his mercy endures forever;*

*Give thanks to him who has chosen
the sons of Zadok to be priests,
for his mercy endures forever;*

*Give thanks to the shield of Abraham,
for his mercy endures forever;*

*Give thanks to the rock of Isaac,
for his mercy endures forever;*

*Give thanks to the mighty one of
Jacob,
for his mercy endures forever;*

*Give thanks to him who has chosen
Zion,
for his mercy endures forever;*

*Give thanks to the King of the kings
of kings,
for his mercy endures forever;*

*He has raised up a horn for his
people,
praise for all his loyal ones.*

*For the children of Israel, the people
close to him.
Praise the Lord!*

———————

s Other ancient authorities read *work*   *t* Heb: Gk
the Father of my lord

———————

original ending of the author, who gives his
full name and recommends *this book*.
51.1–30: Two appendices: A psalm of
thanksgiving (vv.1–12) and a 23-line acro-
stic poem about Sirach's love for Wisdom
(vv.13–30). Verses 13–20a have been preserved in a psalms scroll from Qumran
Cave II.

13 While I was still young, before I
   went on my travels,
   I sought wisdom openly in my
   prayer.
14 Before the temple I asked for her,
   and I will search for her until
   the end.

15 From the first blossom to the
   ripening grape
   my heart delighted in her;
   my foot walked on the straight
   path;
   from my youth I followed her
   steps.

16 I inclined my ear a little and
   received her,
   and I found for myself much
   instruction.
17 I made progress in her;
   to him who gives wisdom I will
   give glory.

18 For I resolved to live according to
   wisdom, *u*
   and I was zealous for the good,
   and I shall never be
   disappointed.
19 My soul grappled with wisdom, *u*
   and in my conduct I was strict; *v*

   I spread out my hands to the
   heavens,
   and lamented my ignorance of
   her.
20 I directed my soul to her,
   and in purity I found her.

   With her I gained understanding
   from the first;
   therefore I will never be
   forsaken.
21 My heart was stirred to seek her;

   therefore I have gained a prize
   possession.
22 The Lord gave me my tongue as a
   reward,
   and I will praise him with it.

23 Draw near to me, you who are
   uneducated,
   and lodge in the house of
   instruction.
24 Why do you say you are lacking
   in these things, *w*
   and why do you endure such
   great thirst?
25 I opened my mouth and said,
   Acquire wisdom *x* for yourselves
   without money.

26 Put your neck under her *y* yoke,
   and let your souls receive
   instruction;
   it is to be found close by.

27 See with your own eyes that I
   have labored but little
   and found for myself much
   serenity.
28 Hear but a little of my instruction,
   and through me you will
   acquire silver and gold. *z*

29 May your soul rejoice in God's *a*
   mercy,
   and may you never be ashamed
   to praise him.
30 Do your work in good time,
   and in his own time God *b* will
   give you your reward.

---

u Gk *her*   *v* Meaning of Gk uncertain
w Cn Compare Heb Syr: Meaning of Gk
uncertain   *x* Heb: Gk lacks *wisdom*   *y* Heb:
other ancient authorities read *the*
z Syr Compare Heb: Gk *Get instruction with a
large sum of silver, and you will gain by it much
gold.*   *a* Gk *his*   *b* Gk *he*

Baruch

The book of Baruch was probably written sometime between 200 and 60 B.C.; it is set, however, during the Babylonian exile of the early sixth-century B.C., and attributed to Jeremiah's friend and secretary, Baruch son of Neriah (Jer 32.12; 36.4; 43.3; 45.1). Although Jeremiah and Baruch both are reported (Jer 43.1–7) to have been taken to Egypt in 582 B.C., a tradition developed later, which is reflected in these works, that Baruch went to Babylonia. If the book of Daniel was composed in the first half of the second century B.C., then Baruch would have been written after about 150 B.C., because Bar 1.15–2.19 is largely Dan 9.4–19 rewritten. Most of Baruch is made up of pastiches of biblical passages copied or paraphrased (from, e.g., Dan 9, Job 28, and Isa 40–66). Certainly Baruch himself would not have made the numerous mistakes contained in Bar 1.1–14.

Baruch falls into two main sections, each of which is made up of two parts. The first section, in prose, includes an introduction (1.1–14) and a corporate confession of sin (1.15–3.8) for Jews in Jerusalem to recite at the altar there, along with appropriate sacrifices, on various festival days and seasons. The idea of a letter or scroll written in Babylon to be read aloud in Jerusalem is derived from the exchange of letters recorded in Jer 29 and the scroll of Jeremiah's oracles penned by Baruch and read before King Jehoiakim in 605 B.C. (Jer 36). The corporate confession is modeled on Dan 9.4–19 (compare Ezra 9.6–15; Neh 9.6–37).

The second section is made up of two poems. The first (3.9–4.4) is a paean of praise of Wisdom, which though elusive is largely identified as Torah, God's precious gift to Israel. The second comprises an address by Jerusalem to the people of Israel (4.5–29), and by a rhetorical apostrophe to Jerusalem (4.30–5.9), inspired no doubt by Isa 51.17–52.10; 54; and 60–62, where the speaker is also not always clearly defined.

The basic text of the following translation is the Greek Septuagint; there are also ancient Syriac, Latin, Coptic, Ethiopic, Arabic, and Armenian versions based on the Greek. The prose section (1.1–3.8) has long been viewed as translated from a lost Hebrew original; recent research indicates that the poetic sections also derive from Hebrew originals.

There may have been as many as four different authors contributing to what is now called Baruch, one for each of the three major sections and a final redactor. Different names for God are used in the confession and in the poems. The theologies of the confession and of the second poem are quite compatible, but are both so clearly drawn from biblical passages paraphrased or rewritten that it is difficult to discern the particular thinking of the author(s). The first poem, on Wisdom, is similarly drawn from the Bible (Job 28 largely), and thus conceals the mind of its composer; it has, however, a different tone and style from the second. An argument could be made that there were only two basic contributors, and that one of these was the redactor. As a whole literary piece, Baruch would have well served Jewish communities in Judah and the Dispersion during the Seleucid and later eras of suffering and repression.

1 These are the words of the book that Baruch son of Neriah son of Mahseiah son of Zedekiah son of Hasadiah son of Hilkiah wrote in Babylon, ²in the fifth year, on the seventh day of the month, at the time when the Chaldeans took Jerusalem and burned it with fire.

3 Baruch read the words of this book to Jeconiah son of Jehoiakim, king of Judah, and to all the people who came to hear the book, ⁴and to the nobles and the princes, and to the elders, and to all the people, small and great, all who lived in Babylon by the river Sud.

5 Then they wept, and fasted, and prayed before the Lord; ⁶they collected as much money as each could give, ⁷and sent it to Jerusalem to the high priest*a* Jehoiakim son of Hilkiah son of Shallum, and to the priests, and to all the people who were present with him in Jerusalem. ⁸At the same time, on the tenth day of Sivan, Baruch*b* took the vessels of the house of the Lord, which had been carried away from the temple, to return them to the land of Judah—the silver vessels that Zedekiah son of Josiah, king of Judah, had made, ⁹after King Nebuchadnezzar of Babylon had carried away from Jerusalem Jeconiah and the princes and the prisoners and the nobles and the people of the land, and brought them to Babylon.

10 They said: Here we send you money; so buy with the money burnt offerings and sin offerings and incense, and prepare a grain offering, and offer them on the altar of the Lord our God; ¹¹and pray for the life of King Nebuchadnezzar of Babylon, and for the life of his son

Belshazzar, so that their days on earth may be like the days of heaven. ¹²The Lord will give us strength, and light to our eyes; we shall live under the protection*c* of King Nebuchadnezzar of Babylon, and under the protection of his son Belshazzar, and we shall serve them many days and find favor in their sight. ¹³Pray also for us to the Lord our God, for we have sinned against the Lord our God, and to this day the anger of the Lord and his wrath have not turned away from us. ¹⁴And you shall read aloud this scroll that we are sending you, to make your confession in the house of the Lord on the days of the festivals and at appointed seasons.

15 And you shall say: The Lord our God is in the right, but there is open shame on us today, on the people of Judah, on the inhabitants of Jerusalem, ¹⁶and on our kings, our rulers, our priests, our prophets, and our ancestors, ¹⁷because we have sinned before the Lord. ¹⁸We have disobeyed him, and have not heeded the voice of the Lord our God, to walk in the statutes of the Lord that he set before us. ¹⁹From the time when the Lord brought our ancestors out of the land of Egypt until today, we have been disobedient to the Lord our God, and we have been negligent, in not heeding his voice. ²⁰So to this day there have clung to us the calamities and the curse that the Lord declared through his servant Moses at the time when he brought our ancestors out of the land of Egypt to give to us a land flowing with milk and

a Gk *the priest*   *b* Gk *he*   *c* Gk *in the shadow*

1.1–14: Historical introduction. 1–2: Authorship and date. **1:** *Baruch,* Jeremiah's secretary (Jer 32.12). **2:** *Fifth year,* after the fall of Jerusalem in 587/6 B.C. **3–4:** The book is read before the exiles. **3:** *Jeconiah,* also called Jehoiachin (2 Kings 24.15; Jer 24.1). **4:** *Sud,* unknown.
1.5–14: A gift of money, the temple vessels, and the book are sent to Jerusalem. **5:** The word *Lord* occurs only in the first part of the book (1.1–3.8). **7:** *The high priest Jehoia-*

kim, otherwise unknown. **8:** *Sivan,* the third month (May–June). For the return of gold and *silver vessels,* see Ezra 1.7–11. **9:** Jer 24.1; 2 Kings 24.10–16. **11:** Jer 29.7. *Belshazzar* was actually the son of Nabonidus. *Like the days of heaven,* without end (Deut 11.21).
1.15–3.8: Confession of sin, for the Jerusalem community (1.15–2.5), and for the exiles (2.6–3.8); compare 1.15–16 and 2.6.
1.15–2.5: Disobedience brought the judgment of exile.

honey. 21 We did not listen to the voice of the Lord our God in all the words of the prophets whom he sent to us, 22 but all of us followed the intent of our own wicked hearts by serving other gods and doing what is evil in the sight of the Lord our God.

2 So the Lord carried out the threat he spoke against us: against our judges who ruled Israel, and against our kings and our rulers and the people of Israel and Judah. 2 Under the whole heaven there has not been done the like of what he has done in Jerusalem, in accordance with the threats that were*d* written in the law of Moses. 3 Some of us ate the flesh of their sons and others the flesh of their daughters. 4 He made them subject to all the kingdoms around us, to be an object of scorn and a desolation among all the surrounding peoples, where the Lord has scattered them. 5 They were brought down and not raised up, because our nation*e* sinned against the Lord our God, in not heeding his voice.

6 The Lord our God is in the right, but there is open shame on us and our ancestors this very day. 7 All those calamities with which the Lord threatened us have come upon us. 8 Yet we have not entreated the favor of the Lord by turning away, each of us, from the thoughts of our wicked hearts. 9 And the Lord has kept the calamities ready, and the Lord has brought them upon us, for the Lord is just in all the works that he has commanded us to do. 10 Yet we have not obeyed his voice, to walk in the statutes of the Lord that he set before us.

11 And now, O Lord God of Israel, who brought your people out of the land of Egypt with a mighty hand and with signs and wonders and with great power and outstretched arm, and made yourself a name that continues to this day, 12 we have sinned, we have been ungodly, we have done wrong, O Lord our God, against all your ordinances. 13 Let your anger turn away from us, for we are left, few in number, among the nations where you have scattered us. 14 Hear, O Lord, our prayer and our supplication, and for your own sake deliver us, and grant us favor in the sight of those who have carried us into exile; 15 so that all the earth may know that you are the Lord our God, for Israel and his descendants are called by your name.

16 O Lord, look down from your holy dwelling, and consider us. Incline your ear, O Lord, and hear; 17 open your eyes, O Lord, and see, for the dead who are in Hades, whose spirit has been taken from their bodies, will not ascribe glory or justice to the Lord; 18 but the person who is deeply grieved, who walks bowed and feeble, with failing eyes and famished soul, will declare your glory and righteousness, O Lord.

19 For it is not because of any righteous deeds of our ancestors or our kings that we bring before you our prayer for mercy, O Lord our God. 20 For you have sent your anger and your wrath upon us, as you declared by your servants the prophets, saying: 21 Thus says the Lord: Bend your shoulders and serve the king of Babylon, and you will remain in the land that I gave to your ancestors. 22 But if you will not obey the voice of the Lord and will not serve the king of Babylon, 23 I will make to cease from the towns of Judah and from the region around Jerusalem the voice of mirth and the voice of gladness, the voice of the bridegroom and the voice of the bride, and the whole land will be a desolation without inhabitants.

24 But we did not obey your voice, to

d Gk *in accordance with what is*
e Gk *because we*

1.15–18: Based on Dan 9.7–10. **15:** Ezra 9.7. **20:** Deut ch 28; Jer 11.3–5. **21:** Jer 7.25–26; Dan 9.5.
2.1–2: Dan 9.12–13. **3:** Lev 26.29; Deut 28.53; Jer 19.9; Lam 4.10. **5:** Deut 28.13. **2.6–10:** Confession of guilt. **8:** Dan 9.13.

9: Dan 9.14.
2.11–26: Supplication and confession. **11–14:** Dan 9.15–17. **13:** Deut 4.27; Jer 42.2. **16:** Deut 26.15. **17:** Pss 6.5; 30.9; Isa 38.18; Sir 17.27–28. *Hades,* Sheol. **21:** Jer 27.11–12. **23:** Jer 7.34. **25:** Jer 36.30. **26:** Jer 7.14.

serve the king of Babylon; and you have carried out your threats, which you spoke by your servants the prophets, that the bones of our kings and the bones of our ancestors would be brought out of their resting place; 25 and indeed they have been thrown out to the heat of day and the frost of night. They perished in great misery, by famine and sword and pestilence. 26 And the house that is called by your name you have made as it is today, because of the wickedness of the house of Israel and the house of Judah.

27 Yet you have dealt with us, O Lord our God, in all your kindness and in all your great compassion, 28 as you spoke by your servant Moses on the day when you commanded him to write your law in the presence of the people of Israel, saying, 29 "If you will not obey my voice, this very great multitude will surely turn into a small number among the nations, where I will scatter them. 30 For I know that they will not obey me, for they are a stiff-necked people. But in the land of their exile they will come to themselves 31 and know that I am the Lord their God. I will give them a heart that obeys and ears that hear; 32 they will praise me in the land of their exile, and will remember my name 33 and turn from their stubbornness and their wicked deeds; for they will remember the ways of their ancestors, who sinned before the Lord. 34 I will bring them again into the land that I swore to give to their ancestors, to Abraham, Isaac, and Jacob, and they will rule over it; and I will increase them, and they will not be diminished. 35 I will make an everlasting covenant with them to be their God and they shall be my people; and I will never again remove my people Israel from the land that I have given them."

3 O Lord Almighty, God of Israel, the soul in anguish and the wearied spirit cry out to you. 2 Hear, O Lord, and have mercy, for we have sinned before you. 3 For you are enthroned forever, and we are perishing forever. 4 O Lord Almighty, God of Israel, hear now the prayer of the people*f* of Israel, the children of those who sinned before you, who did not heed the voice of the Lord their God, so that calamities have clung to us. 5 Do not remember the iniquities of our ancestors, but in this crisis remember your power and your name. 6 For you are the Lord our God, and it is you, O Lord, whom we will praise. 7 For you have put the fear of you in our hearts so that we would call upon your name; and we will praise you in our exile, for we have put away from our hearts all the iniquity of our ancestors who sinned against you. 8 See, we are today in our exile where you have scattered us, to be reproached and cursed and punished for all the iniquities of our ancestors, who forsook the Lord our God.

9 Hear the commandments of life,
      O Israel;
      give ear, and learn wisdom!
10 Why is it, O Israel, why is it that
      you are in the land of your
      enemies,
      that you are growing old in a
      foreign country,
      that you are defiled with the dead,
11   that you are counted among
      those in Hades?
12 You have forsaken the fountain of
      wisdom.
13 If you had walked in the way of
      God,

f Gk *dead*

2.27–35: Repentance and restoration under an everlasting covenant. 28–29: Deut 28.58, 62. 30: 1 Kings 8.47. 31: Jer 24.7. 33: Deut 9.6. 34: Lev 26.42; Deut 6.10; Jer 32.37. 35: Jer 32.38–40; Ezek 36.26–29; Am 9.15. 3.1–8: Impassioned plea of repentant exiles ("though penitent we are still in exile!"). 4: The Israelites in exile were as though "dead" (vv. 10–11; Isa 59.10b; Lam 3.6). 7: Jer 32.40b. 8: The ancestors' sins (2.33; 3.4–5) are visited on later generations (Ex 34.7; Lam 5.7; contrast Jer 31.29 and Ezek 18.2–32). 3.9–4.4: **Wisdom, found by God, was given to Israel as Torah.** 3.9–14: Introduction to the poem. 10: *Growing old,* the exile has been long (contrast

you would be living in peace
    forever.
14 Learn where there is wisdom,
    where there is strength,
    where there is understanding,
  so that you may at the same time
    discern
  where there is length of days,
    and life,
  where there is light for the eyes,
    and peace.

15 Who has found her place?
  And who has entered her
    storehouses?
16 Where are the rulers of the
    nations,
  and those who lorded it over
    the animals on earth;
17 those who made sport of the birds
    of the air,
  and who hoarded up silver and
    gold
  in which people trust,
  and there is no end to their
    getting;
18 those who schemed to get silver,
    and were anxious,
  but there is no trace of their
    works?
19 They have vanished and gone
    down to Hades,
  and others have arisen in their
    place.

20 Later generations have seen the
    light of day,
  and have lived upon the earth;
  but they have not learned the way
    to knowledge,
  nor understood her paths,
  nor laid hold of her.
21 Their descendants have strayed far
    from her[g] way.

22 She has not been heard of in
    Canaan,
  or seen in Teman;
23 the descendants of Hagar, who
    seek for understanding on
    the earth,
  the merchants of Merran and
    Teman,
  the story-tellers and the seekers
    for understanding,
  have not learned the way to
    wisdom,
  or given thought to her paths.

24 O Israel, how great is the house of
    God,
  how vast the territory that he
    possesses!
25 It is great and has no bounds;
  it is high and immeasurable.
26 The giants were born there, who
    were famous of old,
  great in stature, expert in war.
27 God did not choose them,
  or give them the way to
    knowledge;
28 so they perished because they had
    no wisdom,
  they perished through their
    folly.

29 Who has gone up into heaven, and
    taken her,
  and brought her down from the
    clouds?
30 Who has gone over the sea, and
    found her,
  and will buy her for pure gold?
31 No one knows the way to her,
  or is concerned about the path
    to her.

g Other ancient authorities read *their*

1.2). **11**: Pss 28.1; 88.4; Isa 53.12. **12**: Prov
18.4; Jer 2.13. **14**: Prov 3.16; 8.14.
  3.15–28: The rulers of the world and the
mighty have not found wisdom. **15**: Job
28.12. **16b–17a**: Jer 27.6; Dan 2.38; Jdt 11.7.
22: *Canaan,* Ezek 28.3–5 associates Tyre (in
Canaan) with wisdom. *Teman,* in Edom, was
reputed for its wisdom (Jer 49.7; Ob 8–9). **23**:

Merran, perhaps a corruption that arose in the
Hebrew text for "Midian," a son of Keturah
(Gen 25.2). **24**: *House of God,* the created
world. **26**: Gen 6.4; Wis 14.6; compare the
book of Enoch 7.1–6.
  3.29–37: God found wisdom and gave her
to Israel (Sir 24.1–12). **29–30**: Deut 30.12–
13; Job 28.13–14.

32 But the one who knows all things
     knows her,
   he found her by his
     understanding.
   The one who prepared the earth
     for all time
   filled it with four-footed
     creatures;
33 the one who sends forth the light,
     and it goes;
   he called it, and it obeyed him,
     trembling;
34 the stars shone in their watches,
     and were glad;
   he called them, and they said,
     "Here we are!"
   They shone with gladness for
     him who made them.
35 This is our God;
     no other can be compared to
     him.
36 He found the whole way to
     knowledge,
   and gave her to his servant
     Jacob
   and to Israel, whom he loved.
37 Afterward she appeared on earth
     and lived with humankind.

4 She is the book of the
     commandments of God,
   the law that endures forever.
   All who hold her fast will live,
     and those who forsake her will
     die.
2 Turn, O Jacob, and take her;
   walk toward the shining of her
     light.
3 Do not give your glory to
     another,
   or your advantages to an alien
     people.
4 Happy are we, O Israel,

   for we know what is pleasing to
     God.
5 Take courage, my people,
   who perpetuate Israel's name!
6 It was not for destruction
     that you were sold to the
     nations,
   but you were handed over to your
     enemies
   because you angered God.
7 For you provoked the one who
     made you
   by sacrificing to demons and
     not to God.
8 You forgot the everlasting God,
     who brought you up,
   and you grieved Jerusalem, who
     reared you.
9 For she saw the wrath that came
     upon you from God,
   and she said:
   Listen, you neighbors of Zion,
   God has brought great sorrow
     upon me;
10 for I have seen the exile of my
     sons and daughters,
   which the Everlasting brought
     upon them.
11 With joy I nurtured them,
   but I sent them away with
     weeping and sorrow.
12 Let no one rejoice over me, a
     widow
   and bereaved of many;
   I was left desolate because of the
     sins of my children,
   because they turned away from
     the law of God.
13 They had no regard for his
     statutes;
   they did not walk in the ways
     of God's commandments,

3.32–34: Job 28.23–26; Prov 8.22–31. **33**: *Light*, Gen 1.3. **34**: *Stars . . . were glad*, Job 38.7. **37**: Many early Christian commentators took this as an allusion to the Incarnation.
   4.1–3: Wisdom is Torah. **1**: Sir 24.23. **2**: Isa 60.3.
   4.5–5.9: **Poem of comfort and restoration.**

4.5–20: Israel provoked God, and Zion now mourns for her captive children. **5**: *Take courage, my people* (compare vv. 21, 27, 30), inspired by Isa 40.1 (compare Deut 31.6). **7**: *Demons*, Deut 32.16–17; Ps 106.37; 1 Cor 10.20. **9b–16**: Jerusalem speaks to her *neighbors* (i.e. neighboring cities). **12**: *Widow*, Lam 1.1. **15**: Deut 28.49–50; Jer 6.15.

or tread the paths his
righteousness showed them.
14 Let the neighbors of Zion come;
remember the capture of my
sons and daughters,
which the Everlasting brought
upon them.
15 For he brought a distant nation
against them,
a nation ruthless and of a
strange language,
which had no respect for the aged
and no pity for a child.
16 They led away the widow's
beloved sons,
and bereaved the lonely woman
of her daughters.

17 But I, how can I help you?
18 For he who brought these
calamities upon you
will deliver you from the hand
of your enemies.
19 Go, my children, go;
for I have been left desolate.
20 I have taken off the robe of peace
and put on sackcloth for my
supplication;
I will cry to the Everlasting all
my days.

21 Take courage, my children, cry to
God,
and he will deliver you from the
power and hand of the
enemy.
22 For I have put my hope in the
Everlasting to save you,
and joy has come to me from
the Holy One,
because of the mercy that will
soon come to you
from your everlasting savior. *h*
23 For I sent you out with sorrow
and weeping,

but God will give you back to
me with joy and gladness
forever.
24 For as the neighbors of Zion have
now seen your capture,
so they soon will see your
salvation by God,
which will come to you with great
glory
and with the splendor of the
Everlasting.
25 My children, endure with patience
the wrath that has come
upon you from God.
Your enemy has overtaken you,
but you will soon see their
destruction
and will tread upon their necks.
26 My pampered children have
traveled rough roads;
they were taken away like a
flock carried off by the
enemy.

27 Take courage, my children, and
cry to God,
for you will be remembered by
the one who brought this
upon you.
28 For just as you were disposed to
go astray from God,
return with tenfold zeal to seek
him.
29 For the one who brought these
calamities upon you
will bring you everlasting joy
with your salvation.

30 Take courage, O Jerusalem,
for the one who named you will
comfort you.
31 Wretched will be those who
mistreated you

h Or *from the Everlasting, your savior*

4.17–29: Jerusalem encourages her exiled
children. 17–18: Only God can help. 20: *Robe
of peace,* garment worn in time of prosperity.
Sackcloth for my supplication, garment worn by
a suppliant. 23: Ps 126.6; Jer 31.12–13. 24: Isa
60.1–3. 25: *The wrath* is only temporary (Isa
54.7–8).

4.30–5.9: Jerusalem encouraged with
promises concerning the destruction of her
enemy and the return of her children.
4.30: *The one who named you,* see 5.4 n. 31–
35: Contrast the attitude toward Babylon in
1.11–12.

and who rejoiced at your fall.
32 Wretched will be the cities that
your children served as
slaves;
wretched will be the city that
received your offspring.
33 For just as she rejoiced at your fall
and was glad for your ruin,
so she will be grieved at her
own desolation.
34 I will take away her pride in her
great population,
and her insolence will be turned
to grief.
35 For fire will come upon her from
the Everlasting for many
days,
and for a long time she will be
inhabited by demons.

36 Look toward the east,
O Jerusalem,
and see the joy that is coming
to you from God.
37 Look, your children are coming,
whom you sent away;
they are coming, gathered from
east and west,
at the word of the Holy One,
rejoicing in the glory of God.

5 Take off the garment of your
sorrow and affliction,
O Jerusalem,
and put on forever the beauty of
the glory from God.
2 Put on the robe of the
righteousness that comes
from God;

put on your head the diadem of
the glory of the Everlasting;
3 for God will show your splendor
everywhere under heaven.
4 For God will give you evermore
the name,
"Righteous Peace, Godly
Glory."

5 Arise, O Jerusalem, stand upon
the height;
look toward the east,
and see your children gathered
from west and east
at the word of the Holy One,
rejoicing that God has
remembered them.
6 For they went out from you on
foot,
led away by their enemies;
but God will bring them back to
you,
carried in glory, as on a royal
throne.
7 For God has ordered that every
high mountain and the
everlasting hills be made
low
and the valleys filled up, to
make level ground,
so that Israel may walk safely in
the glory of God.
8 The woods and every fragrant tree
have shaded Israel at God's
command.
9 For God will lead Israel with joy,
in the light of his glory,
with the mercy and
righteousness that come
from him.

4.35: *Fire,* Jer 51.58. *Demons,* Isa 13.21. **36**: Isa 40.9–11. **37**: Isa 43.5.
5.1–9: Glorification of Jerusalem and return of the exiles. **1–2**: Isa 61.3, 10. **4**: Isa 60.14; 62.4; Jer 33.16; Ezek 48.35. *Righteous Peace,* Isa 32.17. **5**: Isa 49.18; 60.4. **6**: Isa 49.22; 66.20. **7**: Isa 42.16–17.

The Letter of Jeremiah

These seventy-three verses purport to be a letter that Jeremiah composed for those about to be taken into exile from Judah to Babylonia in 597 (or 587) B.C. by Nebuchadnezzar's forces. It was undoubtedly inspired by Jeremiah's letter (Jer 29.1–23) to those who had been taken hostage in 597, a decade before the final defeat of Judah and the destruction of Jerusalem. It is an impassioned sermon against idol worship and polytheism based on Jer 10, and particularly Jer 10.11: "May the gods, who did not make heaven and earth, perish from the earth and from beneath the heavens." This verse is the only one in the book of Jeremiah in Aramaic, and because it is so central to the Letter it has been suggested that the latter too may originally have been composed in Aramaic. The Letter is also influenced, however, by other biblical polemics against idol worship (Pss 115.4–8; 135.15–18; Isa 40.18–20; 41.6–7; 46.1–7; etc.) and may well have been written in Hebrew. A few scholars have suggested that it was originally composed in Greek. The various parts of the sermon cohere as a series of warnings to Jews, who might be attracted to idol worship, to recognize and be wary of the idolatry of their time; each part ends on a common refrain, with variations, insisting that idols are not gods nor to be confused with the one, true God (vv. 16, 23, 29, 40, 44, 52, 56, 65, 69, 72).

Most scholars date the Letter in the hellenistic period. The reference in v. 3 (so some have argued) would yield a date around 317 B.C.; others date the Letter still later. The allusion to the Letter in 2 Macc 2.1–3 would indicate a date at least in the second century B.C., perhaps the third.

The Letter is found at different locations in various manuscripts and versions. It stands as a discrete work between Lamentations and Ezekiel in two major Greek Septuagint manuscripts (fourth-century Vaticanus and fifth-century Alexandrinus), in the Milan Syriac Hexaplar, and in Arabic. In other Greek and Syriac manuscripts, and in the Latin version, it appears as the sixth chapter of Baruch. Since it is, however, clearly independent of Baruch, the New Revised Standard Version includes it as a separate book.

6 *a* A copy of a letter that Jeremiah sent to those who were to be taken to Babylon as exiles by the king of the Babylonians, to give them the message that God had commanded him.

2 Because of the sins that you have committed before God, you will be taken to Babylon as exiles by Nebuchadnezzar, king of the Babylonians. 3 Therefore when you have come to Babylon you will remain there for many years, for a long time, up to seven generations; after

a The King James Version (like the Latin Vulgate) prints The Letter of Jeremiah as Chapter 6 of the Book of Baruch, and the chapter and verse numbers are here retained. In the Greek Septuagint, the Letter is separated from Baruch by the Book of Lamentations.

that I will bring you away from there in peace. [4]Now in Babylon you will see gods made of silver and gold and wood, which people carry on their shoulders, and which cause the heathen to fear. [5]So beware of becoming at all like the foreigners or of letting fear for these gods[b] possess you [6]when you see the multitude before and behind them worshiping them. But say in your heart, "It is you, O Lord, whom we must worship." [7]For my angel is with you, and he is watching over your lives.

8 Their tongues are smoothed by the carpenter, and they themselves are overlaid with gold and silver; but they are false and cannot speak. [9]People[c] take gold and make crowns for the heads of their gods, as they might for a girl who loves ornaments, [10]and make crowns for the heads of their gods. Sometimes the priests secretly take gold and silver from their gods and spend it on themselves, [11]or even give some of it to the prostitutes on the terrace. They deck their gods[d] out with garments like human beings—these gods of silver and gold and wood [12]that cannot save themselves from rust and corrosion. When they have been dressed in purple robes, [13]their faces are wiped because of the dust from the temple, which is thick upon them. [14]One of them holds a scepter, like a district judge, but is unable to destroy anyone who offends it. [15]Another has a dagger in its right hand, and an ax, but cannot defend itself from war and rob-

bers. [16]From this it is evident that they are not gods; so do not fear them.

17 For just as someone's dish is useless when it is broken, [18]so are their gods when they have been set up in the temples. Their eyes are full of the dust raised by the feet of those who enter. And just as the gates are shut on every side against anyone who has offended a king, as though under sentence of death, so the priests make their temples secure with doors and locks and bars, in order that they may not be plundered by robbers. [19]They light more lamps for them than they light for themselves, though their gods[e] can see none of them. [20]They are[f] just like a beam of the temple, but their hearts, it is said, are eaten away when crawling creatures from the earth devour them and their robes. They do not notice [21]when their faces have been blackened by the smoke of the temple. [22]Bats, swallows, and birds alight on their bodies and heads; and so do cats. [23]From this you will know that they are not gods; so do not fear them.

24 As for the gold that they wear for beauty—it[g] will not shine unless someone wipes off the tarnish; for even when they were being cast, they did not feel it. [25]They are bought without regard to cost, but there is no breath in them. [26]Having no feet, they are carried on the shoulders of others, revealing to human-

b Gk *for them*   c Gk *They*   d Gk *them*
e Gk *they*   f Gk *It is*   g Lat Syr: Gk *they*

6.1–7: Historical introduction. 1: The exile of 597 B.C. (2 Kings 24.10–17). *Letter,* according to Jer 29.1 a letter is sent to Babylon. *King of the Babylonians,* but "king of Babylon" in the book of Jeremiah (Jer 20.4; 21.2; etc.). **2:** Jer 10–13; etc. **3:** *Seven generations,* contrast seventy years in Jer 29.10, forty years in Ezek 4.6, seventy weeks of years in Dan 9.24. **4:** *Silver and gold,* overlaid on wood (v. 55); Isa 40.19; Jer 10.3–4). *Which people carry on their shoulders,* perhaps an allusion to the Babylonian New Year procession, or a reflection of Isa 46.7; Jer 10.5. **5:** *Like the foreigners,* Jer 10.2. **7:** *My angel,* Ex 23.23; 32.34; Ps 91.11–12; etc.

8–73: Condemnation of idolatry.

8–16: Idols are decked out like people. 8: *Carpenter,* Isa 40.20; 44.13; Jer 10.3–4; etc. **11:** *Prostitutes,* probably cult prostitutes. **12:** *Purple robes,* Jer 10.9. **14:** *Scepter,* Esth 5.2. *Destroy,* put to death. **15:** *Dagger,* the Hebrew word behind the Greek could also mean "sword." Archaeologists have found representations of deities bearing scepters, swords, daggers, and battle-axes.

17–23: Uselessness and helplessness of idols. 17: *Dish . . . broken,* Isa 30.14; Jer 19.11; 22.28. **18:** *Gates* of the palace or doors of courtyard prison (Jer 32.2). **19:** Ps 115.5. *Lamps* have been found in excavated temples. **22:** This is the earliest Jewish reference to *cats,* which were first domesticated in Egypt.

kind their worthlessness. And those who serve them are put to shame [27] because, if any of these gods falls[h] to the ground, they themselves must pick it up. If anyone sets it upright, it cannot move itself; and if it is tipped over, it cannot straighten itself. Gifts are placed before them just as before the dead. [28] The priests sell the sacrifices that are offered to these gods[i] and use the money themselves. Likewise their wives preserve some of the meat[j] with salt, but give none to the poor or helpless. [29] Sacrifices to them may even be touched by women in their periods or at childbirth. Since you know by these things that they are not gods, do not fear them.

30 For how can they be called gods? Women serve meals for gods of silver and gold and wood; [31] and in their temples the priests sit with their clothes torn, their heads and beards shaved, and their heads uncovered. [32] They howl and shout before their gods as some do at a funeral banquet. [33] The priests take some of the clothing of their gods[k] to clothe their wives and children. [34] Whether one does evil to them or good, they will not be able to repay it. They cannot set up a king or depose one. [35] Likewise they are not able to give either wealth or money; if one makes a vow to them and does not keep it, they will not require it. [36] They cannot save anyone from death or rescue the weak from the strong. [37] They cannot restore sight to the blind; they cannot rescue one who is in distress. [38] They cannot take pity on a widow or do good to an orphan. [39] These things that are made of wood and overlaid with gold and sil-

ver are like stones from the mountain, and those who serve them will be put to shame. [40] Why then must anyone think that they are gods, or call them gods?

Besides, even the Chaldeans themselves dishonor them; for when they see someone who cannot speak, they bring Bel and pray that the mute may speak, as though Bel[l] were able to understand! [41] Yet they themselves cannot perceive this and abandon them, for they have no sense. [42] And the women, with cords around them, sit along the passageways, burning bran for incense. [43] When one of them is led off by one of the passers-by and is taken to bed by him, she derides the woman next to her, because she was not as attractive as herself and her cord was not broken. [44] Whatever is done for these idols[m] is false. Why then must anyone think that they are gods, or call them gods?

45 They are made by carpenters and goldsmiths; they can be nothing but what the artisans wish them to be. [46] Those who make them will certainly not live very long themselves; [47] how then can the things that are made by them be gods? They have left only lies and reproach for those who come after. [48] For when war or calamity comes upon them, the priests consult together as to where they can hide themselves and their gods.[n] [49] How then can one fail to see that these are not gods, for they cannot save themselves from war or calamity?

h Gk *if they fall*   i Gk *to them*   j Gk *of them*
k Gk *some of their clothing*   l Gk *he*
m Gk *them*   n Gk *them*

24–29: Idols are unable to feel or move: Isa 40.20; 44.9; 46.2; Jer 10.4–5. **25:** *Without regard to cost*, great cost. *No breath*, Ps 135.17; Jer 10.14; Hab 2.19. **26:** Isa 46.1, 7. **27:** *Cannot move*, Isa 46.7; Jer 10.4. *Gifts for the dead*, Ps 106.28; Sir 30.18–19. **29:** Lev 12.1–8.

30–40a: Idols cannot repay good or evil, or help worshipers. 30: *Women*, there were only male ministrants in the Jewish temple. **31–32:** Ritual lamentations for dying gods (such as Tammuz, Ezek 8.14; compare Lev 21.5, 10; Ezek 24.17). **34b:** Job 12.18;

Dan 2.21. **35b:** Deut 23.21. **36:** On the contrary, the Lord can do this (Deut 32.39; Ps 49.15). **37:** Ps 146.8. **38:** Deut 10.18; Ps 146.9; Jer 7.6. **39:** Hab 2.19.

40b–44: The Chaldeans dishonor their own idols. 40b: *Bel*, Marduk (Isa 46.1). **43:** A similar Babylonian practice is described by Herodotus (*Hist.* I. 199), according to which cult prostitutes sat among roped-off passageways.

45–52: Idols are but the work of human hands. 45: Ps 115.4; Isa 40.19; Jer 10.9. **47:** Idolaters bequeath lies and reproach, not

50 Since they are made of wood and overlaid with gold and silver, it will afterward be known that they are false. 51 It will be manifest to all the nations and kings that they are not gods but the work of human hands, and that there is no work of God in them. 52 Who then can fail to know that they are not gods?*o*

53 For they cannot set up a king over a country or give rain to people. 54 They cannot judge their own cause or deliver one who is wronged, for they have no power; 55 they are like crows between heaven and earth. When fire breaks out in a temple of wooden gods overlaid with gold or silver, their priests will flee and escape, but the gods*p* will be burned up like timbers. 56 Besides, they can offer no resistance to king or enemy. Why then must anyone admit or think that they are gods?

57 Gods made of wood and overlaid with silver and gold are unable to save themselves from thieves or robbers. 58 Anyone who can will strip them of their gold and silver and of the robes they wear, and go off with this booty, and they will not be able to help themselves. 59 So it is better to be a king who shows his courage, or a household utensil that serves its owner's need, than to be these false gods; better even the door of a house that protects its contents, than these false gods; better also a wooden pillar in a palace, than these false gods.

60 For sun and moon and stars are bright, and when sent to do a service, they are obedient. 61 So also the lightning, when it flashes, is widely seen; and the wind likewise blows in every land.

62 When God commands the clouds to go over the whole world, they carry out his command. 63 And the fire sent from above to consume mountains and woods does what it is ordered. But these idols*q* are not to be compared with them in appearance or power. 64 Therefore one must not think that they are gods, nor call them gods, for they are not able either to decide a case or to do good to anyone. 65 Since you know then that they are not gods, do not fear them.

66 They can neither curse nor bless kings; 67 they cannot show signs in the heavens for the nations, or shine like the sun or give light like the moon. 68 The wild animals are better than they are, for they can flee to shelter and help themselves. 69 So we have no evidence whatever that they are gods; therefore do not fear them.

70 Like a scarecrow in a cucumber bed, which guards nothing, so are their gods of wood, overlaid with gold and silver. 71 In the same way, their gods of wood, overlaid with gold and silver, are like a thorn bush in a garden on which every bird perches; or like a corpse thrown out in the darkness. 72 From the purple and linen*r* that rot upon them you will know that they are not gods; and they will finally be consumed themselves, and be a reproach in the land. 73 Better, therefore, is someone upright who has no idols; such a person will be far above reproach.

o Meaning of Gk uncertain   *p* Gk *they*
q Gk *these things*   *r* Cn: Gk *marble*, Syr *silk*

real gods, to posterity. **50**: *Afterward,* when the veneer has been exposed for what it is. *False,* a fraud.

53–56: **The impotence of idols. 53**: See v. 34b. *Give rain,* Deut 11.14; 28.12; Ps 147.8.

57–65: **Idols are helpless, useless, and not to be compared with celestial phenomena. 60**: Gen 1.14–18. **61–62**: Job 38.24–27; Ps 97.4. **63**: *Fire,* lightning. **64**: *Decide a case,* the true God does this (Ex 18.19; Ps 43.1; Isa 41.21).

66–69: **The helplessness of idols. 67**: *Signs,* portents (Jer 10.2; Joel 2.30; Mt 16.1).

70–73: **Idols are compared with a scarecrow, thorn bush, and corpse. 70**: *Scarecrow,* Jer 10.5. **71**: *Thorn bush,* an ordinary, useless shrub (compare Judg 9.14–15). **72**: The Greek text ("marble," see note *r*) is a misinterpretation of the Hebrew word "shesh," which means both "linen" and "marble" ("alabaster"). **73**: The conclusion of the matter.

The Additions to the Greek
Book of Daniel

As in the case of the Book of Esther, the ancient Greek version of the Book of Daniel is considerably longer than the surviving Hebrew text. The Greek Daniel has, apart from numerous textual differences throughout the book, three extended passages that are lacking in the Masoretic Hebrew text. All Greek witnesses place the Prayer of Azarias and the Song of the Three Jews in Dan ch 3. The Septuagint places the prose stories of Bel and the Dragon and of Susanna, in that order, at the end of Daniel after 12.13.

The Greek translation made by Theodotion, though corrected to the Hebrew and therefore shorter than the Septuagint text of Daniel, nonetheless includes all the outstanding passages in the Greek Daniel as integral parts of the book, with Susanna at the beginning of the book and Bel and the Dragon at the end of Dan 6; in this manner chronology is observed in a semibiographical story starting with the young Daniel's early detective work concerning Susanna, and continuing with further sleuthing triumphs over Bel and his priests and over the Dragon, as happening in the court of Cyrus. The Old Latin, Coptic, and Arabic versions follow Theodotion.

In all the witnesses Azariah's prayer and the song of the three Jews appear quite logically after Dan 3.23 (Theodotion; 3.24 in Septuagint), where we find the three gifted and handsome youths (Dan 1.4) in the burning furnace. In the Hebrew and in Theodotion they are called by the Babylonian names given them by Nebuchadnezzar's chief eunuch (Shadrach, Meshach, and Abednego, Dan 1.7); while in the Septuagint they retain their Hebrew names as pronounced in Greek, Ananias, Azarias, and Misael (see 2.17).

Although Theodotion "corrected" in many particulars the Greek text of Daniel to the emerging proto-Masoretic text of the beginning of the second century B.C., he nonetheless retained all the so-called additions of the Septuagint, albeit in a more suitable order for biographic purposes. Jerome's Latin Vulgate followed Theodotion basically, but made the story of Susanna ch 13, and the account of Bel and the Dragon ch 14, thus inverting the Greek order. As is mentioned in the Preface, "To the Reader" (pp. ix–xiv), the New RSV gives a translation of Theodotion's Greek text of Daniel.

The Prayer of Azariah
and the Song of the Three Jews

The passage that follows Dan 3.23(24) in all the previously mentioned witnesses (see p. 173 AP) except the Hebrew, consists of three parts: the prayer of Azariah, in vv. 1–22; a short report in prose on the welfare of the three Jews in the furnace, in vv. 23–27; and a long hymn sung by the three, untouched while the flames danced around them, in vv. 28–68. Both the prayer and the song are included as numbers 7 and 8 of the fifteen "Odes" appended to the Psalter in a few Septuagint manuscripts (see the Introduction to Ps 151).

We learn in 3.24–25 that Nebuchadnezzar was himself witness to the punishment he had decreed against the three Jews for refusing to worship his gods, including the golden statue he had erected (Dan 3.1) in a plain of the province of Babylon. What he saw in the furnace were four men walking about unharmed (Dan 3.25). The short prose report supplies the necessary information that the fourth was an angel of the Lord (v. 26; see Dan 3.28) who made the inside of the furnace quite bearable for the three. Such a miracle deserved liturgical material as well, and so we find in the Greek and Latin traditions the requisite prayer for deliverance before the report (vv. 3–22), and a song of praise after it (vv. 29–68), as indicated by the biblical pattern in such cases (Ex 15; 1 Sam 2; 2 Sam 23). The song is in two parts: the first a song of thanksgiving for deliverance, and the second a litany exhorting all creation to praise God, in the manner of Pss 136 and 148.

Early Jews composed many such poems, as shown in the abundant non-Masoretic and non-biblical psalmody in the Dead Sea Scrolls. Whether these parts of the Greek Daniel were first composed in Hebrew or in a highly semitized Greek is debated; the balance is in favor of Hebrew originals. When they were composed is also debated, but the second century B.C. is indicated. The interesting question is whether they were a part of a pre-Masoretic Hebrew Daniel, which is usually dated in the first half of the second century B.C.; each, the Septuagint and the Hebrew text of Daniel, has its own integrity, especially if read through from beginning to end. Whether that integrity was in the mind of an original author, early redactor, or late redactor, in Hebrew or Greek, will probably not be determined without further discovery of early manuscript evidence.

(Additions to Daniel, inserted
between 3.23 and 3.24)
1 They[a] walked around in the midst
of the flames, singing hymns to God and
blessing the Lord. 2 Then Azariah stood
still in the fire and prayed aloud:
3 "Blessed are you, O Lord, God of
    our ancestors, and worthy
    of praise;
  and glorious is your name
    forever!
4 For you are just in all you have
    done;
  all your works are true and your
    ways right,
  and all your judgments are true.
5 You have executed true judgments
    in all you have brought
    upon us
  and upon Jerusalem, the holy
    city of our ancestors;
  by a true judgment you have
    brought all this upon us
    because of our sins.
6 For we have sinned and broken
    your law in turning away
    from you;
  in all matters we have sinned
    grievously.
7 We have not obeyed your
    commandments,
  we have not kept them or done
    what you have commanded
    us for our own good.
8 So all that you have brought upon
    us,
  and all that you have done to
    us,
  you have done by a true
    judgment.
9 You have handed us over to our
    enemies, lawless and hateful
    rebels,
  and to an unjust king, the most
    wicked in all the world.

10 And now we cannot open our
    mouths;
  we, your servants who worship
    you, have become a shame
    and a reproach.
11 For your name's sake do not give
    us up forever,
  and do not annul your
    covenant.
12 Do not withdraw your mercy
    from us,
  for the sake of Abraham your
    beloved
  and for the sake of your servant
    Isaac
  and Israel your holy one,
13 to whom you promised
  to multiply their descendants
    like the stars of heaven
  and like the sand on the shore
    of the sea.
14 For we, O Lord, have become
    fewer than any other
    nation,
  and are brought low this day in
    all the world because of our
    sins.
15 In our day we have no ruler, or
    prophet, or leader,
  no burnt offering, or sacrifice,
    or oblation, or incense,
  no place to make an offering
    before you and to find
    mercy.
16 Yet with a contrite heart and a
    humble spirit may we be
    accepted,
17 as though it were with burnt
    offerings of rams and bulls,
  or with tens of thousands of fat
    lambs;

a That is, Hananiah, Mishael, and Azariah (Dan 2.17), the original names of Shadrach, Meshach, and Abednego (Dan 1.6-7)

1–22: **The prayer of Azariah. 1:** *They,* the three men mentioned in Dan 1.6–7; 3.22–23. **3:** 1 Chr 29.10, 20. **4:** Neh 9.33; Rev 16.7; 19.2. **6–7:** Isa 59.12–13; Dan 9.5–8; Bar 1.17–18. **8–10:** Lev 26.14, 38; Deut 28.15, 63–64; 30.1–3. **12:** *Abraham your beloved,* 2 Chr 20.7; Isa 41.8; Jas 2.23. **13:** Gen 15.5; 22.17. **14:** Deut 7.7; Jer 42.2; Bar 2.13. **15:** Lam 2.9; Hos 3.4; 2 Esd 10.21–22. **16:** Ps 51.16–17; Hos 6.6. **19:** Ps 25.3. **21:** Ps 35.26. **22:** Ps 83.18.

such may our sacrifice be in
your sight today,
and may we unreservedly
follow you, *b*
for no shame will come to those
who trust in you.
18 And now with all our heart we
follow you;
we fear you and seek your
presence.
19 Do not put us to shame,
but deal with us in your
patience
and in your abundant mercy.
20 Deliver us in accordance with
your marvelous works,
and bring glory to your name,
O Lord.
21 Let all who do harm to your
servants be put to shame;
let them be disgraced and
deprived of all power,
and let their strength be broken.
22 Let them know that you alone are
the Lord God,
glorious over the whole world."

23 Now the king's servants who
threw them in kept stoking the furnace
with naphtha, pitch, tow, and brush-
wood. 24 And the flames poured out
above the furnace forty-nine cubits,
25 and spread out and burned those Chaldeans who were caught near the furnace.
26 But the angel of the Lord came down
into the furnace to be with Azariah and
his companions, and drove the fiery
flame out of the furnace, 27 and made the
inside of the furnace as though a moist
wind were whistling through it. The fire
did not touch them at all and caused them
no pain or distress.
28 Then the three with one voice
praised and glorified and blessed God in
the furnace:
29 "Blessed are you, O Lord, God of
our ancestors,

and to be praised and highly
exalted forever;
30 And blessed is your glorious, holy
name,
and to be highly praised and
highly exalted forever.
31 Blessed are you in the temple of
your holy glory,
and to be extolled and highly
glorified forever.
32 Blessed are you who look into the
depths from your throne on
the cherubim,
and to be praised and highly
exalted forever.
33 Blessed are you on the throne of
your kingdom,
and to be extolled and highly
exalted forever.
34 Blessed are you in the firmament
of heaven,
and to be sung and glorified
forever.

35 "Bless the Lord, all you works of
the Lord;
sing praise to him and highly
exalt him forever.
36 Bless the Lord, you heavens;
sing praise to him and highly
exalt him forever.
37 Bless the Lord, you angels of the
Lord;
sing praise to him and highly
exalt him forever.
38 Bless the Lord, all you waters
above the heavens;
sing praise to him and highly
exalt him forever.
39 Bless the Lord, all you powers of
the Lord;
sing praise to him and highly
exalt him forever.
40 Bless the Lord, sun and moon;
sing praise to him and highly
exalt him forever.

b Meaning of Gk uncertain

**23–27: The continued stoking of the
furnace, and the descent of the angel of
the Lord. 23:** *Naphtha,* a natural petroleum.
28–68: Song of the three young men.

32–37: Ps 148. **35**: Pss 103.22; 145.10. **37**: Pss
103.20; 148.2. **38**: Ps 148.4. **39**: *All you powers,* i.e. heavenly bodies or angels. **40**: Ps
148.3.

41 Bless the Lord, stars of heaven;
   sing praise to him and highly
      exalt him forever.

42 "Bless the Lord, all rain and dew;
   sing praise to him and highly
      exalt him forever.
43 Bless the Lord, all you winds;
   sing praise to him and highly
      exalt him forever.
44 Bless the Lord, fire and heat;
   sing praise to him and highly
      exalt him forever.
45 Bless the Lord, winter cold and
      summer heat;
   sing praise to him and highly
      exalt him forever.
46 Bless the Lord, dews and falling
      snow;
   sing praise to him and highly
      exalt him forever.
47 Bless the Lord, nights and days;
   sing praise to him and highly
      exalt him forever.
48 Bless the Lord, light and darkness;
   sing praise to him and highly
      exalt him forever.
49 Bless the Lord, ice and cold;
   sing praise to him and highly
      exalt him forever.
50 Bless the Lord, frosts and snows;
   sing praise to him and highly
      exalt him forever.
51 Bless the Lord, lightnings and
      clouds;
   sing praise to him and highly
      exalt him forever.

52 "Let the earth bless the Lord;
   let it sing praise to him and
      highly exalt him forever.
53 Bless the Lord, mountains and
      hills;
   sing praise to him and highly
      exalt him forever.
54 Bless the Lord, all that grows in
      the ground;

sing praise to him and highly
   exalt him forever.
55 Bless the Lord, seas and rivers;
   sing praise to him and highly
      exalt him forever.
56 Bless the Lord, you springs;
   sing praise to him and highly
      exalt him forever.
57 Bless the Lord, you whales and all
      that swim in the waters;
   sing praise to him and highly
      exalt him forever.
58 Bless the Lord, all birds of
      the air;
   sing praise to him and highly
      exalt him forever.
59 Bless the Lord, all wild animals
      and cattle;
   sing praise to him and highly
      exalt him forever.

60 "Bless the Lord, all people on
      earth;
   sing praise to him and highly
      exalt him forever.
61 Bless the Lord, O Israel;
   sing praise to him and highly
      exalt him forever.
62 Bless the Lord, you priests of the
      Lord;
   sing praise to him and highly
      exalt him forever.
63 Bless the Lord, you servants of the
      Lord;
   sing praise to him and highly
      exalt him forever.
64 Bless the Lord, spirits and souls of
      the righteous;
   sing praise to him and highly
      exalt him forever.
65 Bless the Lord, you who are holy
      and humble in heart;
   sing praise to him and highly
      exalt him forever.

66 "Bless the Lord, Hananiah,
      Azariah, and Mishael;

44: Ps 148.8. **53**: Ps 148.9.
58–59: Ps 148.10. **61–62**: Ps 135.19. **63**: Ps
134.1. **65**: *Holy and humble in heart*, Pss 18.25,
27; 86.1–2; Zeph 2.3. **67–68**: Pss 106.1;
136.1–2.

sing praise to him and highly
exalt him forever.
For he has rescued us from Hades
and saved us from the
power^c of death,
and delivered us from the midst
of the burning fiery
furnace;
from the midst of the fire he has
delivered us.

67 Give thanks to the Lord, for he is
good,
for his mercy endures forever.
68 All who worship the Lord, bless
the God of gods,
sing praise to him and give
thanks to him,
for his mercy endures forever."

c Gk *hand*

Susanna
(Chapter 13 of the Greek Version of Daniel)

The story of Susanna and the young Daniel in the Septuagint is strikingly different from the same in Theodotion. In Theodotion it reads like a delightful yarn about two wicked elders who falsely accuse the virtuous young Susanna and are exposed by the youthful and sagacious Daniel. In the Septuagint the story reads like a story mirroring all virtuous Jewish youth who are the beloved of Jacob and whose qualities should be sponsored in all Jewish communities. The Septuagint prefers general titles whereas Theodotion provides specific names; the trial takes place in a synagogue in the Septuagint, but in Susanna's home in Theodotion. There is actually little verbatim agreement between the two accounts, though the story is clearly the same. The perverted elders who maligned the young woman, the Septuagint makes clear from the start of its account, were judges corrupted by foreign influence.

Although the Theodotionic account reads better, perhaps, than that in the Septuagint, the story itself is one of the most engaging short stories in world literature. It is a celebration of the triumph of virtue over villainy, and of the innocence of youth over jaded elders corrupted by power and the anxiety of aging. While innocence and vulnerability may be generic to youth itself, it is God (Theodotion) or an angel (Septuagint) who inspires youth with a spirit of insight and understanding, integrity and courage. While the characters, protagonists and antagonists, are Jews, the story is about human strengths and weaknesses, and hence is universal in its appeal.

It is difficult to determine if the account concerning Susanna was composed in Greek or rests upon a Semitic original. Puns based on the Greek in vv. 54–55 and 58–59 might indicate a Greek original, though good translators often try to match puns from original compositions in the receptor language. The Greek text, like other purely Greek portions of Daniel, is full of semitisms; most scholars have thought in terms of a Semitic original, a few thinking of two separate ones lying behind the Theodotionic and the Septuagint versions. The date of composition would have been sometime in the second century B.C.

1 There was a man living in Babylon whose name was Joakim. ²He married the daughter of Hilkiah, named Susanna, a very beautiful woman and one who feared the Lord. ³Her parents were righteous, and had trained their daughter according to the law of Moses. ⁴Joakim was very rich, and had a fine garden adjoining his house; the Jews used to come to him because he was the most honored of them all.

5 That year two elders from the people were appointed as judges. Concerning them the Lord had said: "Wickedness came forth from Babylon, from elders who were judges, who were supposed to govern the people." ⁶These men were frequently at Joakim's house, and all who had a case to be tried came to them there.

7 When the people left at noon, Susanna would go into her husband's garden to walk. ⁸Every day the two elders used to see her, going in and walking about, and they began to lust for her. ⁹They suppressed their consciences and turned away their eyes from looking to Heaven or remembering their duty to administer justice. ¹⁰Both were overwhelmed with passion for her, but they did not tell each other of their distress, ¹¹for they were ashamed to disclose their lustful desire to seduce her. ¹²Day after day they watched eagerly to see her.

13 One day they said to each other, "Let us go home, for it is time for lunch." So they both left and parted from each other. ¹⁴But turning back, they met again; and when each pressed the other for the reason, they confessed their lust.

Then together they arranged for a time when they could find her alone.

15 Once, while they were watching for an opportune day, she went in as before with only two maids, and wished to bathe in the garden, for it was a hot day. ¹⁶No one was there except the two elders, who had hidden themselves and were watching her. ¹⁷She said to her maids, "Bring me olive oil and ointments, and shut the garden doors so that I can bathe." ¹⁸They did as she told them: they shut the doors of the garden and went out by the side doors to bring what they had been commanded; they did not see the elders, because they were hiding.

19 When the maids had gone out, the two elders got up and ran to her. ²⁰They said, "Look, the garden doors are shut, and no one can see us. We are burning with desire for you; so give your consent, and lie with us. ²¹If you refuse, we will testify against you that a young man was with you, and this was why you sent your maids away."

22 Susanna groaned and said, "I am completely trapped. For if I do this, it will mean death for me; if I do not, I cannot escape your hands. ²³I choose not to do it; I will fall into your hands, rather than sin in the sight of the Lord."

24 Then Susanna cried out with a loud voice, and the two elders shouted against her. ²⁵And one of them ran and opened the garden doors. ²⁶When the people in the house heard the shouting in the garden, they rushed in at the side door to see what had happened to her. ²⁷And when the elders told their story,

---

1–4: Introduction. The setting of the story is Babylon during the exile. **1**: The name *Joakim* means "the Lord will establish." **2**: The names *Susanna* and *Hilkiah* mean respectively "lily" and "the Lord is my portion." **4**: Some Jews prospered during the exile (Jer 29.5).

5–14: The two lustful elders. 5: *That year,* apparently the year of Joakim's marriage (v. 2). The *two elders* are identified by Jewish tradition to be the two false prophets mentioned in Jer 29.21–23. The quotation (*"Wickedness . . . people"*) is an unknown prophetic

saying probably based on Jer 23.14–15. **9**: *Heaven,* a metonym, a word associated with another word and used in its place, for God (see 1 Macc 3.18 n. and compare Lk 15.18). Such metonymy was a way of avoiding the pronunciation of God's name.

15–27: The attempted seduction. 17: *Oil and* (perfumed) *ointments* were used after bathing. **22**: The Mosaic law prescribed *death* as punishment for an unfaithful wife (Lev 20.10; Deut 22.22). **23**: See Joseph's reply to his tempter (Gen 39.9).

the servants felt very much ashamed, for nothing like this had ever been said about Susanna.

28 The next day, when the people gathered at the house of her husband Joakim, the two elders came, full of their wicked plot to have Susanna put to death. In the presence of the people they said, 29 "Send for Susanna daughter of Hilkiah, the wife of Joakim." 30 So they sent for her. And she came with her parents, her children, and all her relatives.

31 Now Susanna was a woman of great refinement and beautiful in appearance. 32 As she was veiled, the scoundrels ordered her to be unveiled, so that they might feast their eyes on her beauty. 33 Those who were with her and all who saw her were weeping.

34 Then the two elders stood up before the people and laid their hands on her head. 35 Through her tears she looked up toward Heaven, for her heart trusted in the Lord. 36 The elders said, "While we were walking in the garden alone, this woman came in with two maids, shut the garden doors, and dismissed the maids. 37 Then a young man, who was hiding there, came to her and lay with her. 38 We were in a corner of the garden, and when we saw this wickedness we ran to them. 39 Although we saw them embracing, we could not hold the man, because he was stronger than we, and he opened the doors and got away. 40 We did, however, seize this woman and asked who the young man was, 41 but she would not tell us. These things we testify."

Because they were elders of the people and judges, the assembly believed them and condemned her to death.

42 Then Susanna cried out with a loud voice, and said, "O eternal God,

you know what is secret and are aware of all things before they come to be; 43 you know that these men have given false evidence against me. And now I am to die, though I have done none of the wicked things that they have charged against me!"

44 The Lord heard her cry. 45 Just as she was being led off to execution, God stirred up the holy spirit of a young lad named Daniel, 46 and he shouted with a loud voice, "I want no part in shedding this woman's blood!"

47 All the people turned to him and asked, "What is this you are saying?" 48 Taking his stand among them he said, "Are you such fools, O Israelites, as to condemn a daughter of Israel without examination and without learning the facts? 49 Return to court, for these men have given false evidence against her."

50 So all the people hurried back. And the rest of the*a* elders said to him, "Come, sit among us and inform us, for God has given you the standing of an elder." 51 Daniel said to them, "Separate them far from each other, and I will examine them."

52 When they were separated from each other, he summoned one of them and said to him, "You old relic of wicked days, your sins have now come home, which you have committed in the past, 53 pronouncing unjust judgments, condemning the innocent and acquitting the guilty, though the Lord said, 'You shall not put an innocent and righteous person to death.' 54 Now then, if you really saw this woman, tell me this: Under what tree did you see them being intimate with each other?" He answered, "Under

a Gk lacks *rest of the*

28–43: Susanna falsely accused and condemned to death. 34: The judges play the part of witnesses by laying their hands on the head of the accused (Lev 24.14). **35:** *She looked up toward Heaven,* appealing her cause to a higher tribunal (vv. 42–43). **41:** Since, according to Jewish law, a witness could not be the judge, the sentence of death is passed

by the credulous *assembly.* **42:** *God, you know what is secret,* 1 Sam 16.7; Jer 11.20; 20.12; Ps 33.13–15; Prov 15.11; Heb 4.13.

44–59: Susanna rescued and acquitted. 50: Here *the elders* are obviously not the two who had testified, but their colleagues on the bench. **53:** Ex 23.7. **54–59:** The wordplay of the original (see notes *b* and *c*) may be also

a mastic tree." *b* ⁵⁵ And Daniel said, "Very well! This lie has cost you your head, for the angel of God has received the sentence from God and will immediately cut *b* you in two."

56 Then, putting him to one side, he ordered them to bring the other. And he said to him, "You offspring of Canaan and not of Judah, beauty has beguiled you and lust has perverted your heart. ⁵⁷ This is how you have been treating the daughters of Israel, and they were intimate with you through fear; but a daughter of Judah would not tolerate your wickedness. ⁵⁸ Now then, tell me: Under what tree did you catch them being intimate with each other?" He answered, "Under an evergreen oak." *c* ⁵⁹ Daniel said to him, "Very well! This lie has cost you also your head, for the angel of God is waiting with his sword to split *c* you in two, so as to destroy you both."

60 Then the whole assembly raised a great shout and blessed God, who saves those who hope in him. ⁶¹ And they took action against the two elders, because out of their own mouths Daniel had convicted them of bearing false witness; they did to them as they had wickedly planned to do to their neighbor. ⁶² Acting in accordance with the law of Moses, they put them to death. Thus innocent blood was spared that day.

63 Hilkiah and his wife praised God for their daughter Susanna, and so did her husband Joakim and all her relatives, because she was found innocent of a shameful deed. ⁶⁴ And from that day onward Daniel had a great reputation among the people.

b The Greek words for *mastic tree* and *cut* are similar, thus forming an ironic wordplay
c The Greek words for *evergreen oak* and *split* are similar, thus forming an ironic wordplay

represented in English by the paraphrase, "Under a *clove* tree . . . the angel will *cleave* you"; "under a *yew* tree . . . the angel will *hew* you asunder."

60–62: The two elders condemned to death. 62: *The law of Moses,* concerning false witnesses (Deut 19.16–21).

Bel and the Dragon
(Chapter 14 of the Greek Version of Daniel)

The Septuagint and Theodotionic versions of this story cohere quite well and differ only in details, except that, as noted earlier (p. 173 AP), the version in Theodotion is integrated into the larger book of Daniel in such a fashion that something like a folk-biography is presented. The Septuagint story begins as though the reader knows nothing of Daniel at all. True also to the style of the Theodotionic Daniel, Habakkuk in v. 33 is identified as the biblical prophet, whereas in the Septuagint he is simply a man with the same name as the prophet. Theodotion has in several ways integrated the story into the larger biblical framework.

The story has three distinct episodes: the story of Daniel's exposing the fraud of the priests of Bel; the story of Daniel's proving the vulnerability of the so-called dragon, or snake; and the closing story of Daniel's surviving once more a sojourn in the lions' den, as in Dan 6, but this time for six days (v. 31). After Daniel has proved to the king the fraudulent character of the king's religion, and the king once more is favorably impressed with Daniel and his faith, the Babylonians conspire against the king, even threatening to kill him if he does not hand Daniel over to them. God summons Habakkuk from Judea and again an angel intervenes (as in Dan 6.22) to save him by transporting Habakkuk with the food to the lions' den in Babylon. One is left to assume that the angel had closed the lions' mouths, as in ch 6.

The whole account revolves around the motif of eating—the priests eating the food that the king set out for Bel, the dragon eating the concoction Daniel stirred up that killed the beast, and the focus in the final episode on Daniel's need to eat, which Habakkuk satisfies. All this is apparently set over against the lions' not eating Daniel. Another motif is set in the claim that the king's gods, in contrast to the God of Daniel, were not living gods. The complete conversion of the king occurs between his confession of the greatness of Bel in v. 18 and his confession of the greatness of the God of Daniel in v. 41.

The two genres, one of the favor of the wise courtier in the eyes of a foreign king and the other of court conflict, which are kept distinct in Dan 1–6, are combined in this story. The story reaches beyond the court, however, to the differences between those who, like the king, are open to worshiping the living God and any others who are not. The author was ridiculing, in typical early Jewish literary fashion, the two main characters of the Babylonian creation myth, the *Enuma Elish,* Bel or Marduk, and Tiamat, a sea serpent or monster whom Marduk slew as the major act of creation. By stark contrast, the God of Daniel was "the living God who created heaven and earth and has dominion over all living creatures" (v. 5).

Oppressed folk often ridicule what their malefactors hold dear, and satire is an antidote for the suffering endured. The account of Bel and the Dragon would have had such universal appeal (indeed, still does) that it could have been written anywhere at any time that oppression was severe. It was clearly intended to encourage Jews to remain faithful; it could have been refuted by Babylonian apologists. The original may have been in either Hebrew or Aramaic. Although there are few clues as to when Bel and the Dragon should be dated, the account, like the other portions of the Greek Daniel not in the Hebrew, surely originates in the second century B.C.

1 When King Astyages was laid to rest with his ancestors, Cyrus the Persian succeeded to his kingdom. 2Daniel was a companion of the king, and was the most honored of all his friends.

3 Now the Babylonians had an idol called Bel, and every day they provided for it twelve bushels of choice flour and forty sheep and six measures*a* of wine. 4The king revered it and went every day to worship it. But Daniel worshiped his own God.

So the king said to him, "Why do you not worship Bel?" 5He answered, "Because I do not revere idols made with hands, but the living God, who created heaven and earth and has dominion over all living creatures."

6 The king said to him, "Do you not think that Bel is a living god? Do you not see how much he eats and drinks every day?" 7And Daniel laughed, and said, "Do not be deceived, O king, for this thing is only clay inside and bronze outside, and it never ate or drank anything."

8 Then the king was angry and called the priests of Bel*b* and said to them, "If you do not tell me who is eating these provisions, you shall die. 9But if you prove that Bel is eating them, Daniel shall die, because he has spoken blasphemy against Bel." Daniel said to the king, "Let it be done as you have said."

10 Now there were seventy priests of Bel, besides their wives and children. So the king went with Daniel into the temple of Bel. 11The priests of Bel said, "See, we are now going outside; you yourself, O king, set out the food and prepare the wine, and shut the door and seal it with your signet. 12When you return in the morning, if you do not find that Bel has eaten it all, we will die; otherwise Daniel will, who is telling lies about us." 13They

were unconcerned, for beneath the table they had made a hidden entrance, through which they used to go in regularly and consume the provisions. 14After they had gone out, the king set out the food for Bel. Then Daniel ordered his servants to bring ashes, and they scattered them throughout the whole temple in the presence of the king alone. Then they went out, shut the door and sealed it with the king's signet, and departed. 15During the night the priests came as usual, with their wives and children, and they ate and drank everything.

16 Early in the morning the king rose and came, and Daniel with him. 17The king said, "Are the seals unbroken, Daniel?" He answered, "They are unbroken, O king." 18As soon as the doors were opened, the king looked at the table, and shouted in a loud voice, "You are great, O Bel, and in you there is no deceit at all!"

19 But Daniel laughed and restrained the king from going in. "Look at the floor," he said, "and notice whose footprints these are." 20The king said, "I see the footprints of men and women and children."

21 Then the king was enraged, and he arrested the priests and their wives and children. They showed him the secret doors through which they used to enter to consume what was on the table. 22Therefore the king put them to death, and gave Bel over to Daniel, who destroyed it and its temple.

23 Now in that place*c* there was a great dragon, which the Babylonians revered. 24The king said to Daniel, "You cannot deny that this is a living god; so

a A little more than fifty gallons   *b* Gk *his priests*   *c* Other ancient authorities lack *in that place*

1–2: Introduction. 1: *Cyrus the Persian* (Dan 6.28) became conquering king of Babylon in 538 B.C.

3–22: The story of Bel. 3: *Bel,* or Bel-Marduk (compare Merodach, Jer 50.2; see Isa 46.1 and Letter of Jeremiah 6.41), was the chief god in the Babylonian pantheon. Several ancient sources testify to the enormous quantities of sacrifices presented to Marduk in the daily ritual. **7**: Daniel ridicules the king's argument: clay and bronze do not eat (Sir 30.19). **11**: Dan 6.17. Archaeologists have found many Babylonian signets.

16–22: The fraud detected (compare

worship him." 25 Daniel said, "I worship the Lord my God, for he is the living God. 26 But give me permission, O king, and I will kill the dragon without sword or club." The king said, "I give you permission."

27 Then Daniel took pitch, fat, and hair, and boiled them together and made cakes, which he fed to the dragon. The dragon ate them, and burst open. Then Daniel said, "See what you have been worshiping!"

28 When the Babylonians heard about it, they were very indignant and conspired against the king, saying, "The king has become a Jew; he has destroyed Bel, and killed the dragon, and slaughtered the priests." 29 Going to the king, they said, "Hand Daniel over to us, or else we will kill you and your household." 30 The king saw that they were pressing him hard, and under compulsion he handed Daniel over to them.

31 They threw Daniel into the lions' den, and he was there for six days. 32 There were seven lions in the den, and every day they had been given two human bodies and two sheep; but now they were given nothing, so that they would devour Daniel.

33 Now the prophet Habakkuk was in Judea; he had made a stew and had broken bread into a bowl, and was going into the field to take it to the reapers. 34 But the angel of the Lord said to Habakkuk, "Take the food that you have to Babylon, to Daniel, in the lions' den." 35 Habakkuk said, "Sir, I have never seen Babylon, and I know nothing about the den." 36 Then the angel of the Lord took him by the crown of his head and carried him by his hair; with the speed of the wind[d] he set him down in Babylon, right over the den.

37 Then Habakkuk shouted, "Daniel, Daniel! Take the food that God has sent you." 38 Daniel said, "You have remembered me, O God, and have not forsaken those who love you." 39 So Daniel got up and ate. And the angel of God immediately returned Habakkuk to his own place.

40 On the seventh day the king came to mourn for Daniel. When he came to the den he looked in, and there sat Daniel! 41 The king shouted with a loud voice, "You are great, O Lord, the God of Daniel, and there is no other besides you!" 42 Then he pulled Daniel[e] out, and threw into the den those who had attempted his destruction, and they were instantly eaten before his eyes.

d Or *by the power of his spirit*   e Gk *him*

Dan 2.12; 6.24). **22**: According to ancient historians it was Xerxes who destroyed Bel's temple.

23–42: The story of the dragon. 23: *A great dragon,* that is, a live serpent worshiped as a god (compare Num 21.8–9; 2 Kings 18.4). **26**: *Permission* was granted because the king believed in the immortality of the serpent-god. **31–32**: The second time that Daniel is put in *the lions' den* (Dan 6.16–24).

33–39: The intervention of Habakkuk. 33: The author in the Greek translation made by Theodotion intends to identify this Habakkuk with the Minor Prophet of that name; chronologically, however, such an identification is impossible, nor is it reflected in the Septuagint version. **36**: *Hair,* Ezek 8.3. **37**: 1 Kings 17.4.

40–42: Daniel's liberation. 41: Compare Dan 6.26–27.

1 Maccabees

First Maccabees recounts the origins of the Hasmonean dynasty. This begins with the first appearance of Mattathias (see 2.1n.) and his five sons as leaders of the resistance against Seleucid oppression. It leads to the eventual enthronement of the dynasty at the head of the independent state of Judea. The book begins with the death of Alexander the Great and the rise to power of the Seleucid king, Antiochus IV Epiphanes. When Antiochus attacked Jerusalem and desecrated the temple, Judas Maccabeus (see 2.2–5n.) rallied the Jews to recover and purify it, thereby establishing himself as a powerful leader. The Hasmoneans were as skilled in diplomacy as in warfare, and were able to benefit from the instability of the Seleucid throne. After Judas' death his brother Jonathan was chosen leader of the Jews and was appointed high priest by the Seleucid king Demetrius, who needed help in opposing his rival Alexander Epiphanes. On Jonathan's death his brother Simon was installed as leader and high priest, and Judea was granted independence by Demetrius II. With the accession of Simon's son, John Hyrcanus, the Hasmonean dynasty was in place.

The complex problem of cultural assimilation pervades the book. Since the conquest of Alexander, Greek and Semitic culture had mingled together, and the Hellenistic culture that resulted dominated all the countries of the Mediterranean basin. The books of Sirach and the Wisdom of Solomon, as well as the translation of the Hebrew Scriptures into Greek (the Septuagint), testify to the influence of Greek ideas on Judaism. The balance between adapting to the dominant culture and remaining faithful to the teachings of the Torah was delicate, and with the harsh rule of the Seleucids that delicate balance was tipped.

Before the time of the Maccabees, Jews had usually cooperated peacefully with their foreign rulers, for since the time of Jeremiah they had believed that such rulers were part of God's plan to chastise and redeem Israel. (Paul instructs the early Christians in this theology when he exhorts them in Rom 13.1–7 to support the state.) Not all Jews, therefore, supported the Maccabees in their armed revolt against the Seleucid government. Many tried to adapt to Seleucid demands without abandoning the Torah (1.11–15, 52); others preferred martyrdom (1.62–63; 2.28–38). The author of 1 Maccabees believed that the Hasmonean rebellion and subsequent rule was in accord with the divine will.

Although the order of events sometimes differs from the parallel accounts in 2 Maccabees and the Jewish historian Josephus, 1 Maccabees is generally regarded as an accurate historical source, often corroborated by Polybius and other Greek historians. The diplomatic correspondence and royal pronouncements occurring throughout the book (8.23–32; 9.18–20, 25–45; 11.30–37; 12.5–18, 19–23; 13.36–40; 14.20–23, 27–45; 15.9; 15.16–21) appear to be authentic.

The style echoes the biblical books of Samuel and Kings, giving it the aura of an official history of Israel. Commentary is provided in the form of poetic fragments, whose biblical language provides a theological framework for the narrated events. Frequent allusions to biblical prophecies also help guide the reader to see the Hasmonean dynasty as the fulfillment of the divine will.

All extant manuscripts of 1 Maccabees are in Greek or Latin, the original Hebrew having been lost at an early time. The book was probably written shortly after the death of the Hasmonean king John Hyrcanus I in 104 B.C. (see 16.23–24).

1 After Alexander son of Philip, the Macedonian, who came from the land of Kittim, had defeated *a* King Darius of the Persians and the Medes, he succeeded him as king. (He had previously become king of Greece.) ²He fought many battles, conquered strongholds, and put to death the kings of the earth. ³He advanced to the ends of the earth, and plundered many nations. When the earth became quiet before him, he was exalted, and his heart was lifted up. ⁴He gathered a very strong army and ruled over countries, nations, and princes, and they became tributary to him.

5 After this he fell sick and perceived that he was dying. ⁶So he summoned his most honored officers, who had been brought up with him from youth, and divided his kingdom among them while he was still alive. ⁷And after Alexander had reigned twelve years, he died.

8 Then his officers began to rule, each in his own place. ⁹They all put on crowns after his death, and so did their descendants after them for many years; and they caused many evils on the earth.

10 From them came forth a sinful root, Antiochus Epiphanes, son of King Antiochus; he had been a hostage in Rome. He began to reign in the one hundred thirty-seventh year of the kingdom of the Greeks. *b*

11 In those days certain renegades came out from Israel and misled many, saying, "Let us go and make a covenant with the Gentiles around us, for since we separated from them many disasters have come upon us." ¹²This proposal pleased them, ¹³and some of the people eagerly went to the king, who authorized them to observe the ordinances of the Gentiles. ¹⁴So they built a gymnasium in Jerusalem, according to Gentile custom, ¹⁵and removed the marks of circumcision, and abandoned the holy covenant. They joined with the Gentiles and sold themselves to do evil.

16 When Antiochus saw that his kingdom was established, he determined to become king of the land of Egypt, in order that he might reign over both kingdoms. ¹⁷So he invaded Egypt with a strong force, with chariots and elephants

a Gk adds *and he defeated*   *b* 175 B.C.

1.1–10: Introduction. A summary of history from Alexander to Antiochus IV. **1:** *Alexander* the Great (356–323 B.C.), son of Philip of Macedon, who had conquered *Kittim* (Greece), swept through Asia Minor, and *defeated King Darius* III at Issus (333 B.C.) and at Gaugamela (331 B.C.). **3:** After taking Egypt, Mesopotamia, and Persia he advanced to the *ends of the earth* (to Bactria and India). *He was exalted,* i.e. he was deified. Such pride in rulers is castigated in Isa 2.5–22. **4:** He planned a universal empire dominated by Greek culture. **5:** *He fell sick* in Babylon. **6:** A complex history of power struggles lies behind this statement. **8–9:** By 275 B.C. three dynasties were established, the Antigonids of Macedonia, the Ptolemies of Egypt, and the Seleucids of Syria. **9:** *Crowns,* lit. "diadems"; these were a strip of white cloth decorated on the edges. **10:** *Sinful root,* Isa 11.10; Dan 11.7. *Antiochus* IV, who took the name *Epiphanes* ("god manifest"), reigned 175–164 B.C.; he was *son of King Antiochus* III the Great (223–187 B.C.), who had wrested Palestine from Egypt at the battle of Paneas in 198 B.C. but lost most of Asia Minor to Rome at Magnesia in 190 B.C. (compare Dan 11.18). Because of this defeat the

son *had been a hostage in Rome. One hundred thirty-seventh year* of the Seleucid era; reckoning of this era varied in different places; dates given in the notes (*b, c,* etc.) are approximate.

1.11–15: The paganizing program. Greek culture had penetrated Palestine peacefully, but now enthusiasts introduced Greek religion (2 Macc 4.11–17). **11:** *Certain renegades,* led by Jason, whom Antiochus appointed in place of his brother Onias III (2 Macc 4.7). *Renegades,* lit. "lawless ones," those who compromised the Law of Moses. The term is used throughout 1 Maccabees to describe Jews who did not support the Hasmoneans. *Covenant,* prohibition that was a cornerstone of the Law, because of the danger of idolatry (Ex 34.15–16, Deut 7.1–6). See Jer 44.15–23. *Disasters,* loss of business and prestige because relations with Syria had deteriorated. **14:** *A gymnasium,* see 2 Macc 4.9–10 n.

1.16–40: Antiochus invades Egypt and Palestine. Invasion of Egypt is followed by plundering of the temple in Jerusalem (2 Macc 5.1, 11–26). **17:** The Syrian army had *elephants,* though the treaty of Apamea with

and cavalry and with a large fleet. [18] He engaged King Ptolemy of Egypt in battle, and Ptolemy turned and fled before him, and many were wounded and fell. [19] They captured the fortified cities in the land of Egypt, and he plundered the land of Egypt.

20 After subduing Egypt, Antiochus returned in the one hundred forty-third year.[c] He went up against Israel and came to Jerusalem with a strong force. [21] He arrogantly entered the sanctuary and took the golden altar, the lampstand for the light, and all its utensils. [22] He took also the table for the bread of the Presence, the cups for drink offerings, the bowls, the golden censers, the curtain, the crowns, and the gold decoration on the front of the temple; he stripped it all off. [23] He took the silver and the gold, and the costly vessels; he took also the hidden treasures that he found. [24] Taking them all, he went into his own land.

> He shed much blood,
> and spoke with great arrogance.

25 Israel mourned deeply in every
> community,
26 rulers and elders groaned,
> young women and young men
> became faint,
> the beauty of the women faded.
27 Every bridegroom took up the
> lament;
> she who sat in the bridal
> chamber was mourning.
28 Even the land trembled for its
> inhabitants,
> and all the house of Jacob was
> clothed with shame.

29 Two years later the king sent to the cities of Judah a chief collector of tribute,

and he came to Jerusalem with a large force. [30] Deceitfully he spoke peaceable words to them, and they believed him; but he suddenly fell upon the city, dealt it a severe blow, and destroyed many people of Israel. [31] He plundered the city, burned it with fire, and tore down its houses and its surrounding walls. [32] They took captive the women and children, and seized the livestock. [33] Then they fortified the city of David with a great strong wall and strong towers, and it became their citadel. [34] They stationed there a sinful people, men who were renegades. These strengthened their position; [35] they stored up arms and food, and collecting the spoils of Jerusalem they stored them there, and became a great menace,
36 for the citadel[d] became an ambush
> against the sanctuary,
> an evil adversary of Israel at all
> times.
37 On every side of the sanctuary
> they shed innocent blood;
> they even defiled the sanctuary.
38 Because of them the residents of
> Jerusalem fled;
> she became a dwelling of
> strangers;
> she became strange to her
> offspring,
> and her children forsook her.
39 Her sanctuary became desolate like
> a desert;
> her feasts were turned into
> mourning,
> her sabbaths into a reproach,
> her honor into contempt.
40 Her dishonor now grew as great
> as her glory;

_c_ 169 B.C.   _d_ Gk _it_

Rome (188 B.C.) had forbidden this. **18:** *Ptolemy VI Philometor* reigned 180–145 B.C. **20:** *Antiochus returned* because the Roman envoy, Popilius Laenas, threatened him with war if he annexed Egypt; also, news of internal strife in Jerusalem had reached him, and he feared a revolt (2 Macc ch 5). **21:** See Isa 10.5–11. **1.24–28:** Fragment of a contemporary poem. **28:** *The house of Jacob,* Israel, the Jewish people. **33:** *City of David,* a term with several

different meanings in the Hebrew Scriptures (compare Isa 22.9 and 1 Kings 11.27 with 2 Sam 5.7, 9); the precise location of this fortification within Jerusalem is unknown. **34:** *Sinful people,* like "lawless ones," a biblical term used primarily for evil Israelites (Isa 1.4); it here connotes Jews who supported the Seleucids. **36–40:** Poetic fragment (compare Pss 74; 79). **1.41–64:** **Desecration of the temple.**

her exaltation was turned into mourning.

41 Then the king wrote to his whole kingdom that all should be one people, 42 and that all should give up their particular customs. 43 All the Gentiles accepted the command of the king. Many even from Israel gladly adopted his religion; they sacrificed to idols and profaned the sabbath. 44 And the king sent letters by messengers to Jerusalem and the towns of Judah; he directed them to follow customs strange to the land, 45 to forbid burnt offerings and sacrifices and drink offerings in the sanctuary, to profane sabbaths and festivals, 46 to defile the sanctuary and the priests, 47 to build altars and sacred precincts and shrines for idols, to sacrifice swine and other unclean animals, 48 and to leave their sons uncircumcised. They were to make themselves abominable by everything unclean and profane, 49 so that they would forget the law and change all the ordinances. 50 He added, *ᵉ* "And whoever does not obey the command of the king shall die."

51 In such words he wrote to his whole kingdom. He appointed inspectors over all the people and commanded the towns of Judah to offer sacrifice, town by town. 52 Many of the people, everyone who forsook the law, joined them, and they did evil in the land; 53 they drove Israel into hiding in every place of refuge they had.

54 Now on the fifteenth day of Chis-lev, in the one hundred forty-fifth year,*ᶠ* they erected a desolating sacrilege on the altar of burnt offering. They also built altars in the surrounding towns of Judah, 55 and offered incense at the doors of the houses and in the streets. 56 The books of the law that they found they tore to pieces and burned with fire. 57 Anyone found possessing the book of the covenant, or anyone who adhered to the law, was condemned to death by decree of the king. 58 They kept using violence against Israel, against those who were found month after month in the towns. 59 On the twenty-fifth day of the month they offered sacrifice on the altar that was on top of the altar of burnt offering. 60 According to the decree, they put to death the women who had their children circumcised, 61 and their families and those who circumcised them; and they hung the infants from their mothers' necks.

62 But many in Israel stood firm and were resolved in their hearts not to eat unclean food. 63 They chose to die rather than to be defiled by food or to profane the holy covenant; and they did die. 64 Very great wrath came upon Israel.

2 In those days Mattathias son of John son of Simeon, a priest of the family of Joarib, moved from Jerusalem and settled in Modein. 2 He had five sons, John surnamed Gaddi, 3 Simon called Thassi, 4 Judas called Maccabeus, 5 Eleazar called Avaran, and Jonathan called Apphus.

ᵉ Gk lacks He added   ᶠ 167 B.C.

The first outright religious persecution of the Jews, which is also reflected in Dan 11.29–39 (compare 2 Macc 6.1–11). **41–42:** *His whole kingdom,* Syria, Palestine, Mesopotamia, Persia, and parts of Asia Minor. *One people,* unified in language, religion, culture, and even dress; Judaism, with its revealed law and rejection of other gods, opposed this. **47:** *Unclean animals* were not dirty but ritually impure and unacceptable for sacrifice (Lev 22.17–30).

1.54: *Chislev,* approximately December. The *desolating sacrilege* (Dan 11.31; 12.11; 2 Macc 6.2) was an altar to Olympian Zeus and perhaps a statue of him. **59:** *Offered sacrifice,* probably of swine (2 Macc 6.4–5). **60–**

64: 2 Macc chs 6–7, and 4 Maccabees contain stories of martyrdoms. *Chose to die rather than to be defiled by food,* compare Dan 3.8–18. *Wrath came upon Israel,* as a punishment for sin (2 Macc 6.12–16).

2.1–48: Revolt of Mattathias. 1: The family of *Mattathias* is known as Hasmoneans (see p. xiv AP), from a traditional ancestor Hashmonia, not mentioned in 1 Maccabees but named in Josephus (*Antiquities,* XII.vi.1). *Joarib* was first in the list of divisions of priests (1 Chr 24.7; Neh 11.10). *Modein,* in the mountains on the road to Beth-horon, about seventeen miles northwest of Jerusalem. **2–5:** *Simon,* third of the family to rule (chs 13–16). *Maccabeus,* probably from a Hebrew word

6He saw the blasphemies being committed in Judah and Jerusalem, 7and said,

"Alas! Why was I born to see this,
the ruin of my people, the ruin
of the holy city,
and to live there when it was
given over to the enemy,
the sanctuary given over to
aliens?
8 Her temple has become like a
person without honor;*g*
9 her glorious vessels have been
carried into exile.
Her infants have been killed in her
streets,
her youths by the sword of the
foe.
10 What nation has not inherited her
palaces*h*
and has not seized her spoils?
11 All her adornment has been taken
away;
no longer free, she has become a
slave.
12 And see, our holy place, our
beauty,
and our glory have been laid
waste;
the Gentiles have profaned them.
13 Why should we live any
longer?"

14 Then Mattathias and his sons tore their clothes, put on sackcloth, and mourned greatly.

15 The king's officers who were enforcing the apostasy came to the town of Modein to make them offer sacrifice. 16Many from Israel came to them; and Mattathias and his sons were assembled. 17Then the king's officers spoke to Mattathias as follows: "You are a leader, honored and great in this town, and supported by sons and brothers. 18Now be the first to come and do what the king commands, as all the Gentiles and the people of Judah and those that are left in Jerusalem have done. Then you and your sons will be numbered among the Friends of the king, and you and your sons will be honored with silver and gold and many gifts."

19 But Mattathias answered and said in a loud voice: "Even if all the nations that live under the rule of the king obey him, and have chosen to obey his commandments, everyone of them abandoning the religion of their ancestors, 20I and my sons and my brothers will continue to live by the covenant of our ancestors. 21Far be it from us to desert the law and the ordinances. 22We will not obey the king's words by turning aside from our religion to the right hand or to the left."

23 When he had finished speaking these words, a Jew came forward in the sight of all to offer sacrifice on the altar in Modein, according to the king's command. 24When Mattathias saw it, he burned with zeal and his heart was stirred. He gave vent to righteous anger; he ran and killed him on the altar. 25At the same time he killed the king's officer who was forcing them to sacrifice, and he tore down the altar. 26Thus he burned with zeal for the law, just as Phinehas did against Zimri son of Salu.

27 Then Mattathias cried out in the town with a loud voice, saying: "Let every one who is zealous for the law and supports the covenant come out with me!" 28Then he and his sons fled to the hills and left all that they had in the town.

29 At that time many who were seeking righteousness and justice went down to the wilderness to live there, 30they,

g Meaning of Gk uncertain   *h* Other ancient authorities read *has not had a part in her kingdom*

meaning "hammer." The other surnames are of uncertain derivation. *Jonathan,* successor of Judas (chs 9–12). **7–13:** Poetic fragment; compare Pss 44; 74; 79; and the book of Lamentations.

2.14: *Tore their clothes, put on sackcloth,* signs of mourning (Gen 37.34). **18:** *The Friends of the king* were a special class of potentates and courtiers who wore distinctive purple dress and insignia.

2.23: Elsewhere in chs 1–13, "Israelite" is used instead of the term *Jew,* which here perhaps means "Judean." **24:** *His heart,* literally "his kidneys," which were considered the seat of emotion. **26:** *As Phinehas did,* the whole episode is written to echo Num 25.6–15. **28:**

their sons, their wives, and their livestock, because troubles pressed heavily upon them. 31 And it was reported to the king's officers, and to the troops in Jerusalem the city of David, that those who had rejected the king's command had gone down to the hiding places in the wilderness. 32 Many pursued them, and overtook them; they encamped opposite them and prepared for battle against them on the sabbath day. 33 They said to them, "Enough of this! Come out and do what the king commands, and you will live." 34 But they said, "We will not come out, nor will we do what the king commands and so profane the sabbath day." 35 Then the enemy[i] quickly attacked them. 36 But they did not answer them or hurl a stone at them or block up their hiding places, 37 for they said, "Let us all die in our innocence; heaven and earth testify for us that you are killing us unjustly." 38 So they attacked them on the sabbath, and they died, with their wives and children and livestock, to the number of a thousand persons.

39 When Mattathias and his friends learned of it, they mourned for them deeply. 40 And all said to their neighbors: "If we all do as our kindred have done and refuse to fight with the Gentiles for our lives and for our ordinances, they will quickly destroy us from the earth." 41 So they made this decision that day: "Let us fight against anyone who comes to attack us on the sabbath day; let us not all die as our kindred died in their hiding places."

42 Then there united with them a company of Hasideans, mighty warriors of Israel, all who offered themselves willingly for the law. 43 And all who became fugitives to escape their troubles joined them and reinforced them. 44 They organized an army, and struck down sinners in their anger and renegades in their wrath; the survivors fled to the Gentiles for safety. 45 And Mattathias and his friends went around and tore down the altars; 46 they forcibly circumcised all the uncircumcised boys that they found within the borders of Israel. 47 They hunted down the arrogant, and the work prospered in their hands. 48 They rescued the law out of the hands of the Gentiles and kings, and they never let the sinner gain the upper hand.

49 Now the days drew near for Mattathias to die, and he said to his sons: "Arrogance and scorn have now become strong; it is a time of ruin and furious anger. 50 Now, my children, show zeal for the law, and give your lives for the covenant of our ancestors.

51 "Remember the deeds of the ancestors, which they did in their generations; and you will receive great honor and an everlasting name. 52 Was not Abraham found faithful when tested, and it was reckoned to him as righteousness? 53 Joseph in the time of his distress kept the commandment, and became lord of Egypt. 54 Phinehas our ancestor, because he was deeply zealous, received the covenant of everlasting priesthood. 55 Joshua, because he fulfilled the command, became a judge in Israel. 56 Caleb, because he testified in the assembly, received an inheritance in the land. 57 David, because he was merciful, inherited the throne of the kingdom forever. 58 Elijah, because of great zeal for the law, was taken up into heaven. 59 Hannaniah, Azariah, and Mishael believed and were

i Gk *they*

---

2 Macc 5.27. **29–31**: In *the wilderness* of Judea they found *hiding places* in grottoes and caves (Judg 20.47). **37**: 1.63.

2.41: The earliest statement of the principle that one may profane one sabbath in order to keep all the others. **42**: *Hasideans,* "the pious," a group not concerned for Jewish nationalism but only for the religious law. At first they resisted passively (1.62–63; 2.37), but now turned to violent action.

2.49–70: Death of Mattathias. Mattathias is portrayed like Jacob in Gen ch 49. **52**: *Faithful when tested,* Gen 22.1–18. *Reckoned to him,* Gen 15.6; Rom 4.3. **53**: *Joseph,* Gen chs 39–45. **54**: *Phinehas,* v. 26. **55–56**: *Joshua . . . Caleb,* Num 13.1–14.12; 26.65; Josh 1.1–9.

2.57: *Merciful,* or perhaps "loyal" (2 Sam 7.16; Pss 89.35–37; 132.11–12). **58**: 2 Kings 2.9–12. **59–60**: Dan 3.8–30; 6.1–24. **63**: Ps

saved from the flame. 60 Daniel, because of his innocence, was delivered from the mouth of the lions.

61 "And so observe, from generation to generation, that none of those who put their trust in him will lack strength. 62 Do not fear the words of sinners, for their splendor will turn into dung and worms. 63 Today they will be exalted, but tomorrow they will not be found, because they will have returned to the dust, and their plans will have perished. 64 My children, be courageous and grow strong in the law, for by it you will gain honor.

65 "Here is your brother Simeon who, I know, is wise in counsel; always listen to him; he shall be your father. 66 Judas Maccabeus has been a mighty warrior from his youth; he shall command the army for you and fight the battle against the peoples.*j* 67 You shall rally around you all who observe the law, and avenge the wrong done to your people. 68 Pay back the Gentiles in full, and obey the commands of the law."

69 Then he blessed them, and was gathered to his ancestors. 70 He died in the one hundred forty-sixth year*k* and was buried in the tomb of his ancestors at Modein. And all Israel mourned for him with great lamentation.

3 Then his son Judas, who was called Maccabeus, took command in his place. 2 All his brothers and all who had joined his father helped him; they gladly fought for Israel.

3 He extended the glory of his
  people.
  Like a giant he put on his
    breastplate;
  he bound on his armor of war and
    waged battles,
  protecting the camp by his
    sword.
4 He was like a lion in his deeds,

like a lion's cub roaring for
  prey.
5 He searched out and pursued those
  who broke the law;
  he burned those who troubled
    his people.
6 Law-breakers shrank back for fear
  of him;
  all the evildoers were
    confounded;
  and deliverance prospered by his
    hand.
7 He embittered many kings,
  but he made Jacob glad by his
    deeds,
  and his memory is blessed
    forever.
8 He went through the cities of
  Judah;
  he destroyed the ungodly out of
    the land;*l*
  thus he turned away wrath from
    Israel.
9 He was renowned to the ends of
  the earth;
  he gathered in those who were
    perishing.

10 Apollonius now gathered together Gentiles and a large force from Samaria to fight against Israel. 11 When Judas learned of it, he went out to meet him, and he defeated and killed him. Many were wounded and fell, and the rest fled. 12 Then they seized their spoils; and Judas took the sword of Apollonius, and used it in battle the rest of his life.

13 When Seron, the commander of the Syrian army, heard that Judas had gathered a large company, including a body of faithful soldiers who stayed with him and went out to battle, 14 he said, "I will make a name for myself and win honor in the kingdom. I will make war on Judas and his companions, who scorn

---

j Or *of the people*   *k* 166 B.C.   *l* Gk *it*

37.10, 35–36. **69**: *Gathered to his ancestors,* buried with his ancestors (Judg 2.10).
3.1–12: Defeat of Apollonius. 3–9: From a contemporary poem. **4**: *Like a lion,* Hos 5.14. **8**: *He turned away wrath,* i.e. God's punishment, through his exploits (2 Macc

7.38). **10**: *Apollonius,* according to Josephus (*Antiquities,* XII. v. 5; vii.1), was governor of Samaria.
3.13–26: Battle of Beth-horon. This was Judas' first great victory. **16**: *The ascent of Beth-horon* was a route from the coastal plain

the king's command." [15] Once again a strong army of godless men went up with him to help him, to take vengeance on the Israelites.

16 When he approached the ascent of Beth-horon, Judas went out to meet him with a small company. [17] But when they saw the army coming to meet them, they said to Judas, "How can we, few as we are, fight against so great and so strong a multitude? And we are faint, for we have eaten nothing today." [18] Judas replied, "It is easy for many to be hemmed in by few, for in the sight of Heaven there is no difference between saving by many or by few. [19] It is not on the size of the army that victory in battle depends, but strength comes from Heaven. [20] They come against us in great insolence and lawlessness to destroy us and our wives and our children, and to despoil us; [21] but we fight for our lives and our laws. [22] He himself will crush them before us; as for you, do not be afraid of them."

23 When he finished speaking, he rushed suddenly against Seron and his army, and they were crushed before him. [24] They pursued them[m] down the descent of Beth-horon to the plain; eight hundred of them fell, and the rest fled into the land of the Philistines. [25] Then Judas and his brothers began to be feared, and terror fell on the Gentiles all around them. [26] His fame reached the king, and the Gentiles talked of the battles of Judas.

27 When King Antiochus heard these reports, he was greatly angered; and he sent and gathered all the forces of his kingdom, a very strong army. [28] He opened his coffers and gave a year's pay to his forces, and ordered them to be ready for any need. [29] Then he saw that the money in the treasury was exhausted, and that the revenues from the country were small because of the dissension and disaster that he had caused in the land by abolishing the laws that had existed from the earliest days. [30] He feared that he might not have such funds as he had before for his expenses and for the gifts that he used to give more lavishly than preceding kings. [31] He was greatly perplexed in mind; then he determined to go to Persia and collect the revenues from those regions and raise a large fund.

32 He left Lysias, a distinguished man of royal lineage, in charge of the king's affairs from the river Euphrates to the borders of Egypt. [33] Lysias was also to take care of his son Antiochus until he returned. [34] And he turned over to Lysias[n] half of his forces and the elephants, and gave him orders about all that he wanted done. As for the residents of Judea and Jerusalem, [35] Lysias was to send a force against them to wipe out and destroy the strength of Israel and the remnant of Jerusalem; he was to banish the memory of them from the place, [36] settle aliens in all their territory, and distribute their land by lot. [37] Then the king took the remaining half of his forces and left Antioch his capital in the one hundred and forty-seventh year.[o] He crossed the Euphrates river and went through the upper provinces.

38 Lysias chose Ptolemy son of Dorymenes, and Nicanor and Gorgias, able men among the Friends of the king, [39] and sent with them forty thousand in-

m Other ancient authorities read *him*
n Gk *him*   o 165 B.C.

to the Judean highlands. The town is about twelve miles northwest of Jerusalem. **18**: The word *Heaven* was used to avoid pronouncing God's name (compare "he himself," v. 22, and see Sus 9 n.). *By many or by few,* 1 Sam 14.6. **24**: *Land of the Philistines,* the coastal plain.
3.27–4.35: **Campaigns of Lysias.** Antiochus IV goes to Persia; Judas defeats Lysias at Emmaus and Beth-zur.

3.28: *Any need* implies that Seleucid power was beginning to decline. **30**: Antiochus was noted for his extravagance (see 2 Macc 4.30 n.). **33**: *Antiochus* V Eupator, *his son,* was only nine years old; he reigned 164–162 B.C. **36**: *Settle aliens,* as the Assyrians had done (2 Kings 17.24). **37**: *Antioch,* modern Antakya, was built by Seleucus I in 300 B.C. and expanded by Antiochus IV. *Upper provinces,* Persia.

fantry and seven thousand cavalry to go into the land of Judah and destroy it, as the king had commanded. ⁴⁰So they set out with their entire force, and when they arrived they encamped near Emmaus in the plain. ⁴¹When the traders of the region heard what was said to them, they took silver and gold in immense amounts, and fetters, *p* and went to the camp to get the Israelites for slaves. And forces from Syria and the land of the Philistines joined with them.

42 Now Judas and his brothers saw that misfortunes had increased and that the forces were encamped in their territory. They also learned what the king had commanded to do to the people to cause their final destruction. ⁴³But they said to one another, "Let us restore the ruins of our people, and fight for our people and the sanctuary." ⁴⁴So the congregation assembled to be ready for battle, and to pray and ask for mercy and compassion.
⁴⁵ Jerusalem was uninhabited like a
　　wilderness;
　　not one of her children went in
　　　or out.
　The sanctuary was trampled
　　down,
　　and aliens held the citadel;
　it was a lodging place for the
　　Gentiles.
　Joy was taken from Jacob;
　　the flute and the harp ceased to
　　　play.

46 Then they gathered together and went to Mizpah, opposite Jerusalem, because Israel formerly had a place of prayer in Mizpah. ⁴⁷They fasted that day, put on sackcloth and sprinkled ashes on their heads, and tore their clothes. ⁴⁸And they opened the book of the law

to inquire into those matters about which the Gentiles consulted the likenesses of their gods. ⁴⁹They also brought the vestments of the priesthood and the first fruits and the tithes, and they stirred up the nazirites *q* who had completed their days; ⁵⁰and they cried aloud to Heaven, saying,
　"What shall we do with these?
　　Where shall we take them?
⁵¹ Your sanctuary is trampled down
　　and profaned,
　　and your priests mourn in
　　　humiliation.
⁵² Here the Gentiles are assembled
　　against us to destroy us;
　　you know what they plot
　　　against us.
⁵³ How will we be able to withstand
　　　them,
　　if you do not help us?"

54 Then they sounded the trumpets and gave a loud shout. ⁵⁵After this Judas appointed leaders of the people, in charge of thousands and hundreds and fifties and tens. ⁵⁶Those who were building houses, or were about to be married, or were planting a vineyard, or were fainthearted, he told to go home again, according to the law. ⁵⁷Then the army marched out and encamped to the south of Emmaus. 58 And Judas said, "Arm yourselves and be courageous. Be ready early in the morning to fight with these Gentiles who have assembled against us to destroy us and our sanctuary. ⁵⁹It is better for us to die in battle than to see the misfortunes of our nation and of the sanctuary. ⁶⁰But as his will in heaven may be, so shall he do."

p Syr: Gk Mss, Vg *slaves*　　*q* That is *those separated* or *those consecrated*

3.38: *Ptolemy,* known as Macron (2 Macc 10.12). *Nicanor,* 2 Macc 8.9. *Gorgias,* 2 Macc 10.14. **40**: *Emmaus* (not the Emmaus of Lk 24.13), was about twenty-five miles west of Jerusalem. **41**: Some pro-Syrian Jews joined Antiochus' army. **45**: Compare Ps 74; Isa 24.8.
3.46: *Mizpah,* perhaps en-Nebi Samwil, seven miles northwest of Jerusalem, but sometimes identified with Tell en-Nasbeh, nine miles north of the city. See 1 Sam 7.5–

11. **48**: They expected guidance from *the book of the law,* the Pentateuch, while the Greeks sought oracles from *the likenesses of their gods.* **49**: *Tithes* were brought to Jerusalem and there distributed (Neh 10.35–38). *Nazirites,* Num 6.1–21. **50–53**: Verse 45. **54**: *Trumpets,* to summon the army (Num 10.1–10). **55**: In Moses' day such *leaders* assisted in civic administration (Ex 18.25); here, as in the Essene *War Scroll* from Qumran, they have a military

4 Now Gorgias took five thousand infantry and one thousand picked cavalry, and this division moved out by night ²to fall upon the camp of the Jews and attack them suddenly. Men from the citadel were his guides. ³But Judas heard of it, and he and his warriors moved out to attack the king's force in Emmaus ⁴while the division was still absent from the camp. ⁵When Gorgias entered the camp of Judas by night, he found no one there, so he looked for them in the hills, because he said, "These men are running away from us."

6 At daybreak Judas appeared in the plain with three thousand men, but they did not have armor and swords such as they desired. ⁷And they saw the camp of the Gentiles, strong and fortified, with cavalry all around it; and these men were trained in war. ⁸But Judas said to those who were with him, "Do not fear their numbers or be afraid when they charge. ⁹Remember how our ancestors were saved at the Red Sea, when Pharaoh with his forces pursued them. ¹⁰And now, let us cry to Heaven, to see whether he will favor us and remember his covenant with our ancestors and crush this army before us today. ¹¹Then all the Gentiles will know that there is one who redeems and saves Israel."

12 When the foreigners looked up and saw them coming against them, ¹³they went out from their camp to battle. Then the men with Judas blew their trumpets ¹⁴and engaged in battle. The Gentiles were crushed, and fled into the plain, ¹⁵and all those in the rear fell by the sword. They pursued them to Gazara, and to the plains of Idumea, and to Azotus and Jamnia; and three thousand of

them fell. ¹⁶Then Judas and his force turned back from pursuing them, ¹⁷and he said to the people, "Do not be greedy for plunder, for there is a battle before us; ¹⁸Gorgias and his force are near us in the hills. But stand now against our enemies and fight them, and afterward seize the plunder boldly."

19 Just as Judas was finishing this speech, a detachment appeared, coming out of the hills. ²⁰They saw that their army^r had been put to flight, and that the Jews^r were burning the camp, for the smoke that was seen showed what had happened. ²¹When they perceived this, they were greatly frightened, and when they also saw the army of Judas drawn up in the plain for battle, ²²they all fled into the land of the Philistines. ²³Then Judas returned to plunder the camp, and they seized a great amount of gold and silver, and cloth dyed blue and sea purple, and great riches. ²⁴On their return they sang hymns and praises to Heaven—"For he is good, for his mercy endures forever." ²⁵Thus Israel had a great deliverance that day.

26 Those of the foreigners who escaped went and reported to Lysias all that had happened. ²⁷When he heard it, he was perplexed and discouraged, for things had not happened to Israel as he had intended, nor had they turned out as the king had ordered. ²⁸But the next year he mustered sixty thousand picked infantry and five thousand cavalry to subdue them. ²⁹They came into Idumea and encamped at Beth-zur, and Judas met them with ten thousand men.

30 When he saw that their army was strong, he prayed, saying, "Blessed are

r Gk *they*

---

function (2 Macc 8.22–23). **56:** Deut 20.5–8.
4.2: *Men from the citadel,* Jewish refugees opposed to Judas. **9:** Ex 14.21–29. **15:** The pursuit went in all directions. *Gazara,* or Gezer (Josh 21.21; 1 Kings 9.17), was five miles northwest of Emmaus. *Idumea* was far to the south. *Azotus,* or Ashdod, and *Jamnia,* lay west and southwest. **17–18:** Judas maintained discipline (2 Macc 8.26).
4.19: *The hills,* the Judean highland. **24:**

Heaven, see 3.18 n. See Ps 118.1; 136.1. **26–35:** The account in 2 Macc 11.1–12 puts the rout of Lysias after the death of Timothy. **28:** *The next year,* perhaps as late as autumn, 164 B.C. **29:** *Beth-zur,* about twenty miles south of Jerusalem on the road to Hebron. Lysias decided to attack Jerusalem from the south.
4.30–35: The account in 2 Macc 11.6–15

you, O Savior of Israel, who crushed the attack of the mighty warrior by the hand of your servant David, and gave the camp of the Philistines into the hands of Jonathan son of Saul, and of the man who carried his armor. [31] Hem in this army by the hand of your people Israel, and let them be ashamed of their troops and their cavalry. [32] Fill them with cowardice; melt the boldness of their strength; let them tremble in their destruction. [33] Strike them down with the sword of those who love you, and let all who know your name praise you with hymns."

34 Then both sides attacked, and there fell of the army of Lysias five thousand men; they fell in action.[s] [35] When Lysias saw the rout of his troops and observed the boldness that inspired those of Judas, and how ready they were either to live or to die nobly, he withdrew to Antioch and enlisted mercenaries in order to invade Judea again with an even larger army.

36 Then Judas and his brothers said, "See, our enemies are crushed; let us go up to cleanse the sanctuary and dedicate it." [37] So all the army assembled and went up to Mount Zion. [38] There they saw the sanctuary desolate, the altar profaned, and the gates burned. In the courts they saw bushes sprung up as in a thicket, or as on one of the mountains. They saw also the chambers of the priests in ruins. [39] Then they tore their clothes and mourned with great lamentation; they sprinkled themselves with ashes [40] and fell face down on the ground. And when the signal was given with the trumpets, they cried out to Heaven.

41 Then Judas detailed men to fight against those in the citadel until he had cleansed the sanctuary. [42] He chose blameless priests devoted to the law, [43] and they cleansed the sanctuary and removed the defiled stones to an unclean place. [44] They deliberated what to do about the altar of burnt offering, which had been profaned. [45] And they thought it best to tear it down, so that it would not be a lasting shame to them that the Gentiles had defiled it. So they tore down the altar, [46] and stored the stones in a convenient place on the temple hill until a prophet should come to tell what to do with them. [47] Then they took unhewn[t] stones, as the law directs, and built a new altar like the former one. [48] They also rebuilt the sanctuary and the interior of the temple, and consecrated the courts. [49] They made new holy vessels, and brought the lampstand, the altar of incense, and the table into the temple. [50] Then they offered incense on the altar and lit the lamps on the lampstand, and these gave light in the temple. [51] They placed the bread on the table and hung up the curtains. Thus they finished all the work they had undertaken.

52 Early in the morning on the twenty-fifth day of the ninth month, which is the month of Chislev, in the one hundred forty-eighth year,[u] [53] they rose and offered sacrifice, as the law directs, on the new altar of burnt offering that they had built. [54] At the very season and on the very day that the Gentiles had profaned it, it was dedicated with songs and harps and lutes and cymbals. [55] All the people fell on their faces and wor-

s Or and some fell on the opposite side
t Gk whole   u 164 B.C.

---

agrees that Judas won the battle, but states that there was a negotiated peace.
4.36–61: Rededication of the temple.
38: *Chambers of the priests* perhaps surrounded the sanctuary on three sides. **41:** *The citadel* (1.33–35) was occupied by a Syrian garrison until the time of Simon (13.49–52). **46:** Malachi was regarded as the last *prophet;* though such men as John Hyrcanus I and John the Baptist were thought to have prophetic gifts, this was not universally recognized. **47:** Ex

20.25; Deut 27.5–6. **50:** *Offered incense . . . lit the lamps,* Ex 30.7–8. **51:** *The bread,* of the Presence (Ex 25.30).
4.52–59: Judas set the rededication of the temple exactly three years after its pollution (1.54) and three and a half years after Antiochus' capture of Jerusalem (Dan 7.25; but see 2 Macc 10.3). The Hanukkah festival, celebrated *for eight days* like Hezekiah's reconsecration (2 Chr 29.17), commemorates this event.

shiped and blessed Heaven, who had prospered them. [56] So they celebrated the dedication of the altar for eight days, and joyfully offered burnt offerings; they offered a sacrifice of well-being and a thanksgiving offering. [57] They decorated the front of the temple with golden crowns and small shields; they restored the gates and the chambers for the priests, and fitted them with doors. [58] There was very great joy among the people, and the disgrace brought by the Gentiles was removed.

59 Then Judas and his brothers and all the assembly of Israel determined that every year at that season the days of dedication of the altar should be observed with joy and gladness for eight days, beginning with the twenty-fifth day of the month of Chislev.

60 At that time they fortified Mount Zion with high walls and strong towers all around, to keep the Gentiles from coming and trampling them down as they had done before. [61] Judas[v] stationed a garrison there to guard it; he also fortified Beth-zur to guard it, so that the people might have a stronghold that faced Idumea.

5 When the Gentiles all around heard that the altar had been rebuilt and the sanctuary dedicated as it was before, they became very angry, [2] and they determined to destroy the descendants of Jacob who lived among them. So they began to kill and destroy among the people. [3] But Judas made war on the descendants of Esau in Idumea, at Akrabattene, because they kept lying in wait for Israel. He dealt them a heavy blow and humbled them and despoiled them. [4] He also

remembered the wickedness of the sons of Baean, who were a trap and a snare to the people and ambushed them on the highways. [5] They were shut up by him in their[w] towers; and he encamped against them, vowed their complete destruction, and burned with fire their towers and all who were in them. [6] Then he crossed over to attack the Ammonites, where he found a strong band and many people, with Timothy as their leader. [7] He engaged in many battles with them, and they were crushed before him; he struck them down. [8] He also took Jazer and its villages; then he returned to Judea.

9 Now the Gentiles in Gilead gathered together against the Israelites who lived in their territory, and planned to destroy them. But they fled to the stronghold of Dathema, [10] and sent to Judas and his brothers a letter that said, "The Gentiles around us have gathered together to destroy us. [11] They are preparing to come and capture the stronghold to which we have fled, and Timothy is leading their forces. [12] Now then, come and rescue us from their hands, for many of us have fallen, [13] and all our kindred who were in the land of Tob have been killed; the enemy[x] have captured their wives and children and goods, and have destroyed about a thousand persons there."

14 While the letter was still being read, other messengers, with their garments torn, came from Galilee and made a similar report; [15] they said that the people of Ptolemais and Tyre and Sidon, and

v Gk *He*   *w* Gk *her*   *x* Gk *they*

5.1–68: Campaigns in all directions. Judas now attacked Idumea in the south (vv. 3–5, 65), Ammon and Gilead east of the Jordan (vv. 6–13, 24–51), Galilee in the north (vv. 21–23), and the coastal plain. These events may have occurred after the death of Antiochus IV (6.16). **2**: *Descendants of Jacob,* Israelites or Jews. **3**: *Descendants of Esau,* Edomites or Idumeans, south of the Dead Sea. *Akrabattene,* perhaps on the border between Idumea and Judea. **4**: *Baean,* probably in Transjordan (Num 32.3). **6**: *Ammonites,* a

Semitic people east of the Jordan near the present Amman. **8**: *Jazer,* west of Amman, fifteen miles north of Heshbon (Num 32.3).

5.9: *Gilead,* east of the Jordan between the Yarmuk and the Arnon (Josh 22.9). *Dathema,* possibly el-Hosn, in Gilead opposite Beisan; or Ramtha, now near the Syrian border. **13**: *Land of Tob,* possibly Hippos, twelve miles southeast of the Sea of Galilee (Judg 11.3; 2 Macc 12.17). **15**: *Ptolemais,* or Acco (Judg 1.31), now Acre, north of Haifa on the coast. *Tyre and Sidon,* farther north in Lebanon. As

all Galilee of the Gentiles,[y] had gathered together against them "to annihilate us." [16]When Judas and the people heard these messages, a great assembly was called to determine what they should do for their kindred who were in distress and were being attacked by enemies.[z] [17]Then Judas said to his brother Simon, "Choose your men and go and rescue your kindred in Galilee; Jonathan my brother and I will go to Gilead." [18]But he left Joseph, son of Zechariah, and Azariah, a leader of the people, with the rest of the forces, in Judea to guard it; [19]and he gave them this command, "Take charge of this people, but do not engage in battle with the Gentiles until we return." [20]Then three thousand men were assigned to Simon to go to Galilee, and eight thousand to Judas for Gilead.

21 So Simon went to Galilee and fought many battles against the Gentiles, and the Gentiles were crushed before him. [22]He pursued them to the gate of Ptolemais; as many as three thousand of the Gentiles fell, and he despoiled them. [23]Then he took the Jews[a] of Galilee and Arbatta, with their wives and children, and all they possessed, and led them to Judea with great rejoicing.

24 Judas Maccabeus and his brother Jonathan crossed the Jordan and made three days' journey into the wilderness. [25]They encountered the Nabateans, who met them peaceably and told them all that had happened to their kindred in Gilead: [26]"Many of them have been shut up in Bozrah and Bosor, in Alema and Chaspho, Maked and Carnaim"—all these towns were strong and large— [27]"and some have been shut up in the other towns of Gilead; the enemy[b] are getting ready to attack the strongholds tomorrow and capture and destroy all these people in a single day."

28 Then Judas and his army quickly turned back by the wilderness road to Bozrah; and he took the town, and killed every male by the edge of the sword; then he seized all its spoils and burned it with fire. [29]He left the place at night, and they went all the way to the stronghold of Dathema.[c] [30]At dawn they looked out and saw a large company, which could not be counted, carrying ladders and engines of war to capture the stronghold, and attacking the Jews within.[d] [31]So Judas saw that the battle had begun and that the cry of the town went up to Heaven, with trumpets and loud shouts, [32]and he said to the men of his forces, "Fight today for your kindred!" [33]Then he came up behind them in three companies, who sounded their trumpets and cried aloud in prayer. [34]And when the army of Timothy realized that it was Maccabeus, they fled before him, and he dealt them a heavy blow. As many as eight thousand of them fell that day.

35 Next he turned aside to Maapha,[e] and fought against it and took it; and he killed every male in it, plundered it, and burned it with fire. [36]From there he marched on and took Chaspho, Maked, and Bosor, and the other towns of Gilead.

37 After these things Timothy gathered another army and encamped opposite Raphon, on the other side of the stream. [38]Judas sent men to spy out the camp, and they reported to him, "All the Gentiles around us have gathered to him; it is a very large force. [39]They also have hired Arabs to help them, and they are encamped across the stream, ready

y Gk *aliens*   z Gk *them*   a Gk *those*
b Gk *they*   c Gk lacks *of Dathema.* See verse 9
d Gk *and they were attacking them*   e Other
ancient authorities read *Alema*

yet few Jews lived in *Galilee of the Gentiles* (Isa 9.1; Mt 4.15). **23**: *Arbatta,* either near the Sea of Galilee, or the Arabah depression south of the Dead Sea (Deut 1.7; Josh 11.16).
5.25: *Nabateans,* or Nebaioth (Gen 25.13), an Arab people living as nomads in the desert east of Palestine as far north as Palmyra. **26**:

Bozrah, southeast of Dera'a (Isa 63.1; Jer 48.24). *Bosor,* Bezer in the desert (Deut 4.43). Alema, unidentified. *Chaspho* and *Maked,* cities of Gilead (v. 36). *Carnaim,* Gen 14.5; Am 6.13; 2 Macc 12.21, 26. **28**: *Killed every male,* Gen 34.25.
5.37: *The stream,* a tributary of the Yar-

to come and fight against you." And Judas went to meet them.

40 Now as Judas and his army drew near to the stream of water, Timothy said to the officers of his forces, "If he crosses over to us first, we will not be able to resist him, for he will surely defeat us. 41 But if he shows fear and camps on the other side of the river, we will cross over to him and defeat him." 42 When Judas approached the stream of water, he stationed the officers*f* of the army at the stream and gave them this command, "Permit no one to encamp, but make them all enter the battle." 43 Then he crossed over against them first, and the whole army followed him. All the Gentiles were defeated before him, and they threw away their arms and fled into the sacred precincts at Carnaim. 44 But he took the town and burned the sacred precincts with fire, together with all who were in them. Thus Carnaim was conquered; they could stand before Judas no longer.

45 Then Judas gathered together all the Israelites in Gilead, the small and the great, with their wives and children and goods, a very large company, to go to the land of Judah. 46 So they came to Ephron. This was a large and very strong town on the road, and they could not go around it to the right or to the left; they had to go through it. 47 But the people of the town shut them out and blocked up the gates with stones.

48 Judas sent them this friendly message, "Let us pass through your land to get to our land. No one will do you harm; we will simply pass by on foot." But they refused to open to him. 49 Then Judas ordered proclamation to be made to the army that all should encamp where they were. 50 So the men of the forces

encamped, and he fought against the town all that day and all the night, and the town was delivered into his hands. 51 He destroyed every male by the edge of the sword, and razed and plundered the town. Then he passed through the town over the bodies of the dead.

52 Then they crossed the Jordan into the large plain before Beth-shan. 53 Judas kept rallying the laggards and encouraging the people all the way until he came to the land of Judah. 54 So they went up to Mount Zion with joy and gladness, and offered burnt offerings, because they had returned in safety; not one of them had fallen.

55 Now while Judas and Jonathan were in Gilead and their*g* brother Simon was in Galilee before Ptolemais, 56 Joseph son of Zechariah, and Azariah, the commanders of the forces, heard of their brave deeds and of the heroic war they had fought. 57 So they said, "Let us also make a name for ourselves; let us go and make war on the Gentiles around us." 58 So they issued orders to the men of the forces that were with them and marched against Jamnia. 59 Gorgias and his men came out of the town to meet them in battle. 60 Then Joseph and Azariah were routed, and were pursued to the borders of Judea; as many as two thousand of the people of Israel fell that day. 61 Thus the people suffered a great rout because, thinking to do a brave deed, they did not listen to Judas and his brothers. 62 But they did not belong to the family of those men through whom deliverance was given to Israel.

63 The man Judas and his brothers were greatly honored in all Israel and among all the Gentiles, wherever their

f Or *scribes*   *g* Gk *his*

---

muk. **39**: *Arabs* were not usually hostile to the Jews but could be *hired* as mercenaries. **40–41**: Judas heard Timothy's order or decided to make a surprise attack (compare 1 Sam 14.7–10). **43**: *Sacred precincts,* of Atargatis, the Syrian fish goddess (2 Macc 12.26). **46**: *Ephron,* eight miles east of the Jordan, opposite Beth-shan (v. 52), and west of Irbid (Arbela).

5.48–51: Num 21.21–24. **52**: *The large plain,* between the Jordan and Mt. Gilboa. *Beth-shan,* Beisan, about eighteen miles south of the Sea of Galilee (Judg 1.27; 1 Kings 4.12). **58**: *Jamnia,* 4.15. **62**: Only *the family* of the Hasmoneans is regarded as divinely chosen to save Israel.

name was heard. 64 People gathered to them and praised them.

65 Then Judas and his brothers went out and fought the descendants of Esau in the land to the south. He struck Hebron and its villages and tore down its strongholds and burned its towers on all sides. 66 Then he marched off to go into the land of the Philistines, and passed through Marisa. *h* 67 On that day some priests, who wished to do a brave deed, fell in battle, for they went out to battle unwisely. 68 But Judas turned aside to Azotus in the land of the Philistines; he tore down their altars, and the carved images of their gods he burned with fire; he plundered the towns and returned to the land of Judah.

6 King Antiochus was going through the upper provinces when he heard that Elymais in Persia was a city famed for its wealth in silver and gold. 2 Its temple was very rich, containing golden shields, breastplates, and weapons left there by Alexander son of Philip, the Macedonian king who first reigned over the Greeks. 3 So he came and tried to take the city and plunder it, but he could not because his plan had become known to the citizens 4 and they withstood him in battle. So he fled and in great disappointment left there to return to Babylon.

5 Then someone came to him in Persia and reported that the armies that had gone into the land of Judah had been routed; 6 that Lysias had gone first with a strong force, but had turned and fled before the Jews; *i* that the Jews *j* had grown strong from the arms, supplies, and abundant spoils that they had taken from the armies they had cut down; 7 that they had torn down the abomination that he had erected on the altar in Jerusalem; and that they had surrounded the sanctuary with high walls as before, and also Bethzur, his town.

8 When the king heard this news, he was astounded and badly shaken. He took to his bed and became sick from disappointment, because things had not turned out for him as he had planned. 9 He lay there for many days, because deep disappointment continually gripped him, and he realized that he was dying. 10 So he called all his Friends and said to them, "Sleep has departed from my eyes and I am downhearted with worry. 11 I said to myself, 'To what distress I have come! And into what a great flood I now am plunged! For I was kind and beloved in my power.' 12 But now I remember the wrong I did in Jerusalem. I seized all its vessels of silver and gold, and I sent to destroy the inhabitants of Judah without good reason. 13 I know that it is because of this that these misfortunes have come upon me; here I am, perishing of bitter disappointment in a strange land."

14 Then he called for Philip, one of his Friends, and made him ruler over all his kingdom. 15 He gave him the crown and his robe and the signet, so that he

h Other ancient authorities read *Samaria*
i Gk *them*   j Gk *they*

5.65: *Descendants of Esau*, Edomites. *Hebron*, the old capital of David, twenty miles south of Jerusalem (Gen 23.2; 2 Sam 2.11). **66**: *Marisa*, or Mareshah (Josh 15.44), near Beit-Jibrin.
6.1–17: **Death of Antiochus IV and accession of Antiochus V** (2 Macc ch 9). **1**: *The upper provinces*, Persia and Mesopotamia (3.31–37). *Elymais*, biblical Elam or Susiana; but according to 2 Macc 9.2 the incident occurred in Persepolis. **2**: *Its temple* was that of Nanea (2 Macc 1.13–16), or Anahita, identified with Artemis. **5**: *In Persia*, perhaps at Ecbatana (2 Macc 9.3). According to Polybius (*History*, XXXI. 11) the king took sick and died at Tabae (perhaps Gabae, modern Isfahan). **7**: *The abomination*, statue of a pagan god.
6.8–9: *Deep disappointment*, perhaps insanity; according to 2 Macc 9.5–12 he was stricken with a loathsome physical malady. **12**: *Its vessels*, Dan 5.2. **14–15**: *Philip . . . ruler*, Lysias, satrap in the west, had previously been given this commission (3.32). *The signet*, a symbol of transfer of authority to the regent. **16**: 2 Macc 11.33 implies that Antiochus IV had died before the restoration of the temple at Jerusalem. **17**: The word *Eupator* means "of a good father."

might guide his son Antiochus and bring him up to be king. [16] Thus King Antiochus died there in the one hundred forty-ninth year. [k] [17] When Lysias learned that the king was dead, he set up Antiochus the king's [l] son to reign. Lysias [m] had brought him up from boyhood; he named him Eupator.

18 Meanwhile the garrison in the citadel kept hemming Israel in around the sanctuary. They were trying in every way to harm them and strengthen the Gentiles. [19] Judas therefore resolved to destroy them, and assembled all the people to besiege them. [20] They gathered together and besieged the citadel [n] in the one hundred fiftieth year; [o] and he built siege towers and other engines of war. [21] But some of the garrison escaped from the siege and some of the ungodly Israelites joined them. [22] They went to the king and said, "How long will you fail to do justice and to avenge our kindred? [23] We were happy to serve your father, to live by what he said, and to follow his commands. [24] For this reason the sons of our people besieged the citadel [p] and became hostile to us; moreover, they have put to death as many of us as they have caught, and they have seized our inheritances. [25] It is not against us alone that they have stretched out their hands; they have also attacked all the lands on their borders. [26] And see, today they have encamped against the citadel in Jerusalem to take it; they have fortified both the sanctuary and Beth-zur; [27] unless you quickly prevent them, they will do still greater things, and you will not be able to stop them."

28 The king was enraged when he heard this. He assembled all his Friends, the commanders of his forces and those in authority. [q] [29] Mercenary forces also came to him from other kingdoms and from islands of the seas. [30] The number of his forces was one hundred thousand foot soldiers, twenty thousand horsemen, and thirty-two elephants accustomed to war. [31] They came through Idumea and encamped against Beth-zur, and for many days they fought and built engines of war; but the Jews [r] sallied out and burned these with fire, and fought courageously.

32 Then Judas marched away from the citadel and encamped at Beth-zechariah, opposite the camp of the king. [33] Early in the morning the king set out and took his army by a forced march along the road to Beth-zechariah, and his troops made ready for battle and sounded their trumpets. [34] They offered the elephants the juice of grapes and mulberries, to arouse them for battle. [35] They distributed the animals among the phalanxes; with each elephant they stationed a thousand men armed with coats of mail, and with brass helmets on their heads; and five hundred picked horsemen were assigned to each beast. [36] These took their position beforehand wherever the animal was; wherever it went, they went with it, and they never left it. [37] On the elephants [s] were wooden towers, strong and covered; they were fastened on each animal by special harness, and on each were four [t] armed men who fought from there, and also its Indian driver. [38] The rest of the cavalry were stationed on either side, on the two flanks of the

k 163 B.C.   *l* Gk *his*   *m* Gk *He*   *n* Gk *it*
o 162 B.C.   *p* Meaning of Gk uncertain
q Gk *those over the reins*   *r* Gk *they*
s Gk *them*   *t* Cn: Some authorities read *thirty*; others *thirty-two*

6.18–54: Attack on the citadel and second battle at Beth-zur. The citadel was equally important to the Syrians and to Judas, for without it the Seleucid monarchy could not maintain sovereignty in Palestine. **21:** *Ungodly,* i.e. pro-Greek.
6.28–30: Lysias' second campaign is here dated 162 B.C. (v. 20), but in 2 Macc 13.1 a year earlier. **31:** Judas had won the first battle at *Beth-zur* (4.29–34) and had fortified it

(4.61). **32:** *Beth-zechariah* was six miles from Beth-zur and ten miles southwest of Jerusalem. **34–35:** *The juice* may have been to simulate blood; but *elephants* were sometimes given wine to madden them. Here the animals were used to force an opening in the ranks. *Phalanxes,* the Greek infantry formation, eight to eighteen men deep, highly disciplined and mobile. The Seleucids could muster twenty thousand of such infantry.

army, to harass the enemy while being themselves protected by the phalanxes. ³⁹When the sun shone on the shields of gold and brass, the hills were ablaze with them and gleamed like flaming torches.

40 Now a part of the king's army was spread out on the high hills, and some troops were on the plain, and they advanced steadily and in good order. ⁴¹All who heard the noise made by their multitude, by the marching of the multitude and the clanking of their arms, trembled, for the army was very large and strong. ⁴²But Judas and his army advanced to the battle, and six hundred of the king's army fell. ⁴³Now Eleazar, called Avaran, saw that one of the animals was equipped with royal armor. It was taller than all the others, and he supposed that the king was on it. ⁴⁴So he gave his life to save his people and to win for himself an everlasting name. ⁴⁵He courageously ran into the midst of the phalanx to reach it; he killed men right and left, and they parted before him on both sides. ⁴⁶He got under the elephant, stabbed it from beneath, and killed it; but it fell to the ground upon him and he died. ⁴⁷When the Jews ᵘ saw the royal might and the fierce attack of the forces, they turned away in flight.

48 The soldiers of the king's army went up to Jerusalem against them, and the king encamped in Judea and at Mount Zion. ⁴⁹He made peace with the people of Beth-zur, and they evacuated the town because they had no provisions there to withstand a siege, since it was a sabbatical year for the land. ⁵⁰So the king took Beth-zur and stationed a guard there to hold it. ⁵¹Then he encamped before the sanctuary for many days. He set up siege towers, engines of war to throw fire and stones, machines to shoot ar-

rows, and catapults. ⁵²The Jews ᵘ also made engines of war to match theirs, and fought for many days. ⁵³But they had no food in storage, ᵛ because it was the seventh year; those who had found safety in Judea from the Gentiles had consumed the last of the stores. ⁵⁴Only a few men were left in the sanctuary; the rest scattered to their own homes, for the famine proved too much for them.

55 Then Lysias heard that Philip, whom King Antiochus while still living had appointed to bring up his son Antiochus to be king, ⁵⁶had returned from Persia and Media with the forces that had gone with the king, and that he was trying to seize control of the government. ⁵⁷So he quickly gave orders to withdraw, and said to the king, to the commanders of the forces, and to the troops, men, "Daily we grow weaker, our food supply is scant, the place against which we are fighting is strong, and the affairs of the kingdom press urgently on us. ⁵⁸Now then let us come to terms with these people, and make peace with them and with all their nation. ⁵⁹Let us agree to let them live by their laws as they did before; for it was on account of their laws that we abolished that they became angry and did all these things."

60 The speech pleased the king and the commanders, and he sent to the Jews ʷ an offer of peace, and they accepted it. ⁶¹So the king and the commanders gave them their oath. On these conditions the Jews ᵘ evacuated the stronghold. ⁶²But when the king entered Mount Zion and saw what a strong fortress the place was, he broke the oath he

---

u Gk *they*   v Other ancient authorities read
in the sanctuary   w Gk *them*

6.43: *Eleazar,* brother of Judas (2.5). **48:** *Mount Zion,* south of the temple (1.33). **49:** The garrison was promised immunity if it surrendered. Every seventh year the land had to lie fallow (Ex 23.11; Lev 25.3–7). This *sabbatical year* was apparently 162 B.C. (v. 20) or possibly a year earlier.
6.55–63: Lysias makes peace. The return of Philip caused a diversion; Lysias abandoned the siege and restored Jewish religious

rights. **55:** *Philip* had received the symbols of sovereignty (v. 15), though Antiochus IV had previously appointed Lysias. **59:** Judea had generally accepted Seleucid rule until Antiochus IV began his program of hellenization, though there was always a faction engaged in intrigue with Egypt. **62:** Judas had also built a citadel on *Mount Zion;* its wall was now destroyed.

had sworn and gave orders to tear down the wall all around. ⁶³Then he set off in haste and returned to Antioch. He found Philip in control of the city, but he fought against him, and took the city by force.

7 In the one hundred fifty-first year^x Demetrius son of Seleucus set out from Rome, sailed with a few men to a town by the sea, and there began to reign. ²As he was entering the royal palace of his ancestors, the army seized Antiochus and Lysias to bring them to him. ³But when this act became known to him, he said, "Do not let me see their faces!" ⁴So the army killed them, and Demetrius took his seat on the throne of his kingdom.

5 Then there came to him all the renegade and godless men of Israel; they were led by Alcimus, who wanted to be high priest. ⁶They brought to the king this accusation against the people: "Judas and his brothers have destroyed all your Friends, and have driven us out of our land. ⁷Now then send a man whom you trust; let him go and see all the ruin that Judas^y has brought on us and on the land of the king, and let him punish them and all who help them."

8 So the king chose Bacchides, one of the king's Friends, governor of the province Beyond the River; he was a great man in the kingdom and was faithful to the king. ⁹He sent him, and with him he sent the ungodly Alcimus, whom he

made high priest; and he commanded him to take vengeance on the Israelites. ¹⁰So they marched away and came with a large force into the land of Judah; and he sent messengers to Judas and his brothers with peaceable but treacherous words. ¹¹But they paid no attention to their words, for they saw that they had come with a large force.

12 Then a group of scribes appeared in a body before Alcimus and Bacchides to ask for just terms. ¹³The Hasideans were first among the Israelites to seek peace from them, ¹⁴for they said, "A priest of the line of Aaron has come with the army, and he will not harm us." ¹⁵Alcimus^z spoke peaceable words to them and swore this oath to them, "We will not seek to injure you or your Friends." ¹⁶So they trusted him; but he seized sixty of them and killed them in one day, in accordance with the word that was written,

17 "The flesh of your faithful ones
        and their blood
    they poured out all around
        Jerusalem,
    and there was no one to bury
        them."

¹⁸Then the fear and dread of them fell on all the people, for they said, "There is no truth or justice in them, for they have violated the agreement and the oath that they swore."

^x 161 B.C.   ^y Gk *he*   ^z Gk *He*

7.1–4: Demetrius I becomes king (2 Macc 14.1–2). **1:** *Demetrius* I Soter (reigned 162–150 B.C.) was *son of Seleucus* IV Philopator, elder brother of Antiochus IV. When Rome demanded hostages (1.10), Antiochus IV was sent to Rome; later when Seleucus became king, his son Demetrius replaced Antiochus. On the latter's death, he vainly petitioned the senate to be released. Subsequently he escaped from Rome with a small group of men and landed in Tripolis, *a town by the sea* (2 Macc 14.1). **2:** *Antiochus,* that is, Antiochus V Eupator (6.17). **3:** *Do not let me see their faces,* a signal for the murder. **7.5–25: Alcimus as high priest.** Legitimate high priests were descended from a particular family. Antiochus IV appointed Jason in place of his brother Onias III (2 Macc 4.7);

Jason was in turn supplanted by Menelaus (2 Macc 4.23–26), who was put to death about 162 B.C., after having officiated for ten years (2 Macc 13.1–8). Either Onias III or his son Onias IV, last legitimate claimant, fled to Egypt and established a temple at Heliopolis (Cairo). *Alcimus,* or Jakim (2 Macc 14.3), was not a member of the high-priestly family; he belonged to the hellenizing faction and was willing to further Demetrius' plans. **8:** *Beyond the River,* the province west of the Euphrates (Ezra 4.11).

7.12–14: *The Hasideans* (2.42), probably the same as the *group of scribes,* had no political ambitions and were content to live under Syrian rule if they were permitted to keep the Mosaic law. **17:** Ps 79.2–3. All ancients regarded an unburied dead body with horror,

19 Then Bacchides withdrew from Jerusalem and encamped in Beth-zaith. And he sent and seized many of the men who had deserted to him,ᵃ and some of the people, and killed them and threw them into a great pit. ²⁰He placed Alcimus in charge of the country and left with him a force to help him; then Bacchides went back to the king.

21 Alcimus struggled to maintain his high priesthood, ²²and all who were troubling their people joined him. They gained control of the land of Judah and did great damage in Israel. ²³And Judas saw all the wrongs that Alcimus and those with him had done among the Israelites; it was more than the Gentiles had done. ²⁴So Judasᵇ went out into all the surrounding parts of Judea, taking vengeance on those who had deserted and preventing those in the cityᶜ from going out into the country. ²⁵When Alcimus saw that Judas and those with him had grown strong, and realized that he could not withstand them, he returned to the king and brought malicious charges against them.

26 Then the king sent Nicanor, one of his honored princes, who hated and detested Israel, and he commanded him to destroy the people. ²⁷So Nicanor came to Jerusalem with a large force, and treacherously sent to Judas and his brothers this peaceable message, ²⁸"Let there be no fighting between you and me; I shall come with a few men to see you face to face in peace."

29 So he came to Judas, and they greeted one another peaceably; but the enemy were preparing to kidnap Judas. ³⁰It became known to Judas that Nicanorᵇ had come to him with treacherous intent, and he was afraid of him and

would not meet him again. ³¹When Nicanor learned that his plan had been disclosed, he went out to meet Judas in battle near Caphar-salama. ³²About five hundred of the army of Nicanor fell, and the restᵈ fled into the city of David.

33 After these events Nicanor went up to Mount Zion. Some of the priests from the sanctuary and some of the elders of the people came out to greet him peaceably and to show him the burnt offering that was being offered for the king. ³⁴But he mocked them and derided them and defiled them and spoke arrogantly, ³⁵and in anger he swore this oath, "Unless Judas and his army are delivered into my hands this time, then if I return safely I will burn up this house." And he went out in great anger. ³⁶At this the priests went in and stood before the altar and the temple; they wept and said,
³⁷ "You chose this house to be called
       by your name,
    and to be for your people a
       house of prayer and
       supplication.
³⁸ Take vengeance on this man and
       on his army,
    and let them fall by the sword;
    remember their blasphemies,
    and let them live no longer."

39 Now Nicanor went out from Jerusalem and encamped in Beth-horon, and the Syrian army joined him. ⁴⁰Judas encamped in Adasa with three thousand men. Then Judas prayed and said, ⁴¹"When the messengers from the king spoke blasphemy, your angel went out and struck down one hundred eighty-

ᵃ Or *many of his men who had deserted*
ᵇ Gk *he*   ᶜ Gk *and they were prevented*
ᵈ Gk *they*

and to leave foes unburied was the ultimate outrage. **19**: *Beth-zaith,* perhaps three miles north of Beth-zur; or Bezetha, north of the temple area in Jerusalem.
    7.26–50: Defeat of Nicanor. The last of Judas' great victories (2 Macc 14.12–15.36). **26**: According to Josephus (*Antiquities,* XII. x. 4), *Nicanor* was one of the men who had escaped from Rome with Demetrius (see

7.1 n.). **30**: Judas never trusted the Syrians (vv. 10–11). **31**: *Capharsalama,* perhaps Khirbet Deir Sellam, about five miles northeast of Jerusalem. **33**: The Jews customarily offered sacrifices to God for the welfare of their rulers. **37–38**: Compare 1 Kings 8.29, 43; Pss 68.16; 87.1–2.
    7.40: *Adasa,* about seven miles from Bethhoron on the road to Jerusalem. **41**: 2 Kings

five thousand of the Assyrians.*e* ⁴²So also crush this army before us today; let the rest learn that Nicanor*f* has spoken wickedly against the sanctuary, and judge him according to this wickedness."

43 So the armies met in battle on the thirteenth day of the month of Adar. The army of Nicanor was crushed, and he himself was the first to fall in the battle. ⁴⁴When his army saw that Nicanor had fallen, they threw down their arms and fled. ⁴⁵The Jews*g* pursued them a day's journey, from Adasa as far as Gazara, and as they followed they kept sounding the battle call on the trumpets. ⁴⁶People came out of all the surrounding villages of Judea, and they out-flanked the enemy*h* and drove them back to their pursuers,*i* so that they all fell by the sword; not even one of them was left. ⁴⁷Then the Jews*g* seized the spoils and the plunder; they cut off Nicanor's head and the right hand that he had so arrogantly stretched out, and brought them and displayed them just outside Jerusalem. ⁴⁸The people rejoiced greatly and celebrated that day as a day of great gladness. ⁴⁹They decreed that this day should be celebrated each year on the thirteenth day of Adar. ⁵⁰So the land of Judah had rest for a few days.

8 Now Judas heard of the fame of the Romans, that they were very strong and were well-disposed toward all who made an alliance with them, that they pledged friendship to those who came to

them, ²and that they were very strong. He had been told of their wars and of the brave deeds that they were doing among the Gauls, how they had defeated them and forced them to pay tribute, ³and what they had done in the land of Spain to get control of the silver and gold mines there, ⁴and how they had gained control of the whole region by their planning and patience, even though the place was far distant from them. They also subdued the kings who came against them from the ends of the earth, until they crushed them and inflicted great disaster on them; the rest paid them tribute every year. ⁵They had crushed in battle and conquered Philip, and King Perseus of the Macedonians,*j* and the others who rose up against them. ⁶They also had defeated Antiochus the Great, king of Asia, who went to fight against them with one hundred twenty elephants and with cavalry and chariots and a very large army. He was crushed by them; ⁷they took him alive and decreed that he and those who would reign after him should pay a heavy tribute and give hostages and surrender some of their best provinces, ⁸the countries of India, Media, and Lydia. These they took from him and gave to King Eumenes. ⁹The Greeks planned to come and destroy them, ¹⁰but this became known to them, and they sent a general against the

e Gk *of them*   *f* Gk *he*   *g* Gk *they*
h Gk *them*   *i* Gk *these*   *j* Or *Kittim*

19.35. **43**: *Adar,* roughly March, in 161 B.C. (see 2 Macc 15.36 n.). **45**: *Gazara,* Gezer (4.15). **47**: *Head . . . right hand,* in punishment for blasphemy and for raising his hand against the temple (2 Macc 15.32). See 1 Sam 17.54. **49**: 2 Macc 15.36. This festival, which came to be called Nicanor Day, was one of the days on which the Jews prohibited mourning (compare 13.52). It is no longer observed.

8.1–32: Treaty with Rome. The author of 1 Maccabees emphasizes friendly relations between Rome and the Jews because the Romans checked the ambitions of the Seleucids. After 190 B.C. Rome steadily increased her influence in the Near East and Syrian power declined. **1**: *The Romans* had made *an alliance*

with kings in Asia Minor and Egypt. **2**: Two nations of *Gauls* were *defeated,* those of upper Italy in 190 B.C., and the Galatians of Asia Minor in 189 B.C. **3–4**: Rome conquered the Carthaginian colonies of *Spain,* not *the whole region,* in the Second Punic War. **5**: *Philip,* defeated at Cynoscephalae in 197 B.C.; *Perseus,* his son, last Macedonian king, beaten at Pydna in 168 B.C. **6–8**: *Antiochus* was not captured, but had to *give hostages* (7.1). *India* was not part of his domain; he kept *Media,* but he surrendered *Lydia* and other parts of Asia Minor. *Eumenes* II of Pergamum was given much of Seleucid Asia Minor. **9**: *The Greeks,* possibly the Macedonians (v. 5), or the Achaean league somewhat later. **12**: This is the

Greeks*k* and attacked them. Many of them were wounded and fell, and the Romans*l* took captive their wives and children; they plundered them, conquered the land, tore down their strongholds, and enslaved them to this day. 11 The remaining kingdoms and islands, as many as ever opposed them, they destroyed and enslaved; 12 but with their friends and those who rely on them they have kept friendship. They have subdued kings far and near, and as many as have heard of their fame have feared them. 13 Those whom they wish to help and to make kings, they make kings, and those whom they wish they depose; and they have been greatly exalted. 14 Yet for all this not one of them has put on a crown or worn purple as a mark of pride, 15 but they have built for themselves a senate chamber, and every day three hundred twenty senators constantly deliberate concerning the people, to govern them well. 16 They trust one man each year to rule over them and to control all their land; they all heed the one man, and there is no envy or jealousy among them.

17 So Judas chose Eupolemus son of John son of Accos, and Jason son of Eleazar, and sent them to Rome to establish friendship and alliance, 18 and to free themselves from the yoke; for they saw that the kingdom of the Greeks was enslaving Israel completely. 19 They went to Rome, a very long journey; and they entered the senate chamber and spoke as follows: 20 "Judas, who is also called Maccabeus, and his brothers and the people of the Jews have sent us to you to establish alliance and peace with you, so

that we may be enrolled as your allies and friends." 21 The proposal pleased them, 22 and this is a copy of the letter that they wrote in reply, on bronze tablets, and sent to Jerusalem to remain with them there as a memorial of peace and alliance:

23 "May all go well with the Romans and with the nation of the Jews at sea and on land forever, and may sword and enemy be far from them. 24 If war comes first to Rome or to any of their allies in all their dominion, 25 the nation of the Jews shall act as their allies wholeheartedly, as the occasion may indicate to them. 26 To the enemy that makes war they shall not give or supply grain, arms, money, or ships, just as Rome has decided; and they shall keep their obligations without receiving any return. 27 In the same way, if war comes first to the nation of the Jews, the Romans shall willingly act as their allies, as the occasion may indicate to them. 28 And to their enemies there shall not be given grain, arms, money, or ships, just as Rome has decided; and they shall keep these obligations and do so without deceit. 29 Thus on these terms the Romans make a treaty with the Jewish people. 30 If after these terms are in effect both parties shall determine to add or delete anything, they shall do so at their discretion, and any addition or deletion that they may make shall be valid.

31 "Concerning the wrongs that King Demetrius is doing to them, we have written to him as follows, 'Why have you made your yoke heavy on our friends and allies the Jews? 32 If now they

k Gk *them*   *l* Gk *they*

---

estimate of a partisan; it is not true that they always *kept friendship.* **14:** *A crown,* Rome wanted no king, but magistrates, senators, and knights wore *purple* borders on their garments. **15:** *Every day,* actually senate meetings were held three times a month, and on the festivals. **16:** *One man,* in reality there were two consuls, and *envy* and *jealousy* were constant. The author of 1 Maccabees idealizes the Romans because their republican institutions were congenial to the Jews.
8.17: *Eupolemus,* 2 Macc 4.11. *Accos,* a priestly family (Ezra 2.61). **19:** *A very long*

journey, emphasizes that this alliance was in accord with the law of Moses, which forbade only covenants with foreigners surrounding Israel. **22:** Important documents were often inscribed *on bronze tablets.* **23–30:** The treaty letter begins with the conventional formula and is drawn up as though the two parties were equals, and Judea a sovereign state. **31–32:** This postscript was not part of the treaty, and is correctly omitted from it by Josephus (*Antiquities,* XII. x. 6); there is no evidence that the Romans helped Judas against Demetrius.

appeal again for help against you, we will defend their rights and fight you on sea and on land.' "

9 When Demetrius heard that Nicanor and his army had fallen in battle, he sent Bacchides and Alcimus into the land of Judah a second time, and with them the right wing of the army. ²They went by the road that leads to Gilgal and encamped against Mesaloth in Arbela, and they took it and killed many people. ³In the first month of the one hundred fifty-second year*ᵐ* they encamped against Jerusalem; ⁴then they marched off and went to Berea with twenty thousand foot soldiers and two thousand cavalry.

5 Now Judas was encamped in Elasa, and with him were three thousand picked men. ⁶When they saw the huge number of the enemy forces, they were greatly frightened, and many slipped away from the camp, until no more than eight hundred of them were left.

7 When Judas saw that his army had slipped away and the battle was imminent, he was crushed in spirit, for he had no time to assemble them. ⁸He became faint, but he said to those who were left, "Let us get up and go against our enemies. We may have the strength to fight them." ⁹But they tried to dissuade him, saying, "We do not have the strength. Let us rather save our own lives now, and let us come back with our kindred and fight them; we are too few." ¹⁰But Judas said, "Far be it from us to do such a thing as to flee from them. If our time has come, let us die bravely for our kindred, and leave no cause to question our honor."

11 Then the army of Bacchides*ⁿ*

marched out from the camp and took its stand for the encounter. The cavalry was divided into two companies, and the slingers and the archers went ahead of the army, as did all the chief warriors. ¹²Bacchides was on the right wing. Flanked by the two companies, the phalanx advanced to the sound of the trumpets; and the men with Judas also blew their trumpets. ¹³The earth was shaken by the noise of the armies, and the battle raged from morning until evening.

14 Judas saw that Bacchides and the strength of his army were on the right; then all the stouthearted men went with him, ¹⁵and they crushed the right wing, and he pursued them as far as Mount Azotus. ¹⁶When those on the left wing saw that the right wing was crushed, they turned and followed close behind Judas and his men. ¹⁷The battle became desperate, and many on both sides were wounded and fell. ¹⁸Judas also fell, and the rest fled.

19 Then Jonathan and Simon took their brother Judas and buried him in the tomb of their ancestors at Modein, ²⁰and wept for him. All Israel made great lamentation for him; they mourned many days and said,

21 "How is the mighty fallen,
    the savior of Israel!"

²²Now the rest of the acts of Judas, and his wars and the brave deeds that he did, and his greatness, have not been recorded, but they were very many.

23 After the death of Judas, the renegades emerged in all parts of Israel; all the wrongdoers reappeared. ²⁴In those days a very great famine occurred, and the

m 160 B.C.   n Gk the army

9.1–22: Death of Judas. Continual Syrian pressure weakened Judas' forces, which were a guerrilla band facing a highly organized army. Judas decided that it was better to fall in battle than to withdraw. 1–2: *Bacchides,* 7.8. *Alcimus,* see 7.5 n. Josephus (*Antiquities,* XII. xi. 1) says that they started from Antioch, camped at Arbela in Galilee (not *Gilgal*), besieged refugees in the caves, and went on toward Jerusalem. *Mesaloth,* perhaps the Hebrew word for "steps," i.e. ascents to *Arbela.*

4: *Berea,* perhaps el-Bireh, opposite Ramallah, ten miles north of Jerusalem. 5: *Elasa* has not been identified.

9.15: *Mount Azotus,* perhaps el'Asur, six miles northeast of el-Bireh. **19:** *Modein,* 2.1, 70; 13.27–30. **21:** 2 Sam 1.19. **22:** The expression *Now the rest of the acts* imitates the style of Hebrew chronicles (1 Kings 11.41).

9.23–73: Jonathan becomes leader and defeats Bacchides. 23: *The renegades,* i.e. the pro-Syrian element. **24:** *The country,* the ma-

country went over to their side. ²⁵ Bacchides chose the godless and put them in charge of the country. ²⁶ They made inquiry and searched for the friends of Judas, and brought them to Bacchides, who took vengeance on them and made sport of them. ²⁷ So there was great distress in Israel, such as had not been since the time that prophets ceased to appear among them.

28 Then all the friends of Judas assembled and said to Jonathan, ²⁹ "Since the death of your brother Judas there has been no one like him to go against our enemies and Bacchides, and to deal with those of our nation who hate us. ³⁰ Now therefore we have chosen you today to take his place as our ruler and leader, to fight our battle." ³¹ So Jonathan accepted the leadership at that time in place of his brother Judas.

32 When Bacchides learned of this, he tried to kill him. ³³ But Jonathan and his brother Simon and all who were with him heard of it, and they fled into the wilderness of Tekoa and camped by the water of the pool of Asphar. ³⁴ Bacchides found this out on the sabbath day, and he with all his army crossed the Jordan.

35 So Jonathan*º* sent his brother as leader of the multitude and begged the Nabateans, who were his friends, for permission to store with them the great amount of baggage that they had. ³⁶ But the family of Jambri from Medeba came out and seized John and all that he had, and left with it.

37 After these things it was reported to Jonathan and his brother Simon, "The family of Jambri are celebrating a great wedding, and are conducting the bride, a daughter of one of the great nobles of Canaan, from Nadabath with a large escort." ³⁸ Remembering how their brother John had been killed, they went up and hid under cover of the mountain. ³⁹ They looked out and saw a tumultuous procession with a great amount of baggage; and the bridegroom came out with his friends and his brothers to meet them with tambourines and musicians and many weapons. ⁴⁰ Then they rushed on them from the ambush and began killing them. Many were wounded and fell, and the rest fled to the mountain; and the Jews*ᵖ* took all their goods. ⁴¹ So the wedding was turned into mourning and the voice of their musicians into a funeral dirge. ⁴² After they had fully avenged the blood of their brother, they returned to the marshes of the Jordan.

43 When Bacchides heard of this, he came with a large force on the sabbath day to the banks of the Jordan. ⁴⁴ And Jonathan said to those with him, "Let us get up now and fight for our lives, for today things are not as they were before. ⁴⁵ For look! the battle is in front of us and behind us; the water of the Jordan is on this side and on that, with marsh and thicket; there is no place to turn. ⁴⁶ Cry out now to Heaven that you may be delivered from the hands of our enemies." ⁴⁷ So the battle began, and Jonathan stretched out his hand to strike Bacchides, but he eluded him and went to the

o Gk *he*   *p* Gk *they*

jority of the nation, or perhaps the rural population; resistance now seemed futile. **25:** *The godless,* i.e. hellenized Jews. **27:** *Prophets ceased,* see 4.46 n. **30–31:** *We have chosen you,* Judas was self-appointed, but *Jonathan* was elected by his peers; he became leader about 160 or 159 B.C. and high priest in 152 (10.21). **33:** *Tekoa,* five miles southeast of Bethlehem (Am 1.1); *the wilderness* reached from here to the Dead Sea. *The pool of Asphar* may be three miles south of Tekoa. **34:** *Bacchides* thought the Jews might be surprised *on the sabbath day.* He apparently came from Jerusalem, *crossed the Jordan,* and camped on the east side.

9.35: *His brother,* John (v. 36; 2.2). *The Nabateans,* see 5.25 n. **36:** *Family of Jambri,* evidently a Nabatean tribe. *Medeba* or Madeba, twelve miles southeast of the north end of the Dead Sea. **37:** *Nadabath,* perhaps Nebo, a little north of Medeba (Num 33.47; Deut 32.49). **38:** *John . . . killed,* the sequel to v. 36 was the murder of John and all his companions (Josephus, *Antiquities,* XIII. i. 2). **45:** The Jews were apparently on the east side of the Jordan, between the river and the Syrian forces. **9.50–53:** Bacchides established forces and garrisons to prevent guerrilla operations. *Em-*

rear. [48]Then Jonathan and the men with him leaped into the Jordan and swam across to the other side, and the enemy[q] did not cross the Jordan to attack them. [49]And about one thousand of Bacchides' men fell that day.

50 Then Bacchides[r] returned to Jerusalem and built strong cities in Judea: the fortress in Jericho, and Emmaus, and Beth-horon, and Bethel, and Timnath, and[s] Pharathon, and Tephon, with high walls and gates and bars. [51]And he placed garrisons in them to harass Israel. [52]He also fortified the town of Beth-zur, and Gazara, and the citadel, and in them he put troops and stores of food. [53]And he took the sons of the leading men of the land as hostages and put them under guard in the citadel at Jerusalem.

54 In the one hundred and fifty-third year,[t] in the second month, Alcimus gave orders to tear down the wall of the inner court of the sanctuary. He tore down the work of the prophets! [55]But he only began to tear it down, for at that time Alcimus was stricken and his work was hindered; his mouth was stopped and he was paralyzed, so that he could no longer say a word or give commands concerning his house. [56]And Alcimus died at that time in great agony. [57]When Bacchides saw that Alcimus was dead, he returned to the king, and the land of Judah had rest for two years.

58 Then all the lawless plotted and said, "See! Jonathan and his men are living in quiet and confidence. So now let us bring Bacchides back, and he will capture them all in one night." [59]And they went and consulted with him. [60]He started to come with a large force, and secret-

ly sent letters to all his allies in Judea, telling them to seize Jonathan and his men; but they were unable to do it, because their plan became known. [61]And Jonathan's men[q] seized about fifty of the men of the country who were leaders in this treachery, and killed them.

62 Then Jonathan with his men, and Simon, withdrew to Bethbasi in the wilderness; he rebuilt the parts of it that had been demolished, and they fortified it. [63]When Bacchides learned of this, he assembled all his forces, and sent orders to the men of Judea. [64]Then he came and encamped against Bethbasi; he fought against it for many days and made machines of war.

65 But Jonathan left his brother Simon in the town, while he went out into the country; and he went with only a few men. [66]He struck down Odomera and his kindred and the people of Phasiron in their tents. [67]Then he[u] began to attack and went into battle with his forces; and Simon and his men sallied out from the town and set fire to the machines of war. [68]They fought with Bacchides, and he was crushed by them. They pressed him very hard, for his plan and his expedition had been in vain. [69]So he was very angry at the renegades who had counseled him to come into the country, and he killed many of them. Then he decided to go back to his own land.

70 When Jonathan learned of this, he sent ambassadors to him to make peace with him and obtain release of the cap-

---

q Gk *they*   *r* Gk *he*   *s* Some authorities omit *and*   *t* 159 B.C.   *u* Other ancient authorities read *they*

---

maus, see 3.40 n. *Beth-horon,* see 3.16 n. *Bethel,* now Beitin, about twelve miles north of Jerusalem. *Timnath,* perhaps twelve miles northwest of Bethel. *Pharathon,* six miles southwest of Shechem or Nablus. *Tephon,* Tappuah, twenty-five miles north of Jerusalem. *Beth-zur,* see 4.29 n. *Gazara,* see 4.15 n. **54:** *The wall of the inner court* separated this part from the rest of the temple mount, which was open to Gentiles. Pagans were now to have access to *the sanctuary. The prophets,* Haggai and Zechariah had built the second

temple. **56:** *Alcimus* had been high priest for about two years (7.5). **57:** *He returned,* believing that with the fortresses garrisoned the situation was stable; his departure gave Jonathan a free hand. **61:** *Fifty . . . leaders,* probably the hellenizers (see v. 25 n.).

9.62: *Bethbasi,* perhaps Khirbet Beit-Bassa, about three miles northeast of Tekoa. **66:** *Odomera . . . people of Phasiron,* probably bedouin sheikhs. **68:** *He was crushed,* for Simon attacked by surprise and *Bacchides* had depended heavily on the war machines

tives. 71 He agreed, and did as he said; and he swore to Jonathan*v* that he would not try to harm him as long as he lived. 72 He restored to him the captives whom he had taken previously from the land of Judah; then he turned and went back to his own land, and did not come again into their territory. 73 Thus the sword ceased from Israel. Jonathan settled in Michmash and began to judge the people; and he destroyed the godless out of Israel.

10 In the one hundred sixtieth year*w* Alexander Epiphanes, son of Antiochus, landed and occupied Ptolemais. They welcomed him, and there he began to reign. 2 When King Demetrius heard of it, he assembled a very large army and marched out to meet him in battle. 3 Demetrius sent Jonathan a letter in peaceable words to honor him; 4 for he said to himself, "Let us act first to make peace with him*x* before he makes peace with Alexander against us, 5 for he will remember all the wrongs that we did to him and to his brothers and his nation." 6 So Demetrius*y* gave him authority to recruit troops, to equip them with arms, and to become his ally; and he commanded that the hostages in the citadel should be released to him.

7 Then Jonathan came to Jerusalem and read the letter in the hearing of all the people and of those in the citadel. 8 They were greatly alarmed when they heard that the king had given him authority to recruit troops. 9 But those in the citadel

released the hostages to Jonathan, and he returned them to their parents.

10 And Jonathan took up residence in Jerusalem and began to rebuild and restore the city. 11 He directed those who were doing the work to build the walls and encircle Mount Zion with squared stones, for better fortification; and they did so.

12 Then the foreigners who were in the strongholds that Bacchides had built fled; 13 all of them left their places and went back to their own lands. 14 Only in Beth-zur did some remain who had forsaken the law and the commandments, for it served as a place of refuge.

15 Now King Alexander heard of all the promises that Demetrius had sent to Jonathan, and he heard of the battles that Jonathan*y* and his brothers had fought, of the brave deeds that they had done, and of the troubles that they had endured. 16 So he said, "Shall we find another such man? Come now, we will make him our friend and ally." 17 And he wrote a letter and sent it to him, in the following words:

18 "King Alexander to his brother Jonathan, greetings. 19 We have heard about you, that you are a mighty warrior and worthy to be our friend. 20 And so we have appointed you today to be the high priest of your nation; you are to be called the king's Friend and you are to

v Gk *him*   *w* 152 B.C.   *x* Gk *them*
y Gk *he*

(v. 67). **72**: Josephus says that there was an exchange of prisoners (*Antiquities*, XIII. i. 6). **73**: *Thus the sword ceased*, for about seven years, until the events of 10.69. *Michmash*, now Mukhmas, eight miles northeast of Jerusalem (1 Sam 14.5–23). *To judge the people*, as a natural leader, like Samuel and those in the book of Judges.
10.1–21: Alexander Balas appoints Jonathan high priest. 1: *Alexander* I *Epiphanes*, who came from Ephesus and whose given name was Balas (or Ba'al), posed as the *son of Antiochus* IV. He claimed the kingship from 150 B.C. onward, and reigned until about 145. Attalus II of Pergamum and Ptolemy VI persuaded the Roman senate to recognize him. **6**:

Gave him authority, as a local prince or governor, but not independence. *The hostages*, 9.53. The Syrians held the citadel at Jerusalem.
10.10: *Jonathan* now left Michmash. **11**: Lysias had ordered the wall of the Jewish fortress torn down (6.62). **14**: *Some*, i.e. hellenized Jews opposed to the Hasmoneans. **18–20**: *Alexander*, hearing of Demetrius' letter, decided to outbid him. Until the time of Antiochus IV, the hereditary high priest had been confirmed but not appointed by the ruler; now Alexander appointed Jonathan and made him one of his *Friends* (see 2.18 n.); the Jews had not elected him. **21**: *The sacred vestments*, Ex 28.1–39; 39.1–26. *Booths*, a seven-day festival held in September (Lev 23.33–43), had

take our side and keep friendship with us." He also sent him a purple robe and a golden crown.

21 So Jonathan put on the sacred vestments in the seventh month of the one hundred sixtieth year, *z* at the festival of booths, *a* and he recruited troops and equipped them with arms in abundance. 22 When Demetrius heard of these things he was distressed and said, 23 "What is this that we have done? Alexander has gotten ahead of us in forming a friendship with the Jews to strengthen himself. 24 I also will write them words of encouragement and promise them honor and gifts, so that I may have their help." 25 So he sent a message to them in the following words:

"King Demetrius to the nation of the Jews, greetings. 26 Since you have kept your agreement with us and have continued your friendship with us, and have not sided with our enemies, we have heard of it and rejoiced. 27 Now continue still to keep faith with us, and we will repay you with good for what you do for us. 28 We will grant you many immunities and give you gifts.

29 "I now free you and exempt all the Jews from payment of tribute and salt tax and crown levies, 30 and instead of collecting the third of the grain and the half of the fruit of the trees that I should receive, I release them from this day and henceforth. I will not collect them from the land of Judah or from the three districts added to it from Samaria and Galilee, from this day and for all time. 31 Jerusalem and its environs, its tithes and its revenues, shall be holy and free from tax. 32 I release also my control of the citadel in Jerusalem and give it to the high priest,

so that he may station in it men of his own choice to guard it. 33 And everyone of the Jews taken as a captive from the land of Judah into any part of my kingdom, I set free without payment; and let all officials cancel also the taxes on their livestock.

34 "All the festivals and sabbaths and new moons and appointed days, and the three days before a festival and the three after a festival—let them all be days of immunity and release for all the Jews who are in my kingdom. 35 No one shall have authority to exact anything from them or annoy any of them about any matter.

36 "Let Jews be enrolled in the king's forces to the number of thirty thousand men, and let the maintenance be given them that is due to all the forces of the king. 37 Let some of them be stationed in the great strongholds of the king, and let some of them be put in positions of trust in the kingdom. Let their officers and leaders be of their own number, and let them live by their own laws, just as the king has commanded in the land of Judah.

38 "As for the three districts that have been added to Judea from the country of Samaria, let them be annexed to Judea so that they may be considered to be under one ruler and obey no other authority than the high priest. 39 Ptolemais and the land adjoining it I have given as a gift to the sanctuary in Jerusalem, to meet the necessary expenses of the sanctuary. 40 I also grant fifteen thousand shekels of silver yearly out of the king's revenues from appropriate places. 41 And all the

z 152 B.C.   *a* Or *tabernacles*

come to be associated with the hope of victory over the Gentiles (Zech 14.16–19).

10.22–50: Demetrius' offer to the Jews; his defeat. 25: The letter was addressed *to the nation,* ignoring Jonathan. Demetrius thought that he could drive a wedge between leader and people. **29–30:** *All the Jews* in the Seleucid realm, not merely in Judea. *Tribute,* direct taxes proportionate to individual wealth. *Salt tax,* on salt from the marshes and the Dead Sea. *Crown levies,* fixed amounts of

money. *The three districts* (11.34) that Alexander the Great had transferred from Samaria to Judea and Antiochus IV had reassigned to Samaria were now restored (v. 38). **32:** *Release* of *control of the citadel* would free Jerusalem from military domination.

10.34: *Appointed days,* other public festivals. **36–37:** Opening the army and the civil service to Jews might strengthen their loyalty to the crown. **39:** *Ptolemais* was in the hands of Alexander (v. 1). This was an invitation to

additional funds that the government officials have not paid as they did in the first years,[b] they shall give from now on for the service of the temple.[c] 42 Moreover, the five thousand shekels of silver that my officials[d] have received every year from the income of the services of the temple, this too is canceled, because it belongs to the priests who minister there. 43 And all who take refuge at the temple in Jerusalem, or in any of its precincts, because they owe money to the king or are in debt, let them be released and receive back all their property in my kingdom.

44 "Let the cost of rebuilding and restoring the structures of the sanctuary be paid from the revenues of the king. 45 And let the cost of rebuilding the walls of Jerusalem and fortifying it all around, and the cost of rebuilding the walls in Judea, also be paid from the revenues of the king."

46 When Jonathan and the people heard these words, they did not believe or accept them, because they remembered the great wrongs that Demetrius[e] had done in Israel and how much he had oppressed them. 47 They favored Alexander, because he had been the first to speak peaceable words to them, and they remained his allies all his days.

48 Now King Alexander assembled large forces and encamped opposite Demetrius. 49 The two kings met in battle, and the army of Demetrius fled, and Alexander[f] pursued him and defeated them. 50 He pressed the battle strongly until the sun set, and on that day Demetrius fell.

51 Then Alexander sent ambassadors to Ptolemy king of Egypt with the following message: 52 "Since I have returned to my kingdom and have taken my seat on the throne of my ancestors, and estab-

lished my rule—for I crushed Demetrius and gained control of our country; 53 I met him in battle, and he and his army were crushed by us, and we have taken our seat on the throne of his kingdom— 54 now therefore let us establish friendship with one another; give me now your daughter as my wife, and I will become your son-in-law, and will make gifts to you and to her in keeping with your position."

55 Ptolemy the king replied and said, "Happy was the day on which you returned to the land of your ancestors and took your seat on the throne of their kingdom. 56 And now I will do for you as you wrote, but meet me at Ptolemais, so that we may see one another, and I will become your father-in-law, as you have said."

57 So Ptolemy set out from Egypt, he and his daughter Cleopatra, and came to Ptolemais in the one hundred sixty-second year.[g] 58 King Alexander met him, and Ptolemy[e] gave him his daughter Cleopatra in marriage, and celebrated her wedding at Ptolemais with great pomp, as kings do.

59 Then King Alexander wrote to Jonathan to come and meet him. 60 So he went with pomp to Ptolemais and met the two kings; he gave them and their Friends silver and gold and many gifts, and found favor with them. 61 A group of malcontents from Israel, renegades, gathered together against him to accuse him; but the king paid no attention to them. 62 The king gave orders to take off Jonathan's garments and to clothe him in purple, and they did so. 63 The king also seated him at his side; and he said to his

b Meaning of Gk uncertain   c Gk *house*
d Gk *they*   e Gk *he*   f Other ancient authorities read *Alexander fled, and Demetrius*
g 150 B.C.

the Jews to help Demetrius recapture it. **41**: *The additional funds* were grants once made to the temple by Ptolemaic and Seleucid kings, but *not paid* since the time of Antiochus IV.
10.44–45: Here Demetrius followed the custom of Persian kings (Ezra 6.8; 7.20). **47**: *Alexander* was also recognized as king by the

Jews' allies, the Romans. **50**: *Demetrius fell* probably in 150 B.C. (v. 57).
10.51–66: **Alexander's relations with Egypt and Judea. 51**: *Ptolemy* VI Philometor (1.18). **55**: *Ptolemy* recognized Alexander as legitimate (see 10.1–21 n.).

officers, "Go out with him into the middle of the city and proclaim that no one is to bring charges against him about any matter, and let no one annoy him for any reason." 64 When his accusers saw the honor that was paid him, in accord with the proclamation, and saw him clothed in purple, they all fled. 65 Thus the king honored him and enrolled him among his chief*ʰ* Friends, and made him general and governor of the province. 66 And Jonathan returned to Jerusalem in peace and gladness.

67 In the one hundred sixty-fifth year*ⁱ* Demetrius son of Demetrius came from Crete to the land of his ancestors. 68 When King Alexander heard of it, he was greatly distressed and returned to Antioch. 69 And Demetrius appointed Apollonius the governor of Coelesyria, and he assembled a large force and encamped against Jamnia. Then he sent the following message to the high priest Jonathan:

70 "You are the only one to rise up against us, and I have fallen into ridicule and disgrace because of you. Why do you assume authority against us in the hill country? 71 If you now have confidence in your forces, come down to the plain to meet us, and let us match strength with each other there, for I have with me the power of the cities. 72 Ask and learn who I am and who the others are that are helping us. People will tell you that you cannot stand before us, for your ancestors were twice put to flight in their own land. 73 And now you will not be able to withstand my cavalry and such an army in the plain, where there is no stone or pebble, or place to flee."

74 When Jonathan heard the words of Apollonius, his spirit was aroused. He chose ten thousand men and set out from Jerusalem, and his brother Simon met him to help him. 75 He encamped before Joppa, but the people of the city closed its gates, for Apollonius had a garrison in Joppa. 76 So they fought against it, and the people of the city became afraid and opened the gates, and Jonathan gained possession of Joppa.

77 When Apollonius heard of it, he mustered three thousand cavalry and a large army, and went to Azotus as though he were going farther. At the same time he advanced into the plain, for he had a large troop of cavalry and put confidence in it. 78 Jonathan*ʲ* pursued him to Azotus, and the armies engaged in battle. 79 Now Apollonius had secretly left a thousand cavalry behind them. 80 Jonathan learned that there was an ambush behind him, for they surrounded his army and shot arrows at his men from early morning until late afternoon. 81 But his men stood fast, as Jonathan had commanded, and the enemy's*ᵏ* horses grew tired.

82 Then Simon brought forward his force and engaged the phalanx in battle (for the cavalry was exhausted); they were overwhelmed by him and fled, 83 and the cavalry was dispersed in the plain. They fled to Azotus and entered Beth-dagon, the temple of their idol, for safety. 84 But Jonathan burned Azotus and the surrounding towns and plundered them; and the temple of Dagon,

h Gk *first*   i 147 B.C.   j Gk *he*   k Gk *their*

10.57: *Cleopatra* III, who later married her uncle, Ptolemy VIII. **62:** A change of *garments* often signified honor or dishonor (Zech 3.3–5; Gen 41.42). **63:** See Esth 6.6–9. **65:** *Chief Friends,* see 2.18 n. *General and governor,* with military and civil authority.
10.67–89: Victories of Jonathan. 67: *Demetrius* II *son of Demetrius* I disputed the throne with Alexander and later with Tryphon and Antiochus VI; in 138 B.C. he was taken captive by the Parthians. He reigned again from 129 till his death in 125 B.C. **69:**

Coelesyria, meaning "hollow Syria," originally designated the country between the Lebanon and anti-Lebanon mountains; here it is Palestine and Transjordan, including the coast. *Jamnia,* 4.15. **72:** *Twice put to flight,* 6.54; 9.18. **74:** Jonathan now had forces for more than guerrilla engagements (v. 65); he had troops organized as phalanxes (v. 82). **75:** *Joppa,* now Jaffa, a seaport near Jamnia and forty miles from Jerusalem.
10.82: *His force* had been held in reserve and was fresh. **83:** *Beth-dagon,* house of Dagon,

and those who had taken refuge in it, he burned with fire. [85] The number of those who fell by the sword, with those burned alive, came to eight thousand.

[86] Then Jonathan left there and encamped against Askalon, and the people of the city came out to meet him with great pomp.

[87] He and those with him then returned to Jerusalem with a large amount of booty. [88] When King Alexander heard of these things, he honored Jonathan still more; [89] and he sent to him a golden buckle, such as it is the custom to give to the King's Kinsmen. He also gave him Ekron and all its environs as his possession.

11 Then the king of Egypt gathered great forces, like the sand by the seashore, and many ships; and he tried to get possession of Alexander's kingdom by trickery and add it to his own kingdom. [2] He set out for Syria with peaceable words, and the people of the towns opened their gates to him and went to meet him, for King Alexander had commanded them to meet him, since he was Alexander's[l] father-in-law. [3] But when Ptolemy entered the towns he stationed forces as a garrison in each town.

[4] When he[m] approached Azotus, they showed him the burnt-out temple of Dagon, and Azotus and its suburbs destroyed, and the corpses lying about, and the charred bodies of those whom Jonathan[n] had burned in the war, for they had piled them in heaps along his route. [5] They also told the king what Jonathan

had done, to throw blame on him; but the king kept silent. [6] Jonathan met the king at Joppa with pomp, and they greeted one another and spent the night there. [7] And Jonathan went with the king as far as the river called Eleutherus; then he returned to Jerusalem.

[8] So King Ptolemy gained control of the coastal cities as far as Seleucia by the sea, and he kept devising wicked designs against Alexander. [9] He sent envoys to King Demetrius, saying, "Come, let us make a covenant with each other, and I will give you in marriage my daughter who was Alexander's wife, and you shall reign over your father's kingdom. [10] I now regret that I gave him my daughter, for he has tried to kill me." [11] He threw blame on Alexander[o] because he coveted his kingdom. [12] So he took his daughter away from him and gave her to Demetrius. He was estranged from Alexander, and their enmity became manifest.

[13] Then Ptolemy entered Antioch and put on the crown of Asia. Thus he put two crowns on his head, the crown of Egypt and that of Asia. [14] Now King Alexander was in Cilicia at that time, because the people of that region were in revolt. [15] When Alexander heard of it, he came against him in battle. Ptolemy marched out and met him with a strong force, and put him to flight. [16] So Alexander fled into Arabia to find protection there, and King Ptolemy was trium-

---

l Gk *his*   *m* Other ancient authorities read *they*   *n* Gk *he*   *o* Gk *him*

---

the Philistine grain god (Judg 16.23). **86:** *Askalon,* about twelve miles north of Gaza. **89:** *A golden buckle,* with which the most select of the Friends of the king fastened their purple robes. *Ekron,* northernmost of the Philistine cities, was given to Jonathan as a personal possession, and its taxes were assigned to him. See 1 Sam 27.6.

11.1–19: Invasion of Ptolemy VI and victory of Demetrius II. 1: Josephus says that Ptolemy came to aid Alexander, his son-in-law, but that the latter plotted against Ptolemy's life (*Antiquities,* XIII. iv. 5–6). **5:** *Kept silent,* he had not yet broken with Alexander, and was not ready to commit himself. **7:** *Eleu-*

therus, now Nahr el-Kebir, north of Tripolis. **11.8:** *Seleucia* in Pieria, the main port for Antioch, near the mouth of the Orontes. **9:** *My daughter,* Cleopatra III (10.57). **13:** According to Josephus, the army proclaimed *Ptolemy* as king, but he persuaded the people of Antioch to support Demetrius. **14:** *Cilicia,* on the south coast of Turkey, always closely related to Syria, and the only section of Asia Minor then part of the Seleucid Empire. **15:** *Ptolemy marched out,* according to Josephus (*Antiquities,* XIII. iv. 8) with his son-in-law, Demetrius, who had already married Cleopatra. **16:** *Arabia* here includes the country east of Aleppo and Damascus. **18:** *Ptolemy died of*

phant. [17]Zabdiel the Arab cut off the head of Alexander and sent it to Ptolemy. [18]But King Ptolemy died three days later, and his troops in the strongholds were killed by the inhabitants of the strongholds. [19]So Demetrius became king in the one hundred sixty-seventh year.[p]

20 In those days Jonathan assembled the Judeans to attack the citadel in Jerusalem, and he built many engines of war to use against it. [21]But certain renegades who hated their nation went to the king and reported to him that Jonathan was besieging the citadel. [22]When he heard this he was angry, and as soon as he heard it he set out and came to Ptolemais; and he wrote Jonathan not to continue the siege, but to meet him for a conference at Ptolemais as quickly as possible.

23 When Jonathan heard this, he gave orders to continue the siege. He chose some of the elders of Israel and some of the priests, and put himself in danger, [24]for he went to the king at Ptolemais, taking silver and gold and clothing and numerous other gifts. And he won his favor. [25]Although certain renegades of his nation kept making complaints against him, [26]the king treated him as his predecessors had treated him; he exalted him in the presence of all his Friends. [27]He confirmed him in the high priesthood and in as many other honors as he had formerly had, and caused him to be reckoned among his chief[q] Friends. [28]Then Jonathan asked the king to free Judea and the three districts of Samaria[r] from tribute, and promised him three hundred talents. [29]The king consented,

and wrote a letter to Jonathan about all these things; its contents were as follows:

30 "King Demetrius to his brother Jonathan and to the nation of the Jews, greetings. [31]This copy of the letter that we wrote concerning you to our kinsman Lasthenes we have written to you also, so that you may know what it says. [32]'King Demetrius to his father Lasthenes, greetings. [33]We have determined to do good to the nation of the Jews, who are our friends and fulfill their obligations to us, because of the goodwill they show toward us. [34]We have confirmed as their possession both the territory of Judea and the three districts of Aphairema and Lydda and Rathamin; the latter, with all the region bordering them, were added to Judea from Samaria. To all those who offer sacrifice in Jerusalem we have granted release from[s] the royal taxes that the king formerly received from them each year, from the crops of the land and the fruit of the trees. [35]And the other payments henceforth due to us of the tithes, and the taxes due to us, and the salt pits and the crown taxes due to us— from all these we shall grant them release. [36]And not one of these grants shall be canceled from this time on forever. [37]Now therefore take care to make a copy of this, and let it be given to Jonathan and put up in a conspicuous place on the holy mountain.'"

38 When King Demetrius saw that the land was quiet before him and that

p 145 B.C.   *q* Gk *first*   *r* Cn: Gk *the three districts and Samaria*
s Or *Samaria, for all those who offer sacrifice in Jerusalem, in place of*

---

wounds suffered in the victory over Alexander. **19:** *Demetrius* had claimed to be *king* since 150 B.C. (see 10.67 n.).

11.20–37: Agreement between Demetrius II and Jonathan. 20: Demetrius I had once promised to turn *the citadel* over to the high priest (10.32), but he refused to recognize Jonathan as such because the latter had supported Alexander. Now Jonathan resolved to attack the citadel and make Judea independent. **23–24:** Jonathan decided to *continue the siege* so as to negotiate from strength, but his dangerous visit and gifts showed that

he was willing to make terms. **27:** 10.20.
11.30–37: The letter repeats earlier promises (10.25–45), but says nothing of the citadel. **31:** *Lasthenes,* probably governor of Coelesyria. **34:** *The three districts,* 10.30, 38. *Aphairema,* probably et-Taiyibeh, four miles northeast of Bethel, the Ephraim of Jn 11.54. *Lydda,* or Lod, east of Jaffa. *Rathamin,* perhaps Ramathaim-zophim (1 Sam 1.1), the Arimathea of Mk 15.43.
11.38–52: Jonathan's aid to Demetrius. 38: *Demetrius* in overconfidence reduced his army, probably to save money. This made

there was no opposition to him, he dismissed all his troops, all of them to their own homes, except the foreign troops that he had recruited from the islands of the nations. So all the troops who had served under his predecessors hated him. ³⁹ A certain Trypho had formerly been one of Alexander's supporters; he saw that all the troops were grumbling against Demetrius. So he went to Imalkue the Arab, who was bringing up Antiochus, the young son of Alexander, ⁴⁰ and insistently urged him to hand Antiochus' over to him, to become king in place of his father. He also reported to Imalkue' what Demetrius had done and told of the hatred that the troops of Demetrius" had for him; and he stayed there many days.

41 Now Jonathan sent to King Demetrius the request that he remove the troops of the citadel from Jerusalem, and the troops in the strongholds; for they kept fighting against Israel. ⁴² And Demetrius sent this message back to Jonathan: "Not only will I do these things for you and your nation, but I will confer great honor on you and your nation, if I find an opportunity. ⁴³ Now then you will do well to send me men who will help me, for all my troops have revolted." ⁴⁴ So Jonathan sent three thousand stalwart men to him at Antioch, and when they came to the king, the king rejoiced at their arrival.

45 Then the people of the city assembled within the city, to the number of a hundred and twenty thousand, and they wanted to kill the king. ⁴⁶ But the king fled into the palace. Then the people of the city seized the main streets of the city and began to fight. ⁴⁷ So the king called the Jews to his aid, and they all rallied around him and then spread out through the city; and they killed on that day about one hundred thousand. ⁴⁸ They set fire to the city and seized a large amount of spoil on that day, and saved the king. ⁴⁹ When the people of the city saw that the Jews had gained control of the city as they pleased, their courage failed and they cried out to the king with this entreaty: ⁵⁰ "Grant us peace, and make the Jews stop fighting against us and our city." ⁵¹ And they threw down their arms and made peace. So the Jews gained glory in the sight of the king and of all the people in his kingdom, and they returned to Jerusalem with a large amount of spoil.

52 So King Demetrius sat on the throne of his kingdom, and the land was quiet before him. ⁵³ But he broke his word about all that he had promised; he became estranged from Jonathan and did not repay the favors that Jonathan ᵛ had done him, but treated him very harshly.

54 After this Trypho returned, and with him the young boy Antiochus who began to reign and put on the crown. ⁵⁵ All the troops that Demetrius had discharged gathered around him; they fought against Demetrius, ᵗ and he fled and was routed. ⁵⁶ Trypho captured the elephants ʷ and gained control of Antioch. ⁵⁷ Then the young Antiochus wrote to Jonathan, saying, "I confirm you in the high priesthood and set you over the four districts and make you one of the king's Friends." ⁵⁸ He also sent him gold plate and a table service, and granted him the right to drink from gold cups and dress in purple and wear a gold buckle. ⁵⁹ He appointed Jonathan'sˣ brother Si-

t Gk *him*   *u* Gk *his troops*
v Gk *he*   *w* Gk *animals*   *x* Gk *his*

---

him unpopular. **42–43:** At last Demetrius seemed to agree (compare v. 53) to evacuate the citadel and other fortresses. **45–47:** *People of the city*, a mob, not an army. *Jews*, Judeans (see 2.23 n.).

11.53–74: Estrangement of Demetrius and Jonathan. 53: Josephus says that Demetrius now demanded tribute as before (*Antiquities*, XIII. v. 3). **54:** *Antiochus* VI Epiphanes, son of Alexander Balas, reigned nominally from about 145 to 142 B.C. **55:** *All the troops*, v. 38. **57:** *The four districts*, the three of v. 34 and probably Ekron (10.89). **58:** *Gold cups*, Esth 1.7. *Gold buckle*, sign of being a *Friend* of the king (see 2.18 n.; 10.89 n.). **59:** *The Ladder of Tyre*, the coastline between Ptolemais and Tyre. *The borders of Egypt*, probably Wadi el-Arish.

mon governor from the Ladder of Tyre to the borders of Egypt.

60 Then Jonathan set out and traveled beyond the river and among the towns, and all the army of Syria gathered to him as allies. When he came to Askalon, the people of the city met him and paid him honor. 61 From there he went to Gaza, but the people of Gaza shut him out. So he besieged it and burned its suburbs with fire and plundered them. 62 Then the people of Gaza pleaded with Jonathan, and he made peace with them, and took the sons of their rulers as hostages and sent them to Jerusalem. And he passed through the country as far as Damascus.

63 Then Jonathan heard that the officers of Demetrius had come to Kadesh in Galilee with a large army, intending to remove him from office. 64 He went to meet them, but left his brother Simon in the country. 65 Simon encamped before Beth-zur and fought against it for many days and hemmed it in. 66 Then they asked him to grant them terms of peace, and he did so. He removed them from there, took possession of the town, and set a garrison over it.

67 Jonathan and his army encamped by the waters of Gennesaret. Early in the morning they marched to the plain of Hazor, 68 and there in the plain the army of the foreigners met him; they had set an ambush against him in the mountains, but they themselves met him face to face. 69 Then the men in ambush emerged from their places and joined battle. 70 All the men with Jonathan fled; not one of them was left except Mattathias son of Absalom and Judas son of Chalphi, commanders of the forces of the army. 71 Jonathan tore his clothes, put dust on his head, and prayed. 72 Then he turned back to the battle against the enemy[y] and routed them, and they fled. 73 When his men who were fleeing saw this, they returned to him and joined him in the pursuit as far as Kadesh, to their camp, and there they encamped. 74 As many as three thousand of the foreigners fell that day. And Jonathan returned to Jerusalem.

12 Now when Jonathan saw that the time was favorable for him, he chose men and sent them to Rome to confirm and renew the friendship with them. 2 He also sent letters to the same effect to the Spartans and to other places. 3 So they went to Rome and entered the senate chamber and said, "The high priest Jonathan and the Jewish nation have sent us to renew the former friendship and alliance with them." 4 And the Romans[z] gave them letters to the people in every place, asking them to provide for the envoys[y] safe conduct to the land of Judah.

5 This is a copy of the letter that Jonathan wrote to the Spartans: 6 "The high priest Jonathan, the senate of the nation, the priests, and the rest of the Jewish people to their brothers the Spartans, greetings. 7 Already in time past a letter was sent to the high priest Onias from Arius,[a] who was king among you, stating that you are our brothers, as the appended copy shows. 8 Onias welcomed the envoy with honor, and received the letter, which contained a clear declaration of alliance and friendship. 9 Therefore, though we have no need of these things, since we have as encouragement the holy books that are in our hands,

y Gk *them*   z Gk *they*   a Vg Compare verse 20: Gk *Darius*

11.60: *The river,* Jordan. 61: *Gaza,* southernmost of the Philistine cities, near the Egyptian border (Judg 16.1). 62: *Damascus,* outside Jonathan's control, but his influence extended nearly that far. 63: *Kadesh,* northwest of Lake Huleh or Merom (Judg 4.9). 67: *The waters of Gennesaret,* the Sea of Galilee. *Hazor,* southwest of Lake Huleh (Josh 11.1).
12.1–23: **Alliances with the Romans** and Spartans (compare ch 8). 2: *The Spartans* had not joined the Achaean league against Rome. 4: *The Romans* continued the old alliance in order to keep Syria weak. 6: *The senate,* over which the high priest presided; it corresponds to the later council or Sanhedrin (Mk 14.55). 7: *Onias* I, high priest 320–290 B.C. *Arius,* king of Sparta 309–265 B.C.

10 we have undertaken to send to renew our family ties and friendship with you, so that we may not become estranged from you, for considerable time has passed since you sent your letter to us. 11 We therefore remember you constantly on every occasion, both at our festivals and on other appropriate days, at the sacrifices that we offer and in our prayers, as it is right and proper to remember brothers. 12 And we rejoice in your glory. 13 But as for ourselves, many trials and many wars have encircled us; the kings around us have waged war against us. 14 We were unwilling to annoy you and our other allies and friends with these wars, 15 for we have the help that comes from Heaven for our aid, and so we were delivered from our enemies, and our enemies were humbled. 16 We therefore have chosen Numenius son of Antiochus and Antipater son of Jason, and have sent them to Rome to renew our former friendship and alliance with them. 17 We have commanded them to go also to you and greet you and deliver to you this letter from us concerning the renewal of our family ties. 18 And now please send us a reply to this."

19 This is a copy of the letter that they sent to Onias: 20 "King Arius of the Spartans, to the high priest Onias, greetings. 21 It has been found in writing concerning the Spartans and the Jews that they are brothers and are of the family of Abraham. 22 And now that we have learned this, please write us concerning your welfare; 23 we on our part write to you that your livestock and your property belong to us, and ours belong to you. We therefore command that our envoys *b* report to you accordingly."

24 Now Jonathan heard that the commanders of Demetrius had returned, with a larger force than before, to wage war against him. 25 So he marched away

from Jerusalem and met them in the region of Hamath, for he gave them no opportunity to invade his own country. 26 He sent spies to their camp, and they returned and reported to him that the enemy *b* were being drawn up in formation to attack the Jews *c* by night. 27 So when the sun had set, Jonathan commanded his troops to be alert and to keep their arms at hand so as to be ready all night for battle, and he stationed outposts around the camp. 28 When the enemy heard that Jonathan and his troops were prepared for battle, they were afraid and were terrified at heart; so they kindled fires in their camp and withdrew. *d* 29 But Jonathan and his troops did not know it until morning, for they saw the fires burning. 30 Then Jonathan pursued them, but he did not overtake them, for they had crossed the Eleutherus river. 31 So Jonathan turned aside against the Arabs who are called Zabadeans, and he crushed them and plundered them. 32 Then he broke camp and went to Damascus, and marched through all that region.

33 Simon also went out and marched through the country as far as Askalon and the neighboring strongholds. He turned aside to Joppa and took it by surprise, 34 for he had heard that they were ready to hand over the stronghold to those whom Demetrius had sent. And he stationed a garrison there to guard it.

35 When Jonathan returned he convened the elders of the people and planned with them to build strongholds in Judea, 36 to build the walls of Jerusalem still higher, and to erect a high barrier between the citadel and the city to separate it from the city, in order to isolate it so that its garrison *b* could neither buy

b Gk *they*   *c* Gk *them*   *d* Other ancient authorities omit *and withdrew*

12.21: *Brothers . . . of the family of Abraham,* compare v. 7; such a tradition was evidently current in the East.
12.24–53: **Jonathan captured by Trypho. 24–25:** Jonathan met the Syrians at the border of Judea to prevent an invasion. *Ha-*

math, on the Orontes, modern Hama in Syria. 28: *Kindled fires,* so that Jonathan would think they were still in camp. 30: *The Eleutherus* is too far north (see 11.7 n.); perhaps the Orontes. 31: *Zabadeans,* perhaps people northwest of Damascus.

nor sell. ³⁷So they gathered together to rebuild the city; part of the wall on the valley to the east had fallen, and he repaired the section called Chaphenatha. ³⁸Simon also built Adida in the Shephelah; he fortified it and installed gates with bolts.

39 Then Trypho attempted to become king in Asia and put on the crown, and to raise his hand against King Antiochus. ⁴⁰He feared that Jonathan might not permit him to do so, but might make war on him, so he kept seeking to seize and kill him, and he marched out and came to Beth-shan. ⁴¹Jonathan went out to meet him with forty thousand picked warriors, and he came to Beth-shan. ⁴²When Trypho saw that he had come with a large army, he was afraid to raise his hand against him. ⁴³So he received him with honor and commended him to all his Friends, and he gave him gifts and commanded his Friends and his troops to obey him as they would himself. ⁴⁴Then he said to Jonathan, "Why have you put all these people to so much trouble when we are not at war? ⁴⁵Dismiss them now to their homes and choose for yourself a few men to stay with you, and come with me to Ptolemais. I will hand it over to you as well as the other strongholds and the remaining troops and all the officials, and will turn around and go home. For that is why I am here."

46 Jonathan*ᵉ* trusted him and did as he said; he sent away the troops, and they returned to the land of Judah. ⁴⁷He kept with himself three thousand men, two thousand of whom he left in Galilee, while one thousand accompanied him. ⁴⁸But when Jonathan entered Ptolemais, the people of Ptolemais closed the gates and seized him, and they killed with the sword all who had entered with him.

49 Then Trypho sent troops and cavalry into Galilee and the Great Plain to destroy all Jonathan's soldiers. ⁵⁰But they realized that Jonathan had been seized and had perished along with his men, and they encouraged one another and kept marching in close formation, ready for battle. ⁵¹When their pursuers saw that they would fight for their lives, they turned back. ⁵²So they all reached the land of Judah safely, and they mourned for Jonathan and his companions and were in great fear; and all Israel mourned deeply. ⁵³All the nations around them tried to destroy them, for they said, "They have no leader or helper. Now therefore let us make war on them and blot out the memory of them from humankind."

13 Simon heard that Trypho had assembled a large army to invade the land of Judah and destroy it, ²and he saw that the people were trembling with fear. So he went up to Jerusalem, and gathering the people together ³he encouraged them, saying to them, "You yourselves know what great things my brothers and I and the house of my father have done for the laws and the sanctuary; you know also the wars and the difficulties that my brothers and I have seen. ⁴By reason of this all my brothers have perished for the sake of Israel, and I alone am left. ⁵And now, far be it from me to spare my life in any time of distress, for I am not better than my brothers. ⁶But I will avenge my nation and the sanctuary and your wives and children, for all the nations have gathered together out of hatred to destroy us."

7 The spirit of the people was rekin-

ᵉ Gk *he*

12.36: The purpose was to starve out the garrison. **37:** *The valley to the east,* the Kidron (1 Kings 2.37; Jn 18.1); here the slope was sometimes steep. The location of *Chaphenatha* is unknown. **38:** *Adida,* about three miles east of Lydda (Ezra 2.33; Neh 7.37). *Shephelah,* the foothill country between the coastal plain and the central highlands. **40:** *Beth-shan,* see 5.52 n. **45:** *The other strongholds,* probably

along the coast. **52:** *They mourned,* because of the supposition that Jonathan had been slain; but see 13.23.

13.1–30: Simon becomes leader; death of Jonathan. 1: *Simon* (2.3) was governor of the coastal area (11.59). **4:** Eleazar, Judas, and John had died (6.46; 9.18, 42), and Simon supposed that Jonathan had been slain. **7–8:** Jonathan had been chosen by his friends

dled when they heard these words, 8 and they answered in a loud voice, "You are our leader in place of Judas and your brother Jonathan. 9 Fight our battles, and all that you say to us we will do." 10 So he assembled all the warriors and hurried to complete the walls of Jerusalem, and he fortified it on every side. 11 He sent Jonathan son of Absalom to Joppa, and with him a considerable army; he drove out its occupants and remained there.

12 Then Trypho left Ptolemais with a large army to invade the land of Judah, and Jonathan was with him under guard. 13 Simon encamped in Adida, facing the plain. 14 Trypho learned that Simon had risen up in place of his brother Jonathan, and that he was about to join battle with him, so he sent envoys to him and said, 15 "It is for the money that your brother Jonathan owed the royal treasury, in connection with the offices he held, that we are detaining him. 16 Send now one hundred talents of silver and two of his sons as hostages, so that when released he will not revolt against us, and we will release him."

17 Simon knew that they were speaking deceitfully to him, but he sent to get the money and the sons, so that he would not arouse great hostility among the people, who might say, 18 "It was because Simon*f* did not send him the money and the sons, that Jonathan*g* perished." 19 So he sent the sons and the hundred talents, but Trypho*g* broke his word and did not release Jonathan.

20 After this Trypho came to invade the country and destroy it, and he circled around by the way to Adora. But Simon and his army kept marching along opposite him to every place he went. 21 Now the men in the citadel kept sending envoys to Trypho urging him to come to them by way of the wilderness and to send them food. 22 So Trypho got all his cavalry ready to go, but that night a very heavy snow fell, and he did not go because of the snow. He marched off and went into the land of Gilead. 23 When he approached Baskama, he killed Jonathan, and he was buried there. 24 Then Trypho turned and went back to his own land.

25 Simon sent and took the bones of his brother Jonathan, and buried him in Modein, the city of his ancestors. 26 All Israel bewailed him with great lamentation, and mourned for him many days. 27 And Simon built a monument over the tomb of his father and his brothers; he made it high so that it might be seen, with polished stone at the front and back. 28 He also erected seven pyramids, opposite one another, for his father and mother and four brothers. 29 For the pyramids*h* he devised an elaborate setting, erecting about them great columns, and on the columns he put suits of armor for a permanent memorial, and beside the suits of armor he carved ships, so that they could be seen by all who sail the sea. 30 This is the tomb that he built in Modein; it remains to this day.

31 Trypho dealt treacherously with the young King Antiochus; he killed him 32 and became king in his place, putting on the crown of Asia; and he brought

f Gk *I*   *g* Gk *he*   *h* Gk *For these*

(9.28–30); *the people now elected Simon leader,* but not yet high priest (compare 14.41). **11:** *Jonathan son of Absalom,* perhaps a brother of Mattathias (11.70). **15–16:** He regarded *Jonathan* as a vassal of Syria who had to pay for *the offices he held* (11.57).

13.20: *Adora,* or Adoraim, now Dura, five miles southwest of Hebron (2 Chr 11.9). **22–23:** *He marched off,* south of the Dead Sea. *Baskama,* possibly northeast of the Sea of Galilee. *He killed Jonathan,* late in 143 or early in 142 B.C. **25:** *Modein,* 2.1; 9.19. **28:** *Pyramids,* combining the Greek custom of building a monument with a suit of armor at the victory site with the Hebrew custom of burial at the ancestral home. **29:** *Carved ships,* symbols claiming domination of the sea, found also on coins of Herod and Archelaus. They were not visible from the sea; *so that they could be seen by all who sail the sea,* they were intended to serve as a warning to potential naval invaders. The Hasmoneans held the seaport of Joppa (13.11; 14.5, 34).

13.31–53: Simon makes Judea independent. 31–32: *He killed him,* probably in 142 B.C. *Antiochus* VI was about seven years

great calamity on the land. 33 But Simon built up the strongholds of Judea and walled them all around, with high towers and great walls and gates and bolts, and he stored food in the strongholds. 34 Simon also chose emissaries and sent them to King Demetrius with a request to grant relief to the country, for all that Trypho did was to plunder. 35 King Demetrius sent him a favorable reply to this request, and wrote him a letter as follows, 36 "King Demetrius to Simon, the high priest and friend of kings, and to the elders and nation of the Jews, greetings. 37 We have received the gold crown and the palm branch that you[i] sent, and we are ready to make a general peace with you and to write to our officials to grant you release from tribute. 38 All the grants that we have made to you remain valid, and let the strongholds that you have built be your possession. 39 We pardon any errors and offenses committed to this day, and cancel the crown tax that you owe; and whatever other tax has been collected in Jerusalem shall be collected no longer. 40 And if any of you are qualified to be enrolled in our bodyguard,[j] let them be enrolled, and let there be peace between us."

41 In the one hundred seventieth year[k] the yoke of the Gentiles was removed from Israel, 42 and the people began to write in their documents and contracts, "In the first year of Simon the great high priest and commander and leader of the Jews."

43 In those days Simon[l] encamped against Gazara[m] and surrounded it with troops. He made a siege engine, brought it up to the city, and battered and captured one tower. 44 The men in the siege engine leaped out into the city, and a great tumult arose in the city. 45 The men in the city, with their wives and children, went up on the wall with their clothes torn, and they cried out with a loud voice, asking Simon to make peace with them; 46 they said, "Do not treat us according to our wicked acts but according to your mercy." 47 So Simon reached an agreement with them and stopped fighting against them. But he expelled them from the city and cleansed the houses in which the idols were located, and then entered it with hymns and praise. 48 He removed all uncleanness from it, and settled in it those who observed the law. He also strengthened its fortifications and built in it a house for himself.

49 Those who were in the citadel at Jerusalem were prevented from going in and out to buy and sell in the country. So they were very hungry, and many of them perished from famine. 50 Then they cried to Simon to make peace with them, and he did so. But he expelled them from there and cleansed the citadel from its pollutions. 51 On the twenty-third day of the second month, in the one hundred seventy-first year,[n] the Jews[o] entered it with praise and palm branches, and with harps and cymbals and stringed instruments, and with hymns and songs, because a great enemy had been crushed and removed from Israel. 52 Simon[p] decreed that every year they should celebrate this day with rejoicing. He strengthened the fortifications of the temple hill alongside the citadel, and he

i The word you in verses 37-40 is plural
j Or court   k 142 B.C.   l Gk he
m Cn: Gk Gaza   n 141 B.C.   o Gk they
p Gk He

old and had reigned since 145 (11.54). *Became king,* about 142 or 141 B.C. **34:** *Demetrius* II (see 10.67 n.) now disputed the throne with Trypho. **36–40:** The letter, addressed to *the elders and nation* and to *Simon* as head of a priestly state, recognizes sovereignty (compare v. 42). The weakness of Demetrius II made possible a great diplomatic victory. **42:** The new era, replacing the Seleucid era, is a mark of sovereignty. It is debated whether Simon was the first of the Hasmoneans to strike coins. **43:** A Greek inscription hostile to Simon has been found at *Gazara. Siege engine,* a tower on wheels, in which men with catapults and battering rams could breach fortified walls. **47–48:** The later Hasmoneans continued the policy of settling Jews in strategic places. **51:** *The second month,* Iyyar or May. *Palm branches* symbolized victory (2 Macc 10.7). **53:** *John* Hyrcanus reigned as high priest 134–104 B.C.

and his men lived there. ⁵³Simon saw that his son John had reached manhood, and so he made him commander of all the forces; and he lived at Gazara.

14 In the one hundred seventy-second year*q* King Demetrius assembled his forces and marched into Media to obtain help, so that he could make war against Trypho. ²When King Arsaces of Persia and Media heard that Demetrius had invaded his territory, he sent one of his generals to take him alive. ³The general*r* went and defeated the army of Demetrius, and seized him and took him to Arsaces, who put him under guard.

⁴ The land*s* had rest all the days of
  Simon.
  He sought the good of his
    nation;
  his rule was pleasing to them,
    as was the honor shown him, all
    his days.
⁵ To crown all his honors he took
    Joppa for a harbor,
  and opened a way to the isles of
    the sea.
⁶ He extended the borders of his
    nation,
  and gained full control of the
    country.
⁷ He gathered a host of captives;
  he ruled over Gazara and
    Beth-zur and the citadel,
  and he removed its uncleanness
    from it;
  and there was none to oppose
    him.
⁸ They tilled their land in peace;
  the ground gave its increase,
  and the trees of the plains their
    fruit.

⁹ Old men sat in the streets;
  they all talked together of good
    things,
  and the youths put on splendid
    military attire.
¹⁰ He supplied the towns with food,
  and furnished them with the
    means of defense,
  until his renown spread to the
    ends of the earth.
¹¹ He established peace in the land,
  and Israel rejoiced with great
    joy.
¹² All the people sat under their own
    vines and fig trees,
  and there was none to make
    them afraid.
¹³ No one was left in the land to
    fight them,
  and the kings were crushed in
    those days.
¹⁴ He gave help to all the humble
    among his people;
  he sought out the law,
  and did away with all the
    renegades and outlaws.
¹⁵ He made the sanctuary glorious,
  and added to the vessels of the
    sanctuary.

16 It was heard in Rome, and as far away as Sparta, that Jonathan had died, and they were deeply grieved. ¹⁷When they heard that his brother Simon had become high priest in his stead, and that he was ruling over the country and the towns in it, ¹⁸they wrote to him on bronze tablets to renew with him the friendship and alliance that they had established with his brothers Judas and

---

q 140 B.C.   *r* Gk *He*   *s* Other ancient
authorities add *of Judah*

14.1–15: Capture of Demetrius II. 1: Other historians date this invasion in 138 B.C., the year in which he was captured. *Media,* lying west of Teheran, was still claimed by the Seleucids. **2–3:** *Arsaces* VI Mithradates I (171–138 B.C.), founder of the Parthian Empire, treated Demetrius kindly and later married him to his sister. **14.4–15:** A contemporary poem of rejoicing, describing the reign of Simon as the fulfillment of biblical prophecies. **4:** 1 Kings 5.5.

5–7: 13.41–53. *A harbor,* important for trade connections with the sea (13.11). *The isles of the sea,* Cyprus, Rhodes, and Crete. **8:** Zech 8.12. **9:** Zech 8.4. **10:** 12.38; 13.33, 52. **12:** 1 Kings 4.25; Mic 4.4; Zech 3.10. **13–14:** Isa 11.3–4. **14:** *Sought out,* he studied Torah to learn God's will, as the kings of Israel had consulted prophets. See Ezra 7.10.

14.16–24: Alliances with Rome and Sparta. Simon was perhaps the first high priest recognized by the Roman senate as rul-

Jonathan. ¹⁹And these were read before the assembly in Jerusalem.

20 This is a copy of the letter that the Spartans sent:

"The rulers and the city of the Spartans to the high priest Simon and to the elders and the priests and the rest of the Jewish people, our brothers, greetings. ²¹The envoys who were sent to our people have told us about your glory and honor, and we rejoiced at their coming. ²²We have recorded what they said in our public decrees, as follows, 'Numenius son of Antiochus and Antipater son of Jason, envoys of the Jews, have come to us to renew their friendship with us. ²³It has pleased our people to receive these men with honor and to put a copy of their words in the public archives, so that the people of the Spartans may have a record of them. And they have sent a copy of this to the high priest Simon.' "

24 After this Simon sent Numenius to Rome with a large gold shield weighing one thousand minas, to confirm the alliance with the Romans.*

25 When the people heard these things they said, "How shall we thank Simon and his sons? ²⁶For he and his brothers and the house of his father have stood firm; they have fought and repulsed Israel's enemies and established its freedom." ²⁷So they made a record on bronze tablets and put it on pillars on Mount Zion.

This is a copy of what they wrote: "On the eighteenth day of Elul, in the one hundred seventy-second year,ᵘ which is the third year of the great high priest Simon, ²⁸in Asaramel,ᵛ in the great as-

sembly of the priests and the people and the rulers of the nation and the elders of the country, the following was proclaimed to us:

29 "Since wars often occurred in the country, Simon son of Mattathias, a priest of the sonsʷ of Joarib, and his brothers, exposed themselves to danger and resisted the enemies of their nation, in order that their sanctuary and the law might be preserved; and they brought great glory to their nation. ³⁰Jonathan rallied theˣ nation, became their high priest, and was gathered to his people. ³¹When their enemies decided to invade their country and lay hands on their sanctuary, ³²then Simon rose up and fought for his nation. He spent great sums of his own money; he armed the soldiers of his nation and paid them wages. ³³He fortified the towns of Judea, and Beth-zur on the borders of Judea, where formerly the arms of the enemy had been stored, and he placed there a garrison of Jews. ³⁴He also fortified Joppa, which is by the sea, and Gazara, which is on the borders of Azotus, where the enemy formerly lived. He settled Jews there, and provided in those townsᵗ whatever was necessary for their restoration.

35 "The people saw Simon's faithfulnessʸ and the glory that he had resolved to win for his nation, and they made him their leader and high priest, because he had done all these things and because of

t Gk *them* *u* 140 B.C. *v* This word resembles the Hebrew words for *the court of the people of God* or *the prince of the people of God* *w* Meaning of Gk uncertain *x* Gk *their* *y* Other ancient authorities read *conduct*

er of the Jews. **19**: *The assembly*, the people as a whole. **22**: *Numenius* and *Antipater*, 12.16. **24**: *Weighing one thousand minas*, an obvious exaggeration; a Greek mina is over 15 ounces (troy).

14.25–49: **Simon elected high priest, military commander, and ruler.** The formal document of vv. 27–49 served as a constitution for the new state of Judea. **27–28**: *Bronze tablets*, see 8.22 n. *Mount Zion*, 1.33; 4.37. *Elul*, August–September. *Third year*, see 13.42 n. *The great assembly* represented all "states" or classes. In theory the high priest

held his office by divine appointment, indicated by descent from a particular family. Since there was no legitimate claimant, Simon was legitimized by a process known in ancient Israel. See Ex ch 19; 2 Kings ch 23; Ezra ch 10; Neh ch 9. **29**: *Sons of Joarib*, see 2.1 n. **30**: The decree recognizes in retrospect the office of *Jonathan*, first Hasmonean *high priest*. **32**: Use of *his own money* had not been previously mentioned. **33–34**: 13.43–48; 14.3–7.

14.35: The high priest must have moral responsibility along with his powers. **36–37**:

the justice and loyalty that he had maintained toward his nation. He sought in
every way to exalt his people. ³⁶In his
days things prospered in his hands, so
that the Gentiles were put out of the ᶻ
country, as were also those in the city of
David in Jerusalem, who had built themselves a citadel from which they used to
sally forth and defile the environs of the
sanctuary, doing great damage to its purity. ³⁷He settled Jews in it and fortified
it for the safety of the country and of the
city, and built the walls of Jerusalem
higher.

38 "In view of these things King Demetrius confirmed him in the high
priesthood, ³⁹made him one of his
Friends, and paid him high honors. ⁴⁰For
he had heard that the Jews were addressed by the Romans as friends and
allies and brothers, and that the Ro-
mansᵈ had received the envoys of Simon
with honor.

41 "The Jews and their priests have
resolved that Simon should be their leader and high priest forever, until a trustworthy prophet should arise, ⁴²and that
he should be governor over them and
that he should take charge of the sanctuary and appoint officials over its tasks
and over the country and the weapons
and the strongholds, and that he should
take charge of the sanctuary, ⁴³and that
he should be obeyed by all, and that all
contracts in the country should be written in his name, and that he should be
clothed in purple and wear gold.

44 "None of the people or priests
shall be permitted to nullify any of these
decisions or to oppose what he says, or

to convene an assembly in the country
without his permission, or to be clothed
in purple or put on a gold buckle.
⁴⁵Whoever acts contrary to these decisions or rejects any of them shall be liable
to punishment."

46 All the people agreed to grant Simon the right to act in accordance with
these decisions. ⁴⁷So Simon accepted and
agreed to be high priest, to be commander and ethnarch of the Jews and priests,
and to be protector of them all. ᵇ ⁴⁸And
they gave orders to inscribe this decree
on bronze tablets, to put them up in a
conspicuous place in the precincts of the
sanctuary, ⁴⁹and to deposit copies of
them in the treasury, so that Simon and
his sons might have them.

15 Antiochus, son of King Demetrius, sent a letter from the islands
of the sea to Simon, the priest and ethnarch of the Jews, and to all the nation;
²its contents were as follows: "King Antiochus to Simon the high priest and ethnarch and to the nation of the Jews,
greetings. ³Whereas certain scoundrels
have gained control of the kingdom of
our ancestors, and I intend to lay claim to
the kingdom so that I may restore it as it
formerly was, and have recruited a host
of mercenary troops and have equipped
warships, ⁴and intend to make a landing
in the country so that I may proceed
against those who have destroyed our
country and those who have devastated
many cities in my kingdom, ⁵now therefore I confirm to you all the tax remis-

z Meaning of Gk uncertain   a Gk *they*
b Or *to preside over them all*

1.34; 4.41, 60; 6.18; 13.49–52. **41–43:** The
office was to be hereditary in Simon's family,
but since this was an act of the nation rather
than of God, a *trustworthy prophet* might annul
or confirm the decision (see 4.46 n.). *Clothed
in purple and wear gold,* borrowing the dress of
the Seleucid kings and courtiers. From Alexander Janneus onwards (103–76 B.C.), the
Hasmoneans assumed the title of king. Little
is known about the political role of high priest
during the period of the Second Temple. A letter written in 408 B.C. from the Jews at Elephantine requesting help from the Judean

government is addressed to the high priest
and the nobles. The power vested in Simon
is probably not entirely new. **46–47:** In
this social contract, both the people and Simon accept the conditions. *Ethnarch,* civil
magistrate. **49:** The *treasury* in the temple
served as a national archive.
15.1–14: Arrival of Antiochus VII. 1:
Antiochus VII (known as Sidetes because
reared at Side in Pamphylia), younger brother
of Demetrius II, reigned 138–129 B.C. After
his brother's capture he married Cleopatra III
(10.57–58; 11.12). **3:** *Scoundrels,* Trypho and

sions that the kings before me have granted you, and a release from all the other payments from which they have released you. 6 I permit you to mint your own coinage as money for your country, 7 and I grant freedom to Jerusalem and the sanctuary. All the weapons that you have prepared and the strongholds that you have built and now hold shall remain yours. 8 Every debt you owe to the royal treasury and any such future debts shall be canceled for you from henceforth and for all time. 9 When we gain control of our kingdom, we will bestow great honor on you and your nation and the temple, so that your glory will become manifest in all the earth."

10 In the one hundred seventy-fourth year *c* Antiochus set out and invaded the land of his ancestors. All the troops rallied to him, so that there were only a few with Trypho. 11 Antiochus pursued him, and Trypho *d* came in his flight to Dor, which is by the sea; 12 for he knew that troubles had converged on him, and his troops had deserted him. 13 So Antiochus encamped against Dor, and with him were one hundred twenty thousand warriors and eight thousand cavalry. 14 He surrounded the town, and the ships joined battle from the sea; he pressed the town hard from land and sea, and permitted no one to leave or enter it.

15 Then Numenius and his companions arrived from Rome, with letters to the kings and countries, in which the following was written: 16 "Lucius, consul of the Romans, to King Ptolemy, greetings. 17 The envoys of the Jews have come to us as our friends and allies to renew our ancient friendship and alli-

ance. They had been sent by the high priest Simon and by the Jewish people 18 and have brought a gold shield weighing one thousand minas. 19 We therefore have decided to write to the kings and countries that they should not seek their harm or make war against them and their cities and their country, or make alliance with those who war against them. 20 And it has seemed good to us to accept the shield from them. 21 Therefore if any scoundrels have fled to you from their country, hand them over to the high priest Simon, so that he may punish them according to their law."

22 The consul *e* wrote the same thing to King Demetrius and to Attalus and Ariarathes and Arsaces, 23 and to all the countries, and to Sampsames, *f* and to the Spartans, and to Delos, and to Myndos, and to Sicyon, and to Caria, and to Samos, and to Pamphylia, and to Lycia, and to Halicarnassus, and to Rhodes, and to Phaselis, and to Cos, and to Side, and to Aradus and Gortyna and Cnidus and Cyprus and Cyrene. 24 They also sent a copy of these things to the high priest Simon.

25 King Antiochus besieged Dor for the second time, continually throwing his forces against it and making engines of war; and he shut Trypho up and kept him from going out or in. 26 And Simon sent to Antiochus *g* two thousand picked troops, to fight for him, and silver and gold and a large amount of military equipment. 27 But he refused to receive them, and broke all the agreements he

c 138 B.C. *d* Gk *he* *e* Gk *He*
f The name is uncertain *g* Gk *him*

his faction. **5**: He reaffirms his brother's grants (13.39). **6**: *To mint your own coinage* was legal recognition of independence. When the Seleucids permitted subject cities to coin money, it bore the king's name. **7–8**: 13.38–39. **10**: He first landed in Seleucia (11.8), where Cleopatra was living. **11**: *Dor,* about nine miles north of Caesarea (Judg 1.27). **13**: The numbers are probably exaggerated.
15.15–24: **Renewal of alliance with Rome.** The letter follows logically after 14.24. **16**: If the letter is genuine, this is *Lucius*

Calpurnius Piso, consul 140–139 B.C. *Ptolemy* VII Physcon reigned 145–116 B.C. **18**: *Shield,* see 14.24 n. **22–23**: *Demetrius* II was still a prisoner in Parthia; the Romans had not recognized Antiochus VII. *Attalus* II, king of Pergamum 159–138 B.C.; *Ariarathes* V, king of Cappadocia 162–130 B.C. *Delos* in the Cyclades and the other localities were free states in Greece, the Greek islands and Asia Minor. *Cyrene,* capital of Libya.
15.25–16.10: **War with Antiochus VII.** **15.27**: Josephus says that Antiochus ac-

formerly had made with Simon, and became estranged from him. [28]He sent to him Athenobius, one of his Friends, to confer with him, saying, "You hold control of Joppa and Gazara and the citadel in Jerusalem; they are cities of my kingdom. [29]You have devastated their territory, you have done great damage in the land, and you have taken possession of many places in my kingdom. [30]Now then, hand over the cities that you have seized and the tribute money of the places that you have conquered outside the borders of Judea; [31]or else pay me five hundred talents of silver for the destruction that you have caused and five hundred talents more for the tribute money of the cities. Otherwise we will come and make war on you."

32 So Athenobius, the king's Friend, came to Jerusalem, and when he saw the splendor of Simon, and the sideboard with its gold and silver plate, and his great magnificence, he was amazed. When he reported to him the king's message, [33]Simon said to him in reply: "We have neither taken foreign land nor seized foreign property, but only the inheritance of our ancestors, which at one time had been unjustly taken by our enemies. [34]Now that we have the opportunity, we are firmly holding the inheritance of our ancestors. [35]As for Joppa and Gazara, which you demand, they were causing great damage among the people and to our land; for them we will give you one hundred talents."

Athenobius[h] did not answer him a word, [36]but returned in wrath to the king and reported to him these words, and also the splendor of Simon and all that he had seen. And the king was very angry.

37 Meanwhile Trypho embarked on a

ship and escaped to Orthosia. [38]Then the king made Cendebeus commander-in-chief of the coastal country, and gave him troops of infantry and cavalry. [39]He commanded him to encamp against Judea, to build up Kedron and fortify its gates, and to make war on the people; but the king pursued Trypho. [40]So Cendebeus came to Jamnia and began to provoke the people and invade Judea and take the people captive and kill them. [41]He built up Kedron and stationed horsemen and troops there, so that they might go out and make raids along the highways of Judea, as the king had ordered him.

16 John went up from Gazara and reported to his father Simon what Cendebeus had done. [2]And Simon called in his two eldest sons Judas and John, and said to them: "My brothers and I and my father's house have fought the wars of Israel from our youth until this day, and things have prospered in our hands so that we have delivered Israel many times. [3]But now I have grown old, and you by Heaven's[i] mercy are mature in years. Take my place and my brother's, and go out and fight for our nation, and may the help that comes from Heaven be with you."

4 So John[j] chose out of the country twenty thousand warriors and cavalry, and they marched against Cendebeus and camped for the night in Modein. [5]Early in the morning they started out and marched into the plain, where a large force of infantry and cavalry was coming to meet them; and a stream lay between them. [6]Then he and his army lined up against them. He saw that the soldiers

---

h Gk *He*   *i* Gk *his*   *j* Other ancient authorities read *he*

---

cepted this aid (*Antiquities,* XIII. vii. 2). **30:** *Outside . . . Judea,* perhaps the districts of 11.34; but compare v. 8. **33:** The Hasmoneans claimed that all Palestine had always belonged by right to the Jews. Greek law recognized the right to reclaim ancestral property that had been seized. **35:** *Joppa and Gazara,* 12.33; 13.43–48. **37:** *Orthosia,* a few

miles north of Tripolis; from there Trypho went to Apamea, where he was besieged and slain. **39–40:** *Kedron,* perhaps Gedereth, southwest of Ekron (Josh 15.41). The plan was to control the coastal plain and recover Gazara and Joppa.

16.1: *John* Hyrcanus I commanded Gazara (13.53). **4:** *Cavalry* are now for the first time

were afraid to cross the stream, so he crossed over first; and when his troops saw him, they crossed over after him. [7] Then he divided the army and placed the cavalry in the center of the infantry, for the cavalry of the enemy were very numerous. [8] They sounded the trumpets, and Cendebeus and his army were put to flight; many of them fell wounded and the rest fled into the stronghold. [9] At that time Judas the brother of John was wounded, but John pursued them until Cendebeus[k] reached Kedron, which he had built. [10] They also fled into the towers that were in the fields of Azotus, and John[k] burned it with fire, and about two thousand of them fell. He then returned to Judea safely.

[11] Now Ptolemy son of Abubus had been appointed governor over the plain of Jericho; he had a large store of silver and gold, [12] for he was son-in-law of the high priest. [13] His heart was lifted up; he determined to get control of the country, and made treacherous plans against Simon and his sons, to do away with them. [14] Now Simon was visiting the towns of the country and attending to their needs, and he went down to Jericho with his sons Mattathias and Judas, in the one hundred seventy-seventh year,[l] in the eleventh month, which is the month of Shebat. [15] The son of Abubus received them treacherously in the little stronghold called Dok, which he had built; he gave them a great banquet, and hid men

there. [16] When Simon and his sons were drunk, Ptolemy and his men rose up, took their weapons, rushed in against Simon in the banquet hall and killed him and his two sons, as well as some of his servants. [17] So he committed an act of great treachery and returned evil for good.

[18] Then Ptolemy wrote a report about these things and sent it to the king, asking him to send troops to aid him and to turn over to him the towns and the country. [19] He sent other troops to Gazara to do away with John; he sent letters to the captains asking them to come to him so that he might give them silver and gold and gifts; [20] and he sent other troops to take possession of Jerusalem and the temple hill. [21] But someone ran ahead and reported to John at Gazara that his father and brothers had perished, and that "he has sent men to kill you also." [22] When he heard this, he was greatly shocked; he seized the men who came to destroy him and killed them, for he had found out that they were seeking to destroy him.

[23] The rest of the acts of John and his wars and the brave deeds that he did, and the building of the walls that he completed, and his achievements, [24] are written in the annals of his high priesthood, from the time that he became high priest after his father.

k Gk he l 134 B.C.

---

part of the Judean army. **7**: The meaning is unclear. The author may refer to the prevailing Roman tactic of providing each unit of infantry with a unit of cavalry. **8**: *The stronghold,* Kedron (15.39). **10**: *Azotus,* destroyed by Jonathan (10.84).

16.11–24: Death of Simon and accession of John Hyrcanus I. 11: *Plain of Jericho,* the fertile region north of the Dead Sea. **12**: *The high priest,* Simon. **14**: *Shebat,* February-March. **15**: *Dok,* 'Ain Duq, three miles northwest of Jericho. **18**: *The king,* Antiochus VII. **23**: *John* was high priest 134–104 B.C. When

Antiochus later besieged Jerusalem, John was defeated but made peace and accompanied the king on an expedition to Parthia, where Antiochus was killed. Afterward he gained control of most of Palestine, and forced the Idumeans to adopt Judaism. Late in his reign the Pharisees turned against him and demanded that he give up the high priesthood. **24**: *The annals* have been lost. The book is concluded in a manner similar to the biblical accounts of the kings of Israel (1 Kings 11.41; 2 Kings 10.34; 12.19; 20.20, etc.).

2 Maccabees

Second Maccabees narrates the events of Jewish history during the persecutions of three Seleucid kings: Seleucus IV, Antiochus IV (Epiphanes), and Antiochus Eupator (from about 180–161 B.C.; see Introduction to First Maccabees). The narrative begins with the author's preface (2.19–32), explaining that the work is an abridgment presenting highlights of a five-volume work by Jason of Cyrene. No evidence of Jason's work has survived. The stories in the first half tell of persecution and martyrdom, and in the second half of the victories won by Judas Maccabeus over the Seleucid oppressors. An eloquent epilogue addresses the reader in a style similar to the preface. Two letters to the Jewish communities in Egypt have been added to the beginning of the book (1.1–2.18) by an unknown author.

Although 2 Maccabees parallels chapters 1–8 of 1 Maccabees, it is distinguished by its literary style and theological point of view. The author of 2 Maccabees addresses the reader directly, in the manner of Greek historians, providing theological guidance. The unforgettable stories are told with dramatic artistry and vivid detail. Like the Greek historians the author guides the reader's interpretation by means of elaborate speeches in the mouths of central characters (6.24–28; 7.27–29, 30–38; 15.22–23).

The stories are unified by the idea that history reflects the divine plan, which can be affected by the prayers and deeds of the faithful. Like the tyrants of Egypt, Assyria, and Babylonia, who oppressed Israel in biblical times, the Seleucid kings are seen as unwitting tools of God, aiding in the chastisement of Israel. The author firmly believed in the sanctity of the Temple, but also held that abuses would bring divine judgment, as the desecrations of Antiochus had proved. The author also believed, however, that the suffering of the martyrs and the prayers of the courageous Judas Maccabeus moved God to intervene and end the time of divine wrath.

Several important theological ideas not found in the Hebrew Scriptures but important in Judaism and Christianity appear in 2 Maccabees. These include resurrection of the dead (hinted at in Dan 12.2, but stated clearly in 2 Macc 7–8); the doctrine that the world was created out of nothing (*creatio ex nihilo,* 7.28); and the efficacy of praying for the dead (12.39–45). The beginning of the later rabbinic principle of measure for measure, which teaches that divine retribution is perfectly just, is graphically portrayed in 3.27–28; 9.28; 13.8 and 15.32–33. The stories of the aged scribe Eleazar going willingly to his death rather than eat food forbidden by the Torah, and of the mother encouraging her seven sons to die for their faith in certain hope of resurrection, became models for later Jewish and Christian martyrologies.

Second Maccabees was written in Greek and was translated into Latin, Syriac and Armenian in antiquity. It was written between 104 and 63 B.C. (see 15.37).

1 The Jews in Jerusalem and those in the land of Judea,

To their Jewish kindred in Egypt,

Greetings and true peace.

2 May God do good to you, and may he remember his covenant with Abraham and Isaac and Jacob, his faithful servants. ³May he give you all a heart to worship him and to do his will with a strong heart and a willing spirit. ⁴May he open your heart to his law and his commandments, and may he bring peace. ⁵May he hear your prayers and be reconciled to you, and may he not forsake you in time of evil. ⁶We are now praying for you here.

7 In the reign of Demetrius, in the one hundred sixty-ninth year,ᵃ we Jews wrote to you, in the critical distress that came upon us in those years after Jason and his company revolted from the holy land and the kingdom ⁸and burned the gate and shed innocent blood. We prayed to the Lord and were heard, and we offered sacrifice and grain offering, and we lit the lamps and set out the loaves. ⁹And now see that you keep the festival of booths in the month of Chislev, in the one hundred eighty-eighth year.ᵇ

10 The people of Jerusalem and of Judea and the senate and Judas,

To Aristobulus, who is of the family of the anointed priests, teacher of King Ptolemy, and to the Jews in Egypt,

Greetings and good health.

11 Having been saved by God out of grave dangers we thank him greatly for taking our side against the king,ᶜ ¹²for he drove out those who fought against the holy city. ¹³When the leader reached Persia with a force that seemed irresistible, they were cut to pieces in the temple of Nanea by a deception employed by the priests of the goddessᵈ Nanea. ¹⁴On the pretext of intending to marry her, Antiochus came to the place together with his Friends, to secure most of its treasures as a dowry. ¹⁵When the priests of the temple of Nanea had set out the treasures and Antiochus had come with a few men inside the wall of the sacred precinct, they closed the temple as soon as he entered it. ¹⁶Opening a secret door in the ceiling, they threw stones and

a 143 B.C.   *b* 124 B.C.   *c* Cn: Gk *as those who array themselves against a king*   *d* Gk lacks *the goddess*

1.1–9: Letter to the Jews in Egypt. The authorship of these letters is uncertain. The first is addressed to the large Jewish community that had lived in Egypt since Alexander the Great (1 Macc 1.1). **1:** Greek letters usually began with the word *greetings,* and Jewish ones with *peace* (Rom 1.7). **2:** Gen 15.18; 26.3; 35.12; Lev 26.27–45. **5:** To live outside Judea was thought of as divine punishment. **7:** The previous letter was in the reign of Demetrius II (see 1 Macc 10.67 n.). *The critical distress* was the capture and murder of the high priest Jonathan (1 Macc 12.48; see 13.23 n.). *Jason and his company,* 4.7–22. *The kingdom,* rule of the legitimate high priests. **8:** *Burned the gate,* 1 Macc 4.38. *Shed innocent blood,* 1 Macc 1.60–61. *We . . . were heard,* i.e. by God, when Simon made Judea independent (1 Macc 13.1–42). **9:** *The festival of booths* would properly be kept in September (Lev 23.33–43). This refers to Hanukkah, celebrated on the 25th of *Chislev* (November-December), commemorating Judas Maccabeus' restoration of the temple (10.1–8; 1 Macc 4.59). Palestinian Jews now wished

the Egyptian Jews to observe the feast in 124 B.C., when they wrote.

1.10–2.18: Letter to Aristobulus. The purpose of the letter is to show why the new eight-day festival should be kept, though it had not been prescribed by the Mosaic law. Keeping the festival implied accepting that Judas, like Nehemiah, was doing God's will. Nehemiah's rededication of the temple was a precedent (1.18–36). **1.10:** *The senate,* see 1 Macc 12.6 n. *The anointed priests,* descendants of Zadok (2 Chr 31.10), from whom high priests were chosen. One branch of these came to Egypt with Ptolemy I. The *king,* Ptolemy VII Physcon, who reigned 145–116 B.C. **11:** *Grave dangers,* in the time of king Antiochus IV (4.7). **13:** *The leader,* Antiochus IV, died later; his forces *were cut to pieces* (9.1–4; 1 Macc 6.1–4). *Nanea,* a Syrian goddess equated with Artemis or Aphrodite and the Persian Anahita. **14:** *Marry her,* the goddess, so as to obtain a large *dowry* from the treasures at her temple (compare 9.2; 1 Macc 6.1–4). **18:** *The festival of booths,* compare 1 Macc 10.21; 1 Kings 8.2; Neh 8.13–18.

struck down the leader and his men; they dismembered them and cut off their heads and threw them to the people outside. [17] Blessed in every way be our God, who has brought judgment on those who have behaved impiously.

18 Since on the twenty-fifth day of Chislev we shall celebrate the purification of the temple, we thought it necessary to notify you, in order that you also may celebrate the festival of booths and the festival of the fire given when Nehemiah, who built the temple and the altar, offered sacrifices.

19 For when our ancestors were being led captive to Persia, the pious priests of that time took some of the fire of the altar and secretly hid it in the hollow of a dry cistern, where they took such precautions that the place was unknown to anyone. [20] But after many years had passed, when it pleased God, Nehemiah, having been commissioned by the king of Persia, sent the descendants of the priests who had hidden the fire to get it. And when they reported to us that they had not found fire but only a thick liquid, he ordered them to dip it out and bring it. [21] When the materials for the sacrifices were presented, Nehemiah ordered the priests to sprinkle the liquid on the wood and on the things laid upon it. [22] When this had been done and some time had passed, and when the sun, which had been clouded over, shone out, a great fire blazed up, so that all marveled. [23] And while the sacrifice was being consumed, the priests offered prayer—the priests and everyone. Jonathan led, and the rest responded, as did Nehemiah. [24] The prayer was to this effect:

"O Lord, Lord God, Creator of all things, you are awe-inspiring and strong and just and merciful, you alone are king and are kind, [25] you alone are bountiful, you alone are just and almighty and eternal. You rescue Israel from every evil; you chose the ancestors and consecrated them. [26] Accept this sacrifice on behalf of all your people Israel and preserve your portion and make it holy. [27] Gather together our scattered people, set free those who are slaves among the Gentiles, look on those who are rejected and despised, and let the Gentiles know that you are our God. [28] Punish those who oppress and are insolent with pride. [29] Plant your people in your holy place, as Moses promised."

30 Then the priests sang the hymns. [31] After the materials of the sacrifice had been consumed, Nehemiah ordered that the liquid that was left should be poured on large stones. [32] When this was done, a flame blazed up; but when the light from the altar shone back, it went out. [33] When this matter became known, and it was reported to the king of the Persians that, in the place where the exiled priests had hidden the fire, the liquid had appeared with which Nehemiah and his associates had burned the materials of the sacrifice, [34] the king investigated the matter, and enclosed the place and made it sacred. [35] And with those persons whom the king favored he exchanged many excellent gifts. [36] Nehemiah and his associates called this "nephthar," which means purification, but by most people it is called naphtha. *e*

e Gk *nephthai*

The festival of the fire, vv. 19–36. Fire and light are associated with Hanukkah, which is celebrated with a nine-branched candlestick. A Talmudic tradition tells of a small amount of oil that burned miraculously for a long time till new oil could be consecrated.

1.19: *Persia,* actually Babylonia (2 Kings 24.14), later part of the Persian empire. **20:** *Nehemiah . . . commissioned,* Neh 2.7–8; his book does not contain the legend of the fire. *Thick liquid,* naphtha or petroleum (v. 36).

22: 1 Kings 18.33–38. **25:** *You chose,* Gen 12.1–3; 22.15–18; Deut 14.2; Mal 1.2. **26:** *Your portion,* Israel (Deut 32.9). *Holy,* Lev 19.2. **27:** *Gather together,* Ps 147.2; Jer 23.8; Sir 36.11; Bar 5.6. **28:** *Punish . . . insolent,* 1 Sam 2.3–4; Lk 1.51–52. **29:** *As Moses promised,* Deut 30.5. **34:** Localities where miracles occurred were *enclosed* as *sacred.* The Persians considered fire holy. **36:** *Nephthar* is an otherwise unknown word.

2 One finds in the records that the prophet Jeremiah ordered those who were being deported to take some of the fire, as has been mentioned, ²and that the prophet, after giving them the law, instructed those who were being deported not to forget the commandments of the Lord, or to be led astray in their thoughts on seeing the gold and silver statues and their adornment. ³And with other similar words he exhorted them that the law should not depart from their hearts.

4 It was also in the same document that the prophet, having received an oracle, ordered that the tent and the ark should follow with him, and that he went out to the mountain where Moses had gone up and had seen the inheritance of God. ⁵Jeremiah came and found a cave-dwelling, and he brought there the tent and the ark and the altar of incense; then he sealed up the entrance. ⁶Some of those who followed him came up intending to mark the way, but could not find it. ⁷When Jeremiah learned of it, he rebuked them and declared: "The place shall remain unknown until God gathers his people together again and shows his mercy. ⁸Then the Lord will disclose these things, and the glory of the Lord and the cloud will appear, as they were shown in the case of Moses, and as Solomon asked that the place should be specially consecrated."

9 It was also made clear that being possessed of wisdom Solomon*f* offered sacrifice for the dedication and completion of the temple. ¹⁰Just as Moses prayed to the Lord, and fire came down from heaven and consumed the sacrifices, so also Solomon prayed, and the fire came down and consumed the whole burnt offerings. ¹¹And Moses said, "They were consumed because the sin offering had not been eaten." ¹²Likewise Solomon also kept the eight days.

13 The same things are reported in the records and in the memoirs of Nehemiah, and also that he founded a library and collected the books about the kings and prophets, and the writings of David, and letters of kings about votive offerings. ¹⁴In the same way Judas also collected all the books that had been lost on account of the war that had come upon us, and they are in our possession. ¹⁵So if you have need of them, send people to get them for you.

16 Since, therefore, we are about to celebrate the purification, we write to you. Will you therefore please keep the days? ¹⁷It is God who has saved all his people, and has returned the inheritance to all, and the kingship and the priesthood and the consecration, ¹⁸as he promised through the law. We have hope in God that he will soon have mercy on us and will gather us from everywhere under heaven into his holy place, for he has

f Gk *he*

2.1: No such *records* are known. *Jeremiah* remained in Judea after the exile (Jer 29.1–23; 40.1–42.7). In the apocryphal Epistle of Jeremiah the writer similarly exhorts the exiles. 4: Solomon brought the *tent* to Jerusalem with the ark (1 Kings 8.4). There is no further record in the Old Testament of the tent, but the ark was kept in the first temple; according to Alexander Polyhistor (first century B.C.), perhaps from the historian Eupolemus, Jeremiah concealed the ark after the temple was destroyed in 587–6 B.C. *The mountain*, Nebo (Deut 32.49). 8: *The glory* and *the cloud* indicate God's direct presence (Ex 16.10; Mk 9.2–8). *Solomon*, 1 Kings 8.11.
2.9: Solomon's *wisdom*, 1 Kings 3.3–28; 4.29–34. *Offered sacrifice*, 1 Kings 8.62–64. 10:

Moses prayed, Lev 9.24. *Solomon*, 2 Chr 7.1. 11: The meaning is obscure, but see Lev 10.16–19. 12: *Eight days*, 1 Kings 8.65; 2 Chr 7.9. 13: *The memoirs of Nehemiah*, the biblical book of Nehemiah does not contain these references. See Ezra 3.14 and 1 Esdras 5.46–50. There is no record that *he founded a library*, but the Pentateuch was canonized in his time, and he may have collected the books of Kings. *Votive offerings*, made to the temple (Ezra 7.15–20). 14: *Judas* Maccabeus may have *collected all the books* remaining after the destruction in the time of Antiochus IV (1 Macc 1.56–57). 16: 1.18. 17: *The kingship*, independence; the Hasmoneans were not yet called kings. 18: 1.27; Deut 30.3.

rescued us from great evils and has purified the place.

19 The story of Judas Maccabeus and his brothers, and the purification of the great temple, and the dedication of the altar, 20 and further the wars against Antiochus Epiphanes and his son Eupator, 21 and the appearances that came from heaven to those who fought bravely for Judaism, so that though few in number they seized the whole land and pursued the barbarian hordes, 22 and regained possession of the temple famous throughout the world, and liberated the city, and re-established the laws that were about to be abolished, while the Lord with great kindness became gracious to them— 23 all this, which has been set forth by Jason of Cyrene in five volumes, we shall attempt to condense into a single book. 24 For considering the flood of statistics involved and the difficulty there is for those who wish to enter upon the narratives of history because of the mass of material, 25 we have aimed to please those who wish to read, to make it easy for those who are inclined to memorize, and to profit all readers. 26 For us who have undertaken the toil of abbreviating, it is no light matter but calls for sweat and loss of sleep, 27 just as it is not easy for one who prepares a banquet and seeks the benefit of others. Nevertheless, to secure the gratitude of many we will gladly endure the uncomfortable

toil, 28 leaving the responsibility for exact details to the compiler, while devoting our effort to arriving at the outlines of the condensation. 29 For as the master builder of a new house must be concerned with the whole construction, while the one who undertakes its painting and decoration has to consider only what is suitable for its adornment, such in my judgment is the case with us. 30 It is the duty of the original historian to occupy the ground, to discuss matters from every side, and to take trouble with details, 31 but the one who recasts the narrative should be allowed to strive for brevity of expression and to forego exhaustive treatment. 32 At this point therefore let us begin our narrative, without adding any more to what has already been said; for it would be foolish to lengthen the preface while cutting short the history itself.

3 While the holy city was inhabited in unbroken peace and the laws were strictly observed because of the piety of the high priest Onias and his hatred of wickedness, 2 it came about that the kings themselves honored the place and glorified the temple with the finest presents, 3 even to the extent that King Seleucus of Asia defrayed from his own revenues all the expenses connected with the service of the sacrifices.

4 But a man named Simon, of the tribe of Benjamin, who had been made

---

2.19–32: The epitomist's preface. Following the custom of Greek histories, the Preface presents highlights and entices readers (see Thucydides i 23.1–3 and Tacitus *Histories* i 2–3). He summarizes parts of the book. **20–21:** *Appearances* (Gr. "epiphaneiai"), true divine manifestations, in contrast to Antiochus' boastful title *Epiphanes,* "god manifest." *Judaism,* first known use of this term for the religion, in contrast to Hellenism (4.13). *Barbarian,* used by the Greeks for all non-Greeks, connotes "one who speaks a foreign language." It can also mean "savage," as in 4.25; 5.22; 10.4; 15.2. **23:** *Jason of Cyrene* is not mentioned in ancient sources, and no work of his survives. Resting one's work on the authority of a purported ancient source is a literary tradition of

antiquity; it is not certain whether the author of 2 Maccabees had an actual source or is using the literary conceit that he had such a document.
3.1–4.6: Simon's plot against Onias.
3.1: Jerusalem was not *in unbroken peace,* though quieter than in later years. *The high priest Onias* III, son of Simon the Just (Sir 50.1–21), ruled before 175 B.C. He turned against Syria and collaborated with Egypt, while his cousins, the family of Tobias, to which Simon (v. 4) belonged, were pro-Syrian. **2:** *The kings,* i.e. the Ptolemies of Egypt and Antiochus III the Great (reigned 233–187 B.C.). **3:** *Seleucus* IV Philopator, son of Antiochus III, reigned 187–175 B.C. The events of 3.1–4.6 were in his reign. He was

captain of the temple, had a disagreement with the high priest about the administration of the city market. 5 Since he could not prevail over Onias, he went to Apollonius of Tarsus,^g who at that time was governor of Coelesyria and Phoenicia, 6 and reported to him that the treasury in Jerusalem was full of untold sums of money, so that the amount of the funds could not be reckoned, and that they did not belong to the account of the sacrifices, but that it was possible for them to fall under the control of the king. 7 When Apollonius met the king, he told him of the money about which he had been informed. The king^h chose Heliodorus, who was in charge of his affairs, and sent him with commands to effect the removal of the reported wealth. 8 Heliodorus at once set out on his journey, ostensibly to make a tour of inspection of the cities of Coelesyria and Phoenicia, but in fact to carry out the king's purpose.

9 When he had arrived at Jerusalem and had been kindly welcomed by the high priest ofⁱ the city, he told about the disclosure that had been made and stated why he had come, and he inquired whether this really was the situation. 10 The high priest explained that there were some deposits belonging to widows and orphans, 11 and also some money of Hyrcanus son of Tobias, a man of very prominent position, and that it totaled in all four hundred talents of silver and two hundred of gold. To such an extent the impious Simon had misrepresented the facts. 12 And he said that it was utterly impossible that wrong should be

done to those people who had trusted in the holiness of the place and in the sanctity and inviolability of the temple that is honored throughout the whole world.

13 But Heliodorus, because of the orders he had from the king, said that this money must in any case be confiscated for the king's treasury. 14 So he set a day and went in to direct the inspection of these funds.

There was no little distress throughout the whole city. 15 The priests prostrated themselves before the altar in their priestly vestments and called toward heaven upon him who had given the law about deposits, that he should keep them safe for those who had deposited them. 16 To see the appearance of the high priest was to be wounded at heart, for his face and the change in his color disclosed the anguish of his soul. 17 For terror and bodily trembling had come over the man, which plainly showed to those who looked at him the pain lodged in his heart. 18 People also hurried out of their houses in crowds to make a general supplication because the holy place was about to be brought into dishonor. 19 Women, girded with sackcloth under their breasts, thronged the streets. Some of the young women who were kept indoors ran together to the gates, and some to the walls, while others peered out of the windows. 20 And holding up their hands to heaven, they all made supplication. 21 There was something pitiable in the prostration of the whole populace

g Gk *Apollonius son of Tharseas*   h Gk *He*
i Other ancient authorities read *and*

---

assassinated by Heliodorus (v. 7). **4:** *Simon* was a grandson of Tobias, who married a sister of Onias II. When Onias II refused to pay tribute to Egypt, Ptolemy III took away his civil authority and appointed Joseph, son of Tobias, *captain of the temple.* His son Simon succeeded him. **5:** *Tarsus,* capital of Cilicia (Acts 9.11), then part of the Seleucid empire. *Coelesyria,* see 1 Macc 10.69 n. *Apollonius* was removed from office at the death of Seleucus IV in 175 B.C. **7:** *Heliodorus,* see v. 3 n.
3.9: *The high priest,* Onias III. **11:** *Hyrcanus,* actually son of Joseph and half-brother of Si-

mon (v. 4), was pro-Egyptian. He fled east of the Jordan after 198 B.C. and built the fortress of 'Araq el-Emir. He committed suicide on the accession of Antiochus IV in 175 B.C. *Simon had misrepresented the facts* only in part; Onias and Hyrcanus probably withheld tribute. **18:** Temples, whether pagan or Jewish, were considered inviolate. **19:** *Sackcloth,* robes of goat hair, a sign of mourning and penitence. Some young women were *kept indoors* until marriage (Sir 42.9–12).
3.20: *Holding up their hands,* the ancient gesture of prayer (1 Kings 8.54; 1 Tim 2.8).

and the anxiety of the high priest in his great anguish.

22 While they were calling upon the Almighty Lord that he would keep what had been entrusted safe and secure for those who had entrusted it, 23 Heliodorus went on with what had been decided. 24 But when he arrived at the treasury with his bodyguard, then and there the Sovereign of spirits and of all authority caused so great a manifestation that all who had been so bold as to accompany him were astounded by the power of God, and became faint with terror. 25 For there appeared to them a magnificently caparisoned horse, with a rider of frightening mien; it rushed furiously at Heliodorus and struck at him with its front hoofs. Its rider was seen to have armor and weapons of gold. 26 Two young men also appeared to him, remarkably strong, gloriously beautiful and splendidly dressed, who stood on either side of him and flogged him continuously, inflicting many blows on him. 27 When he suddenly fell to the ground and deep darkness came over him, his men took him up, put him on a stretcher, 28 and carried him away—this man who had just entered the aforesaid treasury with a great retinue and all his bodyguard but was now unable to help himself. They recognized clearly the sovereign power of God.

29 While he lay prostrate, speechless because of the divine intervention and deprived of any hope of recovery, 30 they praised the Lord who had acted marvelously for his own place. And the temple, which a little while before was full of fear and disturbance, was filled with joy and gladness, now that the Almighty Lord had appeared.

31 Some of Heliodorus' friends quickly begged Onias to call upon the Most High to grant life to one who was lying quite at his last breath. 32 So the high priest, fearing that the king might

get the notion that some foul play had been perpetrated by the Jews with regard to Heliodorus, offered sacrifice for the man's recovery. 33 While the high priest was making an atonement, the same young men appeared again to Heliodorus dressed in the same clothing, and they stood and said, "Be very grateful to the high priest Onias, since for his sake the Lord has granted you your life. 34 And see that you, who have been flogged by heaven, report to all people the majestic power of God." Having said this they vanished.

35 Then Heliodorus offered sacrifice to the Lord and made very great vows to the Savior of his life, and having bidden Onias farewell, he marched off with his forces to the king. 36 He bore testimony to all concerning the deeds of the supreme God, which he had seen with his own eyes. 37 When the king asked Heliodorus what sort of person would be suitable to send on another mission to Jerusalem, he replied, 38 "If you have any enemy or plotter against your government, send him there, for you will get him back thoroughly flogged, if he survives at all; for there is certainly some power of God about the place. 39 For he who has his dwelling in heaven watches over that place himself and brings it aid, and he strikes and destroys those who come to do it injury." 40 This was the outcome of the episode of Heliodorus and the protection of the treasury.

4 The previously mentioned Simon, who had informed about the money against[j] his own country, slandered Onias, saying that it was he who had incited Heliodorus and had been the real cause of the misfortune. 2 He dared to designate as a plotter against the government the man who was the benefactor of the city, the protector of his compatriots, and a zealot for the laws. 3 When his ha-

j Gk *and*

24: *Manifestation,* see 2.21 n. 29: *Speechless,* Lk 1.20. 31: *The Most High* (Gen 14.18), a title often used by non-Jews (Dan 3.26; Mk 5.7).
4.1–6: Intrigues concerning the high

priesthood. *Simon* (see 3.4 n.) was disturbed because *Onias* and *Heliodorus* were now friends. The latter may already have planned to kill Seleucus IV and wanted the high

tred progressed to such a degree that even murders were committed by one of Simon's approved agents, [4] Onias recognized that the rivalry was serious and that Apollonius son of Menestheus,[k] and governor of Coelesyria and Phoenicia, was intensifying the malice of Simon. [5] So he appealed to the king, not accusing his compatriots but having in view the welfare, both public and private, of all the people. [6] For he saw that without the king's attention public affairs could not again reach a peaceful settlement, and that Simon would not stop his folly.

7 When Seleucus died and Antiochus, who was called Epiphanes, succeeded to the kingdom, Jason the brother of Onias obtained the high priesthood by corruption, [8] promising the king at an interview[l] three hundred sixty talents of silver, and from another source of revenue eighty talents. [9] In addition to this he promised to pay one hundred fifty more if permission were given to establish by his authority a gymnasium and a body of youth for it, and to enroll the people of Jerusalem as citizens of Antioch. [10] When the king assented and Jason[m] came to office, he at once shifted his compatriots over to the Greek way of life.

11 He set aside the existing royal concessions to the Jews, secured through John the father of Eupolemus, who went on the mission to establish friendship and

alliance with the Romans; and he destroyed the lawful ways of living and introduced new customs contrary to the law. [12] He took delight in establishing a gymnasium right under the citadel, and he induced the noblest of the young men to wear the Greek hat. [13] There was such an extreme of Hellenization and increase in the adoption of foreign ways because of the surpassing wickedness of Jason, who was ungodly and no true[n] high priest, [14] that the priests were no longer intent upon their service at the altar. Despising the sanctuary and neglecting the sacrifices, they hurried to take part in the unlawful proceedings in the wrestling arena after the signal for the discus-throwing, [15] disdaining the honors prized by their ancestors and putting the highest value upon Greek forms of prestige. [16] For this reason heavy disaster overtook them, and those whose ways of living they admired and wished to imitate completely became their enemies and punished them. [17] It is no light thing to show irreverence to the divine laws—a fact that later events will make clear.

18 When the quadrennial games were being held at Tyre and the king was present, [19] the vile Jason sent envoys,

k Vg Compare verse 21: Meaning of Gk uncertain   l Or by a petition   m Gk he   n Gk lacks true

priest's good will. *Apollonius,* in favor with Seleucus, continued to support Simon. **5:** Before Onias arrived in Antioch, Seleucus had already been assassinated by Heliodorus (175 B.C.). **4.7–22: Jason as high priest. 7:** *Antiochus IV Epiphanes,* "god manifest," called Epimanes, "madman," by his enemies, was brother of Seleucus IV, and *succeeded to the kingdom* despite Heliodorus' attempt at revolution. He reigned 175–164 B.C. He had great ability but intense passion and pride (1 Macc 1.1–10). *Jason the brother of Onias* III (3.1), originally named Joshua, took a Greek name. **9–10:** Like Alexander the Great and his successors, Antiochus promoted *the Greek way of life* in order to strengthen his kingdom through cultural unity; this involved worship of other gods. *A gymnasium and a body of youth for it* were necessary *to enroll the people of Jeru-*

salem as citizens of Antioch, so that the city could coin money and have honors and commercial advantages. The gymnasium was the center of political and cultural education, as well as sports.

4.11: *Royal concessions,* granted by Antiochus III (3.2). The mission of *Eupolemus* (1 Macc 8.17) was later. *Destroyed,* 1 Macc 1.15, 44–50. **12:** The broad-brimmed *Greek hat* was worn by the god Hermes; headgear has usually had national or religious significance in the East. **13:** *Hellenization,* Greek religion and culture (see vv. 9–10 n.). *No true high priest,* because he got the office by bribery and did not keep the Mosaic law. **16–17:** For the interpretation of disaster as the result of forsaking Torah see 1 Kings 17.5–18; 2 Chr 36.11–21; Neh ch 9. **18:** *Tyre,* an important port north of Palestine (Josh 19.29; 1 Kings 7.13); *quadrennial games* had been held

chosen as being Antiochian citizens from
Jerusalem, to carry three hundred silver
drachmas for the sacrifice to Hercules.
Those who carried the money, however,
thought best not to use it for sacrifice,
because that was inappropriate, but to
expend it for another purpose. 20 So this
money was intended by the sender for
the sacrifice to Hercules, but by the decision of its carriers it was applied to the
construction of triremes.

21 When Apollonius son of Menestheus was sent to Egypt for the coronation[o] of Philometor as king, Antiochus
learned that Philometor[p] had become
hostile to his government, and he took
measures for his own security. Therefore
upon arriving at Joppa he proceeded to
Jerusalem. 22 He was welcomed magnificently by Jason and the city, and ushered
in with a blaze of torches and with
shouts. Then he marched his army into
Phoenicia.

23 After a period of three years Jason
sent Menelaus, the brother of the previously mentioned Simon, to carry the
money to the king and to complete the
records of essential business. 24 But he,
when presented to the king, extolled him
with an air of authority, and secured the
high priesthood for himself, outbidding
Jason by three hundred talents of silver.
25 After receiving the king's orders he returned, possessing no qualification for
the high priesthood, but having the hot
temper of a cruel tyrant and the rage of
a savage wild beast. 26 So Jason, who after supplanting his own brother was supplanted by another man, was driven as a
fugitive into the land of Ammon. 27 Although Menelaus continued to hold the
office, he did not pay regularly any of the
money promised to the king. 28 When
Sostratus the captain of the citadel kept
requesting payment—for the collection
of the revenue was his responsibility—
the two of them were summoned by the
king on account of this issue. 29 Menelaus
left his own brother Lysimachus as deputy in the high priesthood, while Sostratus
left Crates, the commander of the Cyprian troops.

30 While such was the state of affairs,
it happened that the people of Tarsus and
of Mallus revolted because their cities
had been given as a present to Antiochis,
the king's concubine. 31 So the king went
hurriedly to settle the trouble, leaving
Andronicus, a man of high rank, to act
as his deputy. 32 But Menelaus, thinking
he had obtained a suitable opportunity,
stole some of the gold vessels of the temple and gave them to Andronicus; other
vessels, as it happened, he had sold to
Tyre and the neighboring cities. 33 When
Onias became fully aware of these acts,
he publicly exposed them, having first
withdrawn to a place of sanctuary at
Daphne near Antioch. 34 Therefore
Menelaus, taking Andronicus aside,
urged him to kill Onias. Andronicus[q]
came to Onias, and resorting to treachery, offered him sworn pledges and gave
him his right hand; he persuaded him,
though still suspicious, to come out from

o Meaning of Gk uncertain *p* Gk *he*
q Gk *He*

there as early as the time of Alexander the Great. **19**: *Hercules,* the Greek name of the god Melkart of Tyre. **20**: *Triremes,* war vessels manned by three benches of rowers. **21**: *Apollonius,* v. 4. *The coronation* of Ptolemy VI *Philometor* occurred about 172 B.C., some time after the death of his mother, Cleopatra I, and he ruled until 146 or 145 B.C. His advisers abandoned Cleopatra's policy, became *hostile* to Syria, and claimed Palestine. *Joppa,* the port forty miles from Jerusalem. **22**: *Phoenicia,* the coastal plain.

4.23–50: Menelaus as high priest. 23: *Menelaus* reigned from about 172 to 162 B.C., when he was executed (13.3–8) and replaced by Alcimus (14.3–14). **26**: *Land of Ammon,* east of the Jordan, near the present Amman. **29**: *The Cyprian troops* were mercenaries. **30**: *Mallus* was on the Pyramus river east of *Tarsus* (3.5). Hellenistic kings often provided a wife or *concubine* with a regular income by giving her a city. Antiochus, being extravagant (see 1 Macc 3.30 n.), was often in need of money. **32**: *Gave them,* either to pay tribute or as a bribe. **33**: *Daphne,* about five miles from *Antioch,* had a *place of sanctuary* to Apollo and Artemis.

the place of sanctuary; then, with no regard for justice, he immediately put him out of the way.

35 For this reason not only Jews, but many also of other nations, were grieved and displeased at the unjust murder of the man. ³⁶When the king returned from the region of Cilicia, the Jews in the city*ʳ* appealed to him with regard to the unreasonable murder of Onias, and the Greeks shared their hatred of the crime. ³⁷Therefore Antiochus was grieved at heart and filled with pity, and wept because of the moderation and good conduct of the deceased. ³⁸Inflamed with anger, he immediately stripped off the purple robe from Andronicus, tore off his purple robe, and led him around the whole city to that very place where he had committed the outrage against Onias, and there he dispatched the bloodthirsty fellow. The Lord thus repaid him with the punishment he deserved.

39 When many acts of sacrilege had been committed in the city by Lysimachus with the connivance of Menelaus, and when report of them had spread abroad, the populace gathered against Lysimachus, because many of the gold vessels had already been stolen. ⁴⁰Since the crowds were becoming aroused and filled with anger, Lysimachus armed about three thousand men and launched an unjust attack, under the leadership of a certain Auranus, a man advanced in years and no less advanced in folly. ⁴¹But when the Jews*ˢ* became aware that Lysimachus was attacking them, some picked up stones, some blocks of wood, and others took handfuls of the ashes that were lying around, and threw them in wild confusion at Lysimachus and his men. ⁴²As a result, they wounded many of them, and killed some, and put all the rest to flight; the temple robber himself they killed close by the treasury.

43 Charges were brought against Menelaus about this incident. ⁴⁴When the king came to Tyre, three men sent by the senate presented the case before him. ⁴⁵But Menelaus, already as good as beaten, promised a substantial bribe to Ptolemy son of Dorymenes to win over the king. ⁴⁶Therefore Ptolemy, taking the king aside into a colonnade as if for refreshment, induced the king to change his mind. ⁴⁷Menelaus, the cause of all the trouble, he acquitted of the charges against him, while he sentenced to death those unfortunate men, who would have been freed uncondemned if they had pleaded even before Scythians. ⁴⁸And so those who had spoken for the city and the villages*ᵗ* and the holy vessels quickly suffered the unjust penalty. ⁴⁹Therefore even the Tyrians, showing their hatred of the crime, provided magnificently for their funeral. ⁵⁰But Menelaus, because of the greed of those in power, remained in office, growing in wickedness, having become the chief plotter against his compatriots.

5 About this time Antiochus made his second invasion of Egypt. ²And it happened that, for almost forty days, there appeared over all the city goldenclad cavalry charging through the air, in companies fully armed with lances and drawn swords— ³troops of cavalry drawn up, attacks and counterattacks

*r Or in each city   s Gk they   t Other
ancient authorities read the people*

4.35: *Unjust murder,* he had been lured from a place protected by the gods. **38**: *Stripped off the purple robe,* degrading him before execution. **39**: *The city,* Jerusalem. *Menelaus* was still in Antioch. **42**: *The temple robber,* Lysimachus. **44**: *The senate,* see 1 Macc 12.6 n. **45**: *Dorymenes* had fought for Ptolemy IV against Antiochus III; his son *Ptolemy* had been governor of Cyprus and deserted to Antiochus IV (see 10.12–13 n.). **47**: The

Scythians (Col 3.11) lived in what is now southern Russia and were proverbial for their brutality.

5.1–27: **Antiochus IV desecrates the temple. 1**: *Second invasion,* in 169 B.C.; perhaps the writer regards the coming of the Seleucid army into Palestine in 171 B.C. (4.21–22) as the first invasion. We would speak of them as the first and second phases of the invasion (compare 1 Macc 1.16–19).

made on this side and on that, brandishing of shields, massing of spears, hurling of missiles, the flash of golden trappings, and armor of all kinds. ⁴Therefore everyone prayed that the apparition might prove to have been a good omen.

5 When a false rumor arose that Antiochus was dead, Jason took no fewer than a thousand men and suddenly made an assault on the city. When the troops on the wall had been forced back and at last the city was being taken, Menelaus took refuge in the citadel. ⁶But Jason kept relentlessly slaughtering his compatriots, not realizing that success at the cost of one's kindred is the greatest misfortune, but imagining that he was setting up trophies of victory over enemies and not over compatriots. ⁷He did not, however, gain control of the government; in the end he got only disgrace from his conspiracy, and fled again into the country of the Ammonites. ⁸Finally he met a miserable end. Accused*u* before Aretas the ruler of the Arabs, fleeing from city to city, pursued by everyone, hated as a rebel against the laws, and abhorred as the executioner of his country and his compatriots, he was cast ashore in Egypt. ⁹There he who had driven many from their own country into exile died in exile, having embarked to go to the Lacedaemonians in hope of finding protection because of their kinship. ¹⁰He who had cast out many to lie unburied had no one to mourn for him; he had no funeral of any sort and no place in the tomb of his ancestors.

11 When news of what had happened reached the king, he took it to mean that Judea was in revolt. So, raging inwardly, he left Egypt and took the city by storm.

¹²He commanded his soldiers to cut down relentlessly everyone they met and to kill those who went into their houses. ¹³Then there was massacre of young and old, destruction of boys, women, and children, and slaughter of young girls and infants. ¹⁴Within the total of three days eighty thousand were destroyed, forty thousand in hand-to-hand fighting, and as many were sold into slavery as were killed.

15 Not content with this, Antiochus*v* dared to enter the most holy temple in all the world, guided by Menelaus, who had become a traitor both to the laws and to his country. ¹⁶He took the holy vessels with his polluted hands, and swept away with profane hands the votive offerings that other kings had made to enhance the glory and honor of the place. ¹⁷Antiochus was elated in spirit, and did not perceive that the Lord was angered for a little while because of the sins of those who lived in the city, and that this was the reason he was disregarding the holy place. ¹⁸But if it had not happened that they were involved in many sins, this man would have been flogged and turned back from his rash act as soon as he came forward, just as Heliodorus had been, whom King Seleucus sent to inspect the treasury. ¹⁹But the Lord did not choose the nation for the sake of the holy place, but the place for the sake of the nation. ²⁰Therefore the place itself shared in the misfortunes that befell the nation and afterward participated in its benefits; and what was forsaken in the wrath of the Almighty was restored again in all its glory when the great Lord became reconciled.

u Cn: Gk *Imprisoned*   *v* Gk *he*

2–4: 3.25–26. *The city*, Jerusalem. **5–8**: *Jason* was an Oniad and pro-Egyptian (see 3.1 n.). Thinking *that Antiochus was dead*, he planned, with Egyptian help, to recover the high priesthood. He was opposed by *Menelaus* the Tobiad (4.23) and also by the Jews loyal to Judaism; he massacred people of both factions. *Ammonites*, 4.26. *Aretas*, king of Nabatean Arabia, south and east of Palestine; his capital was at Petra. **9–10**: Rejected in Egypt,

Jason fled to Sparta (1 Macc 12.7). *Unburied*, see 1 Macc 7.17 n.; 1 Kings 13.22.

5.11–14: So confused was the situation that Antiochus thought all *Judea was in revolt*. He was *raging inwardly* because the Romans had forced him out of Egypt (see 1 Macc 1.20 n.); both his foreign and his domestic programs were collapsing. **11**: *The city*, Jerusalem.

5.15–23a: The temple had been pillaged after the first Egyptian invasion (1 Macc

21 So Antiochus carried off eighteen hundred talents from the temple, and hurried away to Antioch, thinking in his arrogance that he could sail on the land and walk on the sea, because his mind was elated. 22 He left governors to oppress the people: at Jerusalem, Philip, by birth a Phrygian and in character more barbarous than the man who appointed him; 23 and at Gerizim, Andronicus; and besides these Menelaus, who lorded it over his compatriots worse than the others did. In his malice toward the Jewish citizens, *w* 24 Antiochus*x* sent Apollonius, the captain of the Mysians, with an army of twenty-two thousand, and commanded him to kill all the grown men and to sell the women and boys as slaves. 25 When this man arrived in Jerusalem, he pretended to be peaceably disposed and waited until the holy sabbath day; then, finding the Jews not at work, he ordered his troops to parade under arms. 26 He put to the sword all those who came out to see them, then rushed into the city with his armed warriors and killed great numbers of people.

27 But Judas Maccabeus, with about nine others, got away to the wilderness, and kept himself and his companions alive in the mountains as wild animals do; they continued to live on what grew wild, so that they might not share in the defilement.

6 Not long after this, the king sent an Athenian*y* senator*z* to compel the Jews to forsake the laws of their ancestors and no longer to live by the laws of God; 2 also to pollute the temple in Jerusalem and to call it the temple of Olympian Zeus, and to call the one in Gerizim the temple of Zeus-the-Friend-of-Strangers, as did the people who lived in that place.

3 Harsh and utterly grievous was the onslaught of evil. 4 For the temple was filled with debauchery and reveling by the Gentiles, who dallied with prostitutes and had intercourse with women within the sacred precincts, and besides brought in things for sacrifice that were unfit. 5 The altar was covered with abominable offerings that were forbidden by the laws. 6 People could neither keep the sabbath, nor observe the festivals of their ancestors, nor so much as confess themselves to be Jews.

7 On the monthly celebration of the king's birthday, the Jews*a* were taken, under bitter constraint, to partake of the sacrifices; and when a festival of Dionysus was celebrated, they were compelled to wear wreathes of ivy and to walk in the procession in honor of Dionysus. 8 At the suggestion of the people of Ptolemais*b* a decree was issued to the neighboring Greek cities that they should adopt the same policy toward the Jews and

w Or worse than the others did in his malice toward
the Jewish citizens   x Gk he   y Other
ancient authorities read Antiochian
z Or Geron an Athenian   a Gk they
b Cn: Gk suggestion of the Ptolemies (or of Ptolemy)

1.21–28). *Angered for a little while,* not permanently (compare 6.12–16). **21**: *His arrogance* was that of a god manifest (see 4.7 n.). **22–23**: *Philip,* probably not the later regent (9.29). *Andronicus* (4.31) was now made governor of Samaria. **24–26**: *Antiochus sent Apollonius* about two years after the events of vv. 15–23 (see 1 Macc 1.29). Loyal Jews did not yet fight on the *sabbath* (1 Macc 2.32–41). **27**: *Judas Maccabeus,* the third son of Mattathias, of the Hasmonean family (1 Macc 2.1–28). *The defilement,* 4.11; 1 Macc 1.48, 63.

6.1–6: **Campaign against Judaism.** What had been voluntary (4.9–17) was now enforced (see 1 Macc 1.41–64 n.). **2**: *Olympian Zeus* was now identified with the God of

Israel and probably with Antiochus. *To pollute the temple,* they set up a statue or pagan altar (1 Macc 1.54). The Samaritans, descendants of the ten northern tribes and Assyrian settlers (2 Kings 17.6, 24), had built the temple on Mount *Gerizim.* **4**: *Intercourse . . . sacred precincts,* as in Syrian fertility cults (see Let Jer 6.11 n. and 6.43 n.). *Things . . . unfit,* swine (Lev 11.7; 1 Macc 1.47). **6**: 1 Macc 1.45–51. *Jews,* originally "Judeans"; here "those loyal to the religion" (Judaism, 2.21).

6.7–17: **The first martyrdoms.** Chs 6–7 are the earliest martyrologies, a type of writing popular subsequently in Christianity, designed to encourage the faithful when persecuted. **7**: *Dionysus,* god of wine and the grape

make them partake of the sacrifices, 9 and should kill those who did not choose to change over to Greek customs. One could see, therefore, the misery that had come upon them. 10 For example, two women were brought in for having circumcised their children. They publicly paraded them around the city, with their babies hanging at their breasts, and then hurled them down headlong from the wall. 11 Others who had assembled in the caves nearby, in order to observe the seventh day secretly, were betrayed to Philip and were all burned together, because their piety kept them from defending themselves, in view of their regard for that most holy day.

12 Now I urge those who read this book not to be depressed by such calamities, but to recognize that these punishments were designed not to destroy but to discipline our people. 13 In fact, it is a sign of great kindness not to let the impious alone for long, but to punish them immediately. 14 For in the case of the other nations the Lord waits patiently to punish them until they have reached the full measure of their sins; but he does not deal in this way with us, 15 in order that he may not take vengeance on us afterward when our sins have reached their height. 16 Therefore he never withdraws his mercy from us. Although he disciplines us with calamities, he does not forsake his own people. 17 Let what we have said serve as a reminder; we must go on briefly with the story.

18 Eleazar, one of the scribes in high position, a man now advanced in age and of noble presence, was being forced to open his mouth to eat swine's flesh. 19 But he, welcoming death with honor rather than life with pollution, went up to the rack of his own accord, spitting

out the flesh, 20 as all ought to go who have the courage to refuse things that it is not right to taste, even for the natural love of life.

21 Those who were in charge of that unlawful sacrifice took the man aside because of their long acquaintance with him, and privately urged him to bring meat of his own providing, proper for him to use, and to pretend that he was eating the flesh of the sacrificial meal that had been commanded by the king, 22 so that by doing this he might be saved from death, and be treated kindly on account of his old friendship with them. 23 But making a high resolve, worthy of his years and the dignity of his old age and the gray hairs that he had reached with distinction and his excellent life even from childhood, and moreover according to the holy God-given law, he declared himself quickly, telling them to send him to Hades.

24 "Such pretense is not worthy of our time of life," he said, "for many of the young might suppose that Eleazar in his ninetieth year had gone over to an alien religion, 25 and through my pretense, for the sake of living a brief moment longer, they would be led astray because of me, while I defile and disgrace my old age. 26 Even if for the present I would avoid the punishment of mortals, yet whether I live or die I shall not escape the hands of the Almighty. 27 Therefore, by bravely giving up my life now, I will show myself worthy of my old age 28 and leave to the young a noble example of how to die a good death willingly and nobly for the revered and holy laws."

When he had said this, he went[c] at once to the rack. 29 Those who a little

c Other ancient authorities read *was dragged*

---

harvest; *ivy* was one of his symbols. **8**: *Ptolemais,* formerly Accho, or Acco, modern Acre, a coastal city eight miles north of Mt. Carmel. If the correct reading is *Ptolemies* or *Ptolemy* (as in note b), see 4.45 n. *The same policy toward the Jews* living as citizens of the Antiochene republic. **10**: See 1 Macc 1.60–61. **11**: A different interpretation is given in 1 Macc

2.29–41. **12–17**: The victories of Israel's enemies are explained as God's corrective punishment, always followed by mercy (compare Isa 54.7–8; Ps 94.12–15).

6.18–31: **Martyrdom of Eleazar.** The story is told more elaborately in 4 Maccabees. **18**: *Scribes,* scholars learned in the Mosaic law, not necessarily priests. **24–28**: Eleazar's

before had acted toward him with goodwill now changed to ill will, because the words he had uttered were in their opinion sheer madness.*ᵈ* 30 When he was about to die under the blows, he groaned aloud and said: "It is clear to the Lord in his holy knowledge that, though I might have been saved from death, I am enduring terrible sufferings in my body under this beating, but in my soul I am glad to suffer these things because I fear him."

31 So in this way he died, leaving in his death an example of nobility and a memorial of courage, not only to the young but to the great body of his nation.

7 It happened also that seven brothers and their mother were arrested and were being compelled by the king, under torture with whips and thongs, to partake of unlawful swine's flesh. 2 One of them, acting as their spokesman, said, "What do you intend to ask and learn from us? For we are ready to die rather than transgress the laws of our ancestors."

3 The king fell into a rage, and gave orders to have pans and caldrons heated. 4 These were heated immediately, and he commanded that the tongue of their spokesman be cut out and that they scalp him and cut off his hands and feet, while the rest of the brothers and the mother looked on. 5 When he was utterly helpless, the king*ᵉ* ordered them to take him to the fire, still breathing, and to fry him in a pan. The smoke from the pan spread widely, but the brothers*ᶠ* and their mother encouraged one another to die nobly, saying, 6 "The Lord God is watching over us and in truth has compassion on us, as Moses declared in his song that bore witness against the people to their faces, when he said, 'And he will have compassion on his servants.' "*ᵍ*

7 After the first brother had died in this way, they brought forward the second for their sport. They tore off the skin of his head with the hair, and asked him, "Will you eat rather than have your body punished limb by limb?" 8 He replied in the language of his ancestors and said to them, "No." Therefore he in turn underwent tortures as the first brother had done. 9 And when he was at his last breath, he said, "You accursed wretch, you dismiss us from this present life, but the King of the universe will raise us up to an everlasting renewal of life, because we have died for his laws."

10 After him, the third was the victim of their sport. When it was demanded, he quickly put out his tongue and courageously stretched forth his hands, 11 and said nobly, "I got these from Heaven, and because of his laws I disdain them, and from him I hope to get them back again." 12 As a result the king himself and those with him were astonished at the young man's spirit, for he regarded his sufferings as nothing.

13 After he too had died, they maltreated and tortured the fourth in the same way. 14 When he was near death, he said, "One cannot but choose to die at the hands of mortals and to cherish the hope God gives of being raised again by him. But for you there will be no resurrection to life!"

15 Next they brought forward the fifth and maltreated him. 16 But he looked at the king,*ʰ* and said, "Because you have authority among mortals, though you also are mortal, you do what you please. But do not think that God has forsaken our people. 17 Keep on, and see how his mighty power will torture you and your descendants!"

---

d Meaning of Gk uncertain *e* Gk *he*
f Gk *they* *g* Gk *slaves* *h* Gk *at him*

---

speech resembles the last speech of Socrates in the *Apology*. **30**: *Fear,* revere (Job 28.28; Ps 19.9).

7.1–42: Martyrdom of seven brothers and their mother. This story is the principal subject of 4 Maccabees. **2**: Dan 3.16–18. **6**:

Deut 32.36. **9**: God is often addressed in later Jewish prayer as *King of the universe.* The idea of resurrection is now clearly stated (Dan 12.2).

7.11: *Heaven,* a circumlocution for God; used also in v. 34. **17**: Antiochus IV died in

18 After him they brought forward the sixth. And when he was about to die, he said, "Do not deceive yourself in vain. For we are suffering these things on our own account, because of our sins against our own God. Therefore[i] astounding things have happened. 19 But do not think that you will go unpunished for having tried to fight against God!"

20 The mother was especially admirable and worthy of honorable memory. Although she saw her seven sons perish within a single day, she bore it with good courage because of her hope in the Lord. 21 She encouraged each of them in the language of their ancestors. Filled with a noble spirit, she reinforced her woman's reasoning with a man's courage, and said to them, 22 "I do not know how you came into being in my womb. It was not I who gave you life and breath, nor I who set in order the elements within each of you. 23 Therefore the Creator of the world, who shaped the beginning of humankind and devised the origin of all things, will in his mercy give life and breath back to you again, since you now forget yourselves for the sake of his laws."

24 Antiochus felt that he was being treated with contempt, and he was suspicious of her reproachful tone. The youngest brother being still alive, Antiochus[j] not only appealed to him in words, but promised with oaths that he would make him rich and enviable if he would turn from the ways of his ancestors, and that he would take him for his Friend and entrust him with public affairs. 25 Since the young man would not listen to him at all, the king called the mother to him and urged her to advise the youth to save himself. 26 After much urging on his part, she undertook to persuade her son. 27 But, leaning close to him, she spoke in their native language as follows, deriding the cruel tyrant: "My son, have pity on me. I carried you nine months in my womb, and nursed you for three years, and have reared you and brought you up to this point in your life, and have taken care of you.[k] 28 I beg you, my child, to look at the heaven and the earth and see everything that is in them, and recognize that God did not make them out of things that existed.[l] And in the same way the human race came into being. 29 Do not fear this butcher, but prove worthy of your brothers. Accept death, so that in God's mercy I may get you back again along with your brothers."

30 While she was still speaking, the young man said, "What are you[m] waiting for? I will not obey the king's command, but I obey the command of the law that was given to our ancestors through Moses. 31 But you,[n] who have contrived all sorts of evil against the Hebrews, will certainly not escape the hands of God. 32 For we are suffering because of our own sins. 33 And if our living Lord is angry for a little while, to rebuke and discipline us, he will again be reconciled with his own servants.[o] 34 But you, unholy wretch, you most defiled of all mortals, do not be elated in vain and puffed up by uncertain hopes, when you raise your hand against the children of heaven. 35 You have not yet escaped the judgment of the almighty, all-seeing God. 36 For our brothers after enduring a brief suffering have drunk[p] of everflowing life, under God's covenant; but you, by the judgment of God, will receive just punishment for your arrogance. 37 I, like my brothers, give up body and life for the laws of our ancestors, appealing to God to show mercy soon to our nation and by trials and plagues to make you confess that he alone is God, 38 and

---

i Lat: Other ancient authorities lack *Therefore*
j Gk *he*   k Or *have borne the burden of your education*   l Or *God made them out of things that did not exist*   m The Gk here for *you* is plural
n The Gk here for *you* is singular   o Gk *slaves*
p Cn: Gk *fallen*

---

misery and his son was murdered (9.5–28). **18–19:** 6.12–16.
7.28: This is the first appearance in Jewish Scriptures of the idea, borrowed from the Greek philosophers, that God created the universe out of nothing. **33:** 5.17; 6.12–16. **38:** *To bring*

through me and my brothers to bring to an end the wrath of the Almighty that has justly fallen on our whole nation."

39 The king fell into a rage, and handled him worse than the others, being exasperated at his scorn. 40 So he died in his integrity, putting his whole trust in the Lord.

41 Last of all, the mother died, after her sons.

42 Let this be enough, then, about the eating of sacrifices and the extreme tortures.

8 Meanwhile Judas, who was also called Maccabeus, and his companions secretly entered the villages and summoned their kindred and enlisted those who had continued in the Jewish faith, and so they gathered about six thousand. 2 They implored the Lord to look upon the people who were oppressed by all; and to have pity on the temple that had been profaned by the godless; 3 to have mercy on the city that was being destroyed and about to be leveled to the ground; to hearken to the blood that cried out to him; 4 to remember also the lawless destruction of the innocent babies and the blasphemies committed against his name; and to show his hatred of evil.

5 As soon as Maccabeus got his army organized, the Gentiles could not withstand him, for the wrath of the Lord had turned to mercy. 6 Coming without warning, he would set fire to towns and villages. He captured strategic positions and put to flight not a few of the enemy. 7 He found the nights most advantageous

for such attacks. And talk of his valor spread everywhere.

8 When Philip saw that the man was gaining ground little by little, and that he was pushing ahead with more frequent successes, he wrote to Ptolemy, the governor of Coelesyria and Phoenicia, to come to the aid of the king's government. 9 Then Ptolemy*q* promptly appointed Nicanor son of Patroclus, one of the king's chief*r* Friends, and sent him, in command of no fewer than twenty thousand Gentiles of all nations, to wipe out the whole race of Judea. He associated with him Gorgias, a general and a man of experience in military service. 10 Nicanor determined to make up for the king the tribute due to the Romans, two thousand talents, by selling the captured Jews into slavery. 11 So he immediately sent to the towns on the seacoast, inviting them to buy Jewish slaves and promising to hand over ninety slaves for a talent, not expecting the judgment from the Almighty that was about to overtake him.

12 Word came to Judas concerning Nicanor's invasion; and when he told his companions of the arrival of the army, 13 those who were cowardly and distrustful of God's justice ran off and got away. 14 Others sold all their remaining property, and at the same time implored the Lord to rescue those who had been sold by the ungodly Nicanor before he ever met them, 15 if not for their own sake, then for the sake of the covenants made with their ancestors, and because he had called them by his holy and glorious name. 16 But Maccabeus gathered his

q Gk *he*   *r* Gk *one of the first*

---

to an end the wrath of the Almighty, not by atoning for Israel's sins through their deaths (as in 4 Macc 1.11; 17.20–22), but by increasing the suffering of Israel to such a degree that God would be moved to intervene for them. See Deut 32.36; Judg 2.18.

8.1–7: Judas begins the revolt.

8.8–29: First victory over Nicanor. Judas assembled his forces at Mizpah and attacked Gorgias' army at Emmaus (see 1 Macc 3.40 n.). **8:** *Philip,* see 5.22 n. *Ptolemy* (see 4.45 n.), appointed by Lysias after Antiochus

had left for Persia (1 Macc 3.38). **9:** *Gorgias,* not Nicanor, is the principal figure in 1 Macc 3.38–4.25. **10:** Since the battle of Magnesia (see 1 Macc 1.10 n.) the Seleucids had been forced to pay *tribute;* perhaps the *two thousand talents* represented the last installment. **11:** Slave traders accompanied the expedition (compare 8.34 and 1 Macc 3.41). **13:** Compare 1 Macc 3.56. **15:** The idea expressed by these words, echoing Dan 9.19, occurs often in later Jewish prayers. *Covenants,* with the patriarchs and at Sinai (see 1.24–29 n.; Ex 19.5–6). *Called*

forces together, to the number six thousand, and exhorted them not to be frightened by the enemy and not to fear the great multitude of Gentiles who were wickedly coming against them, but to fight nobly, [17] keeping before their eyes the lawless outrage that the Gentiles[s] had committed against the holy place, and the torture of the derided city, and besides, the overthrow of their ancestral way of life. [18] "For they trust to arms and acts of daring," he said, "but we trust in the Almighty God, who is able with a single nod to strike down those who are coming against us, and even, if necessary, the whole world."

19 Moreover, he told them of the occasions when help came to their ancestors; how, in the time of Sennacherib, when one hundred eighty-five thousand perished, [20] and the time of the battle against the Galatians that took place in Babylonia, when eight thousand Jews[t] fought along with four thousand Macedonians; yet when the Macedonians were hard pressed, the eight thousand, by the help that came to them from heaven, destroyed one hundred twenty thousand Galatians[u] and took a great amount of booty.

21 With these words he filled them with courage and made them ready to die for their laws and their country; then he divided his army into four parts. [22] He appointed his brothers also, Simon and Joseph and Jonathan, each to command a division, putting fifteen hundred men under each. [23] Besides, he appointed Eleazar to read aloud[v] from the holy book, and gave the watchword, "The help of God"; then, leading the first division

himself, he joined battle with Nicanor. [24] With the Almighty as their ally, they killed more than nine thousand of the enemy, and wounded and disabled most of Nicanor's army, and forced them all to flee. [25] They captured the money of those who had come to buy them as slaves. After pursuing them for some distance, they were obliged to return because the hour was late. [26] It was the day before the sabbath, and for that reason they did not continue their pursuit. [27] When they had collected the arms of the enemy and stripped them of their spoils, they kept the sabbath, giving great praise and thanks to the Lord, who had preserved them for that day and allotted it to them as the beginning of mercy. [28] After the sabbath they gave some of the spoils to those who had been tortured and to the widows and orphans, and distributed the rest among themselves and their children. [29] When they had done this, they made common supplication and implored the merciful Lord to be wholly reconciled with his servants.[w]

30 In encounters with the forces of Timothy and Bacchides they killed more than twenty thousand of them and got possession of some exceedingly high strongholds, and they divided a very large amount of plunder, giving to those who had been tortured and to the orphans and widows, and also to the aged, shares equal to their own. [31] They collected the arms of the enemy,[x] and carefully stored all of them in strategic places;

s Gk *they*   t Gk lacks *Jews*   u Gk lacks *Galatians*   v Meaning of Gk uncertain   w Gk *slaves*   x Gk *their arms*

---

them by his . . . name, as God's people (Deut 28.10). **17**: *Lawless outrage,* 5.15–16. *Ancestral way of life,* the Torah.

8.19: 2 Kings 19.35. **20**: *The Galatians* from Asia Minor often served as mercenaries. Jewish forces evidently aided Antiochus III and *the Macedonians.* **22**: *Simon,* high priest 142–134 B.C., and *Jonathan,* from 160 to 143 or 142 B.C. *Joseph,* called John in 1 Macc 2.2; 9.36. **23**: *Eleazar,* another brother, was killed at Beth-zechariah (1 Macc 2.5; 6.43–46). The

motto "*The help of God*" is prescribed by the Qumran *War Scroll* for one of the banners of the army returning from battle. **25**: *Slaves,* vv. 11, 34. **26**: Gorgias and his army were in the hills (1 Macc 4.16–18). **27–29**: The victory was a sign of God's favor, but the campaign had not yet been won (6.12–16; 1 Macc 4.19–25).

8.30–36: **Other victories** (1 Macc 5.37–44 tells of a battle against *Timothy* at Raphon). **30**: *Bacchides,* 1 Macc 7.8. **33**: *City of their an-*

the rest of the spoils they carried to Jerusalem. ³²They killed the commander of Timothy's forces, a most wicked man, and one who had greatly troubled the Jews. ³³While they were celebrating the victory in the city of their ancestors, they burned those who had set fire to the sacred gates, Callisthenes and some others, who had fled into one little house; so these received the proper reward for their impiety. ʸ

34 The thrice-accursed Nicanor, who had brought the thousand merchants to buy the Jews, ³⁵having been humbled with the help of the Lord by opponents whom he regarded as of the least account, took off his splendid uniform and made his way alone like a runaway slave across the country until he reached Antioch, having succeeded chiefly in the destruction of his own army! ³⁶So he who had undertaken to secure tribute for the Romans by the capture of the people of Jerusalem proclaimed that the Jews had a Defender, and that therefore the Jews were invulnerable, because they followed the laws ordained by him.

9 About that time, as it happened, Antiochus had retreated in disorder from the region of Persia. ²He had entered the city called Persepolis and attempted to rob the temples and control the city. Therefore the people rushed to the rescue with arms, and Antiochus and his army were defeated, ᶻ with the result that Antiochus was put to flight by the inhabitants and beat a shameful retreat. ³While he was in Ecbatana, news came to him of what had happened to Nicanor and the forces of Timothy. ⁴Transported with rage, he conceived the idea of turning upon the Jews the injury done by those who had put him to flight; so he ordered his charioteer to drive without stopping until he completed the journey. But the judgment of heaven rode with him! For in his arrogance he said, "When I get there I will make Jerusalem a cemetery of Jews."

5 But the all-seeing Lord, the God of Israel, struck him with an incurable and invisible blow. As soon as he stopped speaking he was seized with a pain in his bowels, for which there was no relief, and with sharp internal tortures— ⁶and that very justly, for he had tortured the bowels of others with many and strange inflictions. ⁷Yet he did not in any way stop his insolence, but was even more filled with arrogance, breathing fire in his rage against the Jews, and giving orders to drive even faster. And so it came about that he fell out of his chariot as it was rushing along, and the fall was so hard as to torture every limb of his body. ⁸Thus he who only a little while before had thought in his superhuman arrogance that he could command the waves of the sea, and had imagined that he could weigh the high mountains in a balance, was brought down to earth and carried in a litter, making the power of God manifest to all. ⁹And so the ungodly man's body swarmed with worms, and while he was still living in anguish and pain, his flesh rotted away, and because of the stench the whole army felt revulsion at his decay. ¹⁰Because of his intolerable stench no one was able to carry the man who a little while before had thought that he could touch the stars of

y Meaning of Gk uncertain   z Gk *they were defeated*

---

cestors, Jerusalem, with its *sacred gates,* Judas' ancestral home (1 Macc 2.1). **34**: *Thrice-accursed,* 15.3; Add Est 16.15.
9.1–12: Antiochus' illness (1 Macc 6.1–16). Here this story is placed before the purification of the temple (10.1–8; 1 Macc 4.36–61), Judas' southern campaigns (10.14–38; 1 Macc ch 5), and Lysias' first expedition (11.1–15; 1 Macc 4.26–35). **1**: *Antiochus* went to *Persia* to strengthen his authority there and to get funds. **2**: *Persepolis,* near Shiraz, the capital of Persia, founded by Darius I. **3**: Antiochus was on his way to Babylon (1 Macc 6.4) but went north by way of *Ecbatana,* Hamadan. **4**: 5.11; 7.3. **5**: See 1 Macc 6.9 n. **8**: *Command the waves,* like Xerxes invading Greece. *Weigh the high mountains,* like God (see 5.21 n.; Isa 40.12). **9**: *Worms,* Acts 12.23. **10**: Isa 14.12–19.

heaven. [11] Then it was that, broken in spirit, he began to lose much of his arrogance and to come to his senses under the scourge of God, for he was tortured with pain every moment. [12] And when he could not endure his own stench, he uttered these words, "It is right to be subject to God; mortals should not think that they are equal to God."[a]

13 Then the abominable fellow made a vow to the Lord, who would no longer have mercy on him, stating [14] that the holy city, which he was hurrying to level to the ground and to make a cemetery, he was now declaring to be free; [15] and the Jews, whom he had not considered worth burying but had planned to throw out with their children for the wild animals and for the birds to eat, he would make, all of them, equal to citizens of Athens; [16] and the holy sanctuary, which he had formerly plundered, he would adorn with the finest offerings; and all the holy vessels he would give back, many times over; and the expenses incurred for the sacrifices he would provide from his own revenues; [17] and in addition to all this he also would become a Jew and would visit every inhabited place to proclaim the power of God. [18] But when his sufferings did not in any way abate, for the judgment of God had justly come upon him, he gave up all hope for himself and wrote to the Jews the following letter, in the form of a supplication. This was its content:

19 "To his worthy Jewish citizens, Antiochus their king and general sends hearty greetings and good wishes for their health and prosperity. [20] If you and your children are well and your affairs are as you wish, I am glad. As my hope is in heaven, [21] I remember with affection your esteem and goodwill. On my way back from the region of Persia I suffered an annoying illness, and I have deemed it necessary to take thought for the general security of all. [22] I do not despair of my condition, for I have good hope of recovering from my illness, [23] but I observed that my father, on the occasions when he made expeditions into the upper country, appointed his successor, [24] so that, if anything unexpected happened or any unwelcome news came, the people throughout the realm would not be troubled, for they would know to whom the government was left. [25] Moreover, I understand how the princes along the borders and the neighbors of my kingdom keep watching for opportunities and waiting to see what will happen. So I have appointed my son Antiochus to be king, whom I have often entrusted and commended to most of you when I hurried off to the upper provinces; and I have written to him what is written here. [26] I therefore urge and beg you to remember the public and private services rendered to you and to maintain your present goodwill, each of you, toward me and my son. [27] For I am sure that he will follow my policy and will treat you with moderation and kindness."

28 So the murderer and blasphemer, having endured the more intense suffering, such as he had inflicted on others, came to the end of his life by a most pitiable fate, among the mountains in a strange land. [29] And Philip, one of his courtiers, took his body home; then, fearing the son of Antiochus, he withdrew to Ptolemy Philometor in Egypt.

a Or not think thoughts proper only to God

9.13–29: Repentance and death of Antiochus. 15: *Citizens of Athens* were proud of their heritage, though the city no longer had actual power. **16:** 5.16. **17:** 7.37; Dan 4.31–35.
9.19–27: The letter is no supplication (v. 18); it is addressed to Jews loyal to the king and bids them support his *son Antiochus* V (vv. 25–27). **23:** *My father,* Antiochus III (see 3.3 n.), who *appointed* Seleucus IV as *his successor. The upper country,* Babylonia and Persia (1 Macc 3.37). **28:** Antiochus IV died *among the mountains,* perhaps at Gabae or Isfahan (see 1 Macc 6.5 n.). **29:** *Philip* was perhaps Antiochus V's guardian (see 1 Macc 6.14–15 n.). *Fearing* Lysias, viceroy in the west, rather than *the son of Antiochus,* who was a child, he went over to Syria's enemy, *Ptolemy* VI (see 4.21 n.). Josephus says that Philip took over the Seleucid government and was later killed (*Antiquities,* XII. ix. 7).

10 Now Maccabeus and his followers, the Lord leading them on, recovered the temple and the city; ²they tore down the altars that had been built in the public square by the foreigners, and also destroyed the sacred precincts. ³They purified the sanctuary, and made another altar of sacrifice; then, striking fire out of flint, they offered sacrifices, after a lapse of two years, and they offered incense and lighted lamps and set out the bread of the Presence. ⁴When they had done this, they fell prostrate and implored the Lord that they might never again fall into such misfortunes, but that, if they should ever sin, they might be disciplined by him with forbearance and not be handed over to blasphemous and barbarous nations. ⁵It happened that on the same day on which the sanctuary had been profaned by the foreigners, the purification of the sanctuary took place, that is, on the twenty-fifth day of the same month, which was Chislev. ⁶They celebrated it for eight days with rejoicing, in the manner of the festival of booths, remembering how not long before, during the festival of booths, they had been wandering in the mountains and caves like wild animals. ⁷Therefore, carrying ivy-wreathed wands and beautiful branches and also fronds of palm, they offered hymns of thanksgiving to him who had given success to the purifying of his own holy place. ⁸They decreed by public edict, ratified by vote, that the whole nation of the Jews should observe these days every year.

9 Such then was the end of Antiochus, who was called Epiphanes.

10 Now we will tell what took place under Antiochus Eupator, who was the son of that ungodly man, and will give a brief summary of the principal calamities of the wars. ¹¹This man, when he succeeded to the kingdom, appointed one Lysias to have charge of the government and to be chief governor of Coelesyria and Phoenicia. ¹²Ptolemy, who was called Macron, took the lead in showing justice to the Jews because of the wrong that had been done to them, and attempted to maintain peaceful relations with them. ¹³As a result he was accused before Eupator by the king's Friends. He heard himself called a traitor at every turn, because he had abandoned Cyprus, which Philometor had entrusted to him, and had gone over to Antiochus Epiphanes. Unable to command the respect due his office, ᵇ he took poison and ended his life.

14 When Gorgias became governor of the region, he maintained a force of mercenaries, and at every turn kept attacking the Jews. ¹⁵Besides this, the Idumeans, who had control of important strongholds, were harassing the Jews; they received those who were banished

b Cn: Meaning of Gk uncertain

10.1–9: **Purification of the temple** (compare 1 Macc 4.36–61). **1**: They *recovered the temple*, desecrated by Antiochus (6.2–4; 1 Macc 1.54), *and the city*, except for the citadel (1 Macc 4.60; 6.18). **2**: *The altars* had been used for pagan worship. **3**: They *purified the sanctuary* by removing the desecrated stones (1 Macc 1.44–46). The reference to *striking fire out of flint* ignores the legends of 1.19–2.1. *Two years*, according to 1 Macc 1.54 and 4.52 it was three years. The *incense, lamps,* and *bread of the Presence*, prescribed by Ex 30.7–8; 25.30. **4**: 5.17–20; 6.12–16. **5–6**: *Chislev*, December, 164 B.C. (see 1 Macc 4.52–59 n.). At the normal time of *the festival of booths*, in September, *they had been wandering* like their ancestors (Lev 23.43) and could not celebrate it. **7**: *Ivy-wreathed wands*, here in honor of God (compare 6.7). *Branches* were carried in procession at the festival of booths. *Fronds of palm* symbolize victory (1 Macc 13.51; Jn 12.13).

10.10–13: **Antiochus V and Ptolemy Macron. 10–11**: *Antiochus V Eupator* (9.25), son of Antiochus IV, reigned from 164 to 162 B.C., when he was murdered by order of Demetrius I. He was about nine years old; his father had *appointed . . . Lysias* as regent (1 Macc 3.32–33). **12–13**: *Ptolemy* had changed allegiance from Egypt to Syria (see 4.45 n.; 6.8); now he was friendly *to the Jews*.

10.14–23: **Attacks on the Idumeans** (1 Macc 5.1–3, 9–54). **14**: *Gorgias* succeeded Ptolemy. **15**: *Idumeans*, or Edomites (see 1 Macc 5.3 n.); John Hyrcanus later forced

from Jerusalem, and endeavored to keep up the war. 16 But Maccabeus and his forces, after making solemn supplication and imploring God to fight on their side, rushed to the strongholds of the Idumeans. 17 Attacking them vigorously, they gained possession of the places, and beat off all who fought upon the wall, and slaughtered those whom they encountered, killing no fewer than twenty thousand.

18 When at least nine thousand took refuge in two very strong towers well equipped to withstand a siege, 19 Maccabeus left Simon and Joseph, and also Zacchaeus and his troops, a force sufficient to besiege them; and he himself set off for places where he was more urgently needed. 20 But those with Simon, who were money-hungry, were bribed by some of those who were in the towers, and on receiving seventy thousand drachmas let some of them slip away. 21 When word of what had happened came to Maccabeus, he gathered the leaders of the people, and accused these men of having sold their kindred for money by setting their enemies free to fight against them. 22 Then he killed these men who had turned traitor, and immediately captured the two towers. 23 Having success at arms in everything he undertook, he destroyed more than twenty thousand in the two strongholds.

24 Now Timothy, who had been defeated by the Jews before, gathered a tremendous force of mercenaries and collected the cavalry from Asia in no small number. He came on, intending to take Judea by storm. 25 As he drew near, Maccabeus and his men sprinkled dust on their heads and girded their loins with sackcloth, in supplication to God. 26 Falling upon the steps before the altar, they

implored him to be gracious to them and to be an enemy to their enemies and an adversary to their adversaries, as the law declares. 27 And rising from their prayer they took up their arms and advanced a considerable distance from the city; and when they came near the enemy they halted. 28 Just as dawn was breaking, the two armies joined battle, the one having as pledge of success and victory not only their valor but also their reliance on the Lord, while the other made rage their leader in the fight.

29 When the battle became fierce, there appeared to the enemy from heaven five resplendent men on horses with golden bridles, and they were leading the Jews. 30 Two of them took Maccabeus between them, and shielding him with their own armor and weapons, they kept him from being wounded. They showered arrows and thunderbolts on the enemy, so that, confused and blinded, they were thrown into disorder and cut to pieces. 31 Twenty thousand five hundred were slaughtered, besides six hundred cavalry.

32 Timothy himself fled to a stronghold called Gazara, especially well garrisoned, where Chaereas was commander. 33 Then Maccabeus and his men were glad, and they besieged the fort for four days. 34 The men within, relying on the strength of the place, kept blaspheming terribly and uttering wicked words. 35 But at dawn of the fifth day, twenty young men in the army of Maccabeus, fired with anger because of the blasphemies, bravely stormed the wall and with savage fury cut down everyone they met. 36 Others who came up in the same way wheeled around against the defenders and set fire to the towers; they kindled fires and burned the blasphemers

---

them to adopt Judaism. *Those . . . banished,* supporters of Menelaus. **19:** *Urgently needed,* perhaps in Ammon and Gilead (1 Macc 5.6–13).

10.24–38: Victory over Timothy. 24: They met *Timothy* (8.30) at *dawn* (v. 28) at Dathema east of the Jordan (1 Macc 5.28–34). **26:** Ex 23.22. **29:** 3.24–26. **31:** *Twenty thou-*

sand five hundred, compare the number of fatalities mentioned in 8.30; 10.17, 23. **32–38:** The fort of *Gazara* (1 Macc 4.15; 7.45) was well garrisoned; Simon captured it much later (1 Macc 13.43–48). **37:** *They killed Timothy;* but a Timothy reappears in 12.2, 18–25 (compare 1 Macc 5.11–40).

alive. Others broke open the gates and let in the rest of the force, and they occupied the city. [37]They killed Timothy, who was hiding in a cistern, and his brother Chaereas, and Apollophanes. [38]When they had accomplished these things, with hymns and thanksgivings they blessed the Lord who shows great kindness to Israel and gives them the victory.

11 Very soon after this, Lysias, the king's guardian and kinsman, who was in charge of the government, being vexed at what had happened, [2]gathered about eighty thousand infantry and all his cavalry and came against the Jews. He intended to make the city a home for Greeks, [3]and to levy tribute on the temple as he did on the sacred places of the other nations, and to put up the high priesthood for sale every year. [4]He took no account whatever of the power of God, but was elated with his ten thousands of infantry, and his thousands of cavalry, and his eighty elephants. [5]Invading Judea, he approached Beth-zur, which was a fortified place about five stadia[c] from Jerusalem, and pressed it hard.

[6] When Maccabeus and his men got word that Lysias[d] was besieging the strongholds, they and all the people, with lamentations and tears, prayed the Lord to send a good angel to save Israel. [7]Maccabeus himself was the first to take up arms, and he urged the others to risk their lives with him to aid their kindred. Then they eagerly rushed off together. [8]And there, while they were still near Jerusalem, a horseman appeared at their head, clothed in white and brandishing weapons of gold. [9]And together they all praised the merciful God, and were strengthened in heart, ready to assail not only humans but the wildest animals or walls of iron. [10]They advanced in battle order, having their heavenly ally, for the Lord had mercy on them. [11]They hurled themselves like lions against the enemy, and laid low eleven thousand of them and sixteen hundred cavalry, and forced all the rest to flee. [12]Most of them got away stripped and wounded, and Lysias himself escaped by disgraceful flight.

[13] As he was not without intelligence, he pondered over the defeat that had befallen him, and realized that the Hebrews were invincible because the mighty God fought on their side. So he sent to them [14]and persuaded them to settle everything on just terms, promising that he would persuade the king, constraining him to be their friend. [15]Maccabeus, having regard for the common good, agreed to all that Lysias urged. For the king granted every request in behalf of the Jews which Maccabeus delivered to Lysias in writing.

[16] The letter written to the Jews by Lysias was to this effect:

"Lysias to the people of the Jews, greetings. [17]John and Absalom, who were sent by you, have delivered your signed communication and have asked about the matters indicated in it. [18]I have informed the king of everything that needed to be brought before him, and he has agreed to what was possible. [19]If you will maintain your goodwill toward the government, I will endeavor in the future to help promote your welfare.

c Meaning of Gk uncertain   d Gk he

11.1–15: Victory over Lysias at Beth-zur. This probably occurred before the dedication of the temple (1 Macc 4.26–35). **1:** *Lysias,* see 10.10–13 n. **3:** In many Greek cults the priesthood was *for sale every year;* Antiochus IV had twice disposed of the Jewish high priesthood (4.7, 24). **4:** *Elephants,* see 1 Macc 1.17 n.; 6.34–35 n. **5:** *Beth-zur,* about twenty miles south of Jerusalem on the road to Hebron. **6:** *Good angel,* 15.23; Ex 23.20; Josh 5.13–15; Judg 6.11; 2 Kings 19.35. **13–15:** According to 1 Macc 4.35 no peace was made, but Lysias returned to Antioch for reinforcements. He may have heard of Antiochus' death and hastened home to take control. **11.16–38: Letters of Lysias, Antiochus V, and the Romans.** If Lysias heard of Philip's plot (see 9.29 n.), he may have wished to gain time through friendly gestures to the Jews. **16:** He wrote *to the people;* he did not recognize Judas' authority. **19:** Part of the Jews had *goodwill toward the government.* See Introduction to 1 Maccabees. **21:** The date is early December, 164 B.C., before Judas

20 And concerning such matters and their details, I have ordered these men and my representatives to confer with you. 21 Farewell. The one hundred forty-eighth year, *e* Dioscorinthius twenty-fourth."

22 The king's letter ran thus:

"King Antiochus to his brother Lysias, greetings. 23 Now that our father has gone on to the gods, we desire that the subjects of the kingdom be undisturbed in caring for their own affairs. 24 We have heard that the Jews do not consent to our father's change to Greek customs, but prefer their own way of living and ask that their own customs be allowed them. 25 Accordingly, since we choose that this nation also should be free from disturbance, our decision is that their temple be restored to them and that they shall live according to the customs of their ancestors. 26 You will do well, therefore, to send word to them and give them pledges of friendship, so that they may know our policy and be of good cheer and go on happily in the conduct of their own affairs."

27 To the nation the king's letter was as follows:

"King Antiochus to the senate of the Jews and to the other Jews, greetings. 28 If you are well, it is as we desire. We also are in good health. 29 Menelaus has informed us that you wish to return home and look after your own affairs. 30 Therefore those who go home by the thirtieth of Xanthicus will have our pledge of friendship and full permission 31 for the Jews to enjoy their own food and laws, just as formerly, and none of them shall be molested in any way for what may have been done in ignorance. 32 And I have also sent Menelaus to encourage you. 33 Farewell. The one hundred forty-eighth year, *e* Xanthicus fifteenth."

34 The Romans also sent them a letter, which read thus:

"Quintus Memmius and Titus Manius, envoys of the Romans, to the people of the Jews, greetings. 35 With regard to what Lysias the kinsman of the king has granted you, we also give consent. 36 But as to the matters that he decided are to be referred to the king, as soon as you have considered them, send some one promptly so that we may make proposals appropriate for you. For we are on our way to Antioch. 37 Therefore make haste and send messengers so that we may have your judgment. 38 Farewell. The one hundred forty-eighth year, *e* Xanthicus fifteenth."

12 When this agreement had been reached, Lysias returned to the king, and the Jews went about their farming.

2 But some of the governors in various places, Timothy and Apollonius son of Gennaeus, as well as Hieronymus and Demophon, and in addition to these Nicanor the governor of Cyprus, would not let them live quietly and in peace. 3 And the people of Joppa did so ungodly a deed as this: they invited the Jews who lived among them to embark, with their wives and children, on boats that they had provided, as though there were no ill will to the Jews; *f* 4 and this was done by public vote of the city. When they ac-

e 164 B.C.   *f* Gk *to them*

---

rededicated the temple (1 Macc 4.52). **23:** *Our father,* Antiochus IV, *has gone on to the gods;* in his lifetime he had been worshiped. **25:** 1 Macc 4.36–61 says nothing of this, but Lysias may have instructed the citadel garrison not to interfere with the temple.

11.27: The letter *to the senate* (1.10) and people ignores Judas (compare vv. 16–21). **29:** *Menelaus* had gone to Antioch and advised the king to let the Jews *return* to Jerusalem. He was now sent back (v. 32), hoping to regain the high priesthood. **30:** *Xanthicus,* March–

April. **31:** *Their own food and laws,* 1 Macc 1.47–49. The words *in ignorance* imply that the king still maintained his claims and merely granted pardon (1 Macc 13.39). **34–37:** The *envoys* acted as intermediaries in *matters . . . referred to the king* that were still under negotiation.

12.1–16: **Attacks on Joppa, Jamnia, and Caspin. 2:** *Timothy,* 8.30–33; 10.24–37. *Apollonius,* not the Apollonius of 4.21. *Nicanor* is called *governor of Cyprus;* it was under Egypt's rule till 58 B.C., but Syria may have claimed

cepted, because they wished to live peaceably and suspected nothing, the people of Joppa*g* took them out to sea and drowned them, at least two hundred. [5]When Judas heard of the cruelty visited on his compatriots, he gave orders to his men [6]and, calling upon God, the righteous judge, attacked the murderers of his kindred. He set fire to the harbor by night, burned the boats, and massacred those who had taken refuge there. [7]Then, because the city's gates were closed, he withdrew, intending to come again and root out the whole community of Joppa. [8]But learning that the people in Jamnia meant in the same way to wipe out the Jews who were living among them, [9]he attacked the Jamnites by night and set fire to the harbor and the fleet, so that the glow of the light was seen in Jerusalem, thirty miles*h* distant.

10 When they had gone more than a mile*i* from there, on their march against Timothy, at least five thousand Arabs with five hundred cavalry attacked them. [11]After a hard fight, Judas and his companions, with God's help, were victorious. The defeated nomads begged Judas to grant them pledges of friendship, promising to give him livestock and to help his people*j* in all other ways. [12]Judas, realizing that they might indeed be useful in many ways, agreed to make peace with them; and after receiving his pledges they went back to their tents.

13 He also attacked a certain town that was strongly fortified with earthworks*k* and walls, and inhabited by all sorts of Gentiles. Its name was Caspin. [14]Those who were within, relying on the strength of the walls and on their supply of provisions, behaved most insolently toward Judas and his men, railing at them and even blaspheming and saying unholy things. [15]But Judas and his men, calling against the great Sovereign of the

world, who without battering-rams or engines of war overthrew Jericho in the days of Joshua, rushed furiously upon the walls. [16]They took the town by the will of God, and slaughtered untold numbers, so that the adjoining lake, a quarter of a mile*l* wide, appeared to be running over with blood.

17 When they had gone ninety-five miles*m* from there, they came to Charax, to the Jews who are called Toubiani. [18]They did not find Timothy in that region, for he had by then left there without accomplishing anything, though in one place he had left a very strong garrison. [19]Dositheus and Sosipater, who were captains under Maccabeus, marched out and destroyed those whom Timothy had left in the stronghold, more than ten thousand men. [20]But Maccabeus arranged his army in divisions, set men*j* in command of the divisions, and hurried after Timothy, who had with him one hundred twenty thousand infantry and two thousand five hundred cavalry. [21]When Timothy learned of the approach of Judas, he sent off the women and the children and also the baggage to a place called Carnaim; for that place was hard to besiege and difficult of access because of the narrowness of all the approaches. [22]But when Judas' first division appeared, terror and fear came over the enemy at the manifestation to them of him who sees all things. In their flight they rushed headlong in every direction, so that often they were injured by their own men and pierced by the points of their own swords. [23]Judas pressed the pursuit with the utmost vigor, putting the sinners to the sword, and destroyed as many as thirty thousand.

g Gk *they*   *h* Gk *two hundred forty stadia*
i Gk *nine stadia*   *j* Gk *them*
k Meaning of Gk uncertain   *l* Gk *two stadia*
m Gk *seven hundred fifty stadia*

it after the defection of Ptolemy Macron (10.13). There may have been two Nicanors (see 14.12 n.). **8:** *Jamnia,* about twelve miles south of Joppa. **13:** *Caspin,* perhaps Chaspho (1 Macc 5.36). **15:** Josh 6.1–21.
12.17–31: Battles in the northeast (the

account supplements 1 Macc 5.9–32). **17:** *Toubiani,* perhaps people of Tob (1 Macc 5.13). **18:** *One place,* perhaps Bozrah, southeast of Tob (1 Macc 5.28). **21:** *Carnaim,* a little north of Dera'a in Syria (Gen 14.5; 1 Macc 5.26).

24 Timothy himself fell into the hands of Dositheus and Sosipater and their men. With great guile he begged them to let him go in safety, because he held the parents of most of them, and the brothers of some, to whom no consideration would be shown. 25 And when with many words he had confirmed his solemn promise to restore them unharmed, they let him go, for the sake of saving their kindred.

26 Then Judas[n] marched against Carnaim and the temple of Atargatis, and slaughtered twenty-five thousand people. 27 After the rout and destruction of these, he marched also against Ephron, a fortified town where Lysias lived with multitudes of people of all nationalities.[o] Stalwart young men took their stand before the walls and made a vigorous defense; and great stores of war engines and missiles were there. 28 But the Jews[p] called upon the Sovereign who with power shatters the might of his enemies, and they got the town into their hands, and killed as many as twenty-five thousand of those who were in it.

29 Setting out from there, they hastened to Scythopolis, which is seventy-five miles[q] from Jerusalem. 30 But when the Jews who lived there bore witness to the good will that the people of Scythopolis had shown them and their kind treatment of them in times of misfortune, 31 they thanked them and exhorted them to be well disposed to their race in the future also. Then they went up to Jerusalem, as the festival of weeks was close at hand.

32 After the festival called Pentecost, they hurried against Gorgias, the governor of Idumea, 33 who came out with three thousand infantry and four hundred cavalry. 34 When they joined battle, it happened that a few of the Jews fell. 35 But a certain Dositheus, one of Bacenor's men, who was on horseback and was a strong man, caught hold of Gorgias, and grasping his cloak was dragging him off by main strength, wishing to take the accursed man alive, when one of the Thracian cavalry bore down on him and cut off his arm; so Gorgias escaped and reached Marisa.

36 As Esdris and his men had been fighting for a long time and were weary, Judas called upon the Lord to show himself their ally and leader in the battle. 37 In the language of their ancestors he raised the battle cry, with hymns; then he charged against Gorgias' troops when they were not expecting it, and put them to flight.

38 Then Judas assembled his army and went to the city of Adullam. As the seventh day was coming on, they purified themselves according to the custom, and kept the sabbath there.

39 On the next day, as had now become necessary, Judas and his men went to take up the bodies of the fallen and to bring them back to lie with their kindred in the sepulchres of their ancestors. 40 Then under the tunic of each one of the dead they found sacred tokens of the idols of Jamnia, which the law forbids the Jews to wear. And it became clear to all that this was the reason these men had fallen. 41 So they all blessed the ways of

n Gk *he*   *o* Meaning of Gk uncertain
p Gk *they*   *q* Gk *six hundred stadia*

12.26: *Atargatis,* the Syrian goddess to whom fish were sacred. 27: *He marched* south *against Ephron,* eight miles east of the Jordan, opposite Scythopolis (v. 29; 1 Macc 5.46–51). *War engines* were large catapults. 29: *Scythopolis,* ancient Beth-shan, then and later an important city (see 1 Macc 5.52 n.). 31: The *festival of weeks* or Pentecost was at the time of the wheat harvest, seven weeks after Passover, and was celebrated in Jerusalem (Ex 34.22–24; Deut 16.9–12). 12.32–38: **Battle with Gorgias.** 35:

Marisa, in the foothills southwest of Jerusalem near Beit-Jibrin (see 1 Macc 5.66 n.). 36: *Esdris,* evidently a division leader (v. 20); the author of 2 Maccabees has abbreviated his source. 38: *City of Adullam,* northeast of Marisa (Josh 12.15; 15.35). They *kept the sabbath,* when it was not necessary to fight (8.27; see 1 Macc 2.41 n.).
12.39–45: **Burial of the dead.** The author believed that many had been killed because they wore *sacred tokens* of pagan gods *which the law forbids* (v. 40; Deut 7.25–26), but

the Lord, the righteous judge, who reveals the things that are hidden; 42 and they turned to supplication, praying that the sin that had been committed might be wholly blotted out. The noble Judas exhorted the people to keep themselves free from sin, for they had seen with their own eyes what had happened as the result of the sin of those who had fallen. 43 He also took up a collection, man by man, to the amount of two thousand drachmas of silver, and sent it to Jerusalem to provide for a sin offering. In doing this he acted very well and honorably, taking account of the resurrection. 44 For if he were not expecting that those who had fallen would rise again, it would have been superfluous and foolish to pray for the dead. 45 But if he was looking to the splendid reward that is laid up for those who fall asleep in godliness, it was a holy and pious thought. Therefore he made atonement for the dead, so that they might be delivered from their sin.

13 In the one hundred forty-ninth year *r* word came to Judas and his men that Antiochus Eupator was coming with a great army against Judea, 2 and with him Lysias, his guardian, who had charge of the government. Each of them had a Greek force of one hundred ten thousand infantry, five thousand three hundred cavalry, twenty-two elephants, and three hundred chariots armed with scythes.

3 Menelaus also joined them and with utter hypocrisy urged Antiochus on, not for the sake of his country's welfare, but because he thought that he would be established in office. 4 But the King of kings aroused the anger of Antiochus against the scoundrel; and when Lysias informed him that this man was to blame for all the trouble, he ordered them to take him to Beroea and to put him to death by the method that is customary in that place. 5 For there is a tower there, fifty cubits high, full of ashes, and it has a rim running around it that on all sides inclines precipitously into the ashes. 6 There they all push to destruction anyone guilty of sacrilege or notorious for other crimes. 7 By such a fate it came about that Menelaus the lawbreaker died, without even burial in the earth. 8 And this was eminently just; because he had committed many sins against the altar whose fire and ashes were holy, he met his death in ashes.

9 The king with barbarous arrogance was coming to show the Jews things far worse than those that had been done *s* in his father's time. 10 But when Judas heard of this, he ordered the people to call upon the Lord day and night, now if ever to help those who were on the point of being deprived of the law and their country and the holy temple, 11 and not to let the people who had just begun to revive fall into the hands of the blasphemous Gentiles. 12 When they had all joined in the same petition and had implored the merciful Lord with weeping and fasting and lying prostrate for three days without ceasing, Judas exhorted them and ordered them to stand ready.

13 After consulting privately with the elders, he determined to march out and decide the matter by the help of God before the king's army could enter Judea

r 163 B.C.   *s* Or *the worst of the things that had been done*

Josephus says (*Antiquities*, XII. viii. 6) this reverse befell them because they had disobeyed Judas' instructions not to join battle before his arrival. See also 1 Macc 5.67. This is the first known statement of the doctrine that a *sin offering* and prayer make *atonement* for the sins of *the dead* (v. 45), and it is justified by the hope that *those who had fallen would rise again* (vv. 43–44; 7.11; 14.46). *Fall asleep*, die (1 Cor 15.20).

13.1–8: Death of Menelaus. 1–2: *Antio-chus* and *Lysias*, see 10.10–11 n. *Chariots armed with scythes* to cut down foot soldiers had been used since the days of the Persian Empire. **4:** *The King of kings*, God (Deut 10.17; Ps 136.3; Rev 19.16). What *aroused* his *anger* is not known (but see 4.27). *Beroea*, now Aleppo in northern Syria. *The method* of execution (vv. 5–6) was Persian.

13.9–17: Preliminary skirmish. 12: Jews employed such acts of penitence particularly when there was danger of sacrilege (3.15;

and get possession of the city. ¹⁴So, committing the decision to the Creator of the world and exhorting his troops to fight bravely to the death for the laws, temple, city, country, and commonwealth, he pitched his camp near Modein. ¹⁵He gave his troops the watchword, "God's victory," and with a picked force of the bravest young men, he attacked the king's pavilion at night and killed as many as two thousand men in the camp. He stabbed^t the leading elephant and its rider. ¹⁶In the end they filled the camp with terror and confusion and withdrew in triumph. ¹⁷This happened, just as day was dawning, because the Lord's help protected him.

18 The king, having had a taste of the daring of the Jews, tried strategy in attacking their positions. ¹⁹He advanced against Beth-zur, a strong fortress of the Jews, was turned back, attacked again,^u and was defeated. ²⁰Judas sent in to the garrison whatever was necessary. ²¹But Rhodocus, a man from the ranks of the Jews, gave secret information to the enemy; he was sought for, caught, and put in prison. ²²The king negotiated a second time with the people in Beth-zur, gave pledges, received theirs, withdrew, attacked Judas and his men, was defeated; ²³he got word that Philip, who had been left in charge of the government, had revolted in Antioch; he was dismayed, called in the Jews, yielded and swore to observe all their rights, settled with them and offered sacrifice, honored the sanctuary and showed generosity to the holy place. ²⁴He received Maccabeus, left

Hegemonides as governor from Ptolemais to Gerar, ²⁵and went to Ptolemais. The people of Ptolemais were indignant over the treaty; in fact they were so angry that they wanted to annul its terms.^t ²⁶Lysias took the public platform, made the best possible defense, convinced them, appeased them, gained their goodwill, and set out for Antioch. This is how the king's attack and withdrawal turned out.

14 Three years later, word came to Judas and his men that Demetrius son of Seleucus had sailed into the harbor of Tripolis with a strong army and a fleet, ²and had taken possession of the country, having made away with Antiochus and his guardian Lysias.

3 Now a certain Alcimus, who had formerly been high priest but had willfully defiled himself in the times of separation,^v realized that there was no way for him to be safe or to have access again to the holy altar, ⁴and went to King Demetrius in about the one hundred fifty-first year,^w presenting to him a crown of gold and a palm, and besides these some of the customary olive branches from the temple. During that day he kept quiet. ⁵But he found an opportunity that furthered his mad purpose when he was invited by Demetrius to a meeting of the council and was asked about the attitude and intentions of the Jews. He answered:

6 "Those of the Jews who are called

---

t Meaning of Gk uncertain   u Or *faltered*
v Other ancient authorities read *of mixing*
w 161 B.C.

10.4; 1 Macc 4.40). **14**: The Syrian army had invaded Judea from the south, through Idumea (1 Macc 6.31). Judas first *pitched his camp near Modein* to watch the Syrian line along the coast. The first battle occurred at Beth-zechariah (1 Macc 6.32–47). **15**: *"God's victory,"* see 8.23 n. Eleazar *stabbed the leading elephant* (1 Macc 6.43–46). **16**: According to 1 Macc 6.47 the Jews fled. **17**: Ps 46.6.

13.18–26: **Attack on Beth-zur**. **19**: The Syrians were defeated in the first attempt (1 Macc 6.31). **21–22**: The garrison surrendered because of lack of food (1 Macc 6.49); possibly this was the *secret information*. **23**:

Philip, see 9.29 n.; 1 Macc 6.14–15, 55–56. **24**: *Gerar*, south of Gaza on the coastal plain. **26**: 1 Macc 6.63.

14.1–10: **Accession of Demetrius I** (1 Macc 7.1–7). **1**: *Three years later*, about 161 B.C. *Demetrius* I Soter, *son of Seleucus* IV, reigned 162–150. *Tripolis*, see 1 Macc 7.1 n. **2**: *Antiochus . . . Lysias*, 1 Macc 7.3–4. **3**: *Alcimus* may not have *been high priest. Defiled*, 4.11–15. **4**: 1 Macc 7.5–7 may record an earlier visit. *Crown*, emblem of sovereignty; the *palm*, victory. **6**: *Hasideans*, see 1 Macc 2.42 n. **7**: *Ancestral glory*, he claimed legitimate succession.

Hasideans, whose leader is Judas Maccabeus, are keeping up war and stirring up sedition, and will not let the kingdom attain tranquility. 7 Therefore I have laid aside my ancestral glory—I mean the high priesthood—and have now come here, 8 first because I am genuinely concerned for the interests of the king, and second because I have regard also for my compatriots. For through the folly of those whom I have mentioned our whole nation is now in no small misfortune. 9 Since you are acquainted, O king, with the details of this matter, may it please you to take thought for our country and our hard-pressed nation with the gracious kindness that you show to all. 10 For as long as Judas lives, it is impossible for the government to find peace." 11 When he had said this, the rest of the king's Friends,ˣ who were hostile to Judas, quickly inflamed Demetrius still more. 12 He immediately chose Nicanor, who had been in command of the elephants, appointed him governor of Judea, and sent him off 13 with orders to kill Judas and scatter his troops, and to install Alcimus as high priest of the greatʸ temple. 14 And the Gentiles throughout Judea, who had fled beforeᶻ Judas, flocked to join Nicanor, thinking that the misfortunes and calamities of the Jews would mean prosperity for themselves.

15 When the Jewsᵈ heard of Nicanor's coming and the gathering of the Gentiles, they sprinkled dust on their heads and prayed to him who established his own people forever and always upholds his own heritage by manifesting himself. 16 At the command of the leader, theyᵇ set out from there immediately and engaged them in battle at a village called Dessau. ᶻ 17 Simon, the brother of Judas, had encountered Nicanor, but had been temporarily checked because of the sudden consternation created by the enemy.

18 Nevertheless Nicanor, hearing of the valor of Judas and his troops and their courage in battle for their country, shrank from deciding the issue by bloodshed. 19 Therefore he sent Posidonius, Theodotus, and Mattathias to give and receive pledges of friendship. 20 When the terms had been fully considered, and the leader had informed the people, and it had appeared that they were of one mind, they agreed to the covenant. 21 The leadersᵈ set a day on which to meet by themselves. A chariot came forward from each army; seats of honor were set in place; 22 Judas posted armed men in readiness at key places to prevent sudden treachery on the part of the enemy; so they duly held the consultation.

23 Nicanor stayed on in Jerusalem and did nothing out of the way, but dismissed the flocks of people that had gathered. 24 And he kept Judas always in his presence; he was warmly attached to the man. 25 He urged him to marry and have children; so Judasᵇ married, settled down, and shared the common life.

26 But when Alcimus noticed their good will for one another, he took the covenant that had been made and went to Demetrius. He told him that Nicanor was disloyal to the government, since he had appointed that conspirator against the kingdom, Judas, to be his successor. 27 The king became excited and, provoked by the false accusations of that de-

x Gk *of the Friends*
y Gk *greatest*   z Meaning of Gk uncertain
a Gk *they*   b Gk *he*   c Other ancient
authorities read *slowly*   d Gk *They*

14.11–14: **Appointment of Nicanor and Alcimus.** This story omits the expedition of Bacchides (1 Macc 7.8–25). Josephus says that *Nicanor* had escaped from Rome with Demetrius (*Antiquities,* XII. x. 4); if he is the person in 8.9–36 he must have gone from Syria to Rome to assist the escape.
14.15–36: **Nicanor seeks friendship with Judas. 15:** *Sprinkled dust,* Josh 7.6. **16:**

The leader, Judas, or possibly Nicanor. *Dessau,* perhaps Adasa (1 Macc 7.40–45). **20–21:** *The leader,* Nicanor. *The people,* his army. Afterward *the leaders,* Nicanor and Judas, met. **22:** 1 Macc 7.12–18. **24:** *Warmly attached* only so long as things went well (compare vv. 31–33).

14.26: *Alcimus* failed to get civil power and feared that *Judas* would be made his *successor*

praved man, wrote to Nicanor, stating that he was displeased with the covenant and commanding him to send Maccabeus to Antioch as a prisoner without delay.

28 When this message came to Nicanor, he was troubled and grieved that he had to annul their agreement when the man had done no wrong. 29 Since it was not possible to oppose the king, he watched for an opportunity to accomplish this by a stratagem. 30 But Maccabeus, noticing that Nicanor was more austere in his dealings with him and was meeting him more rudely than had been his custom, concluded that this austerity did not spring from the best motives. So he gathered not a few of his men, and went into hiding from Nicanor. 31 When the latter became aware that he had been cleverly outwitted by the man, he went to the great[e] and holy temple while the priests were offering the customary sacrifices, and commanded them to hand the man over. 32 When they declared on oath that they did not know where the man was whom he wanted, 33 he stretched out his right hand toward the sanctuary, and swore this oath: "If you do not hand Judas over to me as a prisoner, I will level this shrine of God to the ground and tear down the altar, and build here a splendid temple to Dionysus."

34 Having said this, he went away. Then the priests stretched out their hands toward heaven and called upon the constant Defender of our nation, in these words: 35 "O Lord of all, though you have need of nothing, you were pleased that there should be a temple for your habitation among us; 36 so now, O holy One, Lord of all holiness, keep undefiled forever this house that has been so recently purified."

37 A certain Razis, one of the elders of Jerusalem, was denounced to Nicanor as a man who loved his compatriots and was very well thought of and for his goodwill was called father of the Jews. 38 In former times, when there was no mingling with the Gentiles, he had been accused of Judaism, and he had most zealously risked body and life for Judaism. 39 Nicanor, wishing to exhibit the enmity that he had for the Jews, sent more than five hundred soldiers to arrest him; 40 for he thought that by arresting[f] him he would do them an injury. 41 When the troops were about to capture the tower and were forcing the door of the courtyard, they ordered that fire be brought and the doors burned. Being surrounded, Razis[g] fell upon his own sword, 42 preferring to die nobly rather than to fall into the hands of sinners and suffer outrages unworthy of his noble birth. 43 But in the heat of the struggle he did not hit exactly, and the crowd was now rushing in through the doors. He courageously ran up on the wall, and bravely threw himself down into the crowd. 44 But as they quickly drew back, a space opened and he fell in the middle of the empty space. 45 Still alive and aflame with anger, he rose, and though his blood gushed forth and his wounds were severe he ran through the crowd; and standing upon a steep rock, 46 with his blood now completely drained from him, he tore out his entrails, took them in both hands and hurled them at the crowd, calling upon the Lord of life and spirit to give them back to him again. This was the manner of his death.

15 When Nicanor heard that Judas and his troops were in the region of Samaria, he made plans to attack them with complete safety on the day of rest. 2 When the Jews who were compelled to follow him said, "Do not destroy so sav-

e Gk *greatest*   f Meaning of Gk
uncertain   g Gk *he*

---

as high priest. **33**: *Stretched out his right hand . . . and swore,* 15.32–33. *Dionysus,* 6.7 n. **35–36**: 1 Kings 8.27–30. *Purified,* 10.1–8.

14.37–46: **Death of Razis.** A martyrology in the style of 6.18–7.42. **37**: *Elders,* 13.13.

42: See 1 Sam 31.4. **46**: He expected his body to be restored in the resurrection (7.11).

15.1–36: **Death of Nicanor** (1 Macc 7.39–50). **1**: *Nicanor* camped at Beth-horon, and *Judas* was at Adasa, between Beth-horon

agely and barbarously, but show respect for the day that he who sees all things has honored and hallowed above other days," ³the thrice-accursed wretch asked if there were a sovereign in heaven who had commanded the keeping of the sabbath day. ⁴When they declared, "It is the living Lord himself, the Sovereign in heaven, who ordered us to observe the seventh day," ⁵he replied, "But I am a sovereign also, on earth, and I command you to take up arms and finish the king's business." Nevertheless, he did not succeed in carrying out his abominable design.

6 This Nicanor in his utter boastfulness and arrogance had determined to erect a public monument of victory over Judas and his forces. ⁷But Maccabeus did not cease to trust with all confidence that he would get help from the Lord. ⁸He exhorted his troops not to fear the attack of the Gentiles, but to keep in mind the former times when help had come to them from heaven, and so to look for the victory that the Almighty would give them. ⁹Encouraging them from the law and the prophets, and reminding them also of the struggles they had won, he made them the more eager. ¹⁰When he had aroused their courage, he issued his orders, at the same time pointing out the perfidy of the Gentiles and their violation of oaths. ¹¹He armed each of them not so much with confidence in shields and spears as with the inspiration of brave words, and he cheered them all by relating a dream, a sort of vision,ʰ which was worthy of belief.

12 What he saw was this: Onias, who had been high priest, a noble and good man, of modest bearing and gentle manner, one who spoke fittingly and had been trained from childhood in all that belongs to excellence, was praying with outstretched hands for the whole body of the Jews. ¹³Then in the same fashion another appeared, distinguished by his gray hair and dignity, and of marvelous majesty and authority. ¹⁴And Onias spoke, saying, "This is a man who loves the family of Israel and prays much for the people and the holy city—Jeremiah, the prophet of God." ¹⁵Jeremiah stretched out his right hand and gave to Judas a golden sword, and as he gave it he addressed him thus: ¹⁶"Take this holy sword, a gift from God, with which you will strike down your adversaries."

17 Encouraged by the words of Judas, so noble and so effective in arousing valor and awaking courage in the souls of the young, they determined not to carry on a campaignⁱ but to attack bravely, and to decide the matter by fighting hand to hand with all courage, because the city and the sanctuary and the temple were in danger. ¹⁸Their concern for wives and children, and also for brothers and sisters ʲ and relatives, lay upon them less heavily; their greatest and first fear was for the consecrated sanctuary. ¹⁹And those who had to remain in the city were in no little distress, being anxious over the encounter in the open country.

20 When all were now looking forward to the coming issue, and the enemy was already close at hand with their army drawn up for battle, the elephantsᵏ strategically stationed and the cavalry deployed on the flanks, ²¹Maccabeus, observing the masses that were in front of him and the varied supply of arms and the savagery of the elephants, stretched out his hands toward heaven and called

h Meaning of Gk uncertain   i Or *to remain in camp*   j Gk *for brothers*   k Gk *animals*

and Jerusalem. **2:** *The Jews* in Nicanor's army wished to honor the sabbath. **3:** *Thrice-accursed,* 8.34. **4–5:** Ex 20.8–11; Dan 3.16–18. **8:** 1 Macc 7.41. **9:** *The law and the prophets* were now regarded as scripture (compare the Prologue to Sirach); not all the other books had been collected. **10:** *Violation of oaths,* 11.27–32; 14.20–28.

15.12: *Onias,* 3.1–40. **15–16:** The *golden sword* was a sign that God approved the Jews' self-defense on the sabbath. **18:** *First fear,* compare 14.33.

15.20: *Elephants,* to break through the Jewish infantry; the *cavalry* protected the *flanks* of the Syrian infantry. **22–23:** See 11.6 n.; 2 Kings 19.35.

The defeat and
death of Nicanor
2 MACCABEES 15

upon the Lord who works wonders; for he knew that it is not by arms, but as the Lord[l] decides, that he gains the victory for those who deserve it. 22 He called upon him in these words: "O Lord, you sent your angel in the time of King Hezekiah of Judea, and he killed fully one hundred eighty-five thousand in the camp of Sennacherib. 23 So now, O Sovereign of the heavens, send a good angel to spread terror and trembling before us. 24 By the might of your arm may these blasphemers who come against your holy people be struck down." With these words he ended his prayer.

25 Nicanor and his troops advanced with trumpets and battle songs, 26 but Judas and his troops met the enemy in battle with invocations to God and prayers. 27 So, fighting with their hands and praying to God in their hearts, they laid low at least thirty-five thousand, and were greatly gladdened by God's manifestation.

28 When the action was over and they were returning with joy, they recognized Nicanor, lying dead, in full armor. 29 Then there was shouting and tumult, and they blessed the Sovereign Lord in the language of their ancestors. 30 Then the man who was ever in body and soul the defender of his people, the man who maintained his youthful goodwill toward his compatriots, ordered them to cut off Nicanor's head and arm and carry them to Jerusalem. 31 When he arrived there and had called his compatriots together and stationed the priests before the altar, he sent for those who were in the citadel. 32 He showed them the vile Nicanor's head and that profane man's arm, which had been boastfully stretched out against the holy house of the Almighty. 33 He cut out the tongue of the ungodly Nicanor and said that he would feed it piecemeal to the birds and would hang up these rewards of his folly opposite the sanctuary. 34 And they all, looking to heaven, blessed the Lord who had manifested himself, saying, "Blessed is he who has kept his own place undefiled!" 35 Judas[m] hung Nicanor's head from the citadel, a clear and conspicuous sign to everyone of the help of the Lord. 36 And they all decreed by public vote never to let this day go unobserved, but to celebrate the thirteenth day of the twelfth month—which is called Adar in the Aramaic language—the day before Mordecai's day.

37 This, then, is how matters turned out with Nicanor, and from that time the city has been in the possession of the Hebrews. So I will here end my story.

38 If it is well told and to the point, that is what I myself desired; if it is poorly done and mediocre, that was the best I could do. 39 For just as it is harmful to drink wine alone, or, again, to drink water alone, while wine mixed with water is sweet and delicious and enhances one's enjoyment, so also the style of the story delights the ears of those who read the work. And here will be the end.

l Gk *he*   *m* Gk *He*

15.29: *Language of their ancestors,* Hebrew. Palestinian Jews spoke Aramaic, but formal prayer, using the language of Scripture, was often in Hebrew. **30:** 1 Sam 17.54. **31:** *The citadel* on the Ophel hill was held by Syrians (1 Macc 1.33; 6.18); but the Jews had built another fort (1 Macc 4.60). **32:** *Head . . . arm,* 14.33. **35:** 1 Sam 31.9; Jdt 14.1; 1 Macc 7.47. **36:** The *twelfth month* (February–March) and also in Hebrew. If there was but one month of Adar in this year (probably 161 B.C.), it was *the day*

before Mordecai's day, but in some years a second month of Adar was intercalated to harmonize the calendar. Nicanor's day was observed up to A.D. 70.

15.37–39: Conclusion. The epitomist wrote some time before the Jewish war (A.D. 66–70), when Jerusalem was still in Jewish hands. **39:** The strong wine of Greece was usually tempered with water. *The style* will delight *the ears of those who read,* because in antiquity it was the custom to read literary works aloud, even to oneself.

(b) The following books are recognized as Deuterocanonical Scripture by the Greek and the Russian Churches. They are not so recognized by the Roman Catholic Church, but 1 Esdras and the Prayer of Manasseh (together with 2 Esdras) are placed in an appendix to the Latin Vulgate Bible.

1 Esdras

The book that is known in the Apocrypha as 1 Esdras is called 3 Esdras in the Latin Vulgate Bible, where it is now placed (since the Council of Trent) in an appendix after the New Testament. None of the other apocryphal books is so intimately connected with the Old Testament. Beginning somewhat abruptly with a description of the great passover held by King Josiah in Jerusalem (about 621 B.C.), the book reproduces the substance of 2 Chr 35.1–36.23, the whole of Ezra, and Neh 7.38–8.12, breaking off in the middle of a sentence after an account of Ezra's reforms (about 458 B.C.). There are numerous minor discrepancies between the apocryphal and canonical accounts, including a rearrangement of the materials, and the story of the three young men in the court of Darius (3.1–5.6) has no parallel in the Old Testament.

The origin of the work is debated. Is it an earlier form of the Greek translation of biblical Ezra, with the Ezra materials found in Nehemiah (7.38–9.38) partially included? Some interpreters believe that to be the case. Several biblical books are known to have had more than a single Hebrew edition in post-exilic Israel, and 1 Esdras may be a translation of an alternative collection of Ezra memoirs, plus lists and other materials, and including the story of the three young men at the court of Darius.

Or is the book an apocryphal work, a translation of a later Hebrew/Aramaic version of the Ezra story, belonging to the late second century B.C., designed to stress the importance of Josiah, Zerubbabel, and Ezra in the establishment of temple worship and fidelity to the Torah? Both views have their supporters, but the former view is the more probable. The date of 1 Esdras in this Greek translation is probably not later than 100 B.C., since the work in its Greek form was used by Josephus in his *Antiquities of the Jewish People* (A.D. 93–94). See the Introductions to 1 Chronicles and Ezra for the origin and purpose of Ezra.

1 Josiah kept the passover to his Lord in Jerusalem; he killed the passover lamb on the fourteenth day of the first month, [2]having placed the priests according to their divisions, arrayed in their vestments, in the temple of the Lord. [3]He told the Levites, the temple servants of Israel, that they should sanctify themselves to the Lord and put the holy ark of the Lord in the house that King Solomon, son of David, had built; [4]and he said, "You need no longer carry it on your shoulders. Now worship the Lord your God and serve his people Israel; prepare yourselves by your families and kindred, [5]in accordance with the directions of King David of Israel and the magnificence of his son Solomon. Stand in order in the temple according to the groupings of the ancestral houses of you Levites, who minister before your kindred the people of Israel, [6]and kill the passover lamb and prepare the sacrifices for your kindred, and keep the passover according to the commandment of the Lord that was given to Moses."

[7] To the people who were present Josiah gave thirty thousand lambs and kids, and three thousand calves; these were given from the king's possessions, as he promised, to the people and the priests and Levites. [8]Hilkiah, Zechariah, and Jehiel,[a] the chief officers of the temple, gave to the priests for the passover two thousand six hundred sheep and three hundred calves. [9]And Jeconiah and Shemaiah and his brother Nethanel, and Hashabiah and Ochiel and Joram, captains over thousands, gave the Levites for the passover five thousand sheep and seven hundred calves.

[10] This is what took place. The priests and the Levites, having the unleavened bread, stood in proper order according to kindred [11]and the grouping of the ancestral houses, before the people, to make the offering to the Lord as it is written in the book of Moses; this they did in the morning. [12]They roasted the passover lamb with fire, as required; and they boiled the sacrifices in bronze pots and caldrons, with a pleasing odor, [13]and carried them to all the people. Afterward they prepared the passover for themselves and for their kindred the priests, the sons of Aaron, [14]because the priests were offering the fat until nightfall; so the Levites prepared it for themselves and for their kindred the priests, the sons of Aaron. [15]The temple singers, the sons of Asaph, were in their place according to the arrangement made by David, and also Asaph, Zechariah, and Eddinus, who represented the king. [16]The gatekeepers were at each gate; no one needed to interrupt his daily duties, for their kindred the Levites prepared the passover for them.

[17] So the things that had to do with the sacrifices to the Lord were accomplished that day: the passover was kept [18]and the sacrifices were offered on the altar of the Lord, according to the command of King Josiah. [19]And the people of Israel who were present at that time kept the passover and the festival of unleavened bread seven days. [20]No passover like it had been kept in Israel since the times of the prophet Samuel; [21]none of the kings of Israel had kept such a passover as was kept by Josiah and the priests and Levites and the people of Judah and all of Israel who were living in Jerusalem. [22]In the eighteenth year of the reign of Josiah this passover was kept.

[23] And the deeds of Josiah were up-

a Gk Esyelus

1.1–33: Josiah's passover; his effort to intercept the Egyptians at Megiddo, and his death (2 Chr 35.1–27). According to 2 Kings 23.21–23 the passover celebration concluded Josiah's religious reform, the account of which is omitted in 1 Esdras. **7–9:** The list of offerings differs slightly from that in 2 Chr 35.7–9.

1.15: *Zechariah* and *Eddinus* appear in 2 Chr 35.15 as Heman and Jeduthun.
1.17–33: 1 Esdras follows the account in 2 Chr 35.16–27 faithfully, apart from the omission of the Pharaoh's name, Josiah's disguising himself, and his being struck by an arrow.

right in the sight of the Lord, for his heart was full of godliness. ²⁴In ancient times the events of his reign have been recorded—concerning those who sinned and acted wickedly toward the Lord beyond any other people or kingdom, and how they grieved the Lord*ᵇ* deeply, so that the words of the Lord fell upon Israel.

25 After all these acts of Josiah, it happened that Pharaoh, king of Egypt, went to make war at Carchemish on the Euphrates, and Josiah went out against him. ²⁶And the king of Egypt sent word to him saying, "What have we to do with each other, O king of Judea? ²⁷I was not sent against you by the Lord God, for my war is at the Euphrates. And now the Lord is with me! The Lord is with me, urging me on! Stand aside, and do not oppose the Lord."

28 Josiah, however, did not turn back to his chariot, but tried to fight with him, and did not heed the words of the prophet Jeremiah from the mouth of the Lord. ²⁹He joined battle with him in the plain of Megiddo, and the commanders came down against King Josiah. ³⁰The king said to his servants, "Take me away from the battle, for I am very weak." And immediately his servants took him out of the line of battle. ³¹He got into his second chariot; and after he was brought back to Jerusalem he died, and was buried in the tomb of his ancestors.

32 In all Judea they mourned for Josiah. The prophet Jeremiah lamented for Josiah, and the principal men, with the women,*ᶜ* have made lamentation for him to this day; it was ordained that this should always be done throughout the whole nation of Israel. ³³These things are written in the book of the histories of the kings of Judea; and every one of the acts of Josiah, and his splendor, and his understanding of the law of the Lord, and the things that he had done before, and these that are now told, are recorded in the book of the kings of Israel and Judah. ✕ 34 The men of the nation took Jeconiah*ᵈ* son of Josiah, who was twenty-three years old, and made him king in succession to his father Josiah. ³⁵He reigned three months in Judah and Jerusalem. Then the king of Egypt deposed him from reigning in Jerusalem, ³⁶and fined the nation one hundred talents of silver and one talent of gold. ³⁷The king of Egypt made his brother Jehoiakim king of Judea and Jerusalem. ³⁸Jehoiakim put the nobles in prison, and seized his brother Zarius and brought him back from Egypt.

39 Jehoiakim was twenty-five years old when he began to reign in Judea and Jerusalem; he did what was evil in the sight of the Lord. ⁴⁰King Nebuchadnezzar of Babylon came up against him; he bound him with a chain of bronze and took him away to Babylon. ⁴¹Nebuchadnezzar also took some holy vessels of the Lord, and carried them away, and stored them in his temple in Babylon. ⁴²But the things that are reported about Jehoiakim,*ᵇ* and his uncleanness and impiety, are written in the annals of the kings.

43 His son Jehoiachin*ᵉ* became king in his place; when he was made king he

b Gk *him*   *c* Or *their wives*   *d* 2 Kings 23.30; 2 Chr 36.1 *Jehoahaz*   *e* Gk *Jehoiakim*

1.34–58: **The last kings of Judah; Jerusalem's fall to the Babylonians** (2 Chr 36.1–21). **34**: The expression *men of the nation* corresponds to the "people of the land" of 2 Chr 36.1; in pre-exilic times these were conservative landowners who often came to the support of reforming kings or who themselves instituted reforms (2 Kings 12.18, 20; 21.24; 23.30). *Jeconiah,* also called Jehoahaz (2 Kings 23.30–31; 2 Chr 36.1–2) and Shallum (Jer 22.11). **38**: The author has misunderstood 2 Chr 36.4. Neco of Egypt removed Jehoahaz from the throne and installed Josiah's elder son Eliakim as king, changing his name to Jehoiakim. Jehoahaz was taken to Egypt where presumably he died (Jer 22.10–12). 1 Esdras has *Jehoiakim* bring up his brother *Zarius* from Egypt; the name *Zarius* is apparently an orthographic corruption (through confusion of the Hebrew letters *d* and *r*) of Zedekiah, who was a brother of Jehoiakim (2 Kings 24.17). **39**: 1 Esdras omits the length of Jehoiakim's reign, which was eleven years (2 Chr 36.5).

was eighteen years old, [44] and he reigned three months and ten days in Jerusalem. He did what was evil in the sight of the Lord. [45] A year later Nebuchadnezzar sent and removed him to Babylon, with the holy vessels of the Lord, [46] and made Zedekiah king of Judea and Jerusalem.

Zedekiah was twenty-one years old, and he reigned eleven years. [47] He also did what was evil in the sight of the Lord, and did not heed the words that were spoken by the prophet Jeremiah from the mouth of the Lord. [48] Although King Nebuchadnezzar had made him swear by the name of the Lord, he broke his oath and rebelled; he stiffened his neck and hardened his heart and transgressed the laws of the Lord, the God of Israel. [49] Even the leaders of the people and of the priests committed many acts of sacrilege and lawlessness beyond all the unclean deeds of all the nations, and polluted the temple of the Lord in Jerusalem—the temple that God had made holy. [50] The God of their ancestors sent his messenger to call them back, because he would have spared them and his dwelling place. [51] But they mocked his messengers, and whenever the Lord spoke, they scoffed at his prophets, [52] until in his anger against his people because of their ungodly acts he gave command to bring against them the kings of the Chaldeans. [53] These killed their young men with the sword around their holy temple, and did not spare young man or young woman,[f] old man or child, for he gave them all into their hands. [54] They took all the holy vessels of the Lord, great and small, the treasure chests of the Lord, and the royal stores, and carried them away to Babylon. [55] They burned the house of the Lord, broke down the walls of Jerusalem, burned their towers with fire, [56] and utterly destroyed all its glorious things. The survivors he led away to Babylon with the sword, [57] and they were servants to him and to his sons until the Persians began to reign, in fulfillment of the word of the Lord by the mouth of Jeremiah, [58] saying, "Until the land has enjoyed its sabbaths, it shall keep sabbath all the time of its desolation until the completion of seventy years."

2 In the first year of Cyrus as king of the Persians, so that the word of the Lord by the mouth of Jeremiah might be accomplished— [2] the Lord stirred up the spirit of King Cyrus of the Persians, and he made a proclamation throughout all his kingdom and also put it in writing:

3 "Thus says Cyrus king of the Persians: The Lord of Israel, the Lord Most High, has made me king of the world, [4] and he has commanded me to build him a house at Jerusalem, which is in Judea. [5] If any of you, therefore, are of his people, may your Lord be with you; go up to Jerusalem, which is in Judea, and build the house of the Lord of Israel—he is the Lord who dwells in Jerusalem, [6] and let each of you, wherever you may live, be helped by the people of your place with gold and silver, [7] with gifts and with horses and cattle, besides the other things added as votive offerings for the temple of the Lord that is in Jerusalem."

8 Then arose the heads of families of the tribes of Judah and Benjamin, and the priests and the Levites, and all whose spirit the Lord had stirred to go up to build the house in Jerusalem for the Lord; [9] their neighbors helped them with everything, with silver and gold, with

---

f Gk *virgin*

1.43: 1 Esdras mistakenly gives Jehoiakim (see note *e*) as the name of that king's son and successor, rather than Jehoiachin; but the king's age at the beginning of his reign is correctly given (*eighteen years;* not eight, as in 2 Chr 36.9).

1.58: To *keep sabbath* means that the land is to continue in a state of "sabbath" rest (i.e. to lie untended as in the seventh or sabbatical year) until the exiles return (Jer 25.11–12; 29.10; compare Lev 25.1–7; 26.27–39).

2.1–15: **Cyrus of Persia permits the exiles to return** (Ezra 1.1–11). The text is virtually identical with that in Ezra, although the inventory of the sacred vessels appears to be better preserved in 1 Esdras than in Ezra. **1**: *First year of Cyrus,* i.e. 538 B.C.

horses and cattle, and with a very great number of votive offerings from many whose hearts were stirred.

10 King Cyrus also brought out the holy vessels of the Lord that Nebuchadnezzar had carried away from Jerusalem and stored in his temple of idols. 11 When King Cyrus of the Persians brought these out, he gave them to Mithridates, his treasurer, 12 and by him they were given to Sheshbazzar, *g* the governor of Judea. 13 The number of these was: one thousand gold cups, one thousand silver cups, twenty-nine silver censers, thirty gold bowls, two thousand four hundred ten silver bowls, and one thousand other vessels. 14 All the vessels were handed over, gold and silver, five thousand four hundred sixty-nine, 15 and they were carried back by Sheshbazzar with the returning exiles from Babylon to Jerusalem.

16 In the time of King Artaxerxes of the Persians, Bishlam, Mithridates, Tabeel, Rehum, Beltethmus, the scribe Shimshai, and the rest of their associates, living in Samaria and other places, wrote him the following letter, against those who were living in Judea and Jerusalem:

17 "To King Artaxerxes our lord, your servants the recorder Rehum and the scribe Shimshai and the other members of their council, and the judges in Coelesyria and Phoenicia: 18 Let it now be known to our lord the king that the Jews who came up from you to us have gone to Jerusalem and are building that rebellious and wicked city, repairing its

market places and walls and laying the foundations for a temple. 19 Now if this city is built and the walls finished, they will not only refuse to pay tribute but will even resist kings. 20 Since the building of the temple is now going on, we think it best not to neglect such a matter, 21 but to speak to our lord the king, in order that, if it seems good to you, search may be made in the records of your ancestors. 22 You will find in the annals what has been written about them, and will learn that this city was rebellious, troubling both kings and other cities, 23 and that the Jews were rebels and kept setting up blockades in it from of old. That is why this city was laid waste. 24 Therefore we now make known to you, O lord and king, that if this city is built and its walls finished, you will no longer have access to Coelesyria and Phoenicia."

25 Then the king, in reply to the recorder Rehum, Beltethmus, the scribe Shimshai, and the others associated with them and living in Samaria and Syria and Phoenicia, wrote as follows:

26 "I have read the letter that you sent me. So I ordered search to be made, and it has been found that this city from of old has fought against kings, 27 that the people in it were given to rebellion and war, and that mighty and cruel kings ruled in Jerusalem and exacted tribute from Coelesyria and Phoenicia. 28 Therefore I have now issued orders to prevent

g Gk Sanabassaros

2.16–30: Opposition to the rebuilding of the temple and the city walls (Ezra 4.7–24). A misplaced account of opposition to rebuilding the walls of Jerusalem in the time of Artaxerxes I (464–424 B.C.). Cyrus was succeeded by Cambyses (529–521), who was followed by Darius I (521–485). Josephus (*Ant.* XI. ii.1–3) substitutes Cambyses for Artaxerxes, thus providing the correct sequence of Persian kings. The original location of the passage was probably between Ezra ch 10 and Neh ch 1. **16:** The name *Beltethmus* is a Greek transliteration of the Aramaic title of the office held by *Rehum;* the same mistake occurs in v. 25. **17:** The persons named are

officials of the Persian province called "Beyond the River" (Ezra 4.10), which included the lands of Syria, Phoenicia, and Palestine. *Rehum* is designated "the commander" in Ezra 4.8f.; the translation *recorder* is supported by Josephus.
2.20: The account differs considerably from that in Ezra 4.14, which contains no reference to the rebuilding of the *temple* at this point (compare Ezra 4.24, however, where work on the *temple* is said to have stopped).
2.25: *Rehum,* the governor is again identified as the *recorder* rather than as the commander of Persian forces in Samaria (Ezra 4.17). As in v. 16 the name *Beltethmus* is a

these people from building the city and to take care that nothing more be done 29 and that such wicked proceedings go no further to the annoyance of kings."

30 Then, when the letter from King Artaxerxes was read, Rehum and the scribe Shimshai and their associates went quickly to Jerusalem, with cavalry and a large number of armed troops, and began to hinder the builders. And the building of the temple in Jerusalem stopped until the second year of the reign of King Darius of the Persians.

3 Now King Darius gave a great banquet for all that were under him, all that were born in his house, and all the nobles of Media and Persia, 2 and all the satraps and generals and governors that were under him in the hundred twenty-seven satrapies from India to Ethiopia. 3 They ate and drank, and when they were satisfied they went away, and King Darius went to his bedroom; he went to sleep, but woke up again.

4 Then the three young men of the bodyguard, who kept guard over the person of the king, said to one another, 5 "Let each of us state what one thing is strongest; and to the one whose statement seems wisest, King Darius will give rich gifts and great honors of victo-

ry. 6 He shall be clothed in purple, and drink from gold cups, and sleep on a gold bed, *h* and have a chariot with gold bridles, and a turban of fine linen, and a necklace around his neck; 7 and because of his wisdom he shall sit next to Darius and shall be called Kinsman of Darius."

8 Then each wrote his own statement, and they sealed them and put them under the pillow of King Darius, 9 and said, "When the king wakes, they will give him the writing; and to the one whose statement the king and the three nobles of Persia judge to be wisest the victory shall be given according to what is written." 10 The first wrote, "Wine is strongest." 11 The second wrote, "The king is strongest." 12 The third wrote, "Women are strongest, but above all things truth is victor." *i*

13 When the king awoke, they took the writing and gave it to him, and he read it. 14 Then he sent and summoned all the nobles of Persia and Media and the satraps and generals and governors and prefects, 15 and he took his seat in the council chamber, and the writing was read in their presence. 16 He said, "Call

h Gk *on gold*   *i* Or *but truth is victor over all things*

---

transliteration of the Aramaic title of *Rehum* and is not the name of a third addressee. **30:** An erroneous reference (as also in Ezra 4.24) to the halting of work on the *temple*.

3.1–5.6: The three young bodyguards in the court of Darius. This famous story, found only in 1 Esdras among the several works attributed to Ezra, provides sufficient reason for the preservation of the book throughout the centuries. The story probably originated outside the Jewish community as a popular tale praising the relative strength of wine, kings, and women (the original order was perhaps kings, wine, and women). The praise of the strength of truth (4.33–41; compare 3.12) was added later in the transmission of the story, perhaps by a Greek-speaking editor (this part of the story has close parallels to Greek thought and literature). The author of 1 Esdras, adopting the story, needed only to identify the third youth with Zerubbabel (4.13) and to add a sequel to the tale, relating how Darius rewarded Zerubbabel by sup-

porting the rebuilding of Jerusalem and its temple (4.42–5.6). The version of the story found in Josephus (*Ant.* XI. iii.2–9) differs from the one given here in several particulars.

3.1–17a: The contest planned. 1–3: Apparently Darius' banquet was held at Susa, though the location is not explicitly mentioned. **2:** During Darius' reign (521–485 B.C.) there were actually only about twenty provinces (*satrapies*); this number was increased during Seleucid times (after 312 B.C.), and the total one *hundred twenty-seven* became conventional in later literature (Esth 1.1; Josephus, *Ant.* XI. iii.2). **4–12:** The three bodyguards decide upon a form of entertainment for the king that would bring riches and honor to one of them. According to Josephus (*Ant.* XI. iii.2) it was the king who proposed the contest.

3.13–17a: The entire court is assembled to hear the guardsmen defend their respective answers; such a scene is entirely consonant with court practices in the ancient world.

the young men, and they shall explain their statements." So they were summoned, and came in. 17 They said to them, "Explain to us what you have written."

Then the first, who had spoken of the strength of wine, began and said: 18 "Gentlemen, how is wine the strongest? It leads astray the minds of all who drink it. 19 It makes equal the mind of the king and the orphan, of the slave and the free, of the poor and the rich. 20 It turns every thought to feasting and mirth, and forgets all sorrow and debt. 21 It makes all hearts feel rich, forgets kings and satraps, and makes everyone talk in millions.*j* 22 When people drink they forget to be friendly with friends and kindred, and before long they draw their swords. 23 And when they recover from the wine, they do not remember what they have done. 24 Gentlemen, is not wine the strongest, since it forces people to do these things?" When he had said this, he stopped speaking.

4 Then the second, who had spoken of the strength of the king, began to speak: 2 "Gentlemen, are not men strongest, who rule over land and sea and all that is in them? 3 But the king is stronger; he is their lord and master, and whatever he says to them they obey. 4 If he tells them to make war on one another, they do it; and if he sends them out against the enemy, they go, and conquer mountains, walls, and towers. 5 They kill and are killed, and do not disobey the king's command; if they win the victory, they bring everything to the king—whatever spoil they take and everything else. 6 Likewise those who do not serve in the army or make war but till the soil; when-

ever they sow and reap, and bring some to the king; and they compel one another to pay taxes to the king. 7 And yet he is only one man! If he tells them to kill, they kill; if he tells them to release, they release; 8 if he tells them to attack, they attack; if he tells them to lay waste, they lay waste; if he tells them to build, they build; 9 if he tells them to cut down, they cut down; if he tells them to plant, they plant. 10 All his people and his armies obey him. Furthermore, he reclines, he eats and drinks and sleeps, 11 but they keep watch around him, and no one may go away to attend to his own affairs, nor may they disobey him. 12 Gentlemen, why is not the king the strongest, since he is to be obeyed in this fashion?" And he stopped speaking.

13 Then the third, who had spoken of women and truth (and this was Zerubbabel), began to speak: 14 "Gentlemen, is not the king great, and are not men many, and is not wine strong? Who is it, then, that rules them, or has the mastery over them? Is it not women? 15 Women gave birth to the king and to every people that rules over sea and land. 16 From women they came; and women brought up the very men who plant the vineyards from which comes wine. 17 Women make men's clothes; they bring men glory; men cannot exist without women. 18 If men gather gold and silver or any other beautiful thing, and then see a woman lovely in appearance and beauty, 19 they let all those things go, and gape at her, and with open mouths stare at her, and all prefer her to gold or silver or any other beautiful thing. 20 A man leaves his

j Gk *talents*

3.17b–24: In praise of the strength of wine. *Wine* is the great leveler in society; it takes away one's capacity for discernment and remembrance, overpowering king and commoner alike.

4.1–12: In praise of the strength of kings. The arbitrary power of oriental kings here portrayed is quite true to the actual situation in the ancient world. No polemic against kingship need be seen in the passage.

4.13–32: In praise of the strength of women. The third youth, identified for the first time as *Zerubbabel* (v. 13), depicts the strength of *women,* who give birth to kings, who receive from men the treasures won in warfare and heroic deeds, who can humiliate their masters, including kings, and yet are sought after and fawned upon by those whom they humiliate.

own father, who brought him up, and his own country, and clings to his wife. 21 With his wife he ends his days, with no thought of his father or his mother or his country. 22 Therefore you must realize that women rule over you!

"Do you not labor and toil, and bring everything and give it to women? 23 A man takes his sword, and goes out to travel and rob and steal and to sail the sea and rivers; 24 he faces lions, and he walks in darkness, and when he steals and robs and plunders, he brings it back to the woman he loves. 25 A man loves his wife more than his father or his mother. 26 Many men have lost their minds because of women, and have become slaves because of them. 27 Many have perished, or stumbled, or sinned because of women. 28 And now do you not believe me?

"Is not the king great in his power? Do not all lands fear to touch him? 29 Yet I have seen him with Apame, the king's concubine, the daughter of the illustrious Bartacus; she would sit at the king's right hand 30 and take the crown from the king's head and put it on her own, and slap the king with her left hand. 31 At this the king would gaze at her with mouth agape. If she smiles at him, he laughs; if she loses her temper with him, he flatters her, so that she may be reconciled to him. 32 Gentlemen, why are not women strong, since they do such things?"

33 Then the king and the nobles looked at one another; and he began to speak about truth: 34 "Gentlemen, are not women strong? The earth is vast, and heaven is high, and the sun is swift in its course, for it makes the circuit of the heavens and returns to its place in one day. 35 Is not the one who does these things great? But truth is great, and stronger than all things. 36 The whole earth calls upon truth, and heaven blesses her. All God's works[k] quake and tremble, and with him there is nothing unrighteous. 37 Wine is unrighteous, the king is unrighteous, women are unrighteous, all human beings are unrighteous, all their works are unrighteous, and all such things. There is no truth in them and in their unrighteousness they will perish. 38 But truth endures and is strong forever, and lives and prevails forever and ever. 39 With it there is no partiality or preference, but it does what is righteous instead of anything that is unrighteous or wicked. Everyone approves its deeds, 40 and there is nothing unrighteous in its judgment. To it belongs the strength and the kingship and the power and the majesty of all the ages. Blessed be the God of truth!" 41 When he stopped speaking, all the people shouted and said, "Great is truth, and strongest of all!"

42 Then the king said to him, "Ask what you wish, even beyond what is written, and we will give it to you, for you have been found to be the wisest. You shall sit next to me, and be called my Kinsman." 43 Then he said to the king,

k Gk All the works

4.29: The king's concubine *Apame*, daughter of Bartacus, cannot be identified.
4.33–41: In praise of the strength of truth. The strength of *truth*, an addition to the original story probably made prior to the story's adaptation to the Jewish author's purpose, is portrayed in imagery akin to the depiction of truth in Greek literature. The Jewish adapter of the story may have modified the original somewhat to make truth more nearly akin to Hebraic ideas of truth (firmness, reliability). The closing references to truth suggest that it is virtually equivalent to the will of God: "Blessed be the God of truth!" (v. 40). The audience responds (v. 41) with the declaration, "Great is truth, and strongest of all!" The Latin proverb "Magna est

veritas et praevalet" ("Great is truth, and it prevails") is the most famous line from the (Clementine) Vulgate text of 1 Esdras.
4.42–57: Zerubbabel's reward. Darius authorizes Zerubbabel to return to Jerusalem and rebuild the temple, with generous support from the Persian treasury. **43**: The historically improbable vow of Darius to rebuild Jerusalem and its temple upon his accession to the kingship is not otherwise attested; indeed, the author has already recounted Cyrus' proclamation authorizing the return of the exiles and the restoration of the temple vessels (2.1–15). **45**: *The Edomites* are credited with having burned the temple, contrary to 1.55 (see Ob 11–14).

"Remember the vow that you made on the day when you became king, to build Jerusalem, 44 and to send back all the vessels that were taken from Jerusalem, which Cyrus set apart when he began[l] to destroy Babylon, and vowed to send them back there. 45 You also vowed to build the temple, which the Edomites burned when Judea was laid waste by the Chaldeans. 46 And now, O lord the king, this is what I ask and request of you, and this befits your greatness. I pray therefore that you fulfill the vow whose fulfillment you vowed to the King of heaven with your own lips."

47 Then King Darius got up and kissed him, and wrote letters for him to all the treasurers and governors and generals and satraps, that they should give safe conduct to him and to all who were going up with him to build Jerusalem. 48 And he wrote letters to all the governors in Coelesyria and Phoenicia and to those in Lebanon, to bring cedar timber from Lebanon to Jerusalem, and to help him build the city. 49 He wrote in behalf of all the Jews who were going up from his kingdom to Judea, in the interest of their freedom, that no officer or satrap or governor or treasurer should forcibly enter their doors; 50 that all the country that they would occupy should be theirs without tribute; that the Idumeans should give up the villages of the Jews that they held; 51 that twenty talents a year should be given for the building of the temple until it was completed, 52 and an additional ten talents a year for burnt offerings to be offered on the altar every day, in accordance with the commandment to make seventeen offerings; 53 and that all who came from Babylonia to build the city should have their freedom, they and their children and all the priests who came. 54 He wrote also concerning their support and the priests' vestments in which[m] they were to minister. 55 He wrote that the support for the Levites should be provided until the day when the temple would be finished and Jerusalem built. 56 He wrote that land and wages should be provided for all who guarded the city. 57 And he sent back from Babylon all the vessels that Cyrus had set apart; everything that Cyrus had ordered to be done, he also commanded to be done and to be sent to Jerusalem.

58 When the young man went out, he lifted up his face to heaven toward Jerusalem, and praised the King of heaven, saying, 59 "From you comes the victory; from you comes wisdom, and yours is the glory. I am your servant. 60 Blessed are you, who have given me wisdom; I give you thanks, O Lord of our ancestors."

61 So he took the letters, and went to Babylon and told this to all his kindred. 62 And they praised the God of their ancestors, because he had given them release and permission 63 to go up and build Jerusalem and the temple that is called by his name; and they feasted, with music and rejoicing, for seven days.

l Cn: Gk *vowed*   *m* Gk *in what priestly vestments*

4.48–57: Darius magnificently supports the program outlined by Zerubbabel. The historical background is reflected more accurately in the decree issued by Darius after the governor of Samaria had complained about the rebuilding of the temple (Ezra 6.1–13; 1 Esd 6.23–34). The decree of Cyrus allowing the exiles to return and restore the temple and its cult (2.1–15) is no doubt historical, and Darius confirmed this decree (6.23–34); but Zerubbabel's return was hardly supported by Darius in the manner here portrayed. **4.58–60: Zerubbabel's prayer.** The language of this prayer is similar to a prayer of Daniel (Dan 2.20–23) and may be dependent upon it.
4.61–5.6: Preparations for the return. Zerubbabel journeys (perhaps from Susa) to Babylon and there recruits leaders for the returning exiles (5.4–6). The list of the leaders is hopelessly confused. *Jeshua* (5.5) is clearly the leading priest, and *Zerubbabel* is the hero of the story, not his son *Joakim.* In Neh 12.10, 26, Joakim appears as the son of Jeshua; 1 Chr 3.17–24 gives a different genealogy for Zerubbabel (where he is said to be a grandson of Jehoiachin).

5 After this the heads of ancestral houses were chosen to go up, according to their tribes, with their wives and sons and daughters, and their male and female servants, and their livestock. [2]And Darius sent with them a thousand cavalry to take them back to Jerusalem in safety, with the music of drums and flutes; [3]all their kindred were making merry. And he made them go up with them.

4 These are the names of the men who went up, according to their ancestral houses in the tribes, over their groups: [5]the priests, the descendants of Phinehas son of Aaron; Jeshua son of Jozadak son of Seraiah and Joakim son of Zerubbabel son of Shealtiel, of the house of David, of the lineage of Phares, of the tribe of Judah, [6]who spoke wise words before King Darius of the Persians, in the second year of his reign, in the month of Nisan, the first month.

7 These are the Judeans who came up out of their sojourn in exile, whom King Nebuchadnezzar of Babylon had carried away to Babylon [8]and who returned to Jerusalem and the rest of Judea, each to his own town. They came with Zerubbabel and Jeshua, Nehemiah, Seraiah, Resaiah, Eneneus, Mordecai, Beelsarus, Aspharasus, Reeliah, Rehum, and Baanah, their leaders.

9 The number of those of the nation and their leaders: the descendants of Parosh, two thousand one hundred seventy-two. The descendants of Shephatiah, four hundred seventy-two. [10]The descendants of Arah, seven hundred fifty-six. [11]The descendants of Pahathmoab, of the descendants of Jeshua and Joab, two thousand eight hundred twelve. [12]The descendants of Elam, one thousand two hundred fifty-four. The descendants of Zattu, nine hundred

forty-five. The descendants of Chorbe, seven hundred five. The descendants of Bani, six hundred forty-eight. [13]The descendants of Bebai, six hundred twenty-three. The descendants of Azgad, one thousand three hundred twenty-two. [14]The descendants of Adonikam, six hundred sixty-seven. The descendants of Bigvai, two thousand sixty-six. The descendants of Adin, four hundred fifty-four. [15]The descendants of Ater, namely of Hezekiah, ninety-two. The descendants of Kilan and Azetas, sixty-seven. The descendants of Azaru, four hundred thirty-two. [16]The descendants of Annias, one hundred one. The descendants of Arom. The descendants of Bezai, three hundred twenty-three. The descendants of Arsiphurith, one hundred twelve. [17]The descendants of Baiterus, three thousand five. The descendants of Bethlomon, one hundred twenty-three. [18]Those from Netophah, fifty-five. Those from Anathoth, one hundred fifty-eight. Those from Bethasmoth, forty-two. [19]Those from Kiriatharim, twenty-five. Those from Chephirah and Beeroth, seven hundred forty-three. [20]The Chadiasans and Ammidians, four hundred twenty-two. Those from Kirama and Geba, six hundred twenty-one. [21]Those from Macalon, one hundred twenty-two. Those from Betolio, fifty-two. The descendants of Niphish, one hundred fifty-six. [22]The descendants of the other Calamolalus and Ono, seven hundred twenty-five. The descendants of Jerechus, three hundred forty-five. [23]The descendants of Senaah, three thousand three hundred thirty.

24 The priests: the descendants of Jedaiah son of Jeshua, of the descendants of Anasib, nine hundred seventy-two. The descendants of Immer, one thousand and fifty-two. [25]The descendants of Pashur,

---

5.7–46: A list of the returning exiles (Ezra 2.1–70 and Neh 7.6–73a). The list in 1 Esdras differs from that in Ezra at many points, both as to names and numbers. The totals, however, are almost identical. The numbers of the priests and Levites are almost

identical in the three lists, an indication that priestly and levitical genealogies were more carefully preserved than the other lists.
5.24–25: Only four divisions of priests are given, while in 1 Chr ch 24 twenty-four divisions appear.

one thousand two hundred forty-seven. The descendants of Charme, one thousand seventeen.

26 The Levites: the descendants of Jeshua and Kadmiel and Bannas and Sudias, seventy-four. 27 The temple singers: the descendants of Asaph, one hundred twenty-eight. 28 The gatekeepers: the descendants of Shallum, the descendants of Ater, the descendants of Talmon, the descendants of Akkub, the descendants of Hatita, the descendants of Shobai, in all one hundred thirty-nine.

29 The temple servants: the descendants of Esau, the descendants of Hasupha, the descendants of Tabbaoth, the descendants of Keros, the descendants of Sua, the descendants of Padon, the descendants of Lebanah, the descendants of Hagabah, 30 the descendants of Akkub, the descendants of Uthai, the descendants of Ketab, the descendants of Hagab, the descendants of Subai, the descendants of Hana, the descendants of Cathua, the descendants of Geddur, 31 the descendants of Jairus, the descendants of Daisan, the descendants of Noeba, the descendants of Chezib, the descendants of Gazera, the descendants of Uzza, the descendants of Phinoe, the descendants of Hasrah, the descendants of Basthai, the descendants of Asnah, the descendants of Maani, the descendants of Nephisim, the descendants of Acuph, *n* the descendants of Hakupha, the descendants of Asur, the descendants of Pharakim, the descendants of Bazluth, 32 the descendants of Mehida, the descendants of Cutha, the descendants of Charea, the descendants of Barkos, the descendants of Serar, the descendants of Temah, the descendants of Neziah, the descendants of Hatipha.

33 The descendants of Solomon's servants: the descendants of Assaphioth, the descendants of Peruda, the descendants of Jaalah, the descendants of Lozon, the descendants of Isdael, the descendants of Shephatiah, 34 the descendants of Agia, the descendants of Pochereth-hazzebaim, the descendants of Sarothie, the descendants of Masiah, the descendants of Gas, the descendants of Addus, the descendants of Subas, the descendants of Apherra, the descendants of Barodis, the descendants of Shaphat, the descendants of Allon.

35 All the temple servants and the descendants of Solomon's servants were three hundred seventy-two.

36 The following are those who came up from Tel-melah and Tel-harsha, under the leadership of Cherub, Addan, and Immer, 37 though they could not prove by their ancestral houses or lineage that they belonged to Israel: the descendants of Delaiah son of Tobiah, and the descendants of Nekoda, six hundred fifty-two.

38 Of the priests the following had assumed the priesthood but were not found registered: the descendants of Habaiah, the descendants of Hakkoz, and the descendants of Jaddus who had married Agia, one of the daughters of Barzillai, and was called by his name. 39 When a search was made in the register and the genealogy of these men was not found, they were excluded from serving as priests. 40 And Nehemiah and Attharias *o* told them not to share in the holy things until a high priest should appear wearing Urim and Thummim. *p*

41 All those of Israel, twelve or more years of age, besides male and female ser-

---

n Other ancient authorities read *Acub* or *Acum*
o Or *the governor*   *p* Gk *Manifestation and Truth*

5.40: The name *Nehemiah* is not found in the lists in Ezra and Nehemiah; "the governor" (see note *o*) orders the community to await the appearance of a high priest before participating in the holy things. The name is an addition to the text, arising from the circumstance that Nehemiah served as governor of Judah under appointment by Artaxerxes I (Neh 5.14). *Urim and Thummim* are the sacred lots used by the priests to receive oracular decisions (Ex 28.30; Lev 8.8; Deut 33.8; 1 Sam 14.41). **41**: The total exceeds the sum of the several groups listed, it being assumed that others were present who are not specifically mentioned in the list.

vants, were forty-two thousand three hundred sixty; [42] their male and female servants were seven thousand three hundred thirty-seven; there were two hundred forty-five musicians and singers. [43] There were four hundred thirty-five camels, and seven thousand thirty-six horses, two hundred forty-five mules, and five thousand five hundred twenty-five donkeys.

44 Some of the heads of families, when they came to the temple of God that is in Jerusalem, vowed that, to the best of their ability, they would erect the house on its site, [45] and that they would give to the sacred treasury for the work a thousand minas of gold, five thousand minas of silver, and one hundred priests' vestments.

46 The priests, the Levites, and some of the people[q] settled in Jerusalem and its vicinity; and the temple singers, the gatekeepers, and all Israel in their towns.

47 When the seventh month came, and the Israelites were all in their own homes, they gathered with a single purpose in the square before the first gate toward the east. [48] Then Jeshua son of Jozadak, with his fellow priests, and Zerubbabel son of Shealtiel, with his kinsmen, took their places and prepared the altar of the God of Israel, [49] to offer burnt offerings upon it, in accordance with the directions in the book of Moses the man of God. [50] And some joined them from the other peoples of the land. And they erected the altar in its place, for all the peoples of the land were hostile to them and were stronger than they; and they offered sacrifices at the proper times and burnt offerings to the Lord morning and evening. [51] They kept the festival of booths, as it is commanded in the law, and offered the proper sacrifices every day, [52] and thereafter the regular offerings and sacrifices on sabbaths and at new moons and at all the consecrated feasts. [53] And all who had made any vow to God began to offer sacrifices to God, from the new moon of the seventh month, though the temple of God was not yet built. [54] They gave money to the masons and the carpenters, and food and drink [55] and carts[r] to the Sidonians and the Tyrians, to bring cedar logs from Lebanon and convey them in rafts to the harbor of Joppa, according to the decree that they had in writing from King Cyrus of the Persians.

56 In the second year after their coming to the temple of God in Jerusalem, in the second month, Zerubbabel son of Shealtiel and Jeshua son of Jozadak made a beginning, together with their kindred and the levitical priests and all who had come back to Jerusalem from exile; [57] and they laid the foundation of the temple of God on the new moon of the second

q Or *those who were of the people*
r Meaning of Gk uncertain

5.47–73: Work on the temple commences and is interrupted (Ezra 3.1–4.5; compare Josephus, *Ant.* XI. iv.1–3). This section is confused because the building of the temple is placed both in the reign of Cyrus (538–529 B.C.) and that of Darius (521–485 B.C.). A first return of exiles under Sheshbazzar and a second return under Zerubbabel and Jeshua have been merged. The true sequence of events is that Sheshbazzar returned to Judah shortly after 538 B.C., restored the sacrificial altar, resumed the cultic services, and laid the foundation of the temple. The work was halted until the return of additional exiles under Zerubbabel and Jeshua; when the work was resumed, opposition from Samaria, the capital of the province to which Judah belonged, quickly developed. Haggai and Zechariah encouraged the community to complete the temple, and work was begun once more; the temple was finally dedicated in 516 B.C. **47–55:** It is highly doubtful that Zerubbabel and Jeshua were involved in the initial work under Sheshbazzar; the events recorded here belong to the period of rebuilding begun in the second year of Darius, not Cyrus. **51:** The *festival of booths*, a harvest celebration, is observed for one week beginning on the fifteenth day of the seventh month (Lev 23.39). **54:** Minted *money* was in use in the Persian period. **56:** Apparently the *second year* of Cyrus is intended, but the second year of Darius is the correct date.

month in the second year after they came to Judea and Jerusalem. [58] They appointed the Levites who were twenty or more years of age to have charge of the work of the Lord. And Jeshua arose, and his sons and kindred and his brother Kadmiel and the sons of Jeshua Emadabun and the sons of Joda son of Iliadun, with their sons and kindred, all the Levites, pressing forward the work on the house of God with a single purpose.

So the builders built the temple of the Lord. [59] And the priests stood arrayed in their vestments, with musical instruments and trumpets, and the Levites, the sons of Asaph, with cymbals, [60] praising the Lord and blessing him, according to the directions of King David of Israel; [61] they sang hymns, giving thanks to the Lord, "For his goodness and his glory are forever upon all Israel." [62] And all the people sounded trumpets and shouted with a great shout, praising the Lord for the erection of the house of the Lord. [63] Some of the levitical priests and heads of ancestral houses, old men who had seen the former house, came to the building of this one with outcries and loud weeping, [64] while many came with trumpets and a joyful noise, [65] so that the people could not hear the trumpets because of the weeping of the people.

For the multitude sounded the trumpets loudly, so that the sound was heard far away; [66] and when the enemies of the tribe of Judah and Benjamin heard it, they came to find out what the sound of the trumpets meant. [67] They learned that those who had returned from exile were building the temple for the Lord God of Israel. [68] So they approached Zerubbabel

and Jeshua and the heads of the ancestral houses and said to them, "We will build with you. [69] For we obey your Lord just as you do and we have been sacrificing to him ever since the days of King Esarhaddon[s] of the Assyrians, who brought us here." [70] But Zerubbabel and Jeshua and the heads of the ancestral houses in Israel said to them, "You have nothing to do with us in building the house for the Lord our God, [71] for we alone will build it for the Lord of Israel, as Cyrus, the king of the Persians, has commanded us." [72] But the peoples of the land pressed hard[t] upon those in Judea, cut off their supplies, and hindered their building; [73] and by plots and demagoguery and uprisings they prevented the completion of the building as long as King Cyrus lived. They were kept from building for two years, until the reign of Darius.

6 Now in the second year of the reign of Darius, the prophets Haggai and Zechariah son of Iddo prophesied to the Jews who were in Judea and Jerusalem; they prophesied to them in the name of the Lord God of Israel. [2] Then Zerubbabel son of Shealtiel and Jeshua son of Jozadak began to build the house of the Lord that is in Jerusalem, with the help of the prophets of the Lord who were with them.

3 At the same time Sisinnes the governor of Syria and Phoenicia and Sathrabuzanes and their associates came to them and said, [4] "By whose order are you building this house and this roof and finishing all the other things? And who are the builders that are finishing these

---

[s] Gk *Asbasareth*   [t] Meaning of Gk uncertain

5.59–65: The author erroneously speaks of the temple's being built at this time; the ceremony described in Ezra 3.10–13 occurred when the foundation of the temple was laid. **66–73:** Enemies interrupt the work; they hear the sound of celebration, a detail not found in Ezra. **5.69:** Instead of *Esarhaddon,* Josephus (*Ant.* XI. iv.3) reads Shalmaneser (as in 2 Kings ch 17). **73:** The *two years* from the reign of Cyrus to that of Darius (compare 2.30) is a mistake; Ezra lacks this detail, although in

Ezra 4.24 the cessation of work until the time of Darius introduces a similar confusion. **6.1–7.15: The temple completed** (Ezra 4.24–6.22). Haggai and Zechariah encourage the resumption of work on the temple and succeed in gaining support for Zerubbabel and Jeshua (= Joshua; compare Hag 1.1–4; 2.1–4; Zech 4.9; 6.15). **6.3:** *Sisinnes* is Tattenai, governor of the province "Beyond the River"; *Sathrabuzanes* is Shetherbozenai (Ezra 5.3).

things?" [5] Yet the elders of the Jews were dealt with kindly, for the providence of the Lord was over the captives; [6] they were not prevented from building until word could be sent to Darius concerning them and a report made.

[7] A copy of the letter that Sisinnes the governor of Syria and Phoenicia, and Sathrabuzanes, and their associates the local rulers in Syria and Phoenicia, wrote and sent to Darius:

[8] "To King Darius, greetings. Let it be fully known to our lord the king that, when we went to the country of Judea and entered the city of Jerusalem, we found the elders of the Jews, who had been in exile, [9] building in the city of Jerusalem a great new house for the Lord, of hewn stone, with costly timber laid in the walls. [10] These operations are going on rapidly, and the work is prospering in their hands and being completed with all splendor and care. [11] Then we asked these elders, 'At whose command are you building this house and laying the foundations of this structure?' [12] In order that we might inform you in writing who the leaders are, we questioned them and asked them for a list of the names of those who are at their head. [13] They answered us, 'We are the servants of the Lord who created the heaven and the earth. [14] The house was built many years ago by a king of Israel who was great and strong, and it was finished. [15] But when our ancestors sinned against the Lord of Israel who is in heaven, and provoked him, he gave them over into the hands of King Nebuchadnezzar of Babylon, king of the Chaldeans; [16] and they pulled down the house, and burned it, and carried the people away captive to Babylon. [17] But in the first year that Cyrus reigned over the country of Babylonia, King Cyrus wrote that this house should be rebuilt. [18] And the holy vessels of gold and of silver, which Nebuchadnezzar had taken out of the house in Jeru-

salem and stored in his own temple, these King Cyrus took out again from the temple in Babylon, and they were delivered to Zerubbabel and Sheshbazzar[u] the governor [19] with the command that he should take all these vessels back and put them in the temple at Jerusalem, and that this temple of the Lord should be rebuilt on its site. [20] Then this Sheshbazzar, after coming here, laid the foundations of the house of the Lord that is in Jerusalem. Although it has been in process of construction from that time until now, it has not yet reached completion.' [21] Now therefore, O king, if it seems wise to do so, let search be made in the royal archives of our lord[v] the king that are in Babylon; [22] if it is found that the building of the house of the Lord in Jerusalem was done with the consent of King Cyrus, and if it is approved by our lord the king, let him send us directions concerning these things."

[23] Then Darius commanded that search be made in the royal archives that were deposited in Babylon. And in Ecbatana, the fortress that is in the country of Media, a scroll[w] was found in which this was recorded: [24] "In the first year of the reign of King Cyrus, he ordered the building of the house of the Lord in Jerusalem, where they sacrifice with perpetual fire; [25] its height to be sixty cubits and its width sixty cubits, with three courses of hewn stone and one course of new native timber; the cost to be paid from the treasury of King Cyrus; [26] and that the holy vessels of the house of the Lord, both of gold and of silver, which Nebuchadnezzar took out of the house in Jerusalem and carried away to Babylon, should be restored to the house in Jerusalem, to be placed where they had been."

[27] So Darius[x] commanded Sisinnes

---

u Gk *Sanabassarus*   v Other ancient authorities read *of Cyrus*   w Other authorities read *passage*   x Gk *he*

6.14: *A king of Israel,* namely Solomon. **18:** *Zerubbabel* is an addition; only Sheshbazzar is mentioned in Ezra 5.14 and in Josephus (*Ant.*

xi. iv.4). **23:** *Ecbatana* was the summer residence of Darius.

6.32: Ezra 6.11 prescribes that violators of

the governor of Syria and Phoenicia, and Sathrabuzanes, and their associates, and those who were appointed as local rulers in Syria and Phoenicia, to keep away from the place, and to permit Zerubbabel, the servant of the Lord and governor of Judea, and the elders of the Jews to build this house of the Lord on its site. 28 "And I command that it be built completely, and that full effort be made to help those who have returned from the exile of Judea, until the house of the Lord is finished; 29 and that out of the tribute of Coelesyria and Phoenicia a portion be scrupulously given to these men, that is, to Zerubbabel the governor, for sacrifices to the Lord, for bulls and rams and lambs, 30 and likewise wheat and salt and wine and oil, regularly every year, without quibbling, for daily use as the priests in Jerusalem may indicate, 31 in order that libations may be made to the Most High God for the king and his children, and prayers be offered for their lives."

32 He commanded that if anyone should transgress or nullify any of the things herein written, *y* a beam should be taken out of the house of the perpetrator, who then shall be impaled upon it, and all property forfeited to the king.

33 "Therefore may the Lord, whose name is there called upon, destroy every king and nation that shall stretch out their hands to hinder or damage that house of the Lord in Jerusalem.

34 "I, King Darius, have decreed that it be done with all diligence as here prescribed."

7 Then Sisinnes the governor of Coelesyria and Phoenicia, and Sathrabuzanes, and their associates, following the orders of King Darius, 2 supervised the holy work with very great care, assisting the elders of the Jews and the chief officers of the temple. 3 The holy work prospered, while the prophets Haggai and Zechariah prophesied; 4 and they completed it by the command of the Lord God of Israel. So with the consent of Cyrus and Darius and Artaxerxes, kings of the Persians, 5 the holy house was finished by the twenty-third day of the month of Adar, in the sixth year of King Darius. 6 And the people of Israel, the priests, the Levites, and the rest of those who returned from exile who joined them, did according to what was written in the book of Moses. 7 They offered at the dedication of the temple of the Lord one hundred bulls, two hundred rams, four hundred lambs, 8 and twelve male goats for the sin of all Israel, according to the number of the twelve leaders of the tribes of Israel; 9 and the priests and the Levites stood arrayed in their vestments, according to kindred, for the services of the Lord God of Israel in accordance with the book of Moses; and the gatekeepers were at each gate.

10 The people of Israel who came from exile kept the passover on the fourteenth day of the first month, after the priests and the Levites were purified together. 11 Not all of the returned captives were purified, but the Levites were all purified together, *z* 12 and they sacrificed the passover lamb for all the returned captives and for their kindred the priests and for themselves. 13 The people of Israel who had returned from exile ate it, all those who had separated themselves from the abominations of the peoples of the land and sought the Lord. 14 They also kept the festival of unleavened bread seven days, rejoicing before the Lord, 15 because he had changed the will of the king of the Assyrians concerning them,

y Other authorities read *stated above* or *added in writing*   *z* Meaning of Gk uncertain

---

the decree be impaled and their house be made a dunghill (2 Kings 10.27; Dan 2.5). **7.4**: *Artaxerxes* (see 8.1–9.36 n.) is erroneously named here (as also in Ezra 6.14); the name is omitted by Josephus because of the anachronism. **5**: The date intended is February–March, 516 B.C. **7–8**: Compare the account of the dedication of the first temple (1 Kings 8.5, 63). **9**: Compare Ezra 6.18. **7.13**: Contrary to Ezra 6.21 the account here seems to suggest that only the returned exiles participated in the passover. **15**: The expression *king of the Assyrians* may be used because the Persian empire comprised the for-

to strengthen their hands for the service of the Lord God of Israel.

8 After these things, when Artaxerxes, the king of the Persians, was reigning, Ezra came, the son of Seraiah son of Azariah son of Hilkiah son of Shallum ²son of Zadok son of Ahitub son of Amariah son of Uzzi son of Bukki son of Abishua son of Phineas son of Eleazar son of Aaron the high*a* priest. ³This Ezra came up from Babylon as a scribe skilled in the law of Moses, which was given by the God of Israel; ⁴and the king showed him honor, for he found favor before the king*b* in all his requests. ⁵There came up with him to Jerusalem some of the people of Israel and some of the priests and Levites and temple singers and gatekeepers and temple servants, ⁶in the seventh year of the reign of Artaxerxes, in the fifth month (this was the king's seventh year); for they left Babylon on the new moon of the first month and arrived in Jerusalem on the new moon of the fifth month, by the prosperous journey that the Lord gave them.*c* ⁷For Ezra possessed great knowledge, so that he omitted nothing from the law of the Lord or the commandments, but taught all Israel all the ordinances and judgments.

8 The following is a copy of the written commission from King Artaxerxes that was delivered to Ezra the priest and reader of the law of the Lord:

9 "King Artaxerxes to Ezra the priest and reader of the law of the Lord, greeting. ¹⁰In accordance with my gracious decision, I have given orders that those of the Jewish nation and of the priests and Levites and others in our realm, those who freely choose to do so, may go with you to Jerusalem. ¹¹Let as many as are so disposed, therefore, leave with you, just as I and the seven Friends who are my counselors have decided, ¹²in order to look into matters in Judea and Jerusalem, in accordance with what is in the law of the Lord, ¹³and to carry to Jerusalem the gifts for the Lord of Israel that I and my Friends have vowed, and to collect for the Lord in Jerusalem all the gold and silver that may be found in the country of Babylonia, ¹⁴together with what is given by the nation for the temple of their Lord that is in Jerusalem, both gold and silver for bulls and rams and lambs and what goes with them, ¹⁵so as to offer sacrifices on the altar of their Lord that is in Jerusalem. ¹⁶Whatever you and your kindred are minded to do with the gold and silver, perform it in accordance with the will of your God; ¹⁷deliver the holy vessels of the Lord that are given you for the use of the temple of your God that is in Jerusalem. ¹⁸And whatever else occurs to you as necessary for the temple of your God, you may provide out of the royal treasury.

19 "I, King Artaxerxes, have commanded the treasurers of Syria and Phoenicia that whatever Ezra the priest and reader of the law of the Most High God

---

a Gk *the first*   *b* Gk *him*   *c* Other authorities add *for him* or *upon him*

---

mer empire of Assyria. Josephus refers to the Persian king (*Ant.* XI. iv.8).

8.1–9.55: The history of Ezra (Ezra 7.1–10.44 and Neh 7.73–8.12). Ezra, whose name appears as author or central personality in 1 Esdras, is first introduced at this point in the document.

8.1–9.36: Ezra leads a group of exiles from Babylonia. The author ignores the work of Nehemiah (Neh chs 1–7), as Sirach ignores the work of Ezra (Sir 49.13). It is possible that Ezra came to Judea under Artaxerxes II (404–358 B.C.) rather than under Artaxerxes I (464–423 B.C.), but the sequence

Ezra (458–7 B.C.), Nehemiah (445–4 B.C.) is more probable. This sequence is presupposed in Ezra and Nehemiah.

8.1–7: Ezra identified. 1–2: The genealogy is briefer than that in Ezra 7.1–5. **6:** *The seventh year* of Artaxerxes I was 458 or 457 B.C. (If Ezra came in the seventh year of Artaxerxes II, the date would be 398 or 397 B.C.) **7:** Ezra comes specifically as a teacher of *the law of the Lord*.

8.8–24: The letter of Artaxerxes to Ezra (Ezra 7.12–26). **11:** *The seven Friends* or counselors of the king are referred to in Esth 1.14 and Herodotus, *Hist.* III. 84.

sends for, they shall take care to give him, [20]up to a hundred talents of silver, and likewise up to a hundred cors of wheat, a hundred baths of wine, and salt in abundance. [21]Let all things prescribed in the law of God be scrupulously fulfilled for the Most High God, so that wrath may not come upon the kingdom of the king and his sons. [22]You are also informed that no tribute or any other tax is to be laid on any of the priests or Levites or temple singers or gatekeepers or temple servants or persons employed in this temple, and that no one has authority to impose any tax on them.

23 "And you, Ezra, according to the wisdom of God, appoint judges and justices to judge all those who know the law of your God, throughout all Syria and Phoenicia; and you shall teach it to those who do not know it. [24]All who transgress the law of your God or the law of the kingdom shall be strictly punished, whether by death or some other punishment, either fine or imprisonment."

25 Then Ezra the scribe said,[d] "Blessed be the Lord alone, who put this into the heart of the king, to glorify his house that is in Jerusalem, [26]and who honored me in the sight of the king and his counselors and all his Friends and nobles. [27]I was encouraged by the help of the Lord my God, and I gathered men from Israel to go up with me."

28 These are the leaders, according to their ancestral houses and their groups, who went up with me from Babylon, in the reign of King Artaxerxes: [29]Of the descendants of Phineas, Gershom. Of the descendants of Ithamar, Gamael. Of the descendants of David, Hattush son of Shecaniah. [30]Of the descendants of Parosh, Zechariah, and with him a hundred fifty men enrolled. [31]Of the descendants

of Pahath-moab, Eliehoenai son of Zerahiah, and with him two hundred men. [32]Of the descendants of Zattu, Shecaniah son of Jahaziel, and with him three hundred men. Of the descendants of Adin, Obed son of Jonathan, and with him two hundred fifty men. [33]Of the descendants of Elam, Jeshaiah son of Gotholiah, and with him seventy men. [34]Of the descendants of Shephatiah, Zeraiah son of Michael, and with him seventy men. [35]Of the descendants of Joab, Obadiah son of Jehiel, and with him two hundred twelve men. [36]Of the descendants of Bani, Shelomith son of Josiphiah, and with him a hundred sixty men. [37]Of the descendants of Bebai, Zechariah son of Bebai, and with him twenty-eight men. [38]Of the descendants of Azgad, Johanan son of Hakkatan, and with him a hundred ten men. [39]Of the descendants of Adonikam, the last ones, their names being Eliphelet, Jeuel, and Shemaiah, and with them seventy men. [40]Of the descendants of Bigvai, Uthai son of Istalcurus, and with him seventy men.

41 I assembled them at the river called Theras, and we encamped there three days, and I inspected them. [42]When I found there none of the descendants of the priests or of the Levites, [43]I sent word to Eliezar, Iduel, Maasmas, [44]Elnathan, Shemaiah, Jarib, Nathan, Elnathan, Zechariah, and Meshullam, who were leaders and men of understanding; [45]I told them to go to Iddo, who was the leading man at the place of the treasury, [46]and ordered them to tell Iddo and his kindred and the treasurers at that place to send us men to serve as priests in the house of our Lord. [47]And by the mighty

d Other ancient authorities lack Then Ezra the scribe said

8.20: The *talent* was 75.5 U.S. pounds; the *cor* 6.5 bushels; and the *bath* about 6 gallons. **22:** Temple personnel are exempt from all taxes. **23–24:** Ezra is given authority to appoint judges throughout the entire province in order to maintain the Jewish law.

8.25–60: **Ezra leads the exiles to Jerusalem** (Ezra 7.27–8.30). **28–40:** The list of

those who returned differs in a few particulars from that found in Ezra 8.1–14.

8.41: *The river . . . Theras* (Ahava in Ezra 8.21) is probably a tributary of the Euphrates. **42–49:** Because neither priests nor Levites were among the group first assembled by Ezra, special measures had to be taken to secure the required number of both.

hand of our Lord they brought us competent men of the descendants of Mahli son of Levi, son of Israel, namely Sherebiah[e] with his descendants and kinsmen, eighteen; [48]also Hashabiah and Annunus and his brother Jeshaiah, of the descendants of Hananiah, and their descendants, twenty men; [49]and of the temple servants, whom David and the leaders had given for the service of the Levites, two hundred twenty temple servants; the list of all their names was reported.

[50] There I proclaimed a fast for the young men before our Lord, to seek from him a prosperous journey for ourselves and for our children and the livestock that were with us. [51]For I was ashamed to ask the king for foot soldiers and cavalry and an escort to keep us safe from our adversaries; [52]for we had said to the king, "The power of our Lord will be with those who seek him, and will support them in every way." [53]And again we prayed to our Lord about these things, and we found him very merciful.

[54] Then I set apart twelve of the leaders of the priests, Sherebiah and Hashabiah, and ten of their kinsmen with them; [55]and I weighed out to them the silver and the gold and the holy vessels of the house of our Lord, which the king himself and his counselors and the nobles and all Israel had given. [56]I weighed and gave to them six hundred fifty talents of silver, and silver vessels worth a hundred talents, and a hundred talents of gold, [57]and twenty golden bowls, and twelve bronze vessels of fine bronze that glittered like gold. [58]And I said to them, "You are holy to the Lord, and the vessels are holy, and the silver and the gold are vowed to the Lord, the Lord of our ancestors. [59]Be watchful and on guard until you deliver them to the leaders of the priests and the Levites, and to the heads of the ancestral houses of Israel, in Jerusalem, in the chambers of the house of our Lord." [60]So the priests and the Levites who took the silver and the gold and the vessels that had been in Jerusalem carried them to the temple of the Lord.

[61] We left the river Theras on the twelfth day of the first month; and we arrived in Jerusalem by the mighty hand of our Lord, which was upon us; he delivered us from every enemy on the way, and so we came to Jerusalem. [62]When we had been there three days, the silver and the gold were weighed and delivered in the house of our Lord to the priest Meremoth son of Uriah; [63]with him was Eleazar son of Phinehas, and with them were Jozabad son of Jeshua and Moeth son of Binnui,[f] the Levites. [64]The whole was counted and weighed, and the weight of everything was recorded at that very time. [65]And those who had returned from exile offered sacrifices to the Lord, the God of Israel, twelve bulls for all Israel, ninety-six rams, [66]seventy-two lambs, and as a thank offering twelve male goats—all as a sacrifice to the Lord. [67]They delivered the king's orders to the royal stewards and to the governors of Coelesyria and Phoenicia; and these officials[g] honored the people and the temple of the Lord.

[68] After these things had been done, the leaders came to me and said, [69]"The people of Israel and the rulers and the priests and the Levites have not put away

e Gk *Asbebias*   *f* Gk *Sabannus*   *g* Gk *they*

8.50: Fasting prior to an important undertaking was common (2 Chr 20.3; Esth 4.16; Jer 36.9). 58: *Holy* objects could be entrusted only to those who were *holy* themselves.
8.61–67: **Arrival in Jerusalem** (Ezra 8.31–36). The treasures are placed in the temple storehouses (*chambers,* v. 59), sacrifices are offered to God, and the king's orders delivered to the provincial officers; the latter have no choice but to obey.

8.68–9.36: **Mixed marriages in Judah** (Ezra 9.1–10.44). No sooner does Ezra arrive than he is presented with evidence that the community has been corrupted by mixed marriages. The older legislation had warned against marriage with the population of Canaan upon entrance into the land (Deut 7.3) but had not expressly forbidden mixed marriages. Strong warnings had been issued, however, against Israel's adopting the abomi-

from themselves the alien peoples of the land and their pollutions, the Canaanites, the Hittites, the Perizzites, the Jebusites, the Moabites, the Egyptians, and the Edomites. [70] For they and their descendants have married the daughters of these people, [h] and the holy race has been mixed with the alien peoples of the land; and from the beginning of this matter the leaders and the nobles have been sharing in this iniquity."

[71] As soon as I heard these things I tore my garments and my holy mantle, and pulled out hair from my head and beard, and sat down in anxiety and grief. [72] And all who were ever moved at [i] the word of the Lord of Israel gathered around me, as I mourned over this iniquity, and I sat grief-stricken until the evening sacrifice. [73] Then I rose from my fast, with my garments and my holy mantle torn, and kneeling down and stretching out my hands to the Lord [74] I said,

"O Lord, I am ashamed and confused before your face. [75] For our sins have risen higher than our heads, and our mistakes have mounted up to heaven [76] from the times of our ancestors, and we are in great sin to this day. [77] Because of our sins and the sins of our ancestors, we with our kindred and our kings and our priests were given over to the kings of the earth, to the sword and exile and plundering, in shame until this day. [78] And now in some measure mercy has come to us from you, O Lord, to leave to us a root and a name in your holy place, [79] and to uncover a light for us in the house of the Lord our God, and to give us food in the time of our servitude. [80] Even in our bondage we were not forsaken by our Lord, but he brought us into favor with the kings of the Persians, so that they have given us food [81] and glorified the temple of our Lord, and raised Zion from desolation, to give us a stronghold in Judea and Jerusalem.

[82] "And now, O Lord, what shall we say, when we have these things? For we have transgressed your commandments, which you gave by your servants the prophets, saying, [83] 'The land that you are entering to take possession of is a land polluted with the pollution of the aliens of the land, and they have filled it with their uncleanness. [84] Therefore do not give your daughters in marriage to their descendants, and do not take their daughters for your descendants; [85] do not seek ever to have peace with them, so that you may be strong and eat the good things of the land and leave it for an inheritance to your children forever.' [86] And all that has happened to us has come about because of our evil deeds and our great sins. For you, O Lord, lifted the burden of our sins [87] and gave us such a root as this; but we turned back again to transgress your law by mixing with the uncleanness of the peoples of the land. [88] Were you not angry enough with us to destroy us without leaving a root or seed or name? [89] O Lord of Israel, you are faithful; for we are left as a root to this day. [90] See, we are now before you in our iniquities; for we can no longer stand in your presence because of these things."

[91] While Ezra was praying and making his confession, weeping and lying on the ground before the temple, there gathered around him a very great crowd of men and women and youths from Jerusalem; for there was great weeping among the multitude. [92] Then Shecaniah son of Jehiel, one of the men of Israel,

---

h Gk *their daughters*   *i* Or *zealous for*

---

nable practices of the surrounding nations (Lev 18.24–30). During the exile Israel had been able to survive only on the basis of maintaining a relatively high level of racial integrity. The strict separation carried out by Ezra is therefore understandable; in the exile standards were probably higher on this issue than they were in Judah. (Nehemiah also faced the same problem; see Neh 10.28–30; 13.3, 23–30.)

8.74–90: Ezra's prayer (Ezra 9.6–15). Ezra speaks for the entire community, acknowledging the sin of all and the justice of their punishment by God. **82–85:** The prophetic books contain no such statement; the author may have in mind Lev 18.19–30.

called out, and said to Ezra, "We have sinned against the Lord, and have married foreign women from the peoples of the land; but even now there is hope for Israel. 93 Let us take an oath to the Lord about this, that we will put away all our foreign wives, with their children, 94 as seems good to you and to all who obey the law of the Lord. 95 Rise up[j] and take action, for it is your task, and we are with you to take strong measures." 96 Then Ezra rose up and made the leaders of the priests and Levites of all Israel swear that they would do this. And they swore to it.

9 Then Ezra set out and went from the court of the temple to the chamber of Jehohanan son of Eliashib, 2 and spent the night there; and he did not eat bread or drink water, for he was mourning over the great iniquities of the multitude. 3 And a proclamation was made throughout Judea and Jerusalem to all who had returned from exile that they should assemble at Jerusalem, 4 and that if any did not meet there within two or three days, in accordance with the decision of the ruling elders, their livestock would be seized for sacrifice and the men themselves[k] expelled from the multitude of those who had returned from the captivity.

5 Then the men of the tribe of Judah and Benjamin assembled at Jerusalem within three days; this was the ninth month, on the twentieth day of the month. 6 All the multitude sat in the open square before the temple, shivering because of the bad weather that prevailed. 7 Then Ezra stood up and said to them, "You have broken the law and married foreign women, and so have increased

the sin of Israel. 8 Now then make confession and give glory to the Lord the God of our ancestors, 9 and do his will; separate yourselves from the peoples of the land and from your foreign wives."

10 Then all the multitude shouted and said with a loud voice, "We will do as you have said. 11 But the multitude is great and it is winter, and we are not able to stand in the open air. This is not a work we can do in one day or two, for we have sinned too much in these things. 12 So let the leaders of the multitude stay, and let all those in our settlements who have foreign wives come at the time appointed, 13 with the elders and judges of each place, until we are freed from the wrath of the Lord over this matter."

14 Jonathan son of Asahel and Jahzeiah son of Tikvah[l] undertook the matter on these terms, and Meshullam and Levi and Shabbethai served with them as judges. 15 And those who had returned from exile acted in accordance with all this.

16 Ezra the priest chose for himself the leading men of their ancestral houses, all of them by name; and on the new moon of the tenth month they began their sessions to investigate the matter. 17 And the cases of the men who had foreign wives were brought to an end by the new moon of the first month.

18 Of the priests, those who were brought in and found to have foreign wives were: 19 of the descendants of Jeshua son of Jozadak and his kindred, Maaseiah, Eliezar, Jarib, and Jodan. 20 They

j Other ancient authorities read *as seems good to you." And all who obeyed the law of the Lord rose and said to Ezra, "Rise up*   *k* Gk *he himself*   *l* Gk *Thocanos*

8.91–9.36: The people repent and dismiss their foreign wives (Ezra 10.1–44). **9.4:** *The ruling elders* issue orders for the entire community to assemble within two or three days; Ezra is the religious, not the political, authority in the land. **7:** *The law,* i.e. Deut 7.3. **8:** To *give glory to the Lord* is to acknowledge themselves to be in the wrong (compare Josh 7.19).
9.11–13: Because of the severe winter

weather, it is agreed that the separation should take place in the local districts, and the multitude is dismissed. **16–17:** Three months are required to settle the cases, from the first of the *tenth month* (Tebet = December-January) to the first of the *first month* (Nisan = March-April). **18–36:** The list of those who put away foreign wives, including priests, Levites, and the laity. The list was probably preserved in the temple archives.

pledged themselves to put away their wives, and to offer rams in expiation of their error. 21 Of the descendants of Immer: Hanani and Zebadiah and Maaseiah and Shemaiah and Jehiel and Azariah. 22 Of the descendants of Pashhur: Elioenai, Maaseiah, Ishmael, and Nathanael, and Gedaliah, and Salthas.

23 And of the Levites: Jozabad and Shimei and Kelaiah, who was Kelita, and Pethahiah and Judah and Jonah. 24 Of the temple singers: Eliashib and Zaccur. *m* 25 Of the gatekeepers: Shallum and Telem. *n*

26 Of Israel: of the descendants of Parosh: Ramiah, Izziah, Malchijah, Mijamin, and Eleazar, and Asibias, and Benaiah. 27 Of the descendants of Elam: Mattaniah and Zechariah, Jezrielus and Abdi, and Jeremoth and Elijah. 28 Of the descendants of Zamoth: Eliadas, Eliashib, Othoniah, Jeremoth, and Zabad and Zerdaiah. 29 Of the descendants of Bebai: Jehohanan and Hananiah and Zabbai and Emathis. 30 Of the descendants of Mani: Olamus, Mamuchus, Adaiah, Jashub, and Sheal and Jeremoth. 31 Of the descendants of Addi: Naathus and Moossias, Laccunus and Naidus, and Bescaspasmys and Sesthel, and Belnuus and Manasseas. 32 Of the descendants of Annan, Elionas and Asaias and Melchias and Sabbaias and Simon Chosamaeus. 33 Of the descendants of Hashum: Mattenai and Mattattah and Zabad and Eliphelet and Manasseh and Shimei. 34 Of the descendants of Bani: Jeremai, Momdius, Maerus, Joel, Mamdai and Bedeiah and Vaniah, Carabasion and Eliashib and Mamitanemus, Eliasis, Binnui, Elialis, Shimei, Shelemiah, Nethaniah. Of the descendants of Ezora: Shashai, Azarel,

Azael, Samatus, Zambris, Joseph. 35 Of the descendants of Nooma: Mazitias, Zabad, Iddo, Joel, Benaiah. 36 All these had married foreign women, and they put them away together with their children.

37 The priests and the Levites and the Israelites settled in Jerusalem and in the country. On the new moon of the seventh month, when the people of Israel were in their settlements, 38 the whole multitude gathered with one accord in the open square before the east gate of the temple; 39 they told Ezra the chief priest and reader to bring the law of Moses that had been given by the Lord God of Israel. 40 So Ezra the chief priest brought the law, for all the multitude, men and women, and all the priests to hear the law, on the new moon of the seventh month. 41 He read aloud in the open square before the gate of the temple from early morning until midday, in the presence of both men and women; and all the multitude gave attention to the law. 42 Ezra the priest and reader of the law stood on the wooden platform that had been prepared; 43 and beside him stood Mattathiah, Shema, Ananias, Azariah, Uriah, Hezekiah, and Baalsamus on his right, 44 and on his left Pedaiah, Mishael, Malchijah, Lothasubus, Nabariah, and Zechariah. 45 Then Ezra took up the book of the law in the sight of the multitude, for he had the place of honor in the presence of all. 46 When he opened the law, they all stood erect. And Ezra blessed the Lord God Most High, the God of hosts, the Almighty, 47 and the multitude answered, "Amen." They lifted up their hands, and fell to the ground

m Gk *Bacchurus*   *n* Gk *Tolbanes*

9.20: An offering of a ram as a guilt offering (Ezra 10.19) was made *in expiation* of the sin. 22: *Gedaliah,* Greek "Ocidelos" (the parallel in Ezra 10.22 reads "Jozabad"; compare Ezra 10.18).
9.37–55: **Ezra's public reading of the law** (Neh 7.73–8.12). 37: *The new moon* or first day *of the seventh month* was a day of holy convocation (Lev 23.23–24; Num 29.1), the day of the New Year. 39: Ezra is not identi-

fied elsewhere as the *chief priest* (in Neh 8.2 he is called the priest). *The law of Moses* is either the present Pentateuch or (more probably) the major legal portions of it. 42: The *platform* erected for Ezra probably continued the tradition whereby kings would appear before the people to reaffirm the covenant law on the festal occasion at the turn of the year (compare 2 Chr 20.5; 23.13; 29.4).

and worshiped the Lord. 48Jeshua and Anniuth and Sherebiah, Jadinus, Akkub, Shabbethai, Hodiah, Maiannas and Kelita, Azariah and Jozabad, Hanan, Pelaiah, the Levites, taught the law of the Lord,° at the same time explaining what was read.

49 Then Attharatesᵖ said to Ezra the chief priest and reader, and to the Levites who were teaching the multitude, and to all, 50"This day is holy to the Lord"— now they were all weeping as they heard the law— 51"so go your way, eat the fat and drink the sweet, and send portions to those who have none; 52for the day is

holy to the Lord; and do not be sorrowful, for the Lord will exalt you." 53The Levites commanded all the people, saying, "This day is holy; do not be sorrowful." 54Then they all went their way, to eat and drink and enjoy themselves, and to give portions to those who had none, and to make great rejoicing; 55because they were inspired by the words which they had been taught. And they came together. q

o Other ancient authorities add *and read the law of the Lord to the multitude*   p Or *the governor*
q The Greek text ends abruptly: compare Neh 8.13

9.48: The Levites explained the law to the people, perhaps translating it (or its difficult portions) into Aramaic for those who may not have been familiar with Hebrew. **49:** *Attharates* is a corruption of "tirshatha," *governor,* in Neh 8.9. 1 Esdras does not intend to indicate that Nehemiah, whom some have identified with Attharates the governor, was a participant in the festivity (in Neh 8.9 the name of Nehemiah is an intrusion). **50–55:**

The people are to rejoice even though the words of the law cause them to recognize their sin. **55:** The book ends abruptly; originally it may have continued with the story of the great celebration of the festival of booths (Neh 8.13–18). This would have been a fitting conclusion to the work, since it begins with the account of Josiah's great passover celebration.

The Prayer of Manasseh

While the Prayer of Manasseh is considered deuterocanonical by Eastern Orthodox communions, it is not so considered by Jews, Protestants, or Roman Catholics. Since the Council of Trent it has been included in an appendix to the Latin Vulgate along with 3 and 4 Ezra (1 and 2 Esdras). In some manuscripts of the Greek Septuagint it stands immediately following the Psalter among a group of fifteen psalms or songs, under the heading "Odes," which, while not in the Psalter itself, are, with the exception of our Prayer and one other, found in some other book in the Old or New Testament (Ex 15, Deut 32, Luke 1, etc.). Most scholars think that it was originally composed in a semitizing Greek probably late in the first century B.C.

King Manasseh is presented in 2 Kings (21.1–18) as the worst possible sinner and the basic cause of the downfall of Judah. In 2 Chronicles, while his wicked deeds are not in any way denied, Manasseh is pictured as praying earnestly and humbly to God during exile. His prayer was heard, and God restored him to the throne in Jerusalem where he instigated a reform program of true worship of God (2 Chr 33.10–17). The account in 2 Chronicles ends with the comment that the whole account of his sins, his penitence, his prayer, God's answer, and his restoration had been written in the records of the seers (33.19). But 2 Chronicles fails to record the prayer. This lack would have been noted by many ancient readers of the biblical Chronicles account; our author filled the obvious gap.

The prayer is a classic of penitential devotion and even has literary value. The theology is consonant with that of early Judaism: God, though clearly the God of justice, is also the God of mercy and repentance. He is the God of those who repent (v. 13). This theme was important to the emerging theology of exilic and post-exilic Judaism, whose existence was always tenuous, living under one repressive régime after another in various parts of the world.

Manasseh, who as king had the power to do all the evil things that brought about Judah's fall, was in the Jewish mind sorely in need of redemption. If he was irredeemable there might be doubt about who could repent and be heard, in other words, doubt about God's measure of mercy being as great as God's measure of justice. God is not only Creator and Sustainer, but also Redeemer—compassionate, long-suffering and very merciful (v. 7). God, therefore, appointed repentance not for the righteous, but ordained it for sinners, even for Manasseh (v. 8).

1 O Lord Almighty,
  God of our ancestors,
  of Abraham and Isaac and Jacob
  and of their righteous offspring;
2 you who made heaven and
        earth
  with all their order;

3 who shackled the sea by your
        word of command,
  who confined the deep
  and sealed it with your terrible
        and glorious name;
4 at whom all things shudder,
  and tremble before your power,

5 for your glorious splendor cannot
   be borne,
   and the wrath of your threat to
      sinners is unendurable;
6 yet immeasurable and unsearchable
   is your promised mercy,
7 for you are the Lord Most High,
   of great compassion,
      long-suffering, and very
         merciful,
   and you relent at human suffering.
   O Lord, according to your great
      goodness
   you have promised repentance and
      forgiveness
   to those who have sinned against
      you,
   and in the multitude of your
      mercies
   you have appointed repentance for
      sinners,
   so that they may be saved.*ᵃ*
8 Therefore you, O Lord, God of
   the righteous,
   have not appointed repentance for
      the righteous,
   for Abraham and Isaac and Jacob,
      who did not sin against
      you,
   but you have appointed repentance
      for me, who am a sinner.
9 For the sins I have committed are
   more in number than the
      sand of the sea;
   my transgressions are multiplied,
      O Lord, they are
      multiplied!
   I am not worthy to look up and
      see the height of heaven
   because of the multitude of my
      iniquities.

10 I am weighted down with many
    an iron fetter,
    so that I am rejected*ᵇ* because of
       my sins,
    and I have no relief;
    for I have provoked your wrath
    and have done what is evil in your
       sight,
    setting up abominations and
       multiplying offenses.
11 And now I bend the knee of my
    heart,
    imploring you for your kindness.
12 I have sinned, O Lord, I have
    sinned,
    and I acknowledge my
       transgressions.
13 I earnestly implore you,
    forgive me, O Lord, forgive me!
    Do not destroy me with my
       transgressions!
    Do not be angry with me forever
       or store up evil for me;
    do not condemn me to the depths
       of the earth.
    For you, O Lord, are the God of
       those who repent,
14 and in me you will manifest your
       goodness;
    for, unworthy as I am, you will
       save me according to your
       great mercy,
15 and I will praise you continually
       all the days of my life.
    For all the host of heaven sings
       your praise,
    and yours is the glory forever.
       Amen.

ᵃ Other ancient authorities lack O Lord, according
. . . be saved   ᵇ Other ancient authorities read
so that I cannot lift up my head

**1–8: Invocation and ascription of
praise to God,** whose majesty is displayed in
creation (vv. 1–4), and whose mercy grants
repentance to sinners (vv. 6–8). **1:** *God of our
ancestors,* Ex 3.15–16; Dan 2.23; Acts 3.13. **2:**
All their order, splendor and orderly array. **3:**
Shackled the sea, Job 38.8–11. **7:** The second
part of this verse (*O Lord . . . may be saved*) is
preserved in the later Greek manuscripts and
in the Latin and Syriac versions. **8:** *Not . . . for
the righteous,* Mk 2.17; Lk 5.32; 1 Tim 1.15.
For me . . . a sinner, Lk 15.7; 18.13.

9–10: Personal confession of sin. For
the background see 2 Kings 21.1–18; 2 Chr
33.1–9.
11–15a: Supplication for pardon. 11:
Knee of my heart, an expression indicating special depth of feeling. See Joel 2.13. **12:** *I acknowledge my transgressions,* compare Ps 19.12.
13: *The depths of the earth,* probably Sheol or
Hades is meant (Ps 63.9; 88.5–6).
15b: Concluding doxology. *Host of
heaven,* multitude of angelic beings (2 Chr
18.18; Lk 2.13).

Psalm 151

Some manuscripts of the Masoretic text of the Hebrew Bible number the psalms in the Psalter sequentially up to 150. The oldest complete Masoretic manuscript of the Bible (Leningradensis), which forms the basis for all current translations into modern languages, numbers them only to 149, combining the "traditional" Ps 115 with 114. Those two psalms are also combined as Ps 113 in Greek Septuagint manuscripts (= "traditional" Ps 114), whereas "traditional" Ps 116 is divided into Pss 114 and 115 in Septuagint manuscripts.

In addition to these rather slight variations in the shape of the "traditional" Psalter, most Greek manuscripts of the Psalter have 151 psalms, the last not appearing in any Hebrew manuscript of the Psalter until the discovery in 1956 of a Psalter manuscript among the Dead Sea Scrolls, from Qumran Cave XI, designated 11QPs^a. The latter contains forty canonical psalms from the last third of the Masoretic or traditional Hebrew Psalter (not all in the traditional sequence) along with eight compositions not in other known Psalters, except for Ps 151 in the Septuagint, and Pss 151, 154 and 155, which are included in a Syriac Psalter. The Hebrew of Ps 151 is subject to more than one interpretation; this is especially the case in vv. 2b–4.

In codex Alexandrinus and most other Septuagint manuscripts Ps 151 is presented as an appendix to the Psalter with a superscription designating it "outside the number" (supposedly of the "traditional" 150 psalms); but it is attached to the Psalter itself and not included among the fifteen "Odes" that in some Septuagint manuscripts (notably codex Alexandrinus) are appended to the Greek Psalter after Ps 151. In codex Sinaiticus, one of the oldest and in some ways the most reliable and almost complete manuscript of the Septuagint, Ps 151 is included as an integral part of the Psalter, for which there is a subscription that reads "The 151 Psalms of David." A translation of the Hebrew text, made by J. A. Sanders, the original editor of the scroll, in *Discoveries in the Judaean Desert of Jordan,* Vol. IV (Oxford, 1965), is given here (with two slight modifications) for purposes of comparison with the Septuagint form of the psalm. It should be mentioned that the Hebrew script presents several palaeographical and philological uncertainties.

A Hallelujah of David the Son of Jesse

[1] Smaller was I than my brothers
  and the youngest of the sons of my father,
Yet he made me shepherd of his flock
  and ruler over his kids.

[2] My hands have made an instrument
  and my fingers a lyre;
And [so] have I rendered glory to the Lord,
  thought I, within my soul.

[3] The mountains do not witness to him,
  nor do the hills proclaim;
The trees have cherished my words
  and the flock my works.

[4] For who can proclaim and who can bespeak
  and who can recount the deeds of the Lord?
Everything has God seen,
  everything has he heard and he has heeded.

⁵He sent his prophet to anoint me,
  Samuel to make me great;
My brothers went out to meet him,
  handsome of figure and appearance.

⁶Though they were tall of stature
  and handsome by their hair,

The Lord God chose
  them not.

⁷But he sent and took me from behind the flock
  and anointed me with holy oil,
And he made me leader of his people
  and ruler over the people of his covenant.

In the line following the Hebrew text of this psalm another psalm (with its heading) begins, of which only two poorly preserved lines remain. Apparently they celebrate David's victory over Goliath; Sanders's translation is as follows:

> At the beginning of David's power after
>   the prophet of God had anointed him.
>
> ¹Then I [saw] a Philistine
>   uttering defiances from the r[anks of the
>   Philistines].

It thus appears that the Greek text of Ps 151 is a condensed recension of what was originally two separate psalms in Hebrew.

This psalm is ascribed to David as his own composition (though it is outside the number^a), after he had fought in single combat with Goliath.

¹ I was small among my brothers,
  and the youngest in my father's
    house;
I tended my father's sheep.

² My hands made a harp;
  my fingers fashioned a lyre.

³ And who will tell my Lord?
  The Lord himself; it is he who
    hears.^b

⁴ It was he who sent his messenger^c
  and took me from my father's
    sheep,

and anointed me with his
  anointing oil.

⁵ My brothers were handsome and
  tall,
but the Lord was not pleased
  with them.

⁶ I went out to meet the Philistine,^d
  and he cursed me by his idols.

⁷ But I drew his own sword;
  I beheaded him, and took away
    disgrace from the people of
    Israel.

a Other ancient authorities add *of the one hundred fifty* (psalms) b Other ancient authorities add *everything*; others add *me*; others read *who will hear me* c Or *angel* d Or *foreigner*

1: *Small . . . youngest*, 1 Sam 16.7 and 11. *Tended . . . sheep*, 1 Sam 16.11. One form of the Syriac version continues, "and I met a lion and also a wolf, and I killed them and tore them in pieces" (compare 1 Sam 17.34–36). **2**: *My hands made a harp*, 2 Chr 29.26. **4**: *Anointed me*, 1 Sam 16.13; Ps 89.20. *Took me from my father's sheep*, Ps 78.70. **5**: *The Lord was not pleased with them*, 1 Sam 16.7–10. **6**: *He cursed* . . . *by his idols*, 1 Sam 17.43. Certain manuscripts of the Old Latin, Arabic, and Ethiopic versions continue, with minor deviations: "And I slung three stones at him in the middle of his forehead, and laid him low by the might of the Lord." According to 1 Sam 17.49–50 David felled Goliath with only one stone. **7**: *His own sword*, 1 Sam 17.51.

3 Maccabees

The title of the book known as 3 Maccabees is a misnomer, for the contents deal not with the exploits of the Maccabean heroes, but with the struggles of Egyptian Jews who suffered under Ptolemy IV Philopator (221–203 B.C.), half a century prior to the Maccabean period with its persecution of Palestinian Jewry under Antiochus IV Epiphanes (175–164 B.C.). The book has been transmitted in manuscripts of the Greek Septuagint and the Syriac Peshitta, as well as in most manuscripts of the Armenian Bible. It is not, however, included in the Latin Vulgate. This may explain why the book has been accorded deuterocanonical status in Eastern Christendom (i.e. of lesser authority than canonical works), while both the Roman and Reformed Churches of the West regard it as apocryphal.

After a brief introduction, 3 Maccabees begins by describing the attempt of King Ptolemy of Egypt to enter the holy of holies in the Jerusalem temple. The desecration is averted by divine intervention in response to the prayer of the high priest Simon (1.1–2.24). Upon his return to Egypt, the king determines to wreak vengeance on the Jews for his humiliation in Jerusalem. He alters their civic status and attempts to impose upon them by force the pagan cult of Dionysus, promising to those who comply equal citizenship with the Alexandrians (2.25–33). The vast majority of Jews resist, and with great cruelty they are herded together to be registered, tortured, and put to death. Again through divine intervention, after forty days the registration remains incomplete because writing materials have been exhausted (3.1–4.21). A third miracle occurs in answer to the prayer of the aged priest Eleazar, and the Jews are spared from being trampled by a great herd of elephants (5.1–6.21). The king, struck with fear as the elephants turn back upon his own forces, repents and becomes the patron of the Jews. He addresses a letter of protection on their behalf to his provincial governors, and the Jews return to their homes in safety and with rejoicing (6.22–7.23).

The book was obviously written to console, exhort, and teach Egyptian Jews, who during the first century B.C. were frequently threatened by the efforts of Roman administrators to alter their civic status. The author intends to inspire faith in the providence of God (4.21) by recounting how Jews had been delivered from similar tribulations in the past.

The work was originally drawn up in Greek by an unknown Alexandrian Jew, sometime between the Battle of Raphia in 217 B.C. and the fall of the Jerusalem temple in A.D. 70. A likely date, considering its literary affinities with 2 Maccabees and the Letter of Aristeas, is the early first century B.C. The author has composed his work by using the familiar principles of concentric parallelism, and focusing on the miracle surrounding the registration in 4.14–21.

A: Ptolemy threatens to desecrate the temple [1.1–29]
  B: Simon's prayer of intercession (divine intervention) [2.1–24]
    C: Ptolemy's cruel treatment of the Jews [2.25–4.13]
      D: Thwarting the registration (divine intervention) [4.14–21]
    C': Ptolemy's cruel treatment of the Jews [5.1–51]
  B': Eleazar's prayer of intercession (divine intervention) [6.1–29]
A': Ptolemy delivers and defends the Jews [6.30–7.23]

The style of the book is pseudoclassical, utilizing many uncommon and poetical words. Sentences are awkwardly constructed and frequently repetitious. The author's exaggerated rhetoric aims to drive home his message that God remains faithful to his chosen people, to bless and preserve them throughout the vicissitudes of their experiences.

1 When Philopator learned from those who returned that the regions that he had controlled had been seized by Antiochus, he gave orders to all his forces, both infantry and cavalry, took with him his sister Arsinoë, and marched out to the region near Raphia, where the army of Antiochus was encamped. 2But a certain Theodotus, determined to carry out the plot he had devised, took with him the best of the Ptolemaic arms that had been previously issued to him,*a* and crossed over by night to the tent of Ptolemy, intending single-handed to kill him and thereby end the war. 3But Dositheus, known as the son of Drimylus, a Jew by birth who later changed his religion and apostatized from the ancestral traditions, had led the king away and arranged that a certain insignificant man should sleep in the tent; and so it turned out that this man incurred the vengeance meant for the king.*b* 4When a bitter fight resulted, and matters were turning out rather in favor of Antiochus, Arsinoë went to the troops with wailing and tears, her locks all disheveled, and exhorted them to defend themselves and their children and wives bravely, promising to give them each two minas of gold if they won the battle. 5And so it came about that the enemy was routed in the action, and many captives also were taken. 6Now that he had foiled the plot, Ptolemy*c* decided to visit the neighboring cities and encourage them. 7By doing this, and by endowing their sacred enclosures with gifts, he strengthened the morale of his subjects.

8 Since the Jews had sent some of their council and elders to greet him, to bring him gifts of welcome, and to congratulate him on what had happened, he was all the more eager to visit them as soon as possible. 9After he had arrived in Jerusalem, he offered sacrifice to the supreme God*d* and made thank-offerings and did what was fitting for the holy place.*e* Then, upon entering the place and being impressed by its excellence and its beauty, 10he marveled at the good order of the temple, and conceived a desire to enter the sanctuary. 11When they said that this was not permitted, because not even members of their own nation were allowed to enter, not even all of the priests, but only the high priest who was pre-eminent over all—and he only once a year—the king was by no means persuaded. 12Even after the law had been read to him, he did not cease to maintain that he ought to enter, saying, "Even if those men are deprived of this honor, I ought not to be." 13And he inquired why, when he entered every other temple,*f* no one there had stopped him.

a Or *the best of the Ptolemaic soldiers previously put under his command*   *b* Gk *that one*   *c* Gk *he*
d Gk *the greatest God*   *e* Gk *the place*   *f* Or *entered the temple precincts*

1.1–7: The battle of Raphia (217 B.C.). The abruptness with which the book opens and the use of the Greek conjunctive particle "de" indicate that the introduction to 3 Maccabees has not survived (see also 2.25 n.). **1**: Ptolemy IV *Philopator* was king of Egypt 221–203 B.C. *From those who returned,* fugitives who had escaped. *Antiochus* III, later called the Great, was king of Syria 223–187 B.C. *Raphia,* a city of Palestine, three miles from Gaza and not far from the Egyptian frontier. *Arsinoë,* Ptolemy's sister, who became his wife, was later put to death at the instigation of her husband. **2**: *Theodotus* had been chief commander of the Egyptian forces in Syria, but subsequently became disaffected and deserted to Antiochus III (so Polybius, v. 40). **3**: A *Dositheus* is mentioned in Hibeh papyrus 90 as priest of Alexander in 222 B.C. **5**: According to Polybius (v.86.5–6) Antiochus lost nearly 10,000 infantry, 300 cavalry, and 4,000 prisoners; Ptolemy 1,500 infantry and 700 cavalry.

1.8–15: Ptolemy attempts to enter the sanctuary at Jerusalem. 9: Reference to *the supreme God,* Greek "megistos theos," occurs frequently in 3 Maccabees (1.9, 16; 3.11; 4.16; 5.25; 7.22) as well as in 2 Maccabees (3.36). That the pagan Ptolemy should have offered *sacrifice* to the God of the Jews was not an unusual practice in an age of religious syncretism. *The holy place,* a surrogate for "the temple" in 3 Maccabees and other Jewish literature. **10**: Ptolemy's eagerness to inspect the interior of the temple may have been motivated by his curiosity concerning its architecture, for he considered himself a con-

¹⁴And someone answered thoughtlessly that it was wrong to take that as a portent.*g* ¹⁵"But since this has happened," the king *h* said, "why should not I at least enter, whether they wish it or not?"

¹⁶ Then the priests in all their vestments prostrated themselves and entreated the supreme God *i* to aid in the present situation and to avert the violence of this evil design, and they filled the temple with cries and tears; ¹⁷those who remained behind in the city were agitated and hurried out, supposing that something mysterious was occurring. ¹⁸Young women who had been secluded in their chambers rushed out with their mothers, sprinkled their hair with dust, *j* and filled the streets with groans and lamentations. ¹⁹Those women who had recently been arrayed for marriage abandoned the bridal chambers *k* prepared for wedded union, and, neglecting proper modesty, in a disorderly rush flocked together in the city. ²⁰Mothers and nurses abandoned even newborn children here and there, some in houses and some in the streets, and without a backward look they crowded together at the most high temple. ²¹Various were the supplications of those gathered there because of what the king was profanely plotting. ²²In addition, the bolder of the citizens would not tolerate the completion of his plans or the fulfillment of his intended purpose. ²³They shouted to their compatriots to take arms and die courageously for the ancestral law, and created a considerable disturbance in the holy place; *l* and being barely restrained by the old men and the elders, *m* they resorted to the same

posture of supplication as the others. ²⁴Meanwhile the crowd, as before, was engaged in prayer, ²⁵while the elders near the king tried in various ways to change his arrogant mind from the plan that he had conceived. ²⁶But he, in his arrogance, took heed of nothing, and began now to approach, determined to bring the aforesaid plan to a conclusion. ²⁷When those who were around him observed this, they turned, together with our people, to call upon him who has all power to defend them in the present trouble and not to overlook this unlawful and haughty deed. ²⁸The continuous, vehement, and concerted cry of the crowds *n* resulted in an immense uproar; ²⁹for it seemed that not only the people but also the walls and the whole earth around echoed, because indeed all at that time *o* preferred death to the profanation of the place.

2 Then the high priest Simon, facing the sanctuary, bending his knees and extending his hands with calm dignity, prayed as follows: *p* ²"Lord, Lord, king of the heavens, and sovereign of all creation, holy among the holy ones, the only ruler, almighty, give attention to us who are suffering grievously from an impious and profane man, puffed up in his audacity and power. ³For you, the

---

g Or *to boast of this*   *h* Gk *he*   *i* Gk *the greatest God*   *j* Other ancient authorities add *and ashes*   *k* Or *the canopies*   *l* Gk *the place* *m* Other ancient authorities read *priests* *n* Other ancient authorities read *vehement cry of the assembled crowds*   *o* Other ancient authorities lack *at that time*   *p* Other ancient authorities lack verse 1

---

noisseur of the arts. **11:** *High priest . . . once a year,* Ex 30.10; Lev 16.2, 11–12, 15, 34; Heb 9.7; Josephus, *Ant.* XII.iii.3. **1.16–29: Jewish reaction to Ptolemy's determination to enter the sanctuary.** It is possible that because of religious superstition many regarded Ptolemy's desire as an evil omen of something calamitous that would befall them. **18:** *Young women,* 2 Macc 3.19. **19:** *Bridal chambers,* Joel 2.16; 2 Esd 16.33, 34; Bar 2.23. **21:** *Various* with respect to the persons offering prayer. **23:** *Die courageously for*

the ancestral law, 1 Macc 2.40; 3.21; 13.3–4; 2 Macc 8.21.

2.1–20: The prayer of Simon, the high priest. This was probably Simon II, son of Onias II and high priest about 219–196 B.C. (see Sir 50.1 n.). The prayer is in a classic Jewish form that, like Eleazar's prayer in 6.1–15, follows the pattern of Pss 105 and 106 in addressing God in terms of his power, glory, and great works reflected in historical deliverances of Israel. **2:** *Holy among the holy ones,* Isa 57.15 LXX. **3:** Ex 18.11; Ps 31.23. **4:** *Giants,*

creator of all things and the governor of all, are a just Ruler, and you judge those who have done anything in insolence and arrogance. ⁴ You destroyed those who in the past committed injustice, among whom were even giants who trusted in their strength and boldness, whom you destroyed by bringing on them a boundless flood. ⁵ You consumed with fire and sulfur the people of Sodom who acted arrogantly, who were notorious for their vices;^q and you made them an example to those who should come afterward. ⁶ You made known your mighty power by inflicting many and varied punishments on the audacious Pharaoh who had enslaved your holy people Israel. ⁷ And when he pursued them with chariots and a mass of troops, you overwhelmed him in the depths of the sea, but carried through safely those who had put their confidence in you, the Ruler over the whole creation. ⁸ And when they had seen works of your hands, they praised you, the Almighty. ⁹ You, O King, when you had created the boundless and immeasurable earth, chose this city and sanctified this place for your name, though you have no need of anything; and when you had glorified it by your magnificent manifestation,^r you made it a firm foundation for the glory of your great and honored name. ¹⁰ And because you love the house of Israel, you promised that if we should have reverses and tribulation should overtake us, you would listen to our petition when we come to this place and pray. ¹¹ And indeed you are faithful and true.

¹² And because oftentimes when our fathers were oppressed you helped them in their humiliation, and rescued them from great evils, ¹³ see now, O holy King, that because of our many and great sins we are crushed with suffering, subjected to our enemies, and overtaken by helplessness. ¹⁴ In our downfall this audacious and profane man undertakes to violate the holy place on earth dedicated to your glorious name. ¹⁵ For your dwelling is the heaven of heavens, unapproachable by human beings. ¹⁶ But because you graciously bestowed your glory on your people Israel, you sanctified this place. ¹⁷ Do not punish us for the defilement committed by these men, or call us to account for this profanation, otherwise the transgressors will boast in their wrath and exult in the arrogance of their tongue, saying, ¹⁸ 'We have trampled down the house of the sanctuary as the houses of the abominations are trampled down.' ¹⁹ Wipe away our sins and disperse our errors, and reveal your mercy at this hour. ²⁰ Speedily let your mercies overtake us, and put praises in the mouth of those who are downcast and broken in spirit, and give us peace."

21 Thereupon God, who oversees all things, the first Father of all, holy among the holy ones, having heard the lawful supplication, scourged him who had exalted himself in insolence and audacity. ²² He shook him on this side and that as a reed is shaken by the wind, so that he lay helpless on the ground and, besides being paralyzed in his limbs, was unable

q Other ancient authorities read *secret in their vices*   *r* Or *epiphany*

Jdt 16.7; Wis 14.6; Sir 16.7; Bar 3.26; 1 Enoch 7.2; 15.8. **5**: *Sodom,* Gen 19.24; Deut 29.23; Wis 10.7. *An example,* 2 Pet 2.6.

2.6: *Power,* Ex 9.16; Rom 9.17. *Varied punishments,* Ex chs 5–12. *Your holy people Israel,* Ex 19.6; 1 Pet 2.9. **7**: *Overwhelmed him,* Ex 14.21–28. **8**: *They praised,* Ex 15.1–21; Wis 19.8–9; 1 Macc 4.9. **9**: *Boundless and immeasurable earth,* Bar 3.24–25. *This city,* Jerusalem. *Place,* see 1.9 n.; 1 Kings 9.3. *No need of anything,* Acts 17.25; 2 Macc 14.35–36. **10**: *Promised . . . you would listen,* Deut 4.30; 30.1–6; 1 Kings 8.33–34, 48–50. **12**: *Our fathers . . .*

you . . . rescued, 1 Sam 12.10–11; Ps 22.4–5; 106.43; Neh 9.28.

2.14: *Glorious name,* Jdt 9.8. **15**: *The heaven of heavens,* 1 Kings 8.27; Isa 66.1. *Unapproachable by human beings,* Prov 30.4; Isa 57.15; Bar 3.29. **18**: *Trampled down,* Isa 10.10–11; Dan 8.13. **19**: *Wipe away our sins,* Ps 51.2, 9. **20**: *Mercies,* Ps 79.8, 13. **2.21–24**: **The punishment of Ptolemy.** **21**: *Holy ones,* see Isa 57.15 LXX. **22**: *Paralyzed,* compare the punishment of Heliodorus (2 Macc 3.22–30) and of Antiochus (2 Macc 9.4–7). **23**: *Friends,* the higher officers and

even to speak, since he was smitten[s] by a righteous judgment. 23 Then both friends and bodyguards, seeing the severe punishment that had overtaken him, and fearing that he would lose his life, quickly dragged him out, panic-stricken in their exceedingly great fear. 24 After a while he recovered, and though he had been punished, he by no means repented, but went away uttering bitter threats.

25 When he arrived in Egypt, he increased in his deeds of malice, abetted by the previously mentioned drinking companions and comrades, who were strangers to everything just. 26 He was not content with his uncounted licentious deeds, but even continued with such audacity that he framed evil reports in the various localities; and many of his friends, intently observing the king's purpose, themselves also followed his will. 27 He proposed to inflict public disgrace on the Jewish community,[t] and he set up a stone[u] on the tower in the courtyard with this inscription: 28 "None of those who do not sacrifice shall enter their sanctuaries, and all Jews shall be subjected to a registration involving poll tax and to the status of slaves. Those who object to this are to be taken by force and put to death; 29 those who are registered are also to be branded on their bodies by fire with the ivy-leaf symbol of Dionysus, and they shall also be reduced to their former limited status." 30 In order that he might not appear to be an enemy of all, he inscribed below: "But if any of them prefer to join those who have been initiated into

the mysteries, they shall have equal citizenship with the Alexandrians."

31 Now some, however, with an obvious abhorrence of the price to be exacted for maintaining the religion of their city,[v] readily gave themselves up, since they expected to enhance their reputation by their future association with the king. 32 But the majority acted firmly with a courageous spirit and did not abandon their religion; and by paying money in exchange for life they confidently attempted to save themselves from the registration. 33 They remained resolutely hopeful of obtaining help, and they abhorred those who separated themselves from them, considering them to be enemies of the Jewish nation,[t] and depriving them of companionship and mutual help.

3 When the impious king comprehended this situation, he became so infuriated that not only was he enraged against those Jews who lived in Alexandria, but was still more bitterly hostile toward those in the countryside; and he ordered that all should promptly be gathered into one place, and put to death by the most cruel means. 2 While these matters were being arranged, a hostile rumor was circulated against the Jewish nation by some who conspired to do them ill, a pretext being given by a report that they hindered others[w] from the observance of their customs. 3 The Jews, however, con-

s Other ancient authorities read *pierced*
t Gk *the nation*   u Gk *stele*   v Meaning of Gk uncertain   w Gk *them*

---

courtiers of the king (see 4 Macc 8.5 n.). *Lose his life,* 2 Macc 3.31. **24:** *By no means repented,* 2 Macc 9.7.

2.25–33: Hostile measures against the Jews of Alexandria. 25: Inasmuch as these *companions* have not, in fact, been *previously mentioned* in the present text of 3 Maccabees, we have additional evidence that the opening section has been lost (see 1.1–7 n.). **26:** *Friends,* see v. 23 n. **28:** *Registration,* a rare Greek word ("laographia"), which has been found in Greek papyri from Egypt, refers to a list of all people of the lower classes and of

the slaves. **29:** Such branding in honor of a deity was not uncommon in ancient times (compare Rev 7.3; 13.16–17). According to 2 Macc 6.7 Antiochus introduced the worship of Dionysus into Jerusalem. **32:** *Paying money,* as bribes. **33:** *Depriving them of companionship,* 2 Jn 10–11.

3.1–10: The Jews and their neighbors. 1: The distinction between Jews in *Alexandria* and those in the *countryside* is made also in 4.11–12. **2:** The *rumor* (Esth 3.8) maliciously represents the Jews as hostile to the best interests of the state. **4:** *Separateness with respect to*

tinued to maintain goodwill and unswerving loyalty toward the dynasty; 4 but because they worshiped God and conducted themselves by his law, they kept their separateness with respect to foods. For this reason they appeared hateful to some; 5 but since they adorned their style of life with the good deeds of upright people, they were established in good repute with everyone. 6 Nevertheless those of other races paid no heed to their good service to their nation, which was common talk among all; 7 instead they gossiped about the differences in worship and foods, alleging that these people were loyal neither to the king nor to his authorities, but were hostile and greatly opposed to his government. So they attached no ordinary reproach to them.

8 The Greeks in the city, though wronged in no way, when they saw an unexpected tumult around these people and the crowds that suddenly were forming, were not strong enough to help them, for they lived under tyranny. They did try to console them, being grieved at the situation, and expected that matters would change; 9 for such a great community ought not be left to its fate when it had committed no offense. 10 And already some of their neighbors and friends and business associates had taken some of them aside privately and were pledging to protect them and to exert more earnest efforts for their assistance.

11 Then the king, boastful of his present good fortune, and not considering the might of the supreme God, *x* but assuming that he would persevere constantly in his same purpose, wrote this letter against them:

12 "King Ptolemy Philopator to his generals and soldiers in Egypt and all its districts, greetings and good health:

13 "I myself and our government are faring well. 14 When our expedition took place in Asia, as you yourselves know, it was brought to conclusion, according to plan, by the gods' deliberate alliance with us in battle, 15 and we considered that we should not rule the nations inhabiting Coelesyria and Phoenicia by the power of the spear, but should cherish them with clemency and great benevolence, gladly treating them well. 16 And when we had granted very great revenues to the temples in the cities, we came on to Jerusalem also, and went up to honor the temple of those wicked people, who never cease from their folly. 17 They accepted our presence by word, but insincerely by deed, because when we proposed to enter their inner temple and honor it with magnificent and most beautiful offerings, 18 they were carried away by their traditional arrogance, and excluded us from entering; but they were spared the exercise of our power because of the benevolence that we have toward all. 19 By maintaining their manifest ill-will toward us, they become the only people among all nations who hold their heads high in defiance of kings and their own benefactors, and are unwilling to regard any action as sincere.

20 "But we, when we arrived in Egypt victorious, accommodated ourselves to their folly and did as was proper, since we treat all nations with benevolence. 21 Among other things, we made known to all our amnesty toward their compatriots here, both because of their

---

x Gk *the greatest God*

---

foods, for a defense of the observance of Jewish dietary rules, see the *Letter of Aristeas,* §§128–166. **5**: Deut 4.5–6; Col 4.5; 1 Thess 4.12. **7**: For similar charges see Esth 3.8; Add Esth 13.4–5. **8**: *The Greeks,* the nobler, cultivated class, in distinction from *those of other races* (v. 6).

3.11–30: **Ptolemy orders the arrest of all Jews in his kingdom. 11**: *Assuming that he*

would persevere, a reference to the calamity that came upon him by which he forgot his own previous commands (5.27–28).

3.15: *Benevolence,* Greek "philanthropia" (see vv. 18, 20), was regarded as a major political virtue during the Hellenistic (and Byzantine) period. **18**: *Excluded,* 1.10–12. **21**: For the confidence placed in Jews, see 6.25 and Josephus, *Ant.* XIX.v.2.

alliance with us and the myriad affairs liberally entrusted to them from the beginning; and we ventured to make a change, by deciding both to deem them worthy of Alexandrian citizenship and to make them participants in our regular religious rites. *y* 22 But in their innate malice they took this in a contrary spirit, and disdained what is good. Since they incline constantly to evil, 23 they not only spurn the priceless citizenship, but also both by speech and by silence they abominate those few among them who are sincerely disposed toward us; in every situation, in accordance with their infamous way of life, they secretly suspect that we may soon alter our policy. 24 Therefore, fully convinced by these indications that they are ill-disposed toward us in every way, we have taken precautions so that, if a sudden disorder later arises against us, we shall not have these impious people behind our backs as traitors and barbarous enemies. 25 Therefore we have given orders that, as soon as this letter arrives, you are to send to us those who live among you, together with their wives and children, with insulting and harsh treatment, and bound securely with iron fetters, to suffer the sure and shameful death that befits enemies. 26 For when all of these have been punished, we are sure that for the remaining time the government will be established for ourselves in good order and in the best state. 27 But those who shelter any of the Jews, whether old people or children or even infants, will be tortured to death with the most hateful torments, together with their families. 28 Any who are willing to give information will receive the property of those who incur the punishment, and also two thousand drachmas from the royal treasury, and will be awarded their freedom. *z* 29 Every place detected sheltering a Jew is to be made unapproachable and burned with fire, and shall become useless for all time to any mortal creature." 30 The letter was written in the above form.

4 In every place, then, where this decree arrived, a feast at public expense was arranged for the Gentiles with shouts and gladness, for the inveterate enmity that had long ago been in their minds was now made evident and outspoken. 2 But among the Jews there was incessant mourning, lamentation, and tearful cries; everywhere their hearts were burning, and they groaned because of the unexpected destruction that had suddenly been decreed for them. 3 What district or city, or what habitable place at all, or what streets were not filled with mourning and wailing for them? 4 For with such a harsh and ruthless spirit were they being sent off, all together, by the generals in the several cities, that at the sight of their unusual punishments, even some of their enemies, perceiving the common object of pity before their eyes, reflected on the uncertainty of life and shed tears at the most miserable expulsion of these people. 5 For a multitude of gray-headed old men, sluggish and bent with age, was being led away, forced to march at a swift pace by the violence with which they were driven in such a shameful manner. 6 And young women who had just entered the bridal chamber *a* to share married life exchanged joy for wailing, their myrrh-perfumed hair sprinkled with ashes, and were carried away unveiled, all together raising a lament instead of a wedding song, as they were torn by the harsh treatment of the heathen. *b* 7 In bonds and in public view they were violently dragged along as far

y Other ancient authorities read *partners of our regular priests*   z Gk *crowned with freedom*   a Or *the canopy*   b Other ancient authorities read *as though torn by heathen whelps*

3.24: *Behind our backs,* Ex 1.10. **28:** *Awarded their freedom,* another rendering is "crowned at the Eleutheria" (a festival of Dionysus; see 2.29 n.). **29:** *Useless for all time,* Add Esth 16.24.
4.1–21: The Jews brought to Alexan- dria and imprisoned. **1:** *Enmity* on the part of native-born Egyptians for the Jews is assumed in 3 Maccabees; contrast 3.8. **2:** *Mourning, lamentation, and tearful cries,* Esth 4.3. **4:** *Unusual punishments,* 2 Macc 9.6. **6:** *Young women,* 1 Macc 1.26–27.

as the place of embarkation. [8] Their husbands, in the prime of youth, their necks encircled with ropes instead of garlands, spent the remaining days of their marriage festival in lamentations instead of good cheer and youthful revelry, seeing death immediately before them. [c] [9] They were brought on board like wild animals, driven under the constraint of iron bonds; some were fastened by the neck to the benches of the boats, others had their feet secured by unbreakable fetters, [10] and in addition they were confined under a solid deck, so that, with their eyes in total darkness, they would undergo treatment befitting traitors during the whole voyage.

[11] When these people had been brought to the place called Schedia, and the voyage was concluded as the king had decreed, he commanded that they should be enclosed in the hippodrome that had been built with a monstrous perimeter wall in front of the city, and that was well suited to make them an obvious spectacle to all coming back into the city and to those from the city [d] going out into the country, so that they could neither communicate with the king's forces nor in any way claim to be inside the circuit of the city. [e] [12] And when this had happened, the king, hearing that the Jews' compatriots from the city frequently went out in secret to lament bitterly the ignoble misfortune of their kindred, [13] ordered in his rage that these people be dealt with in precisely the same fashion as the others, not omitting any detail of their punishment. [14] The entire race was to be registered individually, not for the hard labor that has been briefly mentioned before, but to be tortured with the outrages that he had ordered, and at the end to be destroyed in the space of a single day. [15] The registration of these people was therefore conducted with bitter haste and zealous intensity from the rising of the sun until its setting, coming to an end after forty days but still uncompleted.

[16] The king was greatly and continually filled with joy, organizing feasts in honor of all his idols, with a mind alienated from truth and with a profane mouth, praising speechless things that are not able even to communicate or to come to one's help, and uttering improper words against the supreme God. [f] [17] But after the previously mentioned interval of time the scribes declared to the king that they were no longer able to take the census of the Jews because of their immense number, [18] though most of them were still in the country, some still residing in their homes, and some at the place; [g] the task was impossible for all the generals in Egypt. [19] After he had threatened them severely, charging that they had been bribed to contrive a means of escape, he was clearly convinced about the matter [20] when they said and proved that both the paper [h] and the pens they used for writing had already given out. [21] But this was an act of the invincible providence of him who was aiding the Jews from heaven.

5 Then the king, completely inflexible, was filled with overpowering anger and wrath; so he summoned Her-

c Gk *seeing Hades already lying at their feet*
d Gk *those of them*   *e* Or *claim protection of the walls;* meaning of Gk uncertain   *f* Gk *the greatest God*   *g* Other ancient authorities read *on the way*   *h* Or *paper factory*

4.11: *Schedia,* a promontory about three miles from Alexandria. *The hippodrome* was situated at the east or Canobic gate of Alexandria; according to Strabo (XVII.1.10, 16) a canal joined Schedia and the Canobic gate. *Inside . . . the city,* implies that Jews living in Alexandria (see v. 12, *compatriots from the city*) had been thus far unmolested (yet compare 3.1). **14:** *Mentioned before,* see 2.28. The registration for poll tax and slave status is transformed into an instrument to serve the execution of *the entire race* of Jews. **15:** *Forty days,* see 2 Macc 5.2. **16:** *Feasts,* Dan 5.4. *Supreme God,* see 1.9 n. **4.17:** *Their immense number,* an obvious hyperbole. **19:** *Bribed,* see 2.32. **21:** *An act of the invincible providence* prevents the registration and serves as the focal point of the entire narrative. As in the past, the Jews will be saved from destruction by *him* who aids them *from heaven.*
5.1–51: Ptolemy orders the execution

mon, keeper of the elephants, ²and ordered him on the following day to drug all the elephants—five hundred in number—with large handfuls of frankincense and plenty of unmixed wine, and to drive them in, maddened by the lavish abundance of drink, so that the Jews might meet their doom. ³When he had given these orders he returned to his feasting, together with those of his Friends and of the army who were especially hostile toward the Jews. ⁴And Hermon, keeper of the elephants, proceeded faithfully to carry out the orders. ⁵The servants in charge of the Jews*i* went out in the evening and bound the hands of the wretched people and arranged for their continued custody through the night, convinced that the whole nation would experience its final destruction. ⁶For to the Gentiles it appeared that the Jews were left without any aid, ⁷because in their bonds they were forcibly confined on every side. But with tears and a voice hard to silence they all called upon the Almighty Lord and Ruler of all power, their merciful God and Father, praying ⁸that he avert with vengence the evil plot against them and in a glorious manifestation rescue them from the fate now prepared for them. ⁹So their entreaty ascended fervently to heaven.

10 Hermon, however, when he had drugged the pitiless elephants until they had been filled with a great abundance of wine and satiated with frankincense, presented himself at the courtyard early in the morning to report to the king about these preparations. ¹¹But the Lord*j* sent upon the king a portion of sleep, that beneficence that from the beginning, night and day, is bestowed by him who

grants it to whomever he wishes. ¹²And by the action of the Lord he was overcome by so pleasant and deep a sleep*k* that he quite failed in his lawless purpose and was completely frustrated in his inflexible plan. ¹³Then the Jews, since they had escaped the appointed hour, praised their holy God and again implored him who is easily reconciled to show the might of his all-powerful hand to the arrogant Gentiles.

14 But now, since it was nearly the middle of the tenth hour, the person who was in charge of the invitations, seeing that the guests were assembled, approached the king and nudged him. ¹⁵And when he had with difficulty roused him, he pointed out that the hour of the banquet was already slipping by, and he gave him an account of the situation. ¹⁶The king, after considering this, returned to his drinking, and ordered those present for the banquet to recline opposite him. ¹⁷When this was done he urged them to give themselves over to revelry and to make the present*l* portion of the banquet joyful by celebrating all the more. ¹⁸After the party had been going on for some time, the king summoned Hermon and with sharp threats demanded to know why the Jews had been allowed to remain alive through the present day. ¹⁹But when he, with the corroboration of his Friends, pointed out that while it was still night he had carried out completely the order given him, ²⁰the king,*j* possessed by a savagery worse than that of Phalaris, said that the

---

i Gk *them*   *j* Gk *he*   *k* Other ancient authorities add *from evening until the ninth hour*
l Other ancient authorities read *delayed* (Gk *untimely*)

---

of the Jews, but is twice thwarted (vv. 12, 27–28). **2**: *Five hundred elephants* is an exaggeration; Ptolemy had seventy-three elephants at the battle of Raphia. **3**: *Returned to his feasting,* 4.16. **5**: *Bound the hands,* according to 3.25 they had already been bound securely, but perhaps their hands had been loosened when the Jews were enclosed within the hippodrome (see 5.49 n.). **6**: *It appeared,* although the reader understands the Jews are constantly

aided by divine Providence. **7**: The title *Father* is also given to God in Tob 13.4; Wis 11.10.
5.8: *Glorious manifestation,* 2 Macc 2.21. **11**: The divine gift of *sleep* is extolled in the Latin poets (Seneca, *Hercules Furens* 1066 ff.; Statius, *Silvae* v. 4); compare Ps 127.2. **14**: *Middle of the tenth hour,* 3:30 P.M. **19**: *Friends,* see 2.23 n. **20**: *Phalaris,* tyrant of Agrigentum (c. 570–554 B.C.) whose cruelty was proverbial (Polybius XII.25).

Jews[m] were benefited by today's sleep, "but," he added, "tomorrow without delay prepare the elephants in the same way for the destruction of the lawless Jews!" [21] When the king had spoken, all those present readily and joyfully with one accord gave their approval, and all went to their own homes. [22] But they did not so much employ the duration of the night in sleep as in devising all sorts of insults for those they thought to be doomed.

[23] Then, as soon as the cock had crowed in the early morning, Hermon, having equipped[n] the animals, began to move them along in the great colonnade. [24] The crowds of the city had been assembled for this most pitiful spectacle and they were eagerly waiting for daybreak. [25] But the Jews, at their last gasp—since the time had run out—stretched their hands toward heaven and with most tearful supplication and mournful dirges implored the supreme God[o] to help them again at once. [26] The rays of the sun were not yet shed abroad, and while the king was receiving his Friends, Hermon arrived and invited him to come out, indicating that what the king desired was ready for action. [27] But he, on receiving the report and being struck by the unusual invitation to come out—since he had been completely overcome by incomprehension—inquired what the matter was for which this had been so zealously completed for him. [28] This was the act of God who rules over all things, for he had implanted in the king's mind a forgetfulness of the things he had previously devised. [29] Then Hermon and all the king's Friends[p] pointed out that the animals and the armed forces were ready, "O king, according to your eager purpose."[q] [30] But at these words he was filled with an overpowering wrath, because by the providence of God his whole mind had been deranged concern-

ing these matters; and with a threatening look he said, [31] "If your parents or children were present, I would have prepared them to be a rich feast for the savage animals instead of the Jews, who give me no ground for complaint and have exhibited to an extraordinary degree a full and firm loyalty to my ancestors. [32] In fact you would have been deprived of life instead of these, if it were not for an affection arising from our nurture in common and your usefulness." [33] So Hermon suffered an unexpected and dangerous threat, and his eyes wavered and his face fell. [34] The king's Friends one by one sullenly slipped away and dismissed[r] the assembled people to their own occupations. [35] Then the Jews, on hearing what the king had said, praised the manifest Lord God, King of kings, since this also was his aid that they had received.

[36] The king, however, reconvened the party in the same manner and urged the guests to return to their celebrating. [37] After summoning Hermon he said in a threatening tone, "How many times, you poor wretch, must I give you orders about these things? [38] Equip[s] the elephants now once more for the destruction of the Jews tomorrow!" [39] But the officials who were at table with him, wondering at his instability of mind, remonstrated as follows: [40] "O king, how long will you put us to the test, as though we are idiots, ordering now for a third time that they be destroyed, and again revoking your decree in the matter?[t] [41] As a result the city is in a tumult because of its expectation; it is crowded

m Gk *they*   n Or *armed*   o Gk *the greatest God*   p Gk *all the Friends*   q Other ancient authorities read *pointed to the beasts and the armed forces, saying, "They are ready, O king, according to your eager purpose."*   r Other ancient authorities read *he dismissed*   s Or *Arm*   t Other ancient authorities read *when the matter is in hand*

5.23: *The great colonnade* was no doubt some well-known place in Alexandria. **28:** *The act of God,* Prov 21.1. **29:** An interpolation in several Greek manuscripts indicates that though Ptolemy was moved by compas-

sion and determined to release the Jews, Hermon influenced him to proceed with his plans to destroy them.
5.41: The revolutionary character of the Alexandrians in ancient times is well known.

with masses of people, and also in constant danger of being plundered."

42 At this the king, a Phalaris in everything and filled with madness, took no account of the changes of mind that had come about within him for the protection of the Jews, and he firmly swore an irrevocable oath that he would send them to death[u] without delay, mangled by the knees and feet of the animals, 43 and would also march against Judea and rapidly level it to the ground with fire and spear, and by burning to the ground the temple inaccessible to him[v] would quickly render it forever empty of those who offered sacrifices there. 44 Then the Friends and officers departed with great joy, and they confidently posted the armed forces at the places in the city most favorable for keeping guard.

45 Now when the animals had been brought virtually to a state of madness, so to speak, by the very fragrant draughts of wine mixed with frankincense and had been equipped with frightful devices, the elephant keeper 46 entered at about dawn into the courtyard—the city now being filled with countless masses of people crowding their way into the hippodrome—and urged the king on to the matter at hand. 47 So he, when he had filled his impious mind with a deep rage, rushed out in full force along with the animals, wishing to witness, with invulnerable heart and with his own eyes, the grievous and pitiful destruction of the aforementioned people.

48 When the Jews saw the dust raised by the elephants going out at the gate and by the following armed forces, as well as by the trampling of the crowd, and heard the loud and tumultuous noise, 49 they thought that this was their last moment of life, the end of their most miserable suspense, and giving way to lamentation and groans they kissed each other, embracing relatives and falling into one another's arms[w]—parents and children, mothers and daughters, and others with babies at their breasts who were drawing their last milk. 50 Not only this, but when they considered the help that they had received before from heaven, they prostrated themselves with one accord on the ground, removing the babies from their breasts, 51 and cried out in a very loud voice, imploring the Ruler over every power to manifest himself and be merciful to them, as they stood now at the gates of death. "

6 Then a certain Eleazar, famous among the priests of the country, who had attained a ripe old age and throughout his life had been adorned with every virtue, directed the elders around him to stop calling upon the holy God, and he prayed as follows: 2 "King of great power, Almighty God Most High, governing all creation with mercy, 3 look upon the descendants of Abraham, O Father, upon the children of the sainted Jacob, a people of your consecrated portion who are perishing as foreigners in a foreign land. 4 Pharaoh with his abundance of chariots, the former ruler of this Egypt, exalted with lawless insolence and boastful tongue, you destroyed

u Gk *Hades*   *v* Gk *us*   *w* Gk *falling upon their necks*

42: *Phalaris,* see v. 20 n. 45: The *frightful devices* were probably scythes, knives, and other military equipment attached to the different parts of the bodies of the elephants. 49: *Embracing,* but according to 6.27 they are still bound.

5.50–51: The author continues to build up his thesis that God was the only resort for the captives, and that their hope would not be frustrated. 51: *Gates of death,* Pss 9.13; 107.18.

6.1–15: **The prayer of Eleazar.** Like Si-

mon's prayer in 2.1–20, it is plainly Jewish in form and style, containing doxology, thanksgiving for God's earlier interventions in Israel's history, and petition for a new miracle. The emphasis is on the exclusiveness and separate standing of Israel before God (v. 3). Eleazar expects God's intervention, not on account of Israel's virtues or merits, but because of divine mercy. 1: *Eleazar,* a favorite name for a Jewish hero (2 Macc 6.18). *Priests,* perhaps those of the Jewish temple at Leonto-

together with his arrogant army by drowning them in the sea, manifesting the light of your mercy on the nation of Israel. [5]Sennacherib exulting in his countless forces, oppressive king of the Assyrians, who had already gained control of the whole world by the spear and was lifted up against your holy city, speaking grievous words with boasting and insolence, you, O Lord, broke in pieces, showing your power to many nations. [6]The three companions in Babylon who had voluntarily surrendered their lives to the flames so as not to serve vain things, you rescued unharmed, even to a hair, moistening the fiery furnace with dew and turning the flame against all their enemies. [7]Daniel, who through envious slanders was thrown down into the ground to lions as food for wild animals, you brought up to the light unharmed. [8]And Jonah, wasting away in the belly of a huge, sea-born monster, you, Father, watched over and restored[x] unharmed to all his family. [9]And now, you who hate insolence, all-merciful and protector of all, reveal yourself quickly to those of the nation of Israel[y]—who are being outrageously treated by the abominable and lawless Gentiles.

10 "Even if our lives have become entangled in impieties in our exile, rescue us from the hand of the enemy, and destroy us, Lord, by whatever fate you choose. [11]Let not the vain-minded praise their vanities[z] at the destruction of your beloved people, saying, 'Not even their god has rescued them.' [12]But you, O Eternal One, who have all might and all power, watch over us now and have mercy on us who by the senseless insolence of the lawless are being deprived of life in the manner of traitors. [13]And let

the Gentiles cower today in fear of your invincible might, O honored One, who have power to save the nation of Jacob. [14]The whole throng of infants and their parents entreat you with tears. [15]Let it be shown to all the Gentiles that you are with us, O Lord, and have not turned your face from us; but just as you have said, 'Not even when they were in the land of their enemies did I neglect them,' so accomplish it, O Lord."

16 Just as Eleazar was ending his prayer, the king arrived at the hippodrome with the animals and all the arrogance of his forces. [17]And when the Jews observed this they raised great cries to heaven so that even the nearby valleys resounded with them and brought an uncontrollable terror upon the army. [18]Then the most glorious, almighty, and true God revealed his holy face and opened the heavenly gates, from which two glorious angels of fearful aspect descended, visible to all but the Jews. [19]They opposed the forces of the enemy and filled them with confusion and terror, binding them with immovable shackles. [20]Even the king began to shudder bodily, and he forgot his sullen insolence. [21]The animals turned back upon the armed forces following them and began trampling and destroying them.

22 Then the king's anger was turned to pity and tears because of the things that he had devised beforehand. [23]For when he heard the shouting and saw them all fallen headlong to destruction, he wept and angrily threatened his Friends, saying, [24]"You are committing

---

x Other ancient authorities read *rescued and restored*; others, *mercifully restored*   y Other ancient authorities read *to the saints of Israel*   z Or *bless their vain gods*

---

polis in Egypt. 4: *Pharaoh,* Ex 14.28. 5: *Sennacherib,* 2 Kings 18.13; 19.35–37. 6: *Three companions in Babylon,* Dan 3.22, 27; Song of Thr 22–27. 7: *Daniel,* Dan 6.22.

6.8: *Jonah,* Jon 2.10. 11: Ps 115.2. 15: *As you have said,* Lev 26.44.

6.16–29: **The Jews are delivered, and the king now favors them. 18:** *Most glorious,* Greek "megalodoxos," compare 1 Enoch

14.20 and Testament of Levi 3.4, where God is called "the Great Glory." *Angels of fearful aspect,* for similar terror-inspiring apparitions, see Wis 17.3, 15; 18.17; 2 Macc 3.25–29; 10.29. *Visible to all but the Jews,* Dan 10.7; Acts 9.7; 22.6–9.

6.21: *The animals turned* upon the king's own *forces,* a detail found also in Josephus's account (*Against Apion,* ii.5), compare Pss

treason and surpassing tyrants in cruelty; and even me, your benefactor, you are now attempting to deprive of dominion and life by secretly devising acts of no advantage to the kingdom. 25 Who has driven from their homes those who faithfully kept our country's fortresses, and foolishly gathered every one of them here? 26 Who is it that has so lawlessly encompassed with outrageous treatment those who from the beginning differed from*d* all nations in their goodwill toward us and often have accepted willingly the worst of human dangers? 27 Loose and untie their unjust bonds! Send them back to their homes in peace, begging pardon for your former actions!*b* 28 Release the children of the almighty and living God of heaven, who from the time of our ancestors until now has granted an unimpeded and notable stability to our government." 29 These then were the things he said; and the Jews, immediately released, praised their holy God and Savior, since they now had escaped death.

30 Then the king, when he had returned to the city, summoned the official in charge of the revenues and ordered him to provide to the Jews both wines and everything else needed for a festival of seven days, deciding that they should celebrate their rescue with all joyfulness in that same place in which they had expected to meet their destruction. 31 Accordingly those disgracefully treated and near to death,*c* or rather, who stood at its gates, arranged for a banquet of deliverance instead of a bitter and lamentable death, and full of joy they apportioned to celebrants the place that had been prepared for their destruction and burial. 32 They stopped their chanting of dirges and took up the song of their ancestors, praising God, their Savior and worker of wonders.*d* Putting an end to all mourn-

ing and wailing, they formed choruses*e* as a sign of peaceful joy. 33 Likewise also the king, after convening a great banquet to celebrate these events, gave thanks to heaven unceasingly and lavishly for the unexpected rescue that he*f* had experienced. 34 Those who had previously believed that the Jews would be destroyed and become food for birds, and had joyfully registered them, groaned as they themselves were overcome by disgrace, and their fire-breathing boldness was ignominiously*g* quenched.

35 The Jews, as we have said before, arranged the aforementioned choral group*h* and passed the time in feasting to the accompaniment of joyous thanksgiving and psalms. 36 And when they had ordained a public rite for these things in their whole community and for their descendants, they instituted the observance of the aforesaid days as a festival, not for drinking and gluttony, but because of the deliverance that had come to them through God. 37 Then they petitioned the king, asking for dismissal to their homes. 38 So their registration was carried out from the twenty-fifth of Pachon to the fourth of Epeiph,*i* for forty days; and their destruction was set for the fifth to the seventh of Epeiph,*j* the three days 39 on which the Lord of all most gloriously revealed his mercy and rescued them all together and unharmed. 40 Then they feasted, being provided with everything by the king, until the fourteenth day,*k* on which also they made the petition for

a Or *excelled above* *b* Other ancient authorities read *revoking your former commands* *c* Gk *Hades* *d* Other ancient authorities read *praising Israel and the wonder-working God*; or *praising Israel's Savior, the wonder-working God* *e* Or *dances* *f* Other ancient authorities read *they* *g* Other ancient authorities read *completely* *h* Or *dance* *i* July 7–August 15 *j* August 16–18 *k* August 25

7.15–16; 9.15–16; 35.8; 57.6. **25**: *Faithfully,* contrast the king's language in 3.24. **28**: *Children of . . . God,* Wis 18.13.

6.30–41: The Jews celebrate their deliverance. 32: *The song of their ancestors,* perhaps Ps 136, which was used earlier as a hymn of thanksgiving (1 Chr 16.41; 2 Chr 5.13; 7.3;

Ezra 3.11). **34**: *Food for birds,* Gen 40.19; Ezek 39.4; 2 Macc 9.15.

6.36: The institution of Jewish festivals is a common feature at this period (compare Esth 9.15; 1 Macc 4.56; 7.49; 13.51; 2 Macc 10.6; 15.36). **38**: *Epeiph,* or Epiphi.

their dismissal. [41] The king granted their request at once and wrote the following letter for them to the generals in the cities, magnanimously expressing his concern:

7 "King Ptolemy Philopator to the generals in Egypt and all in authority in his government, greetings and good health:

2 "We ourselves and our children are faring well, the great God guiding our affairs according to our desire. [3] Certain of our friends, frequently urging us with malicious intent, persuaded us to gather together the Jews of the kingdom in a body and to punish them with barbarous penalties as traitors; [4] for they declared that our government would never be firmly established until this was accomplished, because of the ill-will that these people had toward all nations. [5] They also led them out with harsh treatment as slaves, or rather as traitors, and, girding themselves with a cruelty more savage than that of Scythian custom, they tried without any inquiry or examination to put them to death. [6] But we very severely threatened them for these acts, and in accordance with the clemency that we have toward all people we barely spared their lives. Since we have come to realize that the God of heaven surely defends the Jews, always taking their part as a father does for his children, [7] and since we have taken into account the friendly and firm good will that they had toward us and our ancestors, we justly have acquitted them of every charge of whatever kind. [8] We also have ordered all people to return to their own homes, with no one in any place[l] doing them harm at all or

reproaching them for the irrational things that have happened. [9] For you should know that if we devise any evil against them or cause them any grief at all, we always shall have not a mortal but the Ruler over every power, the Most High God, in everything and inescapably as an antagonist to avenge such acts. Farewell."

10 On receiving this letter the Jews[m] did not immediately hurry to make their departure, but they requested of the king that at their own hands those of the Jewish nation who had willfully transgressed against the holy God and the law of God should receive the punishment they deserved. [11] They declared that those who for the belly's sake had transgressed the divine commandments would never be favorably disposed toward the king's government. [12] The king[n] then, admitting and approving the truth of what they said, granted them a general license so that freely, and without royal authority or supervision, they might destroy those everywhere in his kingdom who had transgressed the law of God. [13] When they had applauded him in fitting manner, their priests and the whole multitude shouted the Hallelujah and joyfully departed. [14] And so on their way they punished and put to a public and shameful death any whom they met of their compatriots who had become defiled. [15] In that day they put to death more than three hundred men; and they kept the day as a joyful festival, since they had destroyed the profaners. [16] But those

l Other ancient authorities read way
m Gk they   n Gk He

7.1–9: Ptolemy's letter on behalf of the Jews. 2: *Children,* Philopator had only one legitimate son, born in 209–8, who reigned later as Ptolemy V Epiphanes (203–181 B.C.). Either the author had no knowledge of Philopator's family life, or the king is referring in general terms to include all members of his court. **3**: The king seeks to exonerate himself, blaming others. **4**: *Ill-will,* 3.2, 7; Esth 3.8; Add Esth 13.4–5. **5**: *Scythian custom,* see 2 Macc 4.47 n.; 4 Macc 10.7 n. **6**: *Threatened them,* that is, the enemies of the Jews. *Father,*

5.7 n.; Ps 103.13. **8**: *In any place* through which the Jews might pass on their return.
7.10–23: The Jews punish the renegades and return home. 10: *They requested of the king,* in the later periods of their history the Jews were obliged to seek permission from their foreign rulers to execute their own laws pertaining to capital punishment (Deut 13.6–18; Esth 8.8–11; Jn 18.31). **13**: *Hallelujah,* Tob 13.18.
7.16: Bar 5.6, 8. **17**: This *Ptolemais* was probably not the city of this name near

who had held fast to God even to death and had received the full enjoyment of deliverance began their departure from the city, crowned with all sorts of very fragrant flowers, joyfully and loudly giving thanks to the one God of their ancestors, the eternal Savior *o* of Israel, in words of praise and all kinds of melodious songs.

17 When they had arrived at Ptolemais, called "rose-bearing" because of a characteristic of the place, the fleet waited for them, in accordance with the common desire, for seven days. 18 There they celebrated their deliverance, *p* for the king had generously provided all things to them for their journey until all of them arrived at their own houses. 19 And when they had all landed in peace with appropriate thanksgiving, there too in like manner they decided to observe these days as a joyous festival during the time of their stay. 20 Then, after inscribing

them as holy on a pillar and dedicating a place of prayer at the site of the festival, they departed unharmed, free, and overjoyed, since at the king's command they had all of them been brought safely by land and sea and river to their own homes. 21 They also possessed greater prestige among their enemies, being held in honor and awe; and they were not subject at all to confiscation of their belongings by any one. 22 Besides, they all recovered all of their property, in accordance with the registration, so that those who held any of it restored it to them with extreme fear. *q* So the supreme God perfectly performed great deeds for their deliverance. 23 Blessed be the Deliverer of Israel through all times! Amen.

o Other ancient authorities read *the holy Savior*; others, *the holy one*   p Gk *they made a cup of deliverance*   q Other ancient authorities read *with a very large supplement*

Thebes in Upper Egypt, but "Ptolemais at the harbor" in the Arsinoite nome (province), about twelve miles from present-day Cairo. *Rose-bearing* is not elsewhere applied to Ptolemais. 20: *And sea,* there was no sea to cross in Egypt.

7.22–23: The book closes with a benediction to the *Supreme God . . . Deliverer;* this suggests that it may have been read liturgically to celebrate the Alexandrian festival described in 6.30–36.

(c) The following book is included in the Slavonic Bible as 3 Esdras, but is not found in the Greek. It is included in the Appendix to the Latin Vulgate Bible as 4 Esdras.

2 Esdras

The book commonly known as 2 Esdras differs from the other fourteen books of the Apocrypha in being an apocalypse (for the characteristics of apocalyptic literature, see p. 362 NT). The main part of 2 Esdras is a series of seven revelations (3.1–5.20; 5.21–6.34; 6.35–9.25; 9.38–10.59; 11.1–12.51; 13.1–58; 14.1–48), in which the seer is instructed by the angel Uriel concerning some of the great mysteries of the moral world.

The problems concerning the composition and transmission of 2 Esdras are extremely complicated. The author of the central portion (chs 3–14) was an unknown Palestinian Jew who probably wrote in Hebrew or Aramaic near the close of the first century A.D. Subsequently the book was translated into Greek. About the middle of the next century an unknown Christian editor added in Greek an introductory section, which now comprises chs 1–2. Nearly a century later another unknown Christian appended chs 15–16, also in Greek.

The Semitic original and almost all of the Greek text have been lost (only 15.57–59 survives on a scrap of Greek papyrus). Before the text of the central section (chs 3–14) perished, however, translations were made into several other languages, namely Syriac, Coptic, Ethiopic, Arabic (two independent versions), Armenian, and Georgian. In the West the entire book (chs 1–16) circulated in several Old Latin versions. A later form of the Latin text is printed, since the Council of Trent, as an appendix to the New Testament in the Roman Catholic Vulgate Bible, where it is called the Fourth Book of Esdras.

The purpose of the original author of 2 Esdras was manifold. The apocalypses that are found in chs 11–12 and 13 are concerned chiefly with denunciation of the wickedness of Rome (under the image of "Babylon"). Chapter 14 contains a most important legend about the preservation of the Scriptures and about the authority of the "hidden" books of the Bible—the Apocrypha and Pseudepigrapha of the Hebrew Scriptures. Chapters 3–10 contain the author's wrestling with some of the central questions confronting the Jewish people in the first century A.D. These include in particular the question of how to affirm God's justice, wisdom, power, and goodness, given the many evils and trials that beset the human community, and the people of Israel in particular. These issues are addressed in a series of questions put to an angel by Ezra, illuminated by visions that the seer Ezra is shown, and followed by interpretations of the visions by the angel. Ezra's laments and questions pose the author's own concerns and hint at his own answers. The answers given by the angel are more conventional responses to the questions than they are definitive teachings of the author of 2 Esdras. Readers of 2 Esdras should therefore give special attention to the content and imagery of the complaints and the visions in order to discern the author's own "answers" to haunting questions that the human community continues to face.

Comprising what is sometimes called 5 Ezra (chapters 1–2), 4 Ezra (chapters 3–14), and 6 Ezra (chapters 15–16)

1 The book[a] of the prophet Ezra son of Seraiah son of Azariah son of Hilkiah son of Shallum son of Zadok son of Ahitub ²son of Ahijah son of Phinehas son of Eli son of Amariah son of Azariah son of Meraimoth son of Arna son of Uzzi son of Borith son of Abishua son of Phinehas son of Eleazar ³son of Aaron, of the tribe of Levi, who was a captive in the country of the Medes in the reign of Artaxerxes, king of the Persians.[b]

4 The word of the Lord came to me, saying, ⁵"Go, declare to my people their evil deeds, and to their children the iniquities that they have committed against me, so that they may tell[c] their children's children ⁶that the sins of their parents have increased in them, for they have forgotten me and have offered sacrifices to strange gods. ⁷Was it not I who brought them out of the land of Egypt, out of the house of bondage? But they have angered me and despised my counsels. ⁸Now you, pull out the hair of your head and hurl[d] all evils upon them, for they have not obeyed my law—they are a rebellious people. ⁹How long shall I endure them, on whom I have bestowed such great benefits? ¹⁰For their sake I have overthrown many kings; I struck down Pharaoh with his servants and all his army. ¹¹I destroyed all nations before them, and scattered in the east the peoples of two provinces,[e] Tyre and Sidon; I killed all their enemies.

12 "But speak to them and say, Thus says the Lord: ¹³Surely it was I who

brought you through the sea, and made safe highways for you where there was no road; I gave you Moses as leader and Aaron as priest; ¹⁴I provided light for you from a pillar of fire, and did great wonders among you. Yet you have forgotten me, says the Lord.

15 "Thus says the Lord Almighty:[f] The quails were a sign to you; I gave you camps for your protection, and in them you complained. ¹⁶You have not exulted in my name at the destruction of your enemies, but to this day you still complain.[g] ¹⁷Where are the benefits that I bestowed on you? When you were hungry and thirsty in the wilderness, did you not cry out to me, ¹⁸saying, 'Why have you led us into this wilderness to kill us? It would have been better for us to serve the Egyptians than to die in this wilderness.' ¹⁹I pitied your groanings and gave you manna for food; you ate the bread of angels. ²⁰When you were thirsty, did I not split the rock so that waters flowed in abundance? Because of the heat I clothed you with the leaves of trees.[h] ²¹I divided fertile lands among you; I drove

a Other ancient authorities read *The second book* b Other ancient authorities, which place chapters 1 and 2 after 16.78, lack verses 1–3 and begin the chapter: *The word of the Lord that came to Ezra son of Chusi in the days of King Nebuchadnezzar, saying, "Go,* c Other ancient authorities read *nourish* d Other ancient authorities read *and shake out* e Other ancient authorities read *Did I not destroy the city of Bethsaida because of you, and to the south burn two cities . . . ?* f Other ancient authorities lack *Almighty* g Other ancient authorities read verse 16, *Your pursuer with his army I sank in the sea, but still the people complain also concerning their own destruction.* h Other ancient authorities read *I made for you trees with leaves*

1.1–2.48: Ezra is commanded to reprove the Jewish people. 1.1–3: The genealogy of Ezra, who is of priestly descent (compare the somewhat different genealogies in Ezra 7.1–5 and 1 Esd 8.1–2). **3:** Either *Artaxerxes* I, who reigned 464–424 B.C., or *Artaxerxes* II, who reigned 404–358 B.C.; the former is more probable.
1.4–11: Ezra receives a prophetic call. 4: The expression, *the word of the Lord came . . .,* so typical of prophetic authorization, is absent from the canonical book of Ezra. **5:** Isa

58.1. **8:** The command to *pull out* his *hair* is to be connected with Ezra's denunciation (*hurl all evils*) of his people. **10:** Ex 14.28. **11:** The author is confused; *Tyre and Sidon,* which were cities, not *provinces,* lay to the west of the land of the Medes (v. 3).
1.12–23: Summary of God's mercies to Israel. 13: Ex 14.29. **14:** Ex 13.21. **15:** Ex 16.13; Ps 105.40. **17–18:** Num 14.3. **19:** *The bread of angels,* Ps 78.25; Wis 16.20. **20:** Num 20.11; Wis 11.4. **22–23:** Ex 15.22–25.

out the Canaanites, the Perizzites, and the Philistines[i] before you. What more can I do for you? says the Lord. 22 Thus says the Lord Almighty:[j] When you were in the wilderness, at the bitter stream, thirsty and blaspheming my name, 23 I did not send fire on you for your blasphemies, but threw a tree into the water and made the stream sweet.

24 "What shall I do to you, O Jacob? You, Judah, would not obey me. I will turn to other nations and will give them my name, so that they may keep my statutes. 25 Because you have forsaken me, I also will forsake you. When you beg mercy of me, I will show you no mercy. 26 When you call to me, I will not listen to you; for you have defiled your hands with blood, and your feet are swift to commit murder. 27 It is not as though you had forsaken me; you have forsaken yourselves, says the Lord.

28 "Thus says the Lord Almighty: Have I not entreated you as a father entreats his sons or a mother her daughters or a nurse her children, 29 so that you should be my people and I should be your God, and that you should be my children and I should be your father? 30 I gathered you as a hen gathers her chicks under her wings. But now, what shall I do to you? I will cast you out from my presence. 31 When you offer oblations to me, I will turn my face from you; for I have rejected your[k] festal days, and new moons, and circumcisions of the flesh.[l] 32 I sent you my servants the prophets, but you have taken and killed them and torn their bodies[m] in pieces; I will require their blood of you, says the Lord.[n]

33 "Thus says the Lord Almighty: Your house is desolate; I will drive you out as the wind drives straw; 34 and your sons will have no children, because with you[o] they have neglected my commandment and have done what is evil in my sight. 35 I will give your houses to a people that will come, who without having heard me will believe. Those to whom I have shown no signs will do what I have commanded. 36 They have seen no prophets, yet will recall their former state.[p] 37 I call to witness the gratitude of the people that is to come, whose children rejoice with gladness;[q] though they do not see me with bodily eyes, yet with the spirit they will believe the things I have said.

38 "And now, father,[r] look with pride and see the people coming from the east; 39 to them I will give as leaders Abraham, Isaac, and Jacob, and Hosea and Amos and Micah and Joel and Obadiah and Jonah 40 and Nahum and Habakkuk, Zephaniah, Haggai, Zechariah and Malachi, who is also called the messenger of the Lord.[s]

2 "Thus says the Lord: I brought this people out of bondage, and I gave

---

i Other ancient authorities read *Perizzites and their children*   j Other ancient authorities lack *Almighty*   k Other ancient authorities read *I have not commanded for you*   l Other ancient authorities lack *of the flesh*   m Other ancient authorities read *the bodies of the apostles*   n Other ancient authorities add *Thus says the Lord Almighty: Recently you also laid hands on me, crying out before the judge's seat for him to deliver me to you. You took me as a sinner, not as a father who freed you from slavery, and you delivered me to death by hanging me on the tree; these are the things you have done. Therefore, says the Lord, let my Father and his angels return and judge between you and me; if I have not kept the commandment of the Father, if I have not nourished you, if I have not done the things my Father commanded, I will contend in judgment with you, says the Lord.*   o Other ancient authorities lack *with you*   p Other ancient authorities read *their iniquities*   q Other ancient authorities read *The apostles bear witness to the coming people with joy*   r Other ancient authorities read *brother*   s Other ancient authorities read *and Jacob, Elijah and Enoch, Zechariah and Hosea, Amos, Joel, Micah, Obadiah, Zephaniah,* 40 *Nahum, Jonah, Mattia (or Mattathias), Habakkuk, and twelve angels with flowers*

1.24–32: The casting off of Israel. 26: Isa 1.15; 59.7. **29:** Jer 24.7; Heb 8.10. **30:** The similarity with Mt 23.37 and Lk 13.34 suggests that the author of this part of 2 Esdras was a Jewish Christian. **31:** The rejection of circumcision also reveals the Christian identity of the author. **32:** Compare Mt 23.34–35. **1.33–40: God will give Israel's houses to another people. 35–36:** Gentile Christians are meant (compare Rom 10.14–20). **37:** *With bodily eyes,* Jn 20.29. **38:** God is represented as addressing Ezra as *father* of the na-

them commandments through my servants the prophets; but they would not listen to them, and made my counsels void. ² The mother who bore them' says to them, 'Go, my children, because I am a widow and forsaken. ³ I brought you up with gladness; but with mourning and sorrow I have lost you, because you have sinned before the Lord God and have done what is evil in my sight. " ⁴ But now what can I do for you? For I am a widow and forsaken. Go, my children, and ask for mercy from the Lord.' ⁵ Now I call upon you, father, as a witness in addition to the mother of the children, because they would not keep my covenant, ⁶ so that you may bring confusion on them and bring their mother to ruin, so that they may have no offspring. ⁷ Let them be scattered among the nations; let their names be blotted out from the earth, because they have despised my covenant.

8 "Woe to you, Assyria, who conceal the unrighteous within you! O wicked nation, remember what I did to Sodom and Gomorrah, ⁹ whose land lies in lumps of pitch and heaps of ashes. ᵛ That is what I will do to those who have not listened to me, says the Lord Almighty."

10 Thus says the Lord to Ezra: "Tell my people that I will give them the kingdom of Jerusalem, which I was going to give to Israel. ¹¹ Moreover, I will take back to myself their glory, and will give to these others the everlasting habitations, which I had prepared for Israel. ʷ ¹² The tree of life shall give them fragrant perfume, and they shall neither toil nor become weary. ¹³ Goˣ and you will re-

ceive; pray that your days may be few, that they may be shortened. The kingdom is already prepared for you; be on the watch! ¹⁴ Call, O call heaven and earth to witness: I set aside evil and created good; for I am the Living One, says the Lord.

15 "Mother, embrace your children; bring them up with gladness, as does a dove; strengthen their feet, because I have chosen you, says the Lord. ¹⁶ And I will raise up the dead from their places, and bring them out from their tombs, because I recognize my name in them. ¹⁷ Do not fear, mother of children, for I have chosen you, says the Lord. ¹⁸ I will send you help, my servants Isaiah and Jeremiah. According to their counsel I have consecrated and prepared for you twelve trees loaded with various fruits, ¹⁹ and the same number of springs flowing with milk and honey, and seven mighty mountains on which roses and lilies grow; by these I will fill your children with joy.

20 "Guard the rights of the widow, secure justice for the ward, give to the needy, defend the orphan, clothe the naked, ²¹ care for the injured and the weak, do not ridicule the lame, protect the maimed, and let the blind have a vision of my splendor. ²² Protect the old and the young within your walls; ²³ When you find any who are dead, commit them to

t Other ancient authorities read *They begat for themselves a mother who*   *u* Other ancient authorities read *in his sight*   *v* Other ancient authorities read *Gomorrah, whoseland descends to hell*   *w* Lat *for those*   *x* Other ancient authorities read *Seek*

tion. **39–40:** The three patriarchs and the twelve minor prophets, arranged in the order of the Septuagint.
2.1–9: The Lord's anger against Israel.
1: *My servants the prophets,* Zech 1.6. **2:** *The mother who bore them,* Jerusalem (Isa 54.1; Gal 4.26–27). *Go . . . ,* Bar 4.19. **3:** Bar 4.11. **5:** Again the author has God address Ezra as *father.* **6:** *To ruin,* in the fall of Jerusalem, A.D. 70. **8:** By the name *Assyria,* Israel's ancient foe, the author refers cryptically to Rome. *Sodom and Gomorrah,* Gen 19.24.
2.10–14: Israel's habitation to be given

to others. 10: *My people,* i.e. the Christians (compare Hos 2.23). **11:** *Everlasting habitations,* Lk 16.9. **12:** Rev 2.7; 22.2, 14. **13:** Mt 7.7–8; Lk 11.9–10; Mt 25.34. **14:** Isa 1.2.
2.15–32: Exhortation to good works. 15: *Mother,* probably a reference to the church.
2.18: *Twelve trees,* Rev 22.2. **19:** *Milk and honey,* Deut 31.20. *Seven mighty mountains,* from 1 Enoch 24.2, showing the author's familiarity with this section of the apocalypse of Enoch. **23:** *Find any . . . dead,* compare Tob 1.17–19. **26:** Jn 17.12.

the grave and mark it, *y* and I will give you the first place in my resurrection. ²⁴Pause and be quiet, my people, because your rest will come.

25 "Good nurse, nourish your children; strengthen their feet. ²⁶Not one of the servants *z* whom I have given you will perish, for I will require them from among your number. ²⁷Do not be anxious, for when the day of tribulation and anguish comes, others shall weep and be sorrowful, but you shall rejoice and have abundance. ²⁸The nations shall envy you, but they shall not be able to do anything against you, says the Lord. ²⁹My power will protect *a* you, so that your children may not see hell. *b*

30 "Rejoice, O mother, with your children, because I will deliver you, says the Lord. ³¹Remember your children that sleep, because I will bring them out of the hiding places of the earth, and will show mercy to them; for I am merciful, says the Lord Almighty. ³²Embrace your children until I come, and proclaim mercy to them; because my springs run over, and my grace will not fail."

33 I, Ezra, received a command from the Lord on Mount Horeb to go to Israel. When I came to them they rejected me and refused the Lord's commandment. ³⁴Therefore I say to you, O nations that hear and understand, "Wait for your shepherd; he will give you everlasting rest, because he who will come at the end of the age is close at hand. ³⁵Be ready for the rewards of the kingdom, because perpetual light will shine on you forevermore. ³⁶Flee from the shadow of this age, receive the joy of your glory; I publicly call on my savior to witness. *c* ³⁷Receive what the Lord has entrusted to you and be joyful, giving thanks to him who has called you to the celestial kingdoms. ³⁸Rise, stand erect and see the number of those who have been sealed at the feast of the Lord. ³⁹Those who have departed

from the shadow of this age have received glorious garments from the Lord. ⁴⁰Take again your full number, O Zion, and close the list of your people who are clothed in white, who have fulfilled the law of the Lord. ⁴¹The number of your children, whom you desired, is now complete; implore the Lord's authority that your people, who have been called from the beginning, may be made holy."

42 I, Ezra, saw on Mount Zion a great multitude that I could not number, and they all were praising the Lord with songs. ⁴³In their midst was a young man of great stature, taller than any of the others, and on the head of each of them he placed a crown, but he was more exalted than they. And I was held spellbound. ⁴⁴Then I asked an angel, "Who are these, my lord?" ⁴⁵He answered and said to me, "These are they who have put off mortal clothing and have put on the immortal, and have confessed the name of God. Now they are being crowned, and receive palms." ⁴⁶Then I said to the angel, "Who is that young man who is placing crowns on them and putting palms in their hands?" ⁴⁷He answered and said to me, "He is the Son of God, whom they confessed in the world." So I began to praise those who had stood valiantly for the name of the Lord. *d* ⁴⁸Then the angel said to me, "Go, tell my people how great and how many are the wonders of the Lord God that you have seen."

3 In the thirtieth year after the destruction of the city, I was in Babylon— I, Salathiel, who am also called Ezra. I was troubled as I lay on my bed, and my

---

y Or *seal it*; or *mark them and commit them to the grave*   *z* Or *slaves*   *a* Lat *hands will cover*   *b* Lat *Gehenna*   *c* Other ancient authorities read *I testify that my savior has been commissioned by the Lord*   *d* Other ancient authorities read *to praise and glorify the Lord*

2.33–41: Rejected by Israel, Ezra turns to the Gentiles. 33: *On Mount Horeb,* like a second Moses (Ex 3.1; 2 Chr 5.10). **35**: *Perpetual light,* Isa 60.20; Rev 21.23; 22.5. **40**: *Zion,* the church is identified as Zion, Heb 12.22–23. *Clothed in white,* Rev 3.4; 6.11; 7.14. **41**: *The number . . . is complete,* see 4.36–37 n.; Rev 6.11. *Called,* Rom 8.29–30.

thoughts welled up in my heart, 2because I saw the desolation of Zion and the wealth of those who lived in Babylon. 3My spirit was greatly agitated, and I began to speak anxious words to the Most High, and said, 4"O sovereign Lord, did you not speak at the beginning when you planted*e* the earth—and that without help—and commanded the dust*f* 5and it gave you Adam, a lifeless body? Yet he was the creation of your hands, and you breathed into him the breath of life, and he was made alive in your presence. 6And you led him into the garden that your right hand had planted before the earth appeared. 7And you laid upon him one commandment of yours; but he transgressed it, and immediately you appointed death for him and for his descendants. From him there sprang nations and tribes, peoples and clans without number. 8And every nation walked after its own will; they did ungodly things in your sight and rejected your commands, and you did not hinder them. 9But again, in its time you brought the flood upon the inhabitants of the world and destroyed them. 10And the same fate befell all of them: just as death came upon Adam, so the flood upon them. 11But you left one of them, Noah with his household, and all the righteous who have descended from him.

12 "When those who lived on earth began to multiply, they produced children and peoples and many nations, and

again they began to be more ungodly than were their ancestors. 13And when they were committing iniquity in your sight, you chose for yourself one of them, whose name was Abraham; 14you loved him, and to him alone you revealed the end of the times, secretly by night. 15You made an everlasting covenant with him, and promised him that you would never forsake his descendants; and you gave him Isaac, and to Isaac you gave Jacob and Esau. 16You set apart Jacob for yourself, but Esau you rejected; and Jacob became a great multitude. 17And when you led his descendants out of Egypt, you brought them to Mount Sinai. 18You bent down the heavens and shook*g* the earth, and moved the world, and caused the depths to tremble, and troubled the times. 19Your glory passed through the four gates of fire and earthquake and wind and ice, to give the law to the descendants of Jacob, and your commandment to the posterity of Israel.

20 "Yet you did not take away their evil heart from them, so that your law might produce fruit in them. 21For the first Adam, burdened with an evil heart, transgressed and was overcome, as were also all who were descended from him. 22Thus the disease became permanent; the law was in the hearts of the people along with the evil root; but what was

e Other ancient authorities read *formed*
f Syr Ethiop: Lat *people* or *world*
g Syr Ethiop Arab 1 Georg: Lat *set fast*

2.42–48: **Ezra's vision of a great multitude. 42:** Rev 7.9. **43:** *A young man,* compare v. 47 and 1 Enoch 46.1.

3.1–5.20: The first vision. 3.1–3: Introduction. 1: *The thirtieth year after the destruction* of Jerusalem by Nebuchadnezzar in 587/6 B.C. (2 Kings 25.1ff.) would be 557/6 B.C. The date specified may imply that the author was writing about A.D. 100 (i.e. thirty years after the fall of Jerusalem in A.D. 70). *Salathiel* is the Greek form of Shealtiel (Ezra 3.2; 5.2; Neh 12.1). The words *who am also called Ezra* are an anachronistic gloss; Ezra lived almost a century later.

3.4–36: The author raises perplexing questions. Whence comes sin with its conse-

quent misery? How can Israel's continuing affliction be reconciled with God's justice? **4–5:** The creation of Adam. **6–8:** Adam's sin brings death on all mortals. **7:** The words *immediately you appointed death* imply that Adam was not originally intended to be mortal (see Gen 3.22 and compare Wis 1.13–14; 2.23–24). **8:** Gen 6.12. **9–11:** The flood (Gen 6.11ff.).

3.12–16: The choice of Abraham (Gen 12.1; 17.5). **14:** *By night,* Gen 15.5, 12, 17. **3.17–19:** The Exodus and the giving of the law. **18:** Compare Ex 19.16–18; Ps 68.7–8. **20–27:** The tendency to sin is universal and permanent. **20:** *Evil heart,* the evil "yeşer" (see Sir 15.14–17 n.).

good departed, and the evil remained. 23 So the times passed and the years were completed, and you raised up for yourself a servant, named David. 24 You commanded him to build a city for your name, and there to offer you oblations from what is yours. 25 This was done for many years; but the inhabitants of the city transgressed, 26 in everything doing just as Adam and all his descendants had done, for they also had the evil heart. 27 So you handed over your city to your enemies.

28 "Then I said in my heart, Are the deeds of those who inhabit Babylon any better? Is that why it has gained dominion over Zion? 29 For when I came here I saw ungodly deeds without number, and my soul has seen many sinners during these thirty years. *h* And my heart failed me, 30 because I have seen how you endure those who sin, and have spared those who act wickedly, and have destroyed your people, and protected your enemies, 31 and have not shown to anyone how your way may be comprehended. *i* Are the deeds of Babylon better than those of Zion? 32 Or has another nation known you besides Israel? Or what tribes have so believed the covenants as these tribes of Jacob? 33 Yet their reward has not appeared and their labor has borne no fruit. For I have traveled widely among the nations and have seen that they abound in wealth, though they are unmindful of your commandments. 34 Now therefore weigh in a balance our iniquities and those of the inhabitants of the world; and it will be found which way the turn of the scale will incline. 35 When have the inhabitants of the earth not sinned in your sight? Or what nation

has kept your commandments so well? 36 You may indeed find individuals who have kept your commandments, but nations you will not find."

4 Then the angel that had been sent to me, whose name was Uriel, answered 2 and said to me, "Your understanding has utterly failed regarding this world, and do you think you can comprehend the way of the Most High?" 3 Then I said, "Yes, my lord." And he replied to me, "I have been sent to show you three ways, and to put before you three problems. 4 If you can solve one of them for me, then I will show you the way you desire to see, and will teach you why the heart is evil."

5 I said, "Speak, my lord."

And he said to me, "Go, weigh for me the weight of fire, or measure for me a blast *j* of wind, or call back for me the day that is past."

6 I answered and said, "Who of those that have been born can do that, that you should ask me about such things?"

7 And he said to me, "If I had asked you, 'How many dwellings are in the heart of the sea, or how many streams are at the source of the deep, or how many streams are above the firmament, or which are the exits of Hades, or which are the entrances *k* of paradise?' 8 perhaps you would have said to me, 'I never went down into the deep, nor as yet into Hades, neither did I ever ascend into heaven.' 9 But now I have asked you only

h Ethiop Arab 1 Arm: Lat Syr *in this thirtieth year*   *i* Syr; compare Ethiop: Lat *how this way should be forsaken*   *j* Syr Ethiop Arab 1 Arab 2 Georg *a measure*   *k* Syr Compare Ethiop Arab 2 Arm: Lat lacks *of Hades, or which are the entrances*

3.27: 2 Kings 25.1–21. 28–36: The deeds of Babylon compared with those of Israel. 28: *Babylon,* i.e. Rome (Rev 14.8). 29: *Came here,* to Rome. The first *thirty years* of the Babylonian exile are meant.

3.30–31: Here the author expresses the essence of the problem: God permits evildoers to continue in their wickedness, does not spare the suffering people of God, and does not let anyone understand why this should be

so. 34: For God's balance, compare Job 31.6; Ps 62.9; Prov 16.2; Dan 5.27; Enoch 41.1; 61.8. 36: *Individuals* among the Gentiles.

4.1–5.19: **The reply: God's ways are beyond human comprehension.**

4.1–12: **The limitations of the human mind** (Wis 9.16). 1: The name *Uriel* in Hebrew means "the fire of God." According to Enoch 20.2 Uriel is a watcher over the world and over Tartarus, the lowest part of hell

about fire and wind and the day—things that you have experienced and from which you cannot be separated, and you have given me no answer about them." [10]He said to me, "You cannot understand the things with which you have grown up; [11]how then can your mind comprehend the way of the Most High? And how can one who is already worn out[l] by the corrupt world understand incorruption?"[m] When I heard this, I fell on my face[n] [12]and said to him, "It would have been better for us not to be here than to come here and live in ungodliness, and to suffer and not understand why."

13 He answered me and said, "I went into a forest of trees of the plain, and they made a plan [14]and said, 'Come, let us go and make war against the sea, so that it may recede before us and so that we may make for ourselves more forests.' [15]In like manner the waves of the sea also made a plan and said, 'Come, let us go up and subdue the forest of the plain so that there also we may gain more territory for ourselves.' [16]But the plan of the forest was in vain, for the fire came and consumed it; [17]likewise also the plan of the waves of the sea was in vain,[o] for the sand stood firm and blocked it. [18]If now you were a judge between them, which would you undertake to justify, and which to condemn?"

19 I answered and said, "Each made a foolish plan, for the land has been assigned to the forest, and the locale of the sea a place to carry its waves."

20 He answered me and said, "You have judged rightly, but why have you not judged so in your own case? [21]For as the land has been assigned to the forest and the sea to its waves, so also those who inhabit the earth can understand only what is on the earth, and he who is[p]

above the heavens can understand what is above the height of the heavens."

22 Then I answered and said, "I implore you, my lord, why[q] have I been endowed with the power of understanding? [23]For I did not wish to inquire about the ways above, but about those things that we daily experience: why Israel has been given over to the Gentiles in disgrace; why the people whom you loved has been given over to godless tribes, and the law of our ancestors has been brought to destruction and the written covenants no longer exist. [24]We pass from the world like locusts, and our life is like a mist,[r] and we are not worthy to obtain mercy. [25]But what will he do for his[s] name that is invoked over us? It is about these things that I have asked."

26 He answered me and said, "If you are alive, you will see, and if you live long,[t] you will often marvel, because the age is hurrying swiftly to its end. [27]It will not be able to bring the things that have been promised to the righteous in their appointed times, because this age is full of sadness and infirmities. [28]For the evil about which[u] you ask me has been sown, but the harvest of it has not yet come. [29]If therefore that which has been sown is not reaped, and if the place where the evil has been sown does not pass away, the field where the good has been sown will not come. [30]For a grain of evil seed was sown in Adam's heart from the beginning, and how much ungodliness it has produced until now—and will produce until the time of thresh-

l Meaning of Lat uncertain   *m* Syr Ethiop *the way of the incorruptible?*   *n* Syr Ethiop Arab 1: Meaning of Lat uncertain   *o* Lat lacks *was in vain* *p* Or *those who are*   *q* Syr Ethiop Arm: Meaning of Lat uncertain   *r* Syr Ethiop Arab Georg: Lat *a trembling*   *s* Ethiop adds *holy* *t* Syr: Lat *live*   *u* Syr Ethiop: Meaning of Lat uncertain

---

(compare 2 Pet 2.4 note *l*). **12**: For the seer, to live without understanding of life's meaning is intolerable.

4.13–21: Parable of the conflict between the forest and the sea. 21: Isa 55.8–9; Ps 104.5–9; Jn 3.31; 1 Cor 2.14.

4.22–32: Additional questions. 26–32: Ezra protests that he is inquiring only about the meaning of earthly, historical happenings, not about cosmic events. The angel answers that the new age, soon to dawn, will solve all problems; but first the evil that is sown must be reaped. **30**: *A grain of evil seed,* the evil "yeṣer" (see Sir 15.14–17 n.).

ing comes! 31 Consider now for yourself how much fruit of ungodliness a grain of evil seed has produced. 32 When heads of grain without number are sown, how great a threshing floor they will fill!"

33 Then I answered and said, "How long?" When will these things be? Why are our years few and evil?" 34 He answered me and said, "Do not be in a greater hurry than the Most High. You, indeed, are in a hurry for yourself," but the Highest is in a hurry on behalf of many. 35 Did not the souls of the righteous in their chambers ask about these matters, saying, 'How long are we to remain here?" And when will the harvest of our reward come? 36 And the archangel Jeremiel answered and said, 'When the number of those like yourselves is completed;" for he has weighed the age in the balance, 37 and measured the times by measure, and numbered the times by number; and he will not move or arouse them until that measure is fulfilled.' "

38 Then I answered and said, "But, O sovereign Lord, all of us also are full of ungodliness. 39 It is perhaps on account of us that the time of threshing is delayed for the righteous—on account of the sins of those who inhabit the earth."

40 He answered me and said, "Go and ask a pregnant woman whether, when her nine months have been completed, her womb can keep the fetus within her any longer."

41 And I said, "No, lord, it cannot."

He said to me, "In Hades the chambers of the souls are like the womb. 42 For just as a woman who is in labor makes haste to escape the pangs of birth, so also do these places hasten to give back those things that were committed to them from the beginning. 43 Then the things that you desire to see will be disclosed to you."

44 I answered and said, "If I have found favor in your sight, and if it is possible, and if I am worthy, 45 show me this also: whether more time is to come than has passed, or whether for us the greater part has gone by. 46 For I know what has gone by, but I do not know what is to come."

47 And he said to me, "Stand at my right side, and I will show you the interpretation of a parable."

48 So I stood and looked, and lo, a flaming furnace passed by before me, and when the flame had gone by I looked, and lo, the smoke remained. 49 And after this a cloud full of water passed before me and poured down a heavy and violent rain, and when the violent rainstorm had passed, drops still remained in the cloud.

50 He said to me, "Consider it for yourself; for just as the rain is more than the drops, and the fire is greater than the smoke, so the quantity that passed was far greater; but drops and smoke remained."

51 Then I prayed and said, "Do you think that I shall live until those days? Or who will be alive in those days?"

52 He answered me and said, "Concerning the signs about which you ask me, I can tell you in part; but I was not sent to tell you concerning your life, for I do not know.

5 "Now concerning the signs: lo, the days are coming when those who inhabit the earth shall be seized with great terror," and the way of truth shall be hidden, and the land shall be barren of

v Syr Ethiop: Meaning of Lat uncertain
w Syr Ethiop Arab Arm: Meaning of Lat uncertain   x Syr Ethiop Arab 2 Georg: Lat *How long do I hope thus?*   y Syr Ethiop Arab 2: Lat *number of seeds is completed for you*
z Lat *in it*

4.33–43: **The seer asks when the new age will come;** he is told that first the predetermined number of the righteous must be completed. **35:** *The righteous,* i.e. the righteous dead. *Chambers,* literally "storehouses" or "garners"; according to rabbinical teaching the souls of the righteous dead are beneath the throne of God (compare Rev 6.9f.). **36:** *Jeremiel,* probably the same as Remiel, the seventh of seven archangels mentioned in 1 Enoch 20.1–8. *Completed,* 2.41; Rev 6.11. **36–37:** *Weighed . . . measured . . . numbered,* God has determined the times and periods of history (see Sir 36.10 n.). There may be an

faith. ²Unrighteousness shall be increased beyond what you yourself see, and beyond what you heard of formerly. ³And the land that you now see ruling shall be a trackless waste, and people shall see it desolate. ⁴But if the Most High grants that you live, you shall see it thrown into confusion after the third period;ᵃ

and the sun shall suddenly begin
to shine at night,
and the moon during the day.

⁵ Blood shall drip from wood,
and the stone shall utter its
voice;
the peoples shall be troubled,
and the stars shall fall.ᵇ

⁶And one shall reign whom those who inhabit the earth do not expect, and the birds shall fly away together; ⁷and the Dead Seaᶜ shall cast up fish; and one whom the many do not know shall make his voice heard by night, and all shall hear his voice.ᵈ ⁸There shall be chaos also in many places, fire shall often break out, the wild animals shall roam beyond their haunts, and menstruous women shall bring forth monsters. ⁹Salt waters shall be found in the sweet, and all friends shall conquer one another; then shall reason hide itself, and wisdom shall withdraw into its chamber, ¹⁰and it shall be sought by many but shall not be found, and unrighteousness and unrestraint shall increase on earth. ¹¹One country shall ask its neighbor, 'Has righteousness, or anyone who does right, passed through you?' And it will answer, 'No.' ¹²At that time people shall hope

but not obtain; they shall labor, but their ways shall not prosper. ¹³These are the signs that I am permitted to tell you, and if you pray again, and weep as you do now, and fast for seven days, you shall hear yet greater things than these."

14 Then I woke up, and my body shuddered violently, and my soul was so troubled that it fainted. ¹⁵But the angel who had come and talked with me held me and strengthened me and set me on my feet.

16 Now on the second night Phaltiel, a chief of the people, came to me and said, "Where have you been? And why is your face sad? ¹⁷Or do you not know that Israel has been entrusted to you in the land of their exile? ¹⁸Rise therefore and eat some bread, and do not forsake us, like a shepherd who leaves the flock in the power of savage wolves."

19 Then I said to him, "Go away from me and do not come near me for seven days; then you may come to me." He heard what I said and left me. ²⁰So I fasted seven days, mourning and weeping, as the angel Uriel had commanded me.

21 After seven days the thoughts of my heart were very grievous to me again. ²²Then my soul recovered the spirit of understanding, and I began once

a Literally after the third; Ethiop after three months; Arm after the third vision; Georg after the third day
b Ethiop Compare Syr and Arab: Meaning of Lat uncertain   c Lat Sea of Sodom
d Cn: Lat fish; and it shall make its voice heard by night, which the many have not known, but all shall hear its voice.

---

allusion to Dan 5.24–28, the handwriting on the wall. **41**: *Chambers,* see v. 35 n.

4.44–50: The seer asks what proportion of time remains; he is told by a parable that the end is near.

4.51–5.13: The seer asks whether the end will come during his own lifetime; he is given a description of the signs that will precede the end (compare Mt 24.4–31; Mk 13.5–27; Lk 21.8–28). **5.2**: Mt 24.12. **3**: *The land that you now see ruling,* i.e. the Roman Empire. **4**: The reference to *the third period* is cryptic (compare 14.11–13). **5**: *The stone shall utter its voice,* Hab 2.11; Lk 19.40. **6**: *The birds,*

foreseeing impending disasters, *shall fly away.* **5.8a**: Syriac, "a fissure shall arise over wide regions" (compare Zech 14.4). *Shall often break out,* or "shall burst forth for a long period." **10–11**: Isa 59.14–15. **13**: For the author, fasting prepared one to receive a divine revelation; he refers to three fasts each of seven days (5.20; 6.35; 12.51).

5.14–20: Conclusion of the vision. 14: *Then I woke up,* from the dream-vision. *My soul . . . fainted,* Pss 84.2; 107.5; Jon 2.7; compare Isa 6.5; Dan 10.17b. **16**: *Phaltiel,* the historical reference is uncertain; compare Paltiel in Num 34.26; 2 Sam 3.15.

more to speak words in the presence of the Most High. 23 I said, "O sovereign Lord, from every forest of the earth and from all its trees you have chosen one vine, 24 and from all the lands of the world you have chosen for yourself one region, *e* and from all the flowers of the world you have chosen for yourself one lily, 25 and from all the depths of the sea you have filled for yourself one river, and from all the cities that have been built you have consecrated Zion for yourself, 26 and from all the birds that have been created you have named for yourself one dove, and from all the flocks that have been made you have provided for yourself one sheep, 27 and from all the multitude of peoples you have gotten for yourself one people; and to this people, whom you have loved, you have given the law that is approved by all. 28 And now, O Lord, why have you handed the one over to the many, and dishonored *f* the one root beyond the others, and scattered your only one among the many? 29 And those who opposed your promises have trampled on those who believed your covenants. 30 If you really hate your people, they should be punished at your own hands."

31 When I had spoken these words, the angel who had come to me on a previous night was sent to me. 32 He said to me, "Listen to me, and I will instruct you; pay attention to me, and I will tell you more."

33 Then I said, "Speak, my lord." And he said to me, "Are you greatly disturbed in mind over Israel? Or do you love him more than his Maker does?"

34 I said, "No, my lord, but because of my grief I have spoken; for every hour I suffer agonies of heart, while I strive to understand the way of the Most High and to search out some part of his judgment."

35 He said to me, "You cannot." And I said, "Why not, my lord? Why then was I born? Or why did not my mother's womb become my grave, so that I would not see the travail of Jacob and the exhaustion of the people of Israel?"

36 He said to me, "Count up for me those who have not yet come, and gather for me the scattered raindrops, and make the withered flowers bloom again for me; 37 open for me the closed chambers, and bring out for me the winds shut up in them, or show me the picture of a voice; and then I will explain to you the travail that you ask to understand." *g*

38 I said, "O sovereign Lord, who is able to know these things except he whose dwelling is not with mortals? 39 As for me, I am without wisdom, and how can I speak concerning the things that you have asked me?"

40 He said to me, "Just as you cannot do one of the things that were mentioned, so you cannot discover my judgment, or the goal of the love that I have promised to my people."

41 I said, "Yet, O Lord, you have charge of those who are alive at the end, but what will those do who lived before me, or we, ourselves, or those who come after us?"

42 He said to me, "I shall liken my judgment to a circle; *h* just as for those who are last there is no slowness, so for those who are first there is no haste."

e Ethiop: Lat *pit*　　*f* Syr Ethiop Arab: Lat *prepared*　　*g* Lat *see*　　*h* Or *crown*

5.21–6.34: **The second vision. 5.21–30: The seer reiterates his complaints of divine inequity in dealing with Israel. 23–28:** Most of the figures representing Israel have been drawn from the Old Testament: the *vine* (v. 23), Ps 80.8–15; the *lily* (v. 24), Song 2.2 (interpreted allegorically); Hos 14.5; the *river* (v. 25), Isa 8.6; the city of *Zion* (v. 25), Ps 132.13; the *dove* (v. 26), Ps 74.19; the *sheep* (v. 26), Ps 79.13; Isa 53.7; the *root* (v. 28), 1 Enoch 93.8, compare Rom 11.17–18. **33:** It is unthinkable that human beings should love Israel more than God their *Maker does* (8.47). **35:** Job 3.11; 10.18–19. The seer insists that mortals must be able to comprehend some portion of God's ways; if not, life has no purpose at all. **36–40:** If the seer cannot understand the things of earth, how can he expect to fathom the judgments and purpose of God? **40:** *My . . . I,* the angel speaks in God's name.

43 Then I answered and said, "Could you not have created at one time those who have been and those who are and those who will be, so that you might show your judgment the sooner?"

44 He replied to me and said, "The creation cannot move faster than the Creator, nor can the world hold at one time those who have been created in it."

45 I said, "How have you said to your servant that you*i* will certainly give life at one time to your creation? If therefore all creatures will live at one time*j* and the creation will sustain them, it might even now be able to support all of them present at one time."

46 He said to me, "Ask a woman's womb, and say to it, 'If you bear ten*k* children, why one after another?' Request it therefore to produce ten at one time."

47 I said, "Of course it cannot, but only each in its own time."

48 He said to me, "Even so I have given the womb of the earth to those who from time to time are sown in it. 49 For as an infant does not bring forth, and a woman who has become old does not bring forth any longer, so I have made the same rule for the world that I created."

50 Then I inquired and said, "Since you have now given me the opportunity, let me speak before you. Is our mother, of whom you have told me, still young? Or is she now approaching old age?"

51 He replied to me, "Ask a woman who bears children, and she will tell you. 52 Say to her, 'Why are those whom you have borne recently not like those whom you bore before, but smaller in stature?' 53 And she herself will answer you,

'Those born in the strength of youth are different from those born during the time of old age, when the womb is failing.' 54 Therefore you also should consider that you and your contemporaries are smaller in stature than those who were before you, 55 and those who come after you will be smaller than you, as born of a creation that already is aging and passing the strength of youth."

56 I said, "I implore you, O Lord, if I have found favor in your sight, show your servant through whom you will visit your creation."

6 He said to me, "At the beginning of the circle of the earth, before*l* the portals of the world were in place, and before the assembled winds blew, 2 and before the rumblings of thunder sounded, and before the flashes of lightning shone, and before the foundations of paradise were laid, 3 and before the beautiful flowers were seen, and before the powers of movements*m* were established, and before the innumerable hosts of angels were gathered together, 4 and before the heights of the air were lifted up, and before the measures of the firmaments were named, and before the footstool of Zion was established, 5 and before the present years were reckoned and before the imaginations of those who now sin were estranged, and before those who stored

i Syr Ethiop Arab 1: Meaning of Lat uncertain
j Lat lacks *If . . . one time* *k* Syr Ethiop Arab 2 Arm: Meaning of Lat uncertain
l Meaning of Lat uncertain: Compare Syr *The beginning by the hand of humankind, but the end by my own hands. For as before the land of the world existed there, and before;* Ethiop: *At first by the Son of Man, and afterwards I myself. For before the earth and the lands were created, and before*
m Or *earthquakes*

5.41–55: The place of successive generations in the divine plan for the world. The seer inquires about the status of those who have died before the messianic age shall begin (v. 41); he is told, in effect, that the last shall be as the first, and the first as the last (v. 42). He inquires why all human generations could not have lived at the same time, namely at the beginning of the messianic age (v. 43); the reply is that generations must follow one another (vv. 44–49). *Mother earth*

has become old and the last generations are inferior to the early ones (vv. 50–55).
5.52: *Smaller in stature,* compare Gen 6.4 (the Nephilim, "giants"); Num 13.33.
5.56–6.6: The end of the age. As God alone created the world (without an intermediate agency), so he will bring about its end by himself alone (7.39–44). The use of "before . . ." (6.1) is characteristic of creation stories. See the Babylonian creation story "Enuma Elish" and Gen 2.4b–5.

up treasures of faith were sealed— [6]then I planned these things, and they were made through me alone and not through another; just as the end shall come through me alone and not through another."

7 I answered and said, "What will be the dividing of the times? Or when will be the end of the first age and the beginning of the age that follows?"

8 He said to me, "From Abraham to Isaac,[n] because from him were born Jacob and Esau, for Jacob's hand held Esau's heel from the beginning. [9]Now Esau is the end of this age, and Jacob is the beginning of the age that follows. [10]The beginning of a person is the hand, and the end of a person is the heel;[o] seek for nothing else, Ezra, between the heel and the hand, Ezra!"

11 I answered and said, "O sovereign Lord, if I have found favor in your sight, [12]show your servant the last of your signs of which you showed me a part on a previous night."

13 He answered and said to me, "Rise to your feet and you will hear a full, resounding voice. [14]And if the place where you are standing is greatly shaken [15]while the voice is speaking, do not be terrified; because the word concerns the end, and the foundations of the earth will understand [16]that the speech concerns them. They will tremble and be shaken, for they know that their end must be changed."

17 When I heard this, I got to my feet and listened; a voice was speaking, and its sound was like the sound of mighty[p] waters. [18]It said, "The days are coming when I draw near to visit the inhabitants of the earth, [19]and when I require from the doers of iniquity the penalty of their iniquity, and when the humiliation of Zion is complete. [20]When the seal is placed upon the age that is about to pass away, then I will show these signs: the books shall be opened before the face of the firmament, and all shall see my judgment[q] together. [21]Children a year old shall speak with their voices, and pregnant women shall give birth to premature children at three and four months, and these shall live and leap about. [22]Sown places shall suddenly appear unsown, and full storehouses shall suddenly be found to be empty; [23]the trumpet shall sound aloud, and when all hear it, they shall suddenly be terrified. [24]At that time friends shall make war on friends like enemies, the earth and those who inhabit it shall be terrified, and the springs of the fountains shall stand still, so that for three hours they shall not flow.

25 "It shall be that whoever remains after all that I have foretold to you shall be saved and shall see my salvation and the end of my world. [26]And they shall see those who were taken up, who from their birth have not tasted death; and the heart of the earth's[r] inhabitants shall be changed and converted to a different spirit. [27]For evil shall be blotted out, and deceit shall be quenched; [28]faithfulness shall flourish, and corruption shall be overcome, and the truth, which has been so long without fruit, shall be revealed."

29 While he spoke to me, little by lit-

n Other ancient authorities read *to Abraham*
o Syr: Meaning of Lat uncertain   p Lat
many   q Syr: Lat lacks *my judgment*
r Syr Compare Ethiop Arab 1 Arm: Lat lacks
earth's

6.7–10: The dividing of the times. In allegorical language the seer is told that the present corrupt age (symbolized by *Esau*) will be followed immediately, without a break, by the glorious age to come (symbolized by *Jacob*).
6.11–28: The signs of the end of the age. 12: *Of which you showed me a part,* 4.51–5.13. **17:** *I got to my feet,* presumably the author had previously been lying down, experiencing a dream-vision. *Mighty waters,* Rev 1.15; 14.2;

19.6. **20:** *The books shall be opened,* i.e. the celestial books in which are written the deeds of humankind (Dan 7.10; 12.1; Mal 3.16; Rev 20.12; compare Ex 32.32; Ps 69.28; Lk 10.20; Heb 12.23).
6.23: *The trumpet,* 1 Cor 15.52; 1 Thess 4.16. **26:** *Those who were taken up,* such as Enoch (Gen 5.24; Sir 44.16) and Elijah (2 Kings 2.11–12); compare also 14.9. *Shall be . . . converted,* by the preaching of Elijah (Mal 4.6).

tle the place where I was standing began to rock to and fro. [s] 30 And he said to me, "I have come to show you these things this night. [t] 31 If therefore you will pray again and fast again for seven days, I will again declare to you greater things than these, [u] 32 because your voice has surely been heard by the Most High; for the Mighty One has seen your uprightness and has also observed the purity that you have maintained from your youth. 33 Therefore he sent me to show you all these things, and to say to you: 'Believe and do not be afraid! 34 Do not be quick to think vain thoughts concerning the former times; then you will not act hastily in the last times.'"

35 Now after this I wept again and fasted seven days in the same way as before, in order to complete the three weeks that had been prescribed for me. 36 Then on the eighth night my heart was troubled within me again, and I began to speak in the presence of the Most High. 37 My spirit was greatly aroused, and my soul was in distress.

38 I said, "O Lord, you spoke at the beginning of creation, and said on the first day, 'Let heaven and earth be made,' and your word accomplished the work. 39 Then the spirit was blowing, and darkness and silence embraced everything; the sound of human voices was not yet there. [v] 40 Then you commanded a ray of light to be brought out from your store-chambers, so that your works could be seen.

41 "Again, on the second day, you created the spirit of the firmament, and commanded it to divide and separate the waters, so that one part might move upward and the other part remain beneath.

42 "On the third day you commanded the waters to be gathered together in a seventh part of the earth; six parts you dried up and kept so that some of them might be planted and cultivated and be of service before you. 43 For your word went forth, and at once the work was done. 44 Immediately fruit came forth in endless abundance and of varied appeal to the taste, and flowers of inimitable color, and odors of inexpressible fragrance. These were made on the third day.

45 "On the fourth day you commanded the brightness of the sun, the light of the moon, and the arrangement of the stars to come into being; 46 and you commanded them to serve humankind, about to be formed.

47 "On the fifth day you commanded the seventh part, where the water had been gathered together, to bring forth living creatures, birds, and fishes; and so it was done. 48 The dumb and lifeless water produced living creatures, as it was commanded, so that therefore the nations might declare your wondrous works.

49 "Then you kept in existence two living creatures; [w] the one you called Be-

s Syr Ethiop Compare Arab Arm: Meaning of Lat uncertain   t Syr Compare Ethiop: Meaning of Lat uncertain   u Syr Ethiop Arab 1 Arm: Lat adds *by day*   v Syr Ethiop: Lat *was not yet from you*   w Syr Ethiop: Lat *two souls*

6.29–34: **Conclusion of the vision. 34:** The seer is cautioned against being oversolicitous.
6.35–9.25: The third vision. 6.35–37: Introduction. 35: *I . . . fasted seven days,* see 5.13 n. *The three weeks* (compare Dan 10.2–3), so far only two fasts of seven days have been mentioned (here and at 5.20); presumably the author is thinking also of another fast prior to the first vision (3.1–5.20), not mentioned in the present form of the book.
6.38–59: The seer recounts God's work in creation. If the world was created for Israel (v. 55), why has the nation not possessed its inheritance? **38–54:** Gen ch 1. **38:** *Your word accomplished the work,* Ps 33.6; Heb 11.3; 2 Pet 3.5. **40:** God's *store-chambers* are in heaven. **41:** *The spirit of the firmament* is an angel (compare the angel with power over fire, Rev 14.18, and the angel of water, Rev 16.5). **46:** Ps 8.6–8.
6.49–52: *Behemoth* and *Leviathan* are two primeval monsters (compare Job 7.12; 26.12–13; Ps 74.12–15; 89.10–11; Isa 30.7; 51.9–10). **55:** The idea that the world was created for the sake of Israel (7.11) is not found in the Old Testament, but was deduced by Jewish rabbis from such passages as Ex 4.22; Deut

hemoth[x] and the name of the other Leviathan. [50] And you separated one from the other, for the seventh part where the water had been gathered together could not hold them both. [51] And you gave Behemoth[x] one of the parts that had been dried up on the third day, to live in it, where there are a thousand mountains; [52] but to Leviathan you gave the seventh part, the watery part; and you have kept them to be eaten by whom you wish, and when you wish.

[53] "On the sixth day you commanded the earth to bring forth before you cattle, wild animals, and creeping things; [54] and over these you placed Adam, as ruler over all the works that you had made; and from him we have all come, the people whom you have chosen.

[55] "All this I have spoken before you, O Lord, because you have said that it was for us that you created this world.[y] [56] As for the other nations that have descended from Adam, you have said that they are nothing, and that they are like spittle, and you have compared their abundance to a drop from a bucket. [57] And now, O Lord, these nations, which are reputed to be as nothing, domineer over us and devour us. [58] But we your people, whom you have called your firstborn, only begotten, zealous for you,[z] and most dear, have been given into their hands. [59] If the world has indeed been created for us, why do we not possess our world as an inheritance? How long will this be so?"

7 When I had finished speaking these words, the angel who had been sent to me on the former nights was sent to me again. [2] He said to me, "Rise, Ezra, and listen to the words that I have come to speak to you."

[3] I said, "Speak, my lord." And he said to me, "There is a sea set in a wide expanse so that it is deep and vast, [4] but it has an entrance set in a narrow place, so that it is like a river. [5] If there are those who wish to reach the sea, to look at it or to navigate it, how can they come to the broad part unless they pass through the narrow part? [6] Another example: There is a city built and set on a plain, and it is full of all good things; [7] but the entrance to it is narrow and set in a precipitous place, so that there is fire on the right hand and deep water on the left. [8] There is only one path lying between them, that is, between the fire and the water, so that only one person can walk on the path. [9] If now the city is given to someone as an inheritance, how will the heir receive the inheritance unless by passing through the appointed danger?"

[10] I said, "That is right, lord." He said to me, "So also is Israel's portion. [11] For I made the world for their sake, and when Adam transgressed my statutes, what had been made was judged. [12] And so the entrances of this world were made narrow and sorrowful and toilsome; they are few and evil, full of dangers and involved in great hardships. [13] But the entrances of the greater world are broad and safe, and yield the fruit of immortality. [14] Therefore unless the living pass through the difficult and futile experiences, they can never receive those things that have been reserved for them. [15] Now therefore why are you disturbed, seeing that you are to perish? Why are you moved, seeing that you are mortal? [16] Why have you not considered in your mind what is to come, rather than what is now present?"

[17] Then I answered and said,

x Other Lat authorities read *Enoch*
y Syr Ethiop Arab 2: Lat *the firstborn world*
Compare Arab 1 *first world*   z Meaning of Lat uncertain

10.15; 14.2. **56**: *A drop from a bucket,* Isa 40.15.
7.1–25: The angel instructs the seer. The wickedness of this world makes the path to the next world narrow and dangerous. **1**: *The former nights,* at the beginning of each vision. **11**: Though *the world* was created for Israel's *sake,* that inheritance was spoiled *when* *Adam transgressed* (compare Rom 5.18–20). **12** and **13**: *The entrances,* Ethiopic, "the ways," i.e. the paths of life here on earth, and in the world of immortality. **13**: *The greater world,* Syriac, "the future world." **7.14**: *Things . . . reserved for them,* 1 Cor 2.9. **15–16**: The seer should not brood over diffi-

"O sovereign Lord, you have ordained in your law that the righteous shall inherit these things, but that the ungodly shall perish. 18 The righteous, therefore, can endure difficult circumstances while hoping for easier ones; but those who have done wickedly have suffered the difficult circumstances and will never see the easier ones."

19 He said to me, "You are not a better judge than the Lord,^a or wiser than the Most High! 20 Let many perish who are now living, rather than that the law of God that is set before them be disregarded! 21 For the Lord^b strictly commanded those who came into the world, when they came, what they should do to live, and what they should observe to avoid punishment. 22 Nevertheless they were not obedient, and spoke against him;

> they devised for themselves vain
>   thoughts,
23 and proposed to themselves
>   wicked frauds;
> they even declared that the Most
>   High does not exist,
> and they ignored his ways.
24 They scorned his law,
>   and denied his covenants;
> they have been unfaithful to his
>   statutes,
> and have not performed his
>   works.

25 "That is the reason, Ezra, that empty things are for the empty, and full things are for the full.

26 "For indeed the time will come, when the signs that I have foretold to you will come to pass, that the city that now is not seen shall appear,^c and the land that now is hidden shall be disclosed. 27 Everyone who has been delivered from the evils that I have foretold shall see my wonders. 28 For my son the Messiah^d shall be revealed with those who are with him, and those who remain shall rejoice four hundred years. 29 After those years my son the Messiah shall die, and all who draw human breath.^e 30 Then the world shall be turned back to primeval silence for seven days, as it was at the first beginnings, so that no one shall be left. 31 After seven days the world that is not yet awake shall be roused, and that which is corruptible shall perish. 32 The earth shall give up those who are asleep in it, and the dust those who rest there in silence; and the chambers shall give up the souls that have been committed to them. 33 The Most High shall be revealed on the seat of judgment, and compassion shall pass away, and patience shall be withdrawn.^f 34 Only judgment shall remain, truth shall stand, and faithfulness shall grow strong. 35 Recompense shall follow, and the reward shall be manifested; righteous deeds shall awake, and unrighteous

a Other ancient authorities read God; Ethiop Georg the only One   b Other ancient authorities read God   c Arm: Lat Syr that the bride shall appear, even the city appearing   d Syr Arab 1: Ethiop my Messiah; Arab 2 the Messiah; Arm the Messiah of God; Lat my son Jesus   e Arm all who have continued in faith and in patience   f Lat shall gather together

---

culties and death; though inevitable, they are but preliminary to something better (2 Cor 4.18). **17–18**: The seer inquires whether the future bliss is only for the righteous. They, after all, have hope of bliss with God beyond this life. But what of the wicked, who suffer now and are doomed to suffer more in the judgment? **19–25**: The angel replies that those who disregard God's law will be punished; they had fair warning. **25**: Mt 13.12.

7.26–44: The messianic kingdom and the end of the world. 26: *The signs . . . foretold*, 6.20–24. *The city*, the Jerusalem that is to come; see 10.25–54. *The land*, the paradise that is to come. **28**: *Those who remain*, after the

tribulations that will precede the inauguration of the messianic kingdom. *Four hundred years*, so the Latin and Arabic 1; Syriac, "thirty years"; Arabic 2, "one thousand years"; Ethiopic and Armenian omit. **31**: *The world . . . not yet awake*, i.e. the world to come. **32**: Dan 12.2. *Chambers*, see 4.35 n. **33**: *Judgment*, Syriac adds, "and then comes the end." *Away*, Syriac adds, "and pity shall be far off." The final judgment will be conducted in strict accord with justice and truth. **34**: *Grow strong*, i.e. triumph. **35**: *Righteous deeds shall awake*, acts of charity hitherto concealed shall be disclosed (compare Mt 25.35–46).

deeds shall not sleep. *g 36* The pit*h* of torment shall appear, and opposite it shall be the place of rest; and the furnace of hell*i* shall be disclosed, and opposite it the paradise of delight. *37* Then the Most High will say to the nations that have been raised from the dead, 'Look now, and understand whom you have denied, whom you have not served, whose commandments you have despised. *38* Look on this side and on that; here are delight and rest, and there are fire and torments.' Thus he will*j* speak to them on the day of judgment— *39* a day that has no sun or moon or stars, *40* or cloud or thunder or lightning, or wind or water or air, or darkness or evening or morning, *41* or summer or spring or heat or winter*k* or frost or cold, or hail or rain or dew, *42* or noon or night, or dawn or shining or brightness or light, but only the splendor of the glory of the Most High, by which all shall see what has been destined. *43* It will last as though for a week of years. *44* This is my judgment and its prescribed order; and to you alone I have shown these things."

45 I answered and said, "O sovereign Lord, I said then and*l* I say now: Blessed are those who are alive and keep your commandments! *46* But what of those for whom I prayed? For who among the living is there that has not sinned, or who is there among mortals that has not transgressed your covenant? *47* And now I see that the world to come will bring delight to few, but torments to many. *48* For an evil heart has grown up in us, which has alienated us from God,*m* and has brought us into corruption and the ways of death, and has shown us the paths of perdition and removed us far

from life—and that not merely for a few but for almost all who have been created."

49 He answered me and said, "Listen to me, Ezra,*n* and I will instruct you, and will admonish you once more. *50* For this reason the Most High has made not one world but two. *51* Inasmuch as you have said that the righteous are not many but few, while the ungodly abound, hear the explanation for this.

52 "If you have just a few precious stones, will you add to them lead and clay?"*o 53* I said, "Lord, how could that be?" *54* And he said to me, "Not only that, but ask the earth and she will tell you; defer to her, and she will declare it to you. *55* Say to her, 'You produce gold and silver and bronze, and also iron and lead and clay; *56* but silver is more abundant than gold, and bronze than silver, and iron than bronze, and lead than iron, and clay than lead.' *57* Judge therefore which things are precious and desirable, those that are abundant or those that are rare?"

58 I said, "O sovereign Lord, what is plentiful is of less worth, for what is more rare is more precious."

59 He answered me and said, "Consider within yourself*p* what you have thought, for the person who has what is hard to get rejoices more than the person who has what is plentiful. *60* So also will

g The passage from verse *36* to verse *105,* formerly missing, has been restored to the text
h Syr Ethiop: Lat *place*   i Lat Syr Ethiop *Gehenna*   j Syr Ethiop Arab 1: Lat *you shall*
k Or *storm*   l Syr: Lat *And I answered, "I said then, O Lord, and*   m Cn: Lat Syr Ethiop *from these*
n Syr Arab 1 Georg: Lat Ethiop lack *Ezra*
o Arab 1: Meaning of Lat Syr Ethiop uncertain
p Syr Ethiop Arab 1: Meaning of Lat uncertain

7.36–105: These verses are lacking from the standard editions of the Latin Vulgate and from the King James Version. They are present in the Syriac, Ethiopic, Arabic, and Armenian versions, and in two Latin manuscripts. The section was probably deliberately cut out of an ancestor of most extant Latin manuscripts because of dogmatic reasons, for the passage contains an emphatic denial of the value of prayers for the dead (v. *105*). **36:** *Pit,* Rev 9.2. *Opposite,* Lk 16.23–24. **37:** Mt

25.31ff. **39–43:** Description of the day of judgment. **42:** *Only the uncreated light of the Most High* will serve to illuminate the judgment scene (compare Isa 60.19–20; Rev 21.23). **43:** *A week of years,* seven years. **7.45–61:** **The small number of the saved** (contrast Lk 13.23–30). **45–46:** The seer's chief concern has only been deepened. What hope is there for sinners? And are not all, or almost all (7.48) sinners? **48:** *An evil heart,* see 3.20 n. **49:** 5.32.

be the judgment*q* that I have promised; for I will rejoice over the few who shall be saved, because it is they who have made my glory to prevail now, and through them my name has now been honored. *61* I will not grieve over the great number of those who perish; for it is they who are now like a mist, and are similar to a flame and smoke—they are set on fire and burn hotly, and are extinguished."

62 I replied and said, "O earth, what have you brought forth, if the mind is made out of the dust like the other created things? *63* For it would have been better if the dust itself had not been born, so that the mind might not have been made from it. *64* But now the mind grows with us, and therefore we are tormented, because we perish and we know it. *65* Let the human race lament, but let the wild animals of the field be glad; let all who have been born lament, but let the cattle and the flocks rejoice. *66* It is much better with them than with us; for they do not look for a judgment, and they do not know of any torment or salvation promised to them after death. *67* What does it profit us that we shall be preserved alive but cruelly tormented? *68* For all who have been born are entangled in*r* iniquities, and are full of sins and burdened with transgressions. *69* And if after death we were not to come into judgment, perhaps it would have been better for us."

70 He answered me and said, "When the Most High made the world and Adam and all who have come from him, he first prepared the judgment and the things that pertain to the judgment. *71* But now, understand from your own words—for you have said that the mind

grows with us. *72* For this reason, therefore, those who live on earth shall be tormented, because though they had understanding, they committed iniquity; and though they received the commandments, they did not keep them; and though they obtained the law, they dealt unfaithfully with what they received. *73* What, then, will they have to say in the judgment, or how will they answer in the last times? *74* How long the Most High has been patient with those who inhabit the world!—and not for their sake, but because of the times that he has foreordained."

75 I answered and said, "If I have found favor in your sight, O Lord, show this also to your servant: whether after death, as soon as everyone of us yields up the soul, we shall be kept in rest until those times come when you will renew the creation, or whether we shall be tormented at once?"

76 He answered me and said, "I will show you that also, but do not include yourself with those who have shown scorn, or number yourself among those who are tormented. *77* For you have a treasure of works stored up with the Most High, but it will not be shown to you until the last times. *78* Now concerning death, the teaching is: When the decisive decree has gone out from the Most High that a person shall die, as the spirit leaves the body to return again to him who gave it, first of all it adores the glory of the Most High. *79* If it is one of those who have shown scorn and have not kept the way of the Most High, who have

q Syr Arab 1: Lat *creation*   *r* Syr *defiled with*

7.52: The question implies that the number of the elect cannot be increased by adding base elements. **61:** The angel will not grieve over the sinners who perish, but Ezra will! (7.62–69).
7.62–74: The seer's lament over the human race. 63: 4.12. **64:** The possession of reasoning powers intensifies sufferings. **67:** Ezra, like the whole human race, is one of the sinners, and thus is worse off than the animals, who cannot know and meditate on their fate. Contrast 6.32–34. **70:** *Things that*

pertain to the judgment, according to rabbinical teaching, before the beginning of the world God created Paradise and Gehenna.
7.75–101: The state of the departed after death and before the judgment. 76: Ezra is not to include himself among the wicked, says the angel. But the seer continues to do so (8.47). **77:** *A treasure of works,* 8.33, 36. *Will not be shown,* see v. 35 n. **78:** Eccl 12.7. The first act of the departed spirit (whether righteous or wicked) is to adore God.

despised his law and hated those who fear God— *80* such spirits shall not enter into habitations, but shall immediately wander about in torments, always grieving and sad, in seven ways. *81* The first way, because they have scorned the law of the Most High. *82* The second way, because they cannot now make a good repentance so that they may live. *83* The third way, they shall see the reward laid up for those who have trusted the covenants of the Most High. *84* The fourth way, they shall consider the torment laid up for themselves in the last days. *85* The fifth way, they shall see how the habitations of the others are guarded by angels in profound quiet. *86* The sixth way, they shall see how some of them will cross over*s* into torments. *87* The seventh way, which is worse*t* than all the ways that have been mentioned, because they shall utterly waste away in confusion and be consumed with shame,*u* and shall wither with fear at seeing the glory of the Most High in whose presence they sinned while they were alive, and in whose presence they are to be judged in the last times.

88 "Now this is the order of those who have kept the ways of the Most High, when they shall be separated from their mortal body.*v* *89* During the time that they lived in it,*w* they laboriously served the Most High, and withstood danger every hour so that they might keep the law of the Lawgiver perfectly. *90* Therefore this is the teaching concerning them: *91* First of all, they shall see with great joy the glory of him who receives them, for they shall have rest in seven orders. *92* The first order, because they have striven with great effort to overcome the evil thought that was formed with them, so that it might not lead them astray from life into death. *93* The second order, because they see the perplexity in which

the souls of the ungodly wander and the punishment that awaits them. *94* The third order, they see the witness that he who formed them bears concerning them, that throughout their life they kept the law with which they were entrusted. *95* The fourth order, they understand the rest that they now enjoy, being gathered into their chambers and guarded by angels in profound quiet, and the glory waiting for them in the last days. *96* The fifth order, they rejoice that they have now escaped what is corruptible and shall inherit what is to come; and besides they see the straits and toil*x* from which they have been delivered, and the spacious liberty that they are to receive and enjoy in immortality. *97* The sixth order, when it is shown them how their face is to shine like the sun, and how they are to be made like the light of the stars, being incorruptible from then on. *98* The seventh order, which is greater than all that have been mentioned, because they shall rejoice with boldness, and shall be confident without confusion, and shall be glad without fear, for they press forward to see the face of him whom they served in life and from whom they are to receive their reward when glorified. *99* This is the order of the souls of the righteous, as henceforth is announced;*y* and the previously mentioned are the ways of torment that those who would not give heed shall suffer hereafter."

100 Then I answered and said, "Will time therefore be given to the souls, after they have been separated from the bodies, to see what you have described to me?"

s Cn: Meaning of Lat uncertain   *t* Lat Syr Ethiop *greater*   *u* Syr Ethiop: Meaning of Lat uncertain   *v* Lat *the corruptible vessel*
w Syr: Meaning of Lat uncertain
x Syr Ethiop: Lat *fullness*   *y* Syr: Meaning of Lat uncertain

---

7.80–87: Seven kinds of torment for the wicked. **80:** *Habitations,* Lk 16.9; elsewhere called "chambers," see 4.35 n. **83:** Compare Lk 16.23. **85:** *The others,* i.e. the righteous. **7.88–99:** Seven kinds of joyous rest for the righteous. The author implies that the *mortal body* has been merely a prison-house for the spirit (contrast 1 Cor 15.53; 2 Cor 5.2–4). **92:** *The evil thought,* the evil "yeṣer" (see Sir 15.14–17 n.). **95:** *Chambers,* see 4.35 n. *In the last days,* better, "at their latter end." **97:** *Shine,* v. *125;* Dan 12.3; Mt 13.43. **98:** *To see*

101 He said to me, "They shall have freedom for seven days, so that during these seven days they may see the things of which you have been told, and afterwards they shall be gathered in their habitations."

102 I answered and said, "If I have found favor in your sight, show further to me, your servant, whether on the day of judgment the righteous will be able to intercede for the ungodly or to entreat the Most High for them— *103* fathers for sons or sons for parents, brothers for brothers, relatives for their kindred, or friends for those who are most dear."

104 He answered me and said, "Since you have found favor in my sight, I will show you this also. The day of judgment is decisive *z* and displays to all the seal of truth. Just as now a father does not send his son, or a son his father, or a master his servant, or a friend his dearest friend, to be ill *a* or sleep or eat or be healed in his place, *105* so no one shall ever pray for another on that day, neither shall anyone lay a burden on another; *b* for then all shall bear their own righteousness and unrighteousness."

36 *106* I answered and said, "How then do we find that first Abraham prayed for the people of Sodom, and Moses for our ancestors who sinned in the desert, 37 *107* and Joshua after him for Israel in the days of Achan, 38 *108* and Samuel in the days of Saul, *c* and David for the plague, and Solomon for those at the dedication, 39 *109* and Elijah for those who received the rain, and for the one who was dead, that he might live, 40 *110* and Hezekiah for the people in the days of Sennacherib, and many others prayed for many? 41 *111* So if now, when corruption has increased and unrighteousness has multiplied, the righteous have prayed for the ungodly, why will it not be so then as well?"

42 *112* He answered me and said, "This present world is not the end; the full glory does not *d* remain in it; *e* therefore those who were strong prayed for the weak. 43 *113* But the day of judgment will be the end of this age and the beginning *f* of the immortal age to come, in which corruption has passed away, 44 *114* sinful indulgence has come to an end, unbelief has been cut off, and righteousness has increased and truth has appeared. 45 *115* Therefore no one will then be able to have mercy on someone who has been condemned in the judgment, or to harm *g* someone who is victorious."

46 *116* I answered and said, "This is my first and last comment: it would have been better if the earth had not produced Adam, or else, when it had produced him, had restrained him from sinning. 47 *117* For what good is it to all that they live in sorrow now and expect punishment after death? 48 *118* O Adam, what have you done? For though it was you who sinned, the fall was not yours alone, but ours also who are your descendants. 49 *119* For what good is it to us, if an immortal time has been promised to us, but we have done deeds that bring death? 50 *120* And what good is it that an everlasting hope has been promised to us, but we

---

z Lat *bold* *a* Syr Ethiop Arm: Lat *to understand*   *b* Syr Ethiop: Lat lacks *on that . . . another*   *c* Syr Ethiop Arab 1: Lat Arab 2 Arm lack *in the days of Saul*   *d* Lat lacks *not*   *e* Or *the glory does not continuously abide in it*   *f* Syr Ethiop: Lat lacks *the beginning*   *g* Syr Ethiop: Lat *overwhelm*

---

the face of God (Mt 5.8; Heb 12.14; 1 Jn 3.2; Rev 22.4). *Reward*, 1 Cor 3.14; Rev 22.12. *101: Habitations*, see v. *80* n.

7.102–115: No intercession for the wicked on the day of judgment (compare Deut 24.16; Jer 31.30; Ezek 18.1–32). *106:* At verse *106* we come to the continuation of chapter 7 as preserved in the standard editions of the Latin Vulgate; NRSV resumes the Latin numbering here, designating verses *106–140* as 36–70, but with the numbers *106–140* added as well. Gen 18.23; Ex 32.11. *107:* Josh 7.6–7. *108:* *Samuel*, 1 Sam 7.9; 12.23. *David*, 2 Sam 24.17. *Solomon*, 1 Kings 8.22–23, 30. *109:* 1 Kings 18.42, 45; 17.20–21. *110:* 2 Kings 19.15–19.

7.112–115: During the present order, intercession *for the weak* is possible, but the day of judgment means the closing of all accounts on the basis of strict justice (see v. 33 n.).

7.116–131: The seer laments the fate of the mass of humanity. 116: *My first . . . comment*, 3.5ff. *118:* 4.30–31.

The seer laments the
fate of humankind
2 ESDRAS 7, 8

have miserably failed? 51 *121* Or that safe and healthful habitations have been reserved for us, but we have lived wickedly? 52 *122* Or that the glory of the Most High will defend those who have led a pure life, but we have walked in the most wicked ways? 53 *123* Or that a paradise shall be revealed, whose fruit remains unspoiled and in which are abundance and healing, but we shall not enter it 54 *124* because we have lived in perverse ways? *h* 55 *125* Or that the faces of those who practiced self-control shall shine more than the stars, but our faces shall be blacker than darkness? 56 *126* For while we lived and committed iniquity we did not consider what we should suffer after death."

57 *127* He answered and said, "This is the significance of the contest that all who are born on earth shall wage: 58 *128* if they are defeated they shall suffer what you have said, but if they are victorious they shall receive what I have said. *i* 59 *129* For this is the way of which Moses, while he was alive, spoke to the people, saying, 'Choose life for yourself, so that you may live!' 60 *130* But they did not believe him or the prophets after him, or even myself who have spoken to them. 61 *131* Therefore there shall not be *j* grief at their destruction, so much as joy over those to whom salvation is assured."

62 *132* I answered and said, "I know, O Lord, that the Most High is now called merciful, because he has mercy on those who have not yet come into the world; 63 *133* and gracious, because he is gracious to those who turn in repentance to his law; 64 *134* and patient, because he

shows patience toward those who have sinned, since they are his own creatures; 65 *135* and bountiful, because he would rather give than take away; *k* 66 *136* and abundant in compassion, because he makes his compassions abound more and more to those now living and to those who are gone and to those yet to come— 67 *137* for if he did not make them abound, the world with those who inhabit it would not have life— 68 *138* and he is called the giver, because if he did not give out of his goodness so that those who have committed iniquities might be relieved of them, not one ten-thousandth of humankind could have life; 69 *139* and the judge, because if he did not pardon those who were created by his word and blot out the multitude of their sins, *l* 70 *140* there would probably be left only very few of the innumerable multitude."

8 He answered me and said, "The Most High made this world for the sake of many, but the world to come for the sake of only a few. 2 But I tell you a parable, Ezra. Just as, when you ask the earth, it will tell you that it provides a large amount of clay from which earthenware is made, but only a little dust from which gold comes, so is the course of the present world. 3 Many have been created, but only a few shall be saved."

4 I answered and said, "Then drink your fill of understanding, *m* O my soul, and drink wisdom, O my heart. 5 For

h Cn: Lat Syr *places*   *i* Syr Ethiop Arab 1: Lat *what I say*   *j* Syr: Lat *there was not*   *k* Or he *is ready to give according to requests*   *l* Lat *contempts*   *m* Syr: Lat *Then release understanding*

7.123: *Fruit,* compare Ezek 47.12; Rev 22.2. **125:** *Shine more than the stars,* Dan 12.3; compare Mt 13.43. *Darkness,* Mt 8.12; 22.13; Jude 13. **127–129:** Human beings are responsible for their choices (Deut 30.19; Ezek 18.1–32).

7.132–8.3: The seer acknowledges (and implicitly appeals to) God's mercy. Will a merciful God permit so many to perish? Ezra is told that nothing can alter their doom, for *many have been created, but only a few shall be saved* (8.3). **132–139:** For the sevenfold attributes of God, compare Ex 34.6–7. **132:**

O Lord, better, "sir." **135:** Acts 20.35. **138:** *Life,* i.e. eternal life.

8.2: *A parable,* an analogous illustration (as in 7.54–57). **3:** Mt 22.14.

8.4–36: The seer implores God to show mercy upon his creation. 4–19a: Why should God wonderfully fashion and sustain all humankind, only to destroy a great majority? **4–5:** The pre-existence of the soul is implied here (Wis 8.19). **7:** Isa 44.6; 45.11; 60.21. **14:** *Was fashioned by your command,* Ps 139.14–15. **15–16:** The seer leaves the fate of humankind in God's hands, and speaks partic-

not of your own will did you come into the world,[n] and against your will you depart, for you have been given only a short time to live. [6] O Lord above us, grant to your servant that we may pray before you, and give us a seed for our heart and cultivation of our understanding so that fruit may be produced, by which every mortal who bears the likeness[o] of a human being may be able to live. [7] For you alone exist, and we are a work of your hands, as you have declared. [8] And because you give life to the body that is now fashioned in the womb, and furnish it with members, what you have created is preserved amid fire and water, and for nine months the womb[p] endures your creature that has been created in it. [9] But that which keeps and that which is kept shall both be kept by your keeping.[n] And when the womb gives up again what has been created in it, [10] you have commanded that from the members themselves (that is, from the breasts) milk, the fruit of the breasts, should be supplied, [11] so that what has been fashioned may be nourished for a time; and afterwards you will still guide it in your mercy. [12] You have nurtured it in your righteousness, and instructed it in your law, and reproved it in your wisdom. [13] You put it to death as your creation, and make it live as your work. [14] If then you will suddenly and quickly[q] destroy what with so great labor was fashioned by your command, to what purpose was it made? [15] And now I will speak out: About all humankind you know best; but I will speak about your people, for whom I am grieved, [16] and about your inheritance, for whom I lament, and about Israel, for whom I am sad, and about the seed of Jacob, for whom I am

troubled. [17] Therefore I will pray before you for myself and for them, for I see the failings of us who inhabit the earth; [18] and now also[r] I have heard of the swiftness of the judgment that is to come. [19] Therefore hear my voice and understand my words, and I will speak before you."

The beginning of the words of Ezra's prayer,[s] before he was taken up. He said: [20] "O Lord, you who inhabit eternity,[t] whose eyes are exalted[u] and whose upper chambers are in the air, [21] whose throne is beyond measure and whose glory is beyond comprehension, before whom the hosts of angels stand trembling [22] and at whose command they are changed to wind and fire,[v] whose word is sure and whose utterances are certain, whose command is strong and whose ordinance is terrible, [23] whose look dries up the depths and whose indignation makes the mountains melt away, and whose truth is established[w] forever— [24] hear, O Lord, the prayer of your servant, and give ear to the petition of your creature; attend to my words. [25] For as long as I live I will speak, and as long as I have understanding I will answer. [26] O do not look on the sins of your people, but on those who serve you in truth. [27] Do not take note of the endeavors of those who act wickedly, but of the endeavors of those who have kept your covenants amid afflictions. [28] Do not think of those who have lived wickedly in your sight,

n Syr: Meaning of Lat uncertain   o Syr: Lat place   p Lat what you have formed   q Syr: Lat will with a light command   r Syr: Lat but   s Syr Ethiop; Lat beginning of Ezra's words   t Or you who abide forever   u Another Lat text reads whose are the highest heavens   v Syr: Lat they whose service takes the form of wind and fire   w Arab 2: Other authorities read truth bears witness

---

ularly about Israel, God's *inheritance* (Ps 28.9).

8.19b–36: A beautiful and liturgically structured prayer (invocation to God, whose attributes are recalled, vv. 20–23; petitions, interspersed with confession and intercessions, vv. 24–35; concluding ascription of praise, v. 36). This prayer also occurs separately, with the title "Confessio Esdrae," in the section of canticles and hymns contained in many manuscripts of the Latin Vulgate

Bible. This circumstance accounts for the presence (in v. 19b) of a superscription in the third person. **19b:** The words, *before he was taken up,* indicate that the belief was current that Ezra, like Enoch and Elijah, was translated to heaven without dying.

8.22: *Wind and fire,* Ps 104.4; Heb 1.7. **23:** *Dries up,* Isa 50.2; 51.10. *Mountains melt,* Mic 1.4; Sir 16.18–19. **32:** Rom 3.19–26. **33:** 7.77.

but remember those who have willingly acknowledged that you are to be feared. 29 Do not will the destruction of those who have the ways of cattle, but regard those who have gloriously taught your law. *x* 30 Do not be angry with those who are deemed worse than wild animals, but love those who have always put their trust in your glory. 31 For we and our ancestors have passed our lives in ways that bring death; *y* but it is because of us sinners that you are called merciful. 32 For if you have desired to have pity on us, who have no works of righteousness, then you will be called merciful. 33 For the righteous, who have many works laid up with you, shall receive their reward in consequence of their own deeds. 34 But what are mortals, that you are angry with them; or what is a corruptible race, that you are so bitter against it? 35 For in truth there is no one among those who have been born who has not acted wickedly; among those who have existed *z* there is no one who has not done wrong. 36 For in this, O Lord, your righteousness and goodness will be declared, when you are merciful to those who have no store of good works."

37 He answered me and said, "Some things you have spoken rightly, and it will turn out according to your words. 38 For indeed I will not concern myself about the fashioning of those who have sinned, or about their death, their judgment, or their destruction; 39 but I will rejoice over the creation of the righteous,

over their pilgrimage also, and their salvation, and their receiving their reward. 40 As I have spoken, therefore, so it shall be.

41 "For just as the farmer sows many seeds in the ground and plants a multitude of seedlings, and yet not all that have been sown will come up *a* in due season, and not all that were planted will take root; so also those who have been sown in the world will not all be saved."

42 I answered and said, "If I have found favor in your sight, let me speak. 43 If the farmer's seed does not come up, because it has not received your rain in due season, or if it has been ruined by too much rain, it perishes. *b* 44 But people, who have been formed by your hands and are called your own image because they are made like you, and for whose sake you have formed all things—have you also made them like the farmer's seed? 45 Surely not, O Lord *c* above! But spare your people and have mercy on your inheritance, for you have mercy on your own creation."

46 He answered me and said, "Things that are present are for those who live now, and things that are future are for those who will live hereafter. 47 For you

x Syr *have received the brightness of your law*
y Syr Ethiop: Meaning of Lat uncertain
z Syr: Meaning of Lat uncertain   *a* Syr Ethiop *will live*; Lat *will be saved*   *b* Cn: Compare Syr Arab 1 Arm Georg 2: Meaning of Lat uncertain
c Ethiop Arab Compare Syr: Lat lacks *O Lord*

8.37–40: The divine reply to the seer's prayer: God will rejoice in the righteous and forget the sinners (the central petition of the prayer—mercy on the wicked—is ignored). **39:** *Their pilgrimage,* i.e. their return home to God (compare 2 Cor 5.6–8). **40:** Instead of *I have spoken,* the reading of the Ethiopic, "you have spoken," is to be preferred in view of v. 37 and the irony of the divine reply: "it is to be as you have *spoken,* but not as you had intended" (in vv. 26–36 the seer prayed God to ignore the wicked and their doings and pay attention to the righteous only; this, the Almighty replies, he will do, but in the sense of being unconcerned about the *destruction* of the wicked, v. 38).

8.41–45: Humankind is like the farmer's seed; only a few individuals will escape destruction. **45:** An anguished entreaty: *spare your people,* Joel 2.17.

8.46–62a: The final divine reply: The seer is assured that his lot is with the blessed, and is advised to think no more about sinners, who deserve their doom because they have *despised the Most High* (v. 56). **46–47:** The seer's objection (v. 44) is invalid, for the simile of the seeds suits the *present* corruptible order; the *future* has standards of its own. Moreover, God's love for his *creation* far exceeds human love (see 5.33 n.). **8.47–50:** The angel is almost annoyed with Ezra for insisting upon placing himself

come far short of being able to love my creation more than I love it. But you have often compared yourself[d] to the unrighteous. Never do so! 48 But even in this respect you will be praiseworthy before the Most High, 49 because you have humbled yourself, as is becoming for you, and have not considered yourself to be among the righteous. You will receive the greatest glory, 50 for many miseries will affect those who inhabit the world in the last times, because they have walked in great pride. 51 But think of your own case, and inquire concerning the glory of those who are like yourself, 52 because it is for you that paradise is opened, the tree of life is planted, the age to come is prepared, plenty is provided, a city is built, rest is appointed,[e] goodness is established and wisdom perfected beforehand. 53 The root of evil[f] is sealed up from you, illness is banished from you, and death[g] is hidden; Hades has fled and corruption has been forgotten;[h] 54 sorrows have passed away, and in the end the treasure of immortality is made manifest. 55 Therefore do not ask any more questions about the great number of those who perish. 56 For when they had opportunity to choose, they despised the Most High, and were contemptuous of his law, and abandoned his ways. 57 Moreover, they have even trampled on his righteous ones, 58 and said in their hearts that there is no God—though they knew well that they must die. 59 For just as the things that I have predicted await[i] you, so the thirst and torment that are prepared await them. For the Most High did not intend that anyone should be destroyed; 60 but those who were created

have themselves defiled the name of him who made them, and have been ungrateful to him who prepared life for them now. 61 Therefore my judgment is now drawing near; 62 I have not shown this to all people, but only to you and a few like you."

Then I answered and said, 63 "O Lord, you have already shown me a great number of the signs that you will do in the last times, but you have not shown me when you will do them."

9 He answered me and said, "Measure carefully in your mind, and when you see that some of the predicted signs have occurred, 2 then you will know that it is the very time when the Most High is about to visit the world that he has made. 3 So when there shall appear in the world earthquakes, tumult of peoples, intrigues of nations, wavering of leaders, confusion of princes, 4 then you will know that it was of these that the Most High spoke from the days that were of old, from the beginning. 5 For just as with everything that has occurred in the world, the beginning is evident,[j] and the end manifest; 6 so also are the times of the Most High: the beginnings are manifest in wonders and mighty works, and the end in penalties[k] and in signs.

7 It shall be that all who will be saved and will be able to escape on account of their works, or on account of the faith by

d Syr Ethiop: Lat *brought yourself near*
e Syr Ethiop: Lat *allowed*   f Lat lacks *of evil*
g Syr Ethiop Arm: Lat lacks *death*   h Syr: Lat *Hades and corruption have fled into oblivion*; or *corruption has fled into Hades to be forgotten*
i Syr: Lat *will receive*   j Syr: Ethiop *is in the word*; Meaning of Lat uncertain   k Syr: Lat Ethiop *in effects*

with the wicked. Humility is fine, for pride is dangerous indeed. But Ezra has no need to fear the judgment. The fact that the angel *cannot seem even to understand* that Ezra's concern is not for himself but for the myriads of sinners doomed to perish is a good indication that the author of 2 Esd 3–10 thinks as Ezra does, not as the angel does. **48:** *In this respect,* i.e. the seer's humility (compare Lk 18.13–14). **52:** The future joys of heaven are already in existence and may be contemplated now (1 Pet 1.4). *Tree of life, 7.123*; Rev 2.7; 22.2.

53: *Hades* is personified (as in Rev 6.8). **56:** *Opportunity to choose,* i.e. free will. **58:** Ps 14.1; 53.1. **59:** *The things . . . predicted,* in vv. 52–54. *Thirst,* in the fire of hell (Lk 16.24). *The Most High did not intend* humankind's destruction (Mt 18.14; 1 Tim 2.4). **62:** *A few like you,* i.e. prophets (apocalyptists) like the seer.
8.62b–9.13: The end, and the signs that will precede it (4.51–5.13; 6.11–24). **8.63:** *When,* 4.33; contrast Acts 1.7.
9.3: The messianic woes on earth. **7:** De-

which they have believed, ⁸will survive the dangers that have been predicted, and will see my salvation in my land and within my borders, which I have sanctified for myself from the beginning. ⁹Then those who have now abused my ways shall be amazed, and those who have rejected them with contempt shall live in torments. ¹⁰For as many as did not acknowledge me in their lifetime, though they received my benefits, ¹¹and as many as scorned my law while they still had freedom, and did not understand but despised it*ˡ* while an opportunity of repentance was still open to them, ¹²these must in torment acknowledge it*ˡ* after death. ¹³Therefore, do not continue to be curious about how the ungodly will be punished; but inquire how the righteous will be saved, those to whom the age belongs and for whose sake the age was made."*ᵐ*

14 I answered and said, ¹⁵"I said before, and I say now, and will say it again: there are more who perish than those who will be saved, ¹⁶as a wave is greater than a drop of water."

17 He answered me and said, "As is the field, so is the seed; and as are the flowers, so are the colors; and as is the work, so is the product; and as is the farmer, so is the threshing floor. ¹⁸For there was a time in this age when I was preparing for those who now exist, before the world was made for them to live in, and no one opposed me then, for no one existed; ¹⁹but now those who have been created in this world, which is supplied both with an unfailing table and an inexhaustible pasture,*ⁿ* have become

corrupt in their ways. ²⁰So I considered my world, and saw that it was lost. I saw that my earth was in peril because of the devices of those who*ᵒ* had come into it. ²¹And I saw and spared some*ᵖ* with great difficulty, and saved for myself one grape out of a cluster, and one plant out of a great forest. *q* ²²So let the multitude perish that has been born in vain, but let my grape and my plant be saved, because with much labor I have perfected them.

23 "Now, if you will let seven days more pass—do not, however, fast during them, ²⁴but go into a field of flowers where no house has been built, and eat only of the flowers of the field, and taste no meat and drink no wine, but eat only flowers, ²⁵and pray to the Most High continually. Then I will come and talk with you."

26 So I went, as he directed me, into the field that is called Ardat;*ʳ* there I sat among the flowers and ate of the plants of the field, and the nourishment they afforded satisfied me. ²⁷After seven days, while I lay on the grass, my heart was troubled again as it was before. ²⁸Then my mouth was opened, and I began to speak before the Most High, and said, ²⁹"O Lord, you showed yourself among us, to our ancestors in the wilderness when they came out from Egypt and when they came into the untrodden and unfruitful wilderness; ³⁰and you said, 'Hear me, O Israel, and give heed to my

l Or *me*   *m* Syr: Lat *saved, and whose is the age and for whose sake the age was made and when*
n Cn: Lat *law*   *o* Cn: Lat *devices that*
p Lat *them*   *q* Syr Ethiop Arab 1: Lat *tribe*
r Syr Ethiop *Arpad*; Arm *Ardab*

---

liverance may come on the basis of good deeds or of belief in God (compare Jas 2.14–26 and Gal 2.11–21).
9.9–12: The state of the wicked immediately after death. **11:** Opportunity of repentance (Wis 12.10, 20; Heb 12.17). **12:** *Acknowledge,* their earlier opportunity of repentance; or the word may be translated "be brought to know."
9.14–25: Recapitulation: The seer again deplores the fate of the wicked, and the small number of the saved is explained a last time. **19:** Restore "law" (see note *n*) to the text: the

meaning is that despite God's gracious provision of earthly sustenance and divine law, mortals *have become corrupt.*
9.21–22: The preservation of a small remnant is the result of God's grace. **24:** Likewise Daniel and his companions ate only vegetables (Dan 1.8–16; compare 2 Macc 5.27).
9.26–10.59: The fourth vision. 9.26–28: Introduction. 26: *Ardat,* an unknown location, probably of symbolical or mystic significance.
9.29–37: The abiding glory of the Mosaic law, contrasted with Israel. **29:** Ex 19.9;

words, O descendants of Jacob. 31 For I sow my law in you, and it shall bring forth fruit in you, and you shall be glorified through it forever.' 32 But though our ancestors received the law, they did not keep it and did not observe thes statutes; yet the fruit of the law did not perish—for it could not, because it was yours. 33 Yet those who received it perished, because they did not keep what had been sown in them. 34 Now this is the general rule that, when the ground has received seed, or the sea a ship, or any dish food or drink, and when it comes about that what was sown or what was launched or what was put in is destroyed, 35 they are destroyed, but the things that held them remain; yet with us it has not been so. 36 For we who have received the law and sinned will perish, as well as our hearts that received it; 37 the law, however, does not perish but survives in its glory."

38 When I said these things in my heart, I looked around,ᵗ and on my right I saw a woman; she was mourning and weeping with a loud voice, and was deeply grieved at heart; her clothes were torn, and there were ashes on her head. 39 Then I dismissed the thoughts with which I had been engaged, and turned to her 40 and said to her, "Why are you weeping, and why are you grieved at heart?"

41 She said to me, "Let me alone, my lord, so that I may weep for myself and continue to mourn, for I am greatly embittered in spirit and deeply distressed."

42 I said to her, "What has happened to you? Tell me."

43 And she said to me, "Your servant was barren and had no child, though I lived with my husband for thirty years.

44 Every hour and every day during those thirty years I prayed to the Most High, night and day. 45 And after thirty years God heard your servant, and looked upon my low estate, and considered my distress, and gave me a son. I rejoiced greatly over him, I and my husband and all my neighbors;ᵘ and we gave great glory to the Mighty One. 46 And I brought him up with much care. 47 So when he grew up and I came to take a wife for him, I set a day for the marriage feast.

10 "But it happened that when my son entered his wedding chamber, he fell down and died. 2 So all of us put out our lamps, and all my neighborsᵛ attempted to console me; I remained quiet until the evening of the second day. 3 But when all of them had stopped consoling me, encouraging me to be quiet, I got up in the night and fled, and I came to this field, as you see. 4 And now I intend not to return to the town, but to stay here; I will neither eat nor drink, but will mourn and fast continually until I die."

5 Then I broke off the reflections with which I was still engaged, and answered her in anger and said, 6 "You most foolish of women, do you not see our mourning, and what has happened to us? 7 For Zion, the mother of us all, is in deep grief and great distress. 8 It is most appropriate to mourn now, because we are all mourning, and to be sorrowful, because we are all sorrowing; you are sorrowing for one son, but we, the whole world, for our mother.ʷ 9 Now ask the earth,

---

s Lat *my* t Syr Arab Arm: Lat *I looked about me with my eyes* u Literally *all my citizens*
v Literally *all my citizens* w Compare Syr: Meaning of Lat uncertain

---

24.10; Deut 4.12. **30–37**: The seer draws the contrast between the vessel that contains a precious object and the object it contains. The latter may be used up or destroyed, but normally the former survives. With us it is just the opposite; God keeps alive the divine law, but Israel, its receptacle, is destroyed. Could God not care a bit more for the receptacle? **9.38–10.24: The seer speaks with a dis-**

consolate woman. 38: *Ashes on her head,* a sign of mourning. **47**: It was customary for the father to arrange for the wedding (see Sir 7.25 n.).
10.2: *Lamps,* because weddings took place at night. **2**: *I remained quiet,* shows the depth of her grief, for ordinarily there was loud lamentation. **7**: *Zion, the mother of us all,* Gal 4.26, compare Lam 2.20–22.

and she will tell you that it is she who ought to mourn over so many who have come into being upon her. [10]From the beginning all have been born of her, and others will come; and, lo, almost all go[x] to perdition, and a multitude of them will come to doom. [11]Who then ought to mourn the more, she who lost so great a multitude, or you who are grieving for one alone? [12]But if you say to me, 'My lamentation is not like the earth's, for I have lost the fruit of my womb, which I brought forth in pain and bore in sorrow; [13]but it is with the earth according to the way of the earth—the multitude that is now in it goes as it came'; [14]then I say to you, 'Just as you brought forth in sorrow, so the earth also has from the beginning given her fruit, that is, humankind, to him who made her.' [15]Now, therefore, keep your sorrow to yourself, and bear bravely the troubles that have come upon you. [16]For if you acknowledge the decree of God to be just, you will receive your son back in due time, and will be praised among women. [17]Therefore go into the town to your husband."

18 She said to me, "I will not do so; I will not go into the city, but I will die here."

19 So I spoke again to her, and said, [20]"Do not do that, but let yourself be persuaded—for how many are the adversities of Zion?—and be consoled because of the sorrow of Jerusalem. [21]For you see how our sanctuary has been laid waste, our altar thrown down, our temple destroyed; [22]our harp has been laid low, our song has been silenced, and our rejoicing has been ended; the light of our lampstand has been put out, the ark of our covenant has been plundered, our holy things have been polluted, and the name by which we are called has been almost profaned; our children[y] have suffered abuse, our priests have been burned to death, our Levites have gone into exile, our virgins have been defiled, and our wives have been ravished; our righteous men[z] have been carried off, our little ones have been cast out, our young men have been enslaved and our strong men made powerless. [23]And, worst of all, the seal of Zion has been deprived of its glory, and given over into the hands of those that hate us. [24]Therefore shake off your great sadness and lay aside your many sorrows, so that the Mighty One may be merciful to you again, and the Most High may give you rest, a respite from your troubles."

25 While I was talking to her, her face suddenly began to shine exceedingly; her countenance flashed like lightning, so that I was too frightened to approach her, and my heart was terrified. While[a] I was wondering what this meant, [26]she suddenly uttered a loud and fearful cry, so that the earth shook at the sound. [27]When I looked up, the woman was no longer visible to me, but a city was being built,[b] and a place of huge foundations showed itself. I was afraid, and cried with a loud voice and said, [28]"Where is

x Literally *walk*   *y* Ethiop *free men*
z Syr *our seers*   *a* Syr Ethiop Arab 1: Lat lacks
I was too . . . terrified. While   *b* Lat: Syr
Ethiop Arab 1 Arab 2 Arm *but there was an
established city*

10.16: To *acknowledge* the justice of God's *decree* is equivalent to pious submission to his will. *You will receive your son back in due time,* i.e. in the birth of another son, after returning to her husband (v. 17). **21–23**: A pathetic account of the utter ruin of Israel. **22**: *Harp* symbolizes the service of praise. The extinction of the perpetually burning lamp marked the cessation of temple services. *Our holy things* are enumerated in 1 Macc 4.49–51. *The name* Israel was bestowed by God (Gen 32.28). **23**: *The seal* of a nation is symbolic of its independence.

10.25–28: **A vision of the transformed Jerusalem. 27**: *A city was being built,* Zech 2.1–5; Heb 11.10; Rev 21.9–21. The new or transformed Zion is under construction, but its extent is known only to God. The author of 2 Esd 3–10 here offers hope for the wicked that a place will exist in Zion for them. Mother Zion will not only be restored but will become the city transformed to accommodate all whom God is pleased to redeem. The Latin text of 10.27, 42 is to be preferred, as in NRSV. **28**: *At first,* 4.1.
10.29–59: **Interpretation of the vision.**

the angel Uriel, who came to me at first? For it was he who brought me into this overpowering bewilderment; my end has become corruption, and my prayer a reproach."

29 While I was speaking these words, the angel who had come to me at first came to me, and when he saw me [30]lying there like a corpse, deprived of my understanding, he grasped my right hand and strengthened me and set me on my feet, and said to me, [31]"What is the matter with you? And why are you troubled? And why are your understanding and the thoughts of your mind troubled?"

32 I said, "It was because you abandoned me. I did as you directed, and went out into the field, and lo, what I have seen I saw, and can still see, I am unable to explain."

33 He said to me, "Stand up like a man, and I will instruct you."

34 I said, "Speak, my lord; only do not forsake me, so that I may not die before my time.[c] [35]For I have seen what I did not know, and I hear[d] what I do not understand [36]—or is my mind deceived, and my soul dreaming? [37]Now therefore I beg you to give your servant an explanation of this bewildering vision."

38 He answered me and said, "Listen to me, and I will teach you, and tell you about the things that you fear; for the Most High has revealed many secrets to you. [39]He has seen your righteous conduct, and that you have sorrowed continually for your people and mourned greatly over Zion. [40]This therefore is the meaning of the vision. [41]The woman who appeared to you a little while ago, whom you saw mourning and whom you began to console [42](you do not now see the form of a woman, but there appeared to you a city being built)[e] [43]and who told you about the misfortune of

her son—this is the interpretation: [44]The woman whom you saw is Zion, which you now behold as a city being built.[f] [45]And as for her telling you that she was barren for thirty years, the reason is that there were three thousand[g] years in the world before any offering was offered in it.[h] [46]And after three thousand[i] years Solomon built the city, and offered offerings; then it was that the barren woman bore a son. [47]And as for her telling you that she brought him up with much care, that was the period of residence in Jerusalem. [48]And as for her saying to you, 'My son died as he entered his wedding chamber,' and that misfortune had overtaken her,[j] this was the destruction that befell Jerusalem. [49]So you saw her likeness, how she mourned for her son, and you began to console her for what had happened.[k] [50]For now the Most High, seeing that you are sincerely grieved and profoundly distressed for her, has shown you the brilliance of her glory, and the loveliness of her beauty. [51]Therefore I told you to remain in the field where no house had been built, [52]for I knew that the Most High would reveal these things to you. [53]Therefore I told you to go into the field where there was no foundation of any building, [54]because no work of human construction could endure in a place where the city of the Most High was to be revealed.

55 "Therefore do not be afraid, and do not let your heart be terrified; but go in and see the splendor or[l] the vastness

c Syr Ethiop Arab: Lat *die to no purpose*
d Other ancient authorities read *have heard*
e Lat: Syr Ethiop Arab 1 Arab 2 Arm *an established city*   f Cn: Lat *an established city*
g Most Lat Mss read *three*   h Cn: Lat Syr Arab Arm *her*   i Syr Ethiop Arab Arm: Lat *three*   j Or *him*   k Most Lat Mss and Arab 1 add *these were the things to be opened to you*
l Other ancient authorities read *and*

30: *Like a corpse,* Rev 1.17; compare Dan 8.18; 10.9. 32: *And can still see,* the vision is still before the seer's eyes. *Unable to explain,* compare 2 Cor 12.3–4 (also of an ecstatic experience). 33: *Stand up,* 5.15; 6.13, 17. 44: *Zion,* i.e. the transformed Jerusalem. 45: *In it,* in the world. 46: *A son,* i.e. the historical Jeru-

salem. 49: The *likeness,* or model, of the earthly city is the heavenly Zion, who *mourned for her son* (the ruined earthly Jerusalem). For the idea of a heavenly counterpart or model, compare Ex 25.9, 40; Heb 8.5.
10.55–56: 1 Cor 2.9; 2 Cor 12.4. *Go in and see,* the city is conceived as still present to

of the building, as far as it is possible for your eyes to see it, [56] and afterward you will hear as much as your ears can hear. [57] For you are more blessed than many, and you have been called to be with[m] the Most High as few have been. [58] But tomorrow night you shall remain here, [59] and the Most High will show you in those dream visions what the Most High will do to those who inhabit the earth in the last days."

So I slept that night and the following one, as he had told me.

11 On the second night I had a dream: I saw rising from the sea an eagle that had twelve feathered wings and three heads. [2] I saw it spread its wings over[n] the whole earth, and all the winds of heaven blew upon it, and the clouds were gathered around it. [o] [3] I saw that out of its wings there grew opposing wings; but they became little, puny wings. [4] But its heads were at rest; the middle head was larger than the other heads, but it too was at rest with them. [5] Then I saw that the eagle flew with its wings, and it reigned over the earth and over those who inhabit it. [6] And I saw how all things under heaven were subjected to it, and no one spoke against it—not a single creature that was on the earth. [7] Then I saw the eagle rise upon its talons, and it uttered a cry to its wings, saying, [8] "Do not all watch at the same time; let each sleep in its own place, and watch in its turn; [9] but let the heads be reserved for the last."

10 I looked again and saw that the voice did not come from its heads, but from the middle of its body. [11] I counted its rival wings, and there were eight of them. [12] As I watched, one wing on the right side rose up, and it reigned over all the earth. [13] And after a time its reign came to an end, and it disappeared, so that even its place was no longer visible. Then the next wing rose up and reigned, and it continued to reign a long time. [14] While it was reigning its end came also, so that it disappeared like the first. [15] And a voice sounded, saying to it, [16] "Listen to me, you who have ruled the earth all this time; I announce this to you before you disappear. [17] After you no one shall rule as long as you have ruled, not even half as long."

18 Then the third wing raised itself up, and held the rule as the earlier ones had done, and it also disappeared. [19] And so it went with all the wings; they wielded power one after another and then were never seen again. [20] I kept looking, and in due time the wings that followed[p] also rose up on the right[q] side, in order to rule. There were some of them that ruled, yet disappeared suddenly; [21] and others of them rose up, but did not hold the rule.

22 And after this I looked and saw that the twelve wings and the two little wings had disappeared, [23] and nothing remained on the eagle's body except the three heads that were at rest and six little wings.

24 As I kept looking I saw that two little wings separated from the six and remained under the head that was on the right side; but four remained in their place. [25] Then I saw that these little

---

m Or been named by   n Arab 2 Arm: Lat Syr Ethiop in   o Syr: Compare Ethiop Arab: Lat lacks the clouds and around it   p Syr Arab 2 the little wings   q Some Ethiop Mss read left

---

Ezra. **57**: *You have been called to be with the Most High,* Arabic 1, "your name is known [or recognized] before the Most High," i.e. God has singled you out for honor (Isa 45.3–4).

11.1–12.51: **The fifth vision (the eagle vision). 11.1**: *From the sea,* Dan 7.3; Rev 13.1. *An eagle,* symbol of the Roman Empire. **2**: *Spread its wings,* asserted its dominion. *The winds,* 13.2; Dan 7.2. **3**: *Opposing wings,* symbolizing usurpers who revolted against the

Roman emperors. *But they became little,* i.e. they were subdued. **4**: *Were at rest,* i.e. were not troubled by the opposing wings.

11.13: *Its reign came to an end,* i.e. the ruler perished. **36**: *Look in front of you,* the seer is alerted to the special importance of what follows. **43**: Dan 5.20.

12.3b–39: **The interpretation of the vision. 3b–9**: The seer awakes and asks for an interpretation of the vision.

wings[r] planned to set themselves up and hold the rule. 26 As I kept looking, one was set up, but suddenly disappeared; 27 a second also, and this disappeared more quickly than the first. 28 While I continued to look the two that remained were planning between themselves to reign together; 29 and while they were planning, one of the heads that were at rest (the one that was in the middle) suddenly awoke; it was greater than the other two heads. 30 And I saw how it allied the two heads with itself, 31 and how the head turned with those that were with it and devoured the two little wings[r] that were planning to reign. 32 Moreover this head gained control of the whole earth, and with much oppression dominated its inhabitants; it had greater power over the world than all the wings that had gone before.

33 After this I looked again and saw the head in the middle suddenly disappear, just as the wings had done. 34 But the two heads remained, which also in like manner ruled over the earth and its inhabitants. 35 And while I looked, I saw the head on the right side devour the one on the left.

36 Then I heard a voice saying to me, "Look in front of you and consider what you see." 37 When I looked, I saw what seemed to be a lion roused from the forest, roaring; and I heard how it uttered a human voice to the eagle, and spoke, saying, 38 "Listen and I will speak to you. The Most High says to you, 39 'Are you not the one that remains of the four beasts that I had made to reign in my world, so that the end of my times might come through them? 40 You, the fourth that has come, have conquered all the beasts that have gone before; and you have held sway over the world with great terror, and over all the earth with grievous oppression; and for so long you have lived on the earth with deceit.[s] 41 You have judged the earth, but not with truth, 42 for you have oppressed the meek and injured the peaceable; you have hated those who tell the truth, and have loved liars; you have destroyed the homes of those who brought forth fruit,

and have laid low the walls of those who did you no harm. 43 Your insolence has come up before the Most High, and your pride to the Mighty One. 44 The Most High has looked at his times; now they have ended, and his ages have reached completion. 45 Therefore you, eagle, will surely disappear, you and your terrifying wings, your most evil little wings, your malicious heads, your most evil talons, and your whole worthless body, 46 so that the whole earth, freed from your violence, may be refreshed and relieved, and may hope for the judgment and mercy of him who made it.' "

12 While the lion was saying these words to the eagle, I looked 2 and saw that the remaining head had disappeared. The two wings that had gone over to it rose up and[t] set themselves up to reign, and their reign was brief and full of tumult. 3 When I looked again, they were already vanishing. The whole body of the eagle was burned, and the earth was exceedingly terrified.

Then I woke up in great perplexity of mind and great fear, and I said to my spirit, 4 "You have brought this upon me, because you search out the ways of the Most High. 5 I am still weary in mind and very weak in my spirit, and not even a little strength is left in me, because of the great fear with which I have been terrified tonight. 6 Therefore I will now entreat the Most High that he may strengthen me to the end."

7 Then I said, "O sovereign Lord, if I have found favor in your sight, and if I have been accounted righteous before you beyond many others, and if my prayer has indeed come up before your face, 8 strengthen me and show me, your servant, the interpretation and meaning of this terrifying vision so that you may fully comfort my soul. 9 For you have judged me worthy to be shown the end of the times and the last events of the times."

10 He said to me, "This is the inter-

---

r Syr: Lat *underwings*   s Syr Arab Arm: Lat Ethiop *The fourth came, however, and conquered . . . and held sway . . . and for so long lived*   t Ethiop: Lat lacks *rose up and*

pretation of this vision that you have seen: [11] The eagle that you saw coming up from the sea is the fourth kingdom that appeared in a vision to your brother Daniel. [12] But it was not explained to him as I now explain to you or have explained it. [13] The days are coming when a kingdom shall rise on earth, and it shall be more terrifying than all the kingdoms that have been before it. [14] And twelve kings shall reign in it, one after another. [15] But the second that is to reign shall hold sway for a longer time than any other one of the twelve. [16] This is the interpretation of the twelve wings that you saw.

[17] "As for your hearing a voice that spoke, coming not from the eagle's[u] heads but from the midst of its body, this is the interpretation: [18] In the midst of[v] the time of that kingdom great struggles shall arise, and it shall be in danger of falling; nevertheless it shall not fall then, but shall regain its former power.[w] [19] As for your seeing eight little wings[x] clinging to its wings, this is the interpretation: [20] Eight kings shall arise in it, whose times shall be short and their years swift; [21] two of them shall perish when the middle of its time draws near; and four shall be kept for the time when its end approaches, but two shall be kept until the end.

[22] "As for your seeing three heads at rest, this is the interpretation: [23] In its last days the Most High will raise up three kings,[y] and they[z] shall renew many things in it, and shall rule the earth [24] and its inhabitants more oppressively than all who were before them. Therefore they are called the heads of the eagle, [25] because it is they who shall sum up his wickedness and perform his last actions. [26] As for your seeing that the large head disappeared, one of the kings[a] shall die in his bed, but in agonies. [27] But as for the two who remained, the sword shall devour them. [28] For the sword of one shall devour him who was with him; but he also shall fall by the sword in the last days.

[29] As for your seeing two little wings[b] passing over to[c] the head which was on the right side, [30] this is the interpretation: It is these whom the Most High has kept for the eagle's[d] end; this was the reign which was brief and full of tumult, as you have seen.

[31] "And as for the lion whom you saw rousing up out of the forest and roaring and speaking to the eagle and reproving him for his unrighteousness, and as for all his words that you have heard, [32] this is the Messiah[e] whom the Most High has kept until the end of days, who will arise from the offspring of David, and will come and speak[f] with them. He will denounce them for their ungodliness and for their wickedness, and will display before them their contemptuous dealings. [33] For first he will bring them alive before his judgment seat, and when he has reproved them, then he will destroy them. [34] But in mercy he will set free the remnant of my people, those

u Lat *his*   v Syr Arm: Lat *After*
Arab 1 Arm: Lat Syr *its beginning*   w Ethiop
underwings   x Syr: Lat
kingdoms   y Syr Ethiop Arab Arm: Lat
them   z Syr Ethiop Arm: Lat *he*   a Lat
them   b Arab 1: Lat *underwings*   c Syr
Ethiop: Lat lacks *to*   d Lat *his*   e Literally
anointed one   f Syr: Lat lacks *of days . . . and
speak*

12.11: *The fourth kingdom* in Daniel's vision (Dan 7.7) symbolized the Greek or Macedonian Empire; here, however, it is reinterpreted (compare v. 12) to refer to the Roman Empire (see 11.1 n.). **13**: *The days are coming*, the seer is represented as prophesying during the exile. **17**: 11.10; compare 11.15. **18**: There is nothing in the vision that corresponds to what is said in this verse. The author probably refers to *the time* of *great struggles* for power that followed the death of Nero A.D. 68. **19**: *Little wings*, 11.3, 11. *Clinging to its wings*, Armenian, "sprouting out around its great wings." **20**: *In it*, within the Roman Empire. **21**: *Its time*, the time of the kingdom. *Its end*, the end of the kingdom. **23**: *Its last days*, the last days of the kingdom. **23–24**: 11.30–32.

12.28: *But . . . days*, there is nothing corresponding to this in the vision. **30**: *As you have seen*, v. 3. **31**: *The lion*, 11.37ff. **32**: *Whom the Most High has kept until the end of days*, the hidden Messiah preserved by God for the last days (Dan 7.13–14; Enoch 48.6; 62.7). *He will denounce them*, 13.37. **34**: *He will make them*

who have been saved throughout my borders, and he will make them joyful until the end comes, the day of judgment, of which I spoke to you at the beginning. 35 This is the dream that you saw, and this is its interpretation. 36 And you alone were worthy to learn this secret of the Most High. 37 Therefore write all these things that you have seen in a book, put it *g* in a hidden place; 38 and you shall teach them to the wise among your people, whose hearts you know are able to comprehend and keep these secrets. 39 But as for you, wait here seven days more, so that you may be shown whatever it pleases the Most High to show you." Then he left me.

40 When all the people heard that the seven days were past and I had not returned to the city, they all gathered together, from the least to the greatest, and came to me and spoke to me, saying, 41 "How have we offended you, and what harm have we done you, that you have forsaken us and sit in this place? 42 For of all the prophets you alone are left to us, like a cluster of grapes from the vintage, and like a lamp in a dark place, and like a haven for a ship saved from a storm. 43 Are not the disasters that have befallen us enough? 44 Therefore if you forsake us, how much better it would have been for us if we also had been consumed in the burning of Zion. 45 For we are no better than those who died there." And they wept with a loud voice.

Then I answered them and said, 46 "Take courage, O Israel; and do not be sorrowful, O house of Jacob; 47 for the Most High has you in remembrance, and the Mighty One has not forgotten you in your struggle. 48 As for me, I have neither forsaken you nor withdrawn from

you; but I have come to this place to pray on account of the desolation of Zion, and to seek mercy on account of the humiliation of our *h* sanctuary. 49 Now go to your homes, every one of you, and after these days I will come to you." 50 So the people went into the city, as I told them to do. 51 But I sat in the field seven days, as the angel *i* had commanded me; and I ate only of the flowers of the field, and my food was of plants during those days.

13 After seven days I dreamed a dream in the night. 2 And lo, a wind arose from the sea and stirred up *j* all its waves. 3 As I kept looking the wind made something like the figure of a man come up out of the heart of the sea. And I saw *k* that this man flew *l* with the clouds of heaven; and wherever he turned his face to look, everything under his gaze trembled, 4 and whenever his voice issued from his mouth, all who heard his voice melted as wax melts *m* when it feels the fire.

5 After this I looked and saw that an innumerable multitude of people were gathered together from the four winds of heaven to make war against the man who came up out of the sea. 6 And I looked and saw that he carved out for himself a great mountain, and flew up on to it. 7 And I tried to see the region or place from which the mountain was carved, but I could not. 8 After this I looked and saw that all who had gathered together against him,

g Ethiop Arab 1 Arab 2 Arm: Lat Syr *them*
h Syr Ethiop: Lat *your*   i Literally *he*
j Other ancient authorities read *I saw a wind arise from the sea and stir up*   k Syr: Lat lacks *the wind . . . I saw*   l Syr Ethiop Arab Arm: Lat *grew strong*   m Syr: Lat *burned as the earth rests*

---

joyful, 7.28. **35:** *The dream,* 11.1. **37:** The seer is bidden to compose an esoteric book. **37–38:** To *put* the book *in a hidden place* suggests that it is an apocryphal book, which only the elect (*the wise*) can *comprehend.* **39:** *He,* the angel Uriel (see 4.1 n.).

12.40–51: The seer comforts those who were grieved because of his absence. 40: *The seven days,* 9.23, 27. **42:** *A lamp,* 2 Pet

1.19. **49:** *These days,* v. 39. **51:** 9.24–26.

13.1–58: The sixth vision (the man from the sea). 3: *Something like the figure of a man,* the Messiah (Dan 7.13); compare v. 32 "my Son," i.e. the Son of God. *Flew with the clouds,* Isa 19.1; Dan 7.13; Rev 1.7. **4:** *As wax melts,* Mic 1.4; Jdt 16.15. **6:** *Carved out,* Dan 2.45.

to wage war with him, were filled with fear, and yet they dared to fight. 9 When he saw the onrush of the approaching multitude, he neither lifted his hand nor held a spear or any weapon of war; 10 but I saw only how he sent forth from his mouth something like a stream of fire, and from his lips a flaming breath, and from his tongue he shot forth a storm of sparks.[n] 11 All these were mingled together, the stream of fire and the flaming breath and the great storm, and fell on the onrushing multitude that was prepared to fight, and burned up all of them, so that suddenly nothing was seen of the innumerable multitude but only the dust of ashes and the smell of smoke. When I saw it, I was amazed.

12 After this I saw the same man come down from the mountain and call to himself another multitude that was peaceable. 13 Then many people[o] came to him, some of whom were joyful and some sorrowful; some of them were bound, and some were bringing others as offerings.

Then I woke up in great terror, and prayed to the Most High, and said, 14 "From the beginning you have shown your servant these wonders, and have deemed me worthy to have my prayer heard by you; 15 now show me the interpretation of this dream also. 16 For as I consider it in my mind, alas for those who will be left in those days! And still more, alas for those who are not left! 17 For those who are not left will be sad 18 because they understand the things that are reserved for the last days, but cannot attain them. 19 But alas for those also who are left, and for that very reason! For they shall see great dangers and much distress, as these dreams show. 20 Yet it is better[p]

to come into these things,[q] though incurring peril, than to pass from the world like a cloud, and not to see what will happen in the last days."

He answered me and said, 21 "I will tell you the interpretation of the vision, and I will also explain to you the things that you have mentioned. 22 As for what you said about those who survive, and concerning those who do not survive,[r] this is the interpretation: 23 The one who brings the peril at that time will protect those who fall into peril, who have works and faith toward the Almighty. 24 Understand therefore that those who are left are more blessed than those who have died.

25 "This is the interpretation of the vision: As for your seeing a man come up from the heart of the sea, 26 this is he whom the Most High has been keeping for many ages, who will himself deliver his creation; and he will direct those who are left. 27 And as for your seeing wind and fire and a storm coming out of his mouth, 28 and as for his not holding a spear or weapon of war, yet destroying the onrushing multitude that came to conquer him, this is the interpretation: 29 The days are coming when the Most High will deliver those who are on the earth. 30 And bewilderment of mind shall come over those who inhabit the earth. 31 They shall plan to make war against one another, city against city, place against place, people against people, and kingdom against kingdom. 32 When these things take place and the signs occur that I showed you before, then my

n Meaning of Lat uncertain   o Lat Syr
Arab 2 literally *the faces of many people*   p Ethiop
Compare Arab 2: Lat *easier*   q Syr: Lat *this*
r Syr Arab 1: Lat lacks *and . . . not survive*

13.10: Isa 11.4. 13a: *Some . . . were bound,* Jews who came from captivity. *Others as offerings,* Isa 66.20.

13.13b–20: **The seer prays that God will interpret the vision to him. 14**: *From the beginning,* when the seer first began to have the visions. *My prayer,* 9.25ff. **19**: *For that very reason,* better, "for this reason—" (the reason follows).

13.21–58: **The interpretation of the vision. 21**: *Things . . . mentioned,* in vv. 16–20. **23**: *The one who brings the peril,* the Messiah, whose advent is preceded by the messianic woes. **26**: *He whom the Most High has been keeping for many ages,* the hidden Messiah (v. 52; 12.32). **27–28**: Verses 9–11. **13.31**: Isa 19.2; Mt 24.7. **32**: *Then my Son will be revealed,* 7.28; Mt 24.30; Mk 13.26. **34**:

Son will be revealed, whom you saw as a man coming up from the sea. [s]

33 "Then, when all the nations hear his voice, all the nations shall leave their own lands and the warfare that they have against one another; [34] and an innumerable multitude shall be gathered together, as you saw, wishing to come and conquer him. [35] But he shall stand on the top of Mount Zion. [36] And Zion shall come and be made manifest to all people, prepared and built, as you saw the mountain carved out without hands. [37] Then he, my Son, will reprove the assembled nations for their ungodliness (this was symbolized by the storm), [38] and will reproach them to their face with their evil thoughts and the torments with which they are to be tortured (which were symbolized by the flames), and will destroy them without effort by means of the law [t] (which was symbolized by the fire).

39 "And as for your seeing him gather to himself another multitude that was peaceable, [40] these are the nine [u] tribes that were taken away from their own land into exile in the days of King Hoshea, whom Shalmaneser, king of the Assyrians, made captives; he took them across the river, and they were taken into another land. [41] But they formed this plan for themselves, that they would leave the multitude of the nations and go to a more distant region, where no human beings had ever lived, [42] so that there at least they might keep their statutes that they had not kept in their own land. [43] And they went in by the narrow passages of the Euphrates river. [44] For at that time the Most High performed signs for them, and stopped the channels of the river until they had crossed over. [45] Through that region there was a long way to go, a journey of a year and a half; and that country is called Arzareth. [v]

46 "Then they lived there until the last times; and now, when they are about to come again, [47] the Most High will stop [w] the channels of the river again, so that they may be able to cross over. Therefore you saw the multitude gathered together in peace. [48] But those who are left of your people, who are found within my holy borders, shall be saved. [x] [49] Therefore when he destroys the multitude of the nations that are gathered together, he will defend the people who remain. [50] And then he will show them very many wonders."

51 I said, "O sovereign Lord, explain this to me: Why did I see the man coming up from the heart of the sea?"

52 He said to me, "Just as no one can explore or know what is in the depths of the sea, so no one on earth can see my Son or those who are with him, except in the time of his day. [y] [53] This is the interpretation of the dream that you saw. And you alone have been enlightened about this, [54] because you have forsaken your own ways and have applied yourself to mine, and have searched out my law; [55] for you have devoted your life to wisdom, and called understanding your mother. [56] Therefore I have shown you these things; for there is a reward laid up with the Most High. For it will be that after three more days I will tell you other things, and explain weighty and wondrous matters to you."

s Syr and most Lat Mss lack *from the sea*
t Syr: Lat *effort and the law*   u Other Lat Mss *ten*; Syr Ethiop Arab 1 Arm *nine and a half*
v That is *Another Land*   w Syr: Lat *stops*
x Syr: Lat lacks *shall be saved*   y Syr: Ethiop *except when his time and his day have come.* Lat lacks *his*

Rev 16.16; 19.19. **36**: *Zion,* the heavenly Jerusalem (7.26; Rev 21.2, 9f.). *Without hands,* Dan 2.34, 45. **37**: 12.32. **40**: 2 Kings 17.1–6. *The nine tribes,* the Northern Kingdom (usually "ten tribes"—see note *u*). *The river,* the Euphrates.
   13.44: *Stopped . . . the river,* Josh 3.14–16. **45**: *Arzareth,* Hebrew for "Another Land" (see note *v*; compare Deut 29.28). **47**: *Will stop . . . the river,* Isa 11.15–16. **49**: *The people who remain,* presumably Israel, including the ten tribes who have returned to Palestine (v. 48). **50**: *Then,* in the messianic age. **52**: *Those . . . with him,* perhaps angels (Mt 24.31; 25.31). *Except . . . day,* until the day on which the Messiah appears.

57 Then I got up and walked in the field, giving great glory and praise to the Most High for the wonders that he does^z from time to time, 58 and because he governs the times and whatever things come to pass in their seasons. And I stayed there three days.

14 On the third day, while I was sitting under an oak, suddenly a voice came out of a bush opposite me and said, "Ezra, Ezra!" 2 And I answered, "Here I am, Lord," and I rose to my feet. 3 Then he said to me, "I revealed myself in a bush and spoke to Moses when my people were in bondage in Egypt; 4 and I sent him and led^a my people out of Egypt; and I led him up on Mount Sinai, where I kept him with me many days. 5 I told him many wondrous things, and showed him the secrets of the times and declared to him^b the end of the times. Then I commanded him, saying, 6 'These words you shall publish openly, and these you shall keep secret.' 7 And now I say to you: 8 Lay up in your heart the signs that I have shown you, the dreams that you have seen, and the interpretations that you have heard; 9 for you shall be taken up from among humankind, and henceforth you shall live with my Son and with those who are like you, until the times are ended. 10 The age has lost its youth, and the times begin to grow old. 11 For the age is divided into twelve parts, and nine^c of its parts have already passed, 12 as well as half of the tenth part; so two of its parts remain, besides half of the tenth part.^d 13 Now therefore, set your house in order, and reprove your people; comfort the lowly among them, and instruct those that are wise.^e And now renounce the life that is corruptible, 14 and put away from you mortal thoughts; cast away from you the burdens of humankind, and divest your-

self now of your weak nature; 15 lay to one side the thoughts that are most grievous to you, and hurry to escape from these times. 16 For evils worse than those that you have now seen happen shall take place hereafter. 17 For the weaker the world becomes through old age, the more shall evils be increased upon its inhabitants. 18 Truth shall go farther away, and falsehood shall come near. For the eagle^f that you saw in the vision is already hurrying to come."

19 Then I answered and said, "Let me speak^g in your presence, Lord. 20 For I will go, as you have commanded me, and I will reprove the people who are now living; but who will warn those who will be born hereafter? For the world lies in darkness, and its inhabitants are without light. 21 For your law has been burned, and so no one knows the things which have been done or will be done by you. 22 If then I have found favor with you, send the holy spirit into me, and I will write everything that has happened in the world from the beginning, the things that were written in your law, so that people may be able to find the path, and that those who want to live in the last days may do so."

23 He answered me and said, "Go and gather the people, and tell them not to seek you for forty days. 24 But prepare for yourself many writing tablets, and take with you Sarea, Dabria, Selemia, Ethanus, and Asiel—these five, who are trained to write rapidly; 25 and you shall come here, and I will light in your heart

z Lat *did*   *a* Syr Arab 1 Arab 2 *he led*
b Syr Ethiop Arab Arm: Lat lacks *declared
to him*   *c* Cn: Lat Ethiop *ten*   *d* Syr lacks
verses 11, 12: Ethiop *For the world is divided into
ten parts, and has come to the tenth, and half of the
tenth remains. Now . . .*   *e* Lat lacks *and . . .
wise*   *f* Syr Ethiop Arab Arm: Meaning of Lat
uncertain   *g* Most Lat Mss lack *Let me speak*

14.1–48: The seventh vision (the legend of Ezra and the holy Scriptures). 1–18: God speaks to Ezra. **1:** *A bush,* compare Ex 3.4. **4:** *Many days,* forty days (Ex 34.28). **9:** *My Son,* the hidden Messiah (7.28; 13.32, 52). **14.10:** 5.50–55. **13:** *House,* of Israel. **14:** 2 Cor 5.4. **16:** Mt 24.8. **18:** *The eagle,* ch 11.

14.19–26: Ezra's prayer for inspiration to restore the holy Scriptures. 20: *Without light,* without the light of God's law (Ps 19.8b). **21:** 4.23. **22:** *The holy spirit* will guide Ezra in rewriting the law, which has been burned (v. 21). **23:** *Forty days,* Ex 24.18; 34.28; Deut 9.9, 18. **24:** *Many,* compare v. 44.

the lamp of understanding, which shall not be put out until what you are about to write is finished. 26 And when you have finished, some things you shall make public, and some you shall deliver in secret to the wise; tomorrow at this hour you shall begin to write."

27 Then I went as he commanded me, and I gathered all the people together, and said, 28 "Hear these words, O Israel. 29 At first our ancestors lived as aliens in Egypt, and they were liberated from there 30 and received the law of life, which they did not keep, which you also have transgressed after them. 31 Then land was given to you for a possession in the land of Zion; but you and your ancestors committed iniquity and did not keep the ways that the Most High commanded you. 32 And since he is a righteous judge, in due time he took from you what he had given. 33 And now you are here, and your people *h* are farther in the interior. *i* 34 If you, then, will rule over your minds and discipline your hearts, you shall be kept alive, and after death you shall obtain mercy. 35 For after death the judgment will come, when we shall live again; and then the names of the righteous shall become manifest, and the deeds of the ungodly shall be disclosed. 36 But let no one come to me now, and let no one seek me for forty days."

37 So I took the five men, as he commanded me, and we proceeded to the field, and remained there. 38 And on the next day a voice called me, saying, "Ezra, open your mouth and drink what I give you to drink." 39 So I opened my mouth, and a full cup was offered to me;

it was full of something like water, but its color was like fire. 40 I took it and drank; and when I had drunk it, my heart poured forth understanding, and wisdom increased in my breast, for my spirit retained its memory, 41 and my mouth was opened and was no longer closed. 42 Moreover, the Most High gave understanding to the five men, and by turns they wrote what was dictated, using characters that they did not know. *j* They sat forty days; they wrote during the daytime, and ate their bread at night. 43 But as for me, I spoke in the daytime and was not silent at night. 44 So during the forty days, ninety-four *k* books were written. 45 And when the forty days were ended, the Most High spoke to me, saying, "Make public the twenty-four *l* books that you wrote first, and let the worthy and the unworthy read them; 46 but keep the seventy that were written last, in order to give them to the wise among your people. 47 For in them is the spring of understanding, the fountain of wisdom, and the river of knowledge." 48 And I did so. *m*

---

h Lat *brothers*   *i* Syr Ethiop Arm: Lat *are among you*   *j* Syr Compare Ethiop Arab 2 Arm: Meaning of Lat uncertain   *k* Syr Ethiop Arab 1 Arm: Meaning of Lat uncertain
l Syr Arab 1: Lat lacks *twenty-four*   *m* Syr adds *in the seventh year of the sixth week, five thousand years and three months and twelve days after creation. At that time Ezra was caught up, and taken to the place of those who are like him, after he had written all these things. And he was called the scribe of the knowledge of the Most High for ever and ever.* Ethiop Arab 1 Arm have a similar ending

---

26: *Some things . . . make public,* namely, the rewritten books of the Old Testament. *Some . . . deliver in secret,* namely, the apocalypses (see 12.37–38 n.).
   14.27–36: The last words of Ezra. 29: *Aliens,* Gen 47.4. 30: *The law,* which, if observed, would confer *life.* 33: *Farther,* 13.45. 34: *Kept alive,* i.e. spiritually alive. 36: *Forty days,* v. 23.
   14.37–48: The restoration of the holy Scriptures. 37: *The five men,* v. 24. 39: *A full cup* of inspiration, containing the fire of the spirit (v. 22). 41: *Was opened,* in fluent speech.

42: *Using characters that they did not know,* in a new Hebrew script, the (modern) square characters. 43: Apparently Ezra dictated constantly, repeating what the scribes did not hear during their times of rest and sleep. 45: *The twenty-four books* of the Hebrew canon comprise the five books of the Law (Gen, Ex, Lev, Num, Deut), eight books of the Prophets (the former prophets, Josh, Judg, 1 and 2 Sam [as one book], 1 and 2 Kings [as one book]; the latter prophets, Isa, Jer, Ezek, and the Twelve [counted as one book]), and eleven books of the Writings (Ps, Prov, Job,

15 *[n]* Speak in the ears of my people the words of the prophecy that I will put in your mouth, says the Lord, [2]and cause them to be written on paper; for they are trustworthy and true. [3]Do not fear the plots against you, and do not be troubled by the unbelief of those who oppose you. [4]For all unbelievers shall die in their unbelief. *[o]*

5 Beware, says the Lord, I am bringing evils upon the world, the sword and famine, death and destruction, [6]because iniquity has spread throughout every land, and their harmful doings have reached their limit. [7]Therefore, says the Lord, [8]I will be silent no longer concerning their ungodly acts that they impiously commit, neither will I tolerate their wicked practices. Innocent and righteous blood cries out to me, and the souls of the righteous cry out continually. [9]I will surely avenge them, says the Lord, and will receive to myself all the innocent blood from among them. [10]See, my people are being led like a flock to the slaughter; I will not allow them to live any longer in the land of Egypt, [11]but I will bring them out with a mighty hand and with an uplifted arm, and will strike Egypt with plagues, as before, and will destroy all its land.

12 Let Egypt mourn, and its foundations, because of the plague of chastisement and castigation that the Lord will bring upon it. [13]Let the farmers that till the ground mourn, because their seed shall fail to grow*[p]* and their trees shall be ruined by blight and hail and by a terrible tempest. [14]Alas for the world and for those who live in it! [15]For the sword and misery draw near them, and nation shall rise up to fight against nation, with swords in their hands. [16]For there shall be unrest among people; growing strong against one another, they shall in their

might have no respect for their king or the chief of their leaders. [17]For a person will desire to go into a city, and shall not be able to do so. [18]Because of their pride the cities shall be in confusion, the houses shall be destroyed, and people shall be afraid. [19]People shall have no pity for their neighbors, but shall make an assault upon*[q]* their houses with the sword, and plunder their goods, because of hunger for bread and because of great tribulation.

20 See how I am calling together all the kings of the earth to turn to me, says God, from the rising sun and from the south, from the east and from Lebanon; to turn and repay what they have given them. [21]Just as they have done to my elect until this day, so I will do, and will repay into their bosom. Thus says the Lord God: [22]My right hand will not spare the sinners, and my sword will not cease from those who shed innocent blood on earth. [23]And a fire went forth from his wrath, and consumed the foundations of the earth and the sinners, like burnt straw. [24]Alas for those who sin and do not observe my commandments, says the Lord;*[r]* [25]I will not spare them. Depart, you faithless children! Do not pollute my sanctuary. [26]For God*[s]* knows all who sin against him; therefore he will hand them over to death and slaughter. [27]Already calamities have come upon the whole earth, and you shall remain in them; God*[s]* will not deliver you, because you have sinned against him. 28 What a terrifying sight, appearing

n Chapters 15 and 16 (except 15.57-59, which has been found in Greek) are extant only in Lat
o Other ancient authorities add *and all who believe shall be saved by their faith* *p* Lat lacks *to grow* *q* Cn: Lat *shall empty* *r* Other ancient authorities read *God* *s* Other ancient authorities read *the Lord*

Song, Ruth, Lam, Eccl, Esth, Dan, Ezra-Neh [as one book], 1 and 2 Chr [as one book]). **46:** *The seventy* are esoteric, apocalyptic books (see 12.37–38 n.).
15.1–16.78: An appendix. 15.1–4: The certainty of this prophecy. **1:** *That I will put in your mouth,* Isa 51.16; Jer 1.9.

15.5–11: God will take vengeance upon the wicked. 9: *All the innocent blood,* i.e. all the souls of the righteous (compare Rev 6.10; 19.2). **10:** Ps 44.22; Isa 53.7. **11:** *Will strike Egypt . . . as before,* perhaps an allusion to the occurrence during the reign of Gallienus (A.D. 260–268) of a terrible famine, followed

from the east! 29 The nations of the dragons of Arabia shall come out with many chariots, and from the day that they set out, their hissing shall spread over the earth, so that all who hear them will fear and tremble. 30 Also the Carmonians, raging in wrath, shall go forth like wild boars*t* from the forest, and with great power they shall come and engage them in battle, and with their tusks they shall devastate a portion of the land of the Assyrians with their teeth. 31 And then the dragons,*u* remembering their origin, shall become still stronger; and if they combine in great power and turn to pursue them, 32 then these shall be disorganized and silenced by their power, and shall turn and flee.*v* 33 And from the land of the Assyrians an enemy in ambush shall attack them and destroy one of them, and fear and trembling shall come upon their army, and indecision upon their kings.

34 See the clouds from the east, and from the north to the south! Their appearance is exceedingly threatening, full of wrath and storm. 35 They shall clash against one another and shall pour out a heavy tempest on the earth, and their own tempest;*w* and there shall be blood from the sword as high as a horse's belly 36 and a man's thigh and a camel's hock. 37 And there shall be fear and great trembling on the earth; those who see that wrath shall be horror-stricken, and they shall be seized with trembling. 38 After that, heavy storm clouds shall be stirred up from the south, and from the north, and another part from the west. 39 But the winds from the east shall prevail over the cloud that was*x* raised in wrath, and shall dispel it; and the tempest*y* that was to cause destruction by the east wind shall be driven violently toward the south and west. 40 Great and mighty clouds, full of wrath and tempest, shall rise and destroy all the earth and its inhabitants, and shall pour out upon every high and lofty place*z* a terrible tempest, 41 fire and hail and flying swords and floods of water, so that all the fields and all the streams shall be filled with the abundance of those waters. 42 They shall destroy cities and walls, mountains and hills, trees of the forests, and grass of the meadows, and their grain. 43 They shall go on steadily to Babylon and blot it out. 44 They shall come to it and surround it; they shall pour out on it the tempest*y* and all its fury;*a* then the dust and smoke shall reach the sky, and all who are around it shall mourn for it. 45 And those who survive shall serve those who have destroyed it.

46 And you, Asia, who share in the splendor of Babylon and the glory of her person— 47 woe to you, miserable wretch! For you have made yourself like her; you have decked out your daughters for prostitution to please and glory in your lovers, who have always lusted after you. 48 You have imitated that hateful one in all her deeds and devices.*b* Therefore God*c* says, 49 I will send evils upon you: widowhood, poverty, famine, sword, and pestilence, bringing ruin to your houses, bringing destruction and death. 50 And the glory of your strength

t Other ancient authorities lack *like wild boars* *u* Cn: Lat *dragon* *v* Other ancient authorities read *turn their face to the north* *w* Meaning of Lat uncertain *x* Literally *that he* *y* Meaning of Lat uncertain *z* Or *eminent person* *a* Other ancient authorities add *until they destroy it to its foundations* *b* Other ancient authorities add *you have followed after that one about to gratify her magnates and leaders so that you may be made proud and be pleased by her fornications* *c* Other ancient authorities read *the Lord*

by a plague, which killed two-thirds of the population of Alexandria.

15.12–27: The signs of the end. 15: *Nation . . . . against nation,* Mt 24.7; Mk 13.8; Lk 21.10. **18:** Lk 21.26.

15.28–63: A vision of warfare. This section is thought to reflect events of the third century A.D., including the attack of King Sapor I of Persia (A.D. 240–273) upon the Roman province of Syria. **30:** *The Carmonians,* from Carmania (Kirman), the southern province of the Parthian empire. *Like wild boars,* Ps 80.13. **35:** *As high as . . . ,* Rev 14.20. **15.43:** *Babylon,* i.e. Rome. **47–48:** Rev 14.8; 17.4–5. **49:** Rev 18.7–8.

shall wither like a flower when the heat shall rise that is sent upon you. ⁵¹You shall be weakened like a wretched woman who is beaten and wounded, so that you cannot receive your mighty lovers. ⁵²Would I have dealt with you so violently, says the Lord, ⁵³if you had not killed my chosen people continually, exulting and clapping your hands and talking about their death when you were drunk?

54 Beautify your face! ⁵⁵The reward of a prostitute is in your lap; therefore you shall receive your recompense. ⁵⁶As you will do to my chosen people, says the Lord, so God will do to you, and will hand you over to adversities. ⁵⁷Your children shall die of hunger, and you shall fall by the sword; your cities shall be wiped out, and all your people who are in the open country shall fall by the sword. ⁵⁸Those who are in the mountains and highlands*d* shall perish of hunger, and they shall eat their own flesh in hunger for bread and drink their own blood in thirst for water. ⁵⁹Unhappy above all others, you shall come and suffer fresh miseries. ⁶⁰As they pass by they shall crush the hateful*e* city, and shall destroy a part of your land and abolish a portion of your glory, when they return from devastated Babylon. ⁶¹You shall be broken down by them like stubble,*f* and they shall be like fire to you. ⁶²They shall devour you and your cities, your land and your mountains; they shall burn with fire all your forests and your fruitful trees. ⁶³They shall carry your children away captive, plunder your wealth, and mar the glory of your countenance.

16 Woe to you, Babylon and Asia! Woe to you, Egypt and Syria! ²Bind on sackcloth and cloth of goats' hair,*g* and wail for your children, and lament for them; for your destruction is at hand. ³The sword has been sent upon you, and who is there to turn it back? ⁴A fire has been sent upon you, and who is there to quench it? ⁵Calamities have been sent upon you, and who is there to drive them away? ⁶Can one drive off a hungry lion in the forest, or quench a fire in the stubble once it has started to burn?*h* ⁷Can one turn back an arrow shot by a strong archer? ⁸The Lord God sends calamities, and who will drive them away? ⁹Fire will go forth from his wrath, and who is there to quench it? ¹⁰He will flash lightning, and who will not be afraid? He will thunder, and who will not be terrified? ¹¹The Lord will threaten, and who will not be utterly shattered at his presence? ¹²The earth and its foundations quake, the sea is churned up from the depths, and its waves and the fish with them shall be troubled at the presence of the Lord and the glory of his power. ¹³For his right hand that bends the bow is strong, and his arrows that he shoots are sharp and when they are shot to the ends of the world will not miss once. ¹⁴Calamities are sent forth and shall not return until they come over the earth. ¹⁵The fire is kindled, and shall not be put out until it consumes the foundations of the earth. ¹⁶Just as an arrow shot by a mighty archer does not return, so the calamities that are sent upon the earth shall not return. ¹⁷Alas for me! Alas for me! Who will deliver me in those days?

18 The beginning of sorrows, when there shall be much lamentation; the beginning of famine, when many shall perish; the beginning of wars, when the powers shall be terrified; the beginning of calamities, when all shall tremble.

d Gk: Lat omits *and highlands*   *e* Another reading is *idle* or *unprofitable*   *f* Other ancient authorities read *like dry straw*   *g* Other ancient authorities lack *cloth of goats' hair*   *h* Other ancient authorities read *fire when dry straw has been set on fire*

16.1–34: Denunciation of Babylon, Asia, Egypt, and Syria. 1: *Babylon,* i.e. Rome. **2:** *Sackcloth and cloth of goats' hair,* signs of mourning. **16.12:** Ps 18.15. **15:** *Until it consumes . . . the earth,* an apocalyptic idea from Persian eschatology (compare 2 Pet 3.10). **29:** Isa 17.6. **16.35–50: God's people are warned of impending disasters. 38:** 4.40. **41:** 1 Cor 7.29–31. **16.51–67: The impossibility of hiding sin from God.**

What shall they do, when the calamities come? [19] Famine and plague, tribulation and anguish are sent as scourges for the correction of humankind. [20] Yet for all this they will not turn from their iniquities, or ever be mindful of the scourges. [21] Indeed, provisions will be so cheap upon earth that people will imagine that peace is assured for them, and then calamities shall spring up on the earth—the sword, famine, and great confusion. [22] For many of those who live on the earth shall perish by famine; and those who survive the famine shall die by the sword. [23] And the dead shall be thrown out like dung, and there shall be no one to console them; for the earth shall be left desolate, and its cities shall be demolished. [24] No one shall be left to cultivate the earth or to sow it. [25] The trees shall bear fruit, but who will gather it? [26] The grapes shall ripen, but who will tread them? For in all places there shall be great solitude; [27] a person will long to see another human being, or even to hear a human voice. [28] For ten shall be left out of a city; and two, out of the field, those who have hidden themselves in thick groves and clefts in the rocks. [29] Just as in an olive orchard three or four olives may be left on every tree, [30] or just as when a vineyard is gathered, some clusters may be left[i] by those who search carefully through the vineyard, [31] so in those days three or four shall be left by those who search their houses with the sword. [32] The earth shall be left desolate, and its fields shall be plowed up,[j] and its roads and all its paths shall bring forth thorns, because no sheep will go along them. [33] Virgins shall mourn because they have no bridegrooms; women shall mourn because they have no husbands; their daughters shall mourn, because they have no help. [34] Their bridegrooms shall be killed in war, and their husbands shall perish of famine.

35 Listen now to these things, and understand them, you who are servants of the Lord. [36] This is word of the Lord; receive it and do not disbelieve what the Lord says. [k] [37] The calamities draw near, and are not delayed. [38] Just as a pregnant woman, in the ninth month when the time of her delivery draws near, has great pains around her womb for two or three hours beforehand, but when the child comes forth from the womb, there will not be a moment's delay, [39] so the calamities will not delay in coming upon the earth, and the world will groan, and pains will seize it on every side.

40 Hear my words, O my people; prepare for battle, and in the midst of the calamities be like strangers on the earth. [41] Let the one who sells be like one who will flee; let the one who buys be like one who will lose; [42] let the one who does business be like one who will not make a profit; and let the one who builds a house be like one who will not live in it; [43] let the one who sows be like one who will not reap; so also the one who prunes the vines, like one who will not gather the grapes; [44] those who marry, like those who will have no children; and those who do not marry, like those who are widowed. [45] Because of this those who labor, labor in vain; [46] for strangers shall gather their fruits, and plunder their goods, overthrow their houses, and take their children captive; for in captivity and famine they will produce their children. [l] [47] Those who conduct business, do so only to have it plundered; the more they adorn their cities, their houses and possessions, and their persons, [48] the more angry I will be with them for their sins, says the Lord. [49] Just as a respectable and virtuous woman abhors a prostitute, [50] so righteousness shall abhor iniquity, when she decks herself out, and shall accuse her to her face when he comes who will defend the one who searches out every sin on earth.

51 Therefore do not be like her or her works. [52] For in a very short time iniquity will be removed from the earth, and righteousness will reign over us. [53] Sinners must not say that they have not

---

i Other ancient authorities read *a cluster may remain
exposed*   *j* Other ancient authorities read *be for
briers*   *k* Cn: Lat *do not believe the gods of whom the
Lord speaks*   *l* Other ancient authorities read
*therefore those who are married may know that they
will produce children for captivity and famine*

sinned;[m] for God[n] will burn coals of fire on the head of everyone who says, "I have not sinned before God and his glory." [54] The Lord[o] certainly knows everything that people do; he knows their imaginations and their thoughts and their hearts. [55] He said, "Let the earth be made," and it was made, and "Let the heaven be made," and it was made. [56] At his word the stars were fixed in their places, and he knows the number of the stars. [57] He searches the abyss and its treasures; he has measured the sea and its contents; [58] he has confined the sea in the midst of the waters;[p] and by his word he has suspended the earth over the water. [59] He has spread out the heaven like a dome and made it secure upon the waters; [60] he has put springs of water in the desert, and pools on the tops of the mountains, so as to send rivers from the heights to water the earth. [61] He formed human beings and put a heart in the midst of each body, and gave each person breath and life and understanding [62] and the spirit[q] of Almighty God,[r] who surely made all things and searches out hidden things in hidden places. [63] He knows your imaginations and what you think in your hearts! Woe to those who sin and want to hide their sins! [64] The Lord will strictly examine all their works, and will make a public spectacle of all of you. [65] You shall be put to shame when your sins come out before others, and your own iniquities shall stand as your accusers on that day. [66] What will you do? Or how will you hide your sins before the Lord and his glory? [67] Indeed, God[s] is the judge; fear him! Cease from your sins, and forget your iniquities, never to commit them again; so God[s] will lead you forth and deliver you from all tribulation.

[68] The burning wrath of a great multitude is kindled over you; they shall drag some of you away and force you to eat what was sacrificed to idols. [69] And those who consent to eat shall be held in derision and contempt, and shall be trampled under foot. [70] For in many places[t] and in neighboring cities there shall be a great uprising against those who fear the Lord. [71] They shall[u] be like maniacs, sparing no one, but plundering and destroying those who continue to fear the Lord.[v] [72] For they shall destroy and plunder their goods, and drive them out of house and home. [73] Then the tested quality of my elect shall be manifest, like gold that is tested by fire.

[74] Listen, my elect ones, says the Lord; the days of tribulation are at hand, but I will deliver you from them. [75] Do not fear or doubt, for God[w] is your guide. [76] You who keep my commandments and precepts, says the Lord God, must not let your sins weigh you down, or your iniquities prevail over you. [77] Woe to those who are choked by their sins and overwhelmed by their iniquities! They are like a field choked with underbrush and its path[x] overwhelmed with thorns, so that no one can pass through. [78] It is shut off and given up to be consumed by fire.

m Other ancient authorities add *or the unjust done injustice*   *n* Lat *for he*   *o* Other ancient authorities read *Lord God*   *p* Other ancient authorities read *confined the world between the waters and the waters*   *q* Or *breath*   *r* Other ancient authorities read *of the Lord Almighty*   *s* Other ancient authorities read *the Lord*   *t* Meaning of Lat uncertain   *u* Other ancient authorities read *For people, because of their misfortunes, shall*   *v* Other ancient authorities read *fear God*   *w* Other ancient authorities read *the Lord*   *x* Other ancient authorities read *seed*

16.68–78: **Though persecuted, God's elect will be delivered. 73**: Zech 13.9; 1 Pet 1.7.

4 Maccabees

The book known as 4 Maccabees is included in important manuscripts of the Greek Bible, and was early translated into Syriac. Although never canonized, it has deeply influenced the preaching and piety of the Eastern Churches.

At one time 4 Maccabees was attributed to Josephus and given the title *On the Supremacy of Reason*. This describes it well, for it is a diatribe or lecture, or perhaps a panegyric, on the mastery of the passions by religious reason, as exemplified by the story of the martyrdoms of Eleazar, the seven brothers, and their mother. Its traditional title was no doubt adopted because the account is an expansion of 2 Macc 6.12–7.42, and the story belongs to the Maccabean period.

The book is a classic example of the interpretation of Judaism in terms of Greek philosophy. The ideas are Stoic (with some significant differences), and so is the terminology. The numerous Old Testament quotations are taken exclusively from the Greek Septuagint. The treatise was written originally in Greek, and in the florid Asiatic style. Possibly it was first delivered as an oration at a festival commemorating the Maccabean martyrs or at the Feast of Dedication (1.10; 3.19; 14.9; compare Jn 10.22).

The author's theology, with its emphasis on the absolute sovereignty of the Law, is genuinely Jewish but with two special characteristics. The martyrdoms are a substitutionary atonement that expiates the nation's sin and purifies the land (1.11; 17.21; 18.4). The martyrs are immediately immortal, received by the patriarchs and living in God (7.19; 16.25). Whereas 2 Maccabees reflects Persian influence with its emphasis on resurrection of the body, 4 Maccabees echoes the Greek idea of the immortality of the soul (14.5–6; 16.13; 17.12; 18.23; see Lk 16.22).

The book has frequently been assigned to the period A.D. 20–54, when Cilicia was joined to Syria and Phoenicia as a single province (4.2), and it is tempting to date it to the reign of Caligula (A.D. 37–41), who proposed to violate the Jerusalem temple (compare 4.5–14). The fact, however, that its concern is with a philosophical question, rather than with persecution *per se,* makes any such hypothesis conjectural. The most that can be said with certainty is that it was written sometime between the end of the Hasmonean dynasty in 63 B.C. and the destruction of the Jerusalem temple in A.D. 70.

Alexandria has been proposed as the place of composition, and Jerusalem cannot be excluded. Antioch, however, has the best claim, for the martyrs might have been brought to the royal capital (5.1), and in Antioch the Jews were called "Hebrews," as in this book.

1 The subject that I am about to discuss is most philosophical, that is, whether devout reason is sovereign over the emotions. So it is right for me to advise you to pay earnest attention to philosophy. ²For the subject is essential to everyone who is seeking knowledge, and in addition it includes the praise of the highest virtue—I mean, of course, rational judgment. ³If, then, it is evident that reason rules over those emotions that hinder self-control, namely, gluttony and lust, ⁴it is also clear that it masters the emotions that hinder one from justice, such as malice, and those that stand in the way of courage, namely anger, fear, and pain. ⁵Some might perhaps ask, "If reason rules the emotions, why is it not sovereign over forgetfulness and ignorance?" Their attempt at argument is ridiculous!ᵃ ⁶For reason does not rule its own emotions, but those that are opposed to justice, courage, and self-control;ᵇ and it is not for the purpose of destroying them, but so that one may not give way to them.

⁷ I could prove to you from many and various examples that reasonᶜ is dominant over the emotions, ⁸but I can demonstrate it best from the noble bravery of those who died for the sake of virtue, Eleazar and the seven brothers and their mother. ⁹All of these, by despising sufferings that bring death, demonstrated that reason controls the emotions. ¹⁰On this anniversaryᵈ it is fitting for me to praise for their virtues those who, with their mother, died for the sake of nobility and goodness, but I would also call them blessed for the honor in which they are held. ¹¹All people, even their torturers, marveled at their courage and endurance,

and they became the cause of the downfall of tyranny over their nation. By their endurance they conquered the tyrant, and thus their native land was purified through them. ¹²I shall shortly have an opportunity to speak of this; but, as my custom is, I shall begin by stating my main principle, and then I shall turn to their story, giving glory to the all-wise God.

13 Our inquiry, accordingly, is whether reason is sovereign over the emotions. ¹⁴We shall decide just what reason is and what emotion is, how many kinds of emotions there are, and whether reason rules over all these. ¹⁵Now reason is the mind that with sound logic prefers the life of wisdom. ¹⁶Wisdom, next, is the knowledge of divine and human matters and the causes of these. ¹⁷This, in turn, is education in the law, by which we learn divine matters reverently and human affairs to our advantage. ¹⁸Now the kinds of wisdom are rational judgment, justice, courage, and self-control. ¹⁹Rational judgment is supreme over all of these, since by means of it reason rules over the emotions. ²⁰The two most comprehensive typesᵉ of the emotions are pleasure and pain; and each of these is by nature concerned with both body and soul. ²¹The emotions of both pleasure and pain have many consequences. ²²Thus desire precedes pleasure and delight follows it. ²³Fear precedes pain and sorrow comes after. ²⁴Anger, as a person will see by

a Or *They are attempting to make my argument ridiculous!*   *b* Other ancient authorities add *and rational judgment*   *c* Other ancient authorities read *devout reason*   *d* Gk *At this time*   *e* Or *sources*

1.1–3.18: Philosophical introduction. The principal thesis is stated in 1.3–12, which concludes with a short doxology, and is developed further in 1.13–3.18. **1**: *Devout,* Greek "eusebēs," religious or pious; compare 5.7, 31. **2–4**: *Rational judgment . . . self-control . . . justice . . . courage,* the four cardinal virtues of the Platonic and Stoic traditions. **5**: The objection is dealt with in 2.24–3.1. **8**: *Eleazar,* 2 Macc 6.18; 3 Macc 6.1. **10**: Compare 3.19 and see Introduction.

1.11: *Tyranny,* the attempt of Antiochus IV (4.15) to impose pagan worship on the Jewish *nation;* see 5.1 n. *Purified,* the idea of expiation is developed further in 6.28–29; 17.21. **17**: *Education in the law,* Jews regarded the Mosaic law as philosophical and the highest form of education (see 11.21 n.; 18.6–19 n.). *We learn . . . to our advantage,* compare the Stoic definition of wisdom in Cicero's *Tusculan Disputations* iv.25.57. **18**: The four *kinds* are found also in Wis 8.7.

reflecting on this experience, is an emotion embracing pleasure and pain. 25 In pleasure there exists even a malevolent tendency, which is the most complex of all the emotions. 26 In the soul it is boastfulness, covetousness, thirst for honor, rivalry, and malice; 27 in the body, indiscriminate eating, gluttony, and solitary gormandizing.

28 Just as pleasure and pain are two plants growing from the body and the soul, so there are many offshoots of these plants,*f* 29 each of which the master cultivator, reason, weeds and prunes and ties up and waters and thoroughly irrigates, and so tames the jungle of habits and emotions. 30 For reason is the guide of the virtues, but over the emotions it is sovereign.

Observe now, first of all, that rational judgment is sovereign over the emotions by virtue of the restraining power of self-control. 31 Self-control, then, is dominance over the desires. 32 Some desires are mental, others are physical, and reason obviously rules over both. 33 Otherwise, how is it that when we are attracted to forbidden foods we abstain from the pleasure to be had from them? Is it not because reason is able to rule over appetites? I for one think so. 34 Therefore when we crave seafood and fowl and animals and all sorts of foods that are forbidden to us by the law, we abstain because of domination by reason. 35 For the emotions of the appetites are restrained, checked by the temperate mind, and all the impulses of the body are bridled by reason.

2 And why is it amazing that the desires of the mind for the enjoyment of beauty are rendered powerless? 2 It is for this reason, certainly, that the temperate Joseph is praised, because by men-

tal˙ effort*g* he overcame sexual desire. 3 For when he was young and in his prime for intercourse, by his reason he nullified the frenzy*h* of the passions. 4 Not only is reason proved to rule over the frenzied urge of sexual desire, but also over every desire.*i* 5 Thus the law says, "You shall not covet your neighbor's wife or anything that is your neighbor's." 6 In fact, since the law has told us not to covet, I could prove to you all the more that reason is able to control desires.

Just so it is with the emotions that hinder one from justice. 7 Otherwise how could it be that someone who is habitually a solitary gormandizer, a glutton, or even a drunkard can learn a better way, unless reason is clearly lord of the emotions? 8 Thus, as soon as one adopts a way of life in accordance with the law, even though a lover of money, one is forced to act contrary to natural ways and to lend without interest to the needy and to cancel the debt when the seventh year arrives. 9 If one is greedy, one is ruled by the law through reason so that one neither gleans the harvest nor gathers the last grapes from the vineyard.

In all other matters we can recognize that reason rules the emotions. 10 For the law prevails even over affection for parents, so that virtue is not abandoned for their sakes. 11 It is superior to love for one's wife, so that one rebukes her when she breaks the law. 12 It takes precedence over love for children, so that one punishes them for misdeeds. 13 It is sovereign over the relationship of friends, so that one rebukes friends when they act wick-

*f Other ancient authorities read these emotions
g Other ancient authorities add in reasoning
h Or gadfly   i Or all covetousness*

1:24: *As a person . . . experience,* the Greek is obscure. **27**: Job 31.17. **33**: *Reason is able to rule over appetites,* in Judaism, desires are not to be extirpated, as Stoics taught, but are to be controlled; compare v. 6; Mishnah *P. Aboth* 4.1. **34**: *Seafood,* Lev 11.1–31; Deut 14.3–21; Acts 10.10–14. **35**: *Emotions . . . restrained . . . impulses bridled;* reason, informed

by the law, dominates the passions of both mind and body.

2.1: *Enjoyment of beauty* refers to sexual desire but also suggests the concept of "eros" in Plato's *Symposium.* **2**: *Joseph,* Gen 39.7–12. **8**: *Lend without interest,* to other Jews, Ex 22.25. *Seventh year,* Deut 15.1–3. **9**: Lev 19.9–10; Deut 20.19–20. **11–12**: Mt 10.37; Lk 14.26.

edly. [14] Do not consider it paradoxical when reason, through the law, can prevail even over enmity. The fruit trees of the enemy are not cut down, but one preserves the property of enemies from marauders and helps raise up what has fallen.[j]

[15] It is evident that reason rules even[k] the more violent emotions: lust for power, vainglory, boasting, arrogance, and malice. [16] For the temperate mind repels all these malicious emotions, just as it repels anger—for it is sovereign over even this. [17] When Moses was angry with Dathan and Abiram, he did nothing against them in anger, but controlled his anger by reason. [18] For, as I have said, the temperate mind is able to get the better of the emotions, to correct some, and to render others powerless. [19] Why else did Jacob, our most wise father, censure the households of Simeon and Levi for their irrational slaughter of the entire tribe of the Shechemites, saying, "Cursed be their anger"? [20] For if reason could not control anger, he would not have spoken thus. [21] Now when God fashioned human beings, he planted in them emotions and inclinations, [22] but at the same time he enthroned the mind among the senses as a sacred governor over them all. [23] To the mind he gave the law; and one who lives subject to this will rule a kingdom that is temperate, just, good, and courageous.

[24] How is it then, one might say, that if reason is master of the emotions, it does not control forgetfulness and ignorance? [1] But this argument is entirely ridiculous; for it is evident that reason rules not over its own emotions, but

over those of the body. [2] No one of us[l] can eradicate that kind of desire, but reason can provide a way for us not to be enslaved by desire. [3] No one of us can eradicate anger from the mind, but reason can help to deal with anger. [4] No one of us can eradicate malice, but reason can fight at our side so that we are not overcome by malice. [5] For reason does not uproot the emotions but is their antagonist.

[6] Now this can be explained more clearly by the story of King David's thirst. [7] David had been attacking the Philistines all day long, and together with the soldiers of his nation had killed many of them. [8] Then when evening fell, he[m] came, sweating and quite exhausted, to the royal tent, around which the whole army of our ancestors had encamped. [9] Now all the rest were at supper, [10] but the king was extremely thirsty, and though springs were plentiful there, he could not satisfy his thirst from them. [11] But a certain irrational desire for the water in the enemy's territory tormented and inflamed him, undid and consumed him. [12] When his guards complained bitterly because of the king's craving, two staunch young soldiers, respecting[n] the king's desire, armed themselves fully, and taking a pitcher climbed over the enemy's ramparts. [13] Eluding the sentinels at the gates, they went searching throughout the enemy camp [14] and found the spring, and from it boldly brought the king a drink. [15] But Da-

j Or *the beasts that have fallen*   *k* Other ancient authorities read *through*   *l* Gk *you*   *m* Other ancient authorities read *he hurried and*   *n* Or *embarrassed because of*

2.14: Deut 20.19–20; Ex 23.4–5; Josephus, *Against Apion* ii.211–212. **17**: *Dathan and Abiram,* Num 16.1–35; Sir 45.18. **19**: Gen 49.7. **21**: According to rabbinic Judaism, God *planted* the good and the evil *inclinations in human beings;* the latter is to be controlled, and in itself is not essentially evil. **23**: *Will rule a kingdom,* according to the Stoics and Philo, the wise man is a king. Compare the different concept of the reign of the saints in 1 Cor 4.8; 6.2–3; 1 Pet 2.9.

3.1: *Those of the body,* but the emotions of

vv. 2–4 are those of the mind; thus 1.6 would fit better here.

3.6–18: **King David's thirst.** Some details are different in 2 Sam 23.13–17; 1 Chr 11.15–19. **7**: *Philistines,* literally "foreigners"; in the Greek Bible this word usually translates the Hebrew word "Philistines." **15**: *Equivalent to blood,* 2 Sam 23.17, "Can I drink the blood . . . ?" **17**: *Frenzied desires,* in Greek mythology the "oistros" was the gadfly that tormented Io, and it became a symbol of uncontrolled sexual desire.

vid, [o] though he was burning with thirst, considered it an altogether fearful danger to his soul to drink what was regarded as equivalent to blood. [16] Therefore, opposing reason to desire, he poured out the drink as an offering to God. [17] For the temperate mind can conquer the drives of the emotions and quench the flames of frenzied desires; [18] it can overthrow bodily agonies even when they are extreme, and by nobility of reason spurn all domination by the emotions.

19 The present occasion now invites us to a narrative demonstration of temperate reason.

20 At a time when our ancestors were enjoying profound peace because of their observance of the law and were prospering, so that even Seleucus Nicanor, king of Asia, had both appropriated money to them for the temple service and recognized their commonwealth— [21] just at that time certain persons attempted a revolution against the public harmony and caused many and various disasters.

4 Now there was a certain Simon, a political opponent of the noble and good man, Onias, who then held the high priesthood for life. When despite all manner of slander he was unable to injure Onias in the eyes of the nation, he fled the country with the purpose of betraying it. [2] So he came to Apollonius, governor of Syria, Phoenicia, and Cilicia, and said, [3] "I have come here because I am loyal to the king's government, to report that in the Jerusalem treasuries there are deposited tens of thousands in private funds, which are not the property of the temple but belong to King Seleucus." [4] When Apollonius learned the de-

tails of these things, he praised Simon for his service to the king and went up to Seleucus to inform him of the rich treasure. [5] On receiving authority to deal with this matter, he proceeded quickly to our country accompanied by the accursed Simon and a very strong military force. [6] He said that he had come with the king's authority to seize the private funds in the treasury. [7] The people indignantly protested his words, considering it outrageous that those who had committed deposits to the sacred treasury should be deprived of them, and did all that they could to prevent it. [8] But, uttering threats, Apollonius went on to the temple. [9] While the priests together with women and children were imploring God in the temple to shield the holy place that was being treated so contemptuously, [10] and while Apollonius was going up with his armed forces to seize the money, angels on horseback with lightning flashing from their weapons appeared from heaven, instilling in them great fear and trembling. [11] Then Apollonius fell down half dead in the temple area that was open to all, stretched out his hands toward heaven, and with tears begged the Hebrews to pray for him and propitiate the wrath of the heavenly army. [12] For he said that he had committed a sin deserving of death, and that if he were spared he would praise the blessedness of the holy place before all people. [13] Moved by these words, the high priest Onias, although otherwise he had scruples about doing so, prayed for him so that King Seleucus would not suppose that Apollo-

o Gk he

3.19–4.14: Attempt on the temple treasury. Compare 2 Macc 3.1–40. **19:** *The present occasion,* perhaps when 4 Maccabees was first read publicly (see Introduction). **20:** *Profound peace,* see 2 Macc 3.1 n. *Seleucus Nicanor,* the author is confused. Seleucus I Nicator ruled 305/304–281/280 B.C.; the king who is meant here is Seleucus IV Philopator, 187–175 B.C. (see 2 Macc 3.3 n.).

4.1: *Simon,* 2 Macc 3.4 n. *Onias* III, 2 Macc 3.1 n. Life tenure of *the high priesthood* was the regular rule until the first century A.D. when

the Roman procurators disregarded it, Jn 18.13 n.; Josephus, *Ant.*XVIII.ii.2; xx.10. **2:** *Cilicia* was joined to Syria and Phoenicia as one province only in A.D. 20–54; 2 Macc 3.5 is more accurate. **3:** *Private funds* were often deposited in temples, as in a bank. **5:** *Authority,* but according to 2 Macc 3.7–8, Heliodorus was put in command. **6:** *Private funds* in the Jerusalem temple, see Josephus, B.J.I.xiii.9; VI.v.2. **10:** Compare 3 Macc 2.21–24; 6.18.

nius had been overcome by human treachery and not by divine justice. [14] So Apollonius, *p* having been saved beyond all expectations, went away to report to the king what had happened to him.

15 When King Seleucus died, his son Antiochus Epiphanes succeeded to the throne, an arrogant and terrible man, [16] who removed Onias from the priesthood and appointed Onias's *q* brother Jason as high priest. [17] Jason *r* agreed that if the office were conferred on him he would pay the king three thousand six hundred sixty talents annually. [18] So the king appointed him high priest and ruler of the nation. [19] Jason *r* changed the nation's way of life and altered its form of government in complete violation of the law, [20] so that not only was a gymnasium constructed at the very citadel *s* of our native land, but also the temple service was abolished. [21] The divine justice was angered by these acts and caused Antiochus himself to make war on them. [22] For when he was warring against Ptolemy in Egypt, he heard that a rumor of his death had spread and that the people of Jerusalem had rejoiced greatly. He speedily marched against them, [23] and after he had plundered them he issued a decree that if any of them were found observing the ancestral law they should die. [24] When, by means of his decrees, he had not been able in any way to put an end to the people's observance of the law, but saw

that all his threats and punishments were being disregarded [25]—even to the extent that women, because they had circumcised their sons, were thrown headlong from heights along with their infants, though they had known beforehand that they would suffer this— [26] when, I say, his decrees were despised by the people, he himself tried through torture to compel everyone in the nation to eat defiling foods and to renounce Judaism.

5 The tyrant Antiochus, sitting in state with his counselors on a certain high place, and with his armed soldiers standing around him, [2] ordered the guards to seize each and every Hebrew and to compel them to eat pork and food sacrificed to idols. [3] If any were not willing to eat defiling food, they were to be broken on the wheel and killed. [4] When many persons had been rounded up, one man, Eleazar by name, leader of the flock, was brought *t* before the king. He was a man of priestly family, learned in the law, advanced in age, and known to many in the tyrant's court because of his philosophy. *u*

5 When Antiochus saw him he said, [6] "Before I begin to torture you, old man, I would advise you to save yourself by eating pork, [7] for I respect your age and

p Gk *he* *q* Gk *his* *r* Gk *He* *s* Or *high place* *t* Or *was the first of the flock to be brought* *u* Other ancient authorities read *his advanced age*

4.15–26: Antiochus' persecution of the Jews. Compare 1 Macc 1.20–64; 2 Macc 5.11–6.11. **15:** *Antiochus IV Epiphanes* was the brother of *Seleucus IV*, and son of Antiochus III; see 1 Macc 1.10 n. **16:** *Jason,* 2 Macc 4.7 n.

4.20: *At the very citadel,* more probably "under the citadel," as in 2 Macc 4.12. **21:** *The divine justice,* a theological interpretation of 2 Macc 4.16–17. **22:** *Ptolemy* VI Philometor (180–145 B.C.), 1 Macc 1.16–19.

5.1–7.23: Martyrdom of Eleazar. Compare 2 Macc 6.18–31. **5.1:** *Tyrant,* in Greek usually with a bad connotation, denoting not a legitimate monarch but one who rules by force. *Sitting in state,* perhaps in Jerusalem; but early Christian tradition located this in Antioch, and a church was erected there in honor of the martyrs. **2:** Jews regarded the

eating of *pork and food sacrificed to idols* as idolatry and profanation of the divine name because it was a public defiance of God's law; compare 1 Cor 10.6–22. **3:** *Defiling,* the Greek word, peculiar to 4 Maccabees, implies that forbidden foods were polluted and particularly odious. **4:** *Eleazar* may mean "God has helped"; it is the same name as Lazarus (Lk 16.20; Jn 11.1) and, as a male name, serves as a symbol for a man of great piety; compare 3 Macc 6.1; 2 Macc 8.23 n. **7–8:** A Stoic *philosopher* regarded the distinctions of national religions and laws, such as those of Judaism, as unimportant, whereas Jews considered the Mosaic law to be the highest philosophy; compare 1.17 n. Stoics also taught that one should live according to *nature.* **7:** *Religion,* Greek "thrēskeia," religious practice or cult; compare v. 31.

your gray hairs. Although you have had them for so long a time, it does not seem to me that you are a philosopher when you observe the religion of the Jews. 8 When nature has granted it to us, why should you abhor eating the very excellent meat of this animal? 9 It is senseless not to enjoy delicious things that are not shameful, and wrong to spurn the gifts of nature. 10 It seems to me that you will do something even more senseless if, by holding a vain opinion concerning the truth, you continue to despise me to your own hurt. 11 Will you not awaken from your foolish philosophy, dispel your futile reasonings, adopt a mind appropriate to your years, philosophize according to the truth of what is beneficial, 12 and have compassion on your old age by honoring my humane advice? 13 For consider this: if there is some power watching over this religion of yours, it will excuse you from any transgression that arises out of compulsion."

14 When the tyrant urged him in this fashion to eat meat unlawfully, Eleazar asked to have a word. 15 When he had received permission to speak, he began to address the people as follows: 16 "We, O Antiochus, who have been persuaded to govern our lives by the divine law, think that there is no compulsion more powerful than our obedience to the law. 17 Therefore we consider that we should not transgress it in any respect. 18 Even if, as you suppose, our law were not truly divine and we had wrongly held it to be divine, not even so would it be right for us to invalidate our reputation for piety. 19 Therefore do not suppose that it would be a petty sin if we were to eat defiling food; 20 to transgress the law in matters either small or great is of equal seriousness, 21 for in either case the law is equally despised. 22 You scoff at our philosophy as though living by it were irrational, 23 but it teaches us self-control, so that we master all pleasures and desires, and it also trains us in courage, so that we endure any suffering willingly; 24 it instructs us in justice, so that in all our dealings we act impartially, *v* and it teaches us piety, so that with proper reverence we worship the only living God.

25 "Therefore we do not eat defiling food; for since we believe that the law was established by God, we know that in the nature of things the Creator of the world in giving us the law has shown sympathy toward us. 26 He has permitted us to eat what will be most suitable for our lives, *w* but he has forbidden us to eat meats that would be contrary to this. 27 It would be tyrannical for you to compel us not only to transgress the law, but also to eat in such a way that you may deride us for eating defiling foods, which are most hateful to us. 28 But you shall have no such occasion to laugh at me, 29 nor will I transgress the sacred oaths of my ancestors concerning the keeping of the law, 30 not even if you gouge out my eyes and burn my entrails. 31 I am not so old and cowardly as not to be young in reason on behalf of piety. 32 Therefore get your torture wheels ready and fan the fire more vehemently! 33 I do not so pity my old age as to break the ancestral law by my own act. 34 I will not play false to you, O law that trained me, nor will I renounce you, beloved self-control. 35 I will not put you to shame, philosophical reason, nor will I reject you, honored priesthood and knowledge of the law. 36 You, O king, *x* shall not defile the honorable mouth of my old age, nor my

v Or *so that we hold in balance all our habitual inclinations*   *w* Or *souls*   *x* Gk lacks *O king*

5.13: *Some power watching over,* a Greek philosophical expression; compare 2 Macc 7.35; 9.5; 3 Macc 2.21. **23–24:** *Self-control . . . courage . . . justice,* cardinal virtues (see 1.2–4 n.). In Xenophon's *Memorabilia,* and sometimes in Philo, *piety* or religion is the fourth virtue.

5.27: *Deride us,* because this would bring discredit on the Jewish people, the Mosaic law, and the God who gave it. God's name must be hallowed (Mt 6.9). **31:** *Piety,* Greek "eusebeia," proper reverence toward God (see v. 7 n.; 1.1 n.). No single Greek word corresponds to the English word "religion."

long life lived lawfully. 37 My ancestors will receive me as pure, as one who does not fear your violence even to death. 38 You may tyrannize the ungodly, but you shall not dominate my religious principles, either by words or through deeds."

6 When Eleazar in this manner had made eloquent response to the exhortations of the tyrant, the guards who were standing by dragged him violently to the instruments of torture. 2 First they stripped the old man, though he remained adorned with the gracefulness of his piety. 3 After they had tied his arms on each side they flogged him, 4 while a herald who faced him cried out, "Obey the king's commands!" 5 But the courageous and noble man, like a true Eleazar, was unmoved, as though being tortured in a dream; 6 yet while the old man's eyes were raised to heaven, his flesh was being torn by scourges, his blood flowing, and his sides were being cut to pieces. 7 Although he fell to the ground because his body could not endure the agonies, he kept his reason upright and unswerving. 8 One of the cruel guards rushed at him and began to kick him in the side to make him get up again after he fell. 9 But he bore the pains and scorned the punishment and endured the tortures. 10 Like a noble athlete the old man, while being beaten, was victorious over his torturers; 11 in fact, with his face bathed in sweat, and gasping heavily for breath, he amazed even his torturers by his courageous spirit.

12 At that point, partly out of pity for his old age, 13 partly out of sympathy from their acquaintance with him, partly out of admiration for his endurance, some of the king's retinue came to him and said, 14 "Eleazar, why are you so irra-

tionally destroying yourself through these evil things? 15 We will set before you some cooked meat; save yourself by pretending to eat pork."

16 But Eleazar, as though more bitterly tormented by this counsel, cried out: 17 "Never may we, the children of Abraham,y think so basely that out of cowardice we feign a role unbecoming to us! 18 For it would be irrational if having lived in accordance with truth up to old age and having maintained in accordance with law the reputation of such a life, we should now change our course 19 and ourselves become a pattern of impiety to the young by setting them an example in the eating of defiling food. 20 It would be shameful if we should survive for a little while and during that time be a laughing stock to all for our cowardice, 21 and be despised by the tyrant as unmanly by not contending even to death for our divine law. 22 Therefore, O children of Abraham, die nobly for your religion! 23 And you, guards of the tyrant, why do you delay?"

24 When they saw that he was so courageous in the face of the afflictions, and that he had not been changed by their compassion, the guards brought him to the fire. 25 There they burned him with maliciously contrived instruments, threw him down, and poured stinking liquids into his nostrils. 26 When he was now burned to his very bones and about to expire, he lifted up his eyes to God and said, 27 "You know, O God, that though I might have saved myself, I am dying in burning torments for the sake of the law. 28 Be merciful to your people, and let our punishment suffice for them. 29 Make my blood their purification, and take my life

y Or O children of Abraham

37: 13.17; 17.12; Mk 12.26–27. Immortality of the martyrs is implied in 9.22; 2 Macc 7.36.
6.5: True Eleazar, see 5.4 n. 6: Eyes . . . to heaven, a natural gesture in prayer, particularly that of a martyr. Compare v. 26 and Stephen's supplication in Acts 7.55. 10: Noble athlete, 1 Cor 9.24–27; Heb 12.1.

6.17–21: See 5.27 n. 23: Why do you delay? Compare 9.1; 2 Macc 7.30. 29: In exchange, Greek "antipsychon," a word used by the martyr Ignatius of Antioch in his letters. Compare 1.11; 9.24; 12.17; 17.21–22; 18.4; Mk 10.45. The idea of expiation derives ultimately from Isa 53.5–12 and is also found in

in exchange for theirs." ³⁰After he said this, the holy man died nobly in his tortures; even in the tortures of death he resisted, by virtue of reason, for the sake of the law.

31 Admittedly, then, devout reason is sovereign over the emotions. ³²For if the emotions had prevailed over reason, we would have testified to their domination. ³³But now that reason has conquered the emotions, we properly attribute to it the power to govern. ³⁴It is right for us to acknowledge the dominance of reason when it masters even external agonies. It would be ridiculous to deny it. *z* ³⁵I have proved not only that reason has mastered agonies, but also that it masters pleasures and in no respect yields to them.

7 For like a most skillful pilot, the reason of our father Eleazar steered the ship of religion over the sea of the emotions, ²and though buffeted by the stormings of the tyrant and overwhelmed by the mighty waves of tortures, ³in no way did he turn the rudder of religion until he sailed into the haven of immortal victory. ⁴No city besieged with many ingenious war machines has ever held out as did that most holy man. Although his sacred life was consumed by tortures and racks, he conquered the besiegers with the shield of his devout reason. ⁵For in setting his mind firm like a jutting cliff, our father Eleazar broke the maddening waves of the emotions. ⁶O priest, worthy of the priesthood, you neither defiled your sacred teeth nor profaned your stomach, which had room only for reverence and purity, by eating defiling foods. ⁷O man in harmony with the law and philosopher of divine life! ⁸Such should be those who are adminis-

trators of the law, shielding it with their own blood and noble sweat in sufferings even to death. ⁹You, father, strengthened our loyalty to the law through your glorious endurance, and you did not abandon the holiness that you praised, but by your deeds you made your words of divine*ᵃ* philosophy credible. ¹⁰O aged man, more powerful than tortures; O elder, fiercer than fire; O supreme king over the passions, Eleazar! ¹¹For just as our father Aaron, armed with the censer, ran through the multitude of the people and conquered the fiery*ᵇ* angel, ¹²so the descendant of Aaron, Eleazar, though being consumed by the fire, remained unmoved in his reason. ¹³Most amazing, indeed, though he was an old man, his body no longer tense and firm, *ᶜ* his muscles flabby, his sinews feeble, he became young again ¹⁴in spirit through reason; and by reason like that of Isaac he rendered the many-headed rack ineffective. ¹⁵O man of blessed age and of venerable gray hair and of law-abiding life, whom the faithful seal of death has perfected!

16 If, therefore, because of piety an aged man despised tortures even to death, most certainly devout reason is governor of the emotions. ¹⁷Some perhaps might say, "Not all have full command of their emotions, because not all have prudent reason." ¹⁸But as many as attend to religion with a whole heart, these alone are able to control the passions of the flesh, ¹⁹since they believe that they, like our patriarchs Abraham

z Syr: Meaning of Gk uncertain   *a* Other ancient authorities lack *divine*   *b* Other ancient authorities lack *fiery*   *c* Gk *the tautness of the body already loosed*

the Qumran *Manual of Discipline.* **31:** The transition from religious language in vv. 27–29 to the philosophical note of *devout reason* is abrupt; but for this author the two are one.

7.1–3: The metaphor of the *pilot* and *the ship,* common in Greek literature, recurs in 13.6–7 and in 15.31–32 as a reference to Noah's ark; compare 1 Pet 3.20. **6:** *Defiled . . . profaned,* the Jewish concept was realistic, as though a physical infection were incurred (see 2 Macc 6.20); contrast Mk 7.15; Acts 10.13–

15. 8: *Administrators,* literally "those who make (or create) something"; the Greek is obscure. A rabbi or priest was responsible for maintenance of the law in the community (Mal 2.7). **9:** *Credible,* in both Judaism and Stoicism, the ultimate test is the conformity of one's deeds to one's profession. **10:** *Eleazar,* see 5.4 n.

7.11: Num 16.46–50. **14:** Compare 2 Cor 4.7–18. *Isaac,* Gen 22.1–14. **19:** *Abraham and Isaac and Jacob* are living (Mk 12.26). *Live to*

and Isaac and Jacob, do not die to God, but live to God. [20] No contradiction therefore arises when some persons appear to be dominated by their emotions because of the weakness of their reason. [21] What person who lives as a philosopher by the whole rule of philosophy, and trusts in God, [22] and knows that it is blessed to endure any suffering for the sake of virtue, would not be able to overcome the emotions through godliness? [23] For only the wise and courageous are masters of their emotions.

8 For this is why even the very young, by following a philosophy in accordance with devout reason, have prevailed over the most painful instruments of torture. [2] For when the tyrant was conspicuously defeated in his first attempt, being unable to compel an aged man to eat defiling foods, then in violent rage he commanded that others of the Hebrew captives be brought, and that any who ate defiling food would be freed after eating, but if any were to refuse, they would be tortured even more cruelly.

3 When the tyrant had given these orders, seven brothers—handsome, modest, noble, and accomplished in every way—were brought before him along with their aged mother. [4] When the tyrant saw them, grouped about their mother as though a chorus, he was pleased with them. And struck by their appearance and nobility, he smiled at them, and summoned them nearer and said, [5] "Young men, with favorable feelings I admire each and every one of you, and greatly respect the beauty and the

number of such brothers. Not only do I advise you not to display the same madness as that of the old man who has just been tortured, but I also exhort you to yield to me and enjoy my friendship. [6] Just as I am able to punish those who disobey my orders, so I can be a benefactor to those who obey me. [7] Trust me, then, and you will have positions of authority in my government if you will renounce the ancestral tradition of your national life. [8] Enjoy your youth by adopting the Greek way of life and by changing your manner of living. [9] But if by disobedience you rouse my anger, you will compel me to destroy each and every one of you with dreadful punishments through tortures. [10] Therefore take pity on yourselves. Even I, your enemy, have compassion for your youth and handsome appearance. [11] Will you not consider this, that if you disobey, nothing remains for you but to die on the rack?"

12 When he had said these things, he ordered the instruments of torture to be brought forward so as to persuade them out of fear to eat the defiling food. [13] When the guards had placed before them wheels and joint-dislocators, rack and hooks[d] and catapults[e] and caldrons, braziers and thumbscrews and iron claws and wedges and bellows, the tyrant resumed speaking: [14] "Be afraid, young fellows; whatever justice you revere will be merciful to you when you transgress under compulsion."

d Meaning of Gk uncertain   e Here and elsewhere in 4 Macc an instrument of torture

---

God, a similar expression is found in Lk 20.38; Rom 6.10; 14.8; Gal 2.19. Compare 16.25. **8.1–9.9: The seven brothers defy the tyrant.** This account is an amplification of 2 Macc 7.1–2. **3:** *Accomplished*, or graceful, the Greek ideal of physical beauty joined to perfect education. **4:** A Greek *chorus* was a company of dancers, who often moved in a circle and spoke lines in unison; compare 14.7. **5:** *Beauty*, see 2.1 n. *Friendship*, almost a technical term, because the "friends" of a Hellenistic king were employed in the government; see v. 7 and 3 Macc 2.23 n. **6:** *Benefac-*

tor, a title often adopted by Hellenistic monarchs; in Lk 22.25 it seems ironical, as here. **8:** *Adopting the Greek way of life*, Antiochus could have believed sincerely that this was the highest civilization and that Judaism was "superstition." Thus it is a tragic conflict between two points of view.

8.13: *Hooks*, these and some of the other instruments of torture cannot be described precisely; compare 11.10. **14:** *Justice*, a philosophical way of speaking of God. **15:** *Nullified his tyranny*, Epictetus the Stoic taught that, while the tyrant might chain a person's leg or

15 But when they had heard the inducements and saw the dreadful devices, not only were they not afraid, but they also opposed the tyrant with their own philosophy, and by their right reasoning nullified his tyranny. 16 Let us consider, on the other hand, what arguments might have been used if some of them had been cowardly and unmanly. Would they not have been the following? 17 "O wretches that we are and so senseless! Since the king has summoned and exhorted us to accept kind treatment if we obey him, 18 why do we take pleasure in vain resolves and venture upon a disobedience that brings death? 19 O men and brothers, should we not fear the instruments of torture and consider the threats of torments, and give up this vain opinion and this arrogance that threatens to destroy us? 20 Let us take pity on our youth and have compassion on our mother's age; 21 and let us seriously consider that if we disobey we are dead! 22 Also, divine justice will excuse us for fearing the king when we are under compulsion. 23 Why do we banish ourselves from this most pleasant life and deprive ourselves of this delightful world? 24 Let us not struggle against compulsion *f* or take hollow pride in being put to the rack. 25 Not even the law itself would arbitrarily put us to death for fearing the instruments of torture. 26 Why does such contentiousness excite us and such a fatal stubbornness please us, when we can live in peace if we obey the king?"

27 But the youths, though about to be tortured, neither said any of these things nor even seriously considered them. 28 For they were contemptuous of the emotions and sovereign over agonies, 29 so that as soon as the tyrant had

ceased counseling them to eat defiling food, all with one voice together, as from one mind, said:

9 "Why do you delay, O tyrant? For we are ready to die rather than transgress our ancestral commandments; 2 we are obviously putting our forebears to shame unless we should practice ready obedience to the law and to Moses *g* our counselor. 3 Tyrant and counselor of lawlessness, in your hatred for us do not pity us more than we pity ourselves. *h* 4 For we consider this pity of yours, which insures our safety through transgression of the law, to be more grievous than death itself. 5 You are trying to terrify us by threatening us with death by torture, as though a short time ago you learned nothing from Eleazar. 6 And if the aged men of the Hebrews because of their religion lived piously *i* while enduring torture, it would be even more fitting that we young men should die despising your coercive tortures, which our aged instructor also overcame. 7 Therefore, tyrant, put us to the test; and if you take our lives because of our religion, do not suppose that you can injure us by torturing us. 8 For we, through this severe suffering and endurance, shall have the prize of virtue and shall be with God, on whose account we suffer; 9 but you, because of your bloodthirstiness toward us, will deservedly undergo from the divine justice eternal torment by fire."

10 When they had said these things, the tyrant was not only indignant, as at those who are disobedient, but also infu-

---

f Or *fate*   *g* Other ancient authorities read *knowledge*   *h* Meaning of Gk uncertain
i Other ancient authorities read *died*

---

cut off one's head, he could neither chain nor cut off one's moral purpose (*Discourses* i.18.17).
8.25: *The law* would not condemn them for *fearing;* but a Jew could not be excused for committing idolatry, even under duress (see 5.2 n.). **29**: *With one voice,* as if they were a chorus (see 8.4 n.).
9.6: *Aged men,* the plural may refer to He-

brew prophets such as Isaiah, who, according to Jewish tradition, were also martyred; compare Heb 11.35–37. **7**: *Do not suppose that you can injure us,* a Stoic principle; suffering cannot affect the essential nature of those who are wise. **8**: *Prize of virtue,* an athletic metaphor; compare 6.10; Wis 10.12; 1 Cor 9.24.
9.10–25: **Martyrdom of the eldest.** The details do not agree with the earlier account

riated, as at those who are ungrateful. [11] Then at his command the guards brought forward the eldest, and having torn off his tunic, they bound his hands and arms with thongs on each side. [12] When they had worn themselves out beating him with scourges, without accomplishing anything, they placed him upon the wheel. [13] When the noble youth was stretched out around this, his limbs were dislocated, [14] and with every member disjointed he denounced the tyrant, saying, [15] "Most abominable tyrant, enemy of heavenly justice, savage of mind, you are mangling me in this manner, not because I am a murderer, or as one who acts impiously, but because I protect the divine law." [16] And when the guards said, "Agree to eat so that you may be released from the tortures," [17] he replied, "You abominable lackeys, your wheel is not so powerful as to strangle my reason. Cut my limbs, burn my flesh, and twist my joints; [18] through all these tortures I will convince you that children of the Hebrews alone are invincible where virtue is concerned." [19] While he was saying these things, they spread fire under him, and while fanning the flames[j] they tightened the wheel further. [20] The wheel was completely smeared with blood, and the heap of coals was being quenched by the drippings of gore, and pieces of flesh were falling off the axles of the machine. [21] Although the ligaments joining his bones were already severed, the courageous youth, worthy of Abraham, did not groan, [22] but as though transformed by fire into immortality, he nobly endured the rackings. [23] "Imitate me, brothers," he said. "Do not leave your post in my struggle[k] or renounce our courageous family ties. [24] Fight the sacred and noble battle for religion. Thereby the just Providence of our ancestors may become merciful to our nation and take vengeance on the accursed tyrant." [25] When he had said this, the saintly youth broke the thread of life.

[26] While all were marveling at his courageous spirit, the guards brought in the next eldest, and after fitting themselves with iron gauntlets having sharp hooks, they bound him to the torture machine and catapult. [27] Before torturing him, they inquired if he were willing to eat, and they heard his noble decision.[l] [28] These leopard-like beasts tore out his sinews with the iron hands, flayed all his flesh up to his chin, and tore away his scalp. But he steadfastly endured this agony and said, [29] "How sweet is any kind of death for the religion of our ancestors!" [30] To the tyrant he said, "Do you not think, you most savage tyrant, that you are being tortured more than I, as you see the arrogant design of your tyranny being defeated by our endurance for the sake of religion? [31] I lighten my pain by the joys that come from virtue, [32] but you suffer torture by the threats that come from impiety. You will not escape, you most abominable tyrant, the judgments of the divine wrath."

j Meaning of Gk uncertain   k Other ancient authorities read *post forever*   l Other ancient authorities read *having heard his noble decision, they tore him to shreds*

---

in 2 Macc 7.3–6; here the author allows himself the freedom of an historical novelist. **17:** See v. 7 n.

9.22: *Transformed,* the same Greek verb is used in Phil 3.21; synonymous verbs in 1 Cor 15.51–52; 2 Cor 3.18. *Immortality,* literally "incorruption," "that which is imperishable," as in 17.12; 1 Cor 15.53. Here the author comes close to the Greek doctrine that the soul is by nature immortal, but puts the emphasis on reward and punishment after this life (compare Lk 16.19–31; 23.43). This is in contrast to the doctrine of the resurrection expressed in 2 Macc 12.44–45. **23:** *Fami-*ly ties, referring to the immediate family, but kinship with the whole Jewish nation may be implied. **24:** *Fight,* compare 2 Tim 4.7. *Accursed,* Greek "alastōr," a word from the Greek tragedies.

9.26–12.19: **Martyrdom of the other brothers.** These stories follow 2 Macc 7.7–40 in general, but are made more vivid and sensational. **28:** *Beasts,* 1 Cor 15.32. **29:** *How sweet,* compare 2 Macc 6.30. One may compare the letter to the Romans by the Christian martyr Ignatius and also the Latin saying, "Dulce et decorum est pro patria mori."

10 When he too had endured a glorious death, the third was led in, and many repeatedly urged him to save himself by tasting the meat. 2 But he shouted, "Do you not know that the same father begot me as well as those who died, and the same mother bore me, and that I was brought up on the same teachings? 3 I do not renounce the noble kinship that binds me to my brothers."[m] 5 Enraged by the man's boldness, they disjointed his hands and feet with their instruments, dismembering him by prying his limbs from their sockets, 6 and breaking his fingers and arms and legs and elbows. 7 Since they were not able in any way to break his spirit,[n] they abandoned the instruments[o] and scalped him with their fingernails in a Scythian fashion. 8 They immediately brought him to the wheel, and while his vertebrae were being dislocated by this, he saw his own flesh torn all around and drops of blood flowing from his entrails. 9 When he was about to die, he said, 10 "We, most abominable tyrant, are suffering because of our godly training and virtue, 11 but you, because of your impiety and bloodthirstiness, will undergo unceasing torments."

12 When he too had died in a manner worthy of his brothers, they dragged in the fourth, saying, 13 "As for you, do not give way to the same insanity as your brothers, but obey the king and save yourself." 14 But he said to them, "You do not have a fire hot enough to make me play the coward. 15 No—by the blessed death of my brothers, by the eternal destruction of the tyrant, and by the everlasting life of the pious, I will not renounce our noble family ties. 16 Contrive tortures, tyrant, so that you may learn

from them that I am a brother to those who have just now been tortured." 17 When he heard this, the bloodthirsty, murderous, and utterly abominable Antiochus gave orders to cut out his tongue. 18 But he said, "Even if you remove my organ of speech, God hears also those who are mute. 19 See, here is my tongue; cut it off, for in spite of this you will not make our reason speechless. 20 Gladly, for the sake of God, we let our bodily members be mutilated. 21 God will visit you swiftly, for you are cutting out a tongue that has been melodious with divine hymns."

11 When he too died, after being cruelly tortured, the fifth leaped up, saying, 2 "I will not refuse, tyrant, to be tortured for the sake of virtue. 3 I have come of my own accord, so that by murdering me you will incur punishment from the heavenly justice for even more crimes. 4 Hater of virtue, hater of humankind, for what act of ours are you destroying us in this way? 5 Is it because[p] we revere the Creator of all things and live according to his virtuous law? 6 But these deeds deserve honors, not tortures."[q] 9 While he was saying these things, the guards bound him and dragged him to the catapult; 10 they tied him to it on his knees, and fitting iron

m Other ancient authorities add verse 4 *So if you have any instrument of torture, apply it to my body; for you cannot touch my soul, even if you wish."*
n Gk *to strangle him* o Other ancient authorities read *they tore off his skin* p Other ancient authorities read *Or does it seem evil to you that* q Other authorities add verses 7 and 8, 7 *If you but understood human feelings and had hope of salvation from God—* 8 *but, as it is, you are a stranger to God and persecute those who serve him."*

10.4: *You cannot touch my soul;* this verse, which does not occur in certain manuscripts, may be a later interpolation. See 9.7 n. and compare Mt 10.28; Lk 12.4–5. **5**: *Boldness,* Acts 4.13; 2 Cor 3.12. Freedom of speech was one of the ideals of Greek democracy. **7**: *Scythian fashion,* the Scythians were notorious for their barbarous cruelty (2 Macc 4.47; 3 Macc 7.5).
10.15: *Everlasting life,* or glorious life; see

9.22 n. *Family ties,* see 9.23; the seven brothers and their mother represent the entire Jewish nation. **19**: 2 Macc 7.10.
11.3: A new idea; he welcomes torture so that the tyrant may be punished the more. **7**: *Human feelings,* ironical because the compassion expressed in 12.2 was genuine but did not go far enough. Verses 7–8 are almost certainly interpolations. **10**: *Wedge on the wheel,* it is not certain how the wheel was constructed.

clamps on them, they twisted his back^r around the wedge on the wheel,^s so that he was completely curled back like a scorpion, and all his members were disjointed. ¹¹In this condition, gasping for breath and in anguish of body, ¹²he said, "Tyrant, they are splendid favors that you grant us against your will, because through these noble sufferings you give us an opportunity to show our endurance for the law."

13 When he too had died, the sixth, a mere boy, was led in. When the tyrant inquired whether he was willing to eat and be released, he said, ¹⁴"I am younger in age than my brothers, but I am their equal in mind. ¹⁵Since to this end we were born and bred, we ought likewise to die for the same principles. ¹⁶So if you intend to torture me for not eating defiling foods, go on torturing!" ¹⁷When he had said this, they led him to the wheel. ¹⁸He was carefully stretched tight upon it, his back was broken, and he was roasted^t from underneath. ¹⁹To his back they applied sharp spits that had been heated in the fire, and pierced his ribs so that his entrails were burned through. ²⁰While being tortured he said, "O contest befitting holiness, in which so many of us brothers have been summoned to an arena of sufferings for religion, and in which we have not been defeated! ²¹For religious knowledge, O tyrant, is invincible. ²²I also, equipped with nobility, will die with my brothers, ²³and I myself will bring a great avenger upon you, you inventor of tortures and enemy of those who are truly devout. ²⁴We six boys have paralyzed your tyranny. ²⁵Since you have not been able to persuade us to change our mind or to force us to eat defiling foods, is not

this your downfall? ²⁶Your fire is cold to us, and the catapults painless, and your violence powerless. ²⁷For it is not the guards of the tyrant but those of the divine law that are set over us; therefore, unconquered, we hold fast to reason."

12 When he too, thrown into the caldron, had died a blessed death, the seventh and youngest of all came forward. ²Even though the tyrant had been vehemently reproached by the brothers, he felt strong compassion for this child when he saw that he was already in fetters. He summoned him to come nearer and tried to persuade him, saying, ³"You see the result of your brothers' stupidity, for they died in torments because of their disobedience. ⁴You too, if you do not obey, will be miserably tortured and die before your time, ⁵but if you yield to persuasion you will be my friend and a leader in the government of the kingdom." ⁶When he had thus appealed to him, he sent for the boy's mother to show compassion on her who had been bereaved of so many sons and to influence her to persuade the surviving son to obey and save himself. ⁷But when his mother had exhorted him in the Hebrew language, as we shall tell a little later, ⁸he said, "Let me loose, let me speak to the king and to all his friends that are with him." ⁹Extremely pleased by the boy's declaration, they freed him at once. ¹⁰Running to the nearest of the braziers, ¹¹he said, "You profane tyrant, most impious of all the wicked, since you have received good things and also your kingdom from God, were you not ashamed to murder his servants and torture on the

r Gk *loins*   *s* Meaning of Gk uncertain
t Other ancient authorities add *by fire*

11.13–27: 2 Macc 7.18–19. **20:** *Contest,* compare 6.10. *Arena,* literally "gymnasium." **21:** *Religious knowledge,* or science. In Greek thought true knowledge almost always leads to virtue; in Judaism, knowledge of the Mosaic law at least predisposes one toward it; see 1.17 n.; 18.6–19 n. **25:** *Downfall,* see 8.15 n. **26:** *Painless,* compare Heb 12.2, "despising the shame."

12.2: *The tyrant could feel strong compassion;* see 8.10. **5:** *Friend,* see 8.5 n. **7:** *Hebrew language,* or perhaps Aramaic, as in Acts 21.40; compare 2 Macc 7.21, 27. Many Palestinians, and certainly the author's first readers, spoke Greek. Her use of Hebrew indicates her devotion to the sacred tongue. *A little later,* for dramatic effect, the author postpones the speech to 16.16–23. **11:** *Those who practice,*

wheel those who practice religion? ¹²Because of this, justice has laid up for you intense and eternal fire and tortures, and these throughout all time*ᵘ* will never let you go. ¹³As a man, were you not ashamed, you most savage beast, to cut out the tongues of men who have feelings like yours and are made of the same elements as you, and to maltreat and torture them in this way? ¹⁴Surely they by dying nobly fulfilled their service to God, but you will wail bitterly for having killed without cause the contestants for virtue." ¹⁵Then because he too was about to die, he said, ¹⁶"I do not desert the excellent example*ᵛ* of my brothers, ¹⁷and I call on the God of our ancestors to be merciful to our nation;*ʷ* ¹⁸but on you he will take vengeance both in this present life and when you are dead." ¹⁹After he had uttered these imprecations, he flung himself into the braziers and so ended his life.*ˣ*

13 Since, then, the seven brothers despised sufferings even unto death, everyone must concede that devout reason is sovereign over the emotions. ²For if they had been slaves to their emotions and had eaten defiling food, we would say that they had been conquered by these emotions. ³But in fact it was not so. Instead, by reason, which is praised before God, they prevailed over their emotions. ⁴The supremacy of the mind over these cannot be overlooked, for the brothers*ʸ* mastered both emotions and pains. ⁵How then can one fail to confess the sovereignty of right reason over emotion in those who were not turned back by fiery agonies? ⁶For just as towers jutting out over harbors hold back the threatening waves and make it calm for those who sail into the inner basin, ⁷so the seven-towered right reason of the youths, by fortifying the harbor of religion, conquered the tempest of the emotions. ⁸For they constituted a holy chorus of religion and encouraged one another, saying, ⁹"Brothers, let us die like brothers for the sake of the law; let us imitate the three youths in Assyria who despised the same ordeal of the furnace. ¹⁰Let us not be cowardly in the demonstration of our piety." ¹¹While one said, "Courage, brother," another said, "Bear up nobly," ¹²and another reminded them, "Remember whence you came, and the father by whose hand Isaac would have submitted to being slain for the sake of religion." ¹³Each of them and all of them together looking at one another, cheerful and undaunted, said, "Let us with all our hearts consecrate ourselves to God, who gave us our lives,*ᶻ* and let us use our bodies as a bulwark for the law. ¹⁴Let us not fear him who thinks he is killing us, ¹⁵for great is the struggle of the soul and the danger of eternal torment lying before those who transgress the commandment of God. ¹⁶Therefore let us put on the full armor of self-control, which is divine reason. ¹⁷For if we so die,*ᵃ* Abraham and Isaac and Jacob will welcome us, and all the fathers will praise us." ¹⁸Those who were left behind said to each of the brothers who were

u Gk *throughout the whole age*   v Other ancient authorities read *the witness*   w Other ancient authorities read *my race*   x Gk *and so gave up;* other ancient authorities read *gave up his spirit* or *his soul*   y Gk *they*   z Or *souls*   a Other ancient authorities read *suffer*

Greek "askētas," almost "the athletes of religion"; compare v. 14 and Philo, *On Dreams* i.59.

12.13: *Feelings like yours,* a Stoic idea, found also in Wis 7.1–6; Acts 14.15. **14:** *Contestants,* see 11.20 n. **19:** *Flung himself,* as the mother does in 17.1. The remaining defenders of Masada at the end of the Jewish War of A.D. 66–73 killed one another. Jews, like Stoics, approved of suicide in certain circumstances.

13.1–14.10: Philosophical interpretation. The martyrdoms attest the supremacy of pious reason. Compare 6.31–35. **13.8:** *Chorus,* see 8.4 n.; 14.7. **9:** Dan ch 3. **12:** *Remember whence you came,* Isa 51.1–2. *The father* and *Isaac,* 15.28; Gen 22.1–19; Wis 10.5. Their story became a favorite theme for Christians (Heb 11.17–19).

13.13: *Each of them and all of them together,* as in a Greek chorus (see 8.4 n.). **14:** Mt 10.28; Lk 12.4. **17:** 5.37 n.; compare Lk 16.22. **19:**

*An encomium on
the seven brothers*

4 MACCABEES 13, 14

being dragged away, "Do not put us to shame, brother, or betray the brothers who have died before us."

19 You are not ignorant of the affection of family ties, which the divine and all-wise Providence has bequeathed through the fathers to their descendants and which was implanted in the mother's womb. 20 There each of the brothers spent the same length of time and was shaped during the same period of time; and growing from the same blood and through the same life, they were brought to the light of day. 21 When they were born after an equal time of gestation, they drank milk from the same fountains. From such embraces brotherly-loving souls are nourished; 22 and they grow stronger from this common nurture and daily companionship, and from both general education and our discipline in the law of God.

23 Therefore, when sympathy and brotherly affection had been so established, the brothers were the more sympathetic to one another. 24 Since they had been educated by the same law and trained in the same virtues and brought up in right living, they loved one another all the more. 25 A common zeal for nobility strengthened their goodwill toward one another, and their concord, 26 because they could make their brotherly love more fervent with the aid of their religion. 27 But although nature and companionship and virtuous habits had augmented the affection of family ties, those who were left endured for the sake of religion, while watching their brothers being maltreated and tortured to death.

14 Furthermore, they encouraged them to face the torture, so that they not only despised their agonies, but also mastered the emotions of brotherly love.

2 O reason,[b] more royal than kings

and freer than the free! 3 O sacred and harmonious concord of the seven brothers on behalf of religion! 4 None of the seven youths proved coward or shrank from death, 5 but all of them, as though running the course toward immortality, hastened to death by torture. 6 Just as the hands and feet are moved in harmony with the guidance of the mind, so those holy youths, as though moved by an immortal spirit of devotion, agreed to go to death for its sake. 7 O most holy seven, brothers in harmony! For just as the seven days of creation move in choral dance around religion, 8 so these youths, forming a chorus, encircled the sevenfold fear of tortures and dissolved it. 9 Even now, we ourselves shudder as we hear of the suffering of these young men; they not only saw what was happening, not only heard the direct word of threat, but also bore the sufferings patiently, and in agonies of fire at that. 10 What could be more excruciatingly painful than this? For the power of fire is intense and swift, and it consumed their bodies quickly.

11 Do not consider it amazing that reason had full command over these men in their tortures, since the mind of woman despised even more diverse agonies, 12 for the mother of the seven young men bore up under the rackings of each one of her children.

13 Observe how complex is a mother's love for her children, which draws everything toward an emotion felt in her inmost parts. 14 Even unreasoning animals, as well as human beings, have a sympathy and parental love for their offspring. 15 For example, among birds, the ones that are tame protect their young by building on the housetops, 16 and the others, by building in precipitous chasms

b Or O minds

Affection, Greek "philtra," a magical charm believed to produce love. *Divine and all-wise Providence,* a Stoic concept (9.24; 17.22).
14.5: 9.8 n.; Heb 12.1. **8:** *Sevenfold fear,* the Greek here is obscure. **9:** *Even now,* see 3.19 n.

14.11–17.1: The mother of the seven. Her death is merely mentioned in 2 Macc 7.41; here it is made the climax of the oration. **14.14:** The analogy between *unreasoning animals* and *human beings* (vv. 14–19) was a theme of popular Greek philosophy. **20:** *Did not sway,* the

356
AP

and in holes and tops of trees, hatch the nestlings and ward off the intruder. [17]If they are not able to keep the intruder[c] away, they do what they can to help their young by flying in circles around them in the anguish of love, warning them with their own calls. [18]And why is it necessary to demonstrate sympathy for children by the example of unreasoning animals, [19]since even bees at the time for making honeycombs defend themselves against intruders and, as though with an iron dart, sting those who approach their hive and defend it even to the death? [20]But sympathy for her children did not sway the mother of the young men; she was of the same mind as Abraham.

15 O reason of the children, tyrant over the emotions! O religion, more desirable to the mother than her children! [2]Two courses were open to this mother, that of religion, and that of preserving her seven sons for a time, as the tyrant had promised. [3]She loved religion more, the religion that preserves them for eternal life according to God's promise.[d] [4]In what manner might I express the emotions of parents who love their children? We impress upon the character of a small child a wondrous likeness both of mind and of form. Especially is this true of mothers, who because of their birthpangs have a deeper sympathy toward their offspring than do the fathers. [5]Considering that mothers are the weaker sex and give birth to many, they are more devoted to their children.[e] [6]The mother of the seven boys, more than any other mother, loved her children. In seven pregnancies she had implanted in herself tender love toward them, [7]and because of the many pains she suffered with each of them she had sympathy for them; [8]yet because of the fear of God she disdained the temporary safety of her children. [9]Not only so, but also because of

the nobility of her sons and their ready obedience to the law, she felt a greater tenderness toward them. [10]For they were righteous and self-controlled and brave and magnanimous, and loved their brothers and their mother, so that they obeyed her even to death in keeping the ordinances.

[11] Nevertheless, though so many factors influenced the mother to suffer with them out of love for her children, in the case of none of them were the various tortures strong enough to pervert her reason. [12]But each child separately and all of them together the mother urged on to death for religion's sake. [13]O sacred nature and affection of parental love, yearning of parents toward offspring, nurture and indomitable suffering by mothers! [14]This mother, who saw them tortured and burned one by one, because of religion did not change her attitude. [15]She watched the flesh of her children being consumed by fire, their toes and fingers scattered[f] on the ground, and the flesh of the head to the chin exposed like masks.

[16] O mother, tried now by more bitter pains than even the birthpangs you suffered for them! [17]O woman, who alone gave birth to such complete devotion! [18]When the firstborn breathed his last, it did not turn you aside, nor when the second in torments looked at you piteously nor when the third expired; [19]nor did you weep when you looked at the eyes of each one in his tortures gazing boldly at the same agonies, and saw in their nostrils the signs of the approach of death. [20]When you saw the flesh of children burned upon the flesh of other children, severed hands upon hands, scalped

---

c Gk it   *d* Gk *according to God*   *e* Or *For to the degree that mothers are weaker and the more children they bear, the more they are devoted to their children.*   *f* Or *quivering*

---

mother's constancy is the supreme proof of the dominance of religious reason. *Abraham* had offered Isaac; see 13.12 n.

15.2: *Two courses,* the two ways of Jer 21.8 became a pattern of Jewish thought. *Religion,*

5.31 n. **4:** *Of mind and of form,* a Stoic idea. **13:** *Indomitable suffering,* actually it is the mother who is *indomitable* in spite of her *love* and *suffering.*

15.17: *Gave birth,* includes the idea of spiri-

heads upon heads, and corpses fallen on other corpses, and when you saw the place filled with many spectators of the torturings, you did not shed tears. 21 Neither the melodies of sirens nor the songs of swans attract the attention of their hearers as did the voices of the children in torture calling to their mother. 22 How great and how many torments the mother then suffered as her sons were tortured on the wheel and with the hot irons! 23 But devout reason, giving her heart a man's courage in the very midst of her emotions, strengthened her to disregard, for the time, her parental love.

24 Although she witnessed the destruction of seven children and the ingenious and various rackings, this noble mother disregarded all these*g* because of faith in God. 25 For as in the council chamber of her own soul she saw mighty advocates—nature, family, parental love, and the rackings of her children— 26 this mother held two ballots, one bearing death and the other deliverance for her children. 27 She did not approve the deliverance that would preserve the seven sons for a short time, 28 but as the daughter of God-fearing Abraham she remembered his fortitude.

29 O mother of the nation, vindicator of the law and champion of religion, who carried away the prize of the contest in your heart! 30 O more noble than males in steadfastness, and more courageous than men in endurance! 31 Just as Noah's ark, carrying the world in the universal flood, stoutly endured the waves, 32 so you, O guardian of the law, overwhelmed from every side by the flood of your emotions and the violent winds, the torture of your sons, endured nobly and withstood the wintry storms that assail religion.

16 If, then, a woman, advanced in years and mother of seven sons, endured seeing her children tortured to death, it must be admitted that devout reason is sovereign over the emotions. 2 Thus I have demonstrated not only that men have ruled over the emotions, but also that a woman has despised the fiercest tortures. 3 The lions surrounding Daniel were not so savage, nor was the raging fiery furnace of Mishael so intensely hot, as was her innate parental love, inflamed as she saw her seven sons tortured in such varied ways. 4 But the mother quenched so many and such great emotions by devout reason.

5 Consider this also: If this woman, though a mother, had been fainthearted, she would have mourned over them and perhaps spoken as follows: 6 "O how wretched am I and many times unhappy! After bearing seven children, I am now the mother of none! 7 O seven childbirths all in vain, seven profitless pregnancies, fruitless nurturings and wretched nursings! 8 In vain, my sons, I endured many birthpangs for you, and the more grievous anxieties of your upbringing. 9 Alas for my children, some unmarried, others married and without offspring.*h* I shall not see your children or have the happiness of being called grandmother. 10 Alas, I who had so many and beautiful children am a widow and alone, with many sorrows.*i* 11 And when I die, I shall have none of my sons to bury me."

12 Yet that holy and God-fearing mother did not wail with such a lament for any of them, nor did she dissuade any of them from dying, nor did she grieve as they were dying. 13 On the contrary, as though having a mind like adamant and giving rebirth for immortality to the whole number of her sons, she implored them and urged them on to death for the sake of religion. 14 O mother, soldier of

g Other ancient authorities read *having bidden them farewell, surrendered them*   h Gk *without benefit*   i Or *much to be pitied*

---

tual birth; compare 16.13 n.; 17.6; Gal 4.19. **25–26:** *Ballots,* as though she were in the *council chamber* of a Greek city. **28:** See 13.12 n. **31:** *Noah's ark,* see 7.1–3 n.; also Wis 14.6.
  16.3: *Daniel,* Dan 6.1–24. *Mishael,* Dan 1.7; 3.19–30. **11:** *None of my sons to bury me,* for both Jews and Greeks a supreme calamity. **13:** *Giving rebirth for immortality,* see 15.17 n.; Jn 3.5. **15:** *Hebrew language,* see 12.7 n.

God in the cause of religion, elder and woman! By steadfastness you have conquered even a tyrant, and in word and deed you have proved more powerful than a man. ¹⁵For when you and your sons were arrested together, you stood and watched Eleazar being tortured, and said to your sons in the Hebrew language, ¹⁶"My sons, noble is the contest to which you are called to bear witness for the nation. Fight zealously for our ancestral law. ¹⁷For it would be shameful if, while an aged man endures such agonies for the sake of religion, you young men were to be terrified by tortures. ¹⁸Remember that it is through God that you have had a share in the world and have enjoyed life, ¹⁹and therefore you ought to endure any suffering for the sake of God. ²⁰For his sake also our father Abraham was zealous to sacrifice his son Isaac, the ancestor of our nation; and when Isaac saw his father's hand wielding a knife[j] and descending upon him, he did not cower. ²¹Daniel the righteous was thrown to the lions, and Hananiah, Azariah, and Mishael were hurled into the fiery furnace and endured it for the sake of God. ²²You too must have the same faith in God and not be grieved. ²³It is unreasonable for people who have religious knowledge not to withstand pain."

24 By these words the mother of the seven encouraged and persuaded each of her sons to die rather than violate God's commandment. ²⁵They knew also that those who die for the sake of God live to God, as do Abraham and Isaac and Jacob and all the patriarchs.

17 Some of the guards said that when she also was about to be seized and put to death she threw herself into the flames so that no one might touch her body.

2 O mother, who with your seven sons nullified the violence of the tyrant, frustrated his evil designs, and showed the courage of your faith! ³Nobly set like a roof on the pillars of your sons, you held firm and unswerving against the earthquake of the tortures. ⁴Take courage, therefore, O holy-minded mother, maintaining firm an enduring hope in God. ⁵The moon in heaven, with the stars, does not stand so august as you, who, after lighting the way of your starlike seven sons to piety, stand in honor before God and are firmly set in heaven with them. ⁶For your children were true descendants of father Abraham.[k]

7 If it were possible for us to paint the history of your religion as an artist might, would not those who first beheld it have shuddered as they saw the mother of the seven children enduring their varied tortures to death for the sake of religion? ⁸Indeed it would be proper to inscribe on their tomb these words as a reminder to the people of our nation:[l]

9 "Here lie buried an aged priest and an aged woman and seven sons, because of the violence of the tyrant who wished to destroy the way of life of the Hebrews. ¹⁰They vindicated their nation,

j Gk *sword*   *k* Gk *For your childbearing was from Abraham the father;* other ancient authorities read *For . . . Abraham the servant*
l Or *as a memorial to the heroes of our people*

16.16–23: Compare this more rhetorical speech with 2 Macc 7.27–29. **16:** *Contest,* 6.10; 11.20. **20:** *Isaac,* see 13.12 n. **21:** *Daniel,* v. 3. *Hananiah, Azariah, and Mishael,* Dan ch 3. **25:** *Live to God,* see 7.19 n.

17.1: *Threw herself,* compare 12.19; 2 Macc 7.41. *Touch her body,* this would be a violation of her chastity.

17.2–18.5: Panegyric on the mother. The author has already pronounced encomiums on Eleazar (7.1–15), the brothers (14.2–10), and the mother (ch 15), sometimes addressing them directly. The oration now comes to its climax. **3:** *Roof . . . pillars . . .*

earthquake, metaphors appropriate to Antioch, where there were frequent earthquakes, but applicable also to Palestine. **5:** Stoics regarded *the stars* as living beings; for Jews the language was metaphorical. *Lighting the way,* mystical language; compare Jn 12.35–36, 46. **6:** *True descendants,* compare 15.28; 13.12 n.; the giving of new birth is like Isaac's return from impending death; compare Heb 11. 17–19. **7:** *Possible,* or "permitted." At this time the Jews may have taken the commandment of Ex 20.4 strictly. **9:** *Way of life,* Greek "politeia," "commonwealth."

looking to God and enduring torture even to death."

11 Truly the contest in which they were engaged was divine, 12 for on that day virtue gave the awards and tested them for their endurance. The prize was immortality in endless life. 13 Eleazar was the first contestant, the mother of the seven sons entered the competition, and the brothers contended. 14 The tyrant was the antagonist, and the world and the human race were the spectators. 15 Reverence for God was victor and gave the crown to its own athletes. 16 Who did not admire the athletes of the divine*m* legislation? Who were not amazed?

17 The tyrant himself and all his council marveled at their*n* endurance, 18 because of which they now stand before the divine throne and live the life of eternal blessedness. 19 For Moses says, "All who are consecrated are under your hands." 20 These, then, who have been consecrated for the sake of God,*o* are honored, not only with this honor, but also by the fact that because of them our enemies did not rule over our nation, 21 the tyrant was punished, and the homeland purified—they having become, as it were, a ransom for the sin of our nation. 22 And through the blood of those devout ones and their death as an atoning sacrifice, divine Providence preserved Israel that previously had been mistreated.

23 For the tyrant Antiochus, when he saw the courage of their virtue and their endurance under the tortures, proclaimed them to his soldiers as an example for their own endurance, 24 and this made them brave and courageous for infantry battle and siege, and he ravaged and conquered all his enemies.

18 O Israelite children, offspring of the seed of Abraham, obey this law and exercise piety in every way, 2 knowing that devout reason is master of all emotions, not only of sufferings from within, but also of those from without.

3 Therefore those who gave over their bodies in suffering for the sake of religion were not only admired by mortals, but also were deemed worthy to share in a divine inheritance. 4 Because of them the nation gained peace, and by reviving observance of the law in the homeland they ravaged the enemy. 5 The tyrant Antiochus was both punished on earth and is being chastised after his death. Since in no way whatever was he able to compel the Israelites to become pagans and to abandon their ancestral customs, he left Jerusalem and marched against the Persians.

6 The mother of seven sons expressed also these principles to her children: 7 "I was a pure virgin and did not go outside my father's house; but I guarded the rib from which woman was made.*p* 8 No seducer corrupted me on a desert plain, nor did the destroyer, the deceitful serpent, defile the purity of my virginity. 9 In the time of my maturity I remained with my husband, and when these sons had grown up their father died. A happy man was he, who lived out his life with

m Other ancient authorities read *true*
n Other ancient authorities add *virtue and*
o Other ancient authorities lack *for the sake of God*   *p* Gk *the rib that was built*

17.11–12: *Contest . . . awards . . . prize,* 6.10; 11.20. **21:** *Ransom,* see 6.29 n. **22:** *Through the blood,* Rom 3.25; *atoning sacrifice,* Greek "hilastērion," as in Rom 3.25; compare Heb 9.11–15; 1 Pet 1.19; 1 Jn 1.7. **24:** *Ravaged and conquered,* but Antiochus was not successful, and died in Babylon (1 Macc 6.1–16).
18.1–5: The exhortation seems repetitious after 17.7–24, but it is the author's method to employ recurrent themes. **5:** *Chastised after his death,* balances the immediate immortality bestowed upon the righteous martyrs. See 18.22–23. *Marched against the Persians,*

17.24 n. The second sentence in this verse does not fit well with the first.
18.6–19: The mother's last words. Compare 2 Macc 7.22–29. The mother is the supreme heroine of the story. This is a quiet passage after the highly emotional parts, designed to move the reader to reflection. Jewish education began in the home, and the mother's influence was always important. **7:** *Rib,* Gen 2.22. **8:** *Desert plain,* Deut 22.25–27. In such places women were in danger from men and also from demons, who were believed to inhabit the wilderness. **11:** *Abel,* Gen

good children, and did not have the grief of bereavement. 10 While he was still with you, he taught you the law and the prophets. 11 He read to you about Abel slain by Cain, and Isaac who was offered as a burnt offering, and about Joseph in prison. 12 He told you of the zeal of Phinehas, and he taught you about Hananiah, Azariah, and Mishael in the fire. 13 He praised Daniel in the den of the lions and blessed him. 14 He reminded you of the scripture of Isaiah, which says, 'Even though you go through the fire, the flame shall not consume you.' 15 He sang to you songs of the psalmist David, who said, 'Many are the afflictions of the righteous.' 16 He recounted to you Solomon's proverb, 'There is a tree of life for those who do his will.' 17 He confirmed the query of Ezekiel, 'Shall these dry bones live?' 18 For he did not forget to teach you the song that Moses taught, which says,

19 'I kill and I make alive: this is your life and the length of your days.' "

20 O bitter was that day—and yet not bitter—when that bitter tyrant of the Greeks quenched fire with fire in his cruel caldrons, and in his burning rage brought those seven sons of the daughter of Abraham to the catapult and back again to more*q* tortures, 21 pierced the pupils of their eyes and cut out their tongues, and put them to death with various tortures. 22 For these crimes divine justice pursued and will pursue the accursed tyrant. 23 But the sons of Abraham with their victorious mother are gathered together into the chorus of the fathers, and have received pure and immortal*r* souls from God, 24 to whom be glory forever and ever. Amen.

q Other ancient authorities read *to all his*
r Other ancient authorities read *victorious*

4.2–15. *Isaac,* Gen 22.1–19. *Joseph,* Gen 39.1–23. **12:** *Phinehas,* Num 25.1–9. *Hananiah,* 16.21. **13:** *Daniel,* Dan 6.1–24. **14:** Isa 43.2. **15:** Ps 34.19. **16:** Prov 3.18, modified slightly. **17:** Ezek 37.2–3. **19:** Deut 32.39; 30.20.

18.20–24: Conclusion. This peroration sums up many previous themes set forth in 4 Maccabees **23:** *Abraham,* 13.12 n. *Chorus,* see 8.4 n. *Immortal,* see 9.22 n. **24:** Compare Rom 11.36; 16.27; 2 Tim 4.18; Heb 13.21.

INDEX TO THE ANNOTATIONS
APOCRYPHAL/DEUTEROCANONICAL BOOKS

The following index lists important persons, places, and ideas that are mentioned in the general introduction and the annotations. In order to gain the fullest information, the verses of the passage of the Apocryphal/Deuterocanonical Books, as well as the annotation itself, should be read, and all cross references should be consulted.

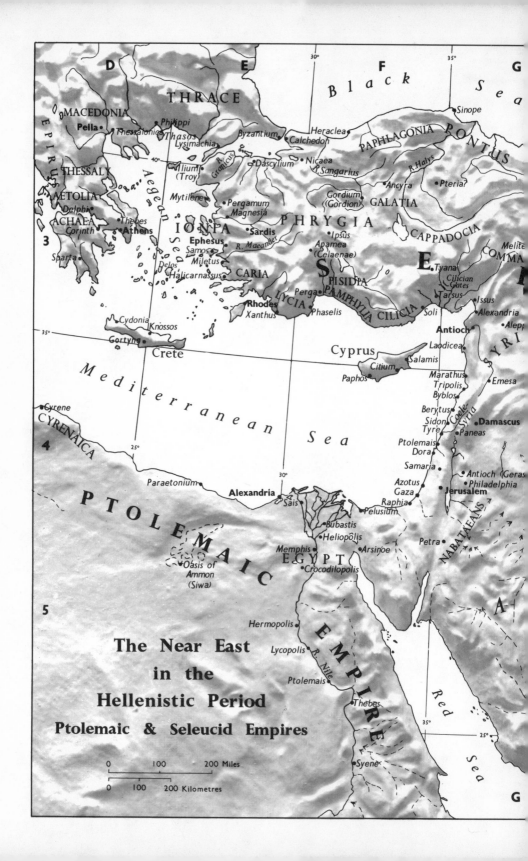

The Near East
in the
Hellenistic Period
Ptolemaic & Seleucid Empires